THE BETRAYAL
kNoWS MY NAME

4

Hotaru Odagiri

Yuki Giou
A first-year high school student. In his previous life, he was a woman and Luka's lover, but he has no memory of this at present. With the ability "Light of God," he can absorb the pain of others and heal their wounds. He's the type to put others before himself.

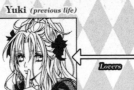

Yuki *(previous life)*

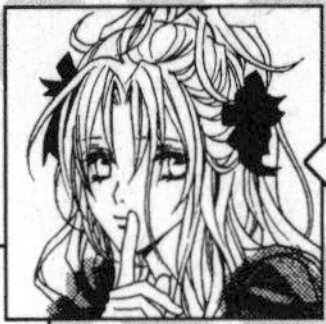
Lovers

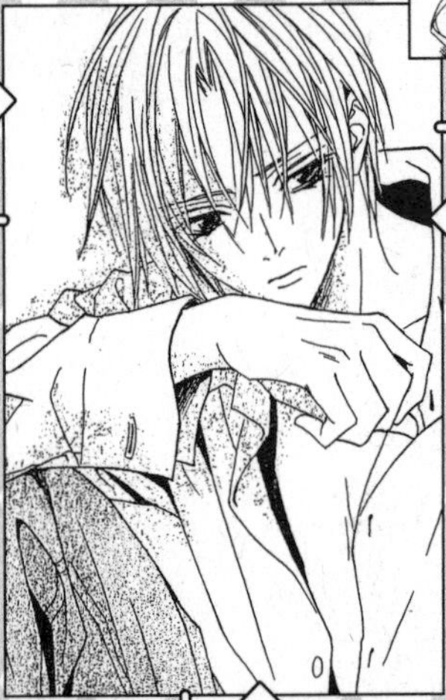
Somehow familiar
Current master
Trusted comrades
Someone to protect

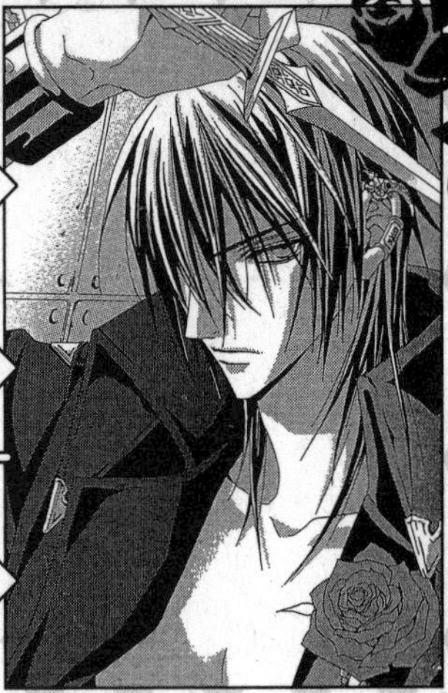

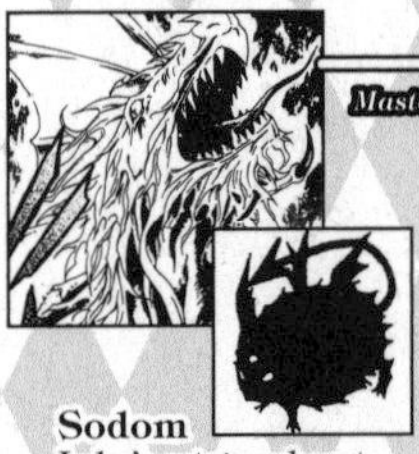
Master

Luka Crosszeria
An Opast. In Infernus, as one of the Zess—the traitor clan—he was apparently treated as a slave. Despite being a Duras, he has joined up with human comrades and currently works with the Giou clan.

Sodom
Luka's retainer beast. It can also take human form.

The Zweilt

Pairs of warriors with particular abilities whose role is to protect Yuki and hunt Duras. They are reincarnated over and over to maintain their abilities and continue the war against the Duras.

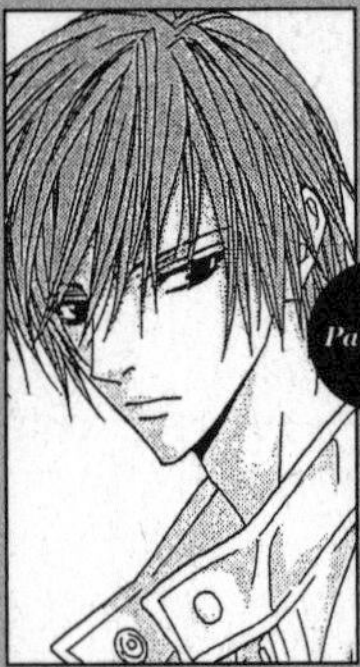

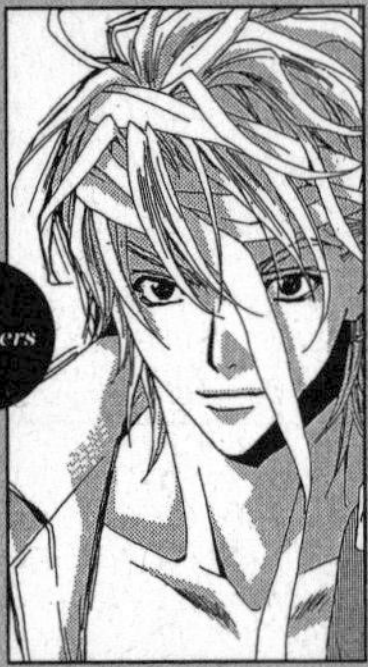
Partners

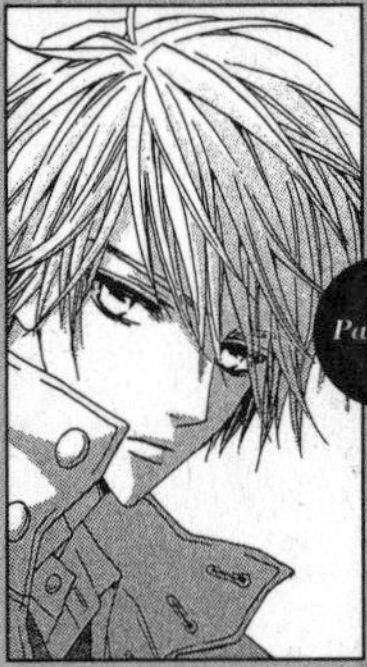

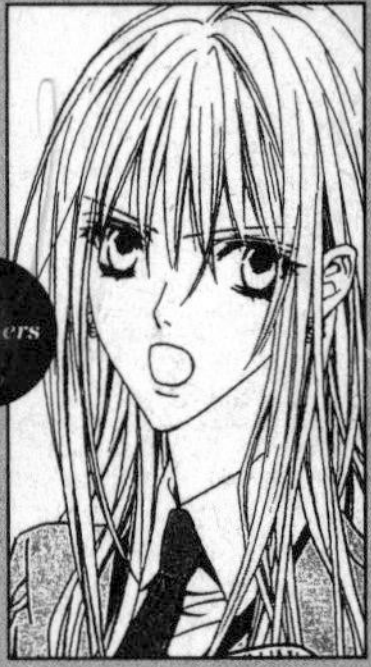
Partners

Shuusei Usui
A second-year high school student. A Zweilt specializing in defense, he summons his two swords "Cry Crow" to "release" the Duras. Has the special ability "Eyes of God." Alias "The One who Sees Through All."

Hotsuma Renjou
A first-year high school student. A Zweilt specializing in offense, he summons his greatsword Master Stroke to fight Duras. Has the special ability "Voice of God." Alias "The One who Burns to Cinders."

Tsukumo Murasame
A first-year high school student. A Zweilt specializing in defense, he summons his gun Knell to "release" Duras. Has the special ability "Ear of God." Alias "The One who Inquires."

Tooko Murasame
A second-year high school student. A Zweilt specializing in offense, she summons her greatsword Eon to fight Duras. Has the special ability "Ear of God." Alias "The One who Inquires."

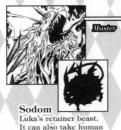

character

The Giou Clan

Betrayed

Not his brother after all, but still important to him

Formerly close friends

Was like an older brother

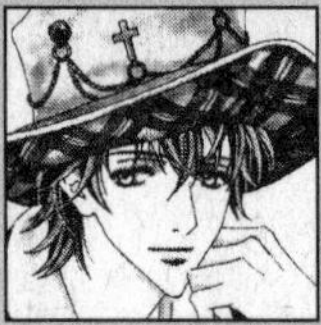

Tachibana Giou
Steward of Twilight Hall. Supervises the Zweilt.

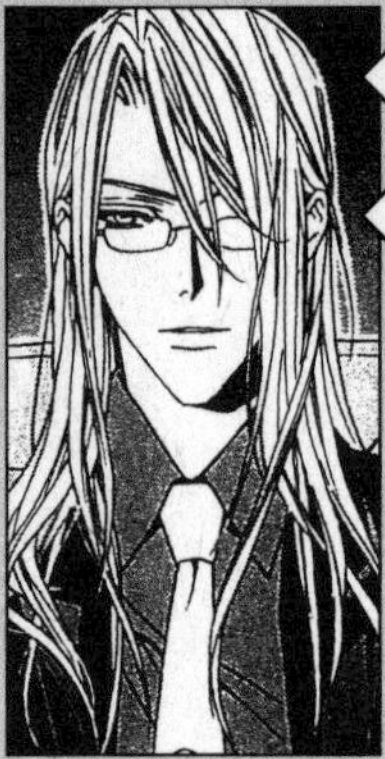

Takashiro Giou
Commander of the Giou clan. He introduced himself as Yuki's brother, but that was a lie, as he has been alive since the "Sunset of the Underworld" a millennium ago. The most powerful of the clan, he is both a wotes and a necromancer. But might he still be hiding things from Yuki...?

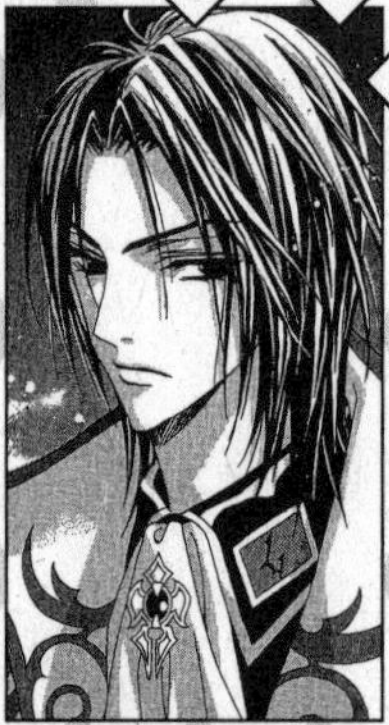

Reiga Giou
As Kanata Wakamiya, he grew up with Yuki at the Morning Sun House and made it to college, but awakened as "Reiga" and became Yuki's enemy. A child of mixed blood, born to an Opast father and a Giou mother. Also a peerless necromancer.

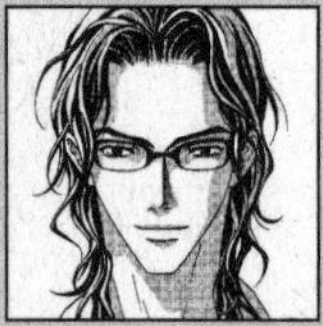

Isuzu Fujiwara
The Giou clan's doctor and permanent staff of the Twilight Hall infirmary. Researching more effective treatments for injuries inflicted by Duras.

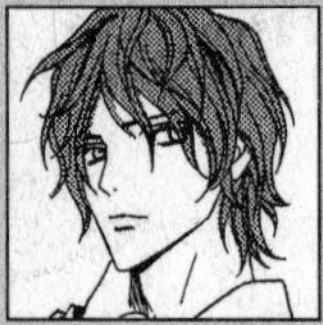

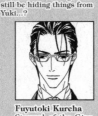

Masamune Shinmei
A second-year high school student and apprentice necromancer residing at the main residence in Kamakura.

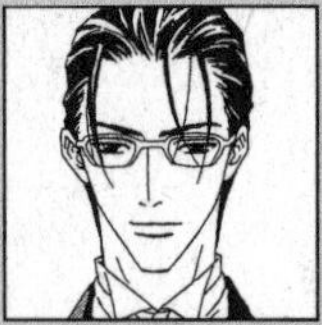

Fuyutoki Kureha
Steward of the Giou main residence in Kamakura. Serves Takashiro.

Sisters

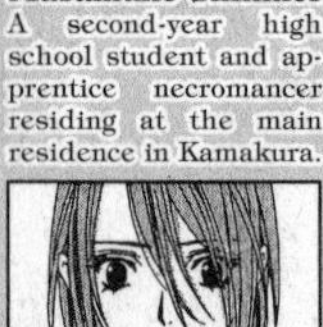

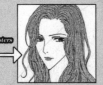

Tsubaki Shikibe
Ibuki's younger sister and Yuki's aunt. Was betrothed to Senshirou.

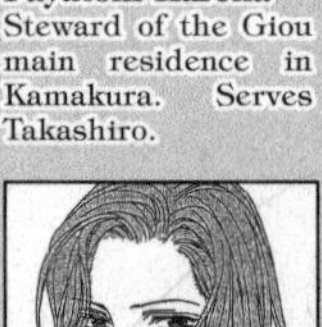

Ibuki Shikibe
Takashiro's very capable secretary and Yuki's aunt.

Partners

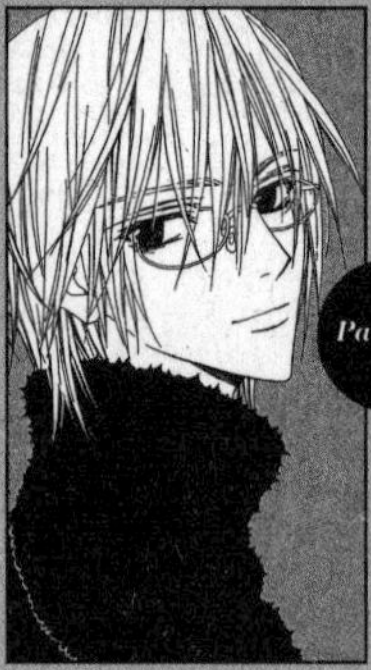

Senshirou Furuori
A first-year in art school. Likes cooking and taking care of people. Completely devoted to Kuroto. A "newbie" Zweilt, who has just joined for this round of the war. He has vowed to take revenge on the Opast Cadenza.

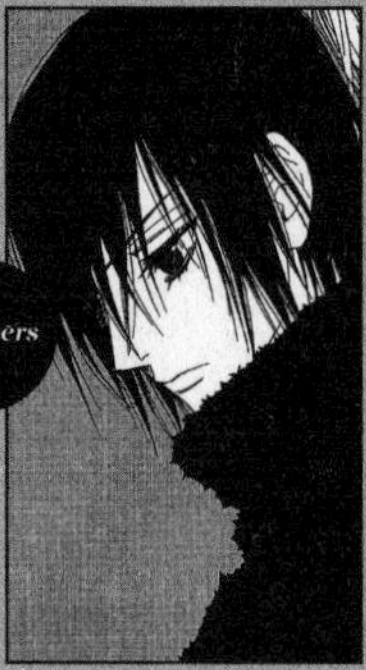

Kuroto Hourai
A first-year high school student. He grew up as a rich boy and has a self-important attitude. He was active as a professional shogi player, but quit to join the fight against the Duras. Has the special ability "Feet of God." Alias "The Swift One."

story

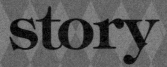

The Giou clan—known as the "descendants of the gods" for the special abilities possessed by many among them—has existed silently in the margins of history. Among those with such abilities, there are "necromancers," who summon and control beings known as Duras from the other world, or Infernus. It was said that these necromancers would bestow great blessings upon the people.

But a day came when the necromancer Reiga betrayed the clan. Using the Duras, he drove the Giou halfway to annihilation, then deserted them for Infernus. That was the beginning of the long war between the Giou clan, led by Takashiro, and the Duras, led by Reiga.

Time rushed onward—and now, over a thousand years later, a new battle is beginning for the Zweilt and for Yuki Giou, the boy who holds the key to a millennium-long struggle...

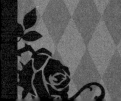

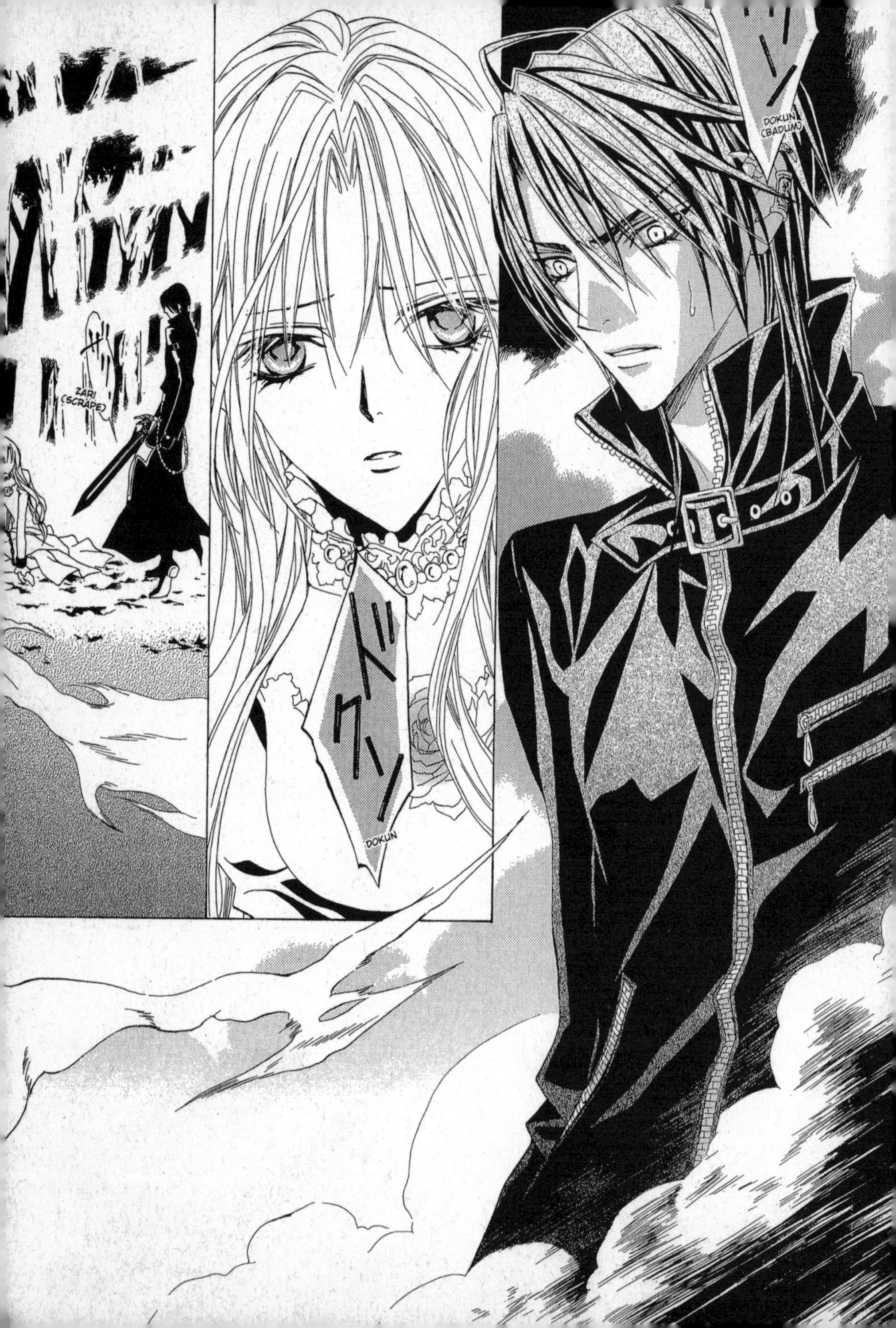
DOKUN (BADUM)
DOKUN
ZARI (SCRAPE)

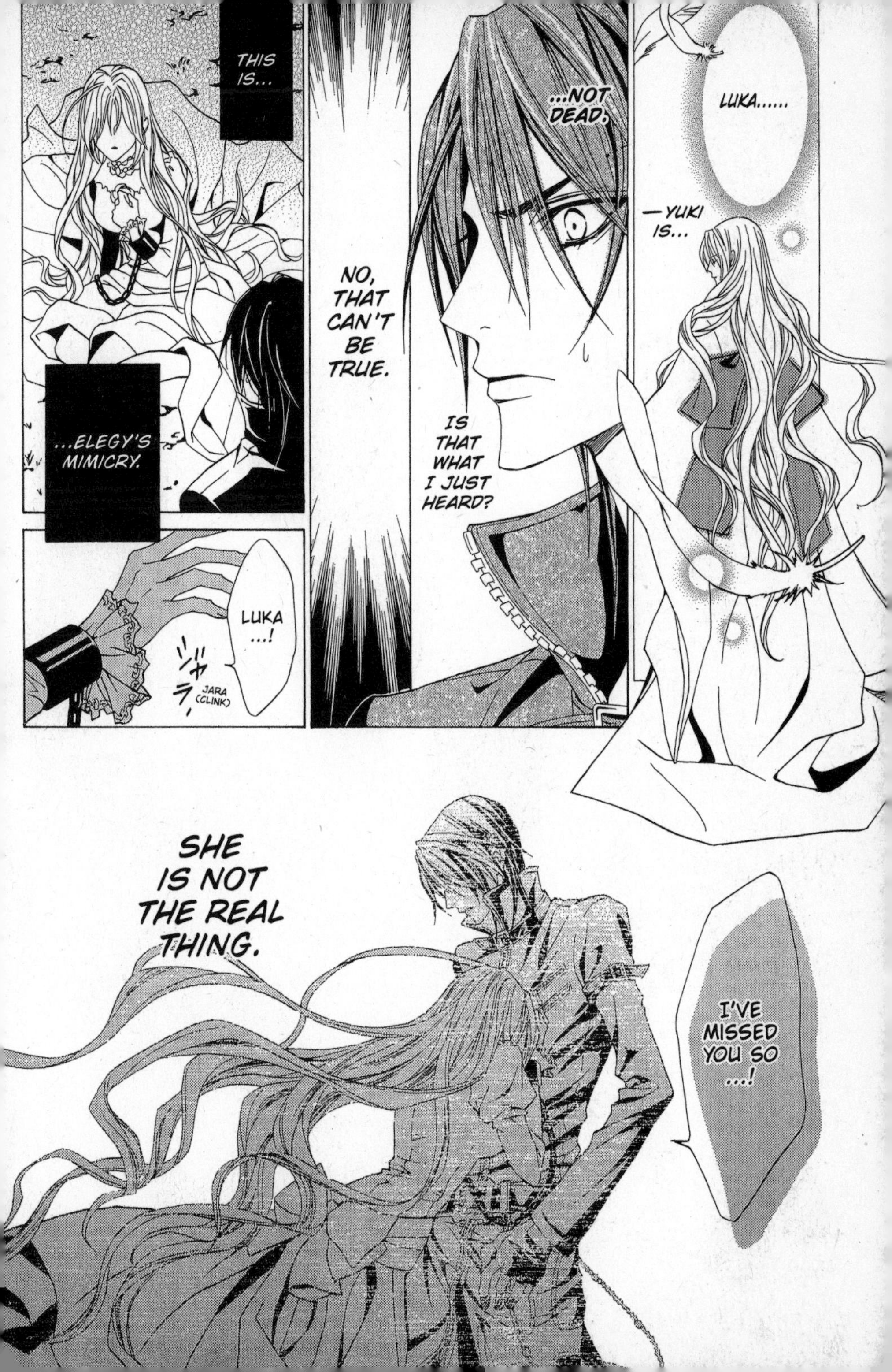
LUKA......
—YUKI IS...
...NOT DEAD.
NO, THAT CAN'T BE TRUE.
IS THAT WHAT I JUST HEARD?
THIS IS...
...ELEGY'S MIMICRY.
LUKA ...!
ジャラ
JARA (CLINK)
I'VE MISSED YOU SO ...!
SHE IS NOT THE REAL THING.

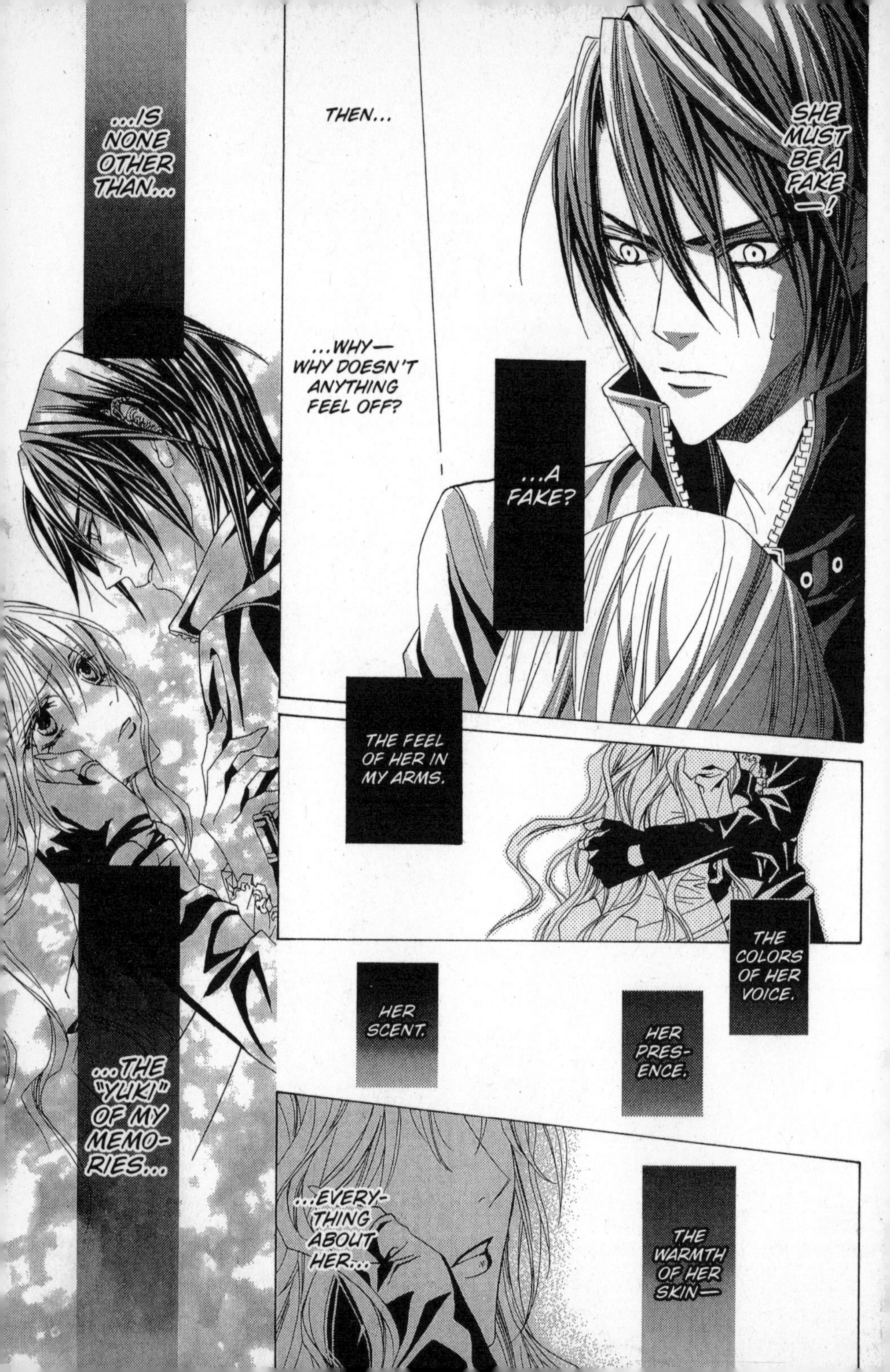

SHE MUST BE A FAKE—!
...A FAKE?
THEN...
...WHY—WHY DOESN'T ANYTHING FEEL OFF?
THE FEEL OF HER IN MY ARMS.
THE COLORS OF HER VOICE.
HER PRESENCE.
HER SCENT.
THE WARMTH OF HER SKIN—
...EVERYTHING ABOUT HER...
...IS NONE OTHER THAN...
...THE "YUKI" OF MY MEMORIES...

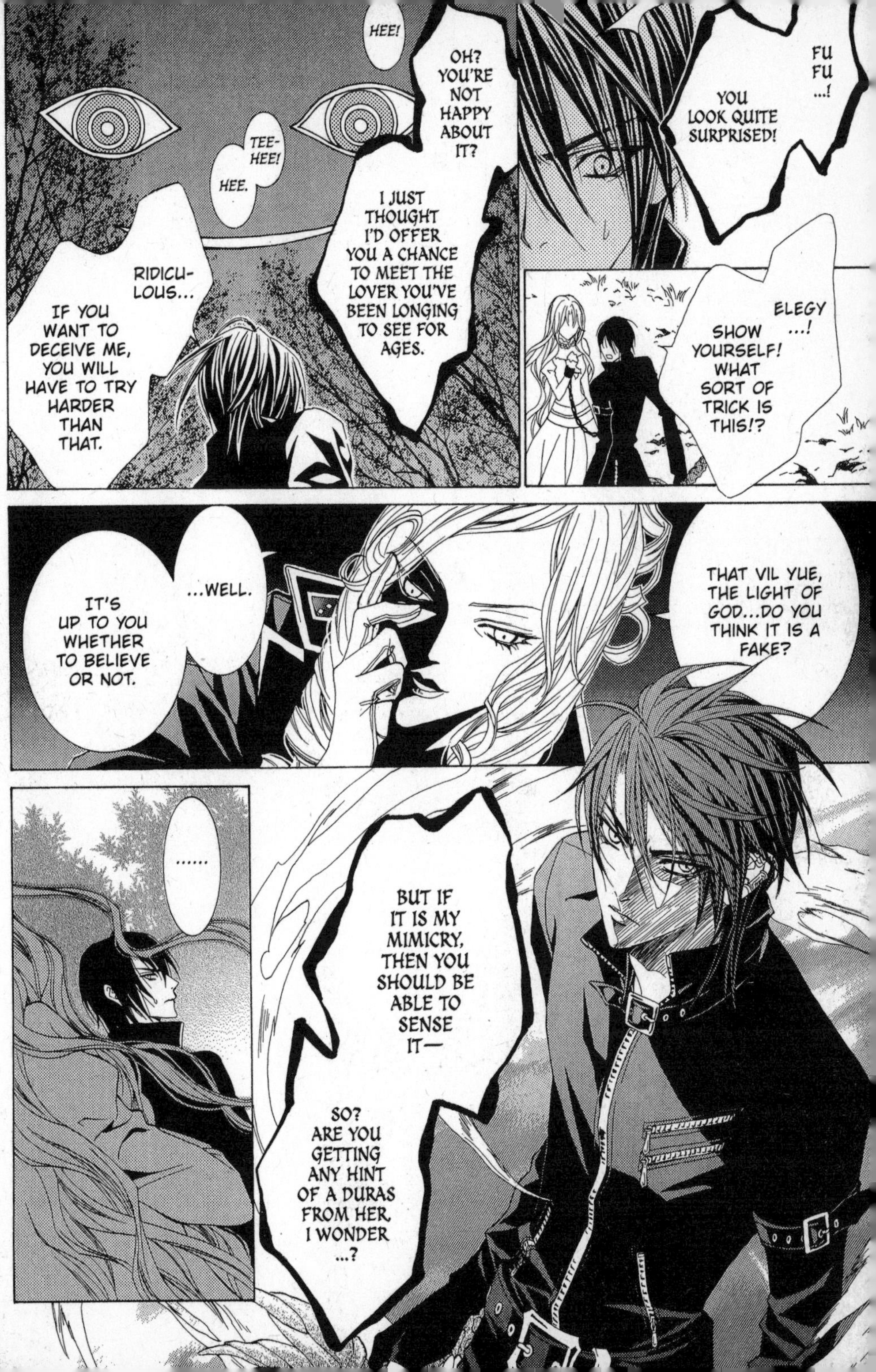
FU FU ...!
YOU LOOK QUITE SURPRISED!
ELEGY ...!
SHOW YOURSELF! WHAT SORT OF TRICK IS THIS!?
HEE!
OH? YOU'RE NOT HAPPY ABOUT IT?
I JUST THOUGHT I'D OFFER YOU A CHANCE TO MEET THE LOVER YOU'VE BEEN LONGING TO SEE FOR AGES.
TEE-HEE!
HEE.
RIDICULOUS...
IF YOU WANT TO DECEIVE ME, YOU WILL HAVE TO TRY HARDER THAN THAT.
THAT VIL YUE, THE LIGHT OF GOD...DO YOU THINK IT IS A FAKE?
...WELL.
IT'S UP TO YOU WHETHER TO BELIEVE OR NOT.
BUT IF IT IS MY MIMICRY, THEN YOU SHOULD BE ABLE TO SENSE IT—
SO? ARE YOU GETTING ANY HINT OF A DURAS FROM HER, I WONDER ...?
......

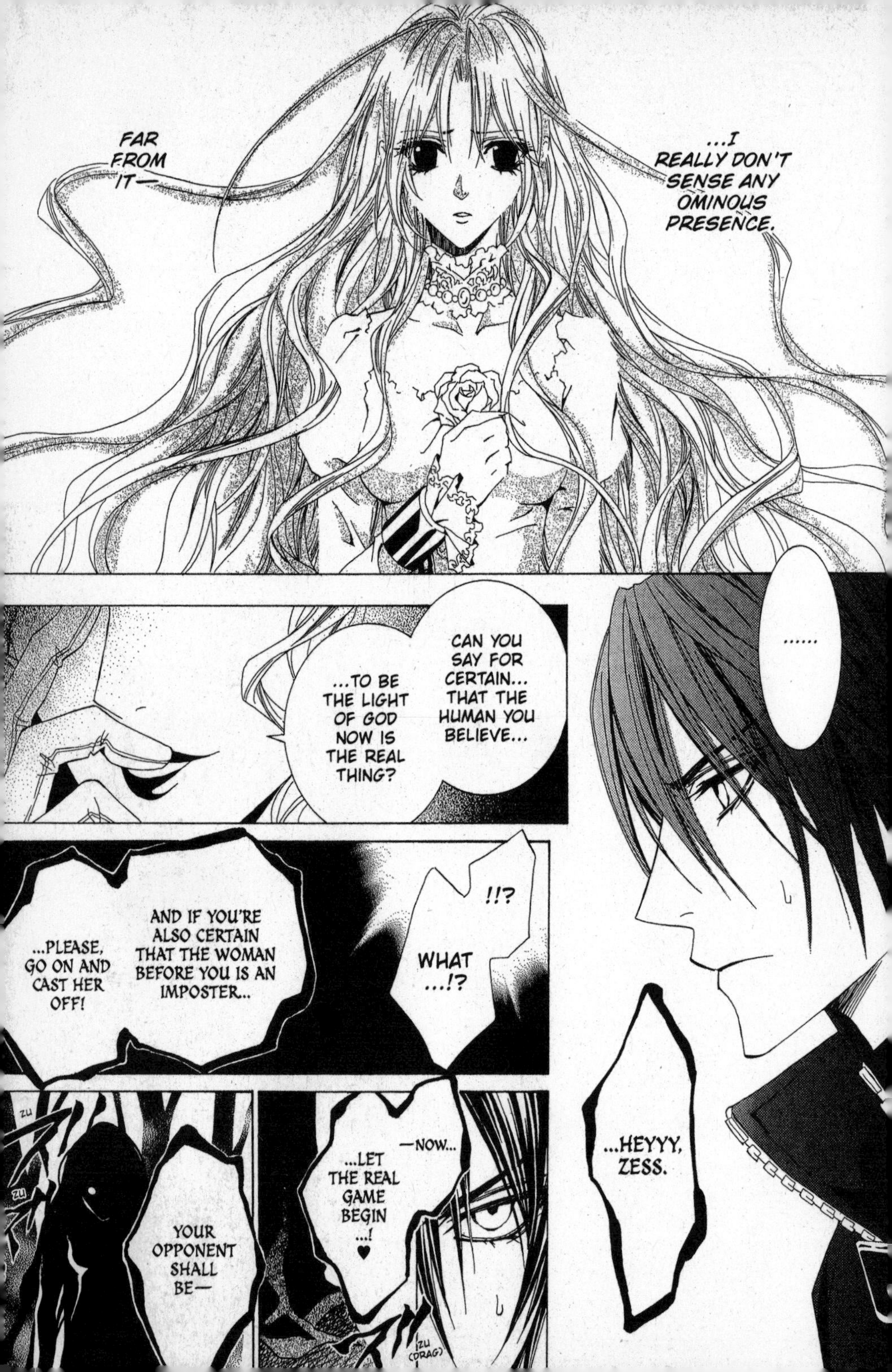
...I REALLY DON'T SENSE ANY OMINOUS PRESENCE.
FAR FROM IT—
......
CAN YOU SAY FOR CERTAIN... THAT THE HUMAN YOU BELIEVE...
...TO BE THE LIGHT OF GOD NOW IS THE REAL THING?
!!?
WHAT ...!?
AND IF YOU'RE ALSO CERTAIN THAT THE WOMAN BEFORE YOU IS AN IMPOSTER...
...PLEASE, GO ON AND CAST HER OFF!
...HEYYY, ZESS.
—NOW...
...LET THE REAL GAME BEGIN ...! ♥
YOUR OPPONENT SHALL BE—
ZU
ZU
ZU (DRAG)

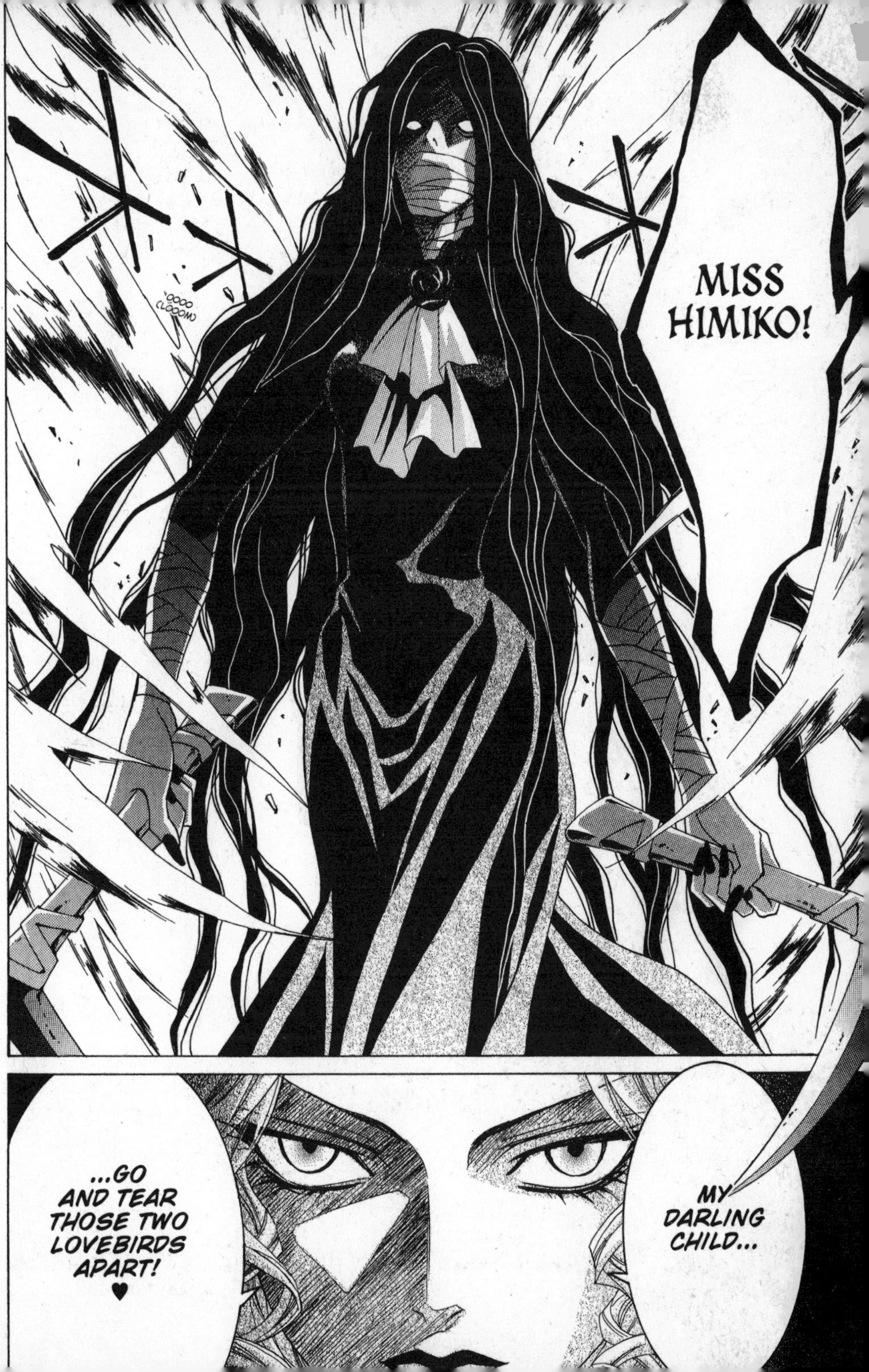
MISS HIMIKO!
OOOO
(LOOOM)
MY DARLING CHILD...
...GO AND TEAR THOSE TWO LOVEBIRDS APART! ♥

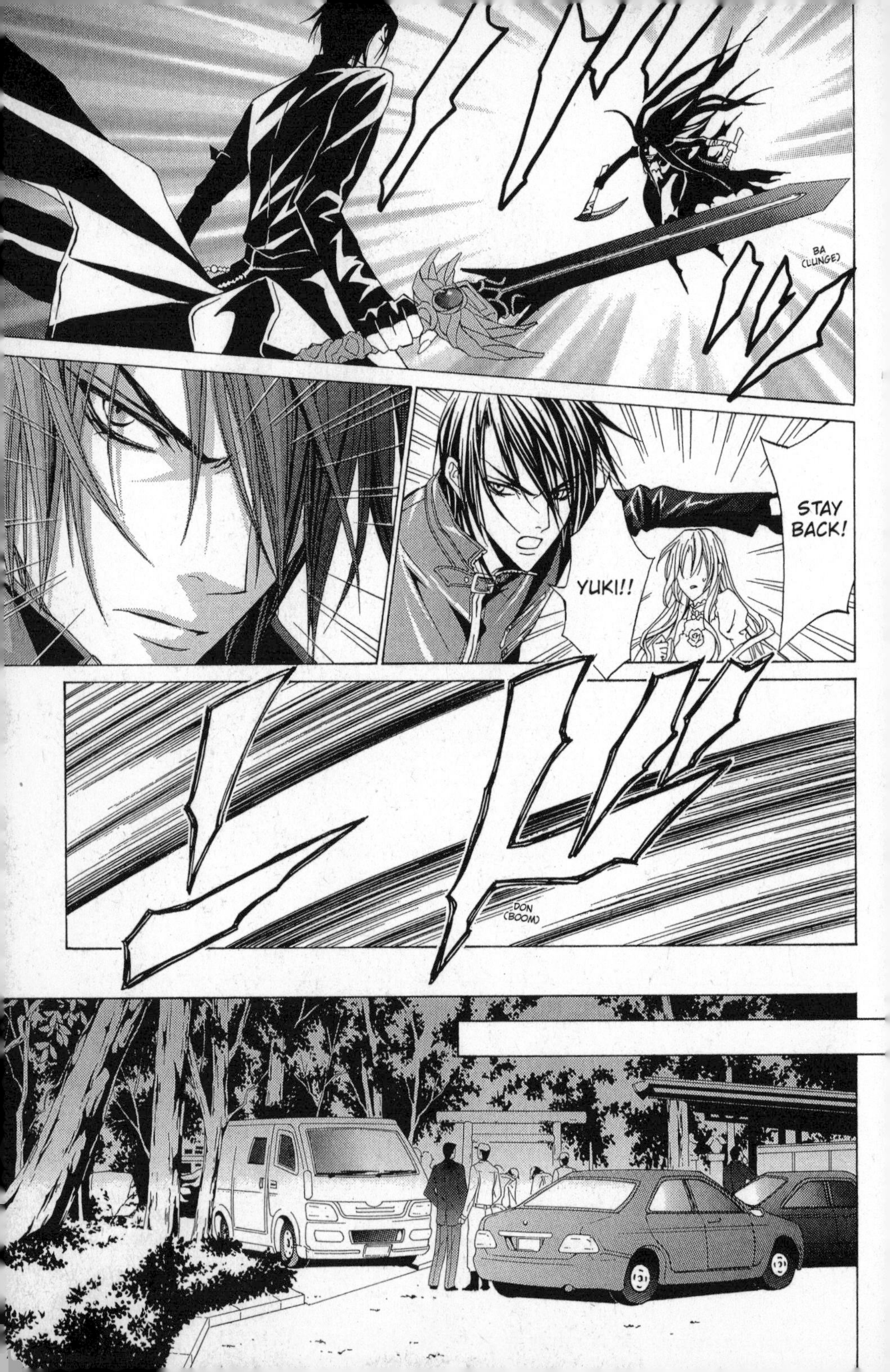
BA (LUNGE)
STAY BACK!
YUKI!!
DON (BOOM)

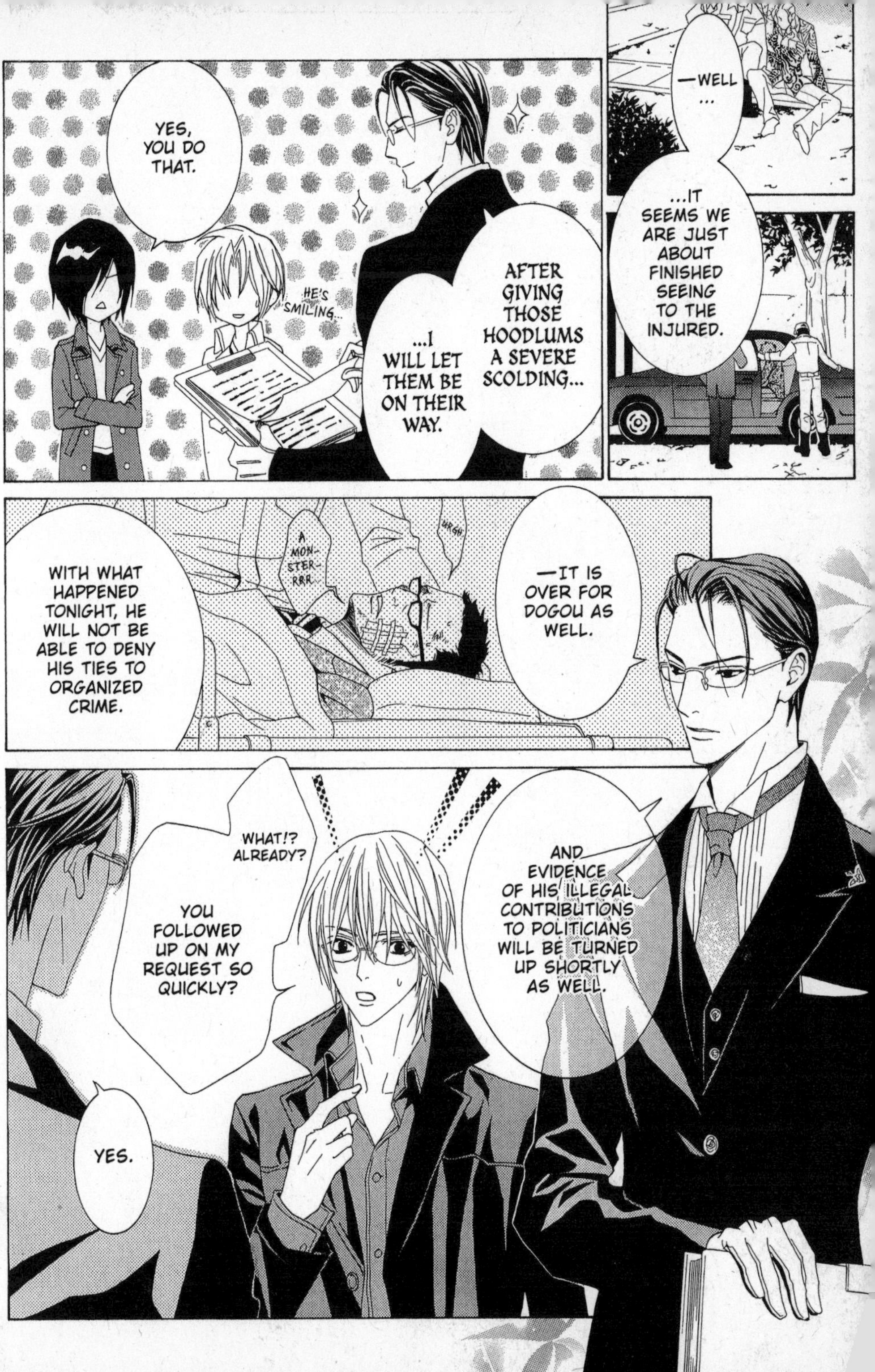
—WELL ...
...IT SEEMS WE ARE JUST ABOUT FINISHED SEEING TO THE INJURED.
AFTER GIVING THOSE HOODLUMS A SEVERE SCOLDING...
...I WILL LET THEM BE ON THEIR WAY.
HE'S SMILING...
YES, YOU DO THAT.
—IT IS OVER FOR DOGOU AS WELL.
URGH
A MON-STER-RRR
WITH WHAT HAPPENED TONIGHT, HE WILL NOT BE ABLE TO DENY HIS TIES TO ORGANIZED CRIME.
AND EVIDENCE OF HIS ILLEGAL CONTRIBUTIONS TO POLITICIANS WILL BE TURNED UP SHORTLY AS WELL.
WHAT!? ALREADY?
YOU FOLLOWED UP ON MY REQUEST SO QUICKLY?
YES.

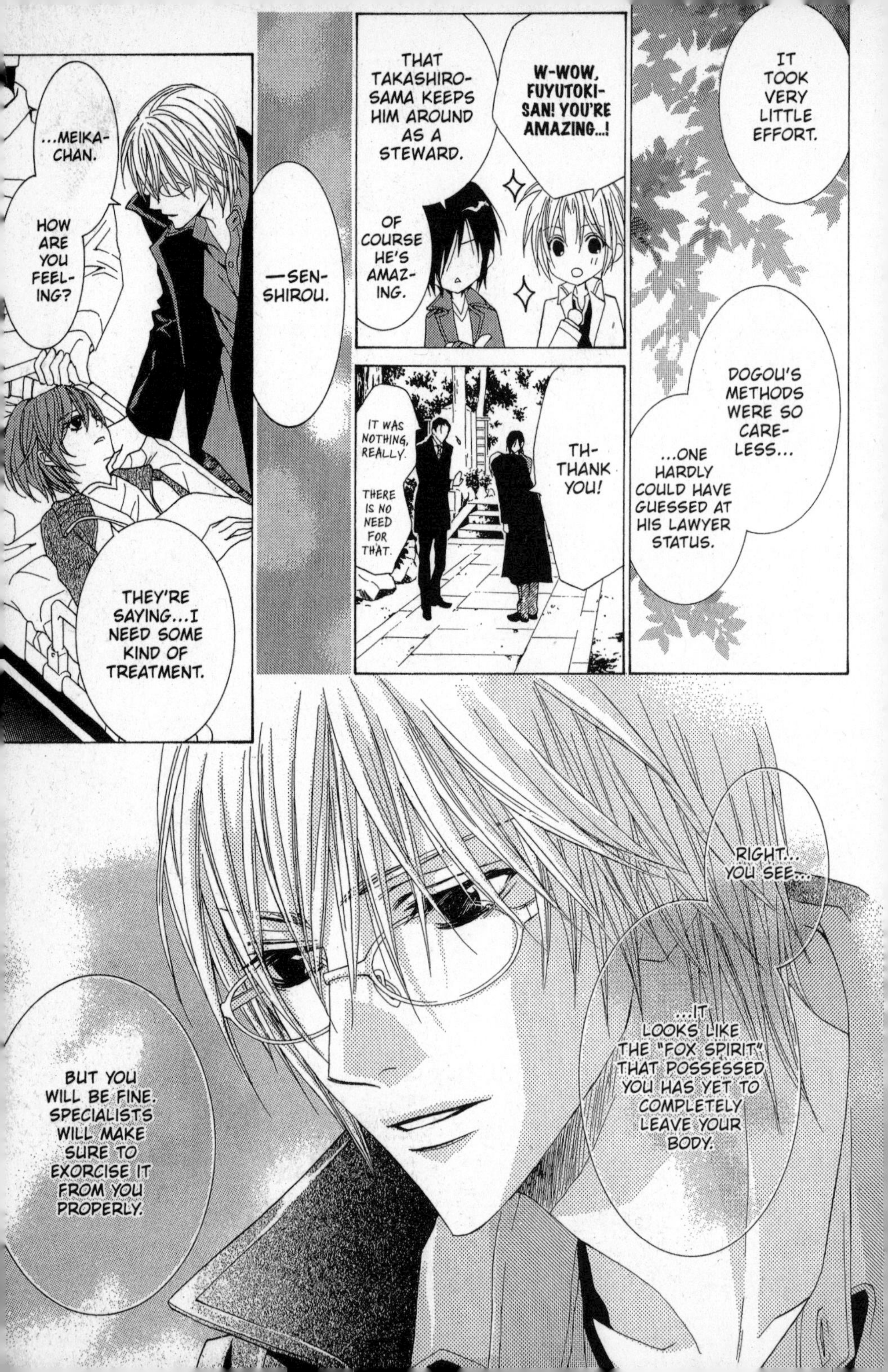
IT TOOK VERY LITTLE EFFORT.
DOGOU'S METHODS WERE SO CARE-LESS...
...ONE HARDLY COULD HAVE GUESSED AT HIS LAWYER STATUS.
W-WOW, FUYUTOKI-SAN! YOU'RE AMAZING...!
THAT TAKASHIRO-SAMA KEEPS HIM AROUND AS A STEWARD.
OF COURSE HE'S AMAZ-ING.
TH-THANK YOU!
IT WAS NOTHING, REALLY.
THERE IS NO NEED FOR THAT.
—SEN-SHIROU.
...MEIKA-CHAN.
HOW ARE YOU FEEL-ING?
THEY'RE SAYING...I NEED SOME KIND OF TREATMENT.
RIGHT... YOU SEE...
...IT LOOKS LIKE THE "FOX SPIRIT" THAT POSSESSED YOU HAS YET TO COMPLETELY LEAVE YOUR BODY.
BUT YOU WILL BE FINE. SPECIALISTS WILL MAKE SURE TO EXORCISE IT FROM YOU PROPERLY.

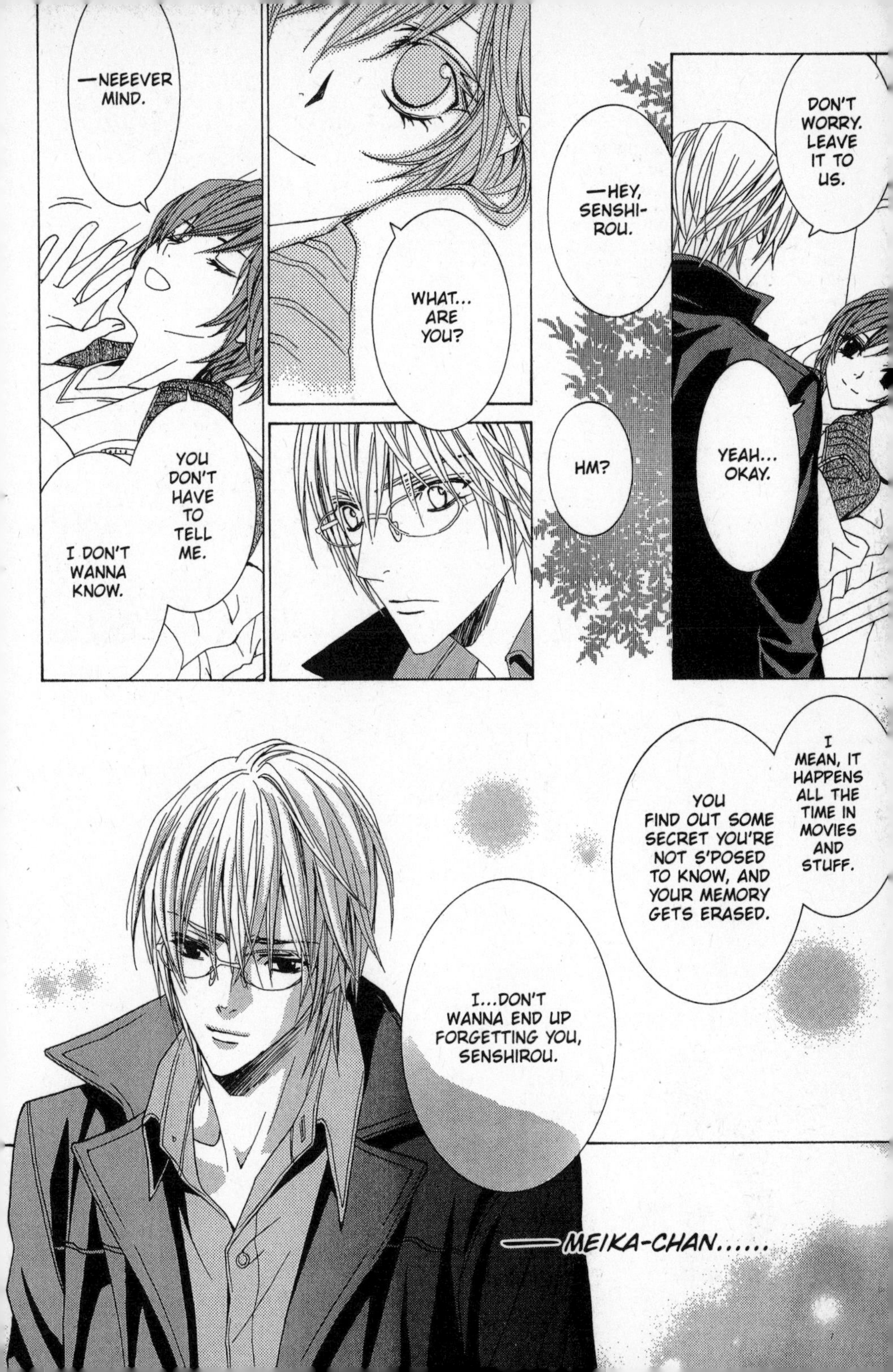
DON'T WORRY. LEAVE IT TO US.
YEAH... OKAY.
—HEY, SENSHIROU.
HM?
WHAT... ARE YOU?
—NEEEVER MIND.
YOU DON'T HAVE TO TELL ME.
I DON'T WANNA KNOW.
I MEAN, IT HAPPENS ALL THE TIME IN MOVIES AND STUFF.
YOU FIND OUT SOME SECRET YOU'RE NOT S'POSED TO KNOW, AND YOUR MEMORY GETS ERASED.
I...DON'T WANNA END UP FORGETTING YOU, SENSHIROU.
—MEIKA-CHAN......

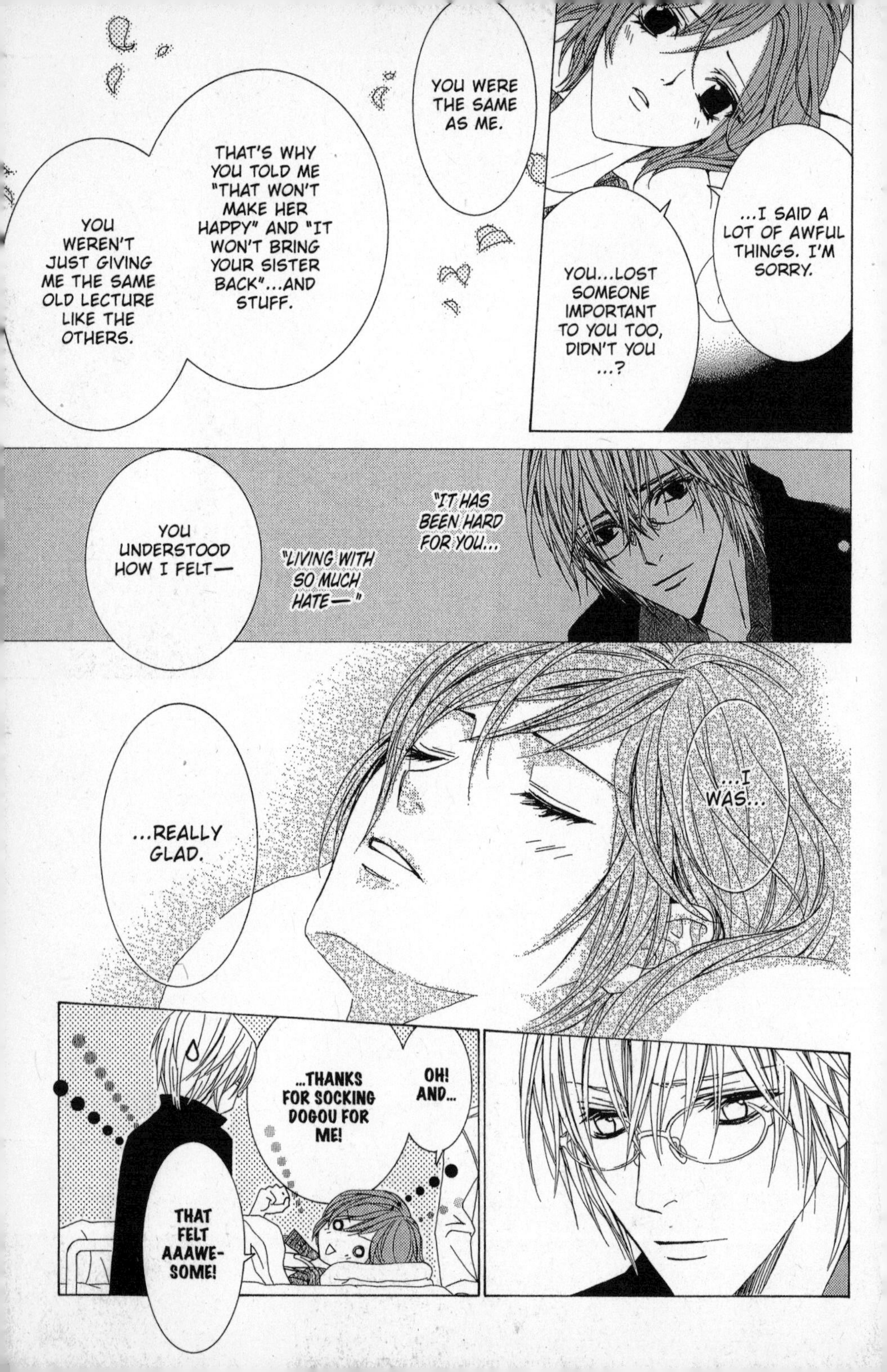
...I SAID A LOT OF AWFUL THINGS. I'M SORRY.
YOU...LOST SOMEONE IMPORTANT TO YOU TOO, DIDN'T YOU ...?
YOU WERE THE SAME AS ME.
THAT'S WHY YOU TOLD ME "THAT WON'T MAKE HER HAPPY" AND "IT WON'T BRING YOUR SISTER BACK"...AND STUFF.
YOU WEREN'T JUST GIVING ME THE SAME OLD LECTURE LIKE THE OTHERS.
"IT HAS BEEN HARD FOR YOU...
"LIVING WITH SO MUCH HATE—"
YOU UNDERSTOOD HOW I FELT—
...I WAS...
...REALLY GLAD.
OH! AND...
...THANKS FOR SOCKING DOGOU FOR ME!
THAT FELT AAAWE-SOME!

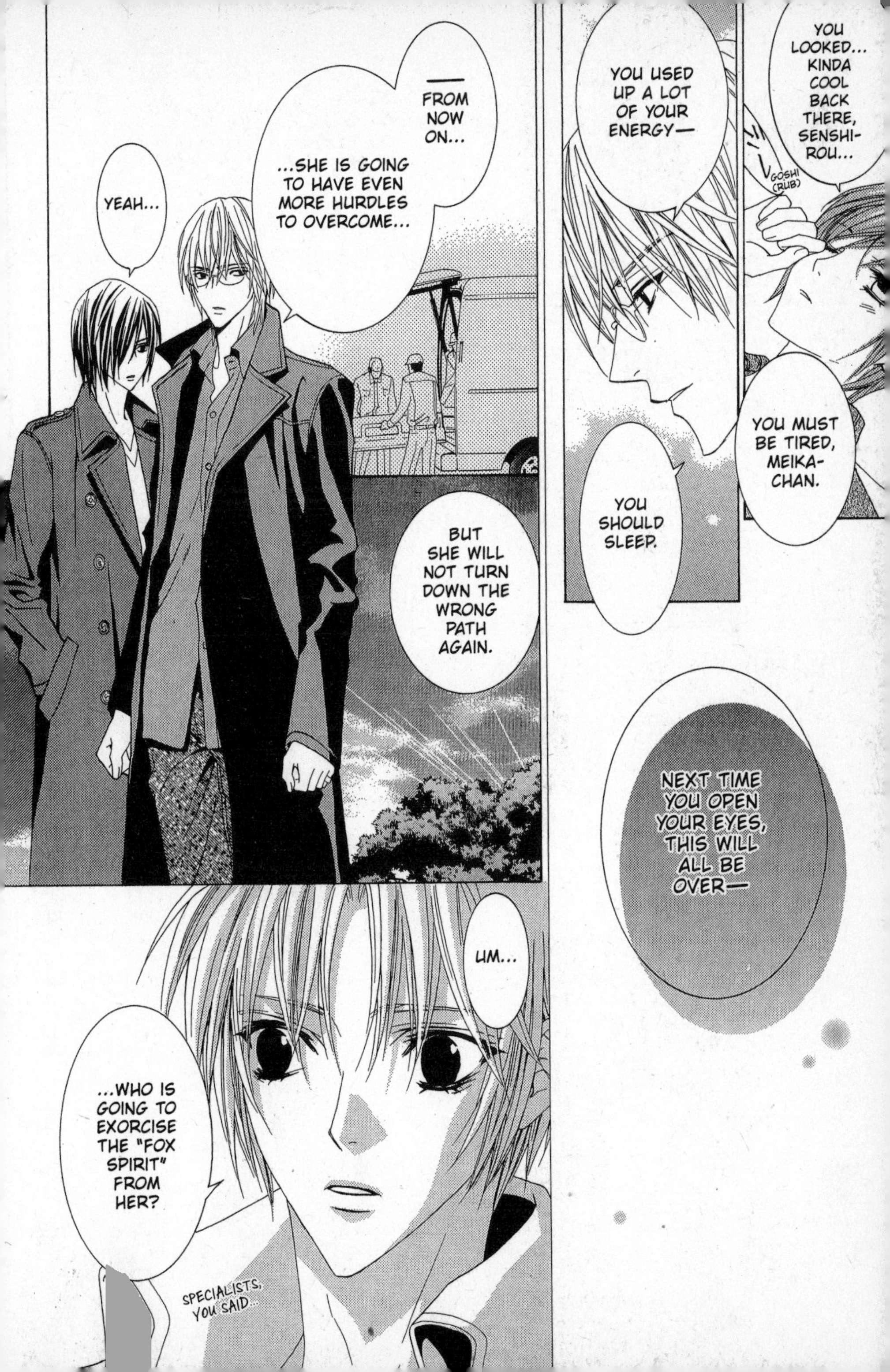
YOU LOOKED... KINDA COOL BACK THERE, SENSHIROU...
GOSHI (RUB)
YOU MUST BE TIRED, MEIKA-CHAN.
YOU USED UP A LOT OF YOUR ENERGY—
YOU SHOULD SLEEP.
NEXT TIME YOU OPEN YOUR EYES, THIS WILL ALL BE OVER—
—FROM NOW ON...
...SHE IS GOING TO HAVE EVEN MORE HURDLES TO OVERCOME...
YEAH...
BUT SHE WILL NOT TURN DOWN THE WRONG PATH AGAIN.
UM...
...WHO IS GOING TO EXORCISE THE "FOX SPIRIT" FROM HER?
SPECIALISTS, YOU SAID...

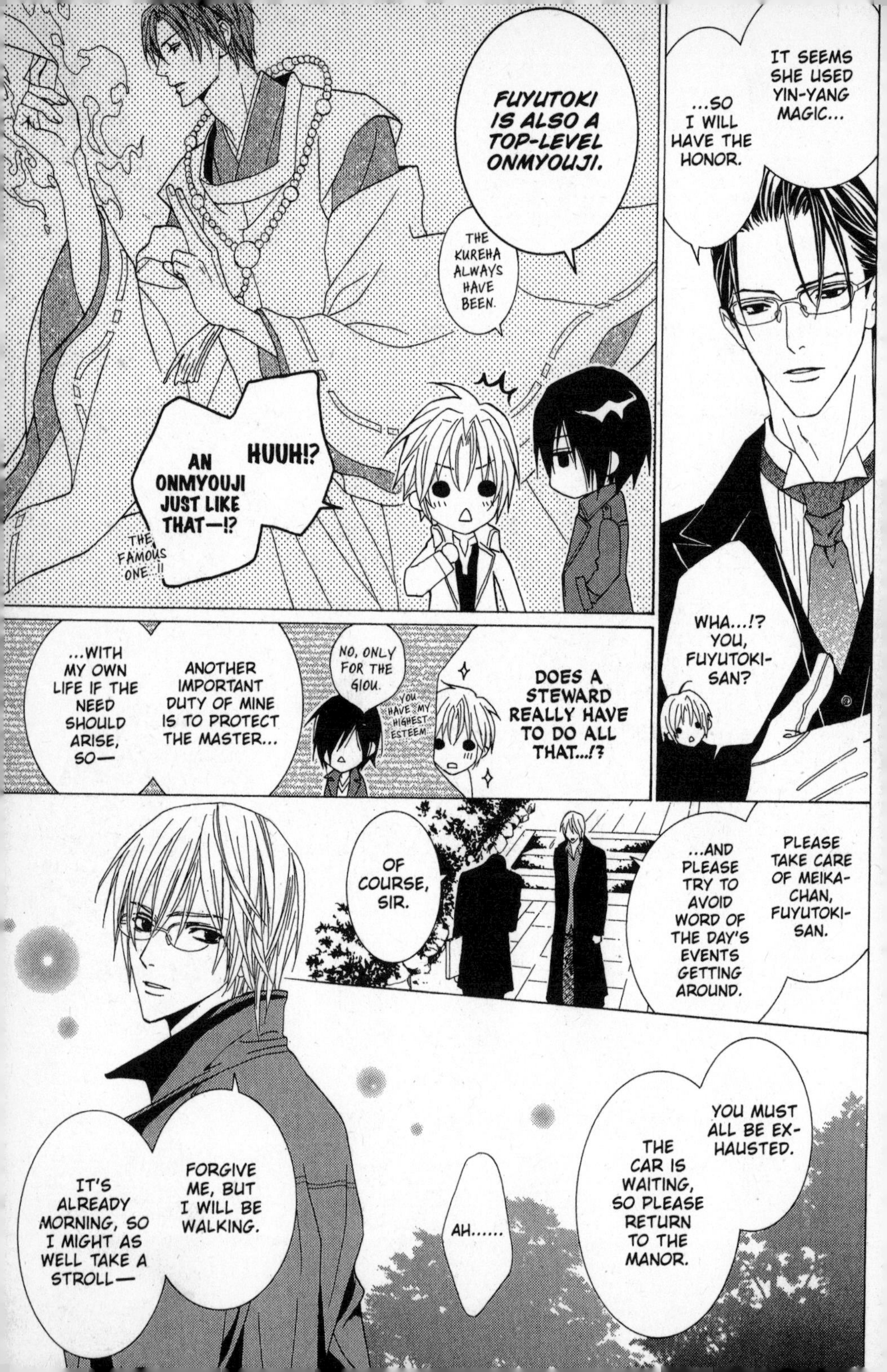
IT SEEMS SHE USED YIN-YANG MAGIC...
...SO I WILL HAVE THE HONOR.
WHA...!? YOU, FUYUTOKI-SAN?
FUYUTOKI IS ALSO A TOP-LEVEL ONMYOUJI.
THE KUREHA ALWAYS HAVE BEEN.
HUUH!? AN ONMYOUJI JUST LIKE THAT—!?
THE FAMOUS ONE!!
DOES A STEWARD REALLY HAVE TO DO ALL THAT...!?
NO, ONLY FOR THE GIOU.
YOU HAVE MY HIGHEST ESTEEM
ANOTHER IMPORTANT DUTY OF MINE IS TO PROTECT THE MASTER...
...WITH MY OWN LIFE IF THE NEED SHOULD ARISE, SO—
PLEASE TAKE CARE OF MEIKA-CHAN, FUYUTOKI-SAN.
...AND PLEASE TRY TO AVOID WORD OF THE DAY'S EVENTS GETTING AROUND.
OF COURSE, SIR.
YOU MUST ALL BE EXHAUSTED.
THE CAR IS WAITING, SO PLEASE RETURN TO THE MANOR.
AH......
FORGIVE ME, BUT I WILL BE WALKING.
IT'S ALREADY MORNING, SO I MIGHT AS WELL TAKE A STROLL—

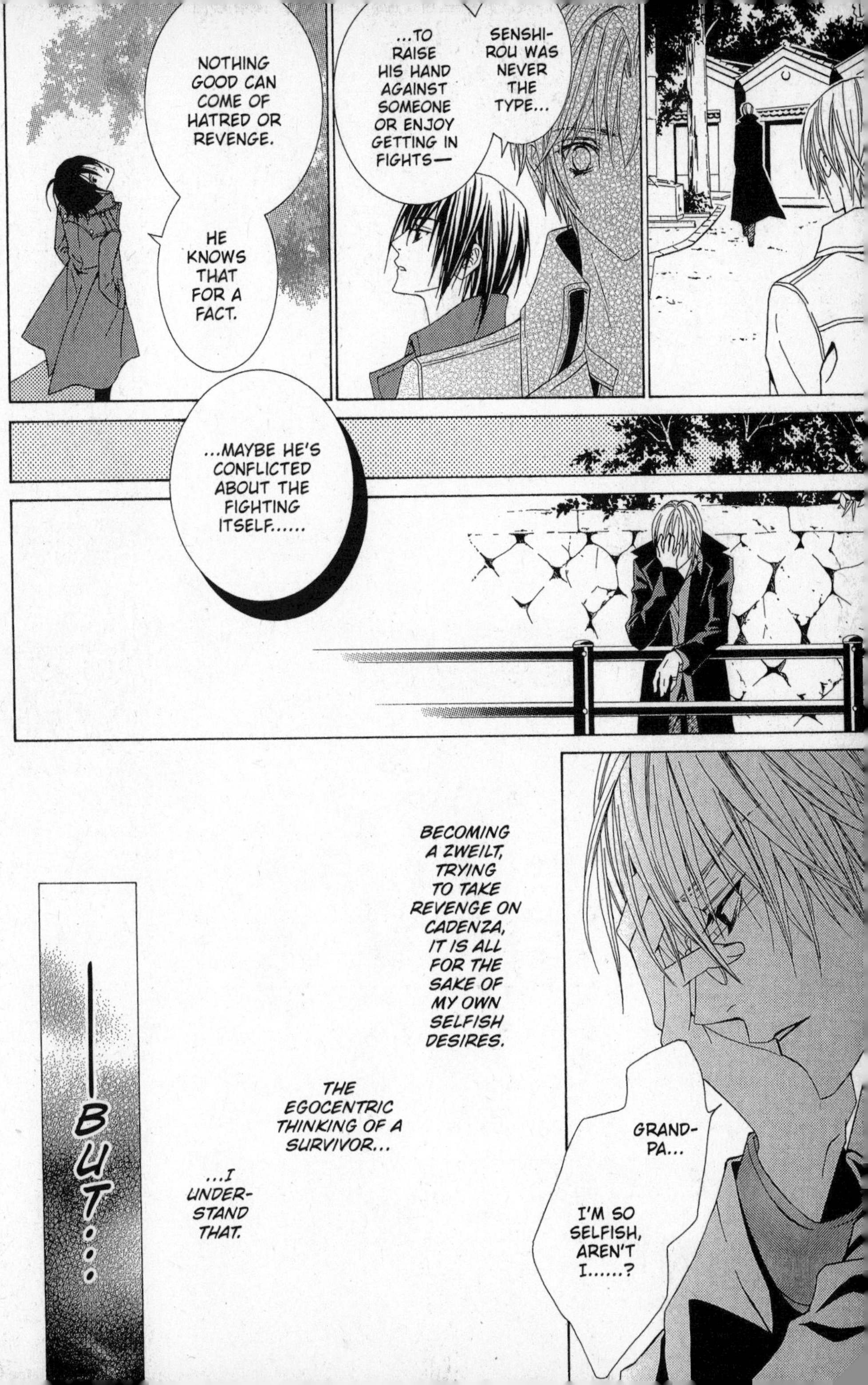
SENSHIROU WAS NEVER THE TYPE...
...TO RAISE HIS HAND AGAINST SOMEONE OR ENJOY GETTING IN FIGHTS—
NOTHING GOOD CAN COME OF HATRED OR REVENGE.
HE KNOWS THAT FOR A FACT.
...MAYBE HE'S CONFLICTED ABOUT THE FIGHTING ITSELF......
BECOMING A ZWEILT, TRYING TO TAKE REVENGE ON CADENZA, IT IS ALL FOR THE SAKE OF MY OWN SELFISH DESIRES.
THE EGOCENTRIC THINKING OF A SURVIVOR...
...I UNDERSTAND THAT.
GRAND-PA...
I'M SO SELFISH, AREN'T I......?
—BUT...

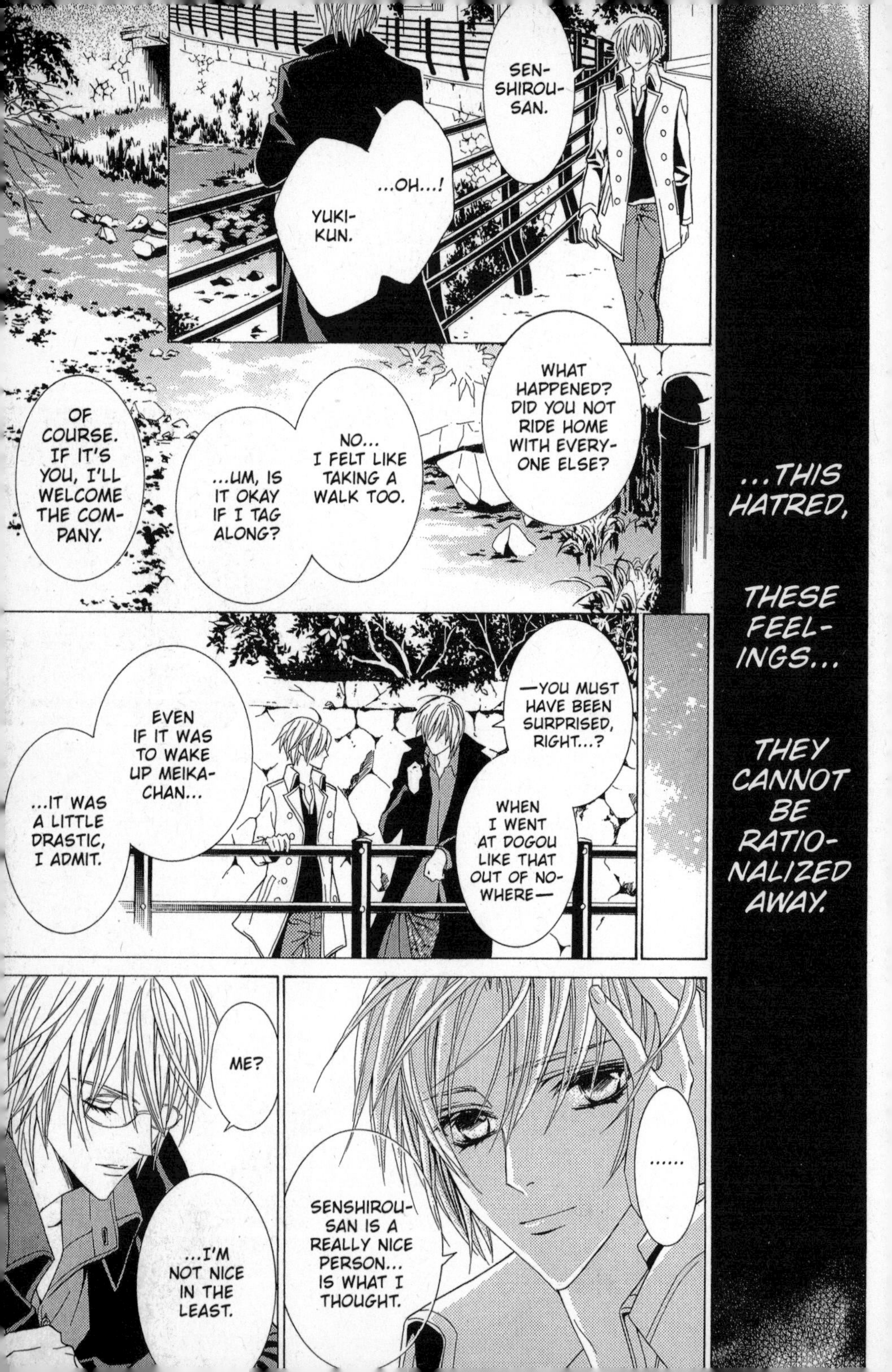
...THIS HATRED,
THESE FEELINGS...
THEY CANNOT BE RATIONALIZED AWAY.
SENSHIROU-SAN.
...OH...! YUKI-KUN.
WHAT HAPPENED? DID YOU NOT RIDE HOME WITH EVERYONE ELSE?
NO... I FELT LIKE TAKING A WALK TOO.
...UM, IS IT OKAY IF I TAG ALONG?
OF COURSE. IF IT'S YOU, I'LL WELCOME THE COMPANY.
—YOU MUST HAVE BEEN SURPRISED, RIGHT...?
WHEN I WENT AT DOGOU LIKE THAT OUT OF NOWHERE—
EVEN IF IT WAS TO WAKE UP MEIKA-CHAN...
...IT WAS A LITTLE DRASTIC, I ADMIT.
......
SENSHIROU-SAN IS A REALLY NICE PERSON... IS WHAT I THOUGHT.
ME?
...I'M NOT NICE IN THE LEAST.

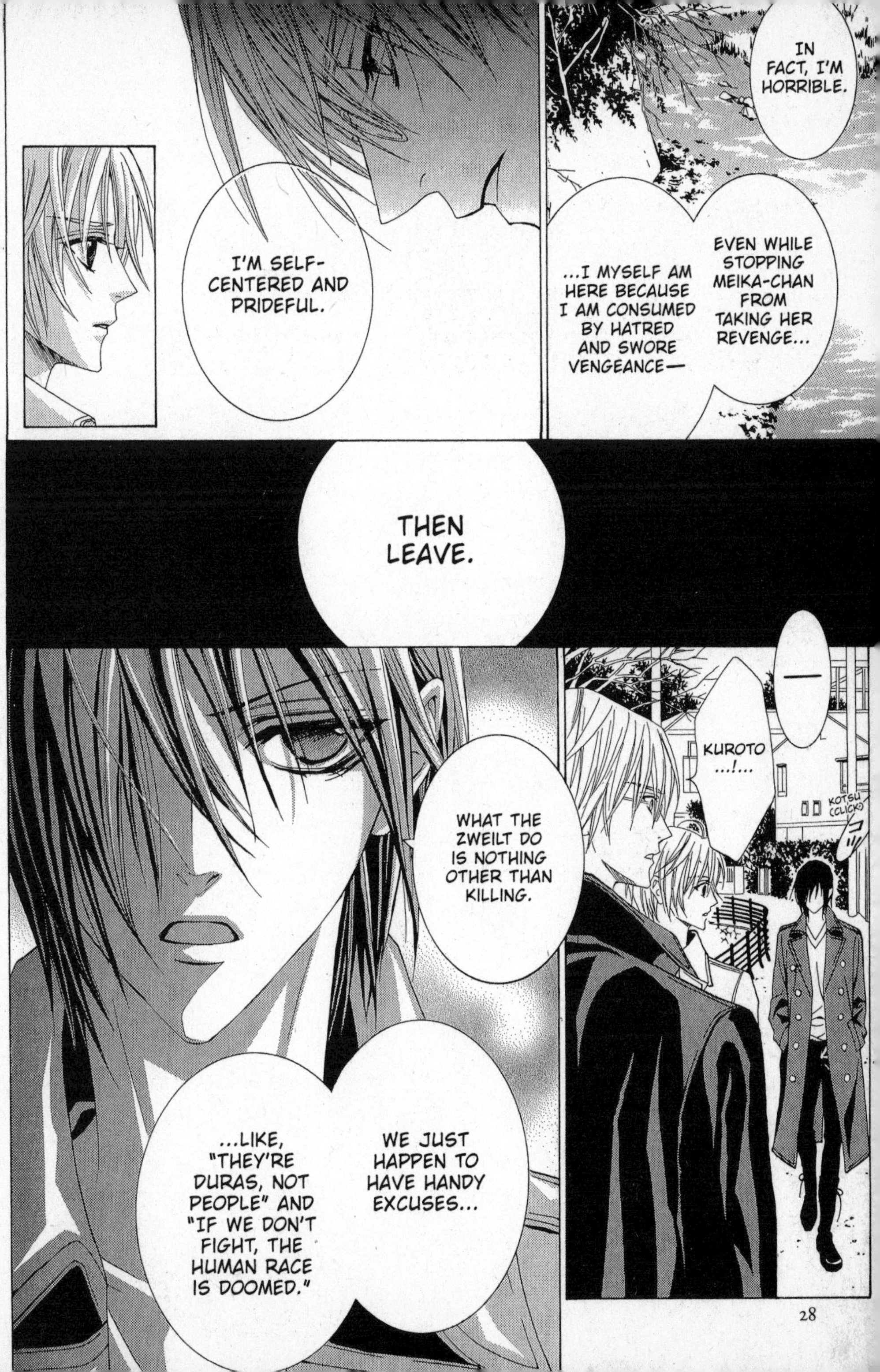
IN FACT, I'M HORRIBLE.
EVEN WHILE STOPPING MEIKA-CHAN FROM TAKING HER REVENGE...
...I MYSELF AM HERE BECAUSE I AM CONSUMED BY HATRED AND SWORE VENGEANCE—
I'M SELF-CENTERED AND PRIDEFUL.
THEN LEAVE.
—
KUROTO ...!...
KOTSU (CLICK)
WHAT THE ZWEILT DO IS NOTHING OTHER THAN KILLING.
WE JUST HAPPEN TO HAVE HANDY EXCUSES...
...LIKE, "THEY'RE DURAS, NOT PEOPLE" AND "IF WE DON'T FIGHT, THE HUMAN RACE IS DOOMED."

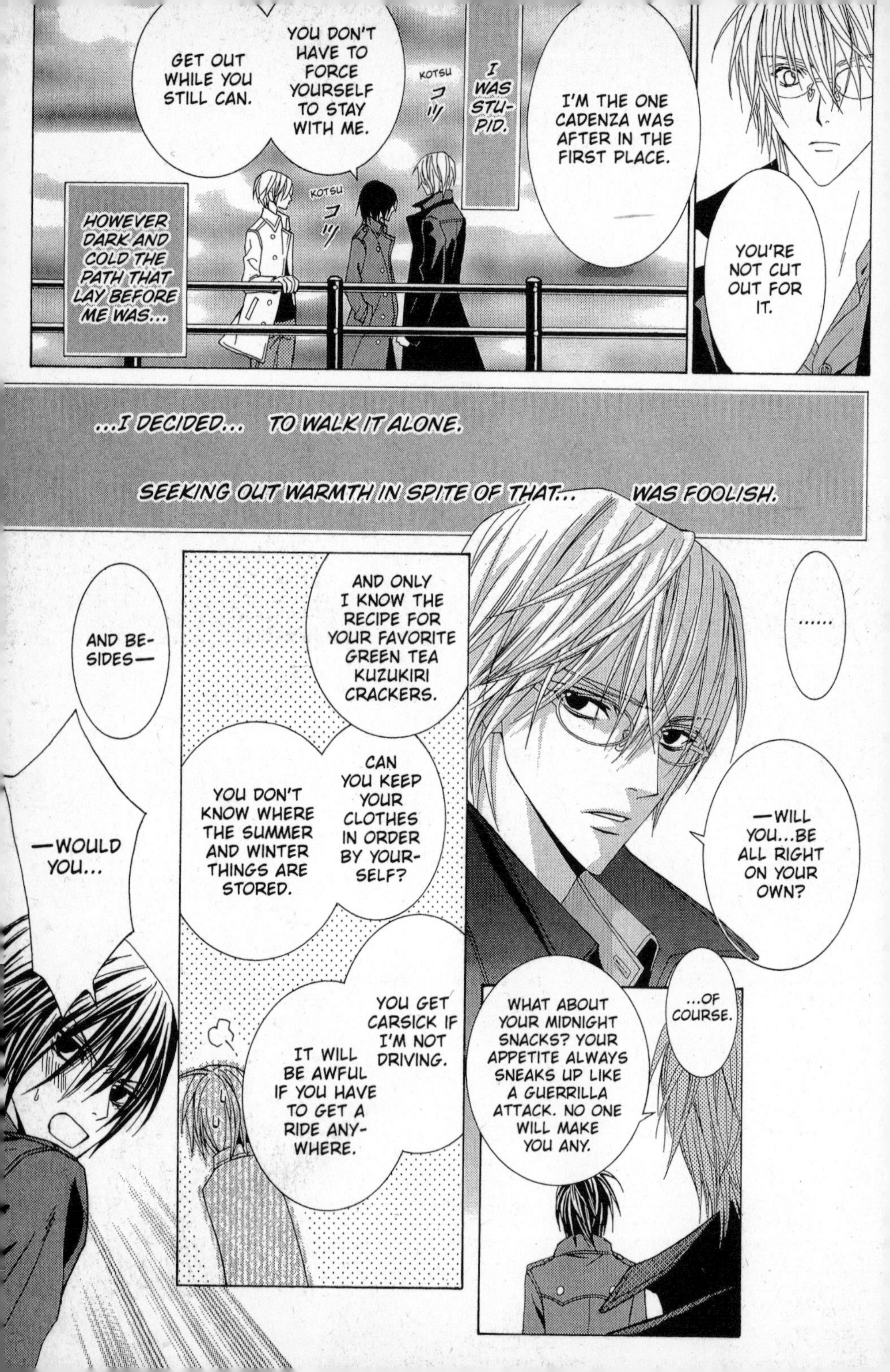
I'M THE ONE CADENZA WAS AFTER IN THE FIRST PLACE.
YOU'RE NOT CUT OUT FOR IT.
I WAS STU-PID.
KOTSU
YOU DON'T HAVE TO FORCE YOURSELF TO STAY WITH ME.
GET OUT WHILE YOU STILL CAN.
KOTSU
HOWEVER DARK AND COLD THE PATH THAT LAY BEFORE ME WAS...
...I DECIDED... TO WALK IT ALONE.
SEEKING OUT WARMTH IN SPITE OF THAT... WAS FOOLISH.
......
—WILL YOU...BE ALL RIGHT ON YOUR OWN?
...OF COURSE.
WHAT ABOUT YOUR MIDNIGHT SNACKS? YOUR APPETITE ALWAYS SNEAKS UP LIKE A GUERRILLA ATTACK. NO ONE WILL MAKE YOU ANY.
AND ONLY I KNOW THE RECIPE FOR YOUR FAVORITE GREEN TEA KUZUKIRI CRACKERS.
CAN YOU KEEP YOUR CLOTHES IN ORDER BY YOUR-SELF?
YOU DON'T KNOW WHERE THE SUMMER AND WINTER THINGS ARE STORED.
YOU GET CARSICK IF I'M NOT DRIVING.
IT WILL BE AWFUL IF YOU HAVE TO GET A RIDE ANY-WHERE.
AND BE-SIDES—
—WOULD YOU...

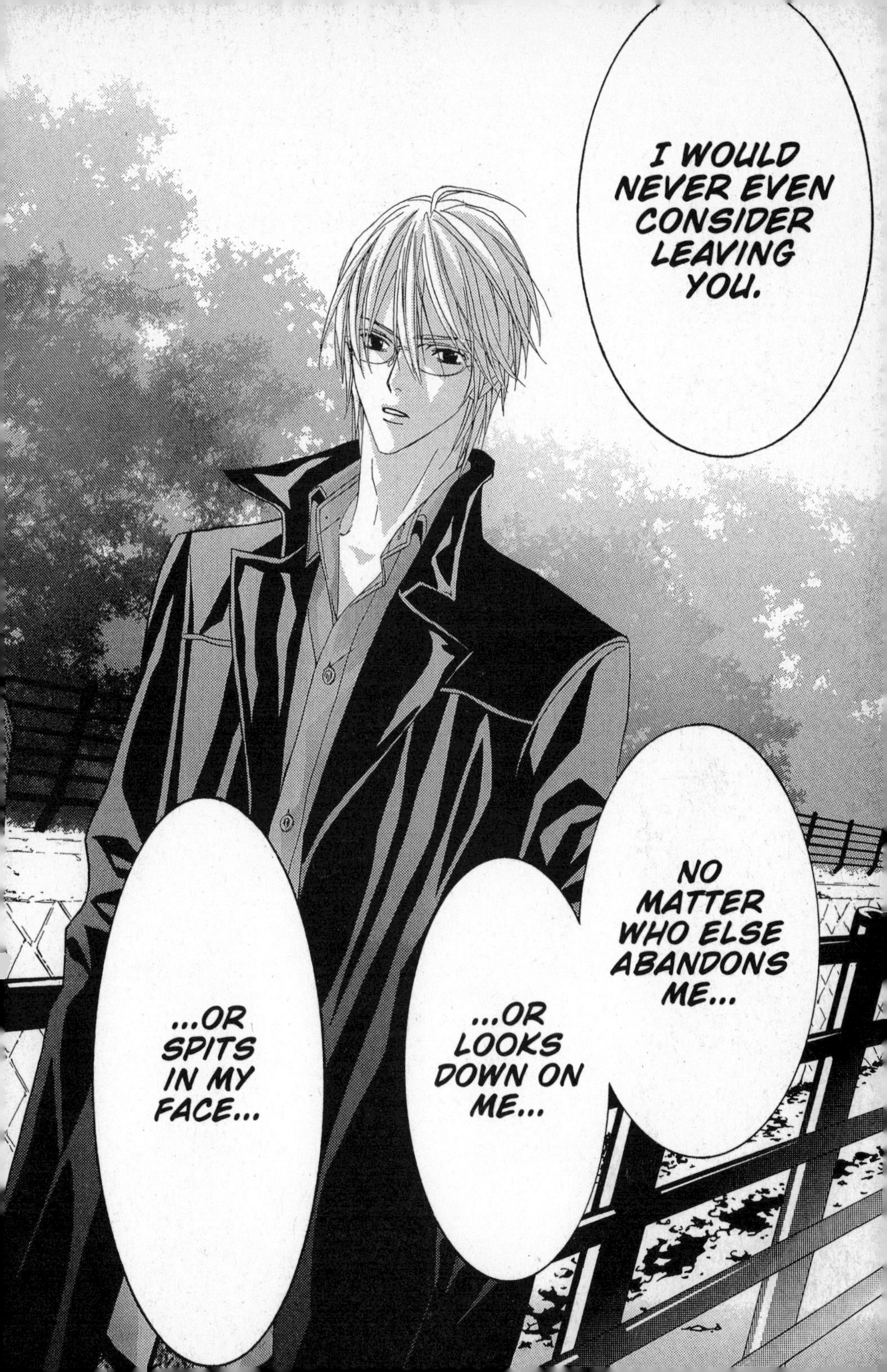
I WOULD NEVER EVEN CONSIDER LEAVING YOU.
NO MATTER WHO ELSE ABANDONS ME...
...OR LOOKS DOWN ON ME...
...OR SPITS IN MY FACE...

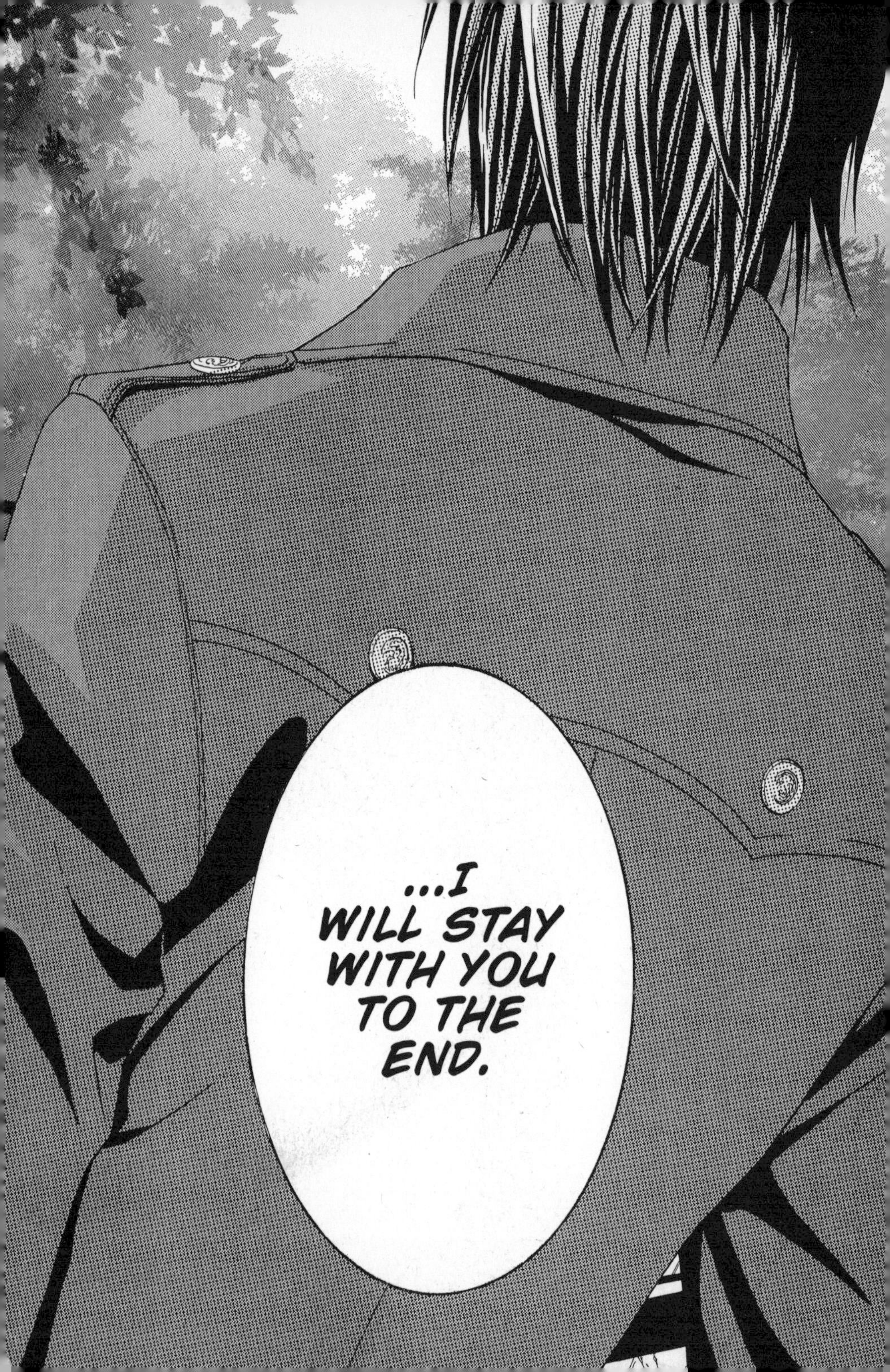
...I WILL STAY WITH YOU TO THE END.

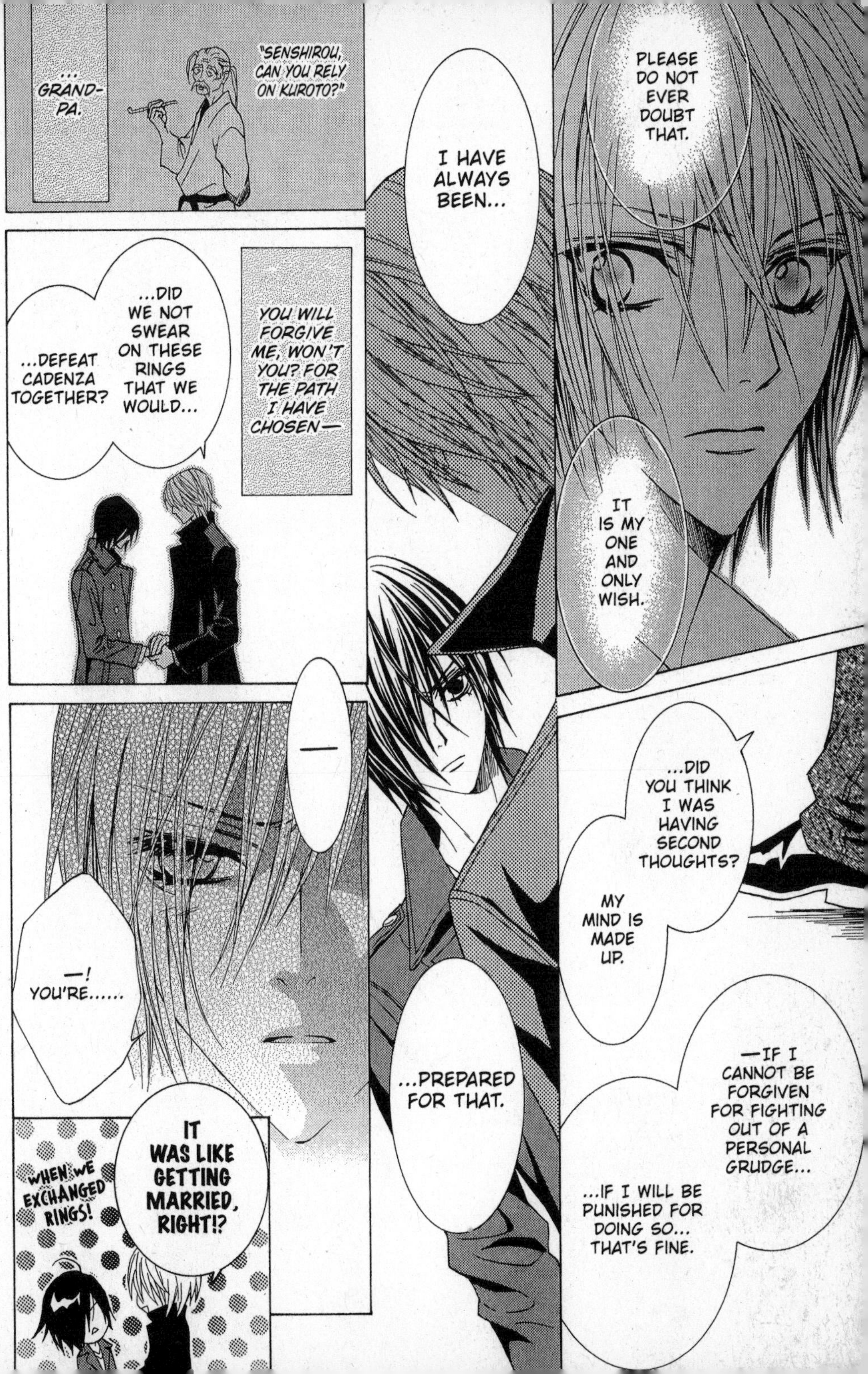
PLEASE DO NOT EVER DOUBT THAT.
IT IS MY ONE AND ONLY WISH.
...DID YOU THINK I WAS HAVING SECOND THOUGHTS?
MY MIND IS MADE UP.
—IF I CANNOT BE FORGIVEN FOR FIGHTING OUT OF A PERSONAL GRUDGE...
...IF I WILL BE PUNISHED FOR DOING SO... THAT'S FINE.
I HAVE ALWAYS BEEN...
...PREPARED FOR THAT.
"SENSHIROU, CAN YOU RELY ON KUROTO?"
...GRAND-PA.
YOU WILL FORGIVE ME, WON'T YOU? FOR THE PATH I HAVE CHOSEN—
...DID WE NOT SWEAR ON THESE RINGS THAT WE WOULD...
...DEFEAT CADENZA TOGETHER?
—
—! YOU'RE......
IT WAS LIKE GETTING MARRIED, RIGHT!?
WHEN WE EXCHANGED RINGS!

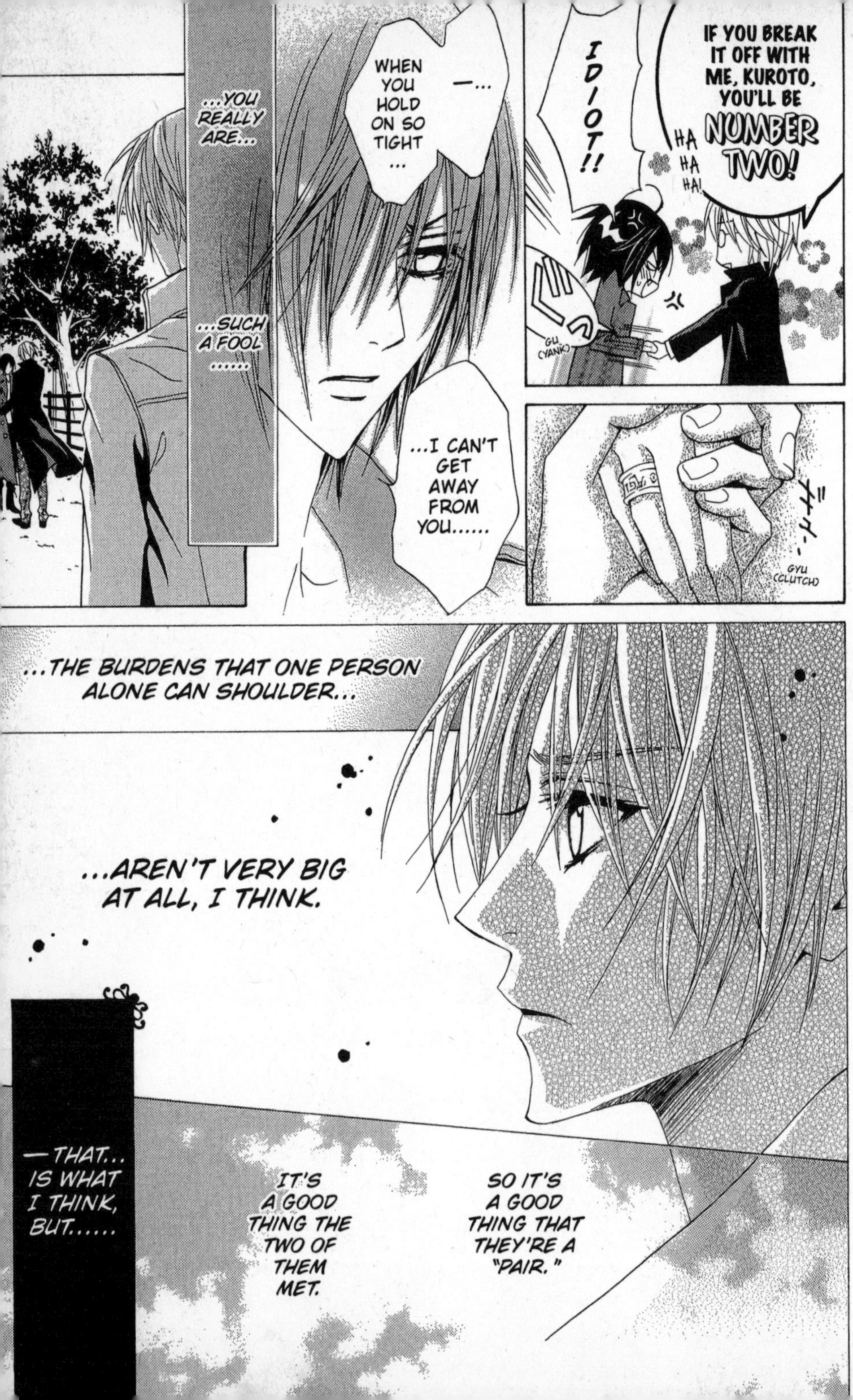
IF YOU BREAK IT OFF WITH ME, KUROTO, YOU'LL BE NUMBER TWO!
HA HA HA!
IDIOT!!
GU (YANK)
GYU (CLUTCH)
—...
WHEN YOU HOLD ON SO TIGHT ...
...YOU REALLY ARE...
...SUCH A FOOL......
...I CAN'T GET AWAY FROM YOU......
...THE BURDENS THAT ONE PERSON ALONE CAN SHOULDER...
...AREN'T VERY BIG AT ALL, I THINK.
SO IT'S A GOOD THING THAT THEY'RE A "PAIR."
IT'S A GOOD THING THE TWO OF THEM MET.
—THAT... IS WHAT I THINK, BUT......

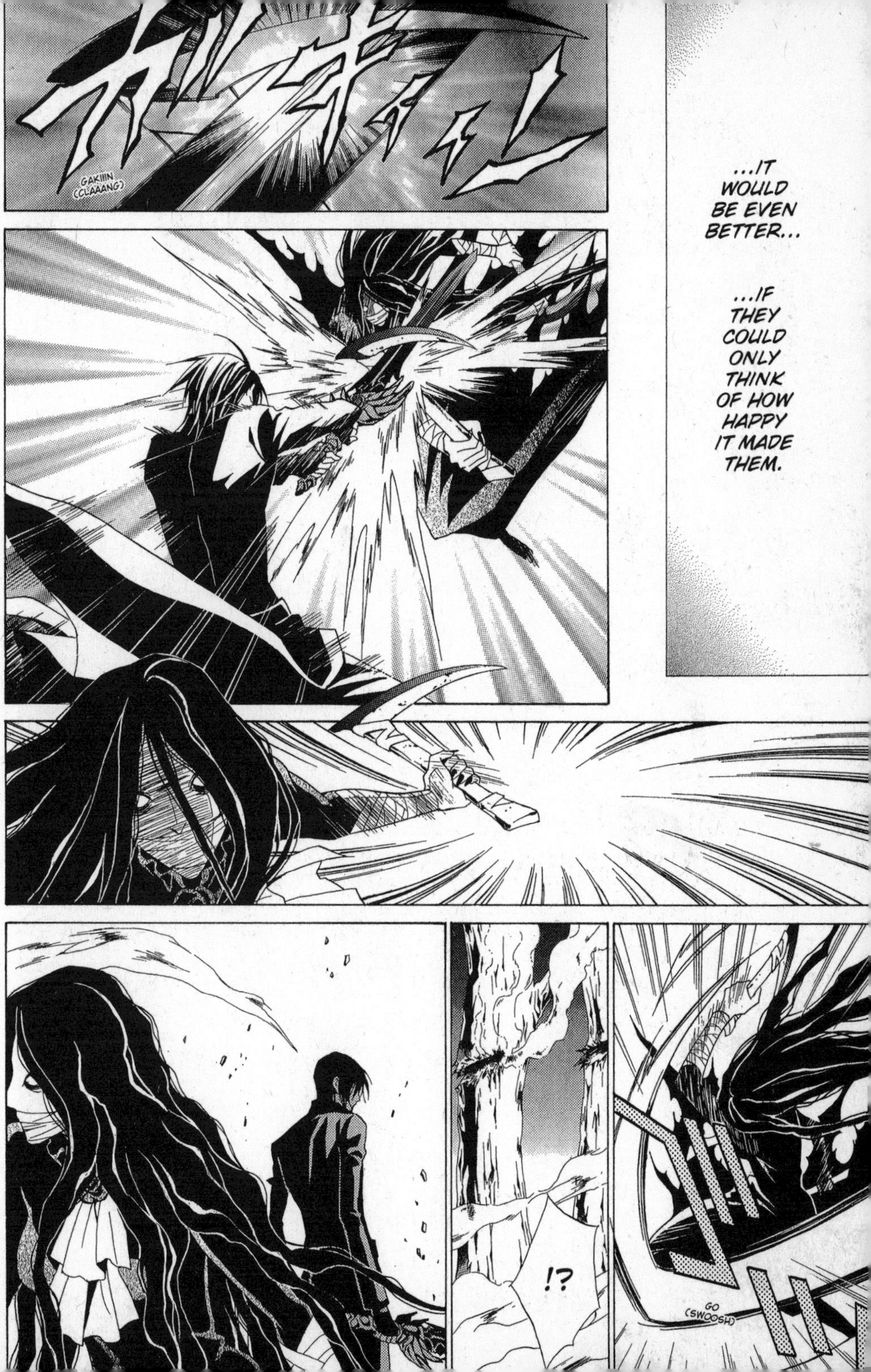
...IT WOULD BE EVEN BETTER...
...IF THEY COULD ONLY THINK OF HOW HAPPY IT MADE THEM.
GAKIIIN (CLAAANG)
GO (SWOOSH)
!?

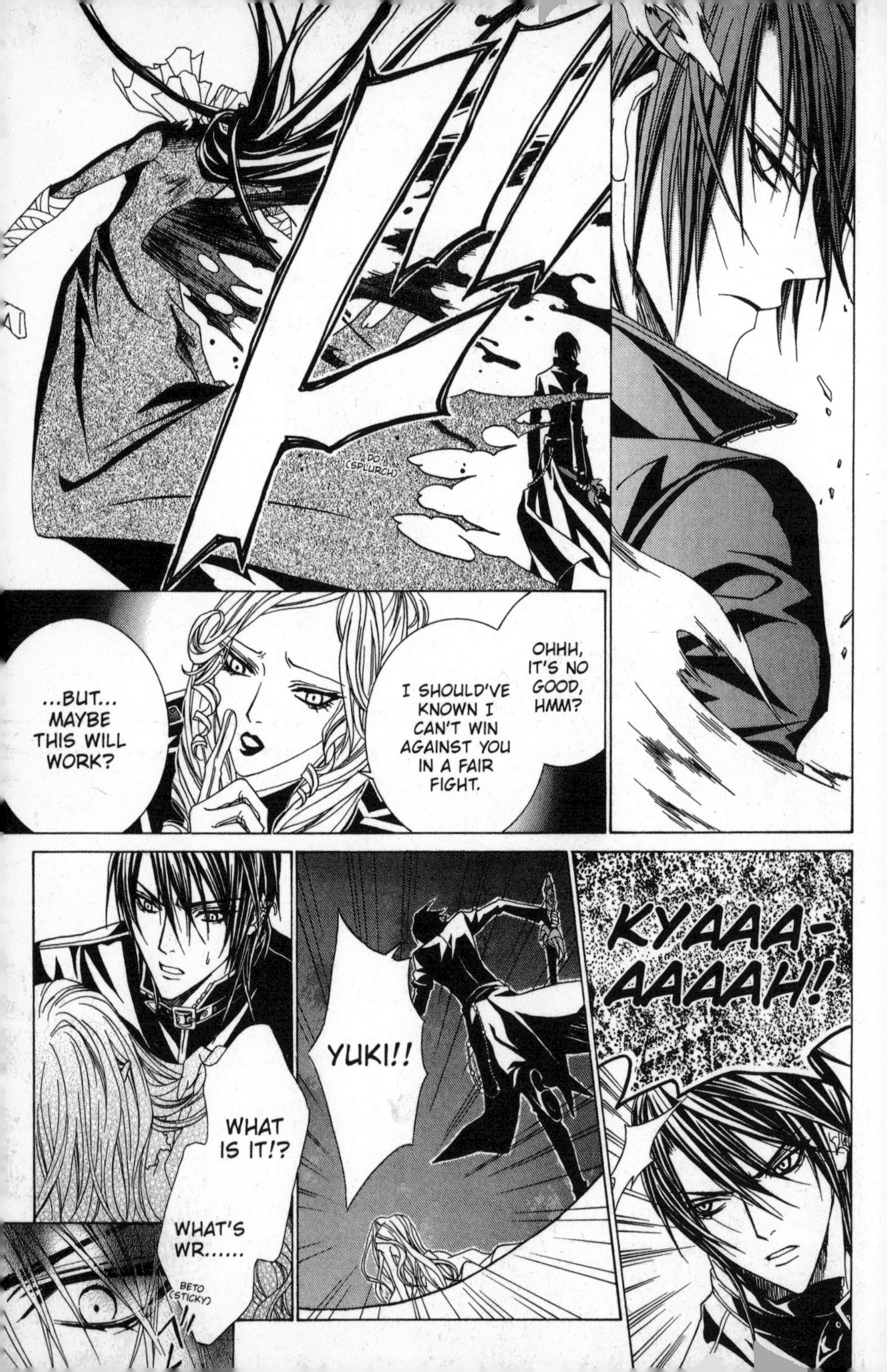
DO! (SPLURCH)
OHHH, IT'S NO GOOD, HMM?
I SHOULD'VE KNOWN I CAN'T WIN AGAINST YOU IN A FAIR FIGHT.
...BUT... MAYBE THIS WILL WORK?
KYAAA-AAAAH!
YUKI!!
WHAT IS IT!?
WHAT'S WR......
BETO (STICKY)

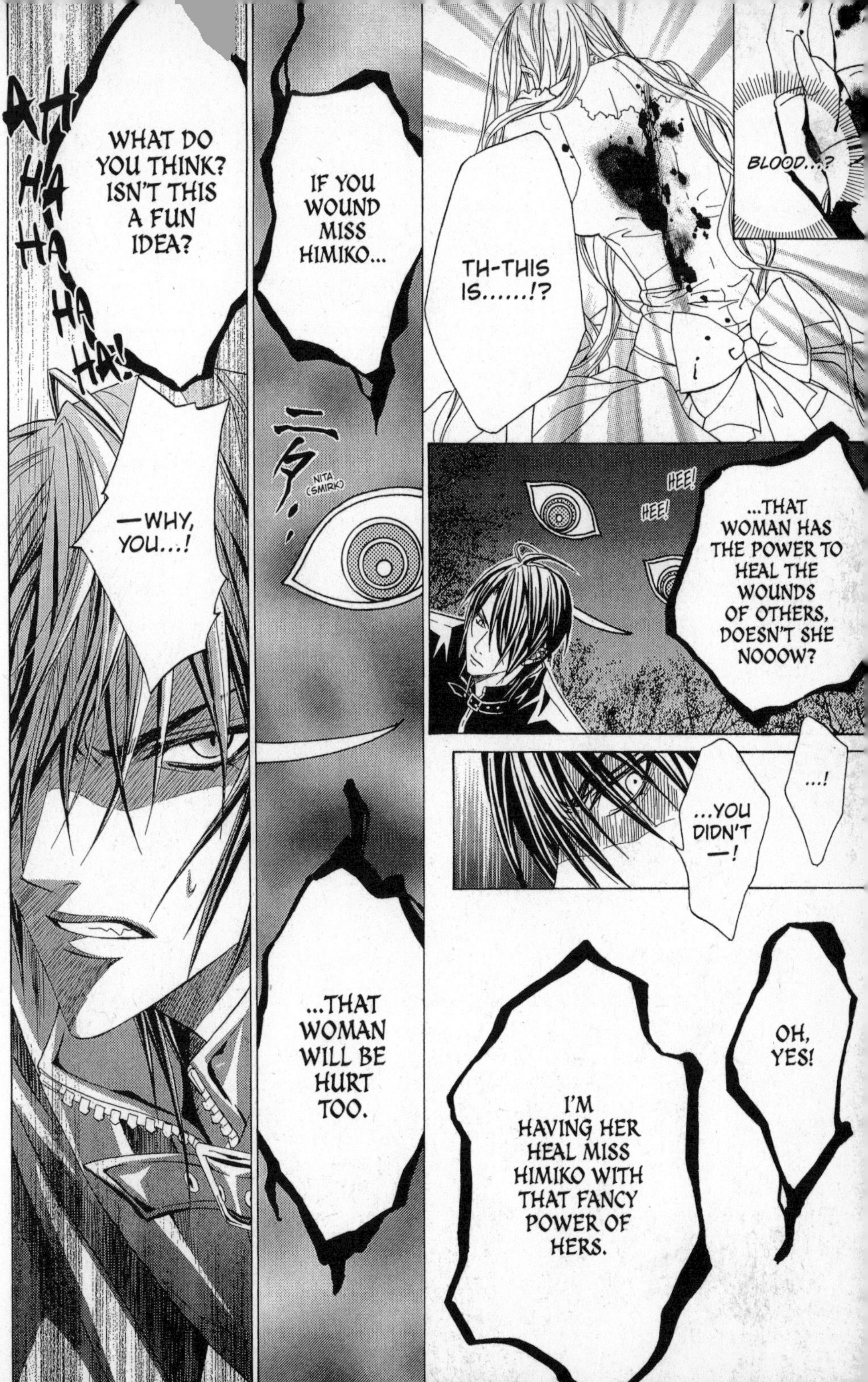
BLOOD...?
TH-THIS IS......!?
HEE! HEE!
...THAT WOMAN HAS THE POWER TO HEAL THE WOUNDS OF OTHERS, DOESN'T SHE NOOOW?
...!
...YOU DIDN'T —!
OH, YES!
I'M HAVING HER HEAL MISS HIMIKO WITH THAT FANCY POWER OF HERS.
IF YOU WOUND MISS HIMIKO...
ニタ
NITA (SMIRK)
...THAT WOMAN WILL BE HURT TOO.
WHAT DO YOU THINK? ISN'T THIS A FUN IDEA?
AH HA HA HA HA HA!
—WHY, YOU...!

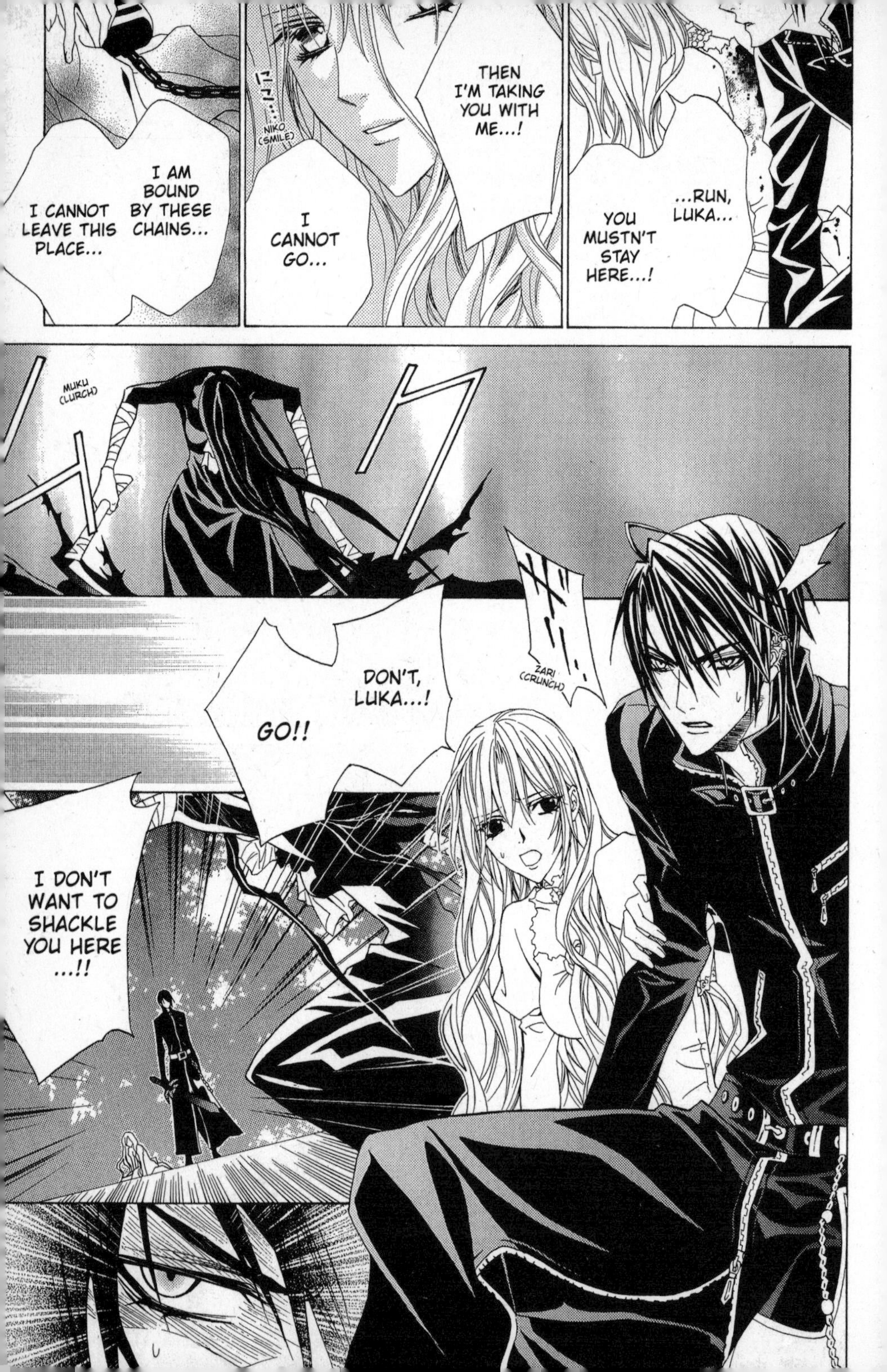
...RUN, LUKA...
YOU MUSTN'T STAY HERE...!
THEN I'M TAKING YOU WITH ME...!
NIKO (SMILE)
I CANNOT GO...
I AM BOUND BY THESE CHAINS...
I CANNOT LEAVE THIS PLACE...
MUKU (LURCH)
ZARI (CRUNCH)
DON'T, LUKA...!
GO!!
I DON'T WANT TO SHACKLE YOU HERE ...!!

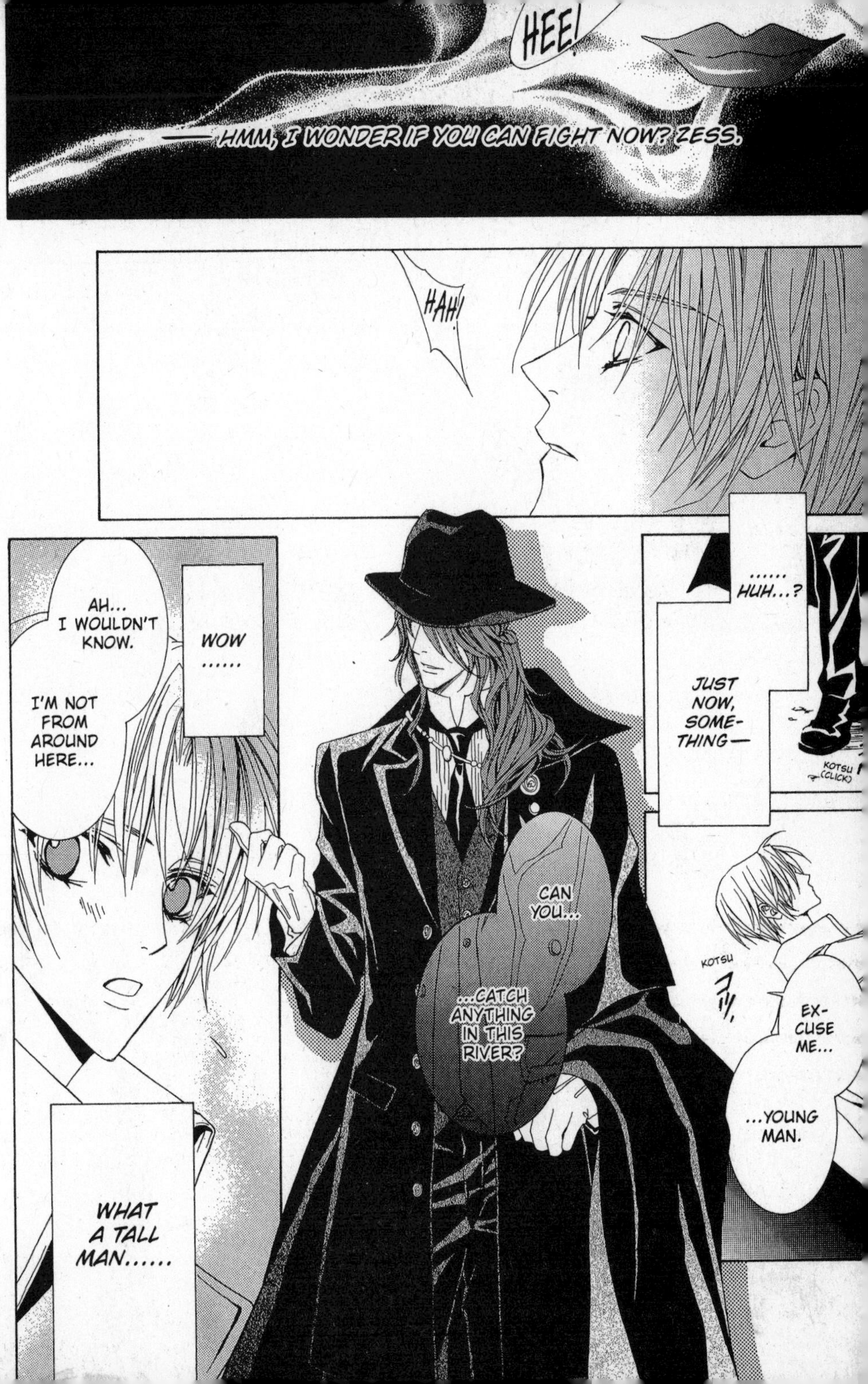
HEE!
——HMM, I WONDER IF YOU CAN FIGHT NOW? ZESS.
HAH!
......HUH...?
JUST NOW, SOME-THING—
KOTSU (CLICK)
KOTSU
EX-CUSE ME...
...YOUNG MAN.
CAN YOU...
...CATCH ANYTHING IN THIS RIVER?
WOW......
AH... I WOULDN'T KNOW.
I'M NOT FROM AROUND HERE...
WHAT A TALL MAN......

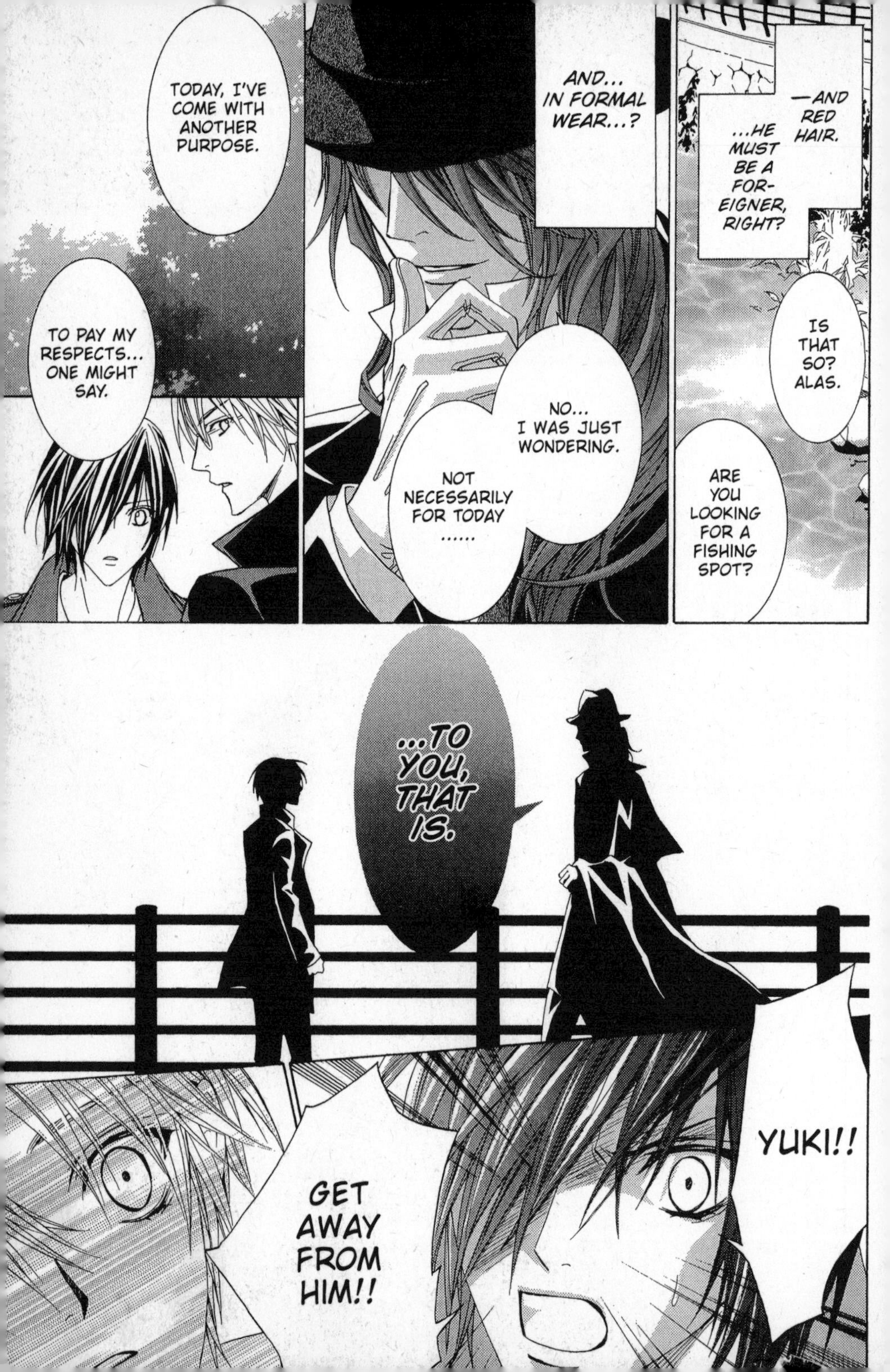
—AND RED HAIR.
...HE MUST BE A FOREIGNER, RIGHT?
IS THAT SO? ALAS.
ARE YOU LOOKING FOR A FISHING SPOT?
AND... IN FORMAL WEAR...?
NO... I WAS JUST WONDERING.
NOT NECESSARILY FOR TODAY ......
TODAY, I'VE COME WITH ANOTHER PURPOSE.
TO PAY MY RESPECTS... ONE MIGHT SAY.
...TO YOU, THAT IS.
YUKI!!
GET AWAY FROM HIM!!

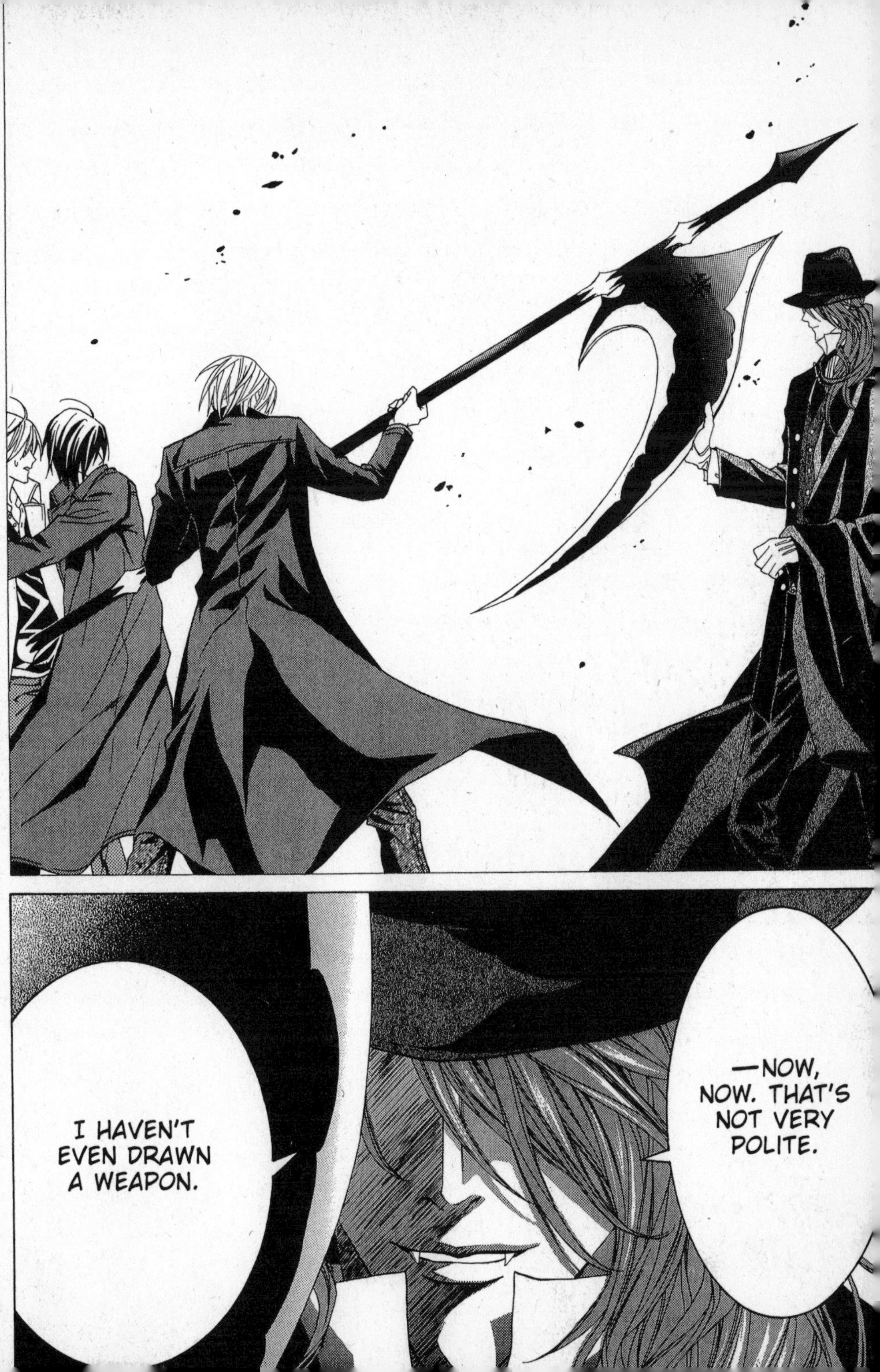
—NOW, NOW. THAT'S NOT VERY POLITE.
I HAVEN'T EVEN DRAWN A WEAPON.

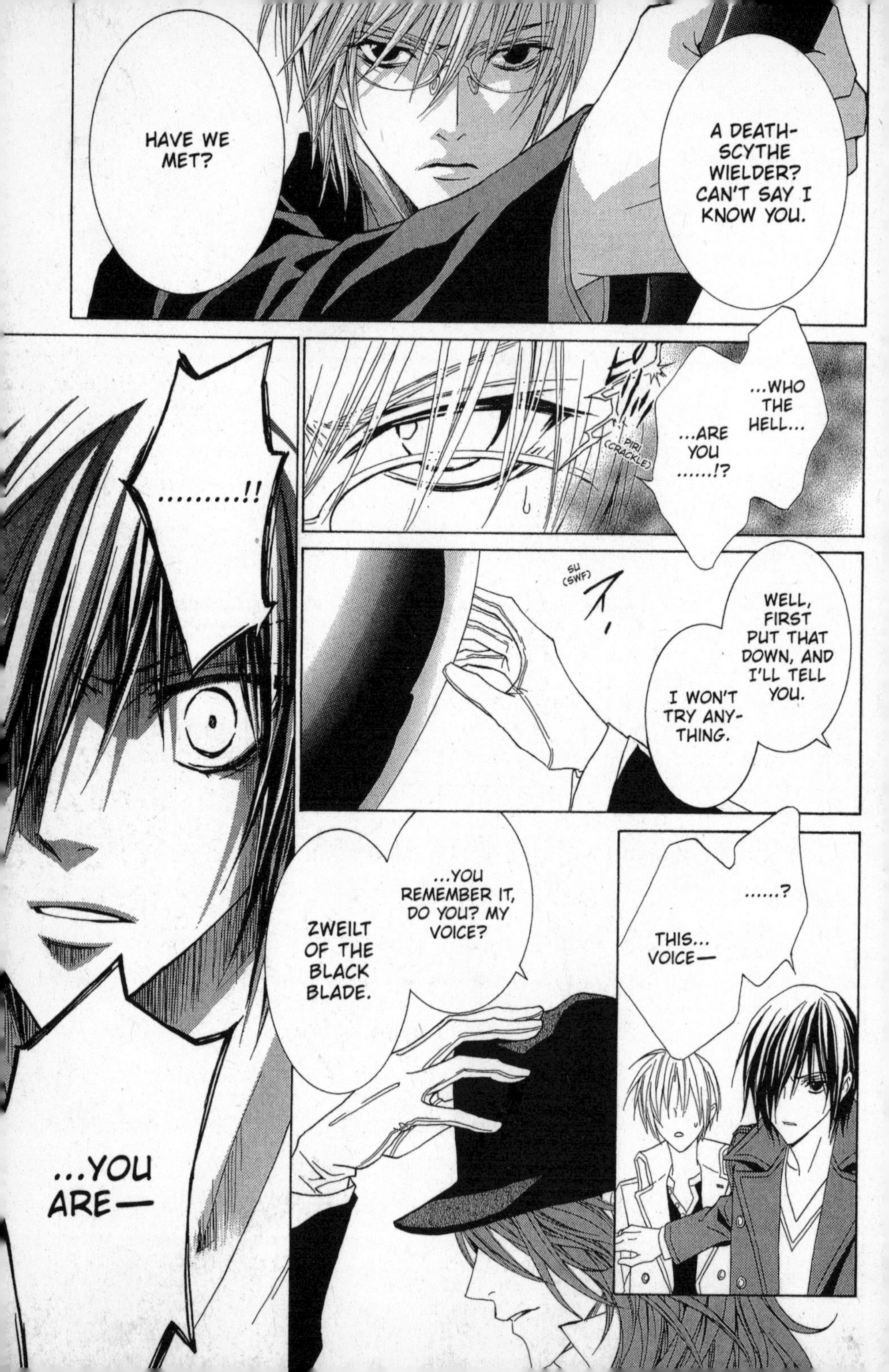
A DEATH-SCYTHE WIELDER? CAN'T SAY I KNOW YOU.
HAVE WE MET?
...WHO THE HELL...
PIRI (CRACKLE)
...ARE YOU ......!?
WELL, FIRST PUT THAT DOWN, AND I'LL TELL YOU.
I WON'T TRY ANYTHING.
SU (SWF)
......?
THIS... VOICE—
...YOU REMEMBER IT, DO YOU? MY VOICE?
ZWEILT OF THE BLACK BLADE.
.........!!
...YOU ARE—

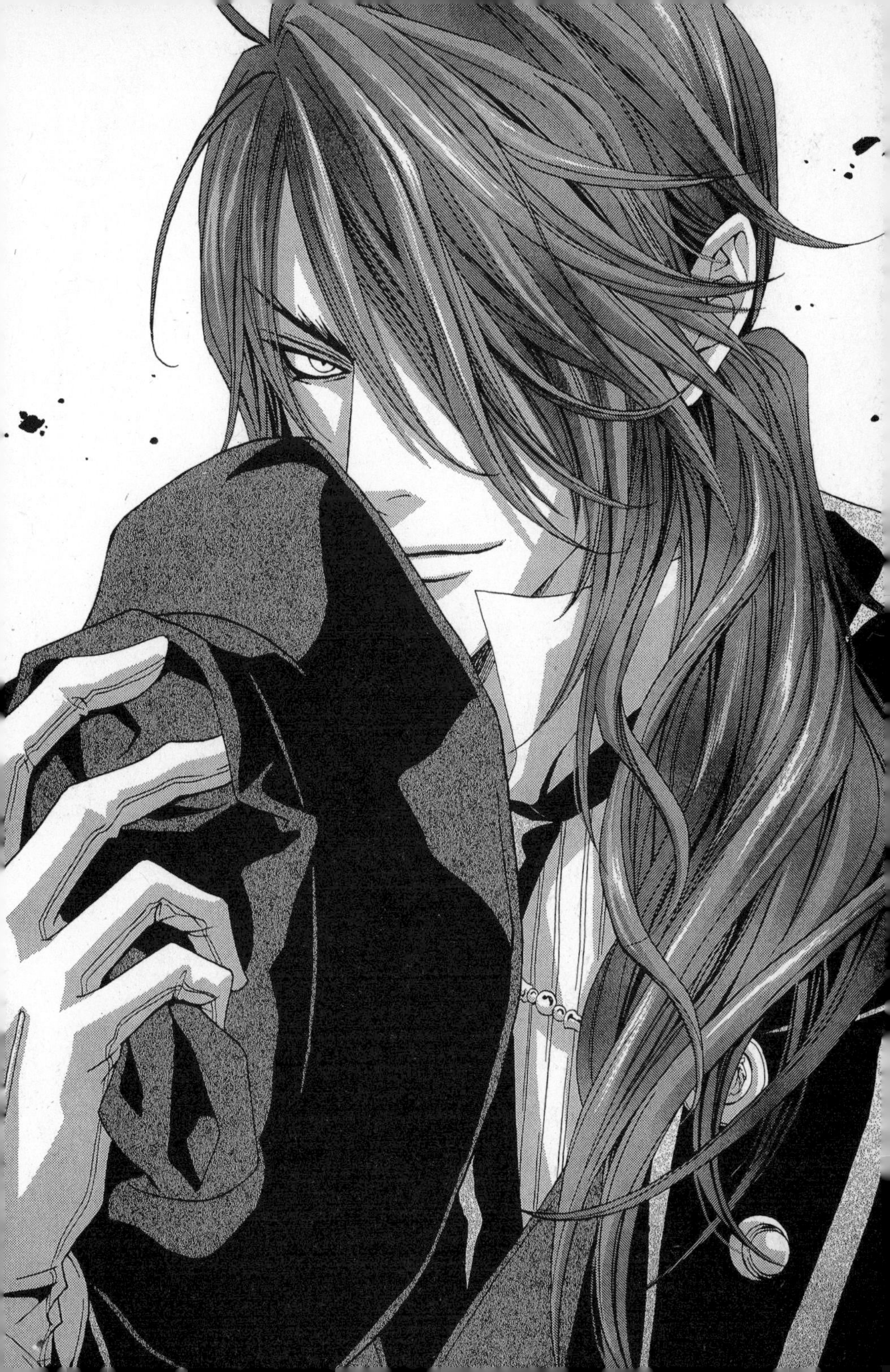

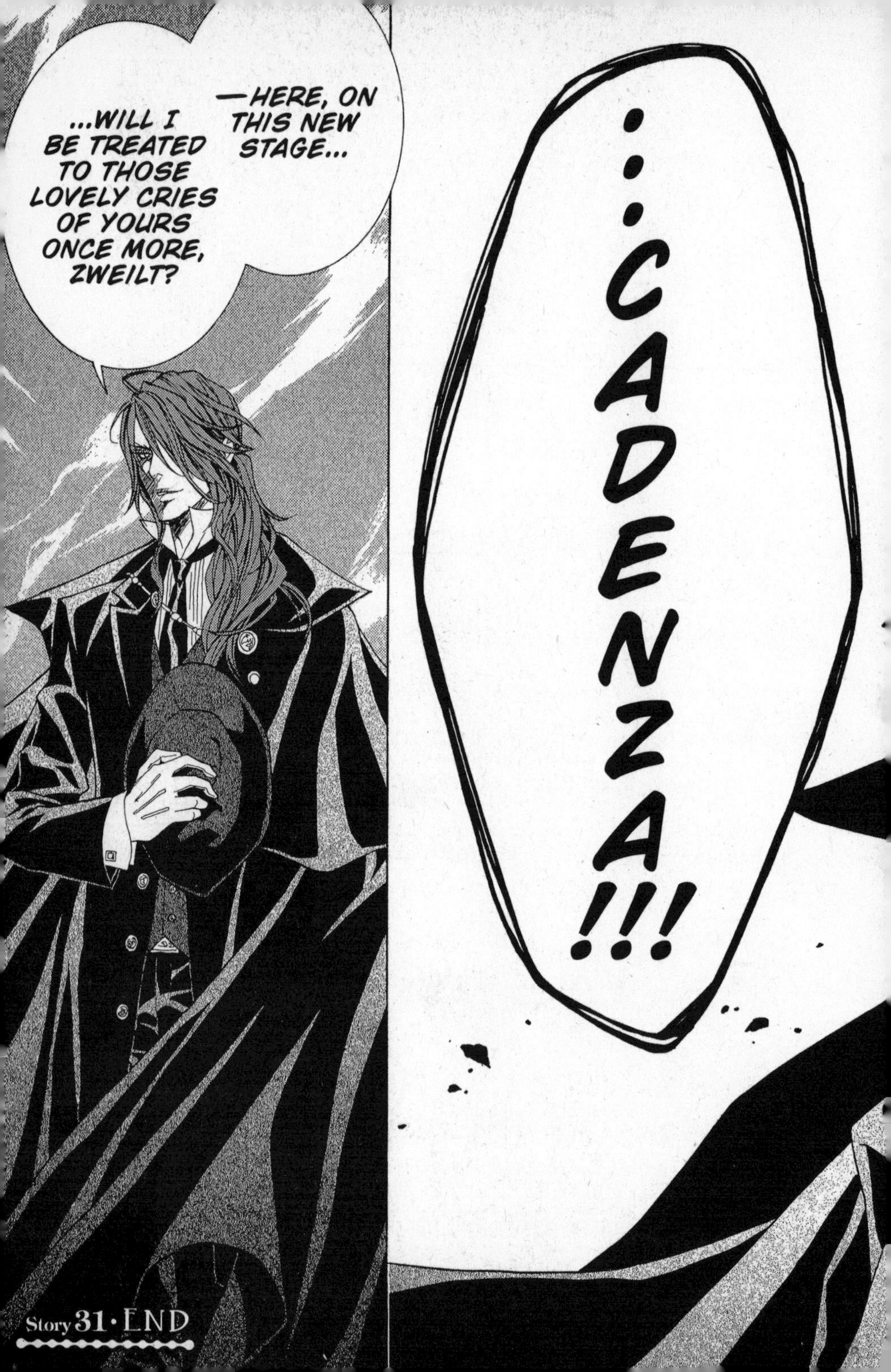
...CADENZA!!!
—HERE, ON THIS NEW STAGE...
...WILL I BE TREATED TO THOSE LOVELY CRIES OF YOURS ONCE MORE, ZWEILT?
Story 31 • END

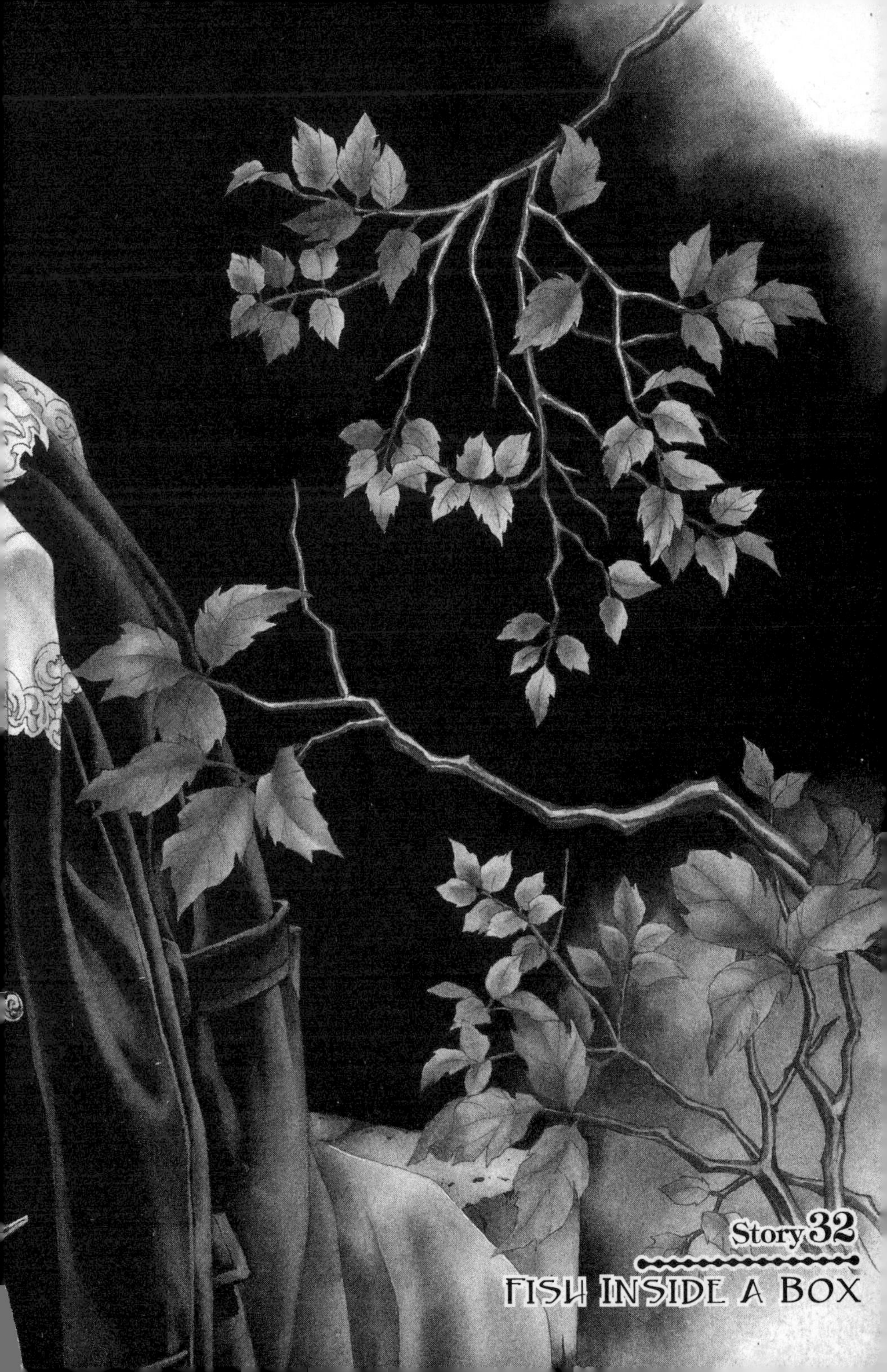
Story 32
FISH INSIDE A BOX

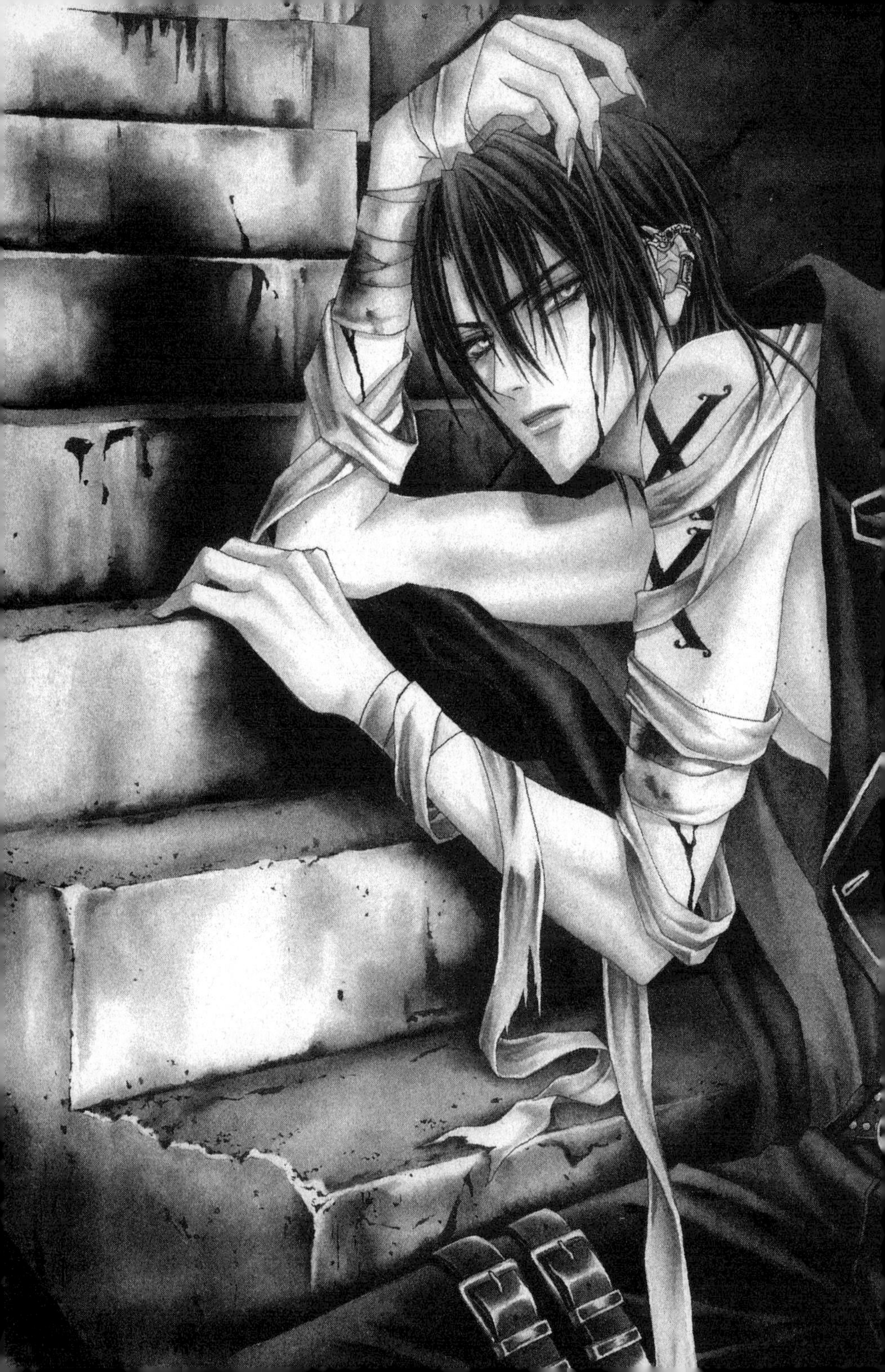

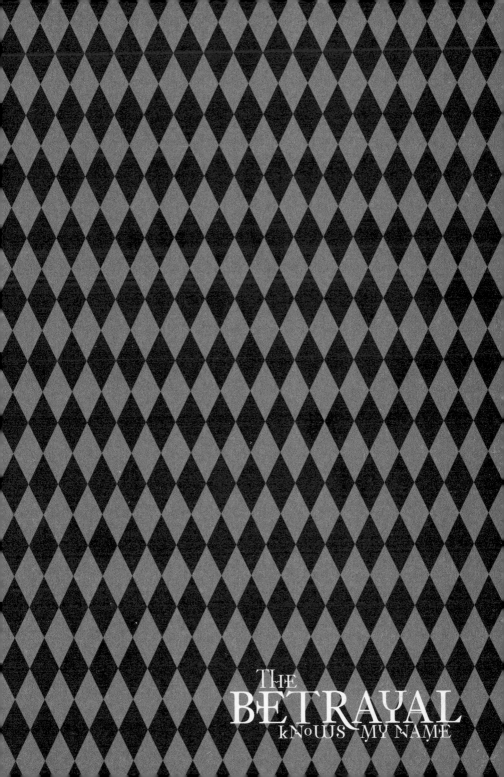

THE
BETRAYAL
kNoWS MY NAME

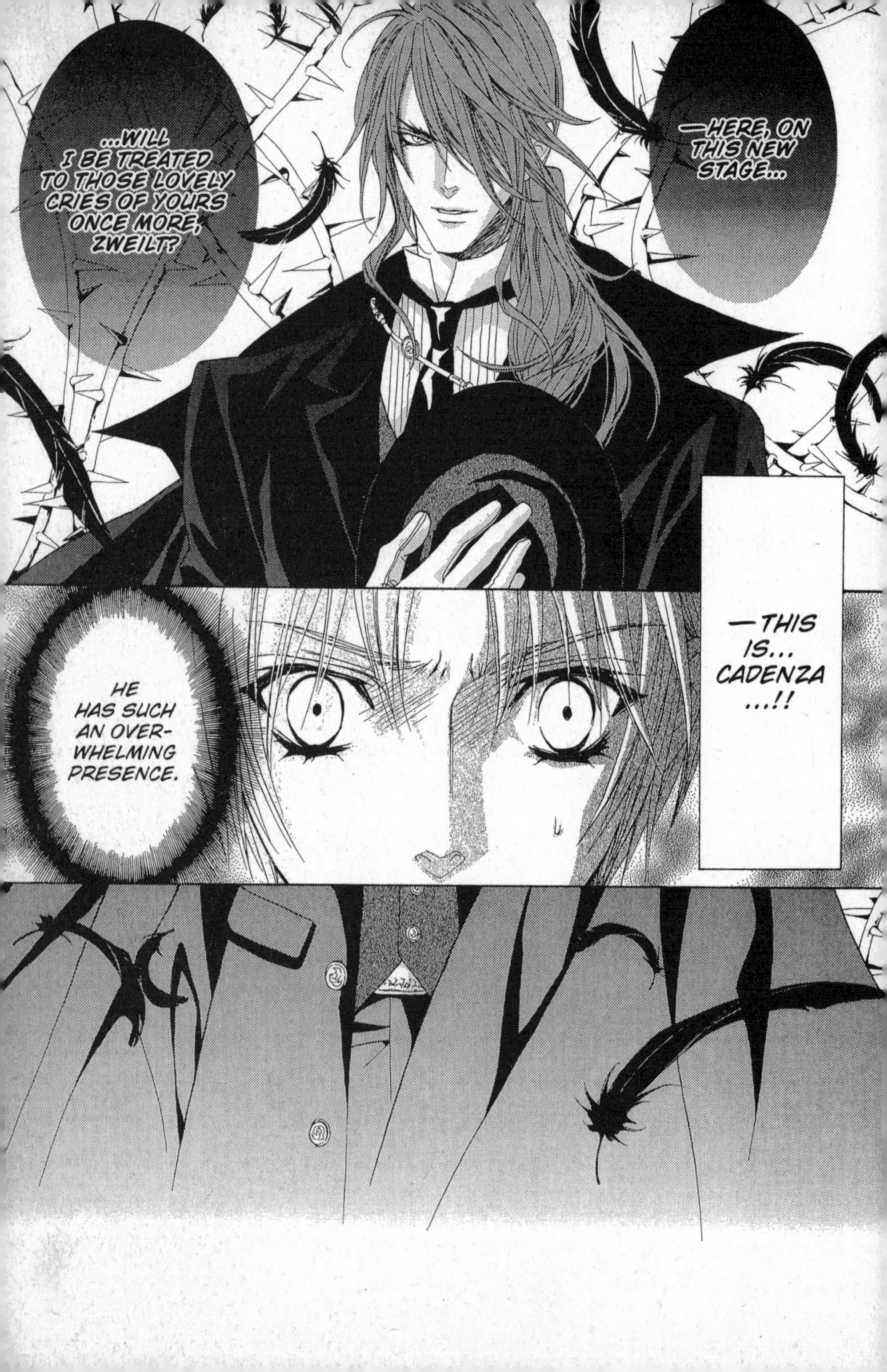
—HERE, ON THIS NEW STAGE...
...WILL I BE TREATED TO THOSE LOVELY CRIES OF YOURS ONCE MORE, ZWEILT?
—THIS IS... CADENZA ...!!
HE HAS SUCH AN OVER-WHELMING PRESENCE.

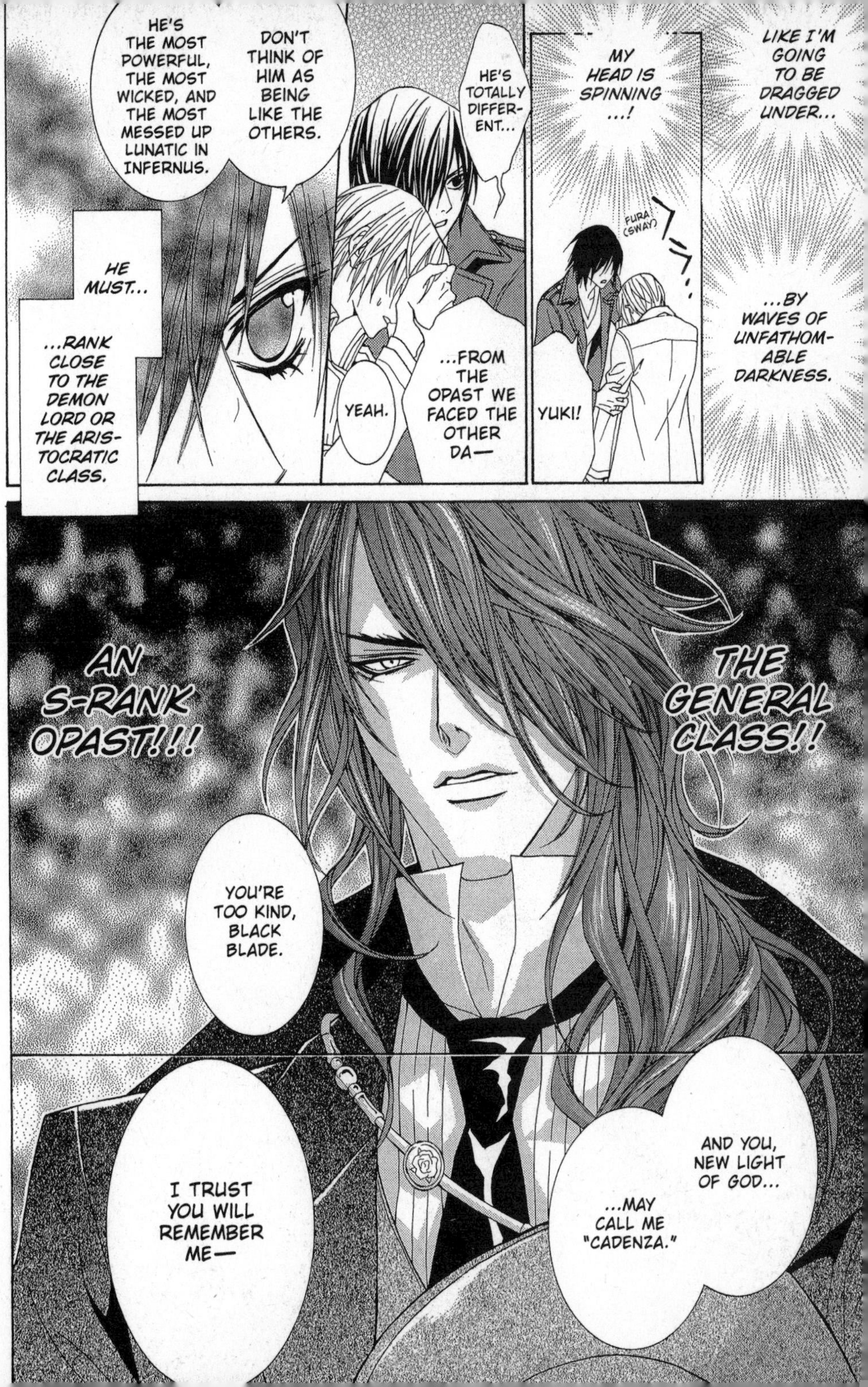
LIKE I'M GOING TO BE DRAGGED UNDER...
MY HEAD IS SPINNING...!
FURA (SWAY)
...BY WAVES OF UNFATHOMABLE DARKNESS.
YUKI!
HE'S TOTALLY DIFFERENT...
DON'T THINK OF HIM AS BEING LIKE THE OTHERS.
HE'S THE MOST POWERFUL, THE MOST WICKED, AND THE MOST MESSED UP LUNATIC IN INFERNUS.
...FROM THE OPAST WE FACED THE OTHER DA—
YEAH.
HE MUST...
...RANK CLOSE TO THE DEMON LORD OR THE ARISTOCRATIC CLASS.
THE GENERAL CLASS!!
AN S-RANK OPAST!!!
YOU'RE TOO KIND, BLACK BLADE.
AND YOU, NEW LIGHT OF GOD...
...MAY CALL ME "CADENZA."
I TRUST YOU WILL REMEMBER ME—

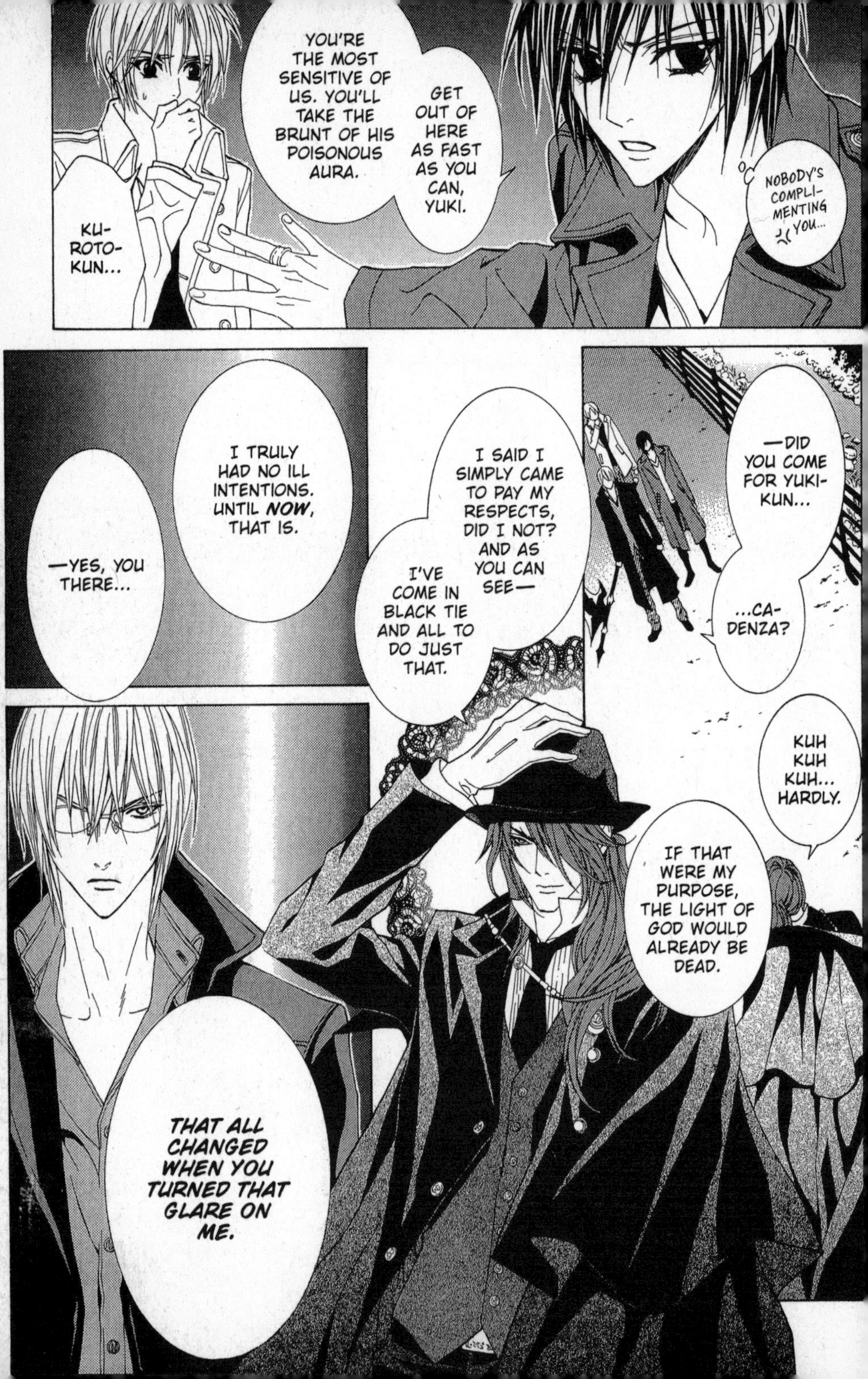
GET OUT OF HERE AS FAST AS YOU CAN, YUKI.
YOU'RE THE MOST SENSITIVE OF US. YOU'LL TAKE THE BRUNT OF HIS POISONOUS AURA.
NOBODY'S COMPLI-MENTING YOU...
KU-ROTO-KUN...
—DID YOU COME FOR YUKI-KUN...
...CA-DENZA?
KUH KUH KUH... HARDLY.
IF THAT WERE MY PURPOSE, THE LIGHT OF GOD WOULD ALREADY BE DEAD.
I SAID I SIMPLY CAME TO PAY MY RESPECTS, DID I NOT? AND AS YOU CAN SEE—
I'VE COME IN BLACK TIE AND ALL TO DO JUST THAT.
I TRULY HAD NO ILL INTENTIONS. UNTIL *NOW*, THAT IS.
—YES, YOU THERE...
THAT ALL CHANGED WHEN YOU TURNED THAT GLARE ON ME.

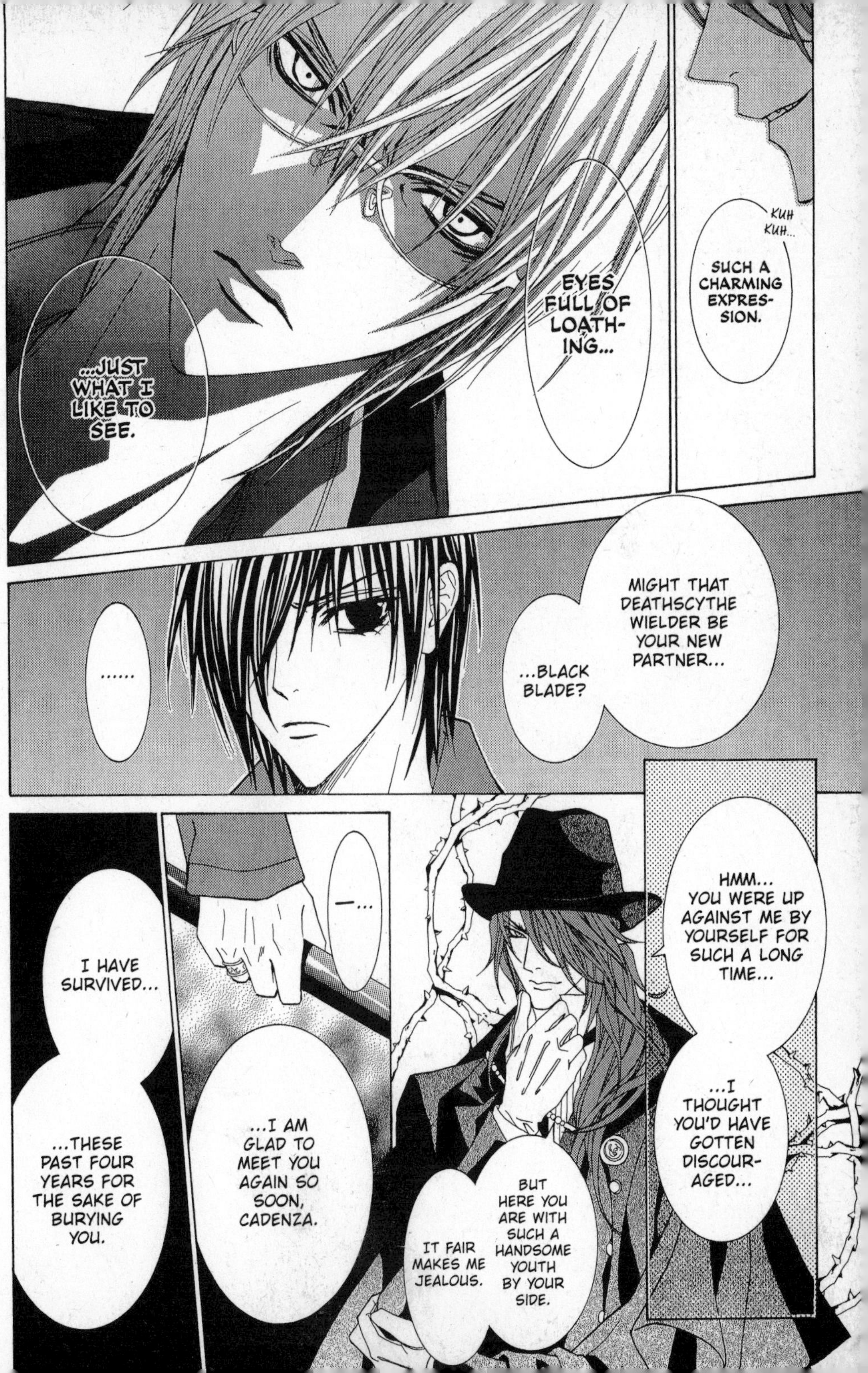
KUH KUH...
SUCH A CHARMING EXPRES-SION.
EYES FULL OF LOATH-ING...
...JUST WHAT I LIKE TO SEE.
MIGHT THAT DEATHSCYTHE WIELDER BE YOUR NEW PARTNER...
...BLACK BLADE?
......
HMM... YOU WERE UP AGAINST ME BY YOURSELF FOR SUCH A LONG TIME...
...I THOUGHT YOU'D HAVE GOTTEN DISCOUR-AGED...
BUT HERE YOU ARE WITH SUCH A HANDSOME YOUTH BY YOUR SIDE.
IT FAIR MAKES ME JEALOUS.
—...
...I AM GLAD TO MEET YOU AGAIN SO SOON, CADENZA.
I HAVE SURVIVED...
...THESE PAST FOUR YEARS FOR THE SAKE OF BURYING YOU.

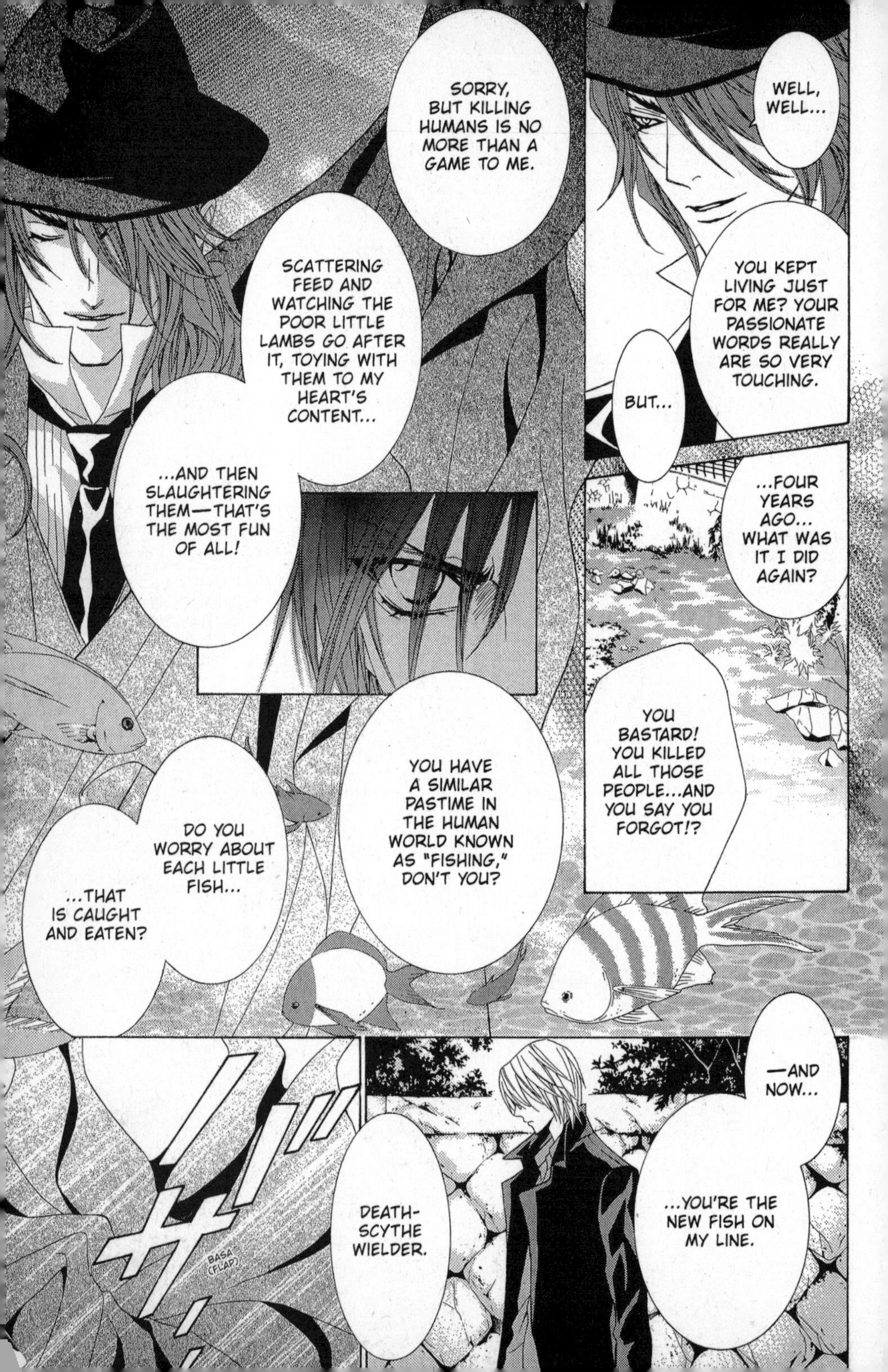
WELL, WELL...
YOU KEPT LIVING JUST FOR ME? YOUR PASSIONATE WORDS REALLY ARE SO VERY TOUCHING.
BUT...
...FOUR YEARS AGO... WHAT WAS IT I DID AGAIN?
YOU BASTARD! YOU KILLED ALL THOSE PEOPLE...AND YOU SAY YOU FORGOT!?
SORRY, BUT KILLING HUMANS IS NO MORE THAN A GAME TO ME.
SCATTERING FEED AND WATCHING THE POOR LITTLE LAMBS GO AFTER IT, TOYING WITH THEM TO MY HEART'S CONTENT...
...AND THEN SLAUGHTERING THEM—THAT'S THE MOST FUN OF ALL!
YOU HAVE A SIMILAR PASTIME IN THE HUMAN WORLD KNOWN AS "FISHING," DON'T YOU?
DO YOU WORRY ABOUT EACH LITTLE FISH...
...THAT IS CAUGHT AND EATEN?
—AND NOW...
...YOU'RE THE NEW FISH ON MY LINE.
DEATH-SCYTHE WIELDER.
BASA (FLAP)

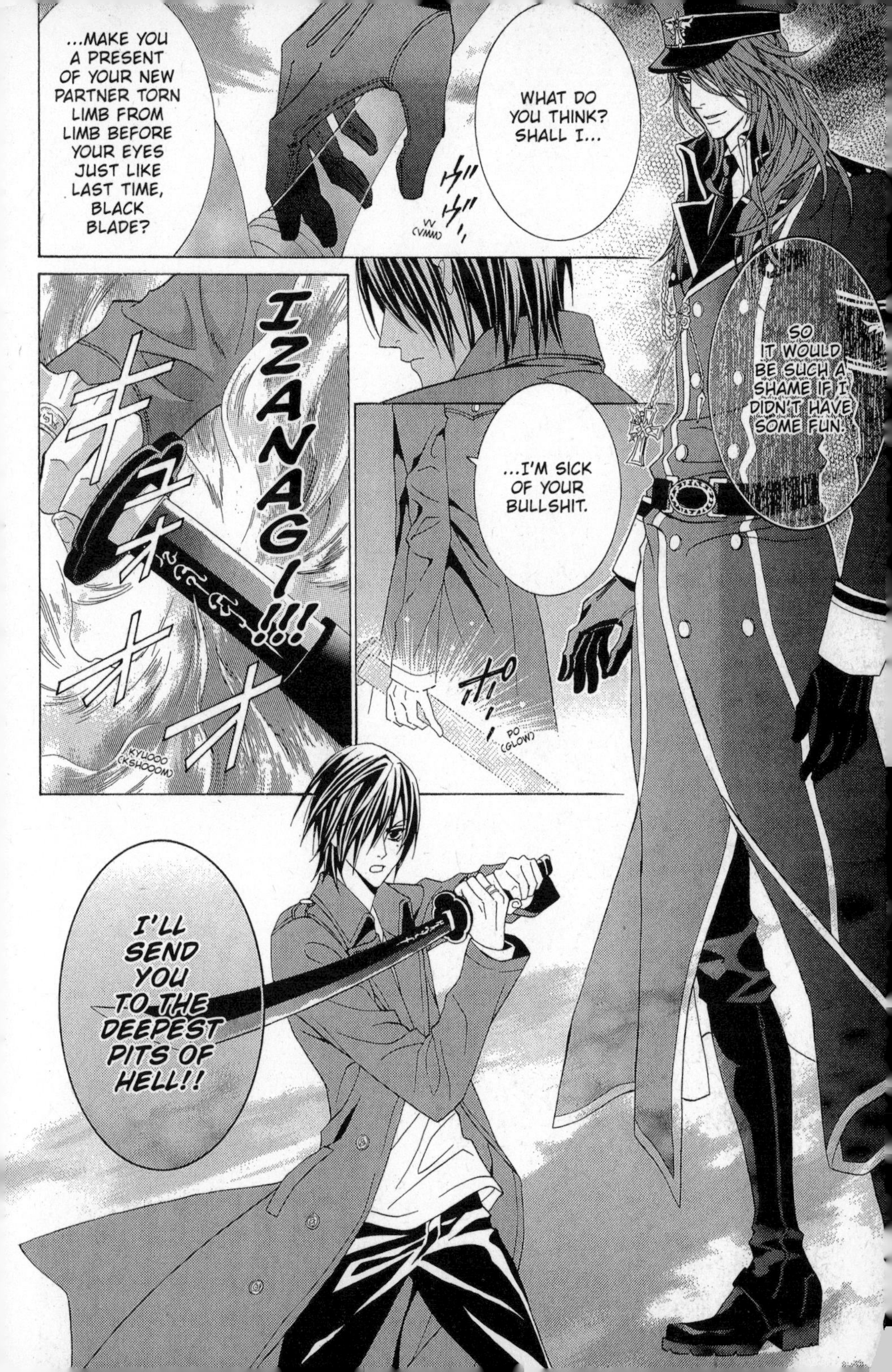
WHAT DO YOU THINK? SHALL I...
VV (VMM)
...MAKE YOU A PRESENT OF YOUR NEW PARTNER TORN LIMB FROM LIMB BEFORE YOUR EYES JUST LIKE LAST TIME, BLACK BLADE?
SO IT WOULD BE SUCH A SHAME IF I DIDN'T HAVE SOME FUN.
...I'M SICK OF YOUR BULLSHIT.
PO (GLOW)
IZANAGI!!!
KYUOOO (KSHOOOM)
I'LL SEND YOU TO THE DEEPEST PITS OF HELL!!

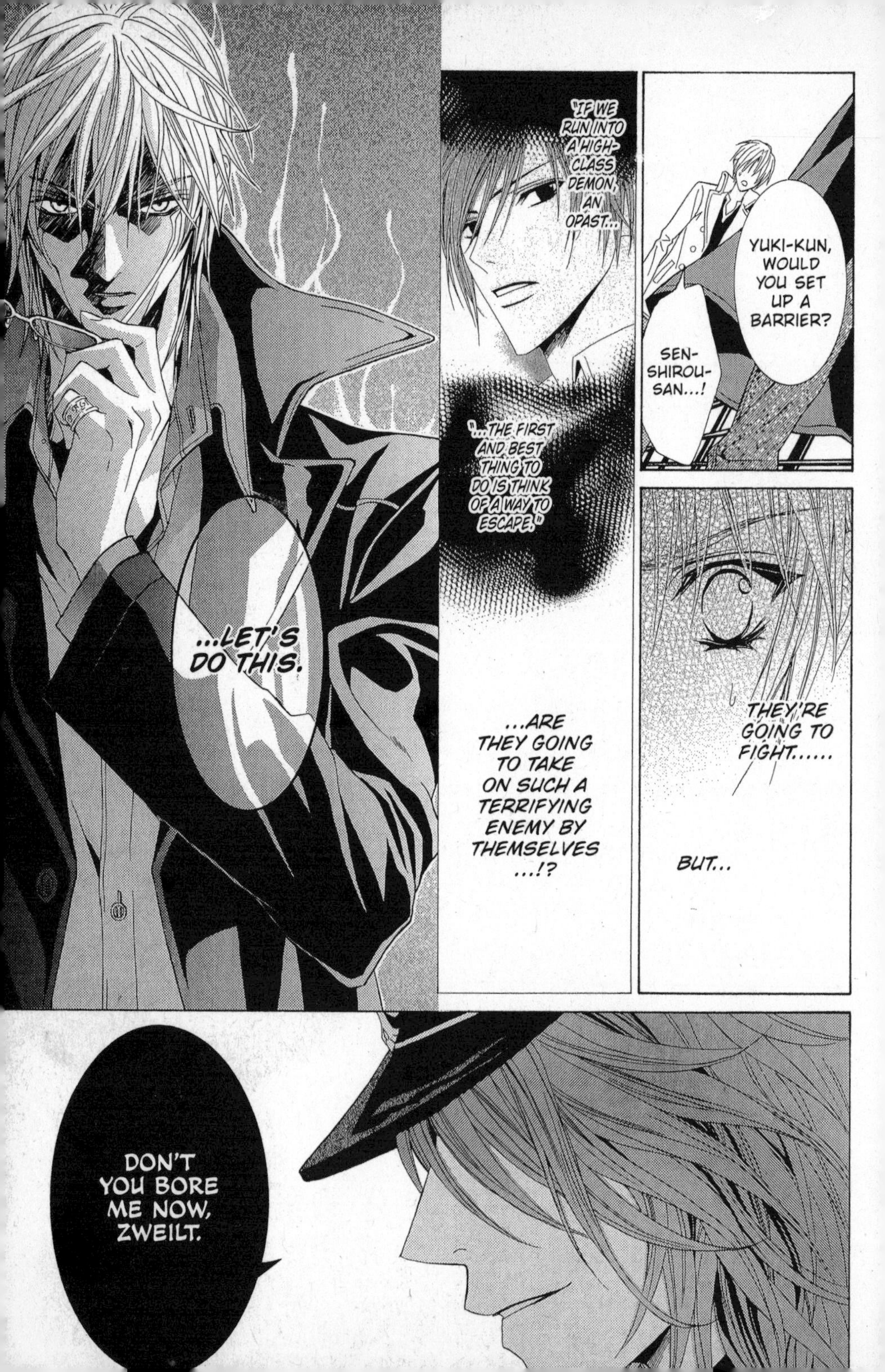
YUKI-KUN, WOULD YOU SET UP A BARRIER?
SEN-SHIROU-SAN...!
THEY'RE GOING TO FIGHT......
BUT...
"IF WE RUN INTO A HIGH-CLASS DEMON, AN OPAST...
"...THE FIRST AND BEST THING TO DO IS THINK OF A WAY TO ESCAPE."
...ARE THEY GOING TO TAKE ON SUCH A TERRIFYING ENEMY BY THEMSELVES ...!?
...LET'S DO THIS.
DON'T YOU BORE ME NOW, ZWEILT.

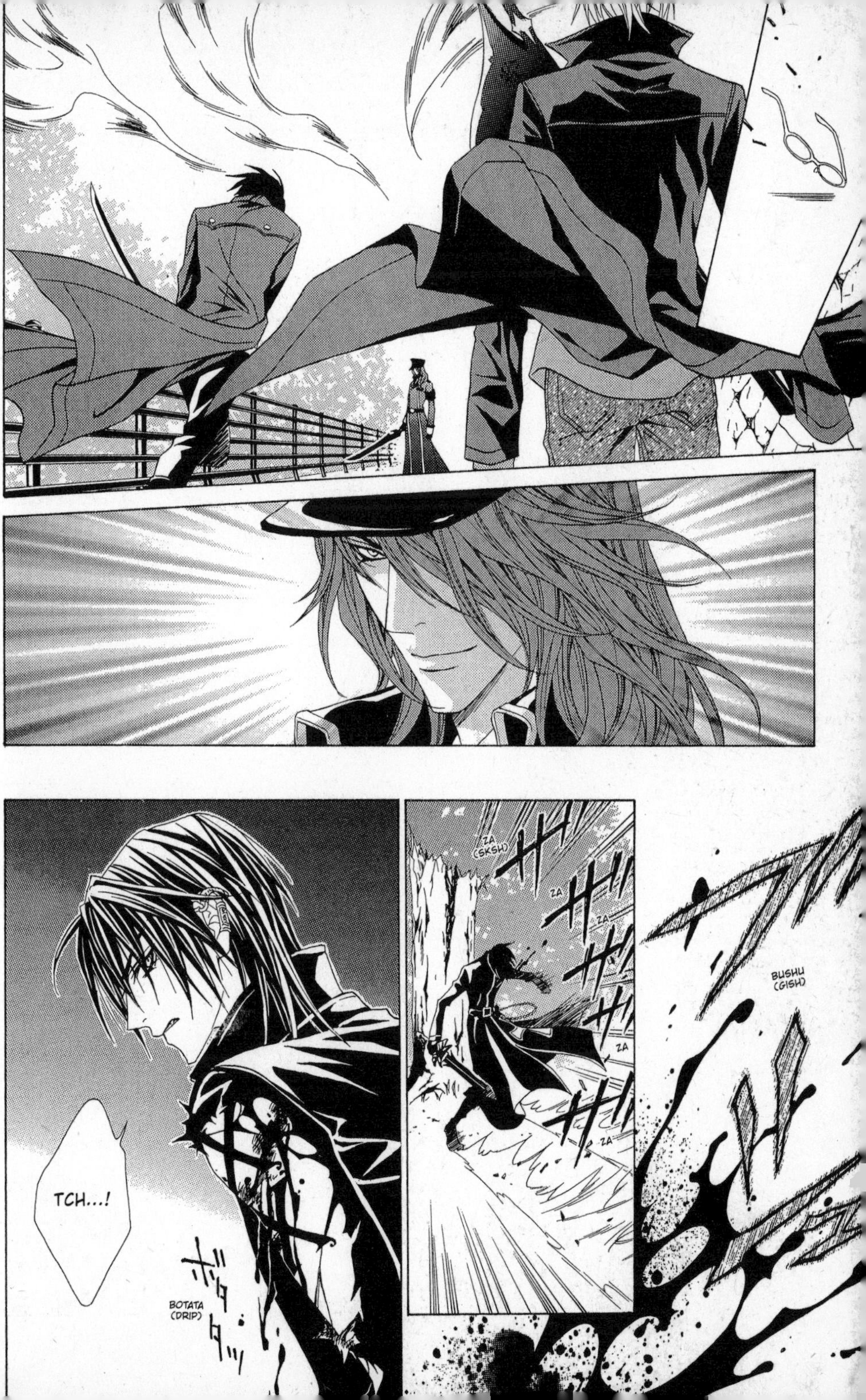
ZA (SKSH)
ZA
ZA
BUSHU (GISH)
ZA
ZA
TCH...!
BOTATA (DRIP)

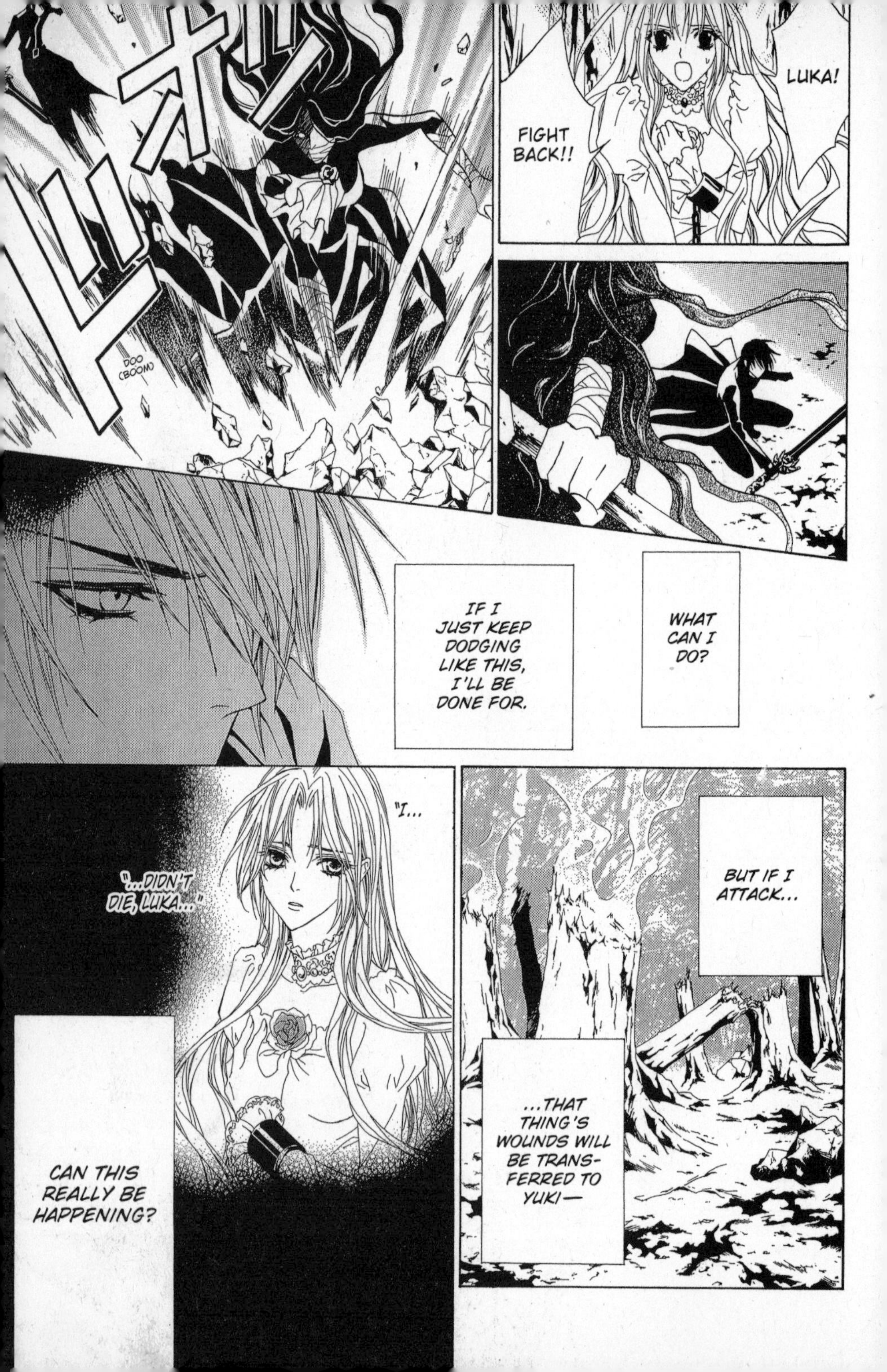
LUKA!
FIGHT BACK!!
DOO (BOOM)
WHAT CAN I DO?
IF I JUST KEEP DODGING LIKE THIS, I'LL BE DONE FOR.
BUT IF I ATTACK...
...THAT THING'S WOUNDS WILL BE TRANS-FERRED TO YUKI—
"I...
"...DIDN'T DIE, LUKA..."
CAN THIS REALLY BE HAPPENING?

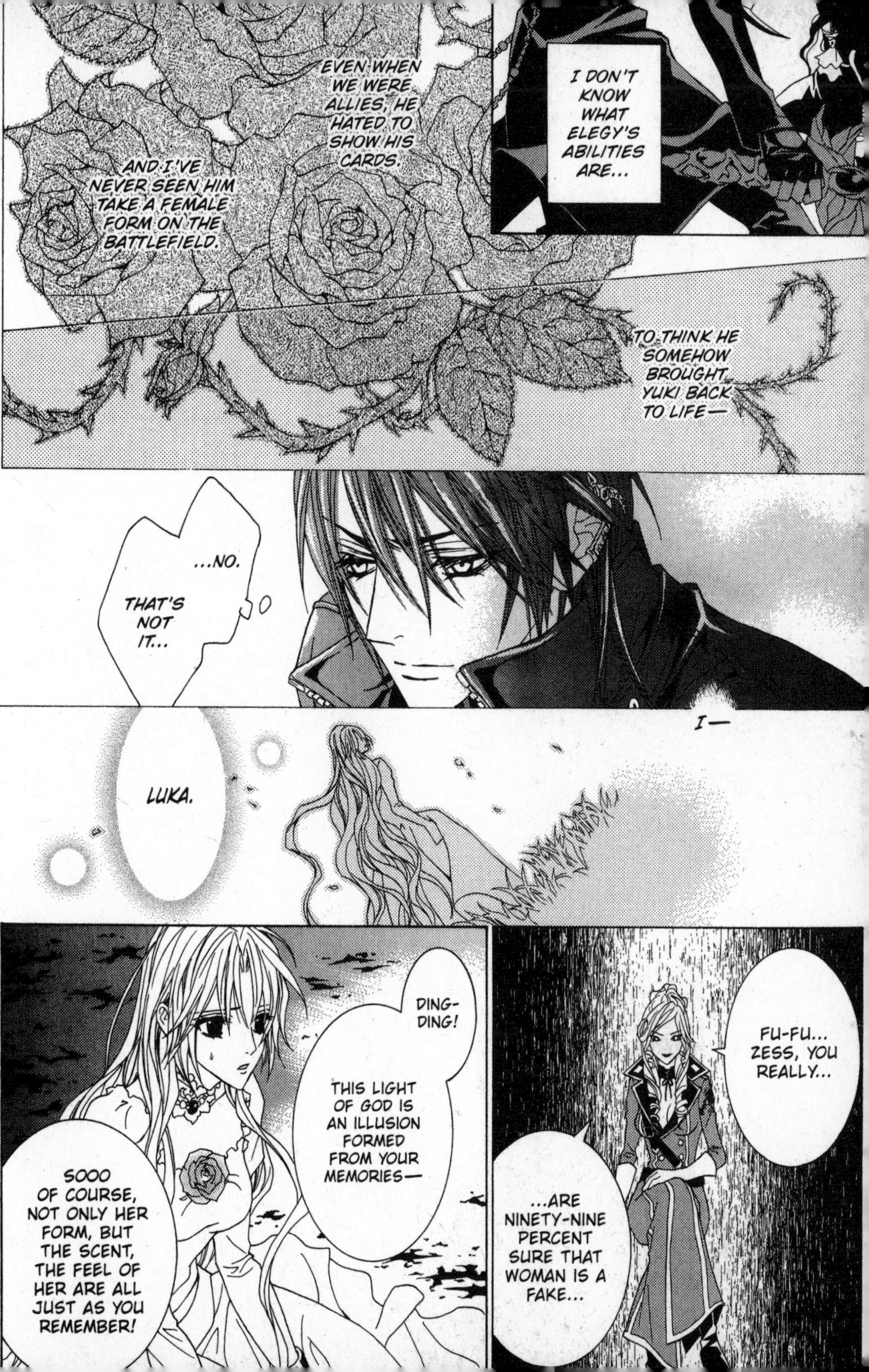
I DON'T KNOW WHAT ELEGY'S ABILITIES ARE...
EVEN WHEN WE WERE ALLIES, HE HATED TO SHOW HIS CARDS.
AND I'VE NEVER SEEN HIM TAKE A FEMALE FORM ON THE BATTLEFIELD.
TO THINK HE SOMEHOW BROUGHT YUKI BACK TO LIFE—
...NO.
THAT'S NOT IT...
I—
LUKA.
FU-FU... ZESS, YOU REALLY...
...ARE NINETY-NINE PERCENT SURE THAT WOMAN IS A FAKE...
DING-DING!
THIS LIGHT OF GOD IS AN ILLUSION FORMED FROM YOUR MEMORIES—
SOOO OF COURSE, NOT ONLY HER FORM, BUT THE SCENT, THE FEEL OF HER ARE ALL JUST AS YOU REMEMBER!

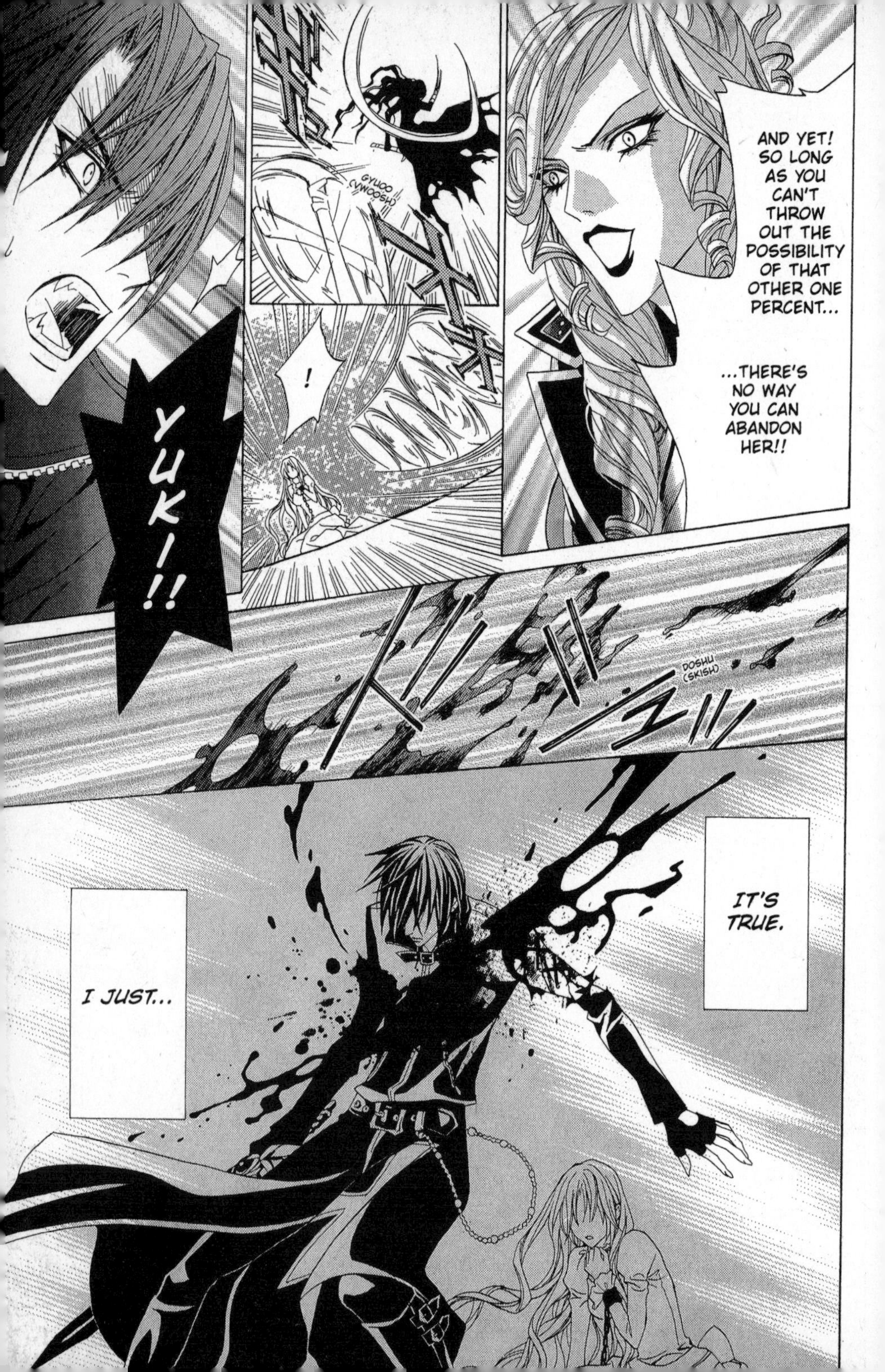
AND YET! SO LONG AS YOU CAN'T THROW OUT THE POSSIBILITY OF THAT OTHER ONE PERCENT...
...THERE'S NO WAY YOU CAN ABANDON HER!!
GYUOO (VWOOSH)
!
YUKI!!
DOSHU (SKISH)
IT'S TRUE.
I JUST...

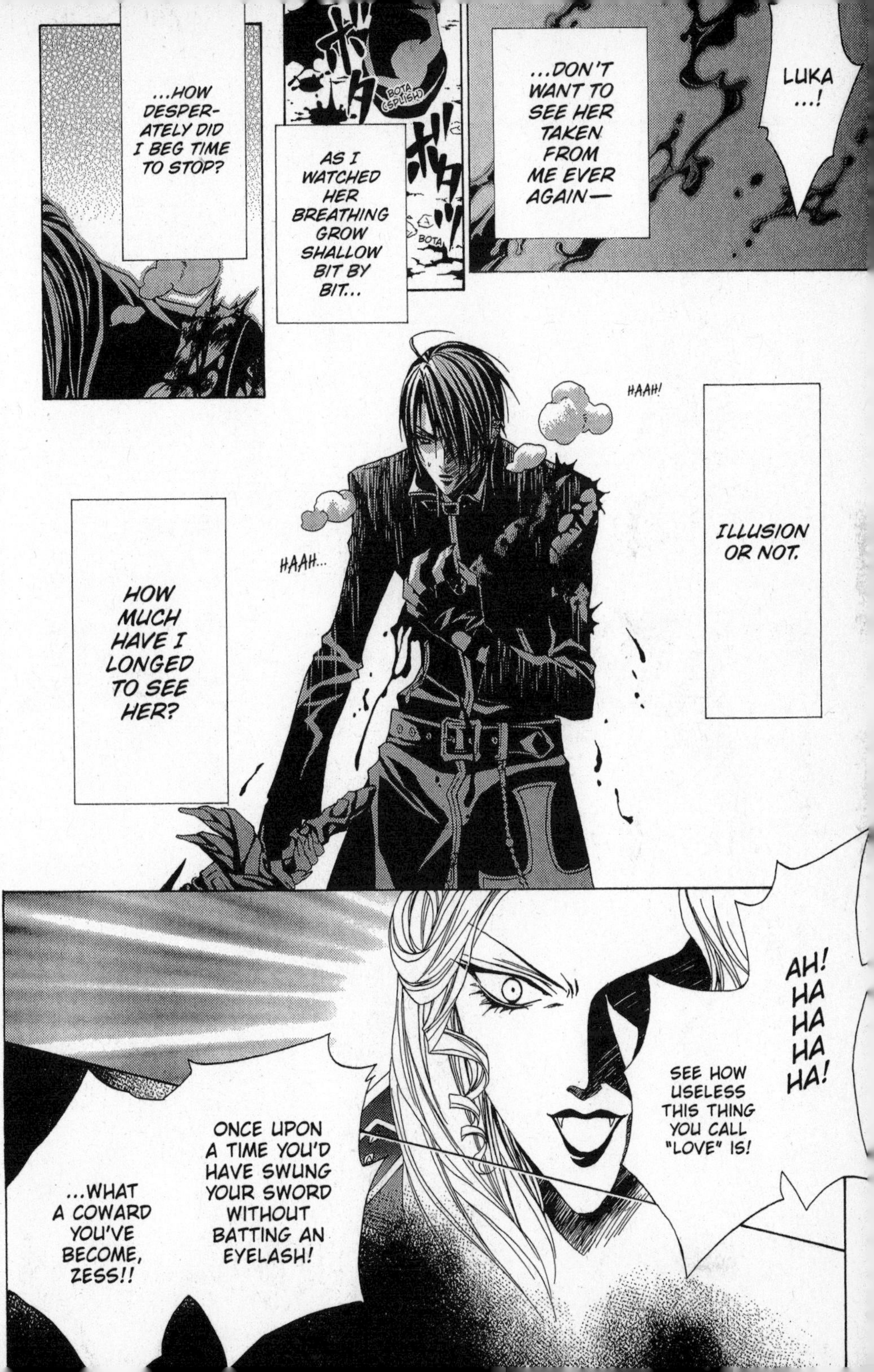
LUKA ...!
...DON'T WANT TO SEE HER TAKEN FROM ME EVER AGAIN—
BOTA (SPLISH)
BOTA
AS I WATCHED HER BREATHING GROW SHALLOW BIT BY BIT...
...HOW DESPERATELY DID I BEG TIME TO STOP?
ILLUSION OR NOT.
HAAH!
HAAH...
HOW MUCH HAVE I LONGED TO SEE HER?
AH! HA HA HA HA!
SEE HOW USELESS THIS THING YOU CALL "LOVE" IS!
ONCE UPON A TIME YOU'D HAVE SWUNG YOUR SWORD WITHOUT BATTING AN EYELASH!
...WHAT A COWARD YOU'VE BECOME, ZESS!!

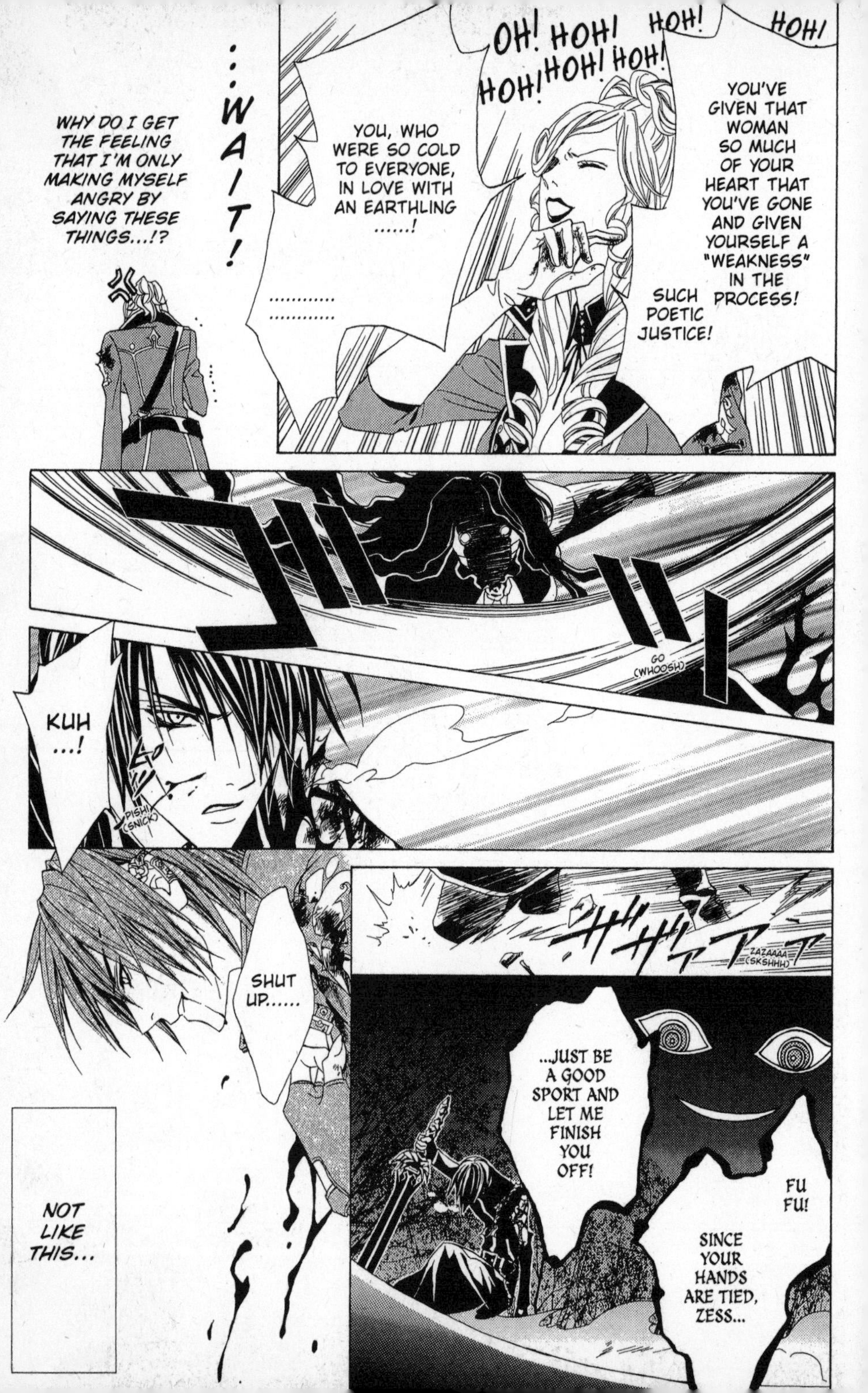
OH! HOH! HOH! HOH! HOH! HOH!
YOU'VE GIVEN THAT WOMAN SO MUCH OF YOUR HEART THAT YOU'VE GONE AND GIVEN YOURSELF A "WEAKNESS" IN THE PROCESS!
SUCH POETIC JUSTICE!
YOU, WHO WERE SO COLD TO EVERYONE, IN LOVE WITH AN EARTHLING ......!
....
...WAIT!
WHY DO I GET THE FEELING THAT I'M ONLY MAKING MYSELF ANGRY BY SAYING THESE THINGS...!?
GO (WHOOSH)
KUH ...!
PISHI (SNICK)
ZAZAAAA (SKSHHH)
FU FU!
SINCE YOUR HANDS ARE TIED, ZESS...
...JUST BE A GOOD SPORT AND LET ME FINISH YOU OFF!
SHUT UP......
NOT LIKE THIS...

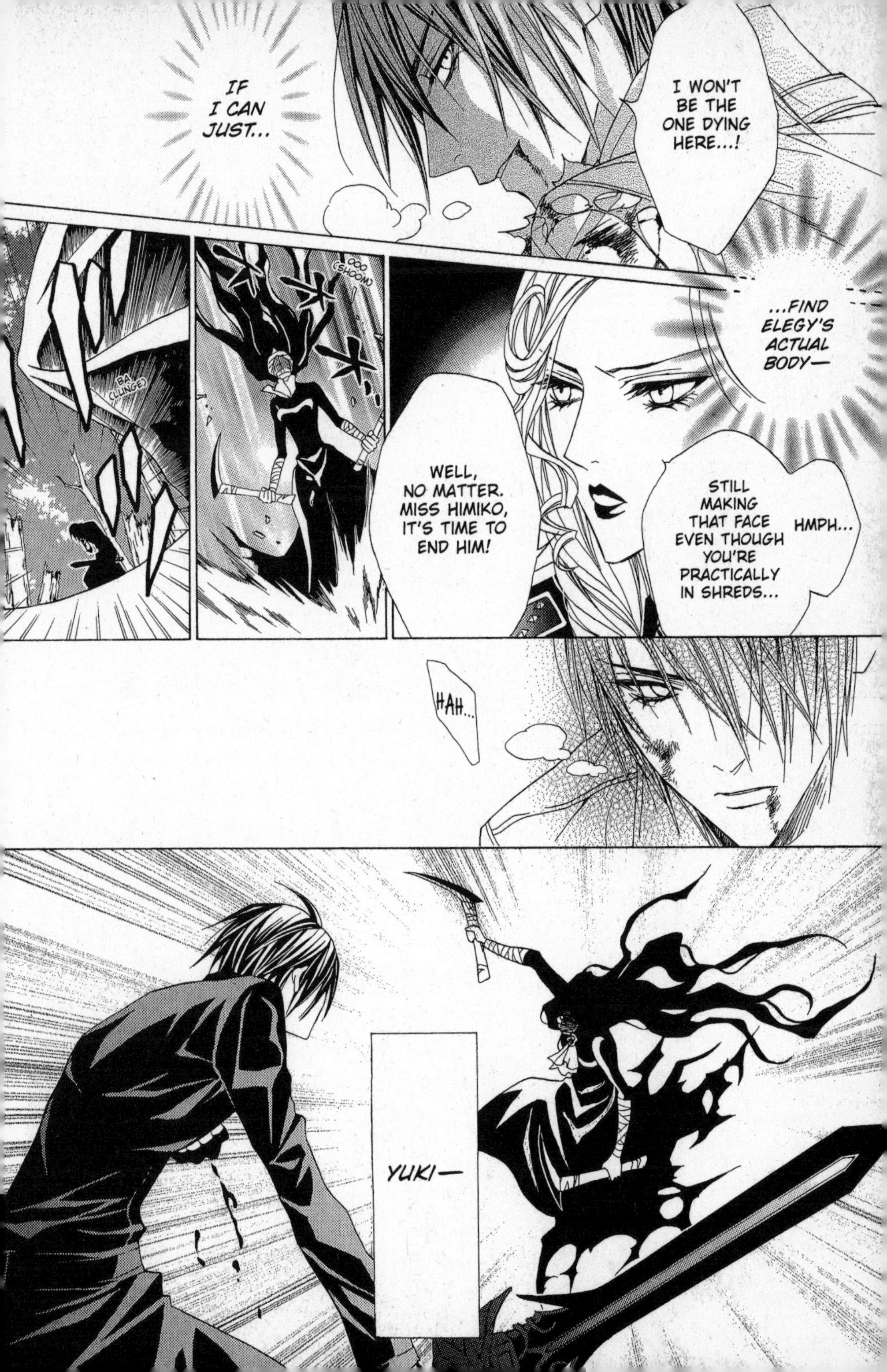
I WON'T BE THE ONE DYING HERE...!
IF I CAN JUST...
...FIND ELEGY'S ACTUAL BODY—
HMPH...
STILL MAKING THAT FACE EVEN THOUGH YOU'RE PRACTICALLY IN SHREDS...
WELL, NO MATTER. MISS HIMIKO, IT'S TIME TO END HIM!
OOO (SHOOM)
BA (LUNGE)
HAH...
YUKI—

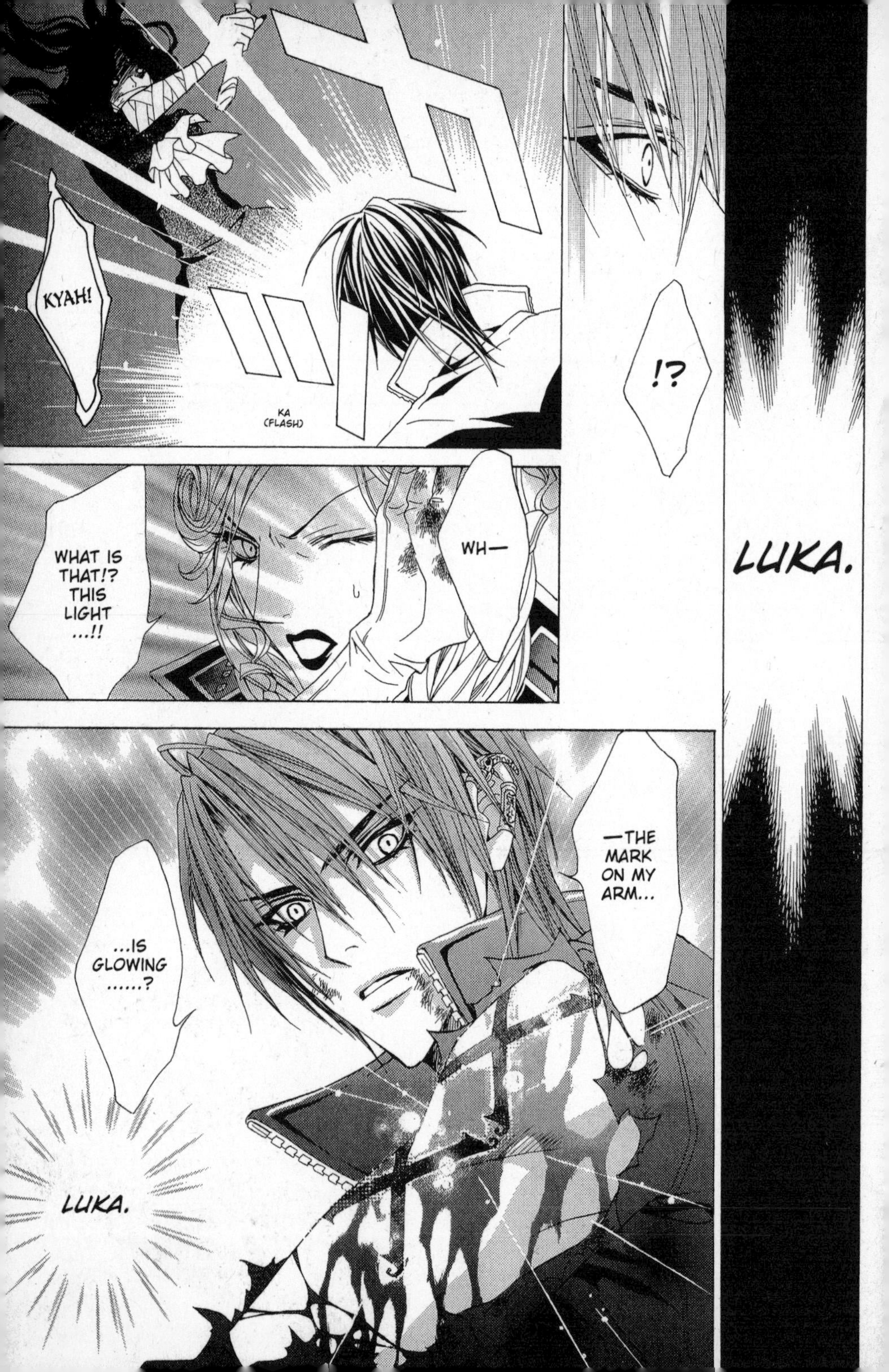
LUKA.
!?
KYAH!
KA (FLASH)
WH—
WHAT IS THAT!? THIS LIGHT ...!!
—THE MARK ON MY ARM...
...IS GLOWING ......?
LUKA.

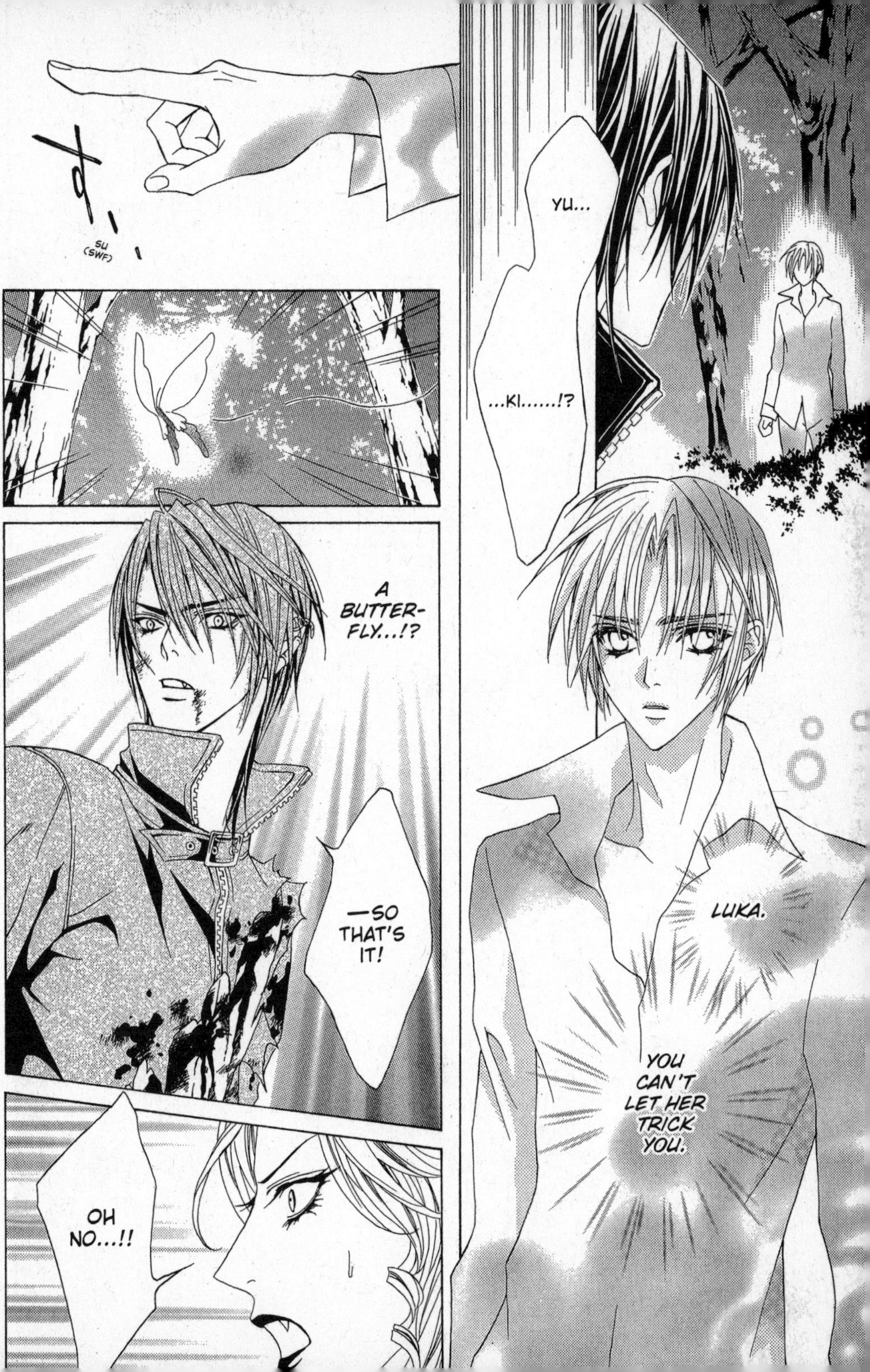
YU...
...KI......!?
LUKA.
YOU CAN'T LET HER TRICK YOU.
SU (SWF)
A BUTTER-FLY...!?
—SO THAT'S IT!
OH NO...!!

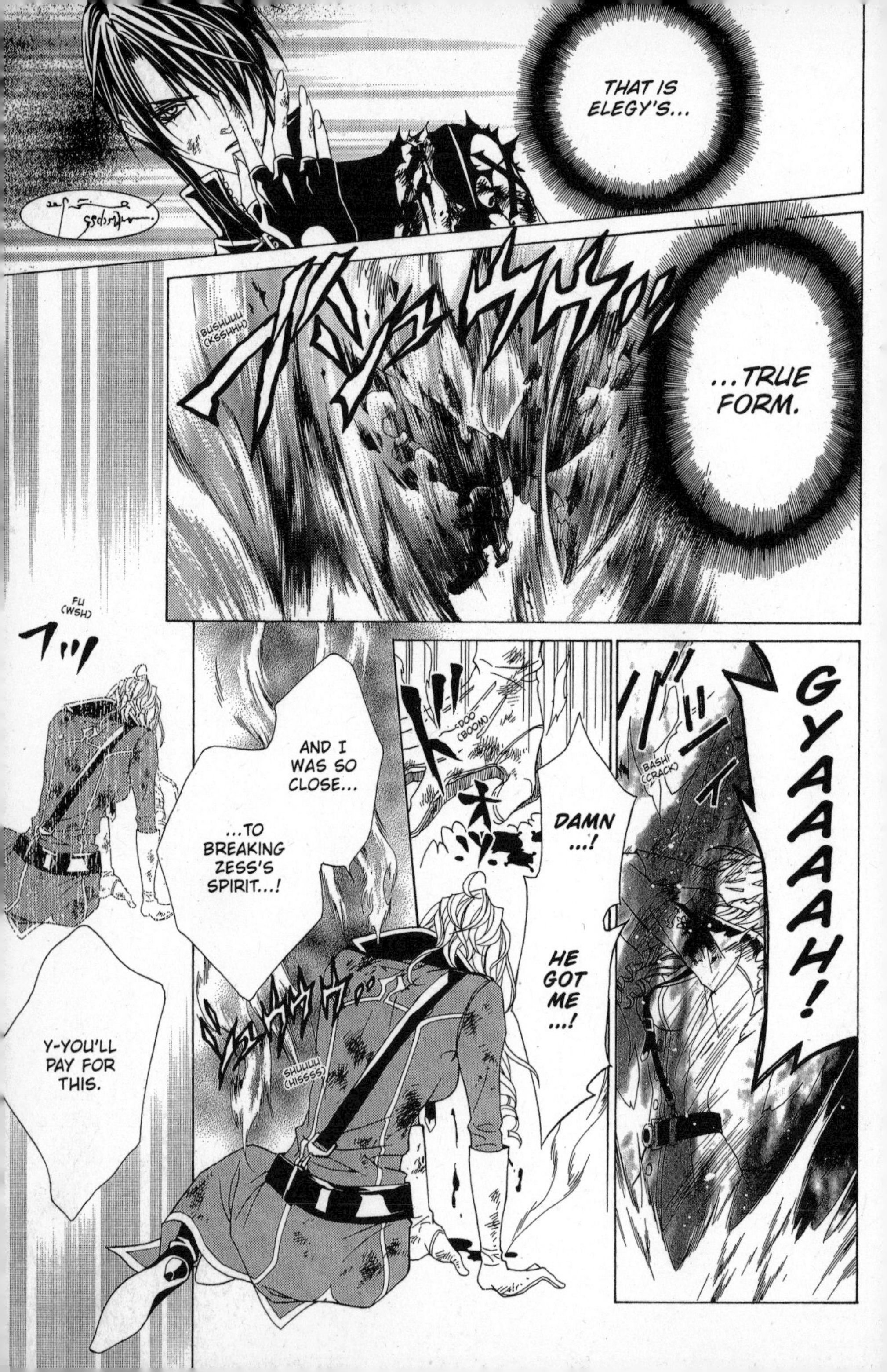
THAT IS ELEGY'S...
...TRUE FORM.
BUSHUUU (KSSHHH)
GYAAAAAH!
BASHI (CRACK)
DOO (BOOM)
DAMN ...!
HE GOT ME ...!
AND I WAS SO CLOSE...
...TO BREAKING ZESS'S SPIRIT...!
SHUUUU (HISSSS)
FU (WSH)
Y-YOU'LL PAY FOR THIS.

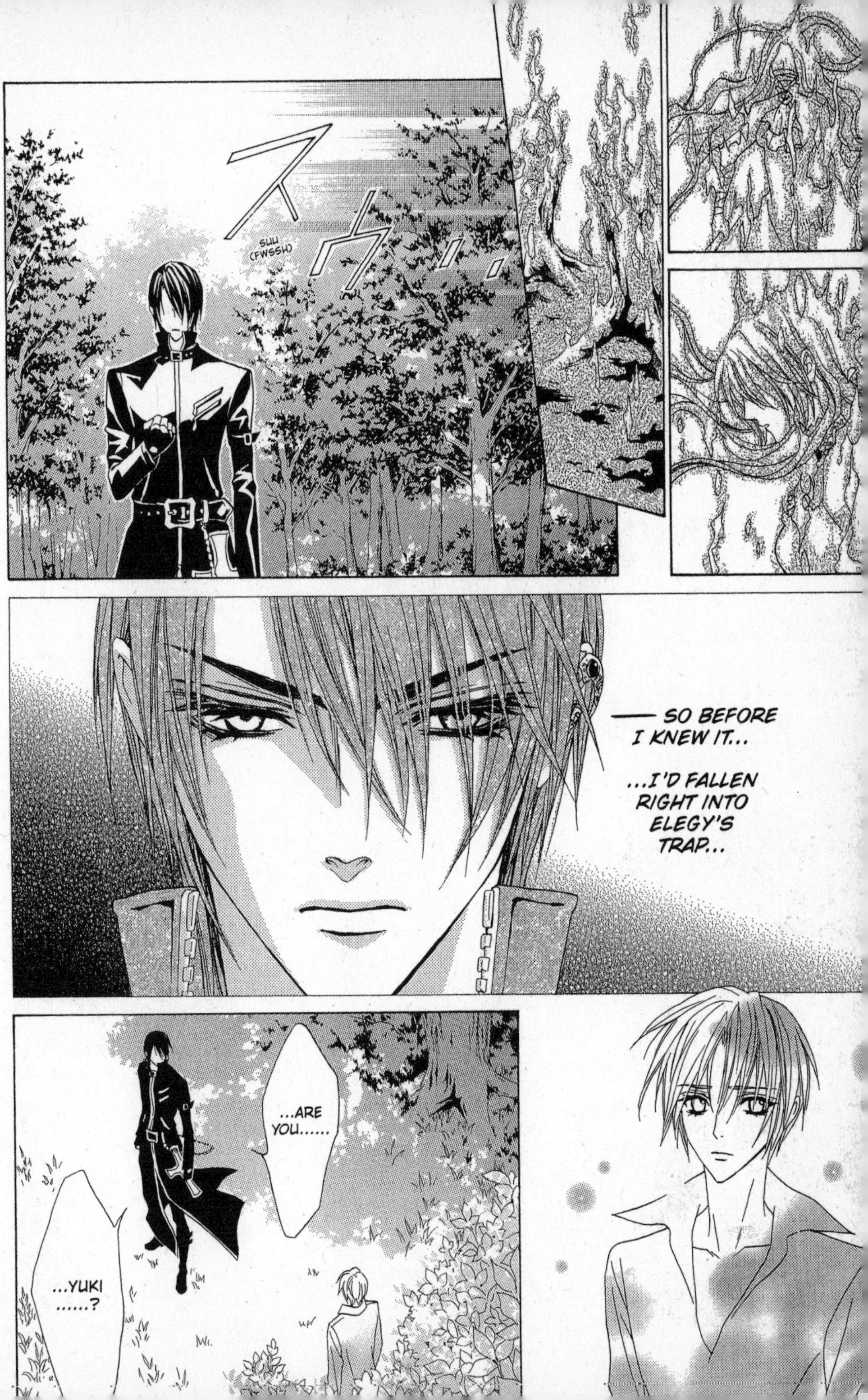
SUU (FWSSH)
— SO BEFORE I KNEW IT...
...I'D FALLEN RIGHT INTO ELEGY'S TRAP...
...ARE YOU......
...YUKI ......?

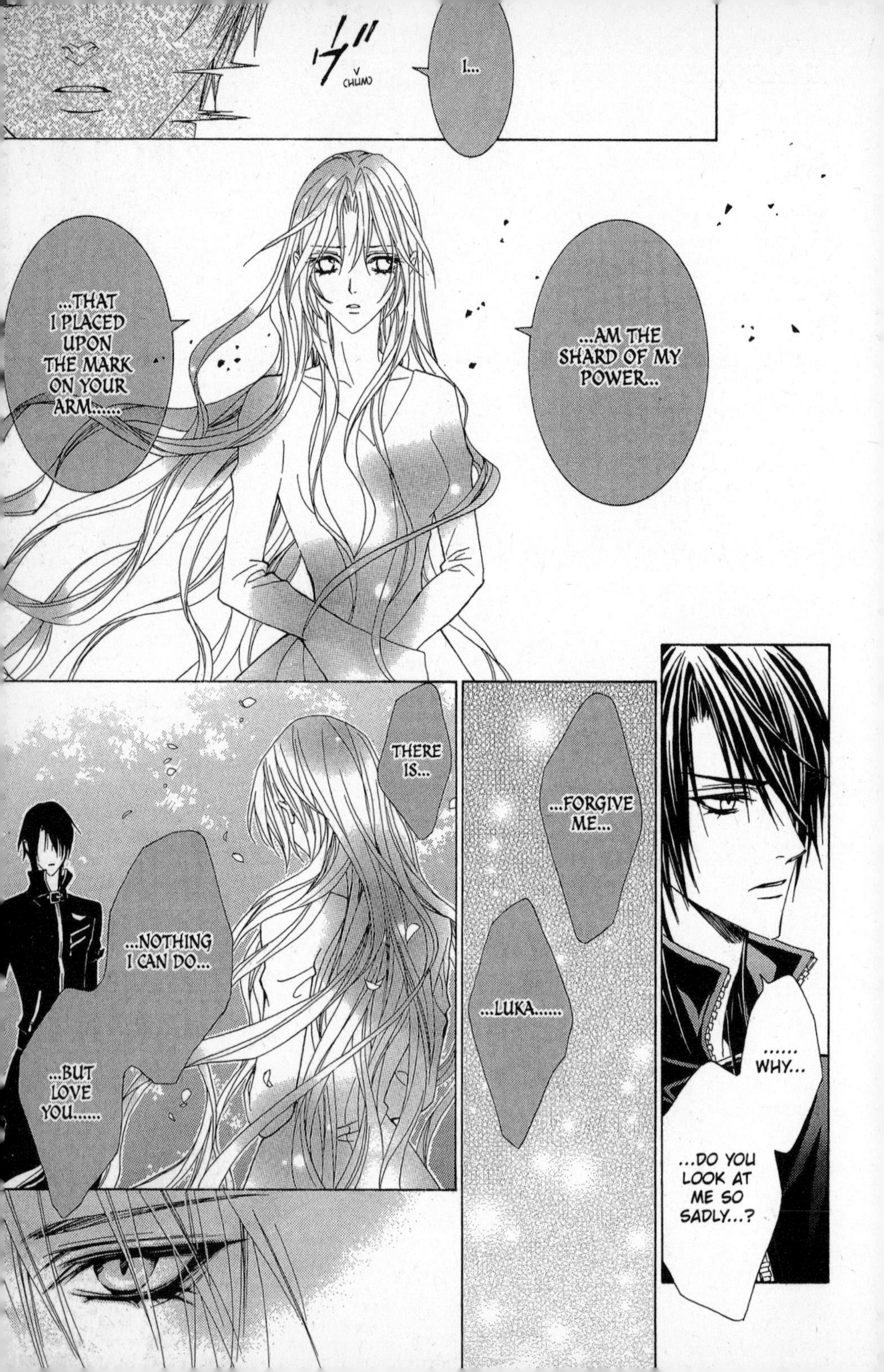
I...
ヴ
(CHUM)
...AM THE SHARD OF MY POWER...
...THAT I PLACED UPON THE MARK ON YOUR ARM......
...... WHY...
...DO YOU LOOK AT ME SO SADLY...?
...FORGIVE ME...
...LUKA......
THERE IS...
...NOTHING I CAN DO...
...BUT LOVE YOU......

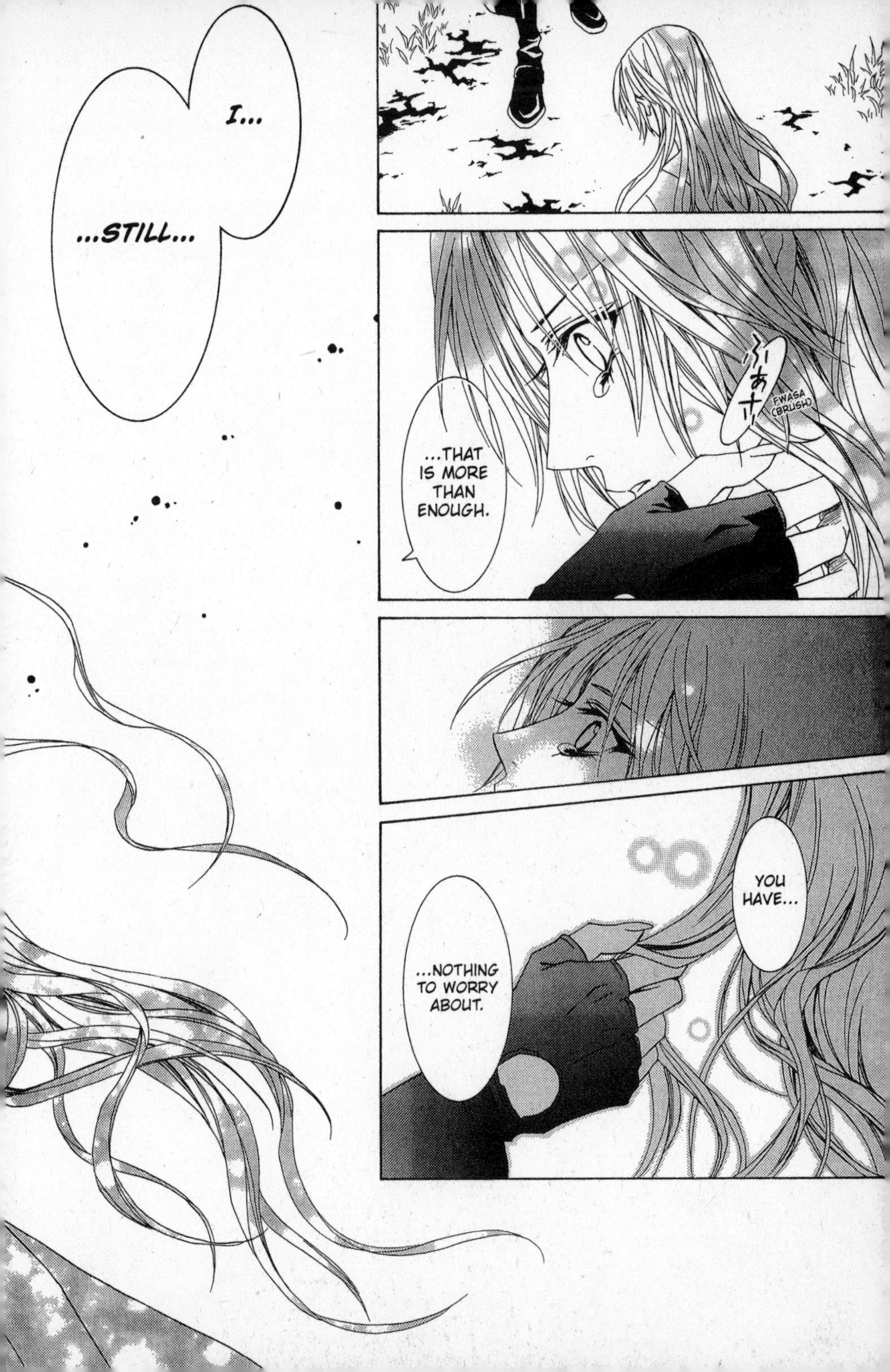
FWASA (BRUSH)
...THAT IS MORE THAN ENOUGH.
YOU HAVE...
...NOTHING TO WORRY ABOUT.
I...
...STILL...

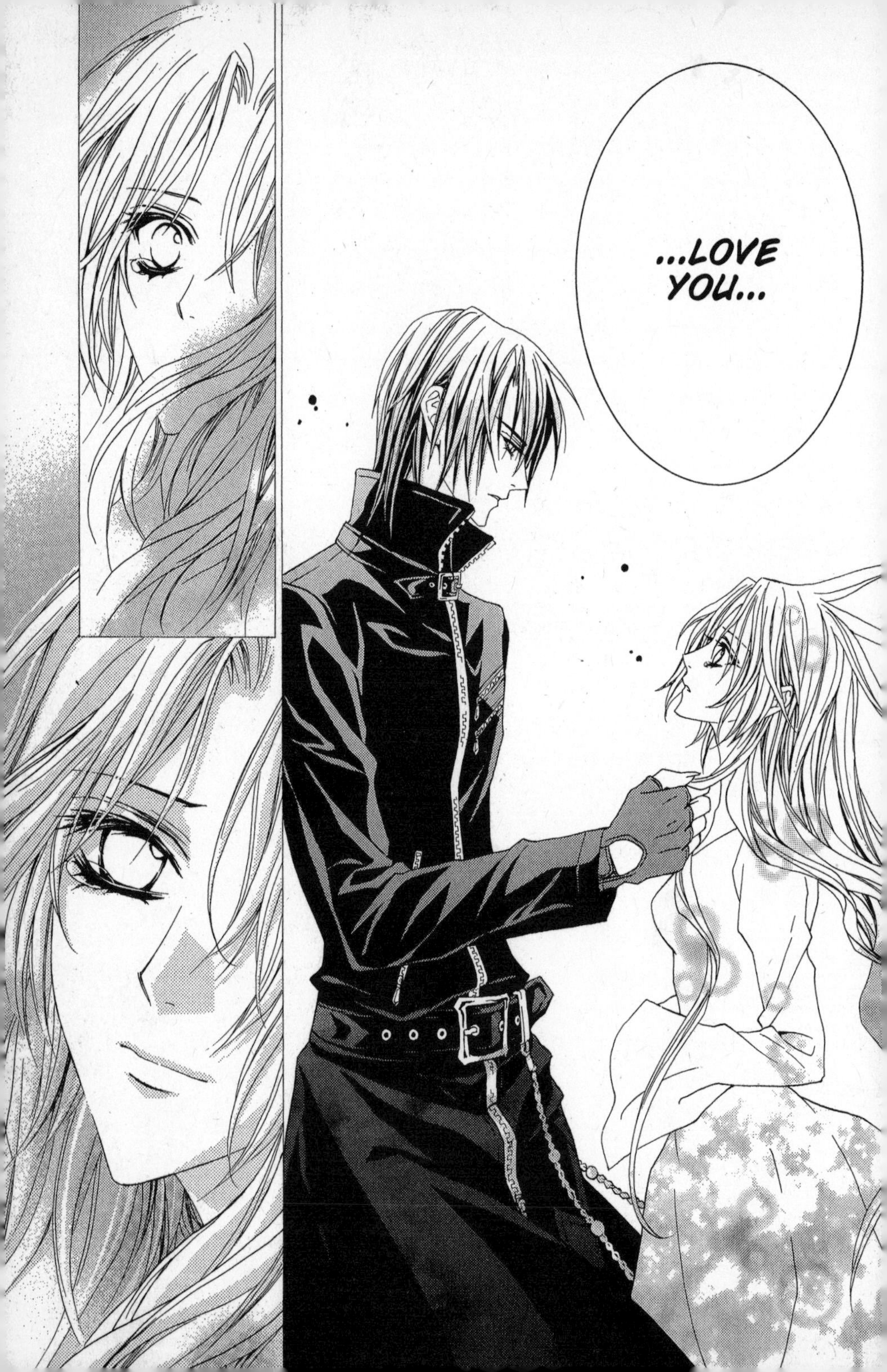
...LOVE YOU...

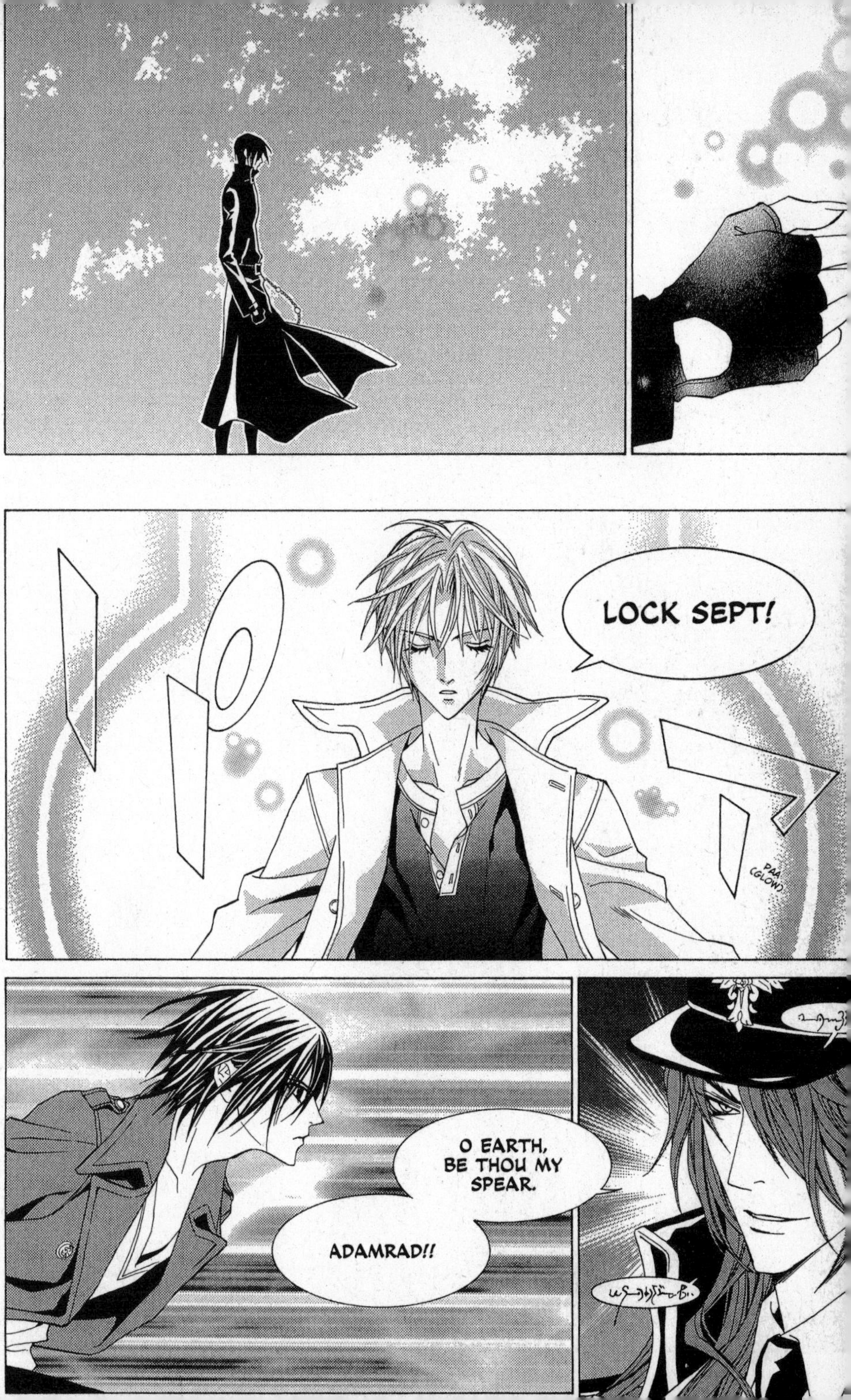
LOCK SEPT!
PAA (GLOW)
O EARTH, BE THOU MY SPEAR.
ADAMRAD!!

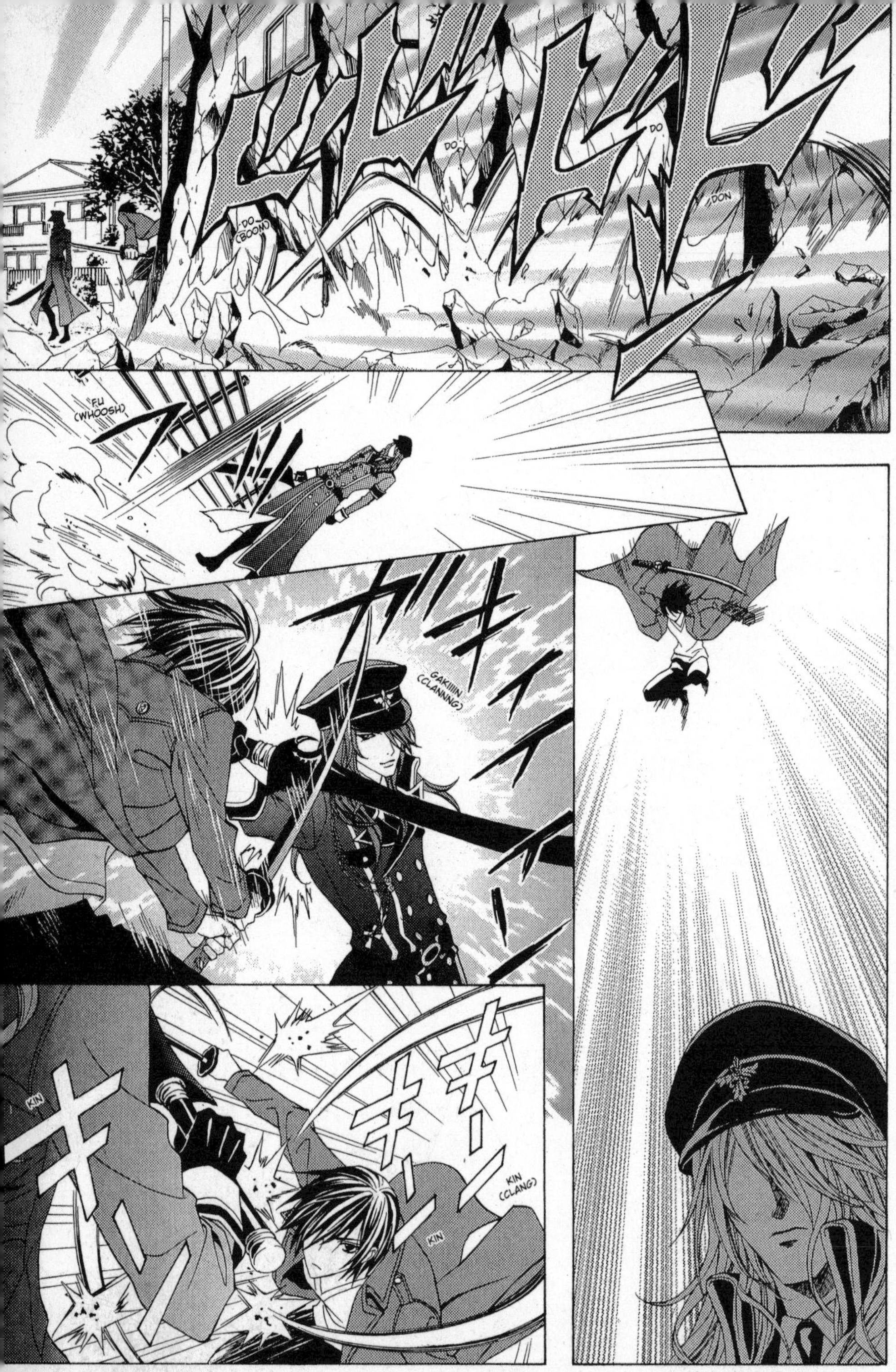
DO
DON
DO
DO (BOOM)
FU (WHOOSH)
GAKIIIIN (CLANNNG)
KIN (CLANG)
KIN
KIN

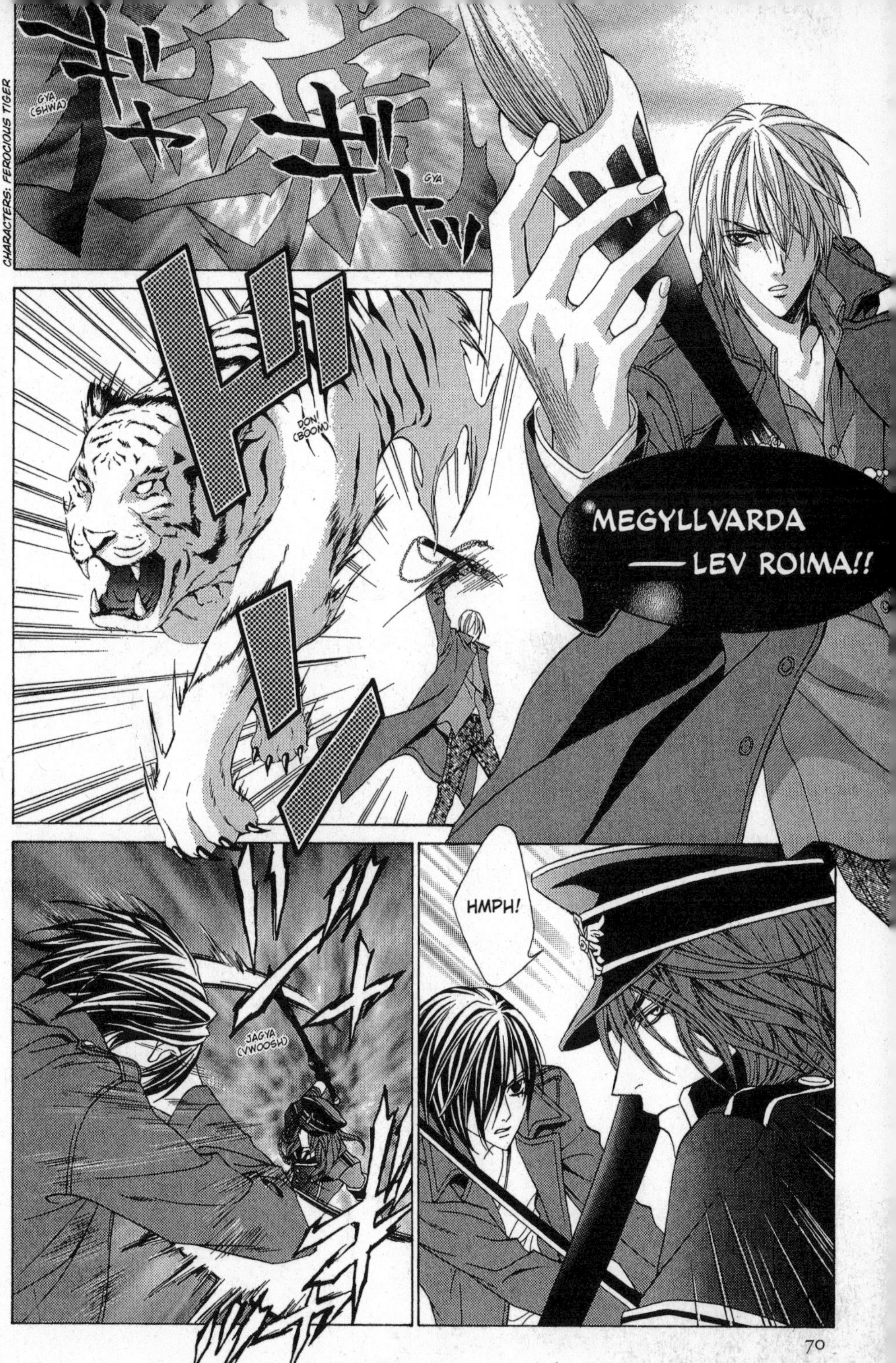

MEGYLLVARDA
——LEV ROIMA!!
GYA (SHWA)
GYA
CHARACTERS: FEROCIOUS TIGER
DON! (BOOM)
HMPH!
JAGYA (VWOOSH)

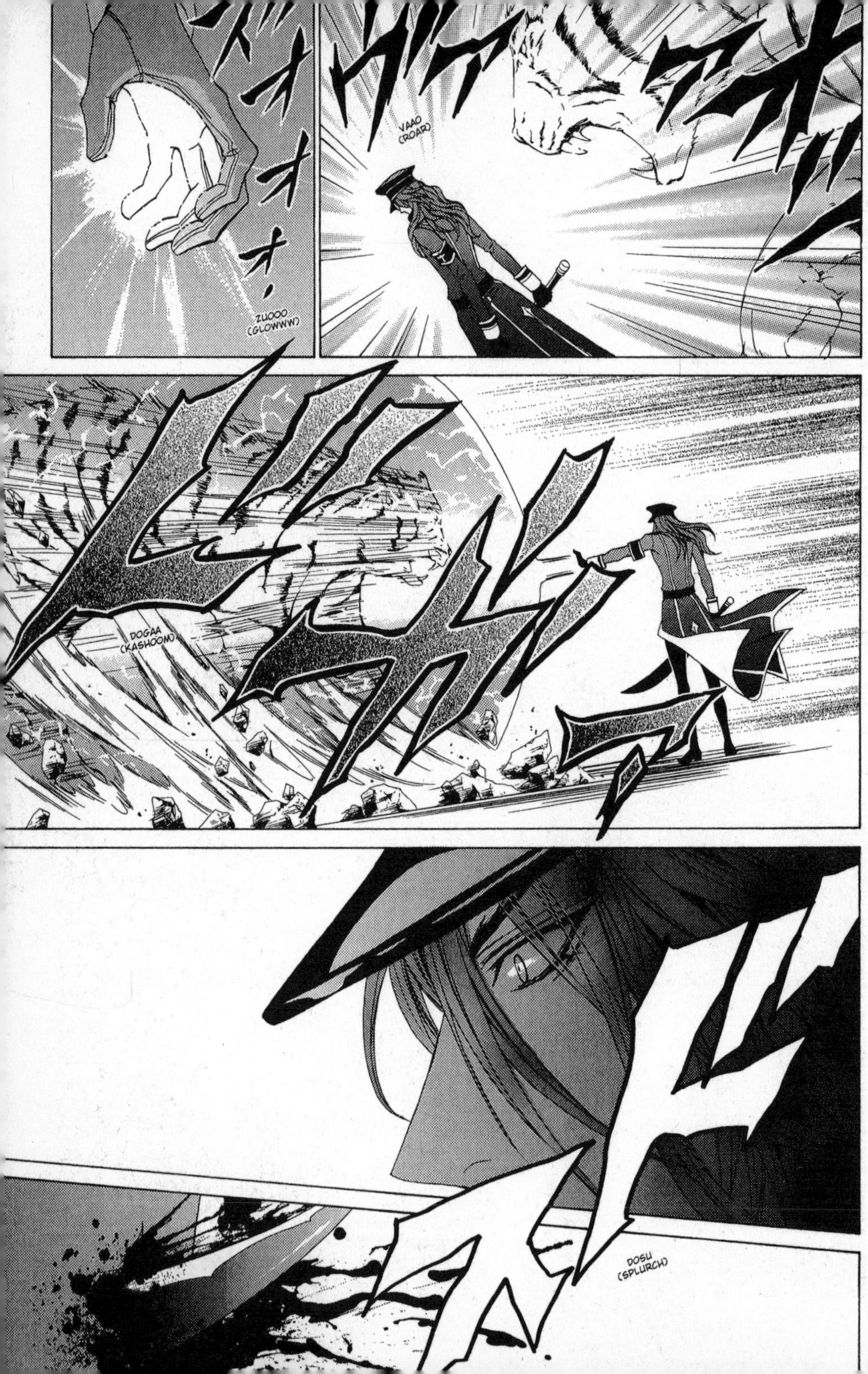
VAAO (ROAR)
ZUOOO (GLOWWW)
DOGAA (KASHOOM)
DOSU (SPLURCH)

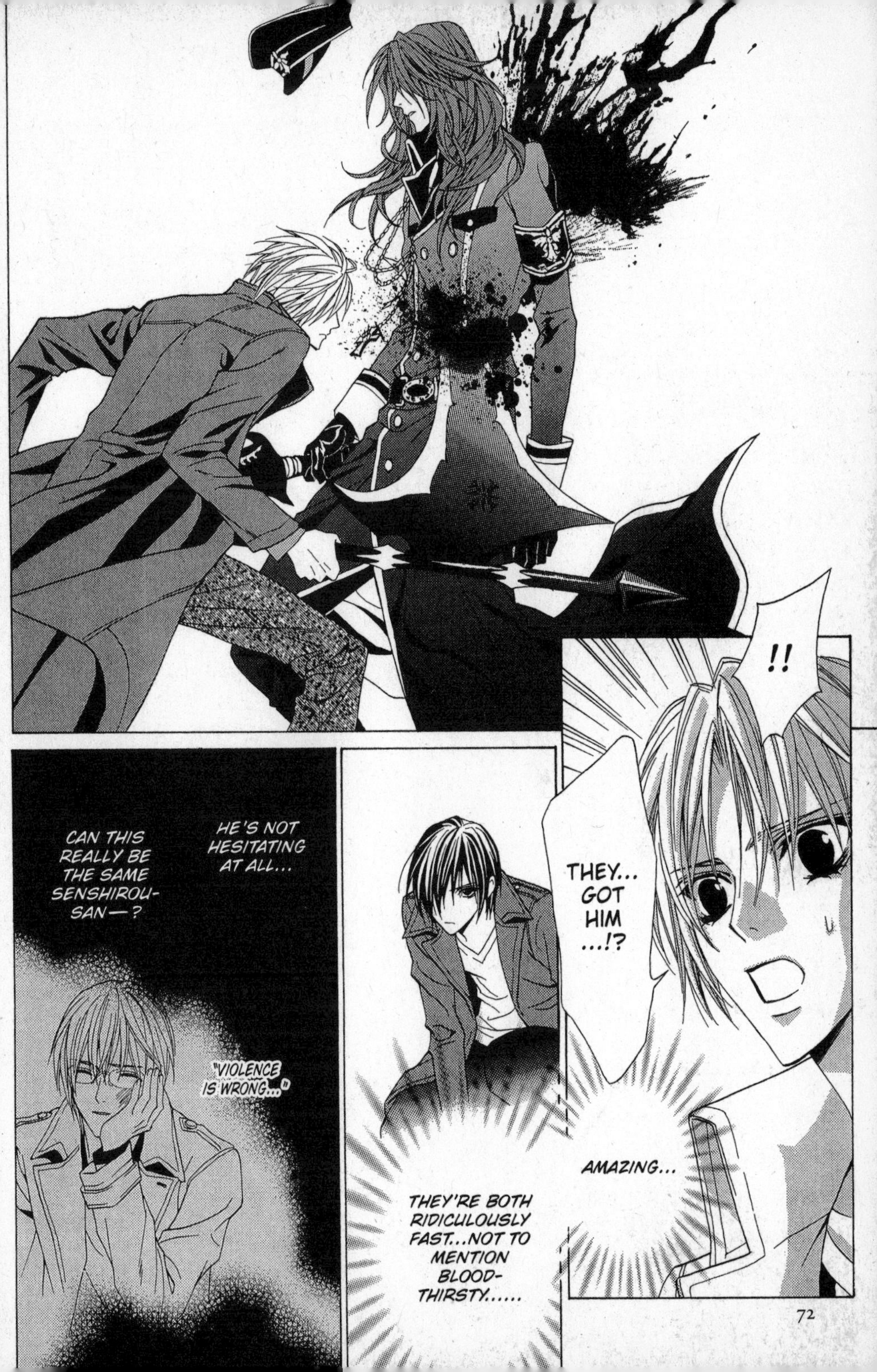
!!
THEY... GOT HIM ...!?
AMAZING...
THEY'RE BOTH RIDICULOUSLY FAST...NOT TO MENTION BLOOD-THIRSTY......
HE'S NOT HESITATING AT ALL...
CAN THIS REALLY BE THE SAME SENSHIROU-SAN—?
"VIOLENCE IS WRONG..."

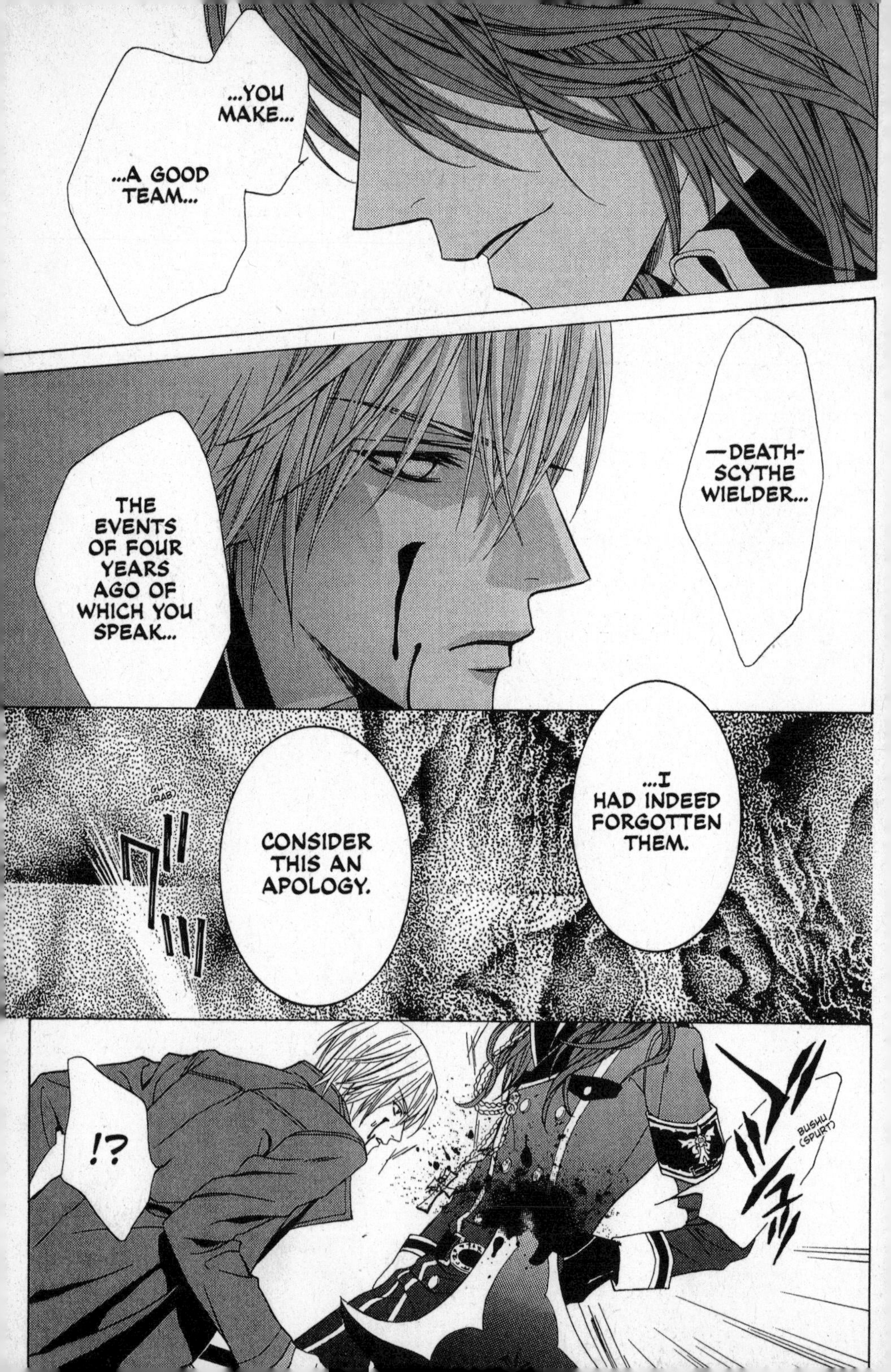
...YOU MAKE...
...A GOOD TEAM...
—DEATH-SCYTHE WIELDER...
THE EVENTS OF FOUR YEARS AGO OF WHICH YOU SPEAK...
...I HAD INDEED FORGOTTEN THEM.
CONSIDER THIS AN APOLOGY.
GU (GRAB)
BUSHU (SPURT)
!?

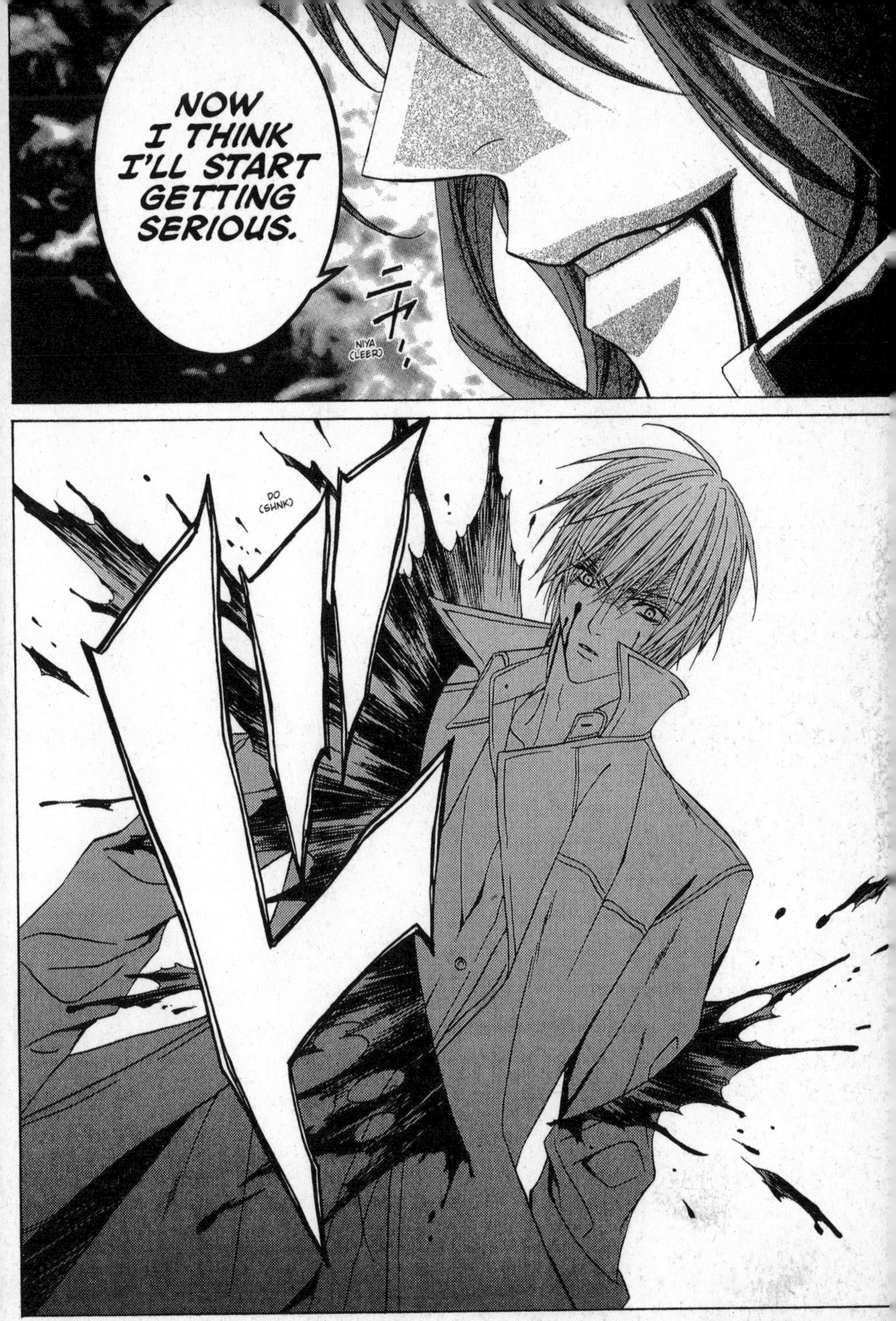
NOW I THINK I'LL START GETTING SERIOUS.
NIYA (LEER)
DO (SHNK)

Story 32 · END

The Betrayal Knows My Name

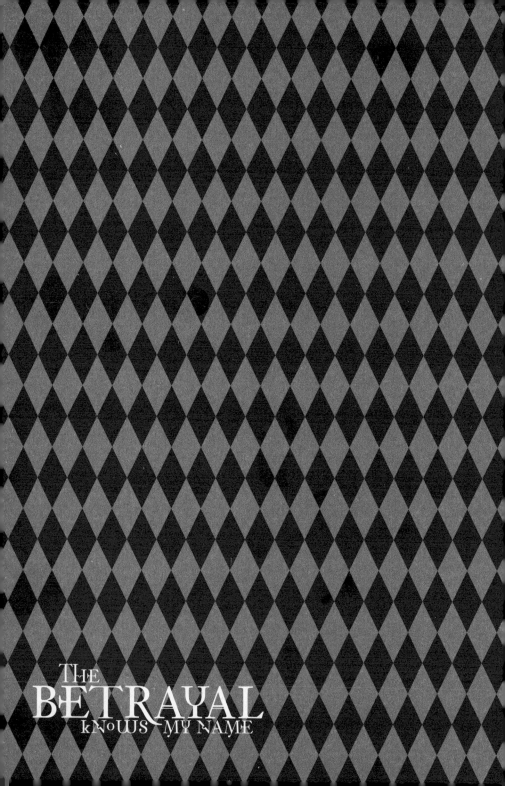

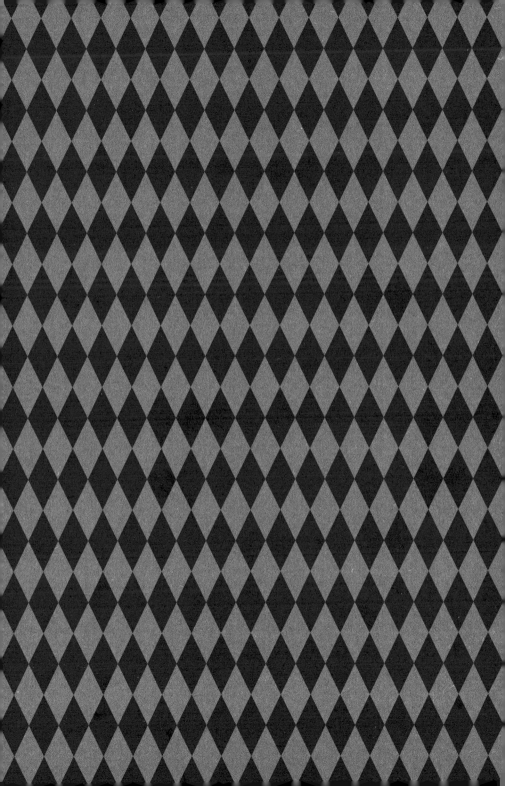

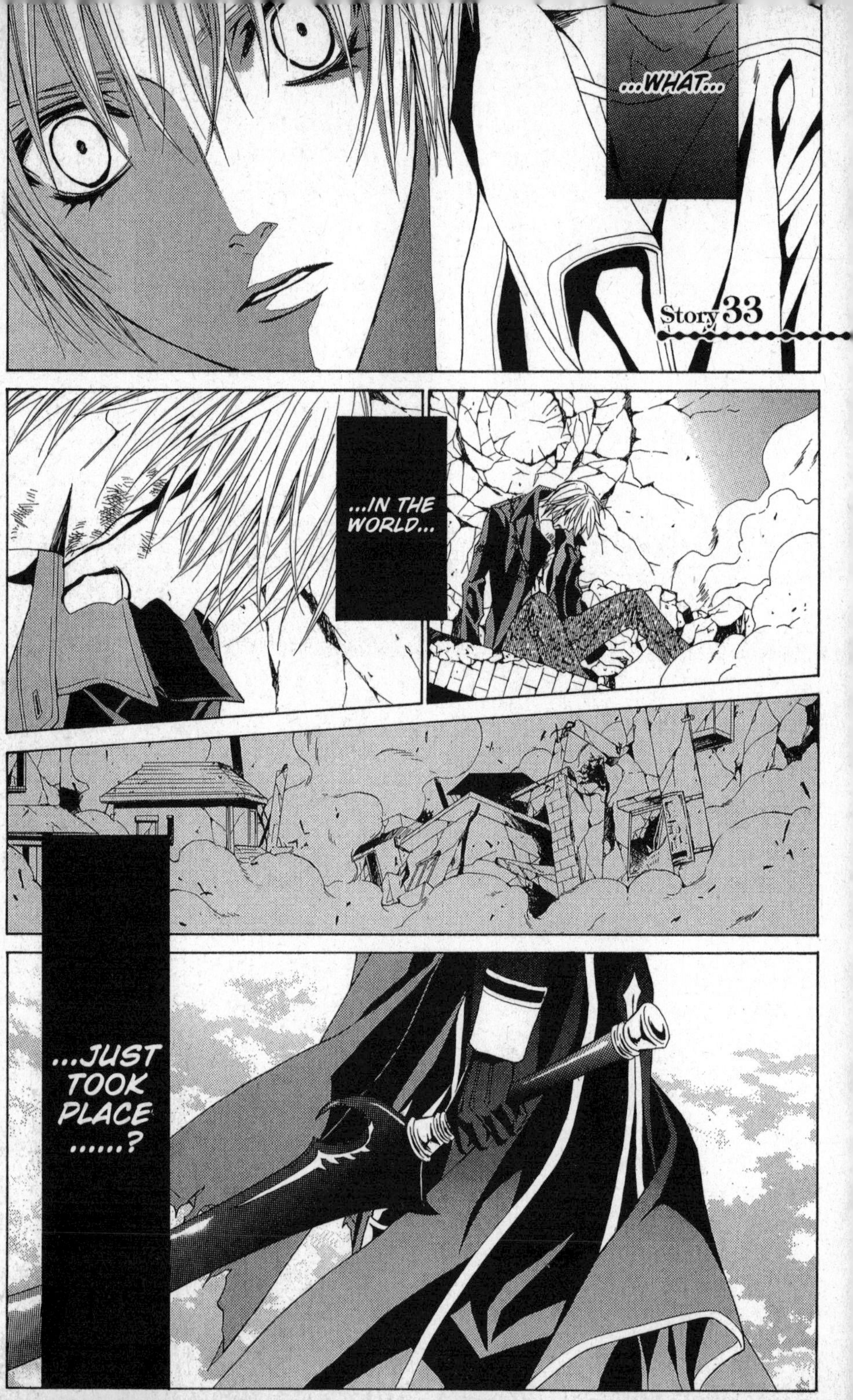

...WHAT...
Story 33
...IN THE WORLD...
...JUST TOOK PLACE ......?

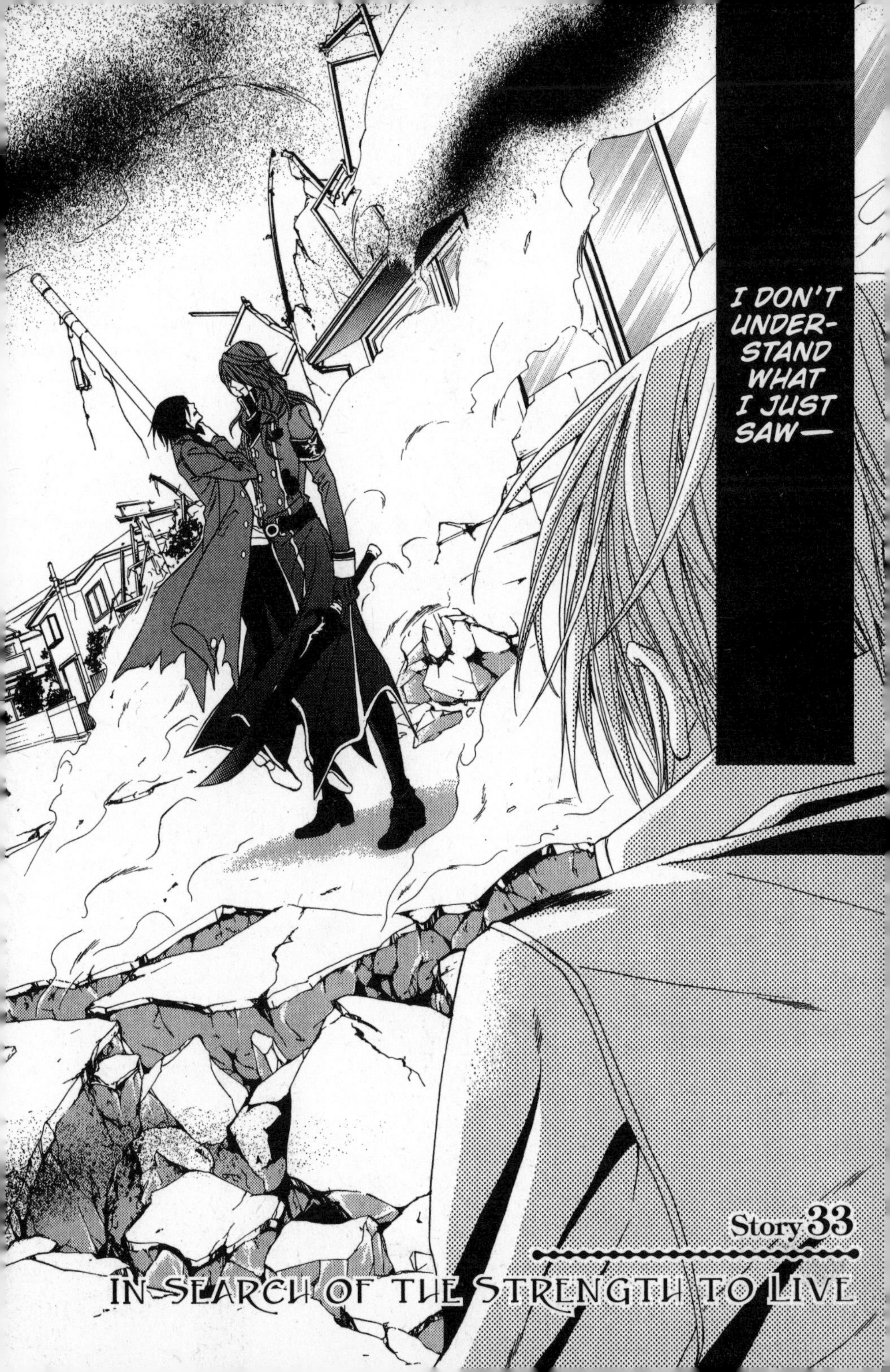
I DON'T UNDERSTAND WHAT I JUST SAW—
Story 33
IN SEARCH OF THE STRENGTH TO LIVE

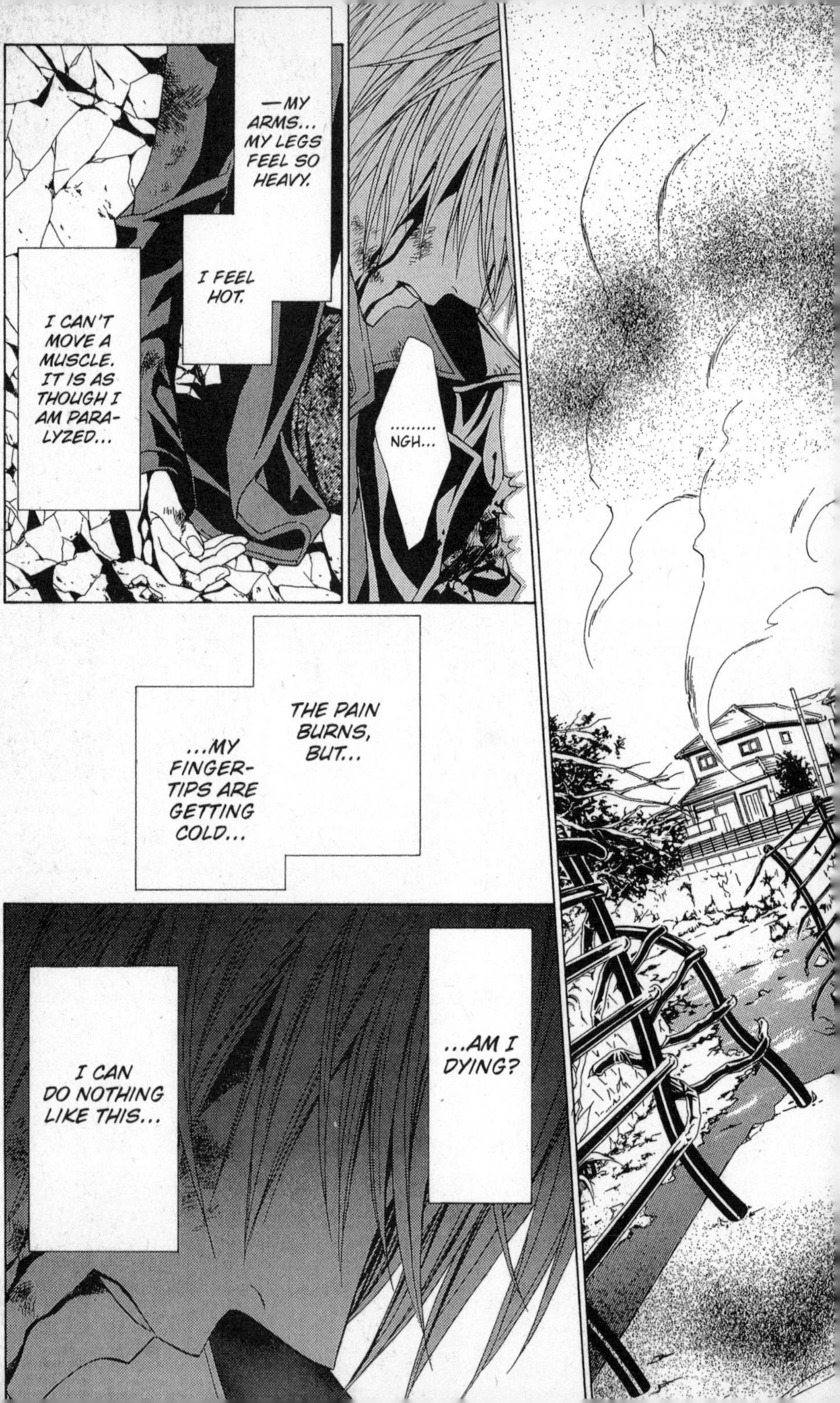
—MY ARMS... MY LEGS FEEL SO HEAVY.
.... NGH...
I FEEL HOT.
I CAN'T MOVE A MUSCLE. IT IS AS THOUGH I AM PARA-LYZED...
THE PAIN BURNS, BUT...
...MY FINGER-TIPS ARE GETTING COLD...
...AM I DYING?
I CAN DO NOTHING LIKE THIS...

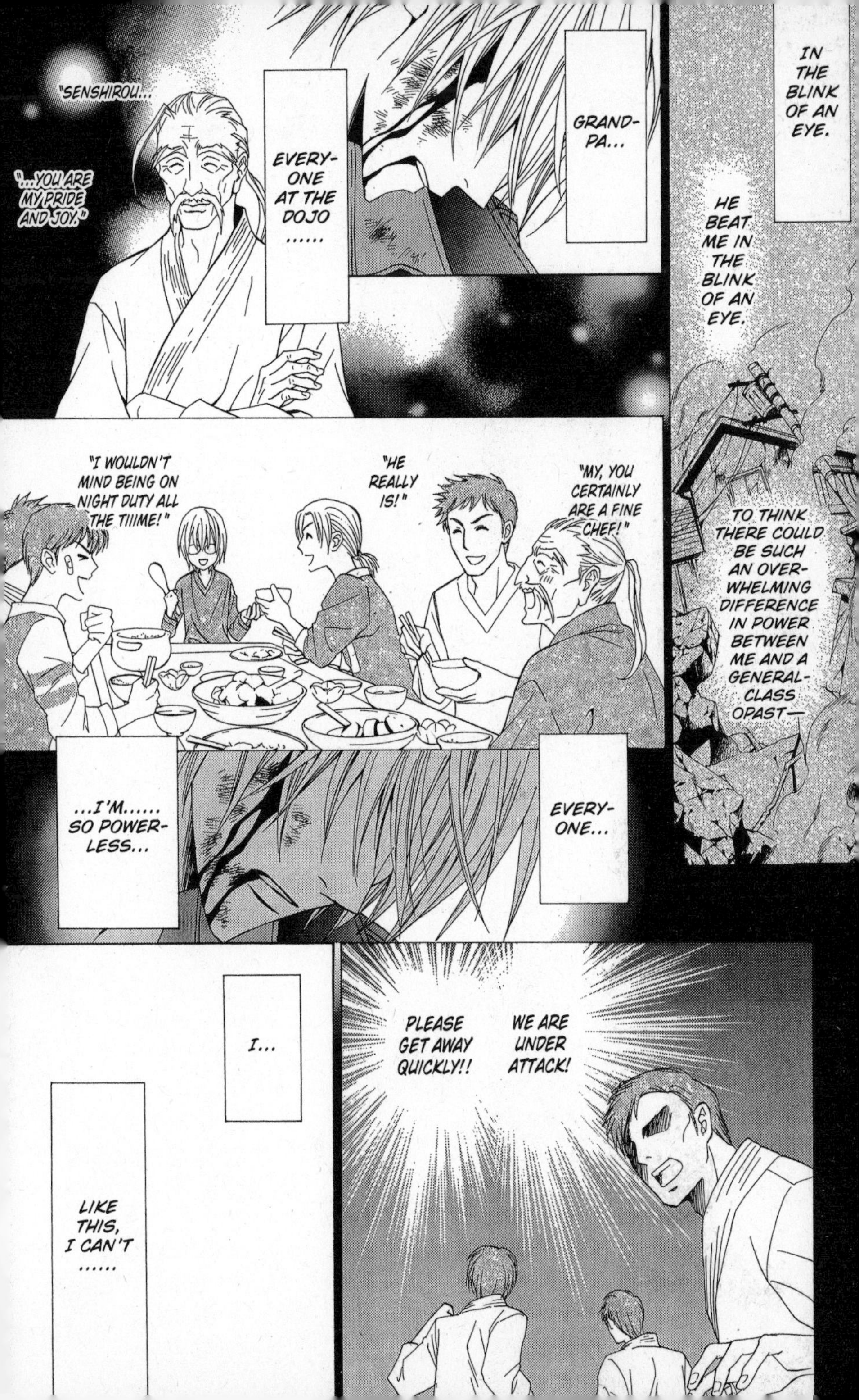
IN THE BLINK OF AN EYE.
HE BEAT ME IN THE BLINK OF AN EYE.
TO THINK THERE COULD BE SUCH AN OVER-WHELMING DIFFERENCE IN POWER BETWEEN ME AND A GENERAL-CLASS OPAST—
GRAND-PA...
EVERY-ONE AT THE DOJO......
"SENSHIROU...
"...YOU ARE MY PRIDE AND JOY."
"MY, YOU CERTAINLY ARE A FINE CHEF!"
"HE REALLY IS!"
"I WOULDN'T MIND BEING ON NIGHT DUTY ALL THE TIIIME!"
EVERY-ONE...
...I'M...... SO POWER-LESS...
WE ARE UNDER ATTACK!
PLEASE GET AWAY QUICKLY!!
I...
LIKE THIS, I CAN'T ......

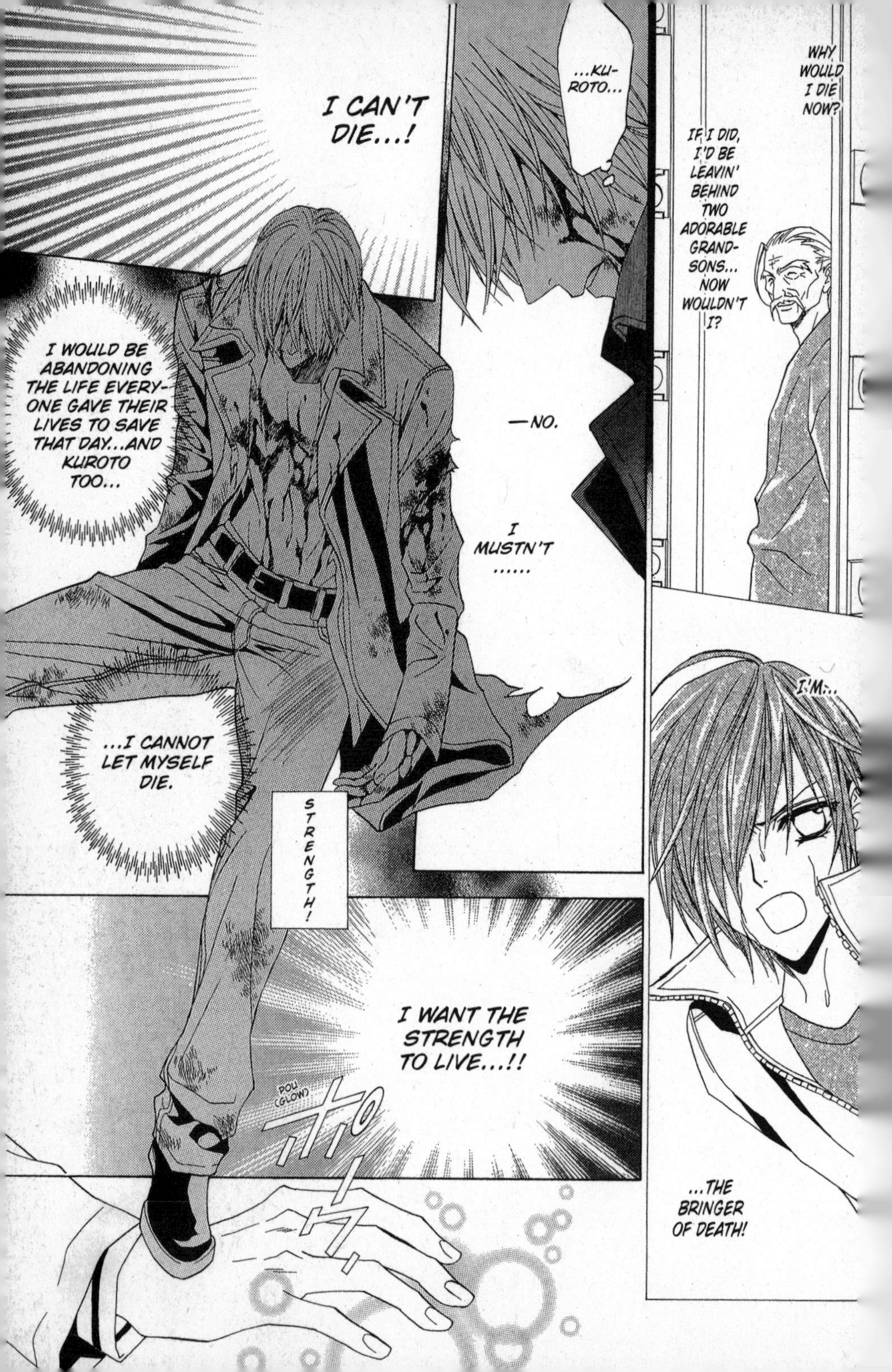
WHY WOULD I DIE NOW?
IF I DID, I'D BE LEAVIN' BEHIND TWO ADORABLE GRAND-SONS... NOW WOULDN'T I?
I'M...
...THE BRINGER OF DEATH!
...KU-ROTO...
—NO.
I MUSTN'T ......
I CAN'T DIE...!
I WOULD BE ABANDONING THE LIFE EVERY-ONE GAVE THEIR LIVES TO SAVE THAT DAY...AND KUROTO TOO...
...I CANNOT LET MYSELF DIE.
STRENGTH!
I WANT THE STRENGTH TO LIVE...!!
POU (GLOW)

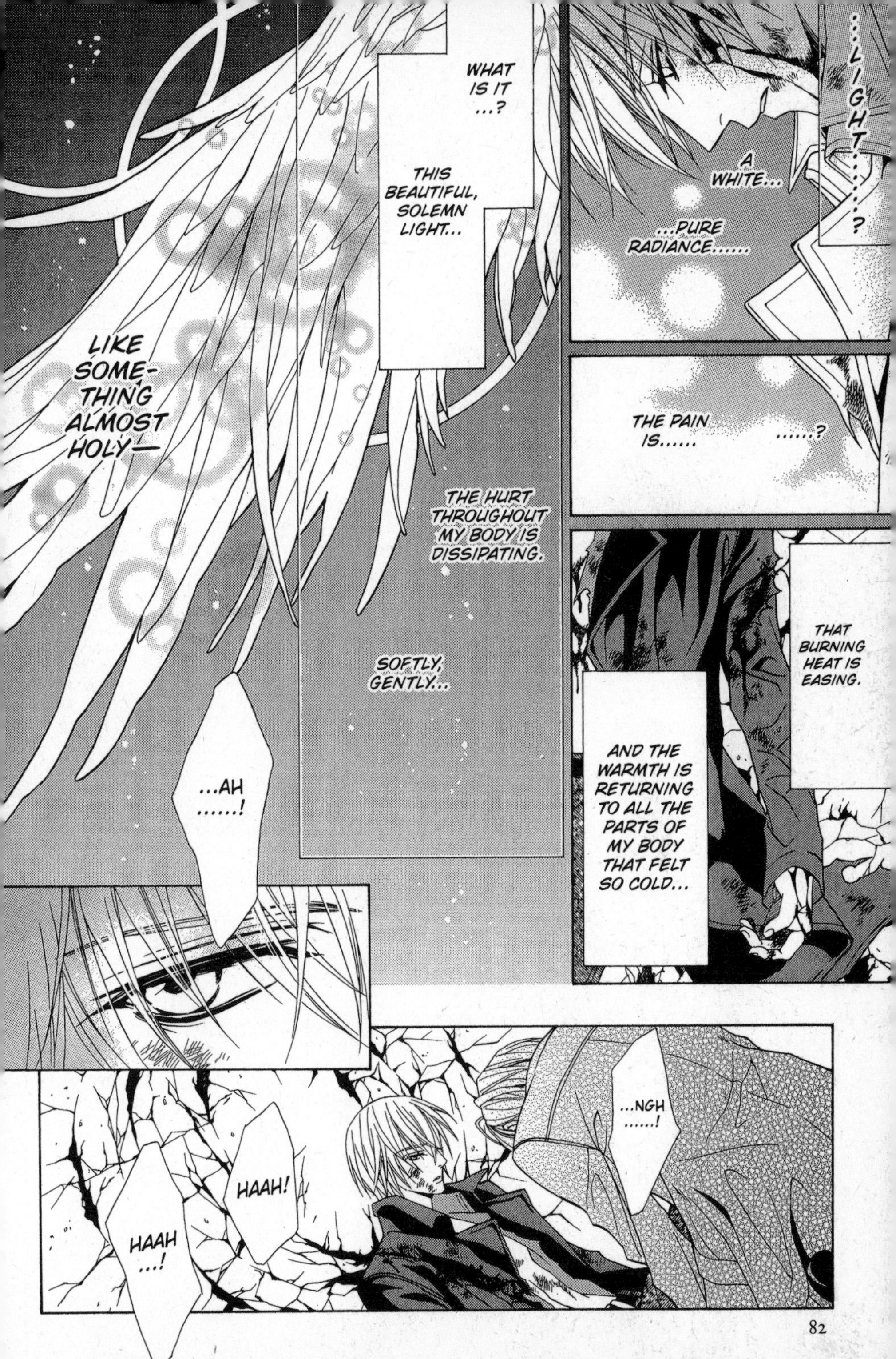
...LIGHT......?
A WHITE...
...PURE RADIANCE......
THE PAIN IS......
......?
THAT BURNING HEAT IS EASING.
AND THE WARMTH IS RETURNING TO ALL THE PARTS OF MY BODY THAT FELT SO COLD...
WHAT IS IT ...?
THIS BEAUTIFUL, SOLEMN LIGHT...
LIKE SOME-THING ALMOST HOLY—
THE HURT THROUGHOUT MY BODY IS DISSIPATING.
SOFTLY, GENTLY...
...AH ......!
...NGH ......!
HAAH!
HAAH ...!

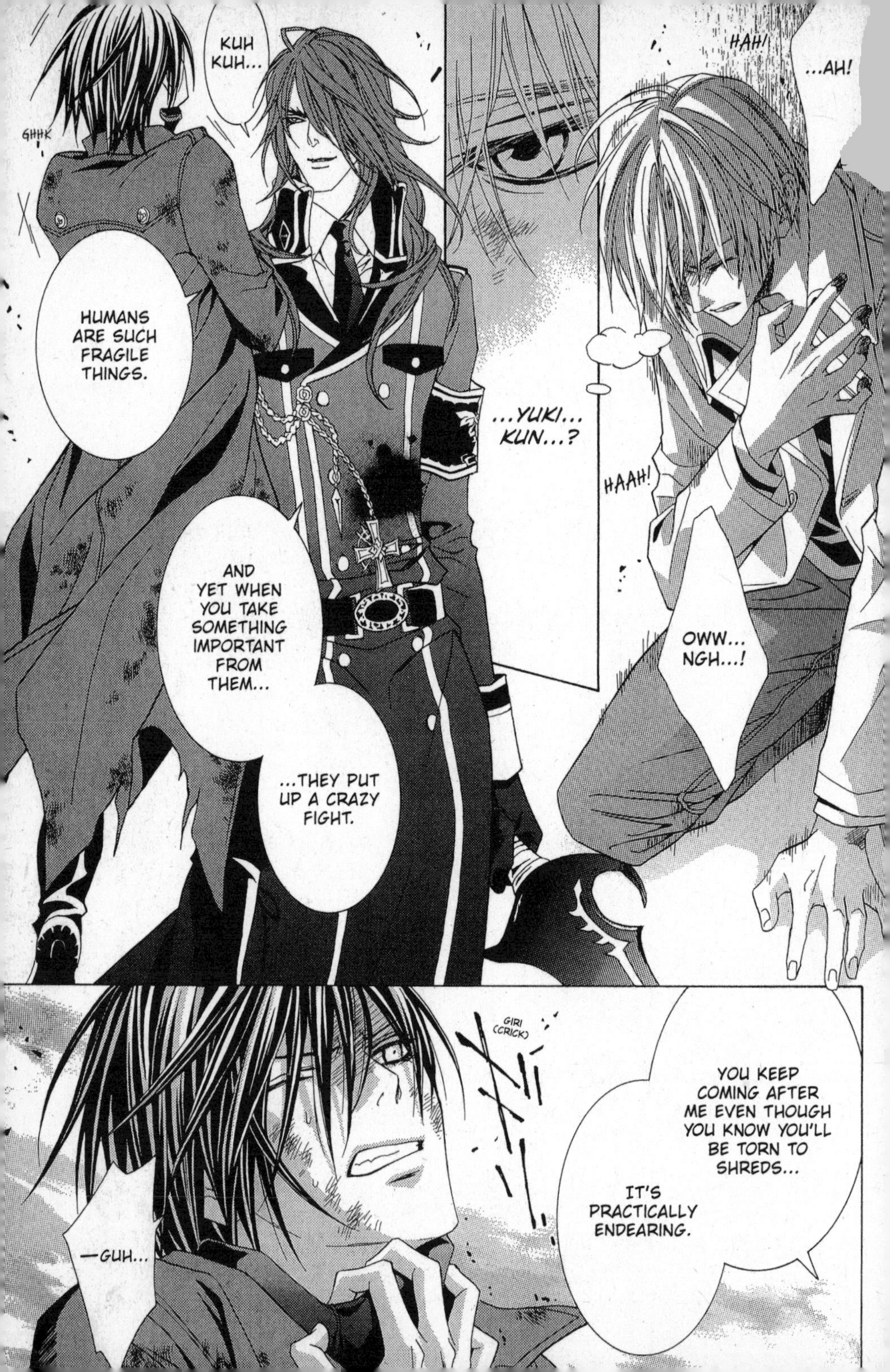

HAH!
...AH!
HAAH!
OWW... NGH...!
...YUKI... KUN...?
KUH KUH...
GHHK
HUMANS ARE SUCH FRAGILE THINGS.
AND YET WHEN YOU TAKE SOMETHING IMPORTANT FROM THEM...
...THEY PUT UP A CRAZY FIGHT.
GIRI (CRICK)
YOU KEEP COMING AFTER ME EVEN THOUGH YOU KNOW YOU'LL BE TORN TO SHREDS...
IT'S PRACTICALLY ENDEARING.
—GUH...

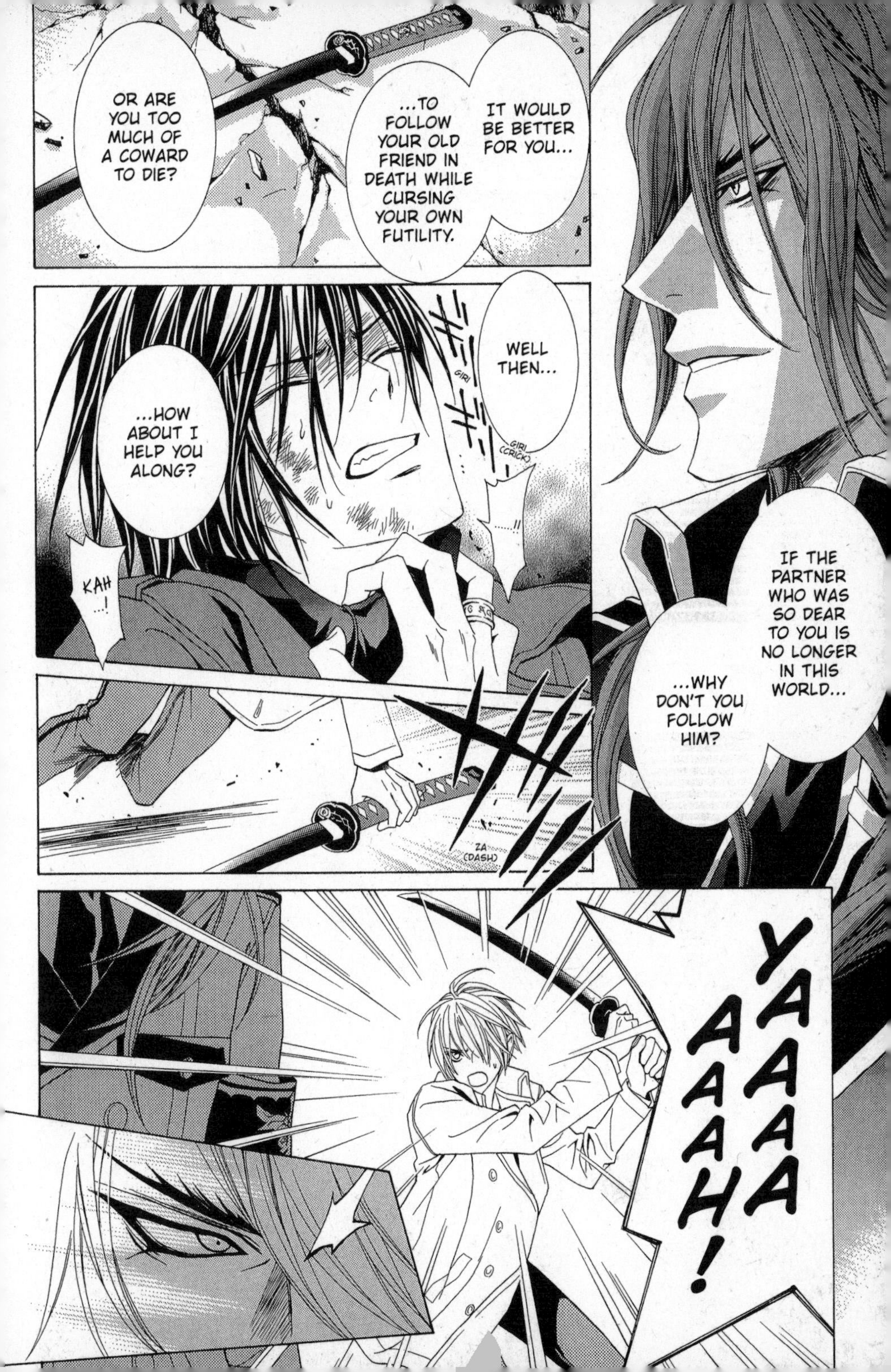
IF THE PARTNER WHO WAS SO DEAR TO YOU IS NO LONGER IN THIS WORLD...
...WHY DON'T YOU FOLLOW HIM?
IT WOULD BE BETTER FOR YOU...
...TO FOLLOW YOUR OLD FRIEND IN DEATH WHILE CURSING YOUR OWN FUTILITY.
OR ARE YOU TOO MUCH OF A COWARD TO DIE?
WELL THEN...
GIRI
GIRI (CRICK)
...!!
...HOW ABOUT I HELP YOU ALONG?
KAH ...!
ZA (DASH)
YAAAAAAAH!

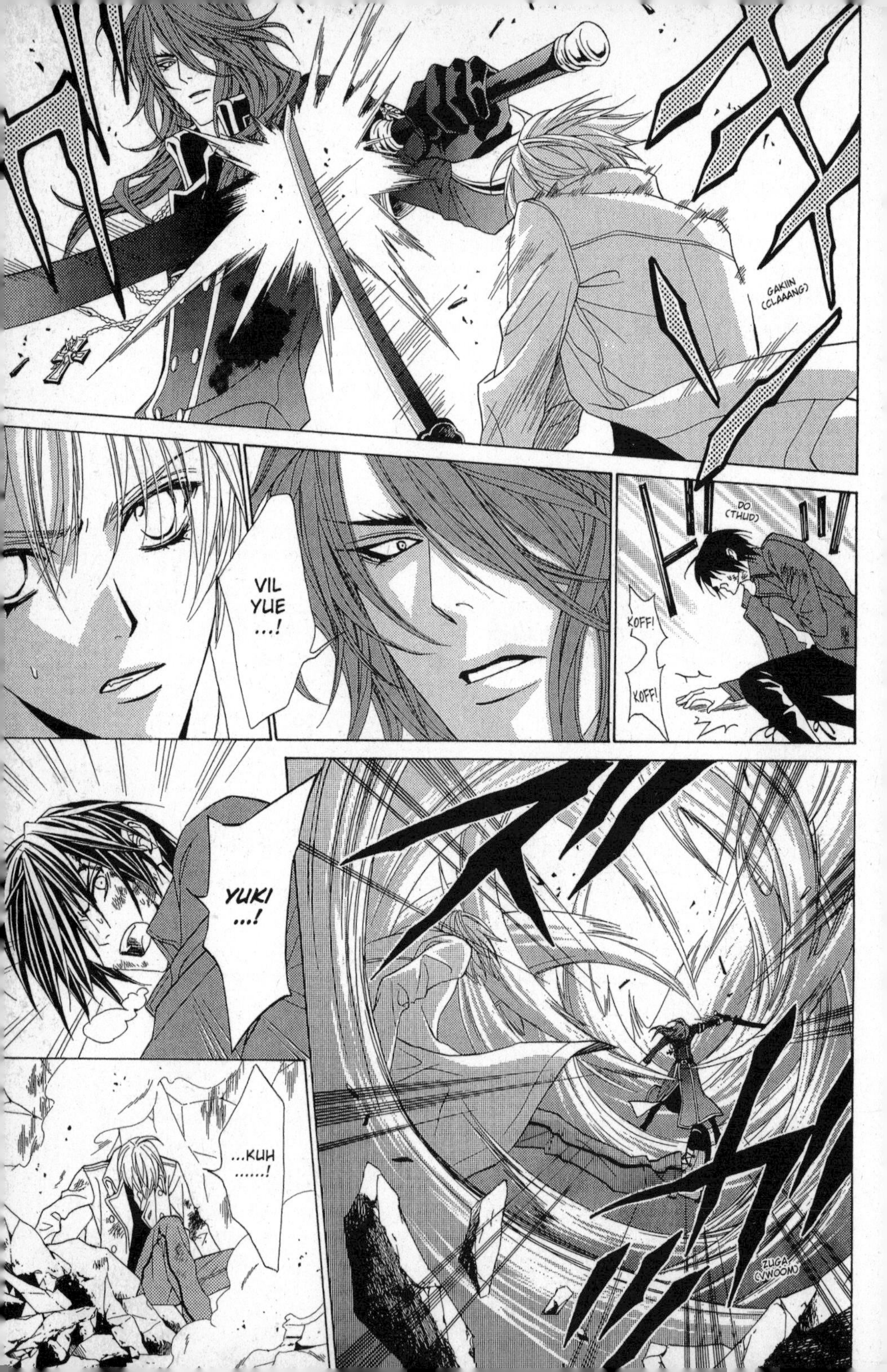
GAKIIN (CLAAANG)
DO (THUD)
KOFF!
KOFF!
VIL YUE ...!
ZUGA (VWOOM)
YUKI ...!
...KUH ......!

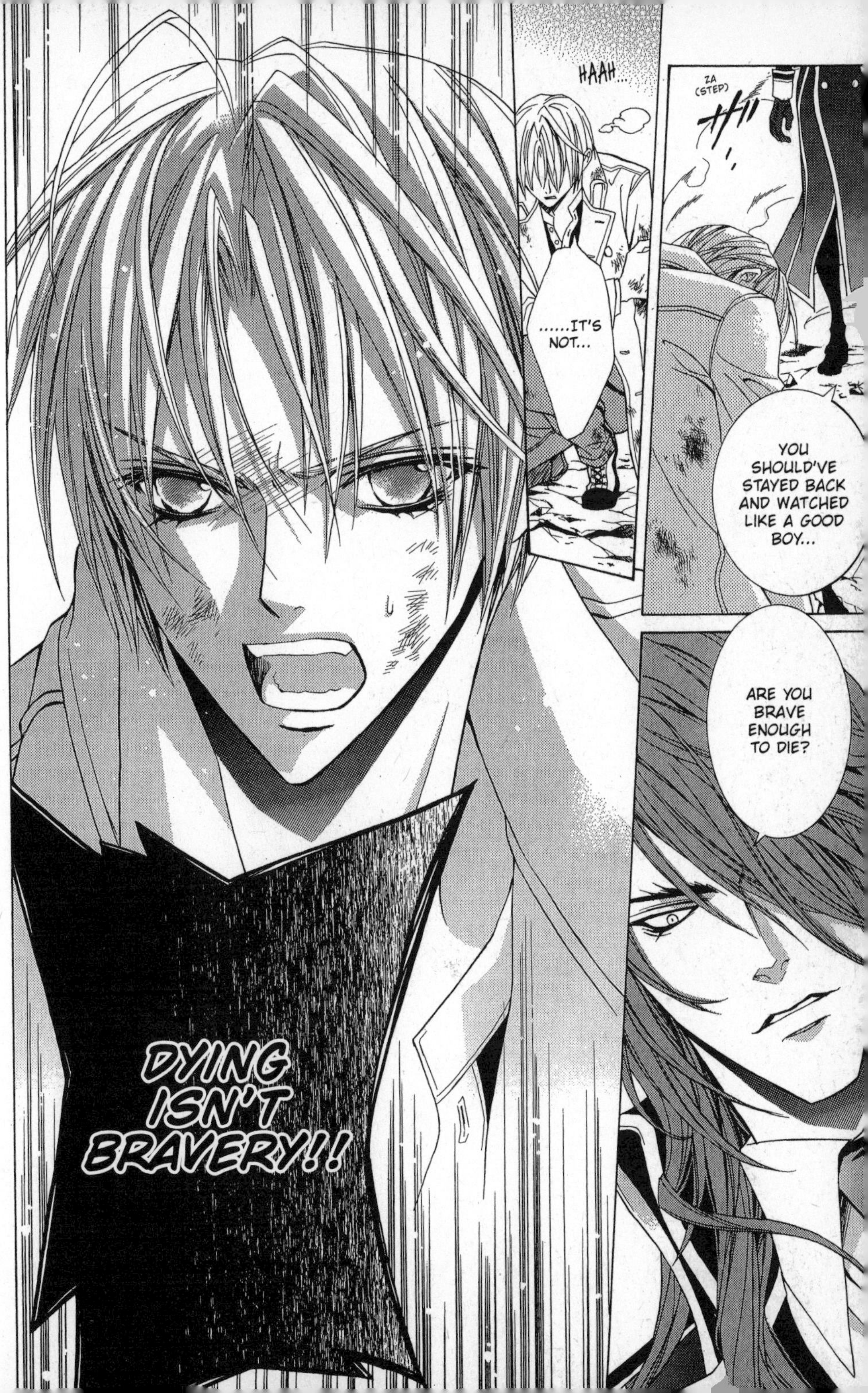
ZA (STEP)
YOU SHOULD'VE STAYED BACK AND WATCHED LIKE A GOOD BOY...
HAAH...
......IT'S NOT...
ARE YOU BRAVE ENOUGH TO DIE?
DYING ISN'T BRAVERY!!

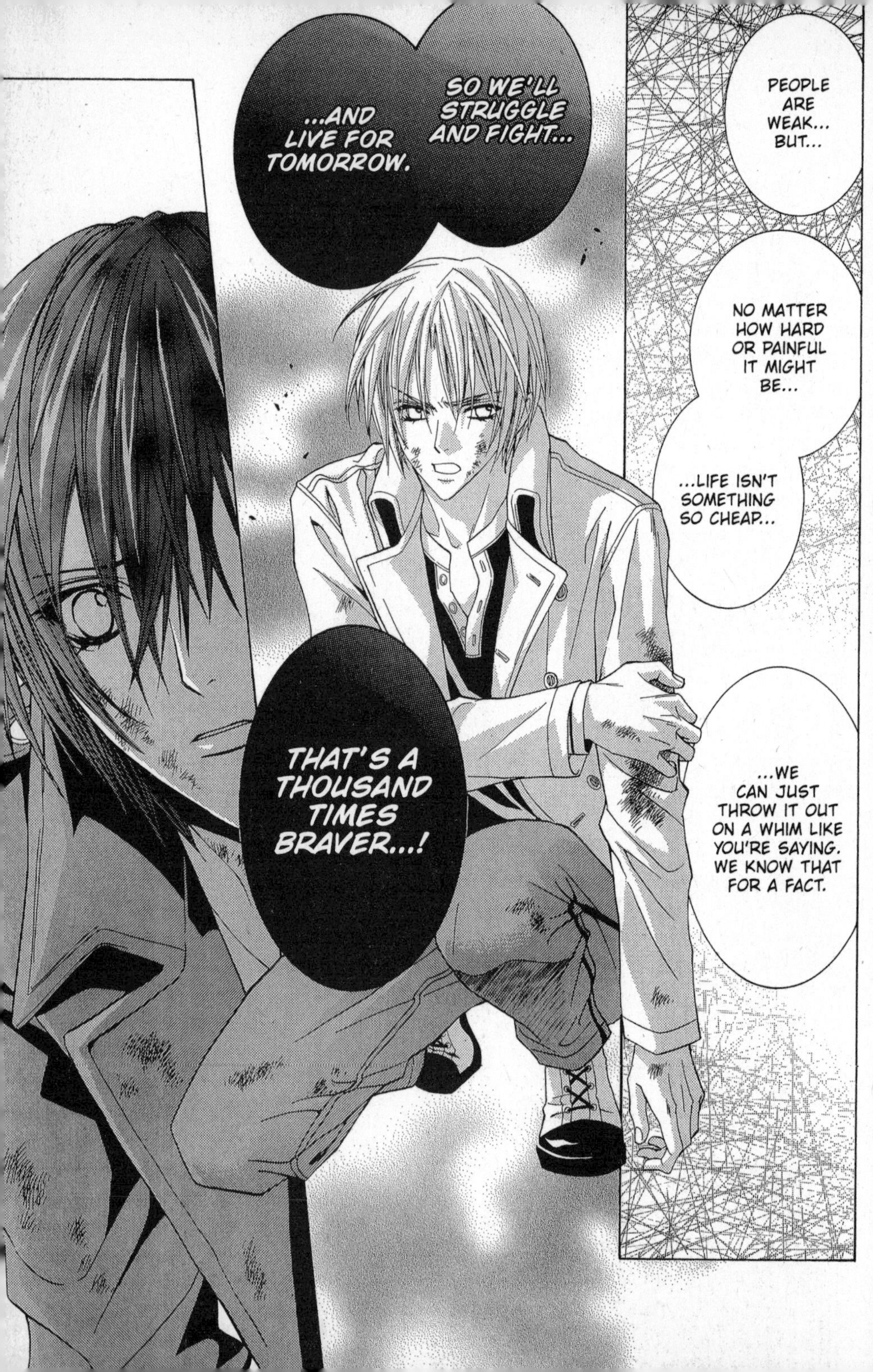
PEOPLE ARE WEAK... BUT...
NO MATTER HOW HARD OR PAINFUL IT MIGHT BE...
...LIFE ISN'T SOMETHING SO CHEAP...
...WE CAN JUST THROW IT OUT ON A WHIM LIKE YOU'RE SAYING. WE KNOW THAT FOR A FACT.
SO WE'LL STRUGGLE AND FIGHT...
...AND LIVE FOR TOMORROW.
THAT'S A THOUSAND TIMES BRAVER...!

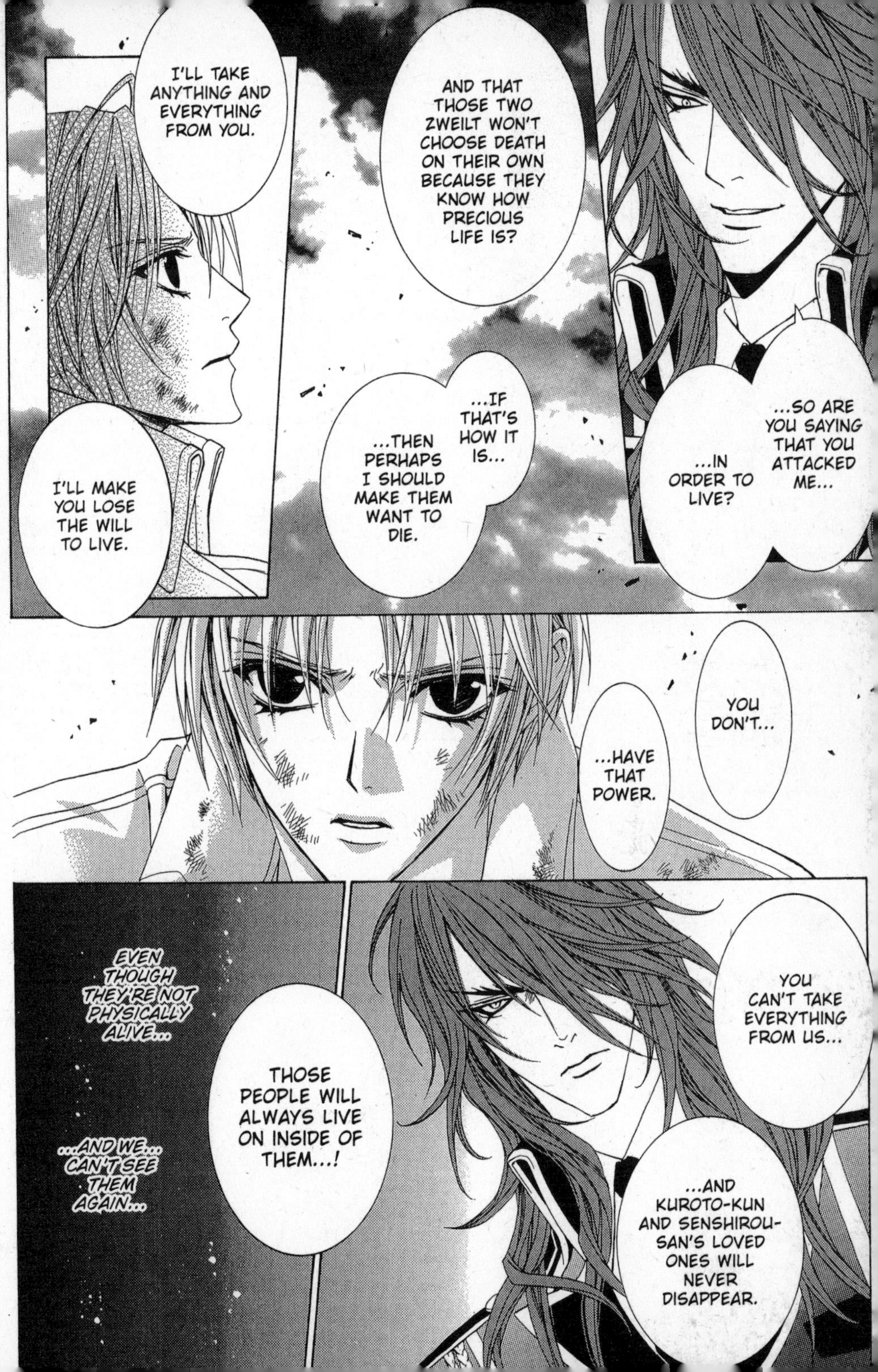
...SO ARE YOU SAYING THAT YOU ATTACKED ME...
...IN ORDER TO LIVE?
AND THAT THOSE TWO ZWEILT WON'T CHOOSE DEATH ON THEIR OWN BECAUSE THEY KNOW HOW PRECIOUS LIFE IS?
...IF THAT'S HOW IT IS...
...THEN PERHAPS I SHOULD MAKE THEM WANT TO DIE.
I'LL TAKE ANYTHING AND EVERYTHING FROM YOU.
I'LL MAKE YOU LOSE THE WILL TO LIVE.
YOU DON'T...
...HAVE THAT POWER.
YOU CAN'T TAKE EVERYTHING FROM US...
...AND KUROTO-KUN AND SENSHIROU-SAN'S LOVED ONES WILL NEVER DISAPPEAR.
THOSE PEOPLE WILL ALWAYS LIVE ON INSIDE OF THEM...!
EVEN THOUGH THEY'RE NOT PHYSICALLY ALIVE...
...AND WE... CAN'T SEE THEM AGAIN...

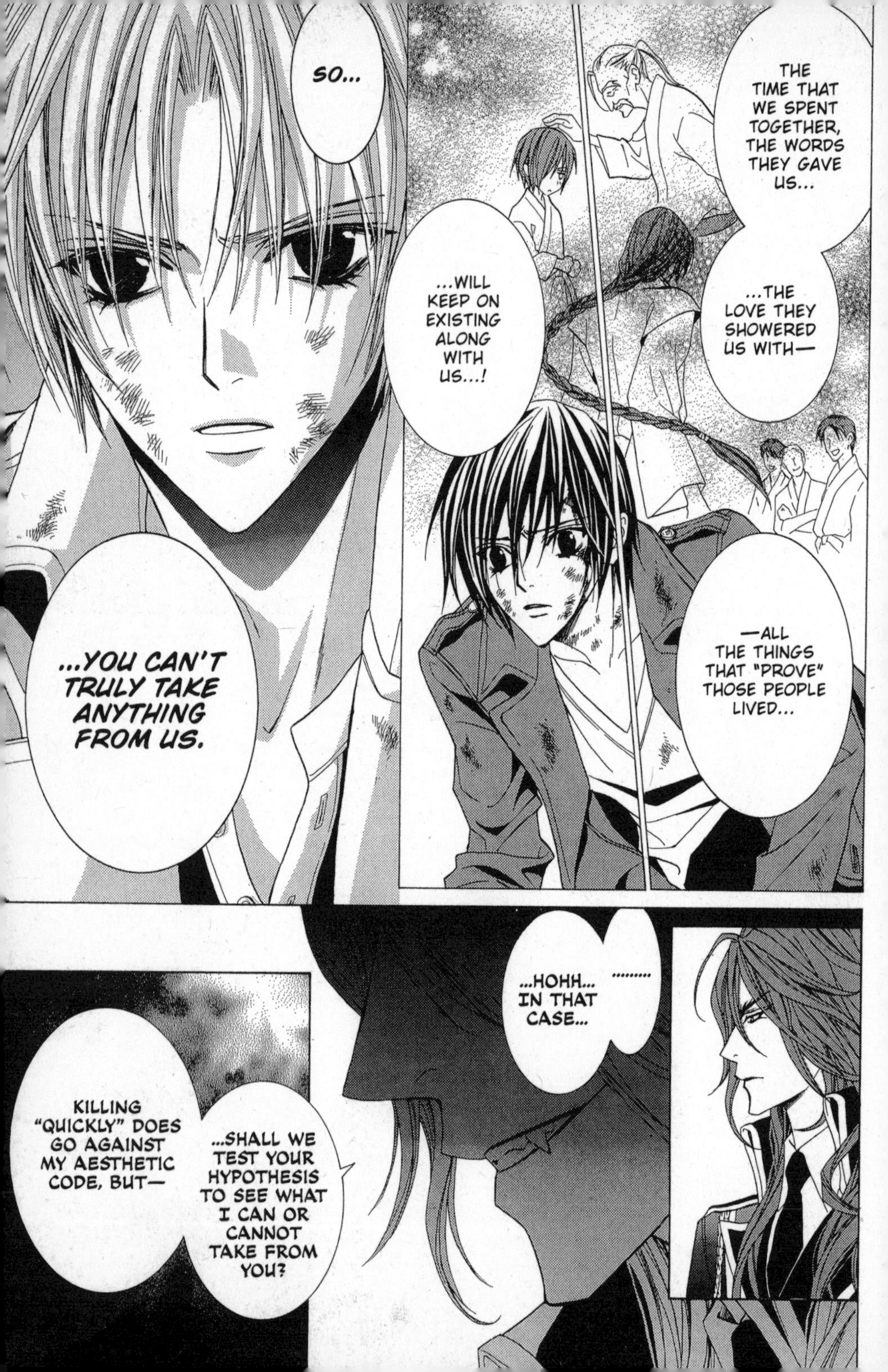
THE TIME THAT WE SPENT TOGETHER, THE WORDS THEY GAVE US...
...THE LOVE THEY SHOWERED US WITH—
—ALL THE THINGS THAT "PROVE" THOSE PEOPLE LIVED...
...WILL KEEP ON EXISTING ALONG WITH US...!
SO...
...YOU CAN'T TRULY TAKE ANYTHING FROM US.
....
...HOHH... IN THAT CASE...
KILLING "QUICKLY" DOES GO AGAINST MY AESTHETIC CODE, BUT—
...SHALL WE TEST YOUR HYPOTHESIS TO SEE WHAT I CAN OR CANNOT TAKE FROM YOU?

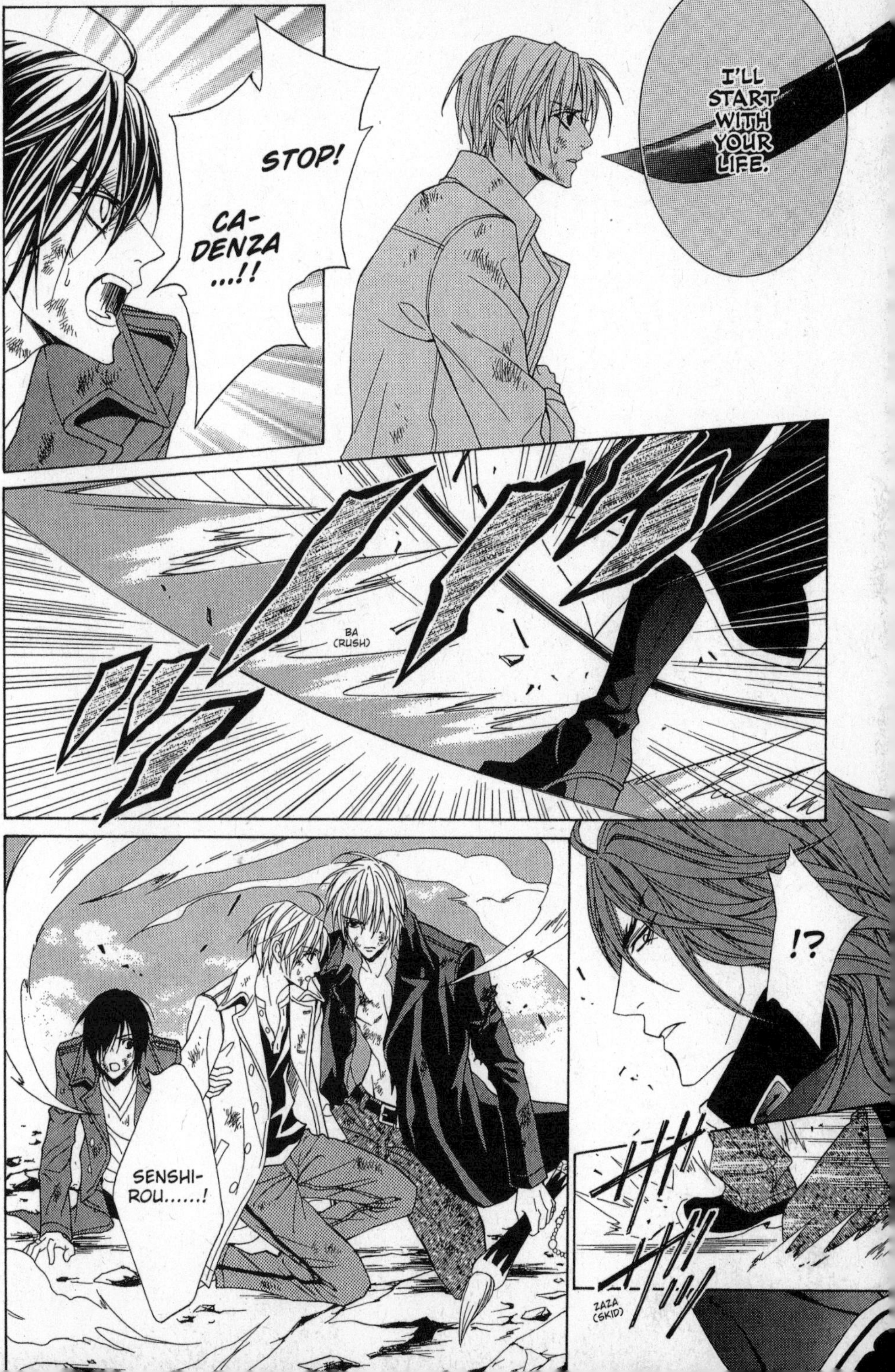
I'LL START WITH YOUR LIFE.
STOP!
CA-DENZA ...!!
BA (RUSH)
!?
ZAZA (SKID)
SENSHIROU......!

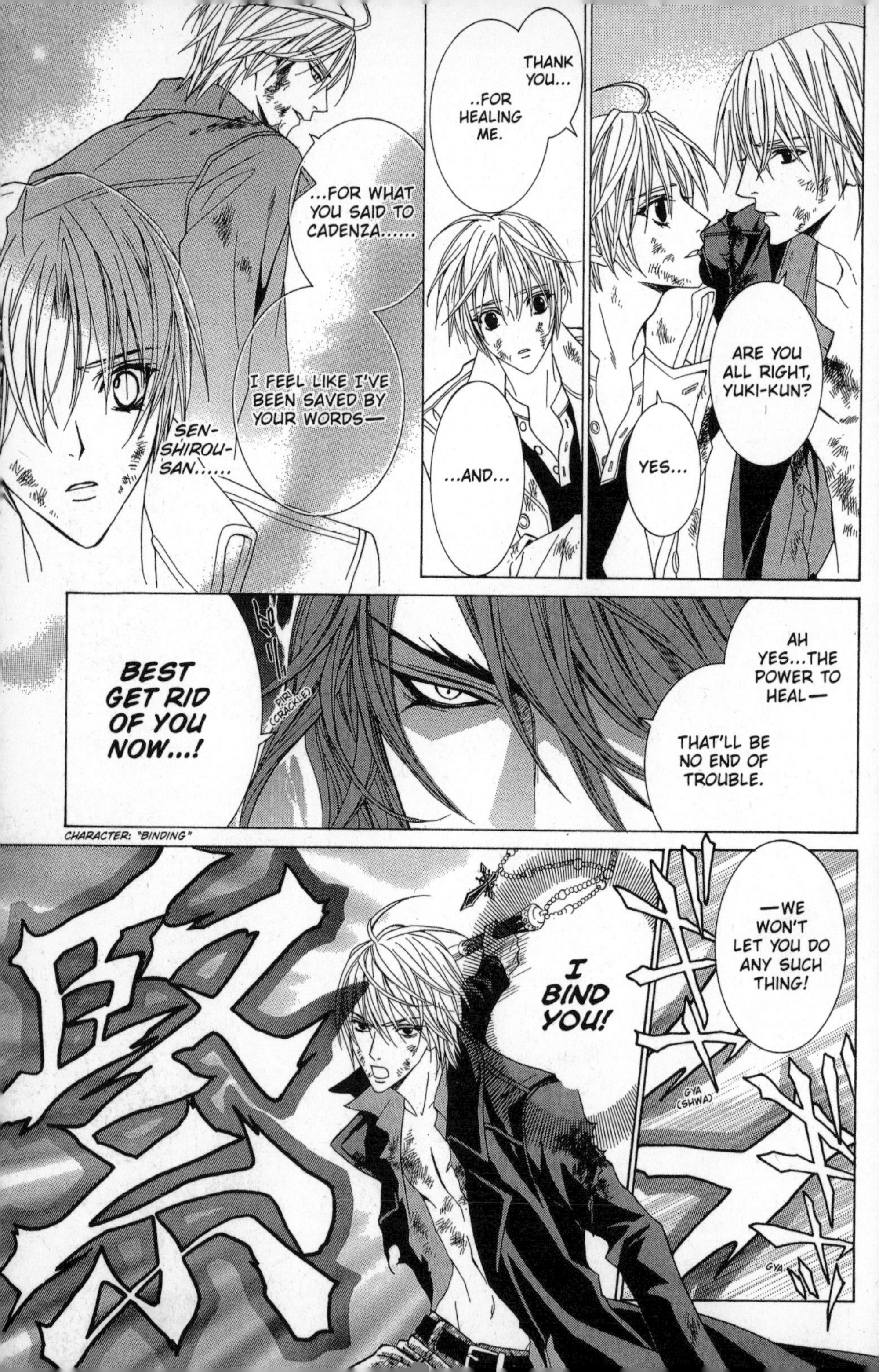
ARE YOU ALL RIGHT, YUKI-KUN?
YES...
THANK YOU...
..FOR HEALING ME.
...AND...
...FOR WHAT YOU SAID TO CADENZA......
I FEEL LIKE I'VE BEEN SAVED BY YOUR WORDS—
SEN-SHIROU-SAN......
AH YES...THE POWER TO HEAL—
THAT'LL BE NO END OF TROUBLE.
PIRI (CRACKLE)
BEST GET RID OF YOU NOW...!
CHARACTER: "BINDING"
—WE WON'T LET YOU DO ANY SUCH THING!
I BIND YOU!
GYA (SHWA)
GYA

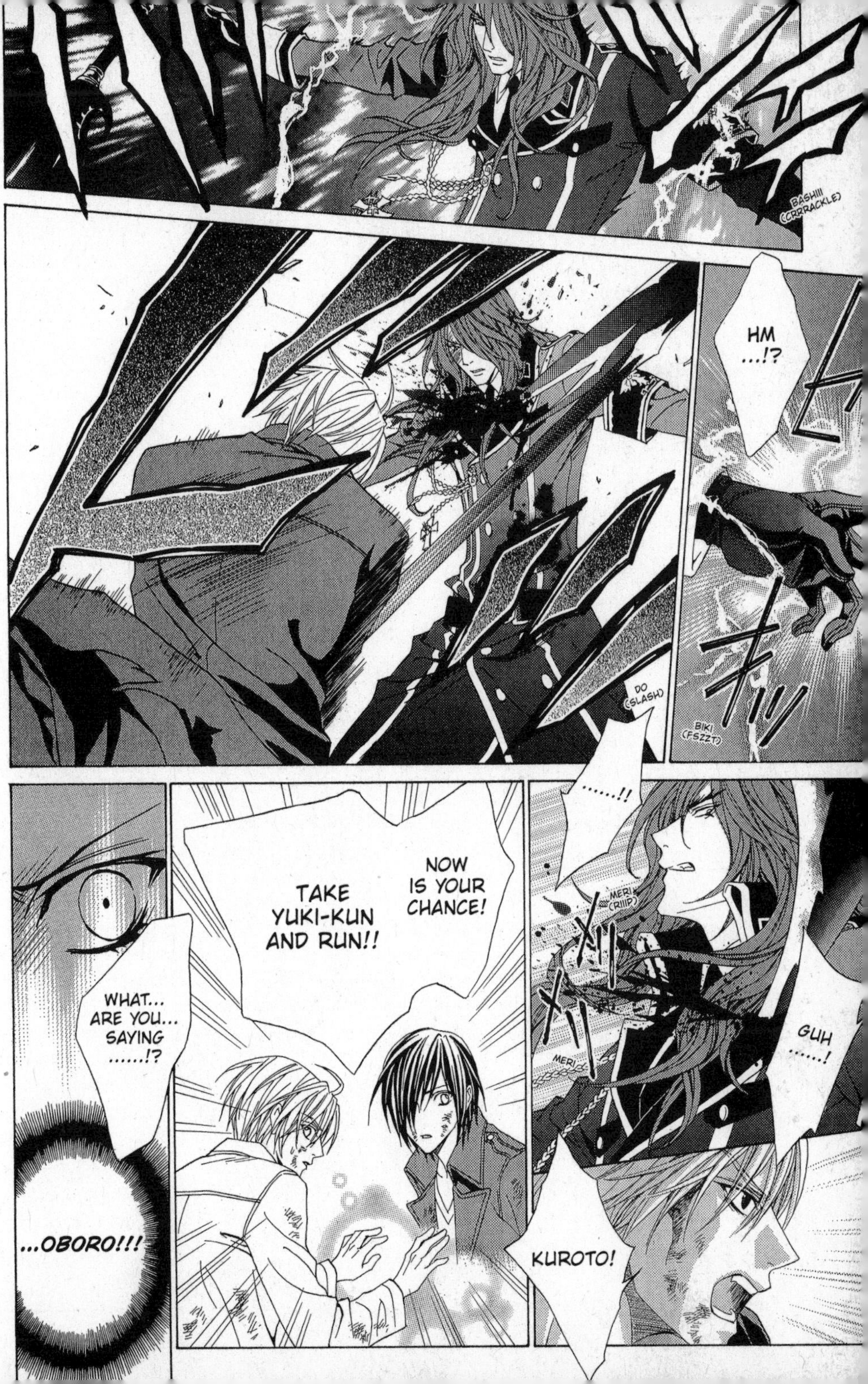
BASHIII (CRRRACKLE)
HM ...!?
BIKI (FSZZT)
DO (SLASH)
......!!
MERI (RIIIP)
MERI
GUH ......!
KUROTO!
NOW IS YOUR CHANCE!
TAKE YUKI-KUN AND RUN!!
WHAT... ARE YOU... SAYING ......!?
...OBORO!!!

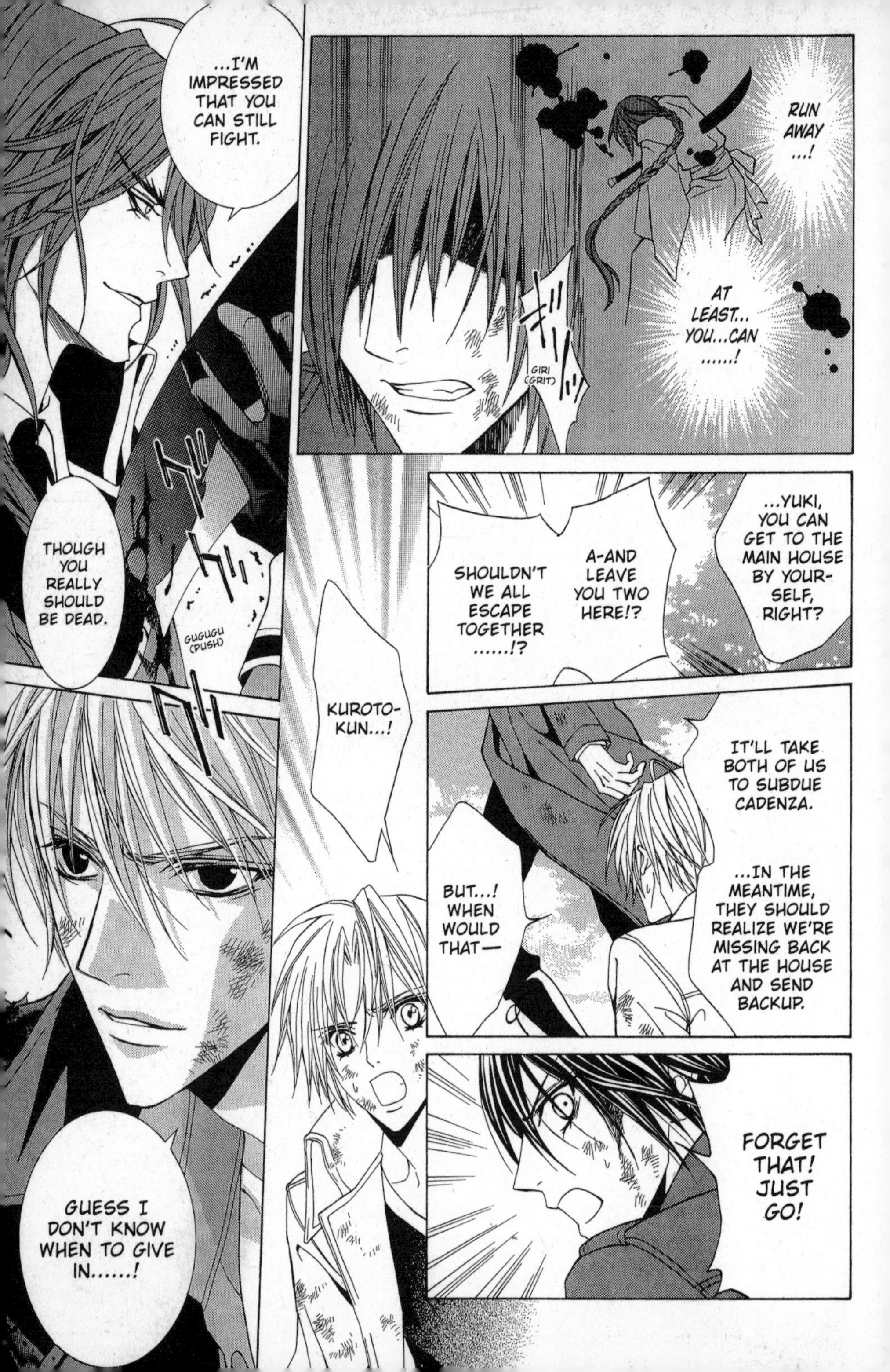
RUN AWAY ...!
AT LEAST... YOU...CAN ......!
GIRI (GRIT)
...I'M IMPRESSED THAT YOU CAN STILL FIGHT.
THOUGH YOU REALLY SHOULD BE DEAD.
GUGUGU (PUSH)
GUESS I DON'T KNOW WHEN TO GIVE IN......!
...YUKI, YOU CAN GET TO THE MAIN HOUSE BY YOUR-SELF, RIGHT?
A-AND LEAVE YOU TWO HERE!?
SHOULDN'T WE ALL ESCAPE TOGETHER ......!?
IT'LL TAKE BOTH OF US TO SUBDUE CADENZA.
...IN THE MEANTIME, THEY SHOULD REALIZE WE'RE MISSING BACK AT THE HOUSE AND SEND BACKUP.
BUT...! WHEN WOULD THAT—
FORGET THAT! JUST GO!
KUROTO-KUN...!

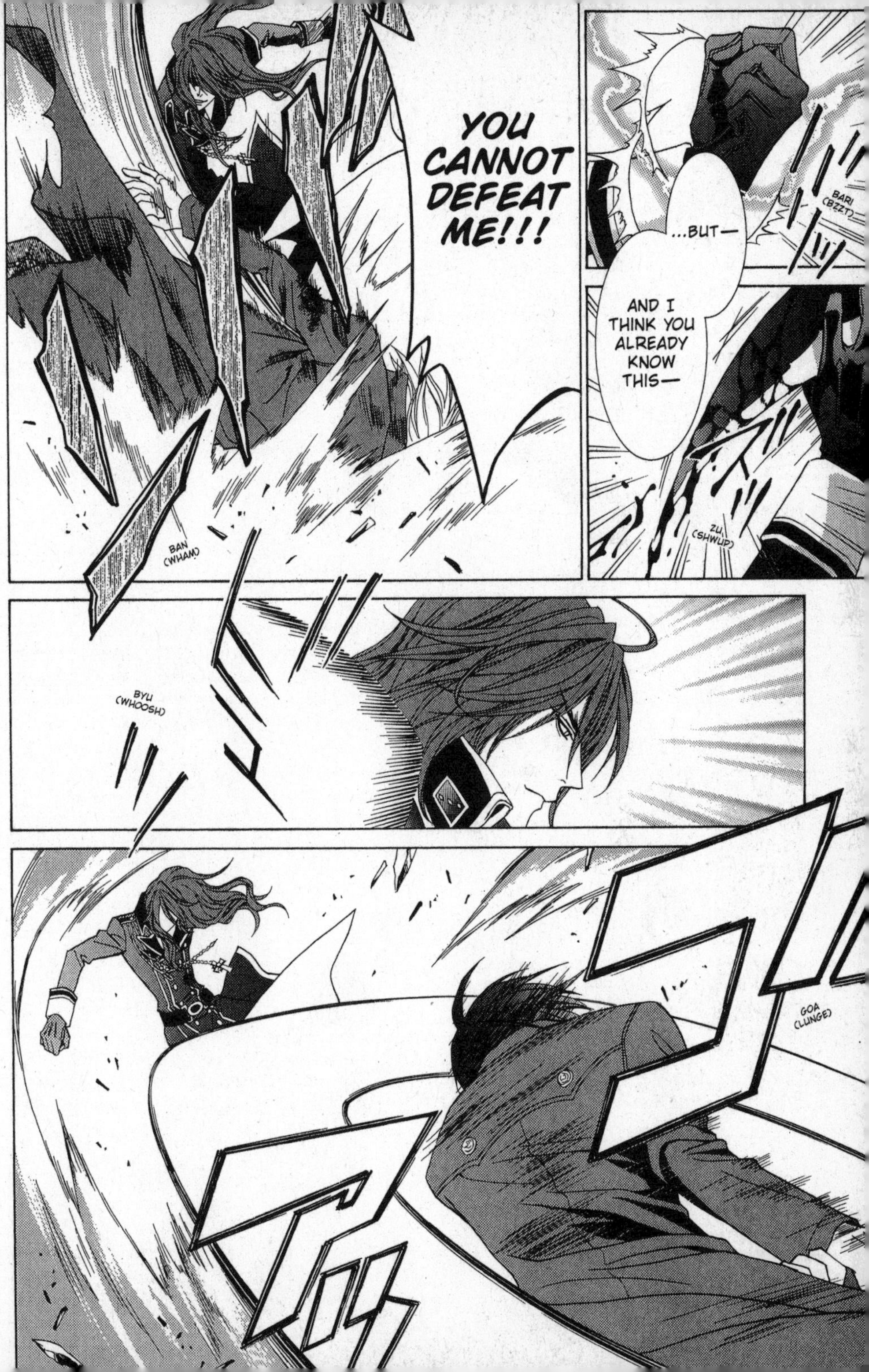
BARI (BZZT)
...BUT—
AND I THINK YOU ALREADY KNOW THIS—
ZU (SHWUP)
YOU CANNOT DEFEAT ME!!!
BAN (WHAM)
BYU (WHOOSH)
GOA (LUNGE)

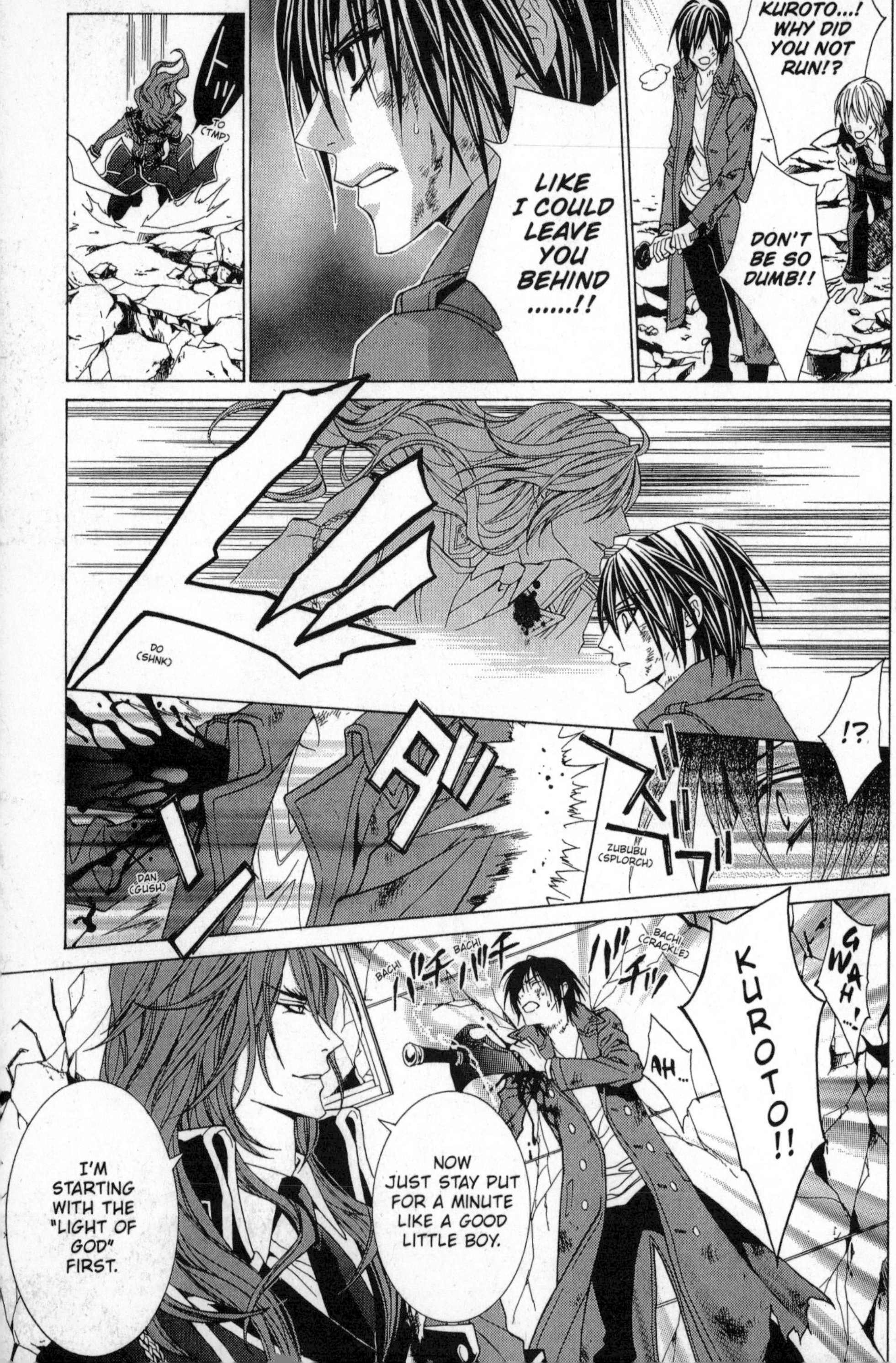
KUROTO...! WHY DID YOU NOT RUN!?
DON'T BE SO DUMB!!
LIKE I COULD LEAVE YOU BEHIND ......!!
TO (TMP)
DO (SHNK)
!?
ZUBUBU (SPLORCH)
DAN (GUSH)
GWAH...!
KUROTO!!
AH...
BACHI (CRACKLE)
BACHI
BACHI
NOW JUST STAY PUT FOR A MINUTE LIKE A GOOD LITTLE BOY.
I'M STARTING WITH THE "LIGHT OF GOD" FIRST.

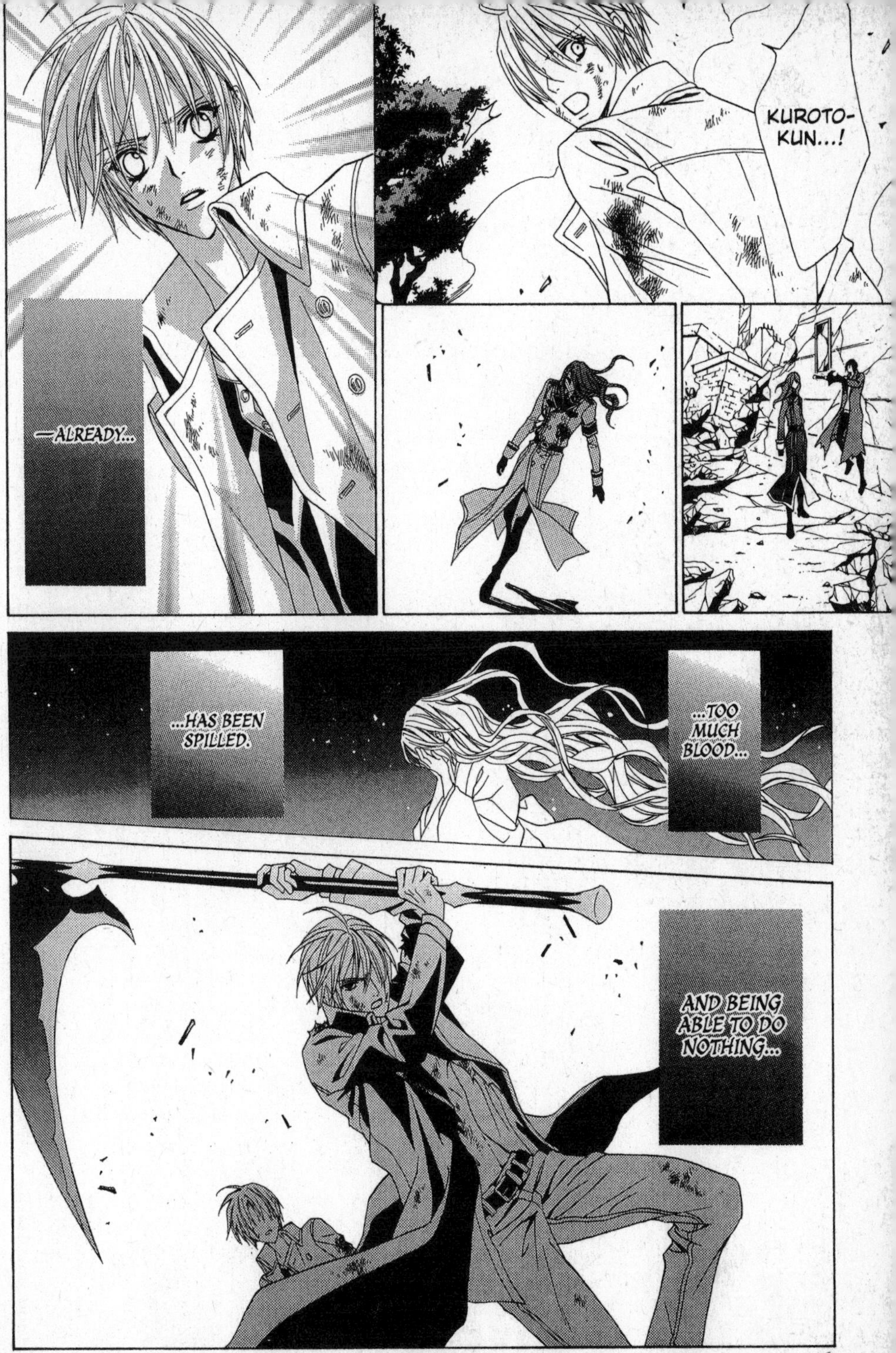
KUROTO-KUN...!
—ALREADY...
...TOO MUCH BLOOD...
...HAS BEEN SPILLED.
AND BEING ABLE TO DO NOTHING...

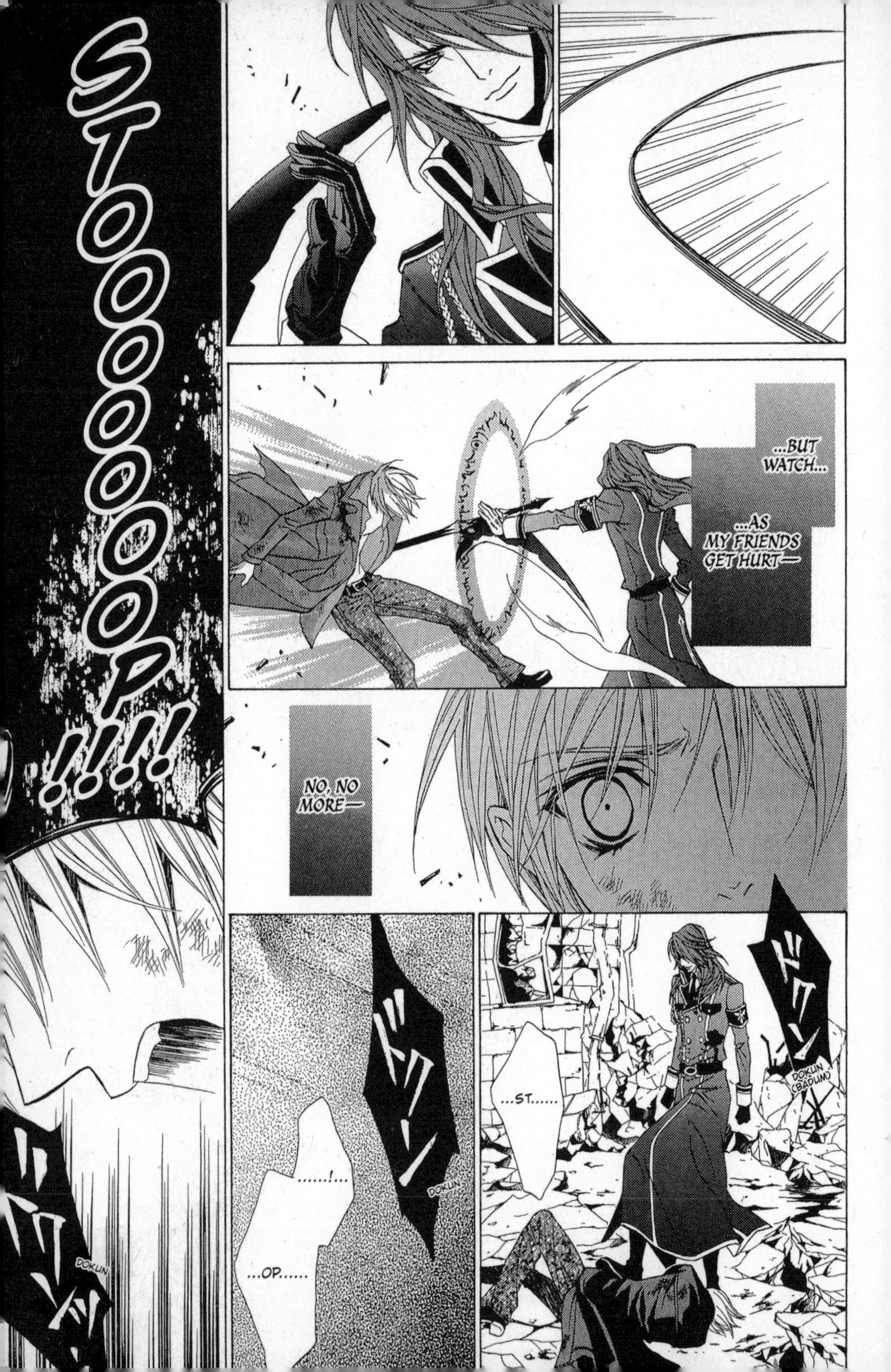
...BUT WATCH...
...AS MY FRIENDS GET HURT—
NO, NO MORE—
ドクン
DOKUN (BADUM)
...ST......
ドクン
DOKUN
......!...
...OP......
STOOOOOOOP!!!!
ドクン
DOKUN

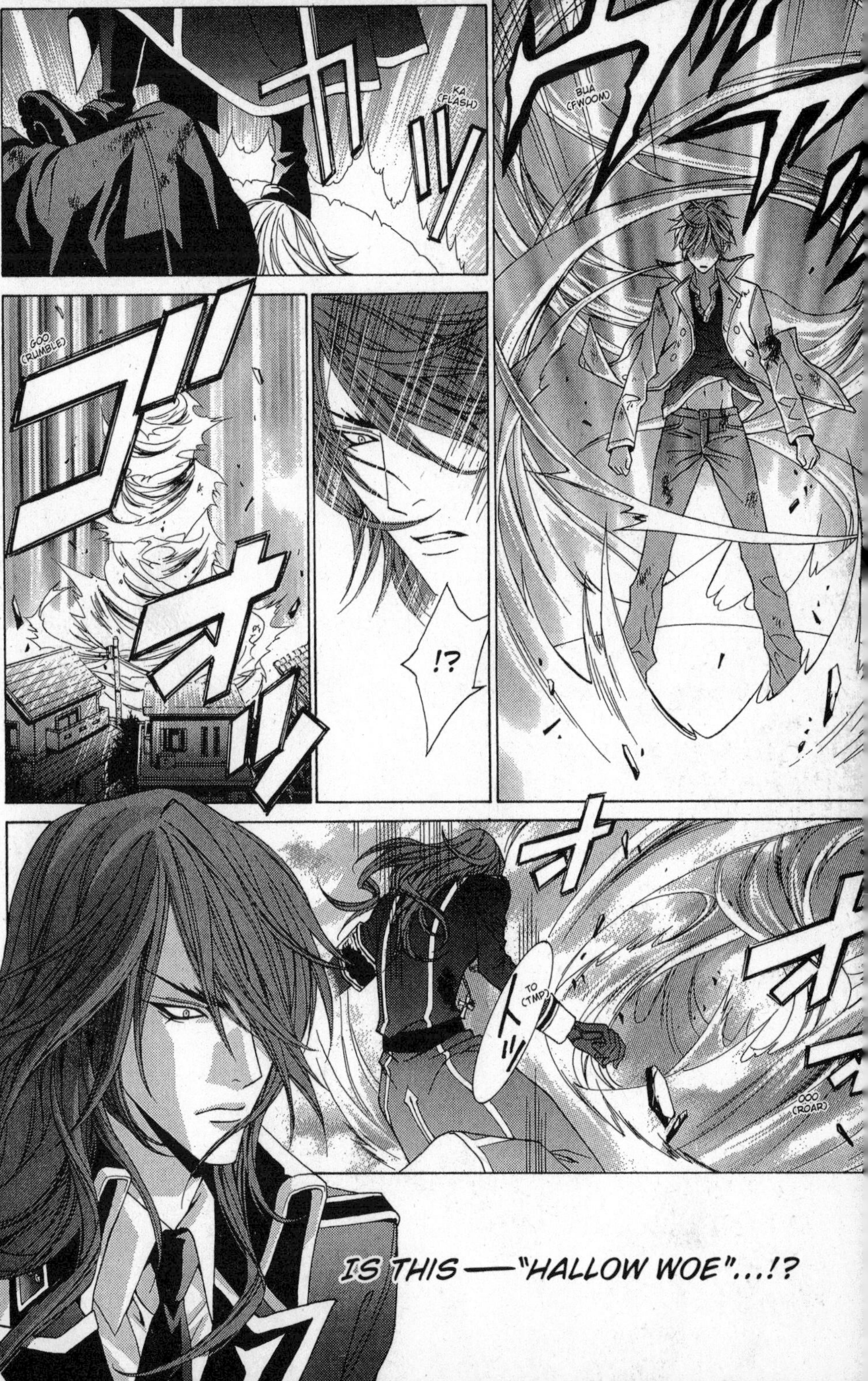
BUA
(FWOOM)
KA
(FLASH)
!?
GOO
(RUMBLE)
OOO
(ROAR)
TO
(TMP)
IS THIS——"HALLOW WOE"...!?

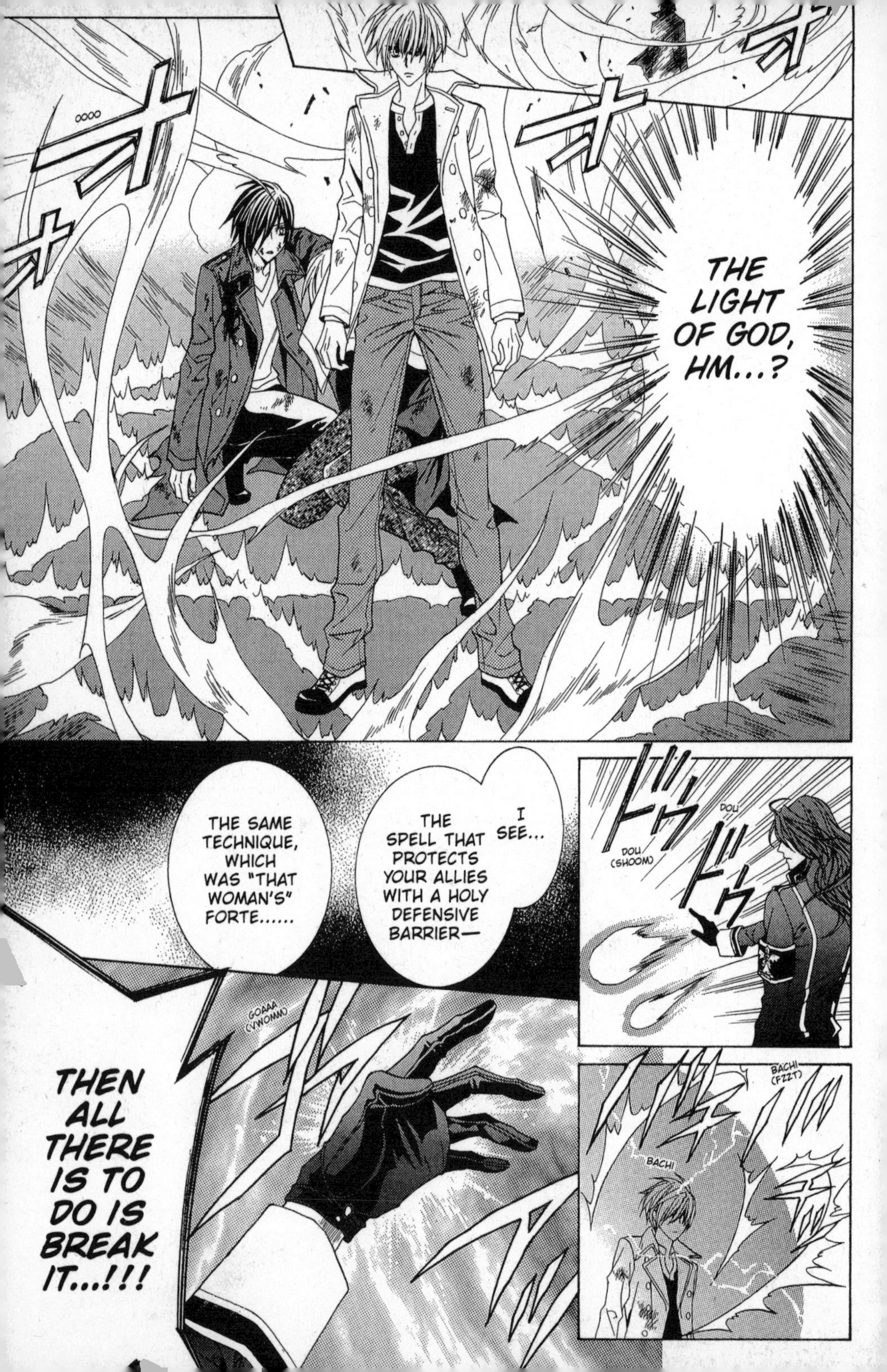
oooo
THE LIGHT OF GOD, HM...?
DOU
DOU (SHOOM)
I SEE...
THE SPELL THAT PROTECTS YOUR ALLIES WITH A HOLY DEFENSIVE BARRIER—
THE SAME TECHNIQUE, WHICH WAS "THAT WOMAN'S" FORTE......
BACHI (FZZT)
BACHI
GOAAA (VWOMM)
THEN ALL THERE IS TO DO IS BREAK IT...!!!

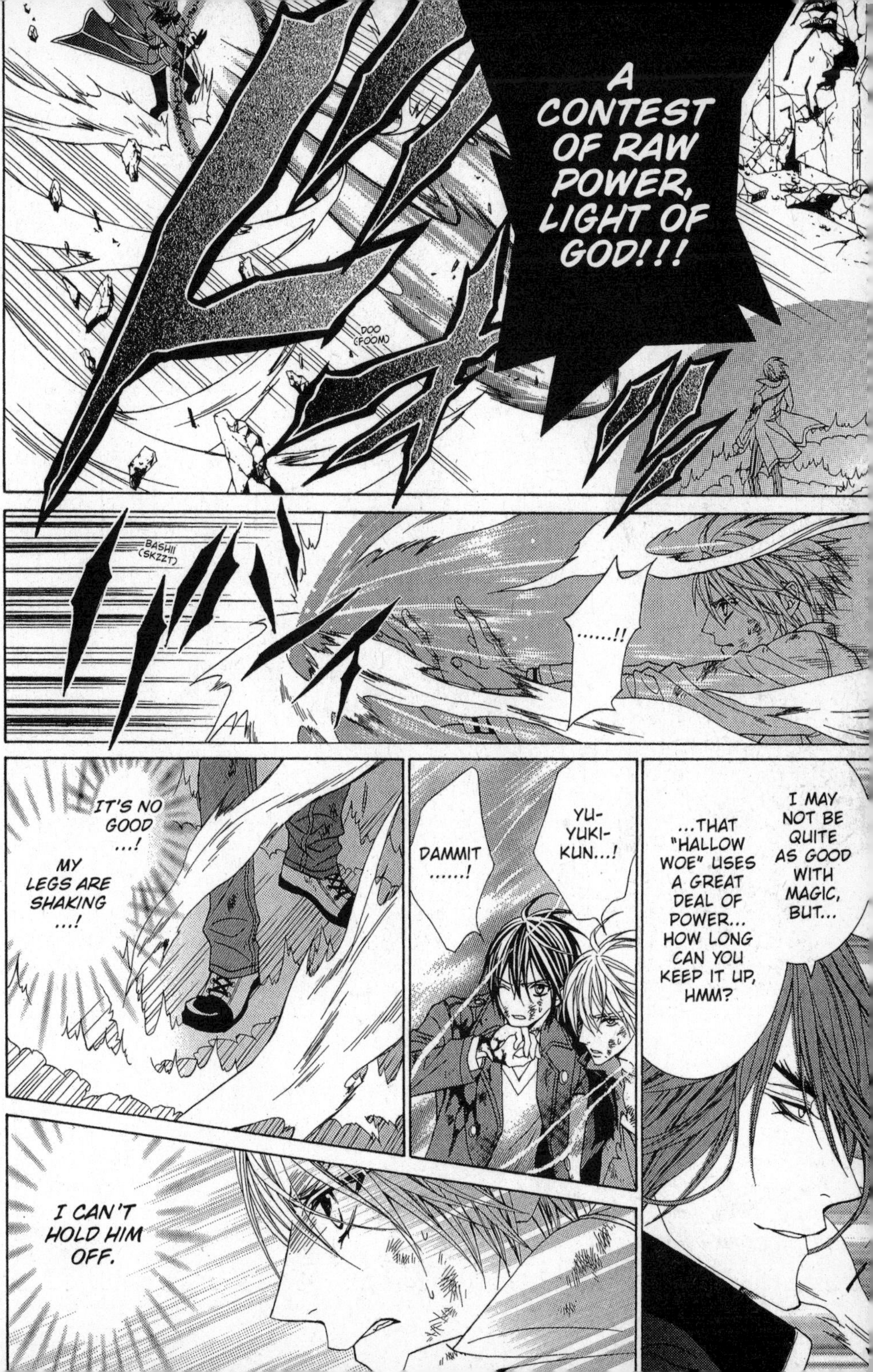
A CONTEST OF RAW POWER, LIGHT OF GOD!!!
DOO (FOOM)
BASHII (SKZZT)
......!!
I MAY NOT BE QUITE AS GOOD WITH MAGIC, BUT...
...THAT "HALLOW WOE" USES A GREAT DEAL OF POWER... HOW LONG CAN YOU KEEP IT UP, HMM?
YU-YUKI-KUN...!
DAMMIT ......!
IT'S NO GOOD ...!
MY LEGS ARE SHAKING ...!
I CAN'T HOLD HIM OFF.

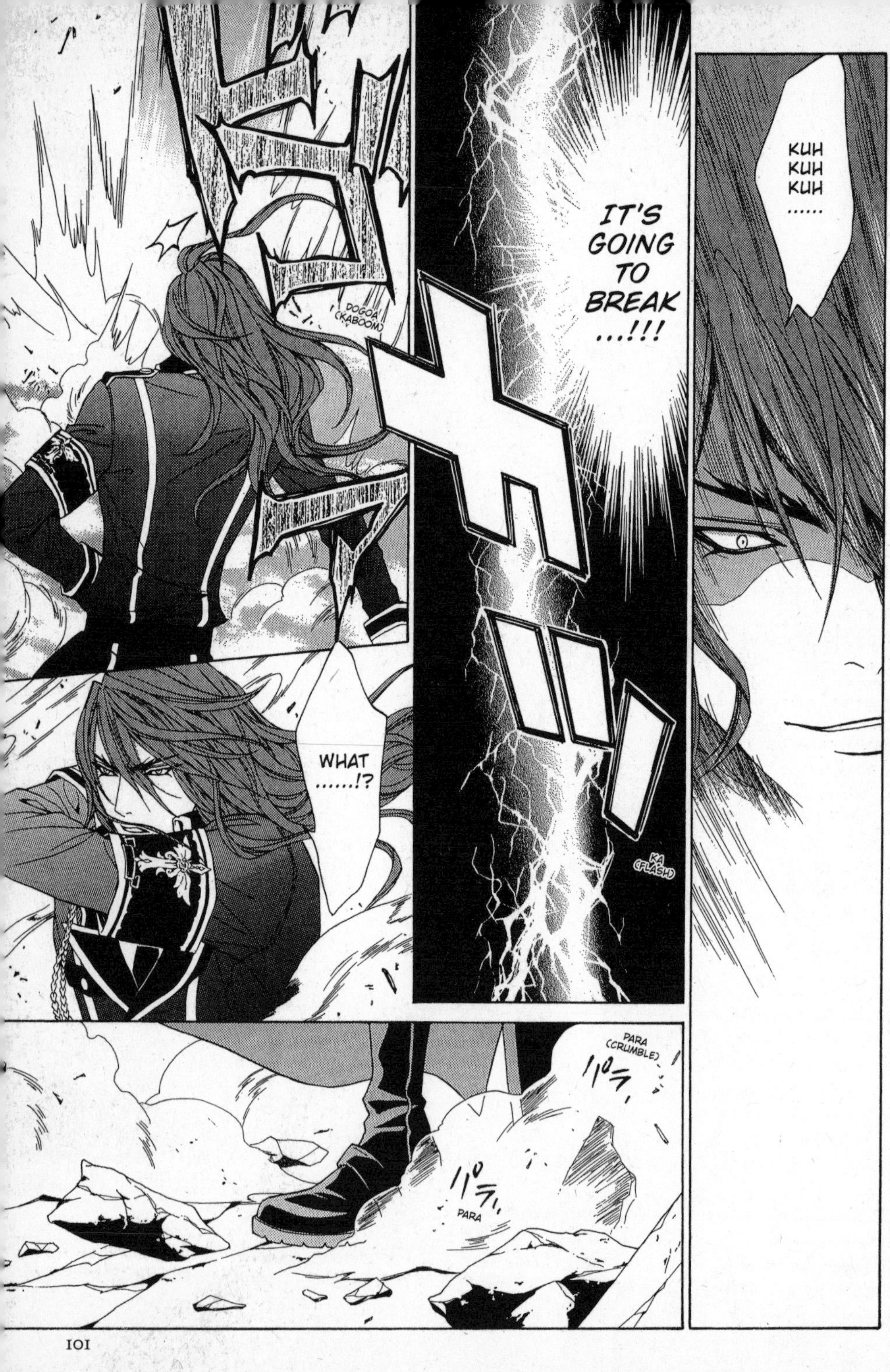
KUH KUH KUH ......
IT'S GOING TO BREAK ...!!!
KA (FLASH)
DOGOA (KABOOM)
WHAT ......!?
PARA (CRUMBLE)
PARA

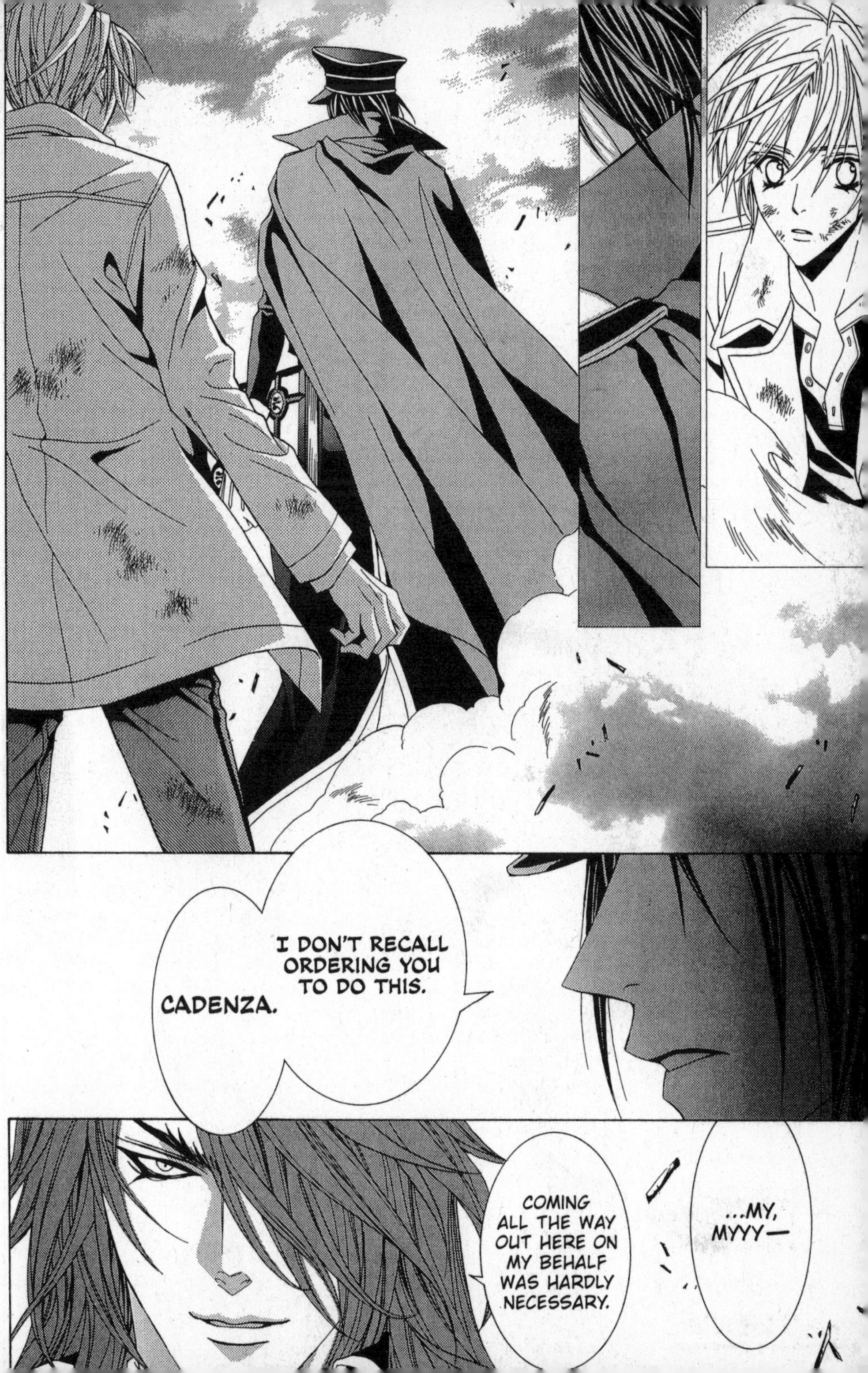
I DON'T RECALL ORDERING YOU TO DO THIS.
CADENZA.
...MY, MYYY—
COMING ALL THE WAY OUT HERE ON MY BEHALF WAS HARDLY NECESSARY.

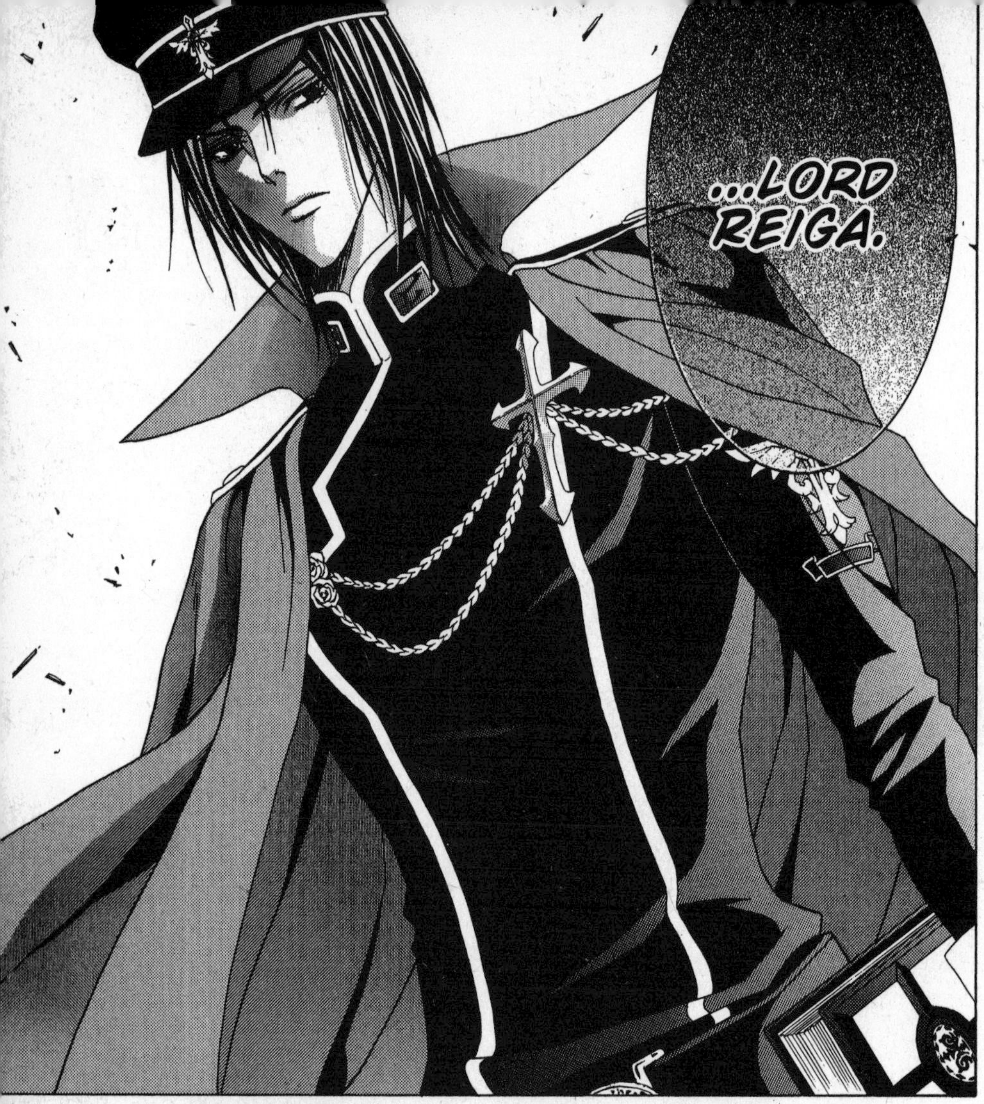
...LORD REIGA.
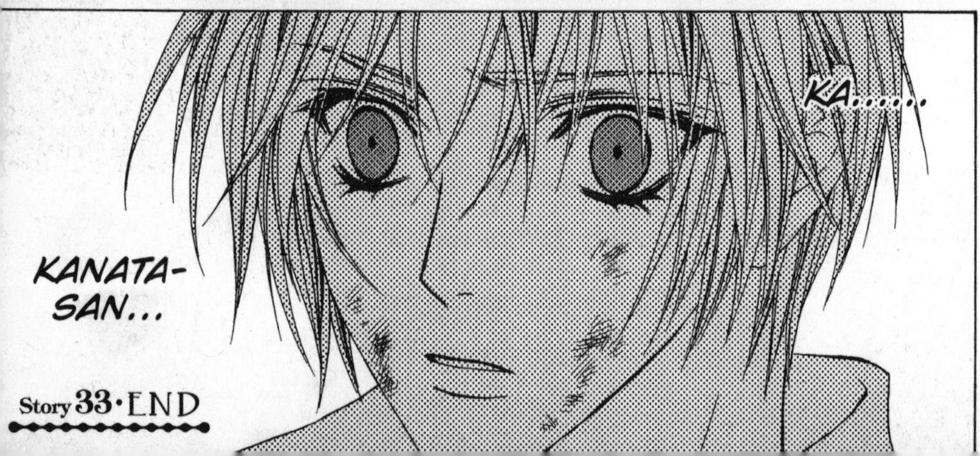
KA......
KANATA-SAN...
Story 33 · END

The
BETRAYAL
knows my name

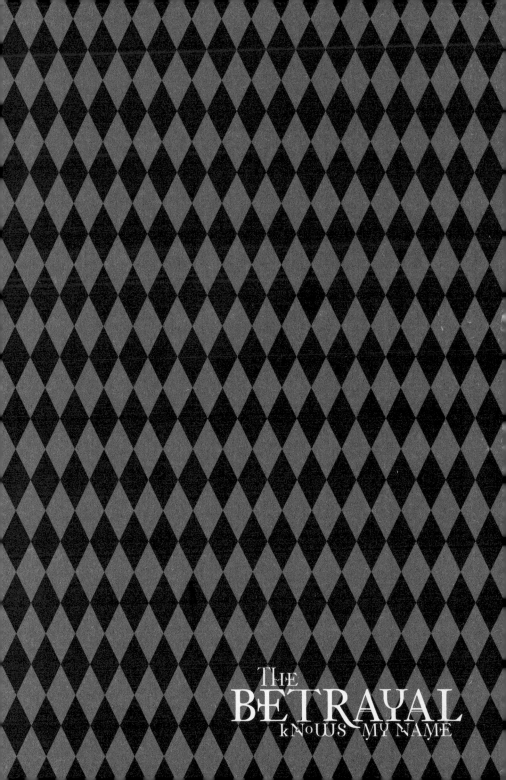

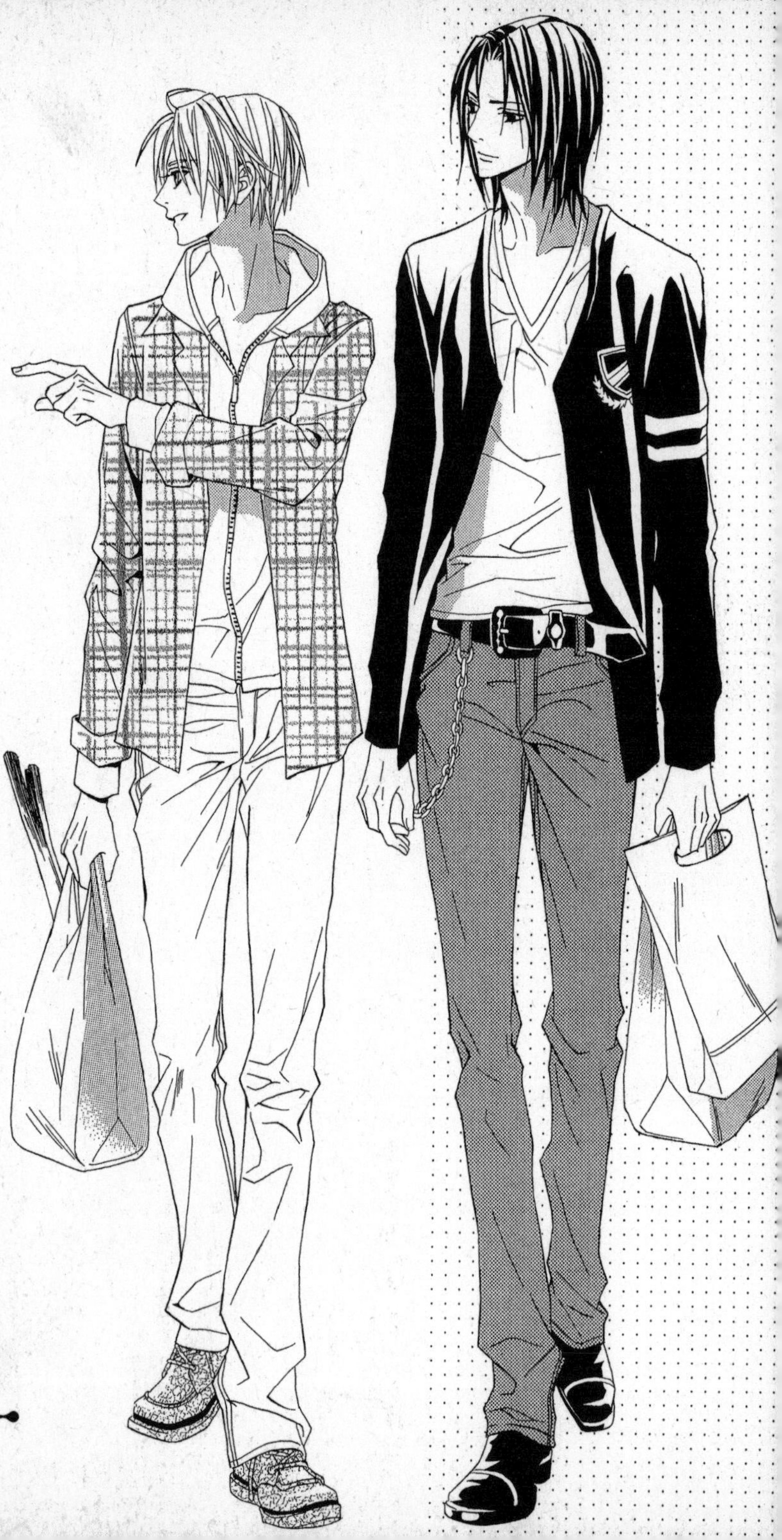

Story 34

REBEL

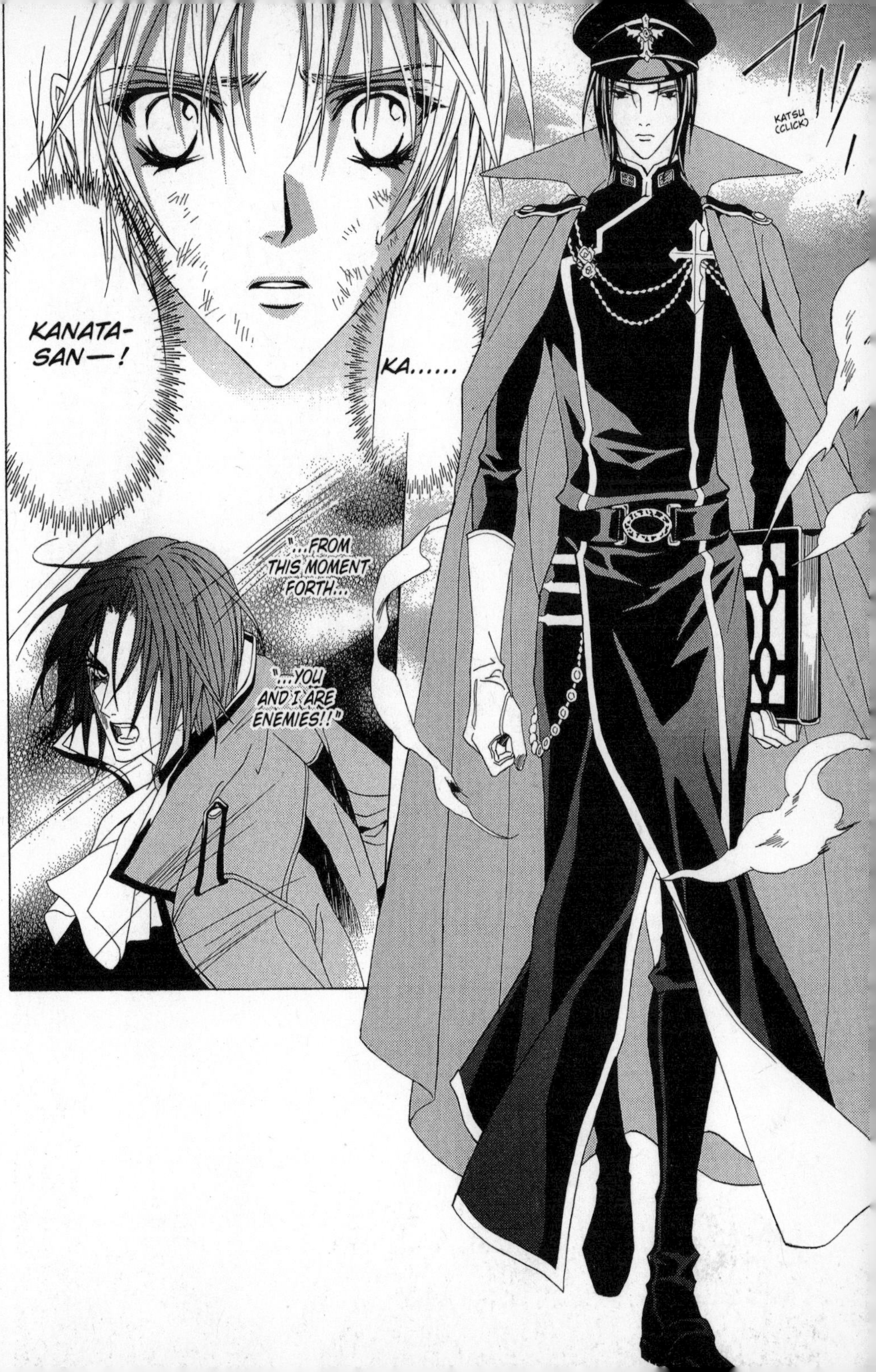
KATSU (CLICK)
KA......
KANATA-SAN—!
"...FROM THIS MOMENT FORTH...
"...YOU AND I ARE ENEMIES!!"

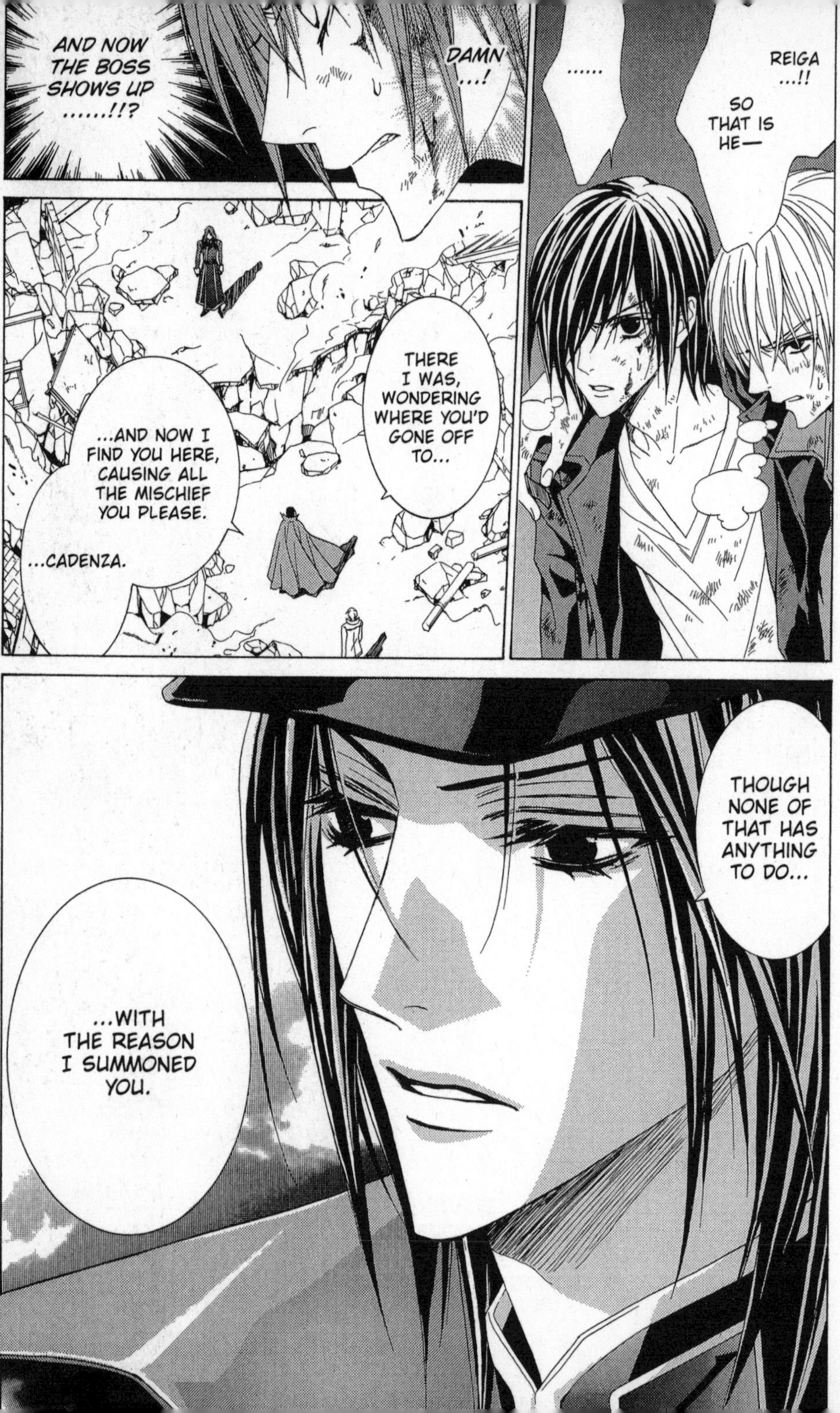
REIGA ...!!
SO THAT IS HE—
......
DAMN ...!
AND NOW THE BOSS SHOWS UP ......!!?
THERE I WAS, WONDERING WHERE YOU'D GONE OFF TO...
...AND NOW I FIND YOU HERE, CAUSING ALL THE MISCHIEF YOU PLEASE.
...CADENZA.
THOUGH NONE OF THAT HAS ANYTHING TO DO...
...WITH THE REASON I SUMMONED YOU.

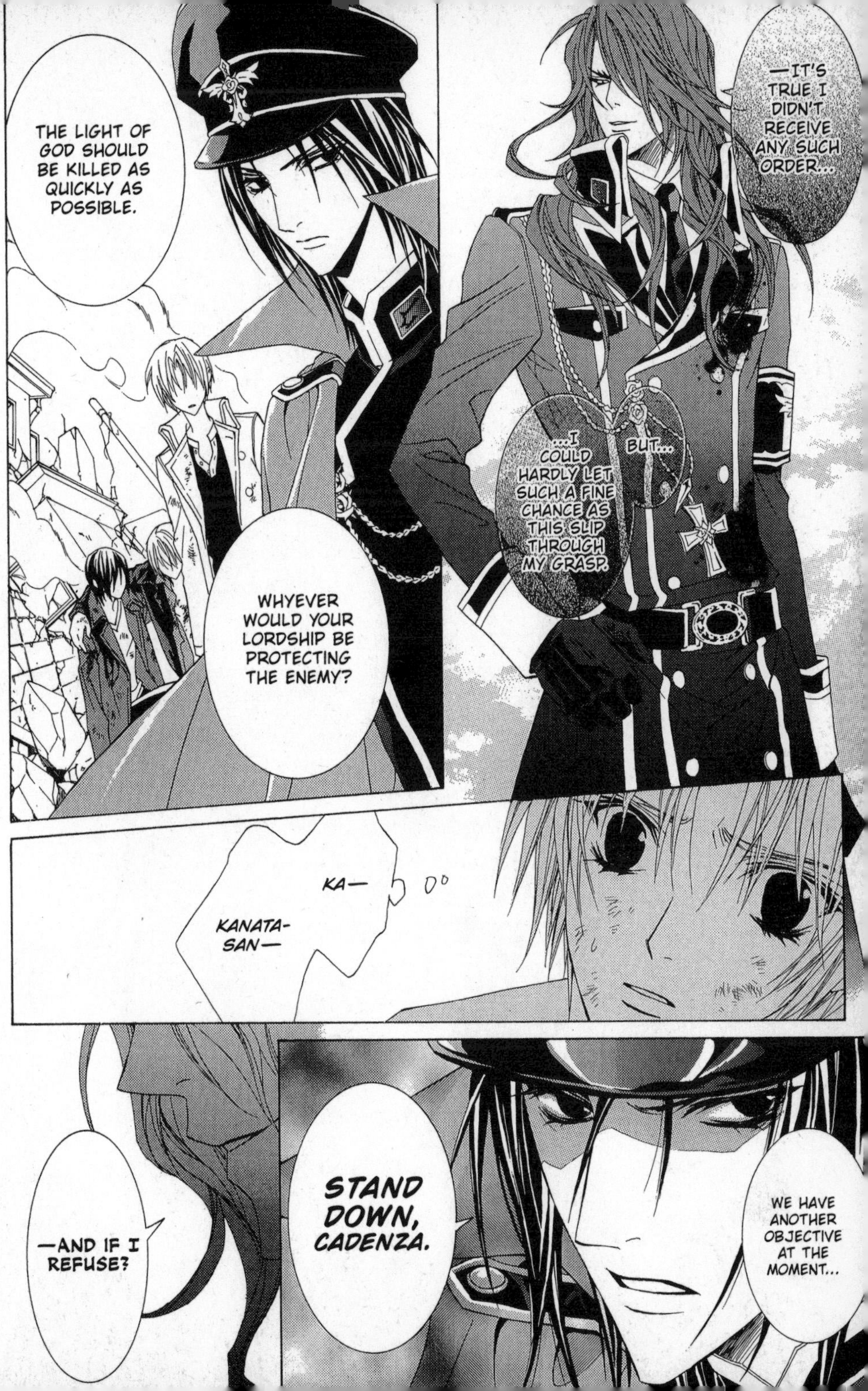
—IT'S TRUE I DIDN'T RECEIVE ANY SUCH ORDER...
BUT...
...I COULD HARDLY LET SUCH A FINE CHANCE AS THIS SLIP THROUGH MY GRASP.
THE LIGHT OF GOD SHOULD BE KILLED AS QUICKLY AS POSSIBLE.
WHYEVER WOULD YOUR LORDSHIP BE PROTECTING THE ENEMY?
KA—
KANATA-SAN—
WE HAVE ANOTHER OBJECTIVE AT THE MOMENT...
STAND DOWN, CADENZA.
—AND IF I REFUSE?

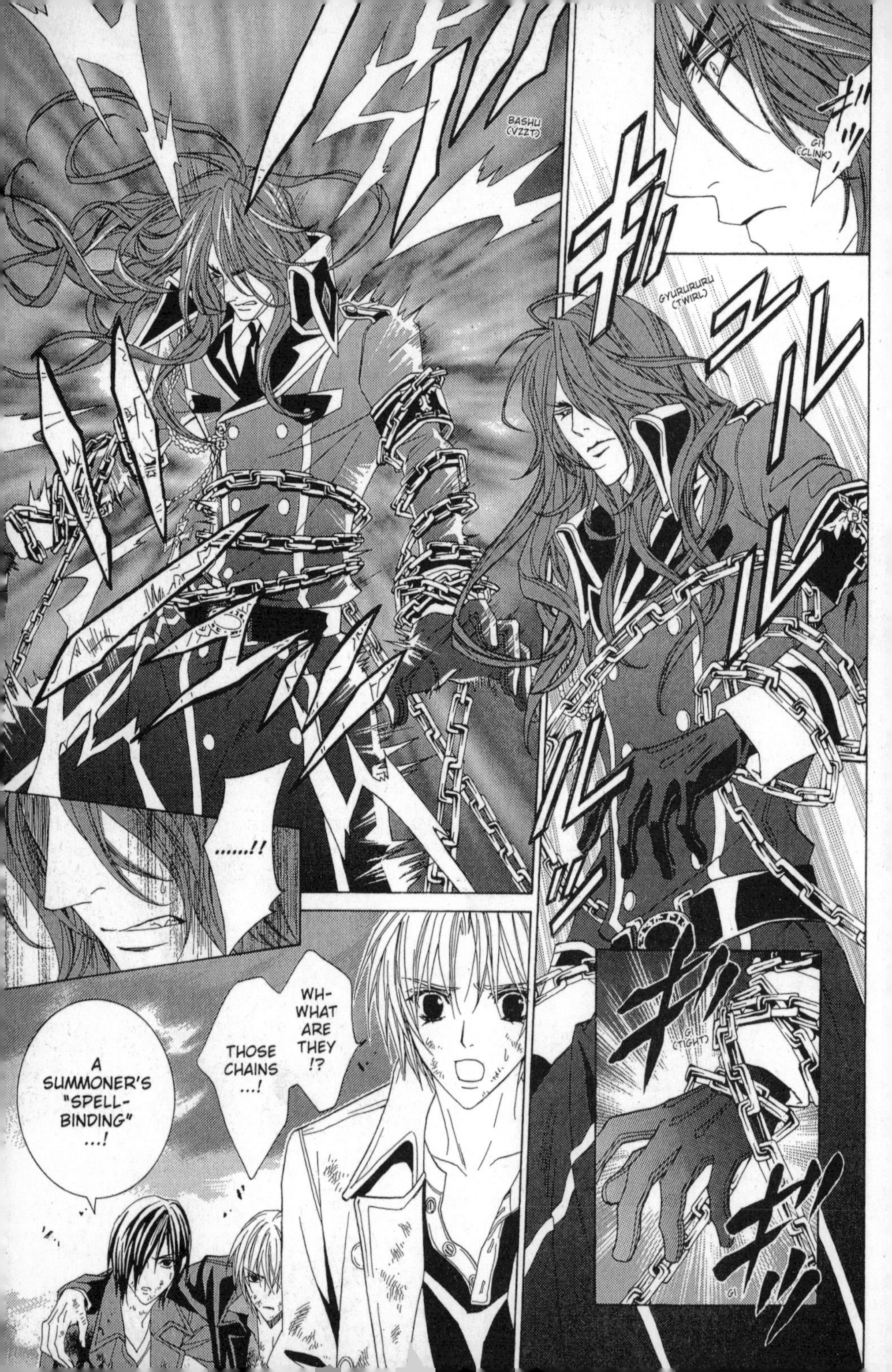
GI (CLINK)
GYURURURU (TWIRL)
BASHU (VZZT)
GI (TIGHT)
GI
......!!
WH-WHAT ARE THEY!?
THOSE CHAINS ...!
A SUMMONER'S "SPELL-BINDING" ...!

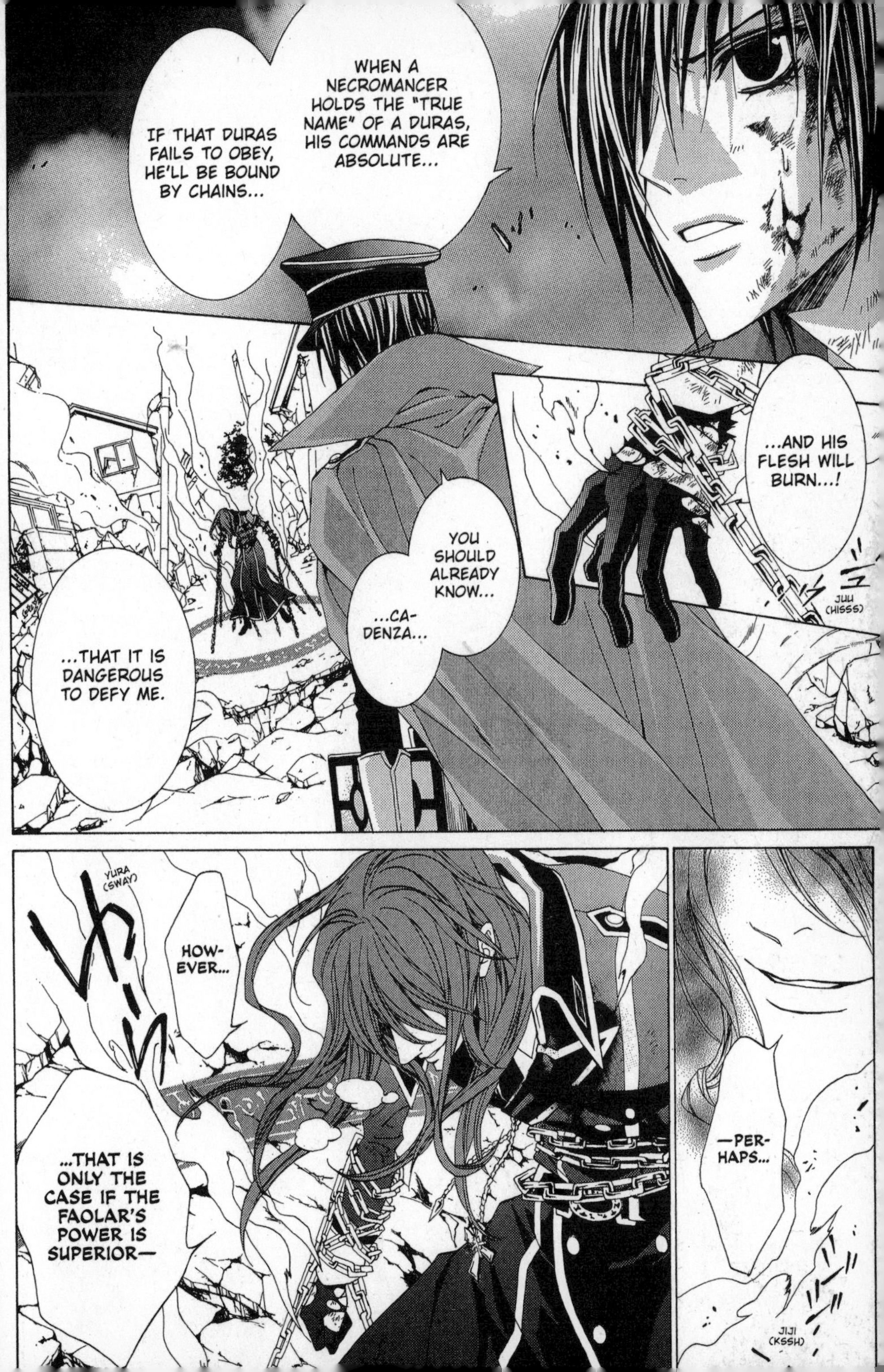
WHEN A NECROMANCER HOLDS THE "TRUE NAME" OF A DURAS, HIS COMMANDS ARE ABSOLUTE...
IF THAT DURAS FAILS TO OBEY, HE'LL BE BOUND BY CHAINS...
...AND HIS FLESH WILL BURN...!
JUU (HISSS)
YOU SHOULD ALREADY KNOW...
...CA-DENZA...
...THAT IT IS DANGEROUS TO DEFY ME.
—PER-HAPS...
JIJI (KSSH)
YURA (SWAY)
HOW-EVER...
...THAT IS ONLY THE CASE IF THE FAOLAR'S POWER IS SUPERIOR—

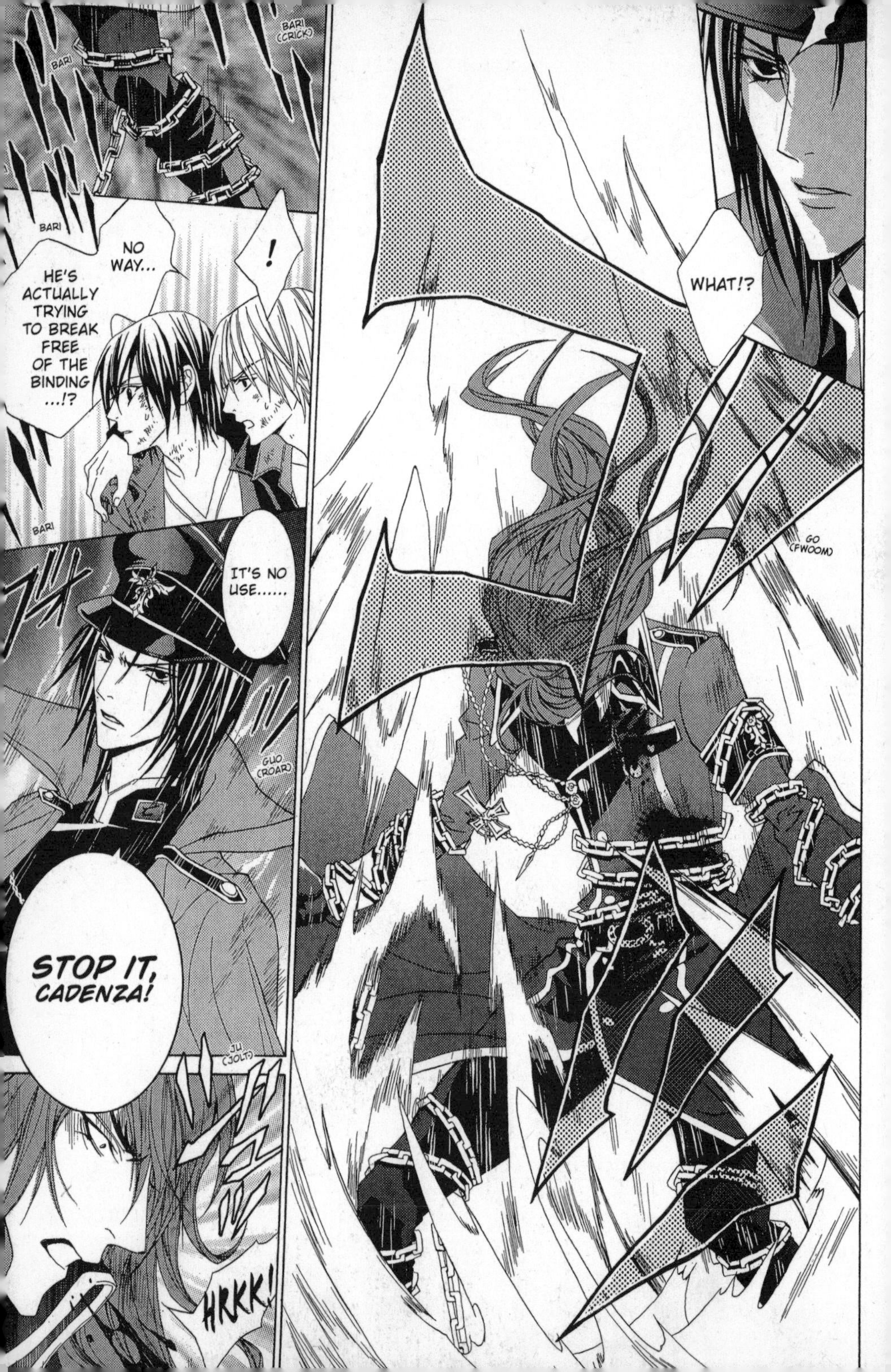
WHAT!?
GO (FWOOM)
BARI (CRICK)
BARI
BARI
!
NO WAY...
HE'S ACTUALLY TRYING TO BREAK FREE OF THE BINDING ...!?
BARI
IT'S NO USE......
GUO (ROAR)
STOP IT, CADENZA!
JU (JOLT)
HRKK!

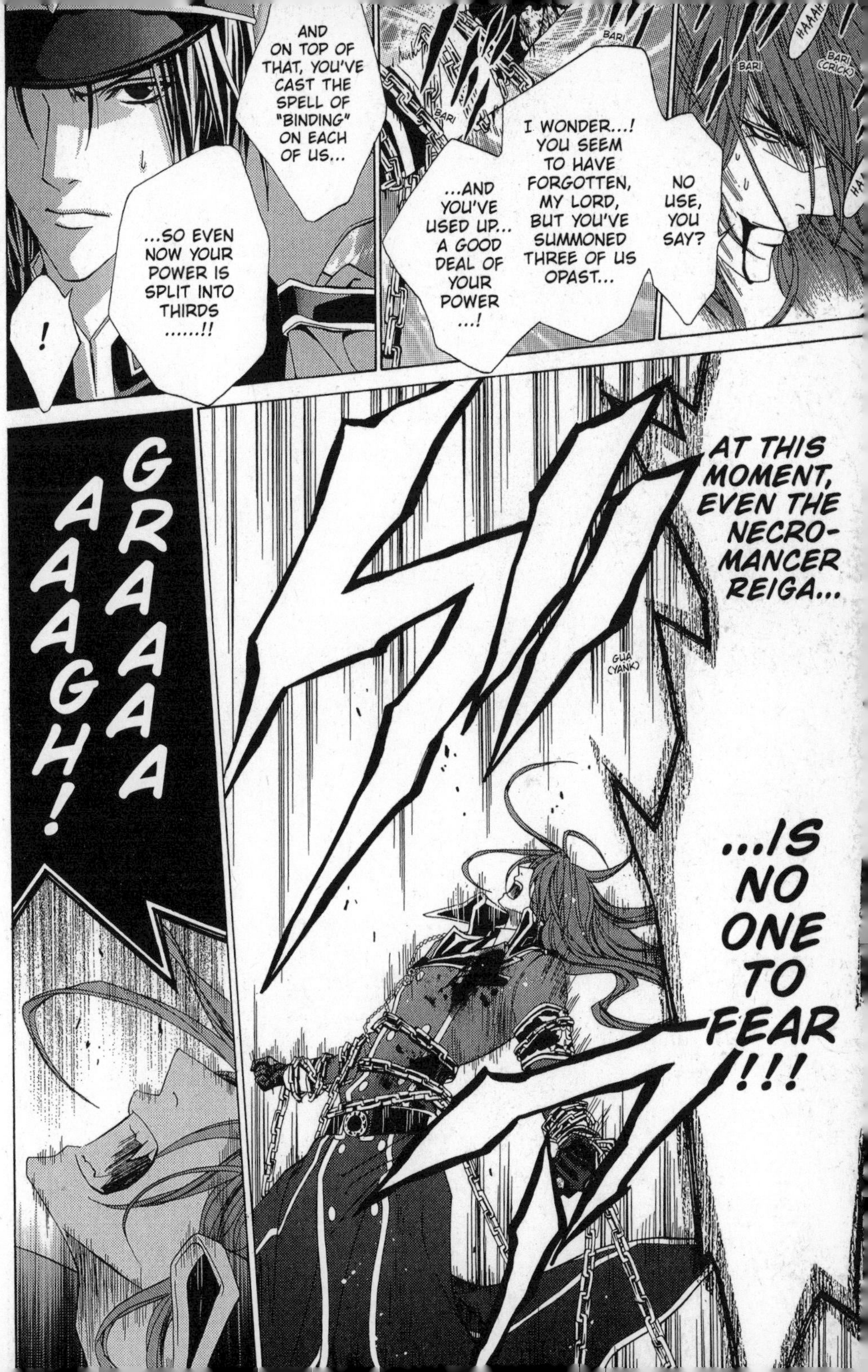
HAAAH
BARI (CRICK)
BARI
BARI
BARI
NO USE, YOU SAY?
I WONDER...! YOU SEEM TO HAVE FORGOTTEN, MY LORD, BUT YOU'VE SUMMONED THREE OF US OPAST...
...AND YOU'VE USED UP... A GOOD DEAL OF YOUR POWER ...!
AND ON TOP OF THAT, YOU'VE CAST THE SPELL OF "BINDING" ON EACH OF US...
...SO EVEN NOW YOUR POWER IS SPLIT INTO THIRDS ......!!
!
AT THIS MOMENT, EVEN THE NECRO-MANCER REIGA...
GUA (YANK)
...IS NO ONE TO FEAR !!!
GRAAAAAAAAGH!

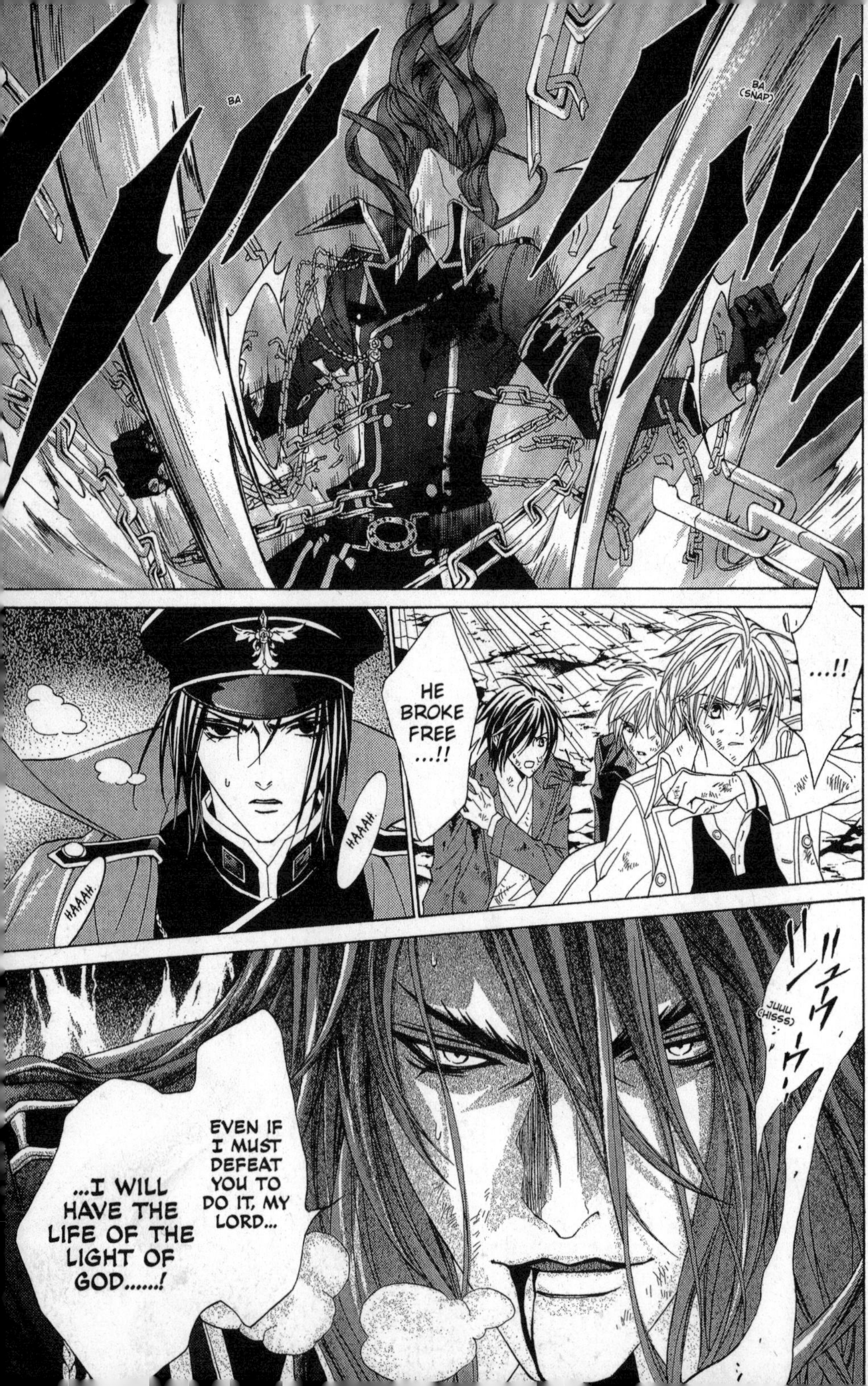
BA (SNAP)
BA
...!!
HE BROKE FREE ...!!
HAAAH.
HAAAH.
JUUU (HISSS)
EVEN IF I MUST DEFEAT YOU TO DO IT, MY LORD...
...I WILL HAVE THE LIFE OF THE LIGHT OF GOD......!

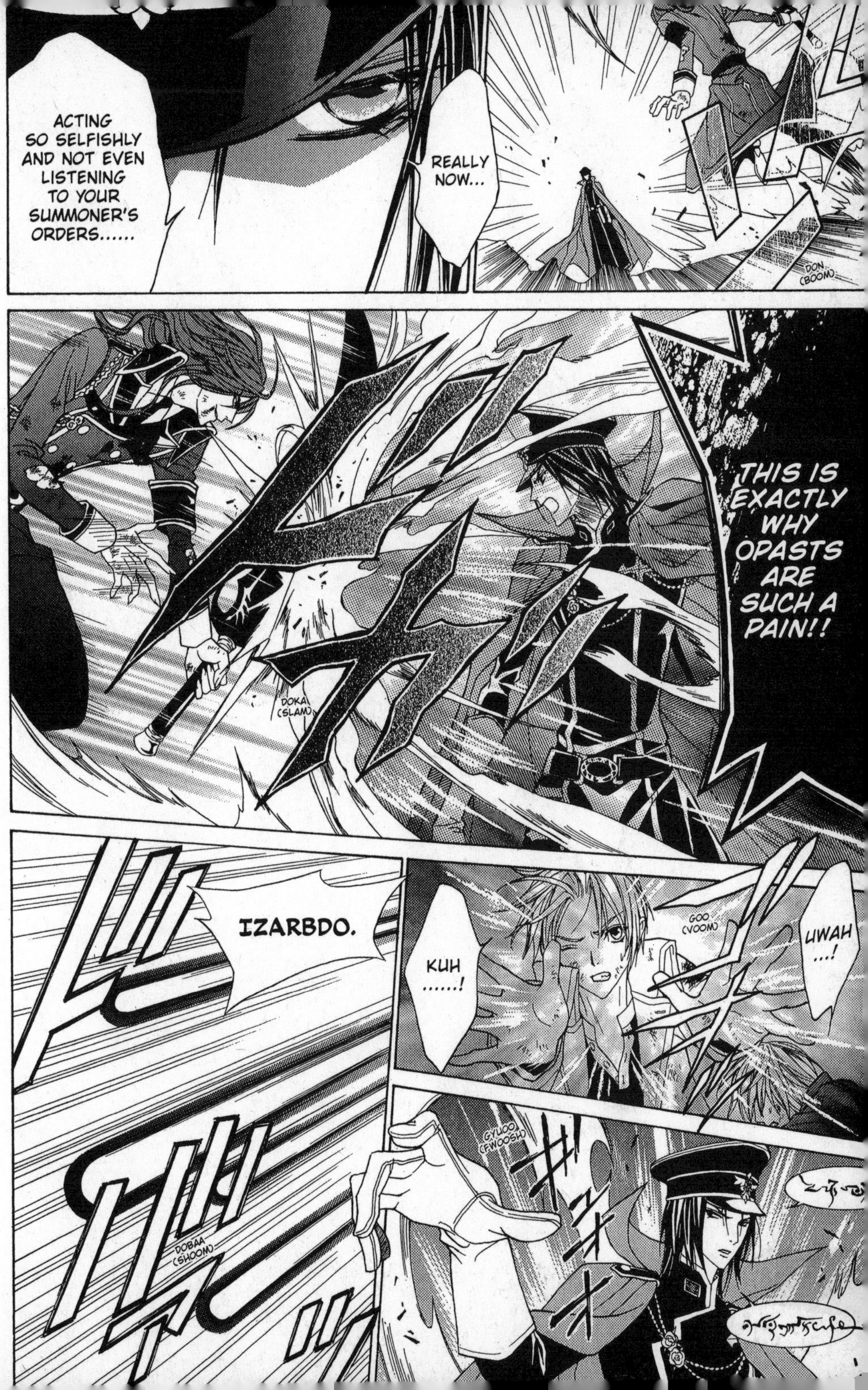
DON (BOOM)
REALLY NOW...
ACTING SO SELFISHLY AND NOT EVEN LISTENING TO YOUR SUMMONER'S ORDERS......
THIS IS EXACTLY WHY OPASTS ARE SUCH A PAIN!!
DOKA (SLAM)
UWAH ...!
GOO (VOOM)
KUH ......!
GYLOO (FWOOSH)
IZARBDO.
DOBAA (SHOOM)

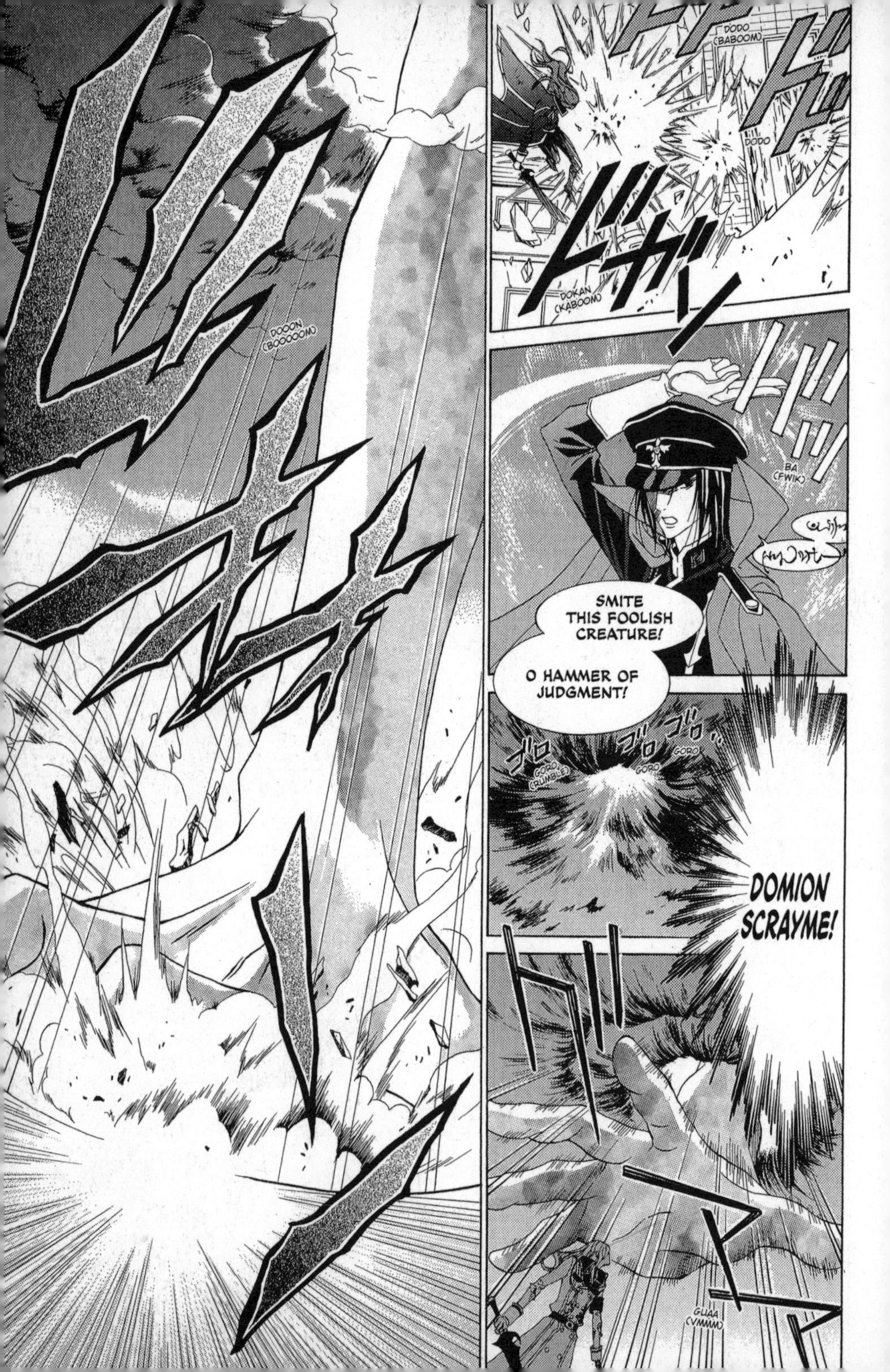
DODO (BABOOM)
DODO
DOKAN (KABOOM)
BA (FWIK)
SMITE THIS FOOLISH CREATURE!
O HAMMER OF JUDGMENT!
GORO (RUMBLE)
GORO
GORO
DOMION SCRAYME!
GUAA (VMMM)
DOOON (BOOOOOM)

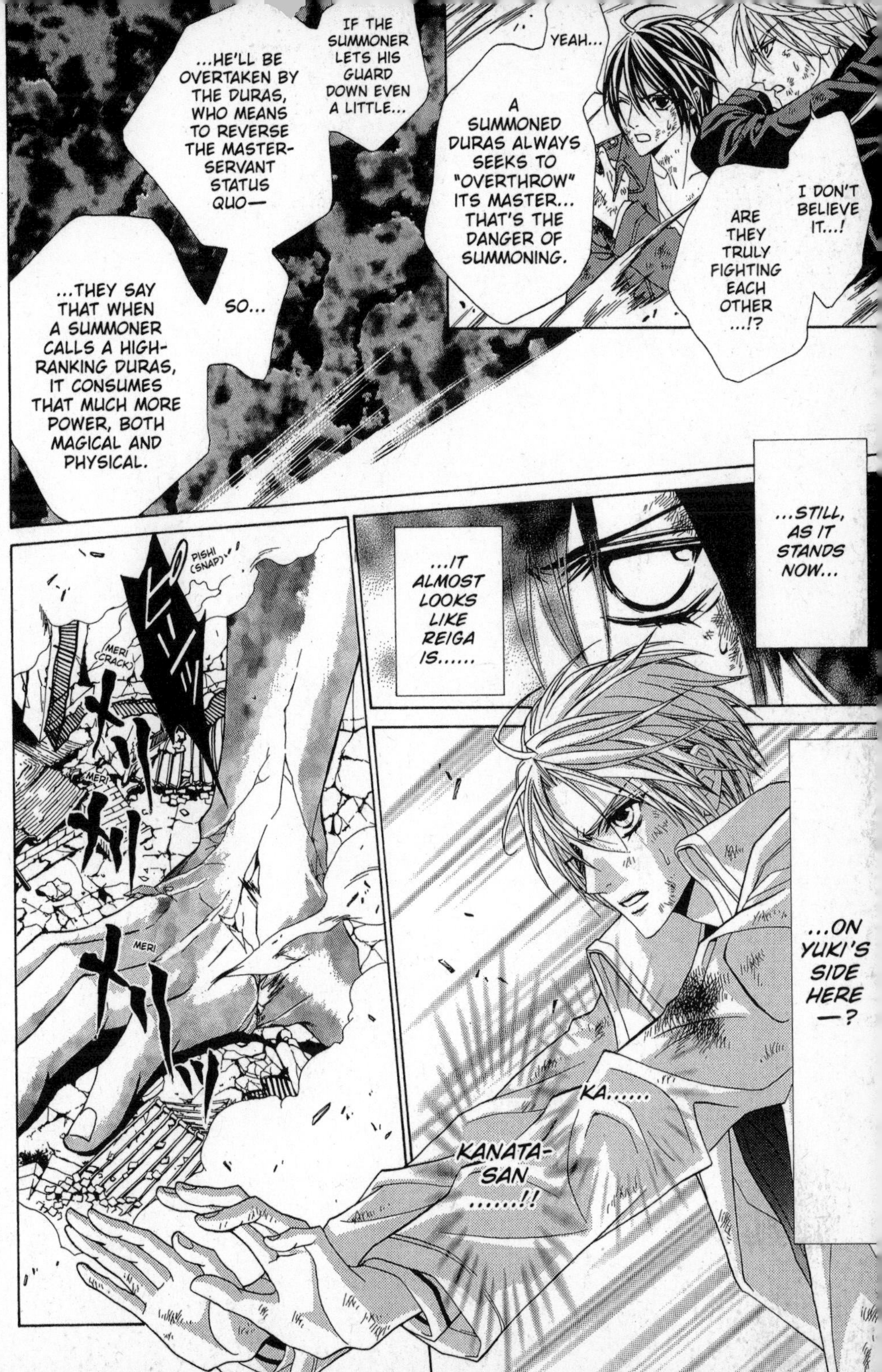

I DON'T BELIEVE IT...!
ARE THEY TRULY FIGHTING EACH OTHER ...!?
YEAH...
A SUMMONED DURAS ALWAYS SEEKS TO "OVERTHROW" ITS MASTER... THAT'S THE DANGER OF SUMMONING.
...THEY SAY THAT WHEN A SUMMONER CALLS A HIGH-RANKING DURAS, IT CONSUMES THAT MUCH MORE POWER, BOTH MAGICAL AND PHYSICAL.
SO...
IF THE SUMMONER LETS HIS GUARD DOWN EVEN A LITTLE...
...HE'LL BE OVERTAKEN BY THE DURAS, WHO MEANS TO REVERSE THE MASTER-SERVANT STATUS QUO—
...STILL, AS IT STANDS NOW...
...IT ALMOST LOOKS LIKE REIGA IS......
...ON YUKI'S SIDE HERE—?
KA......
KANATA-SAN ......!!
PISHI (SNAP)
MERI (CRACK)
MERI
MERI

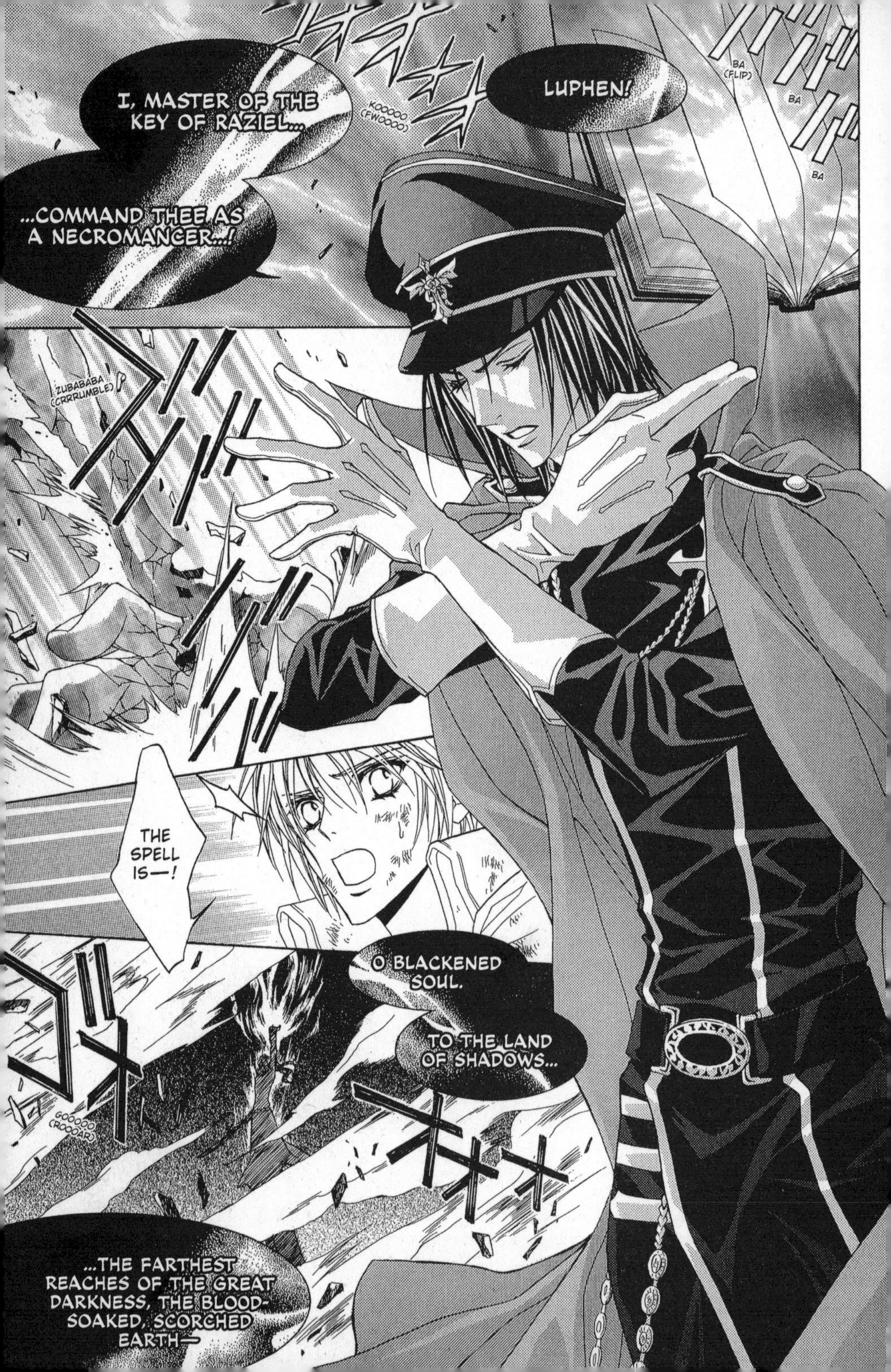
BA (FLIP)
BA
BA
LUPHEN!
KOOOOO (FWOOOO)
I, MASTER OF THE KEY OF RAZIEL...
...COMMAND THEE AS A NECROMANCER...!
ZUBABABA (CRRRUMBLE)
THE SPELL IS—!
O BLACKENED SOUL.
TO THE LAND OF SHADOWS...
GOOOOO (ROOOAR)
...THE FARTHEST REACHES OF THE GREAT DARKNESS, THE BLOOD-SOAKED, SCORCHED EARTH—

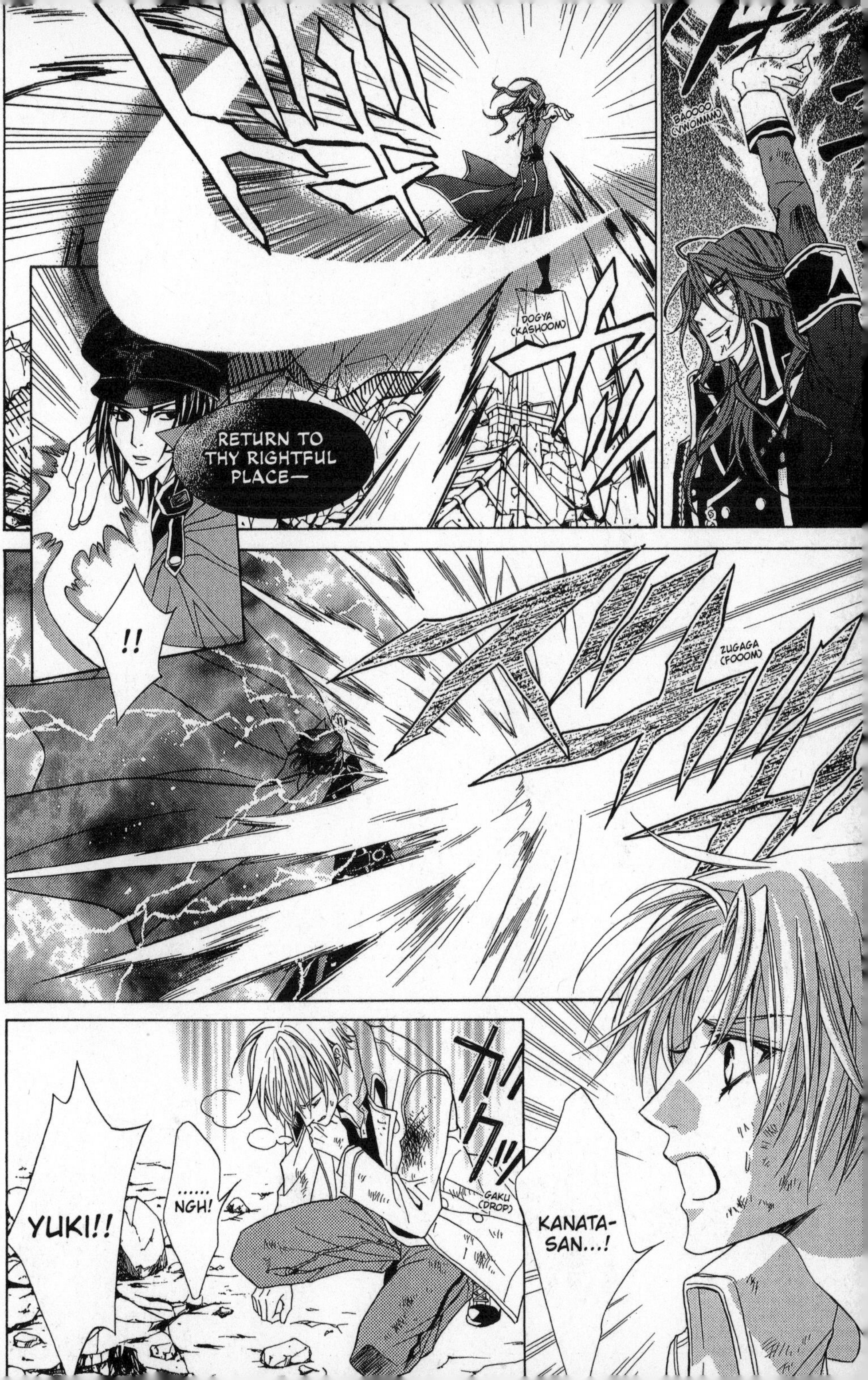
BAOOOO
(VWOMMM)
DOGYA
(KASHOOM)
RETURN TO THY RIGHTFUL PLACE—
ZUGAGA
(FOOOM)
!!
KANATA-SAN...!
GAKU
(DROP)
......NGH!
YUKI!!

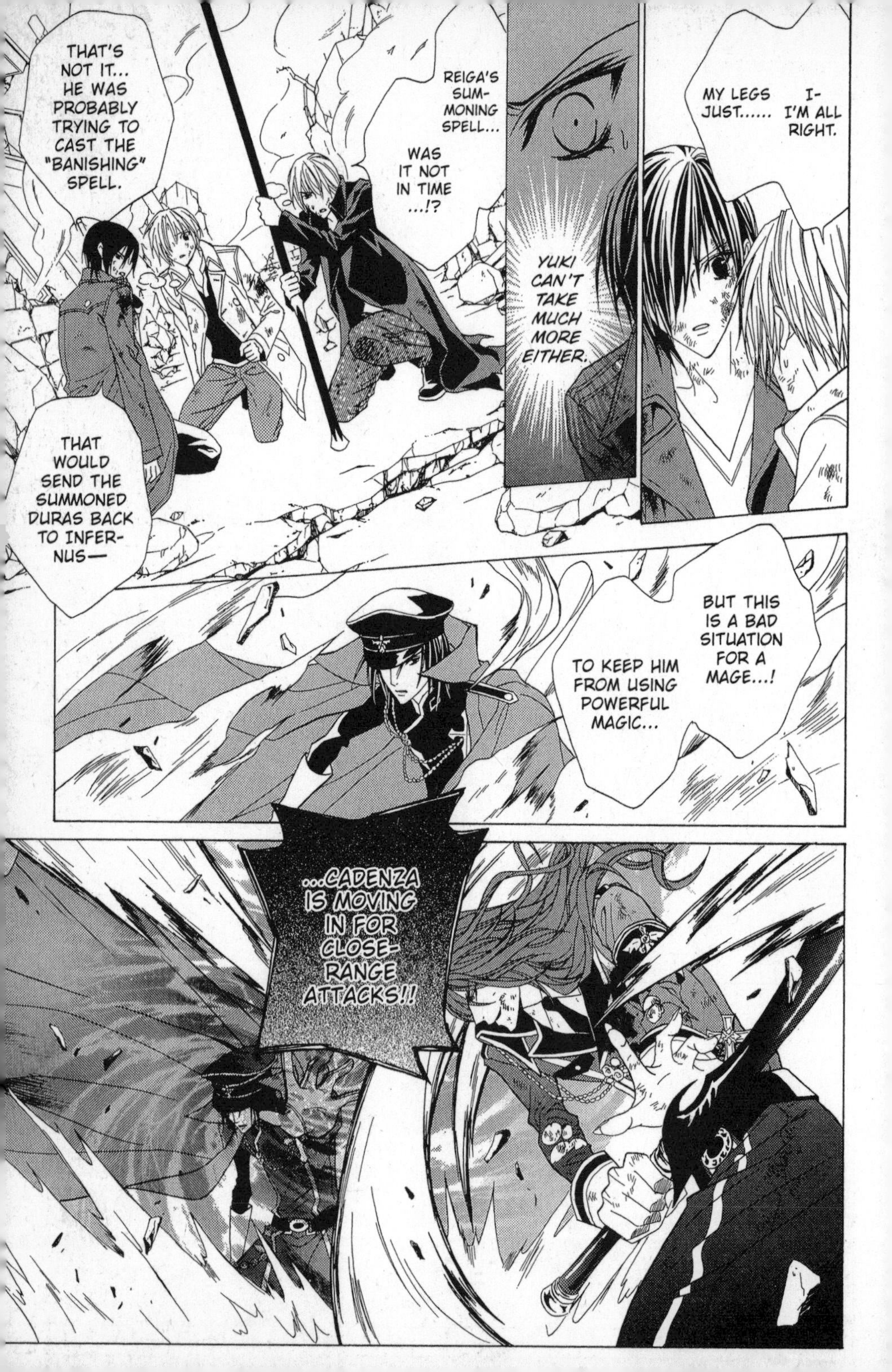
I- I'M ALL RIGHT.
MY LEGS JUST......
YUKI CAN'T TAKE MUCH MORE EITHER.
REIGA'S SUMMONING SPELL...
WAS IT NOT IN TIME ...!?
THAT'S NOT IT... HE WAS PROBABLY TRYING TO CAST THE "BANISHING" SPELL.
THAT WOULD SEND THE SUMMONED DURAS BACK TO INFERNUS—
BUT THIS IS A BAD SITUATION FOR A MAGE...!
TO KEEP HIM FROM USING POWERFUL MAGIC...
...CADENZA IS MOVING IN FOR CLOSE-RANGE ATTACKS!!

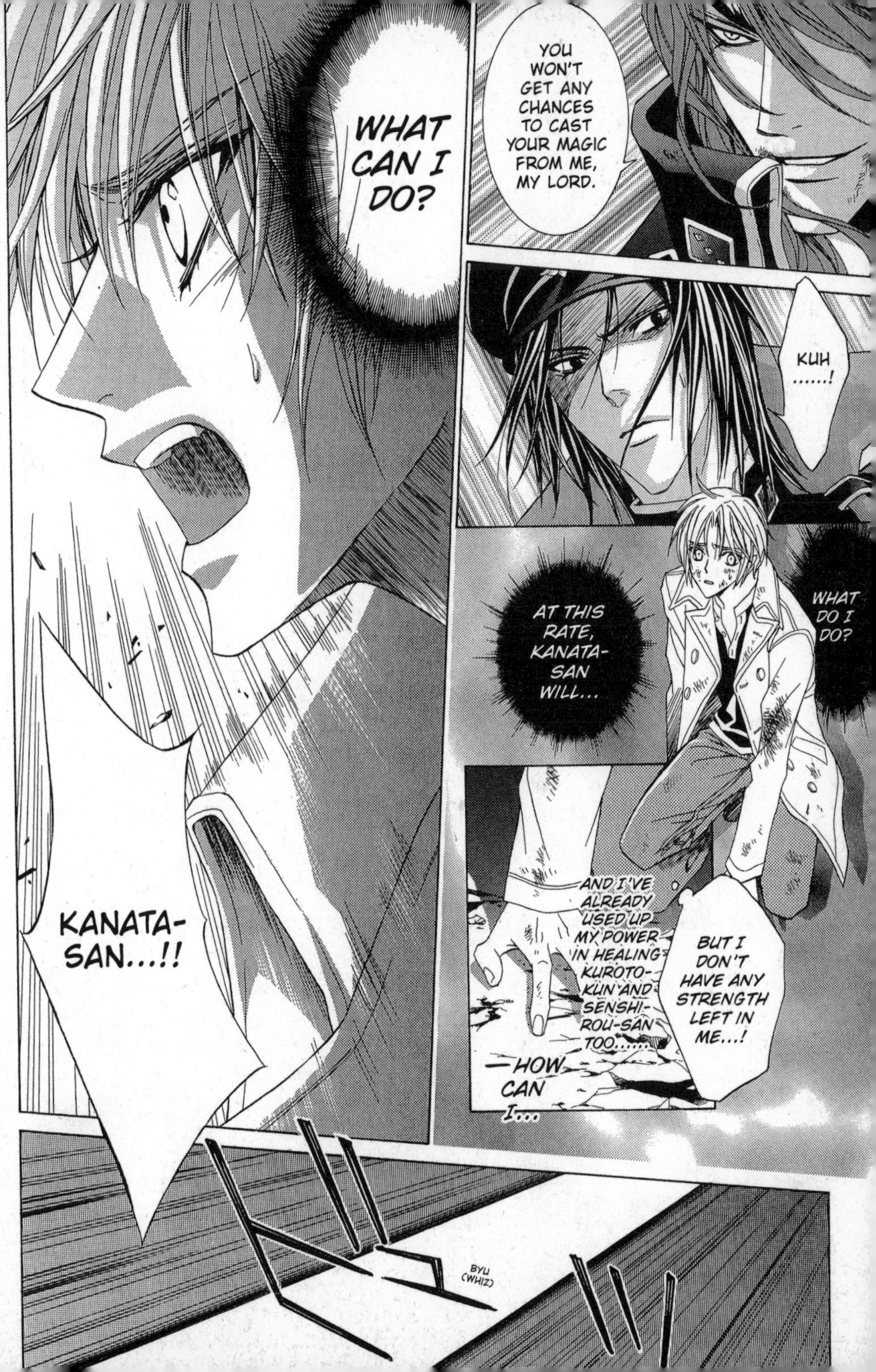
YOU WON'T GET ANY CHANCES TO CAST YOUR MAGIC FROM ME, MY LORD.
KUH ......!
WHAT DO I DO?
AT THIS RATE, KANATA-SAN WILL...
BUT I DON'T HAVE ANY STRENGTH LEFT IN ME...!
AND I'VE ALREADY USED UP MY POWER IN HEALING KUROTO-KUN AND SENSHIROU-SAN TOO......
—HOW CAN I...
WHAT CAN I DO?
KANATA-SAN...!!
BYU (WHIZ)

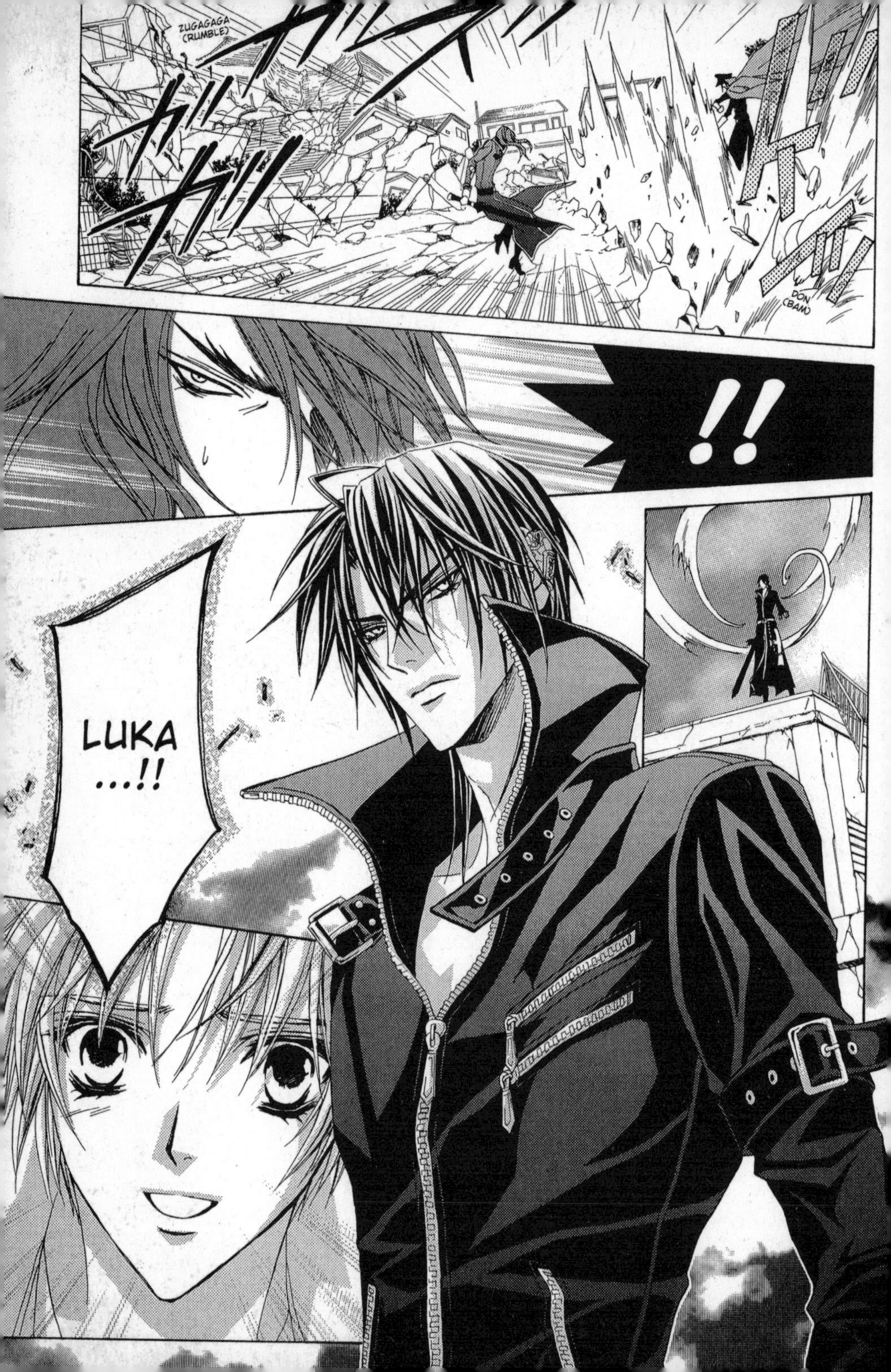
DON (BAM)
ZUGAGAGA (RUMBLE)
!!
LUKA ...!!

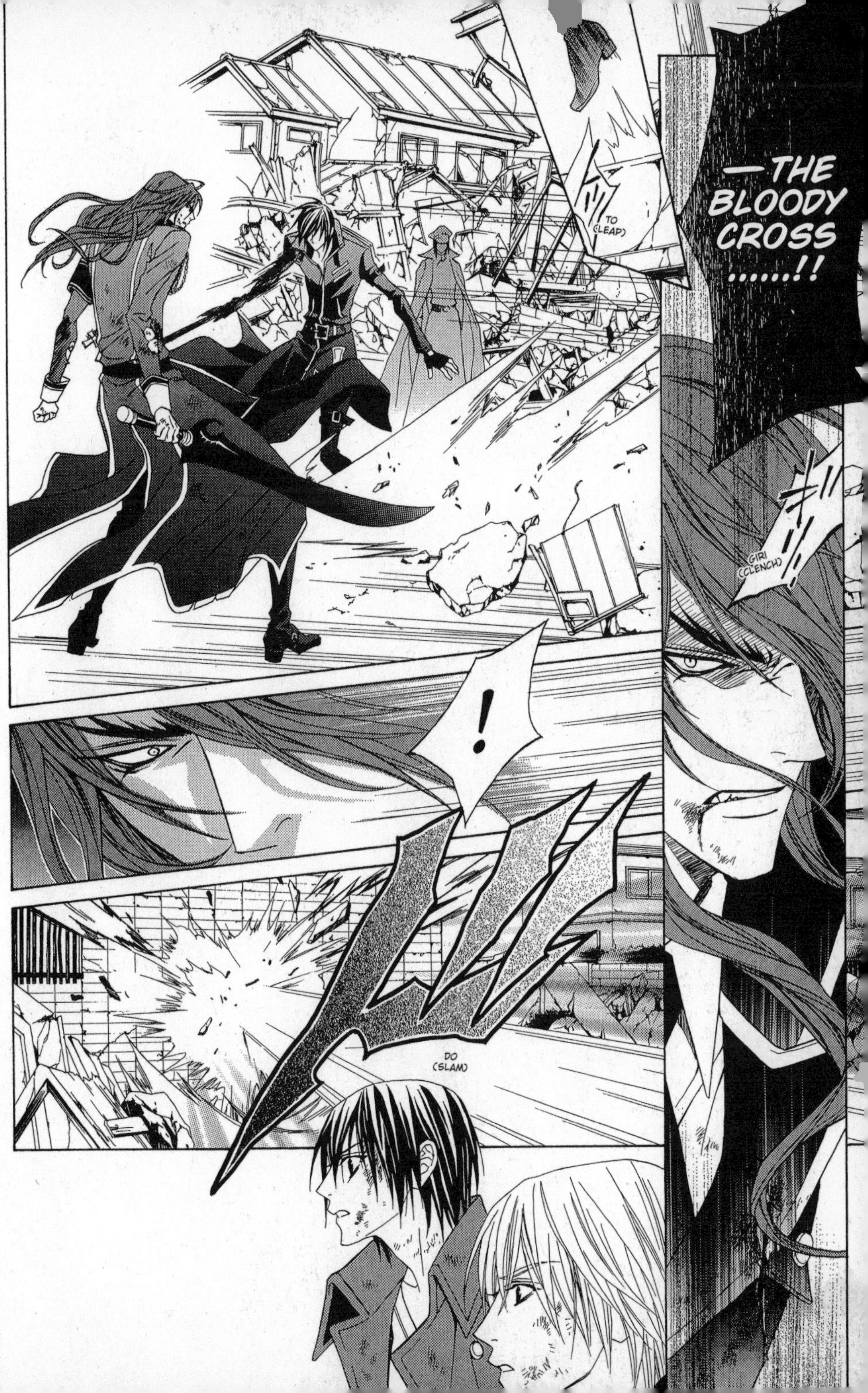
—THE BLOODY CROSS ......!!
GIRI (CLENCH)
TO (LEAP)
!
DO (SLAM)

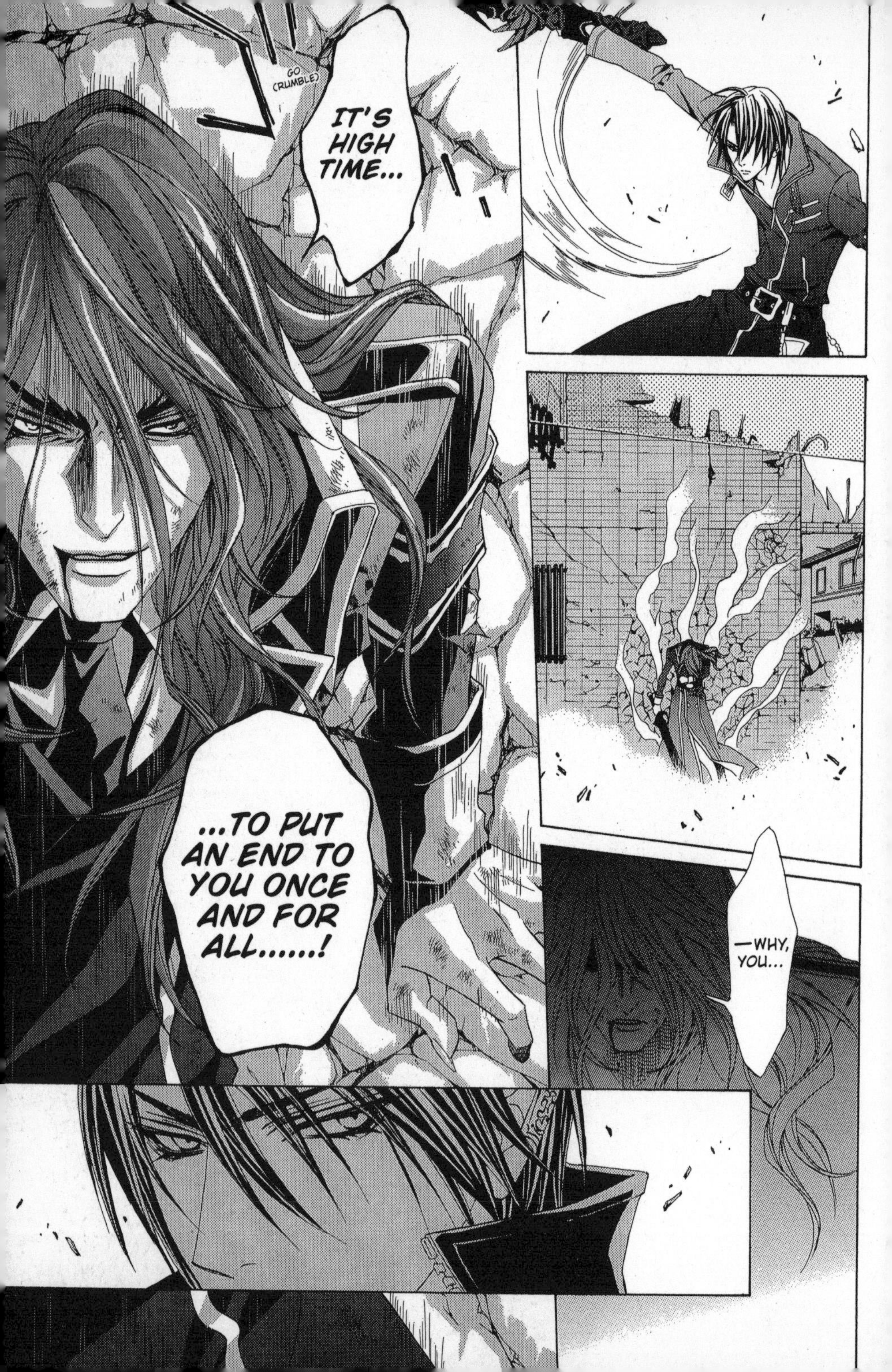
—WHY, YOU...
GO (RUMBLE)
IT'S HIGH TIME...
...TO PUT AN END TO YOU ONCE AND FOR ALL......!

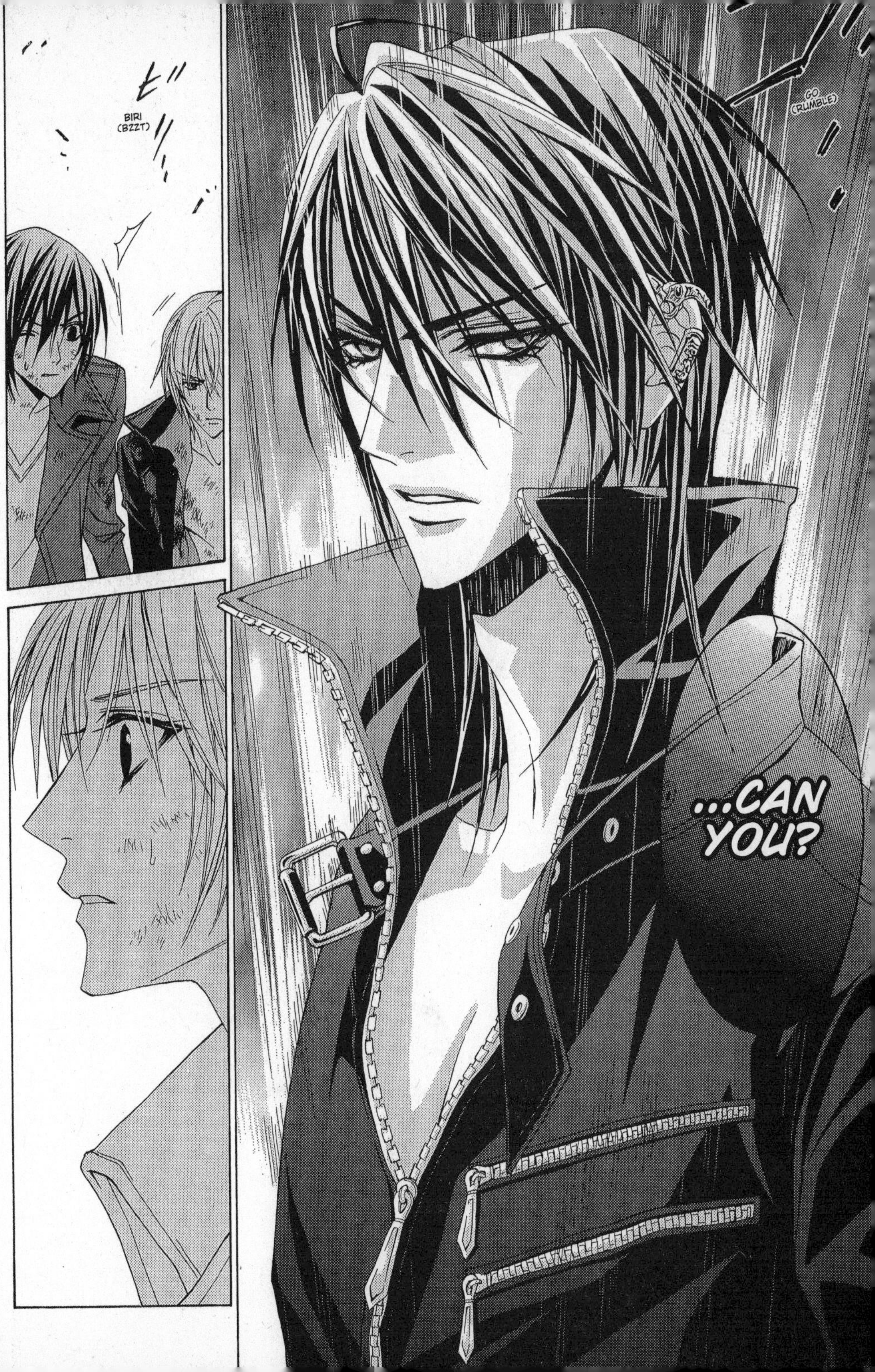
GO
(RUMBLE)
...CAN YOU?
BIRI
(BZZT)

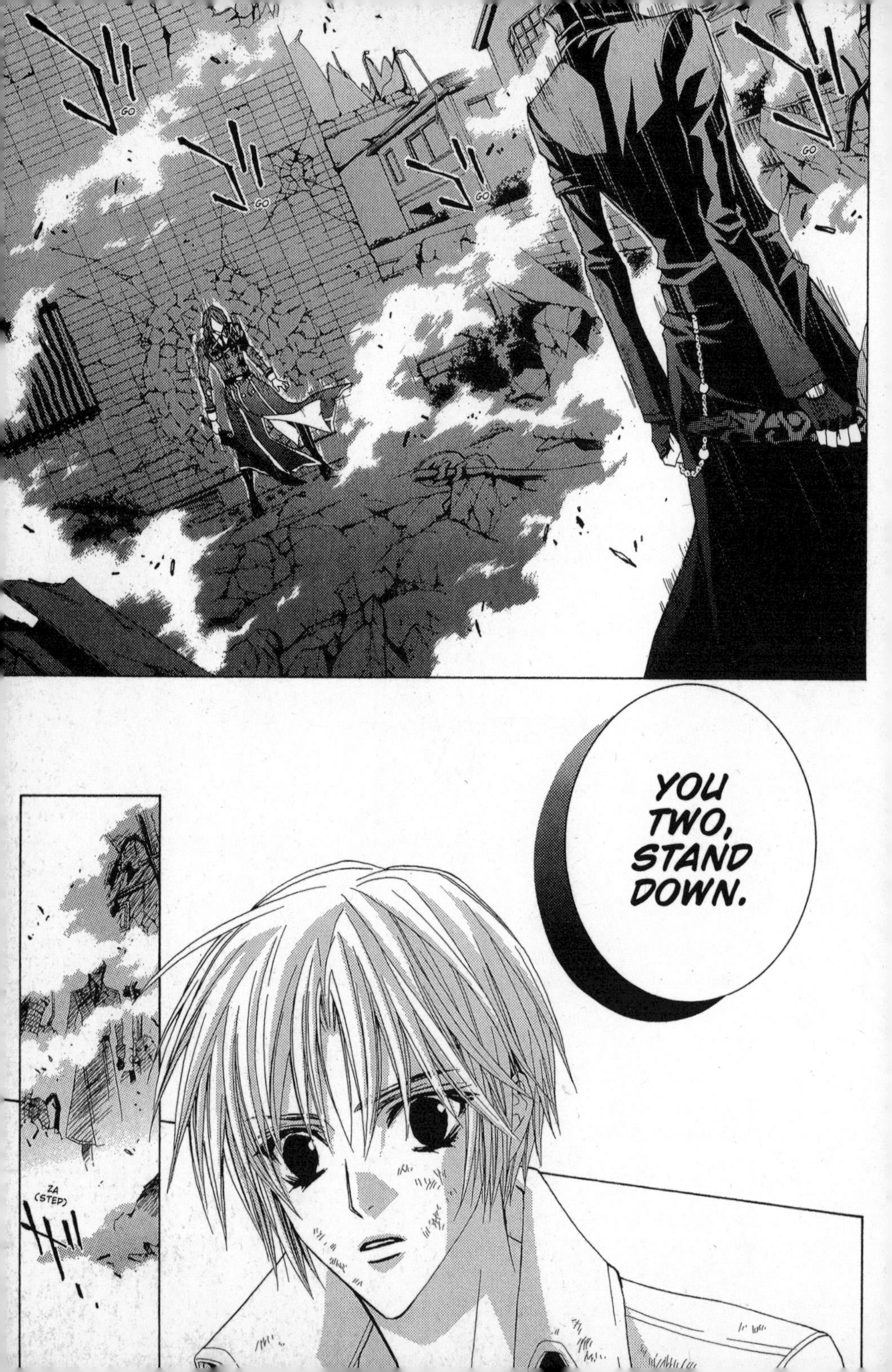
GO
GO
GO
GO
YOU TWO, STAND DOWN.
ZA (STEP)

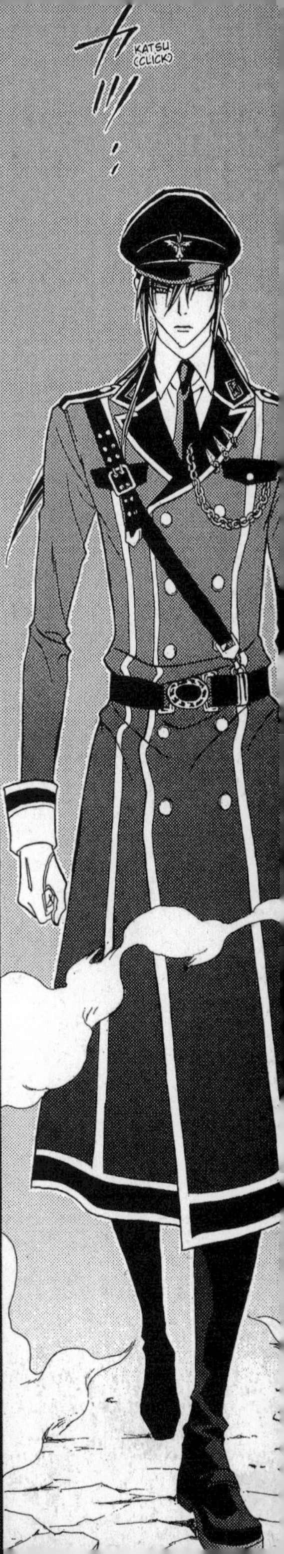
KATSU
(CLICK)
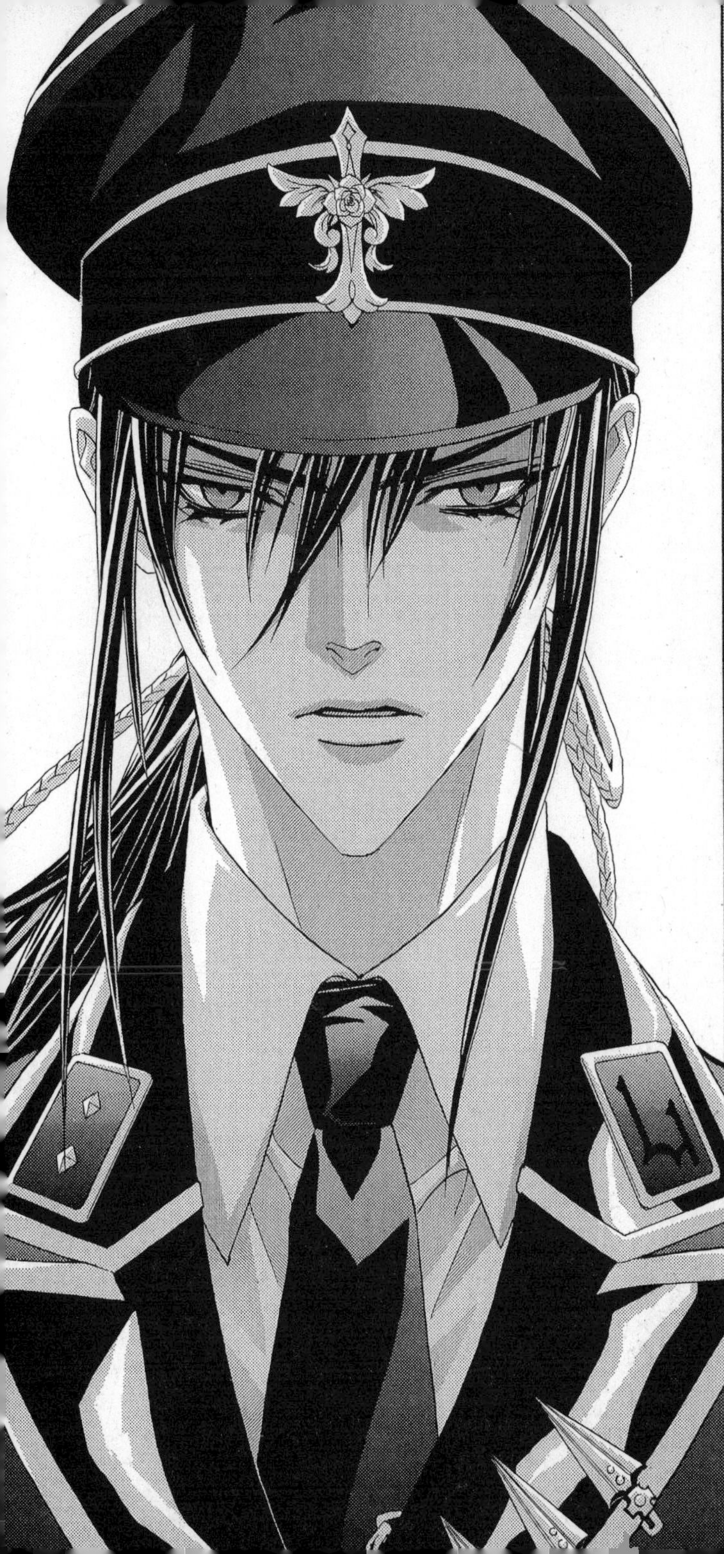

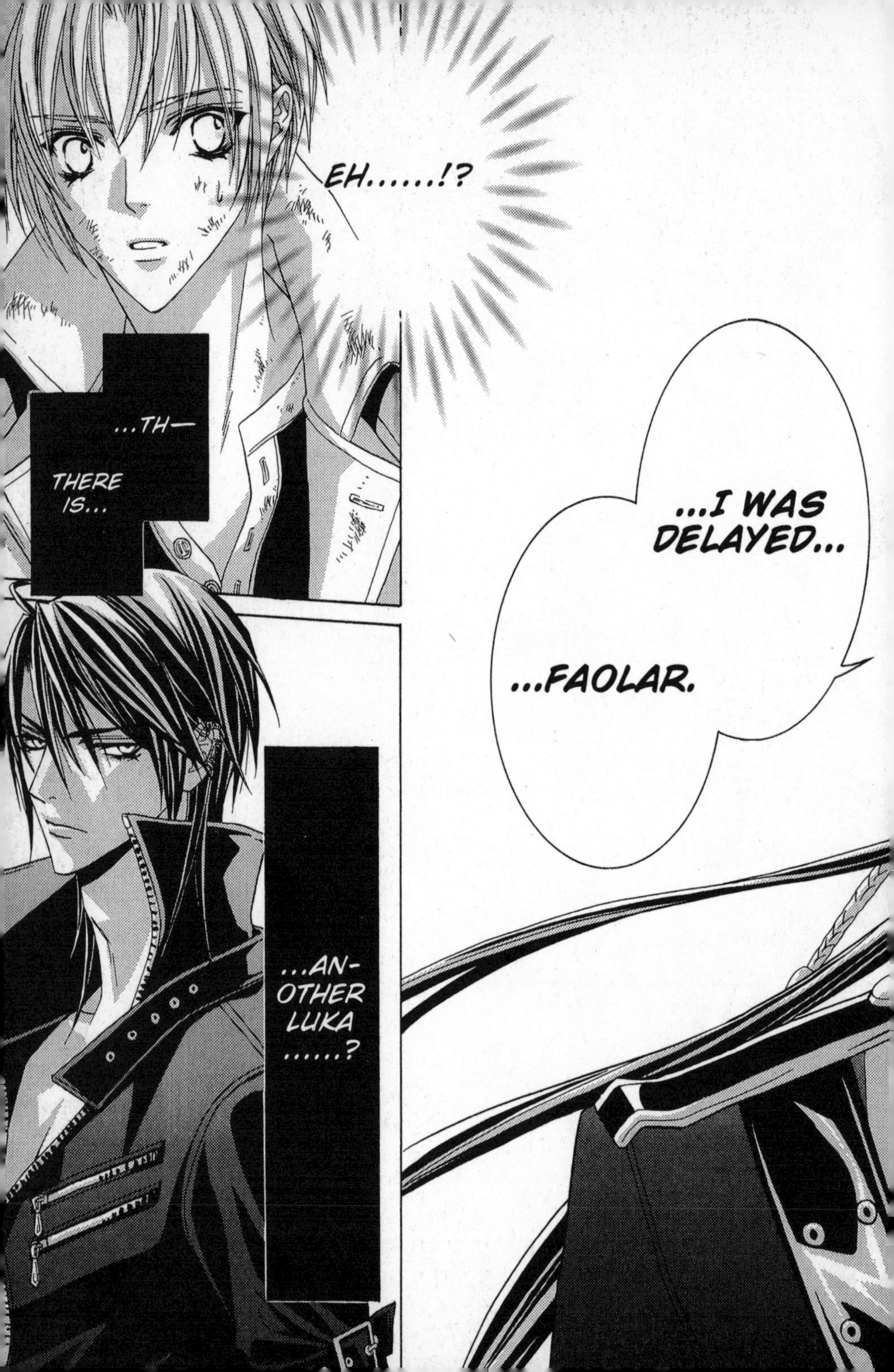
EH......!?
...I WAS DELAYED...
...FAOLAR.
...TH—
THERE IS...
...AN-OTHER LUKA ......?

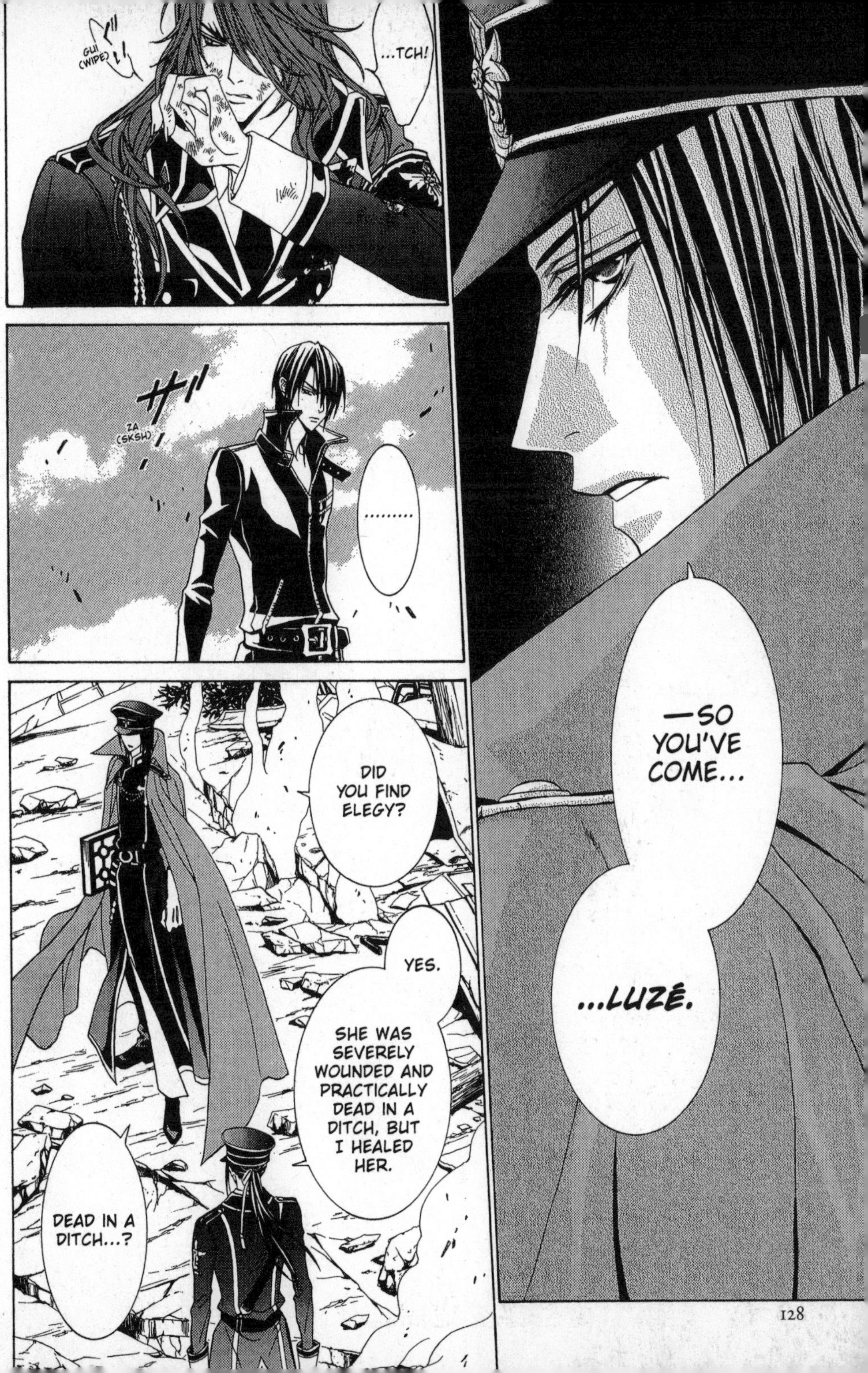
—SO YOU'VE COME...
...LUZE.
...TCH!
GUI (WIPE)
....
ZA (SKSH)
DID YOU FIND ELEGY?
YES.
SHE WAS SEVERELY WOUNDED AND PRACTICALLY DEAD IN A DITCH, BUT I HEALED HER.
DEAD IN A DITCH...?

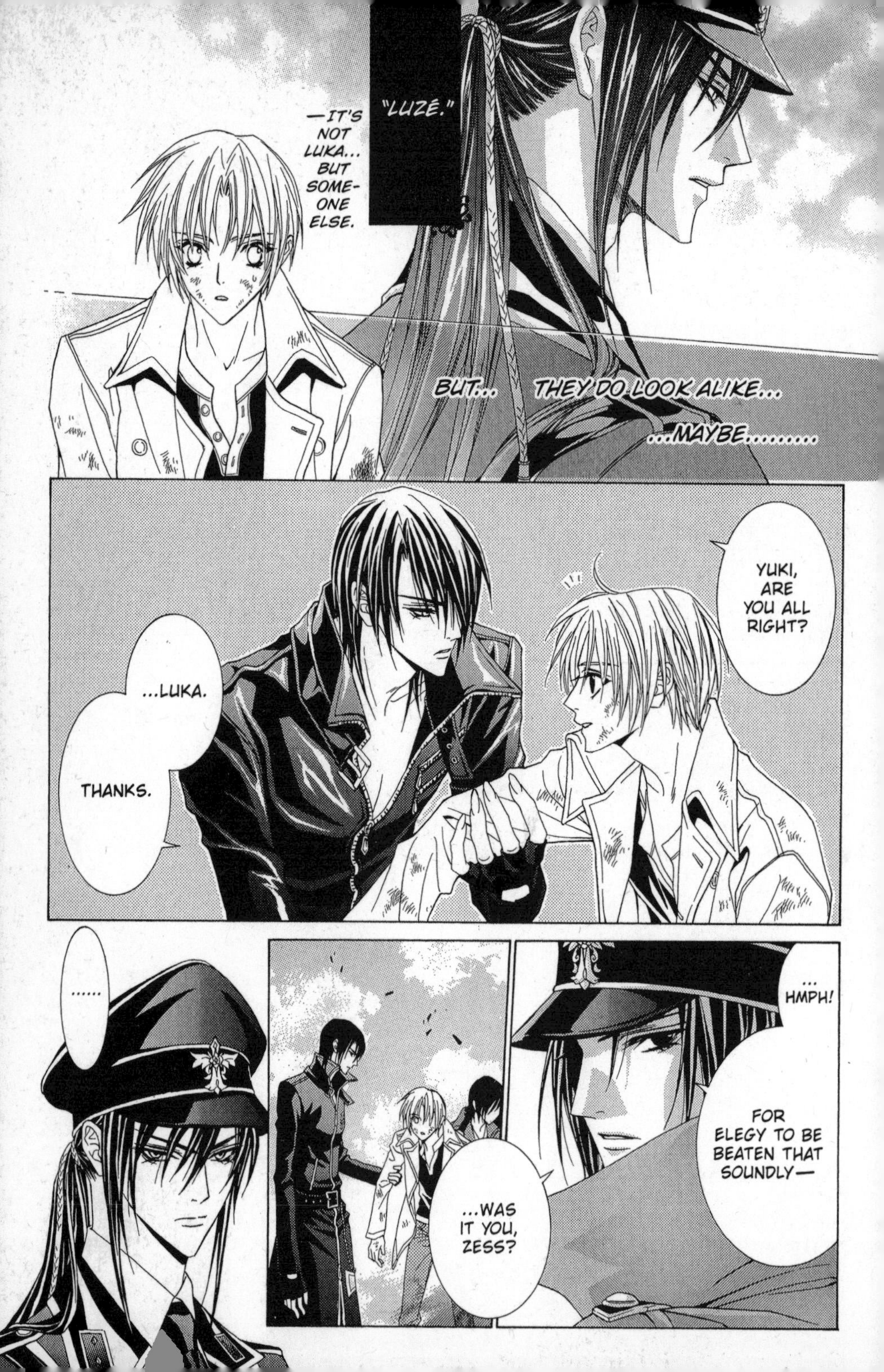
"LUZÉ."
—IT'S NOT LUKA... BUT SOME-ONE ELSE.
BUT... THEY DO LOOK ALIKE...
...MAYBE.........
YUKI, ARE YOU ALL RIGHT?
...LUKA.
THANKS.
...HMPH!
FOR ELEGY TO BE BEATEN THAT SOUNDLY—
...WAS IT YOU, ZESS?
......

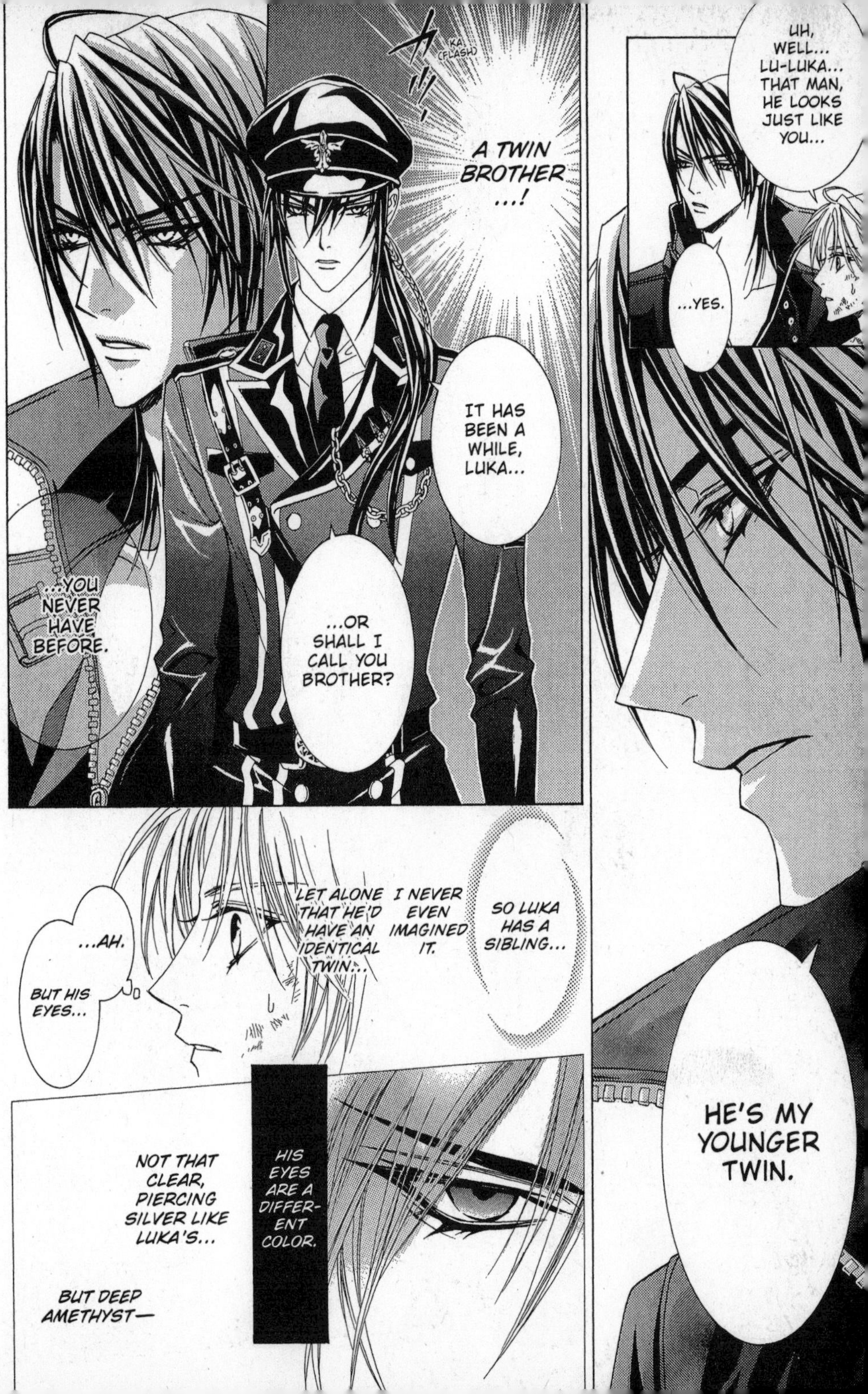

UH, WELL... LU-LUKA... THAT MAN, HE LOOKS JUST LIKE YOU...
...YES.
HE'S MY YOUNGER TWIN.
KA (FLASH)
A TWIN BROTHER ...!
IT HAS BEEN A WHILE, LUKA...
...OR SHALL I CALL YOU BROTHER?
...YOU NEVER HAVE BEFORE.
SO LUKA HAS A SIBLING...
I NEVER EVEN IMAGINED IT.
LET ALONE THAT HE'D HAVE AN IDENTICAL TWIN...
...AH.
BUT HIS EYES...
HIS EYES ARE A DIFFER-ENT COLOR.
NOT THAT CLEAR, PIERCING SILVER LIKE LUKA'S...
BUT DEEP AMETHYST—

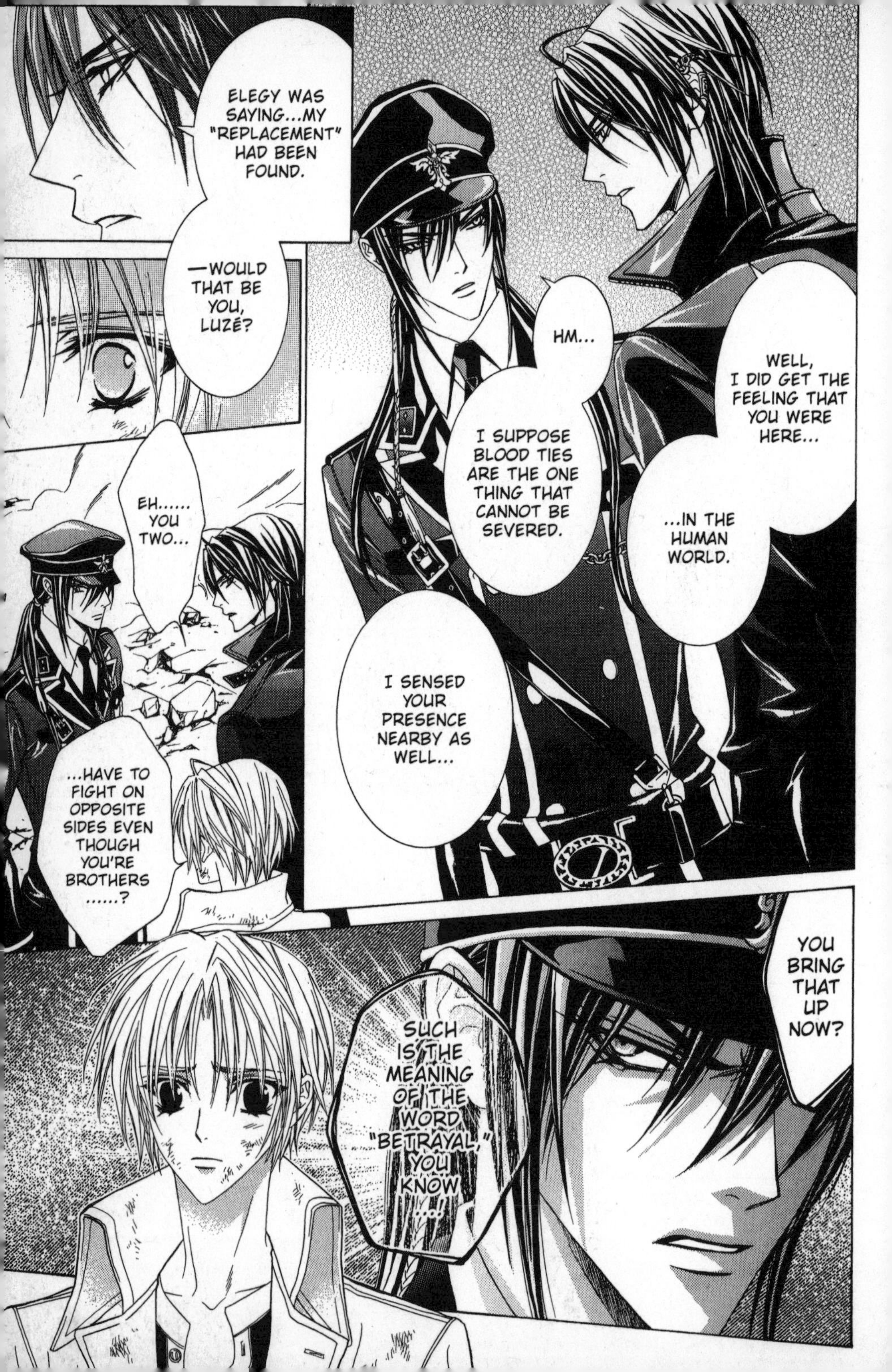
WELL, I DID GET THE FEELING THAT YOU WERE HERE...
...IN THE HUMAN WORLD.
HM...
I SUPPOSE BLOOD TIES ARE THE ONE THING THAT CANNOT BE SEVERED.
I SENSED YOUR PRESENCE NEARBY AS WELL...
ELEGY WAS SAYING...MY "REPLACEMENT" HAD BEEN FOUND.
—WOULD THAT BE YOU, LUZÉ?
EH...... YOU TWO...
...HAVE TO FIGHT ON OPPOSITE SIDES EVEN THOUGH YOU'RE BROTHERS ......?
YOU BRING THAT UP NOW?
SUCH IS THE MEANING OF THE WORD "BETRAYAL," YOU KNOW ...!

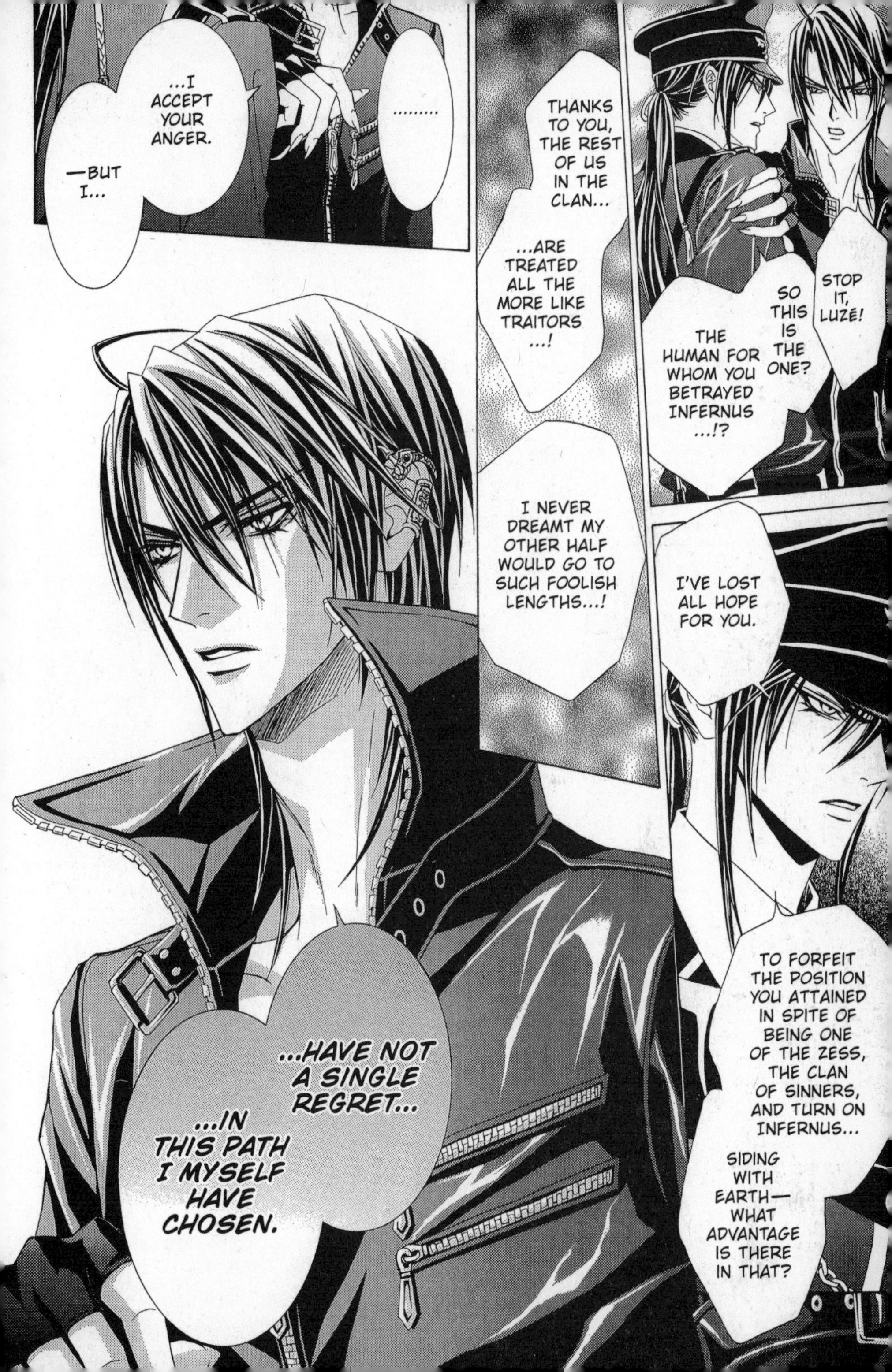
STOP IT, LUZÉ!
SO THIS IS THE ONE?
THE HUMAN FOR WHOM YOU BETRAYED INFERNUS ...!?
THANKS TO YOU, THE REST OF US IN THE CLAN...
...ARE TREATED ALL THE MORE LIKE TRAITORS ...!
I NEVER DREAMT MY OTHER HALF WOULD GO TO SUCH FOOLISH LENGTHS...!
I'VE LOST ALL HOPE FOR YOU.
TO FORFEIT THE POSITION YOU ATTAINED IN SPITE OF BEING ONE OF THE ZESS, THE CLAN OF SINNERS, AND TURN ON INFERNUS...
SIDING WITH EARTH—WHAT ADVANTAGE IS THERE IN THAT?
....
...I ACCEPT YOUR ANGER.
—BUT I...
...HAVE NOT A SINGLE REGRET...
...IN THIS PATH I MYSELF HAVE CHOSEN.

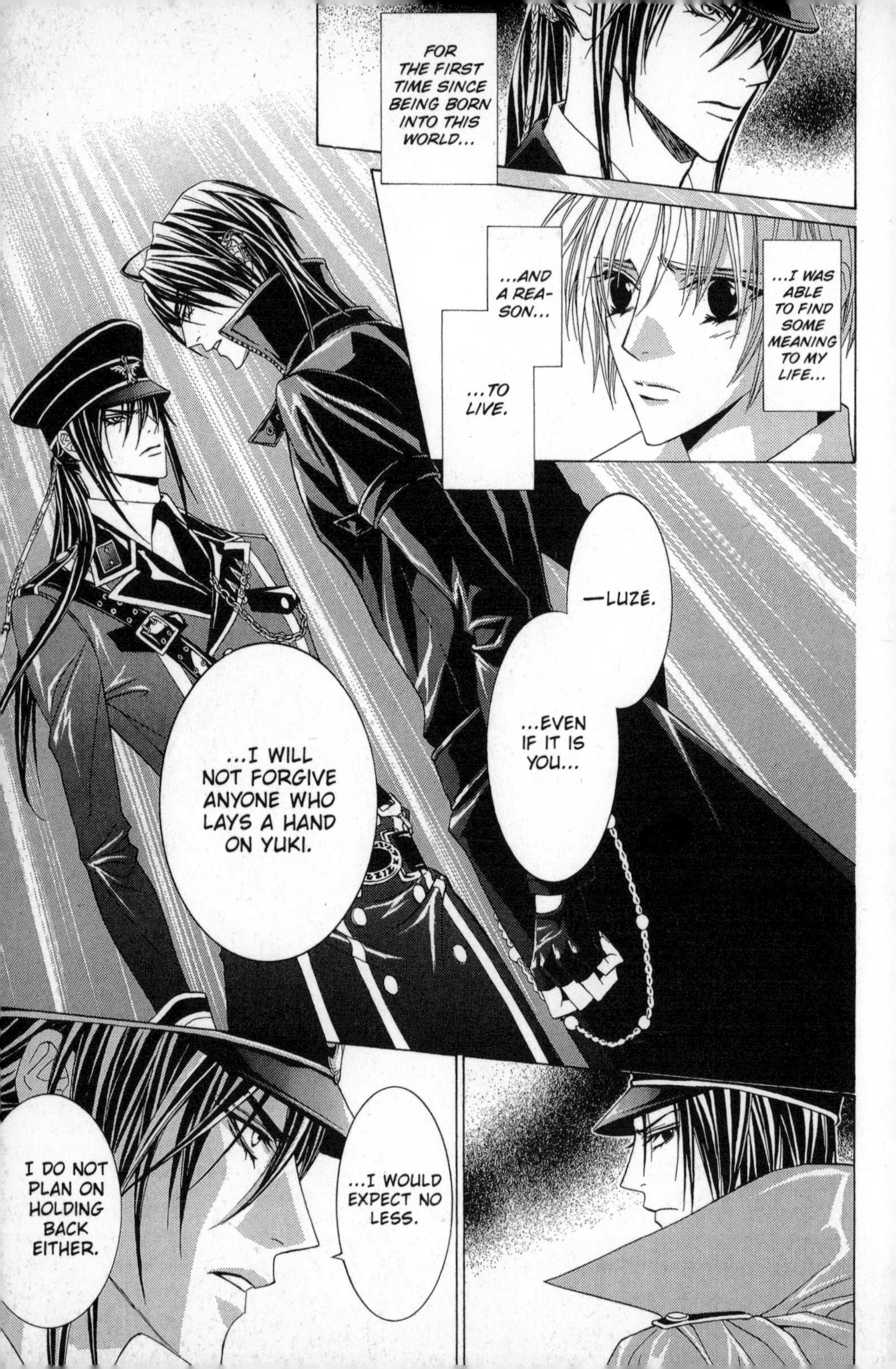
FOR THE FIRST TIME SINCE BEING BORN INTO THIS WORLD...
...I WAS ABLE TO FIND SOME MEANING TO MY LIFE...
...AND A REASON...
...TO LIVE.
—LUZÉ.
...EVEN IF IT IS YOU...
...I WILL NOT FORGIVE ANYONE WHO LAYS A HAND ON YUKI.
...I WOULD EXPECT NO LESS.
I DO NOT PLAN ON HOLDING BACK EITHER.

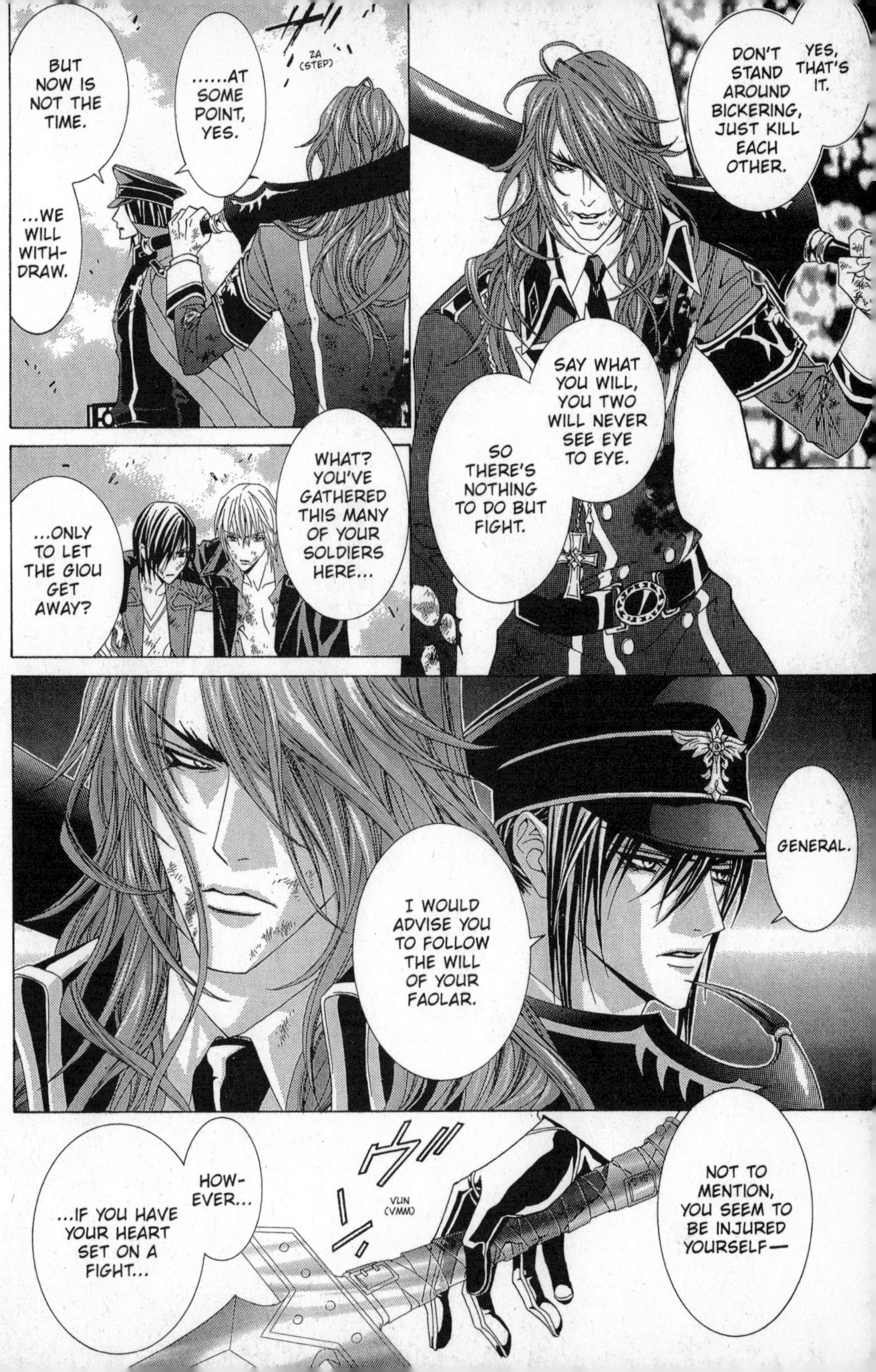
YES, THAT'S IT.
DON'T STAND AROUND BICKERING, JUST KILL EACH OTHER.
SAY WHAT YOU WILL, YOU TWO WILL NEVER SEE EYE TO EYE.
SO THERE'S NOTHING TO DO BUT FIGHT.
ZA (STEP)
......AT SOME POINT, YES.
BUT NOW IS NOT THE TIME.
...WE WILL WITH-DRAW.
WHAT? YOU'VE GATHERED THIS MANY OF YOUR SOLDIERS HERE...
...ONLY TO LET THE GIOU GET AWAY?
GENERAL.
I WOULD ADVISE YOU TO FOLLOW THE WILL OF YOUR FAOLAR.
NOT TO MENTION, YOU SEEM TO BE INJURED YOURSELF—
VUN (VMM)
HOW-EVER...
...IF YOU HAVE YOUR HEART SET ON A FIGHT...

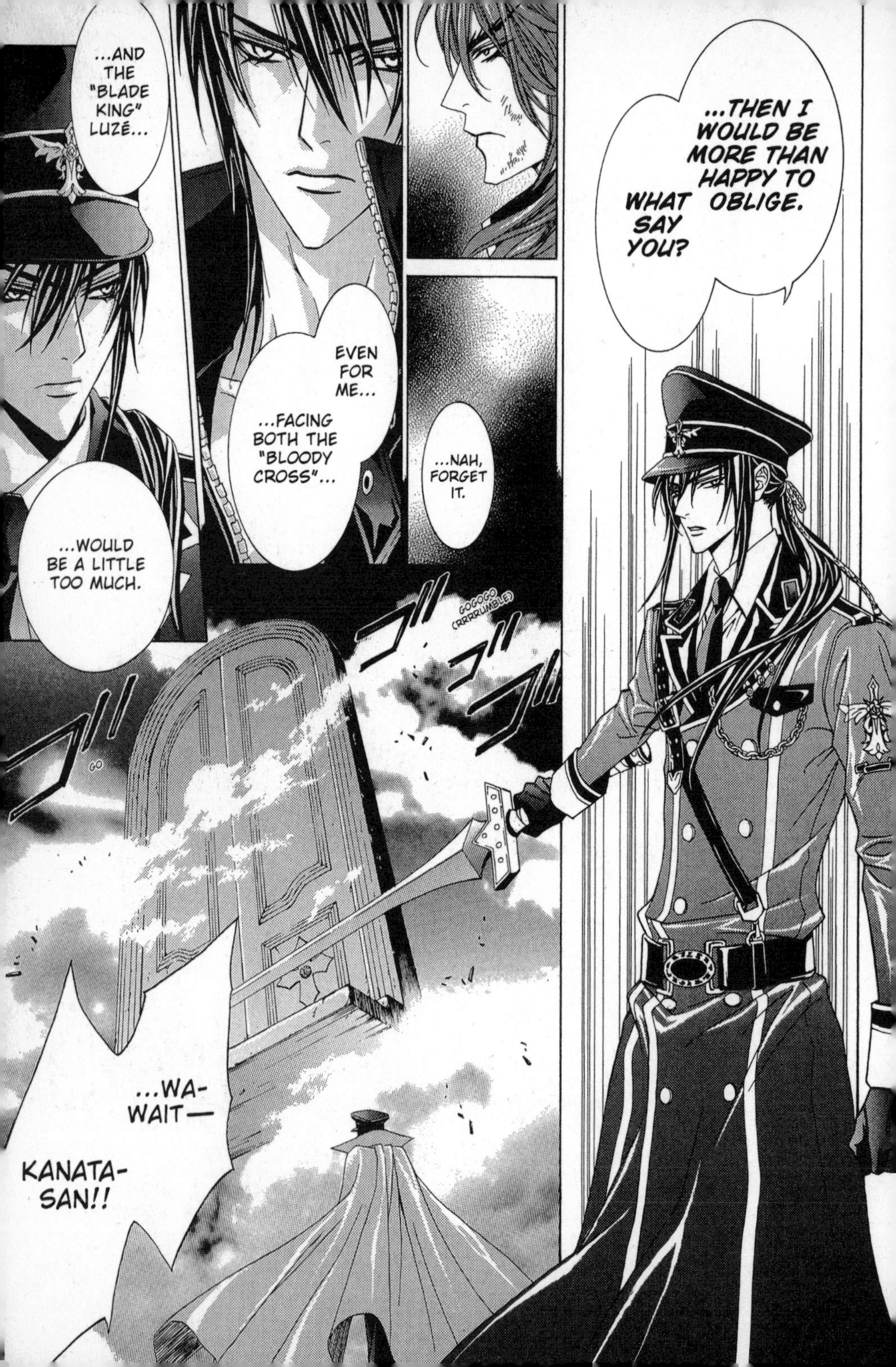
...THEN I WOULD BE MORE THAN HAPPY TO OBLIGE. WHAT SAY YOU?
...NAH, FORGET IT.
EVEN FOR ME...
...FACING BOTH THE "BLOODY CROSS"...
...AND THE "BLADE KING" LUZÉ...
...WOULD BE A LITTLE TOO MUCH.
GOGOGO (RRRRUMBLE)
GO
...WA-WAIT—
KANATA-SAN!!

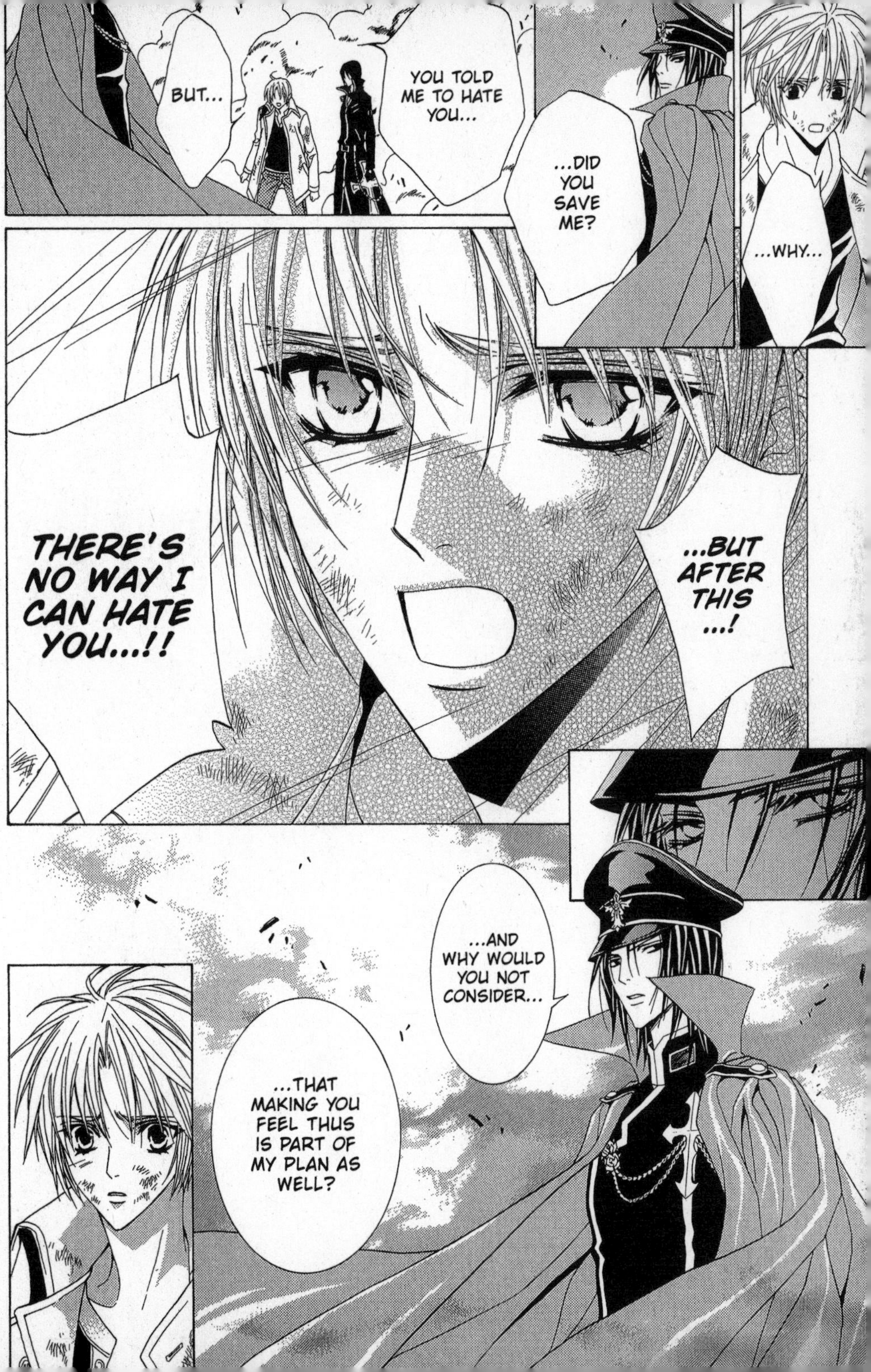
...WHY...
...DID YOU SAVE ME?
YOU TOLD ME TO HATE YOU...
BUT...
...BUT AFTER THIS ...!
THERE'S NO WAY I CAN HATE YOU...!!
...AND WHY WOULD YOU NOT CONSIDER...
...THAT MAKING YOU FEEL THUS IS PART OF MY PLAN AS WELL?

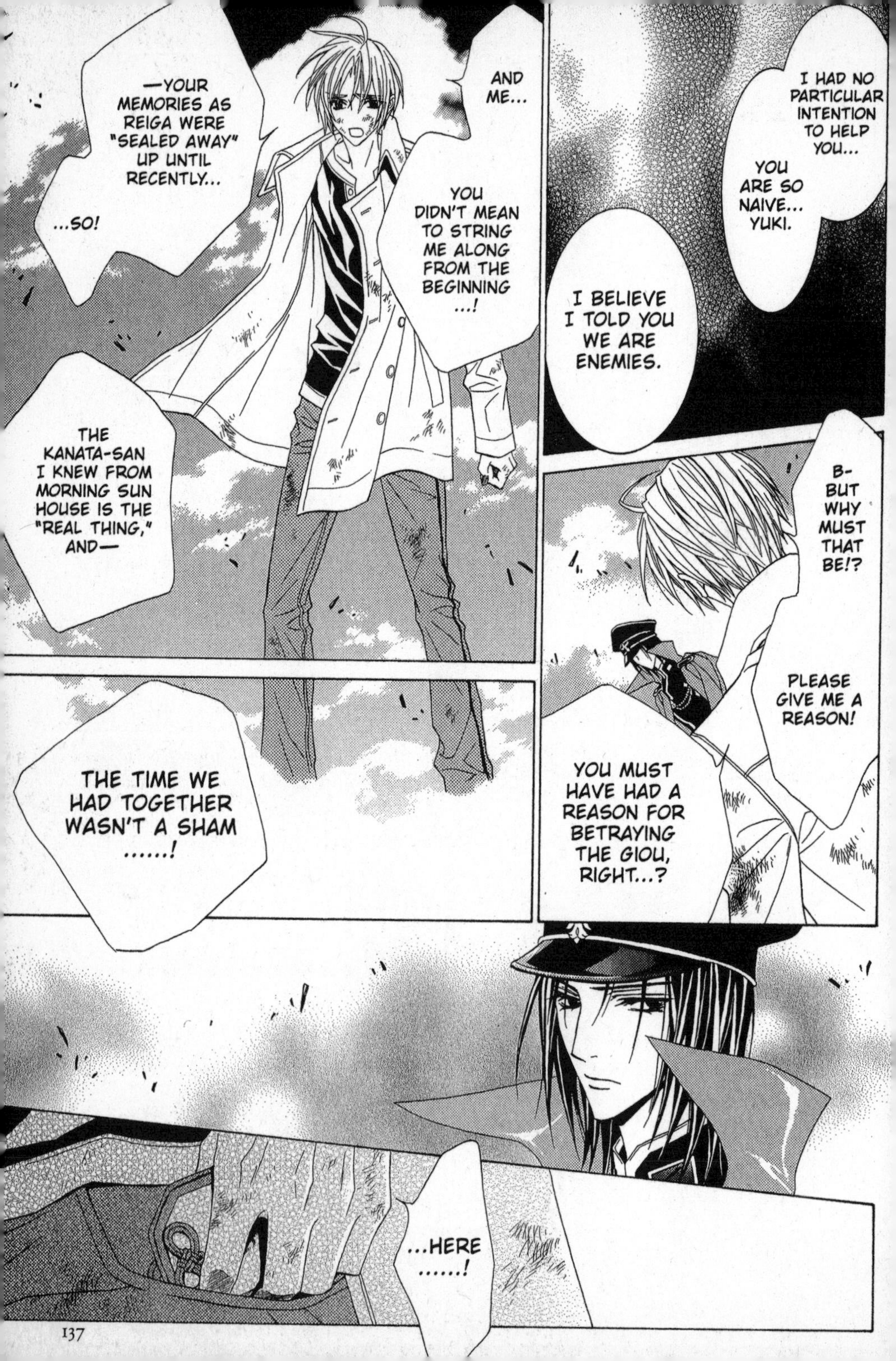
I HAD NO PARTICULAR INTENTION TO HELP YOU...
YOU ARE SO NAIVE... YUKI.
I BELIEVE I TOLD YOU WE ARE ENEMIES.
AND ME...
YOU DIDN'T MEAN TO STRING ME ALONG FROM THE BEGINNING ...!
—YOUR MEMORIES AS REIGA WERE "SEALED AWAY" UP UNTIL RECENTLY...
...SO!
THE KANATA-SAN I KNEW FROM MORNING SUN HOUSE IS THE "REAL THING," AND—
THE TIME WE HAD TOGETHER WASN'T A SHAM ......!
B-BUT WHY MUST THAT BE!?
PLEASE GIVE ME A REASON!
YOU MUST HAVE HAD A REASON FOR BETRAYING THE GIOU, RIGHT...?
...HERE ......!

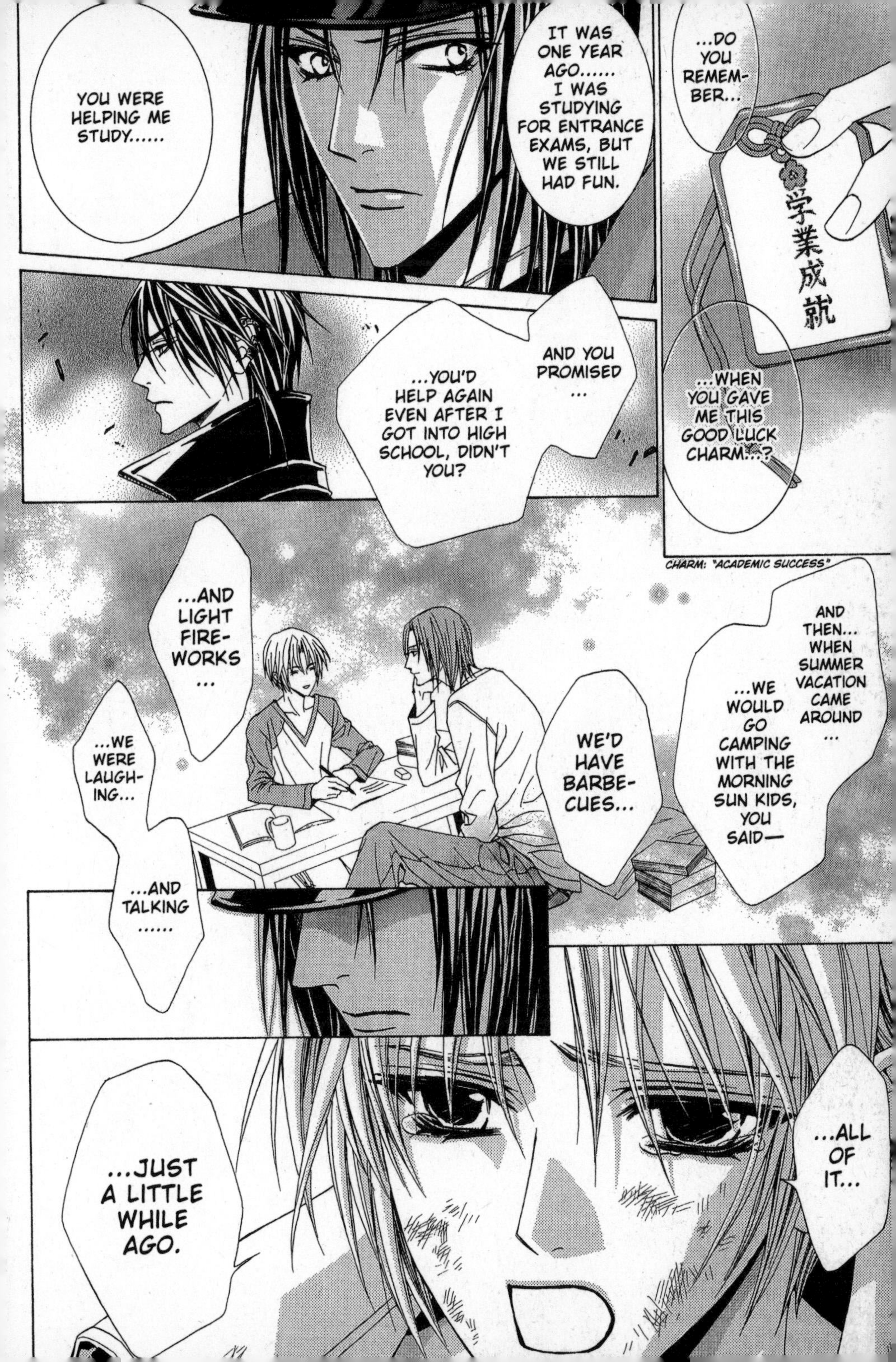
...DO YOU REMEMBER...
学業成就
...WHEN YOU GAVE ME THIS GOOD LUCK CHARM...?
CHARM: "ACADEMIC SUCCESS"
IT WAS ONE YEAR AGO...... I WAS STUDYING FOR ENTRANCE EXAMS, BUT WE STILL HAD FUN.
YOU WERE HELPING ME STUDY......
AND YOU PROMISED ...
...YOU'D HELP AGAIN EVEN AFTER I GOT INTO HIGH SCHOOL, DIDN'T YOU?
AND THEN... WHEN SUMMER VACATION CAME AROUND ...
...WE WOULD GO CAMPING WITH THE MORNING SUN KIDS, YOU SAID—
WE'D HAVE BARBECUES...
...AND LIGHT FIREWORKS ...
...WE WERE LAUGHING...
...AND TALKING ......
...ALL OF IT...
...JUST A LITTLE WHILE AGO.

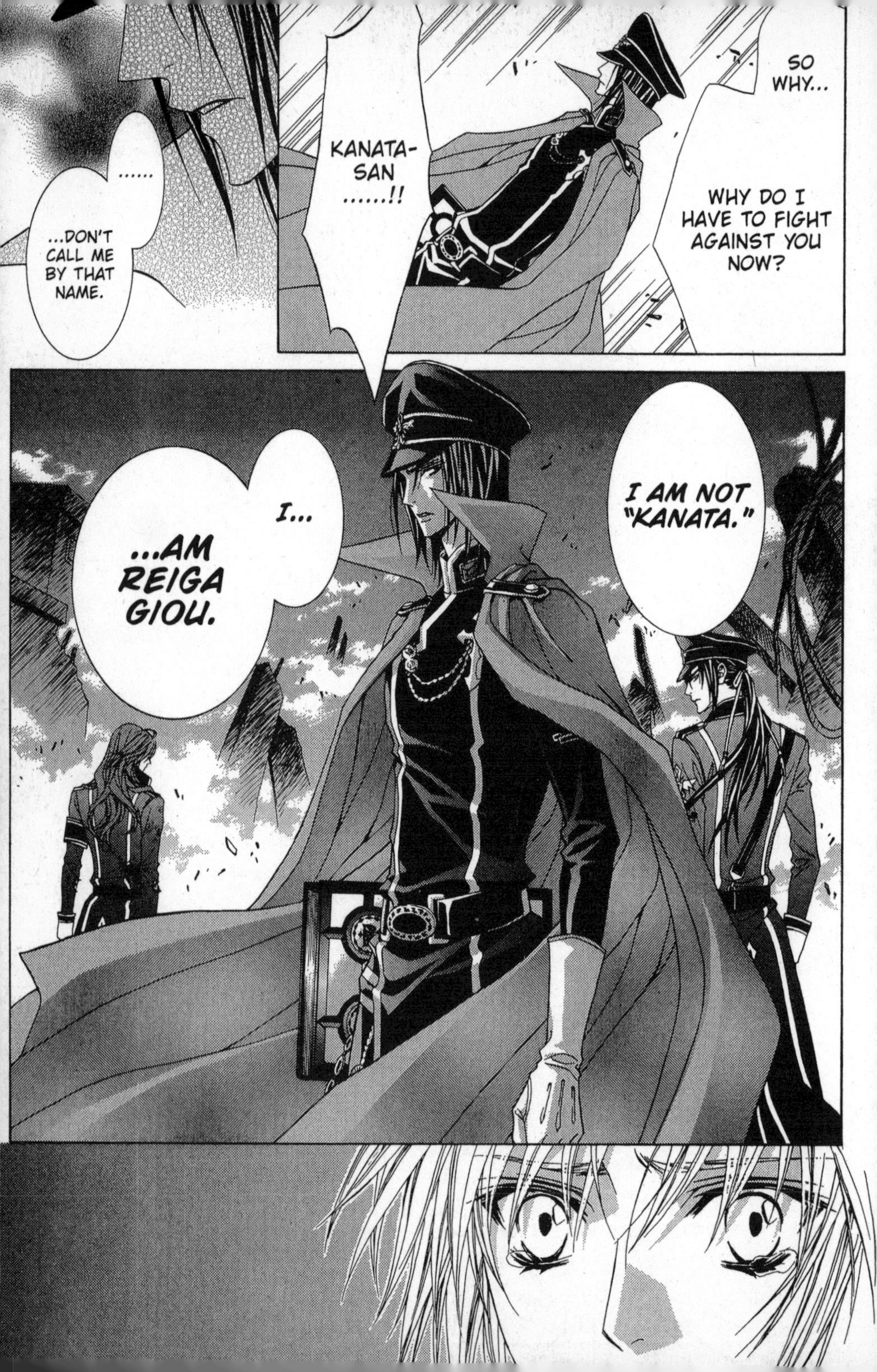
SO WHY...
WHY DO I HAVE TO FIGHT AGAINST YOU NOW?
KANATA-SAN ......!!
......
...DON'T CALL ME BY THAT NAME.
I AM NOT "KANATA."
I...
...AM REIGA GIOU.

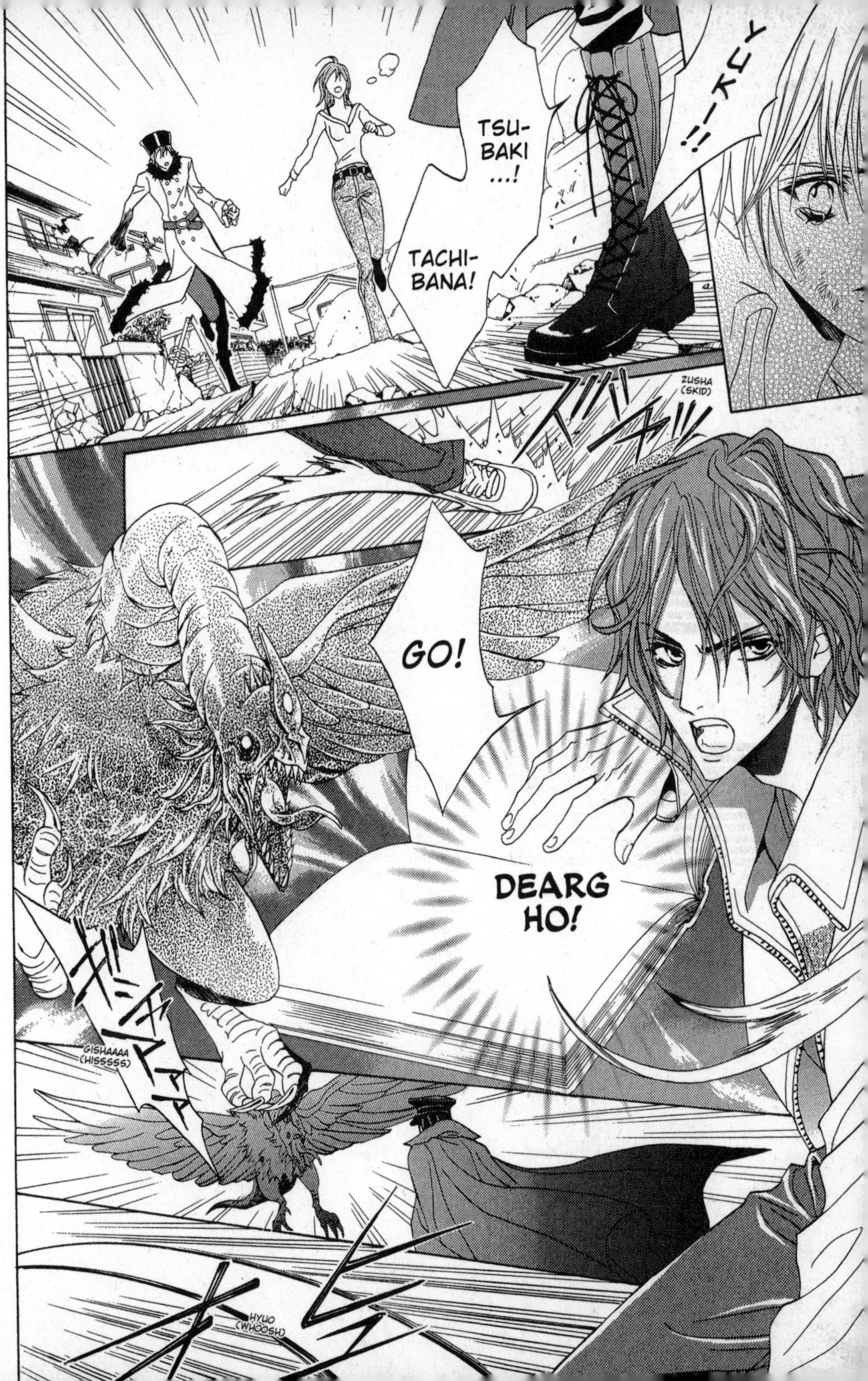
YU-KI--!!
TSU-BAKI ...!
TACHI-BANA!
ZUSHA (SKID)
GO!
DEARG HO!
GISHAAA (HISSSSS)
HYUO (WHOOSH)

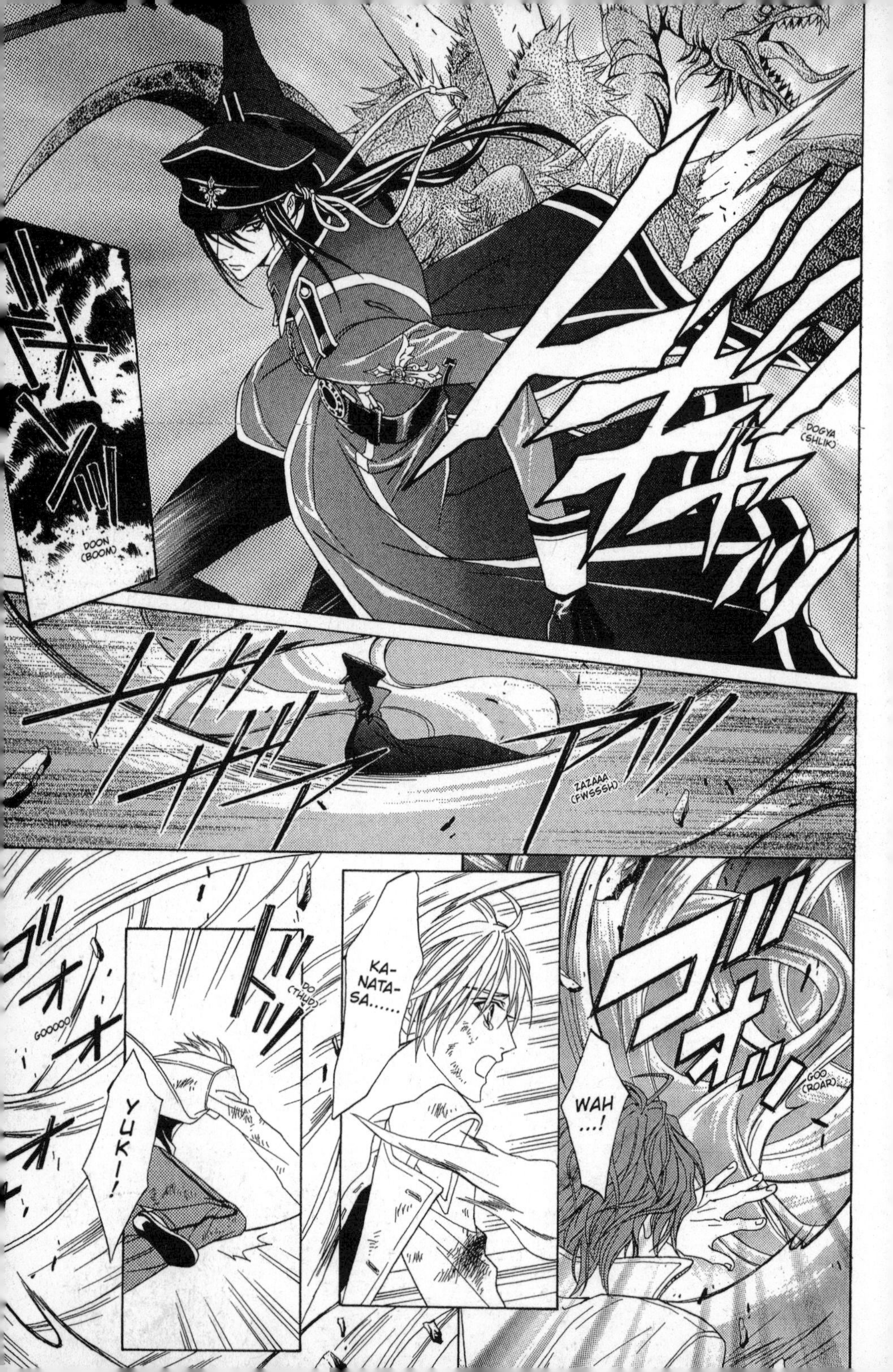
DOGYA (SHLIK)
DOON (BOOM)
ZAZAAA (FWSSSH)
GOO (ROAR)
WAH ...!
KA-NATA-SA......
DO (THUD)
YUKI!
GOOOOO

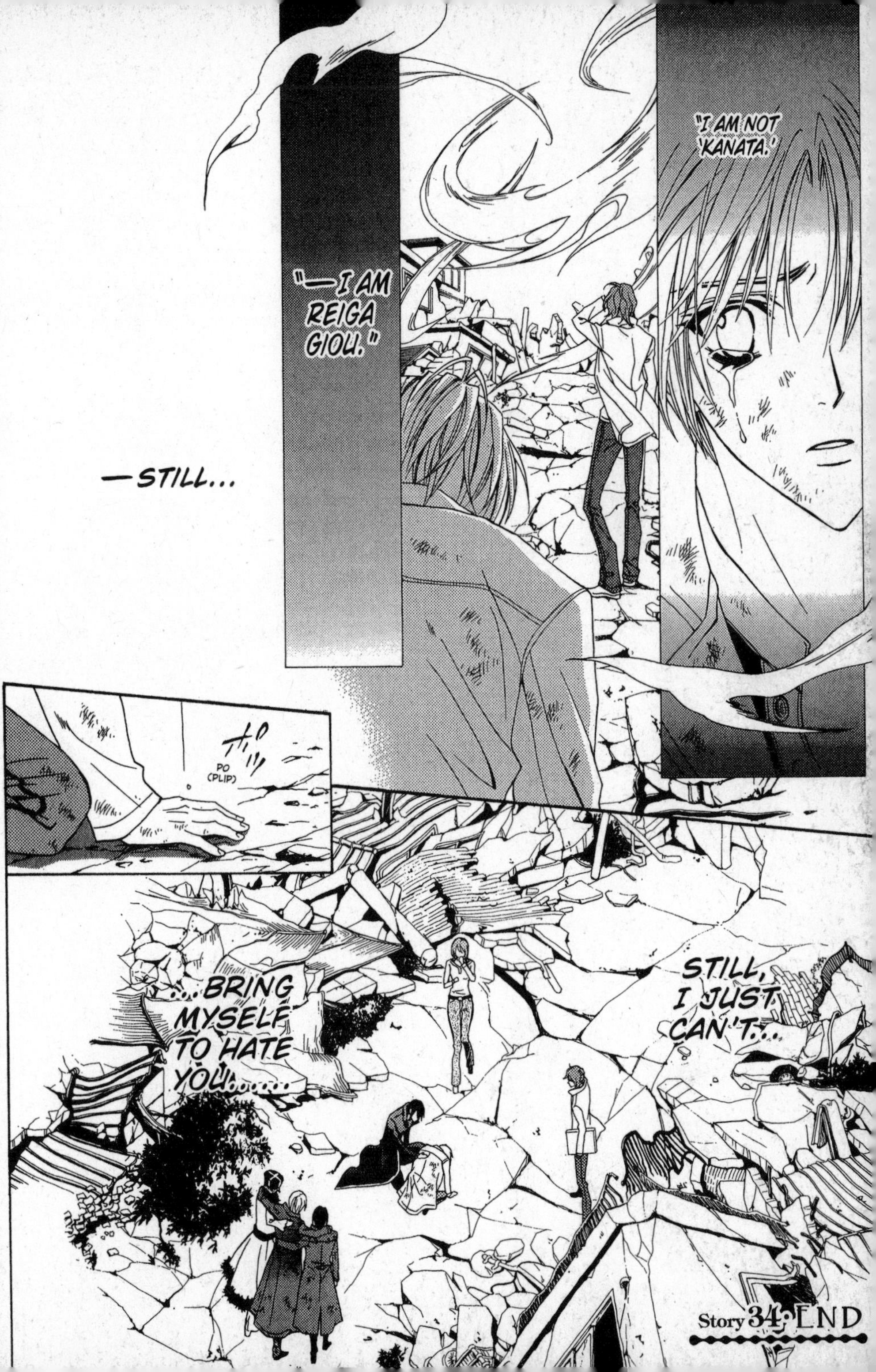
"I AM NOT 'KANATA.'
"—I AM REIGA GIOU."
—STILL...
PO (PLIP)
STILL, I JUST CAN'T...
...BRING MYSELF TO HATE YOU......
Story 34 · END

THE
BETRAYAL
KNOWS MY NAME

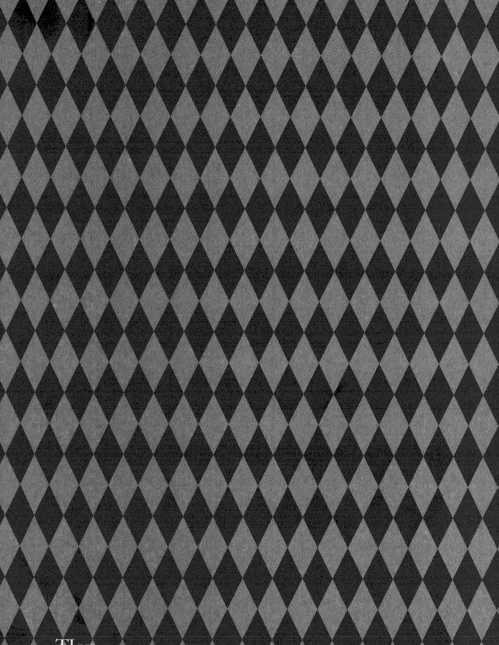

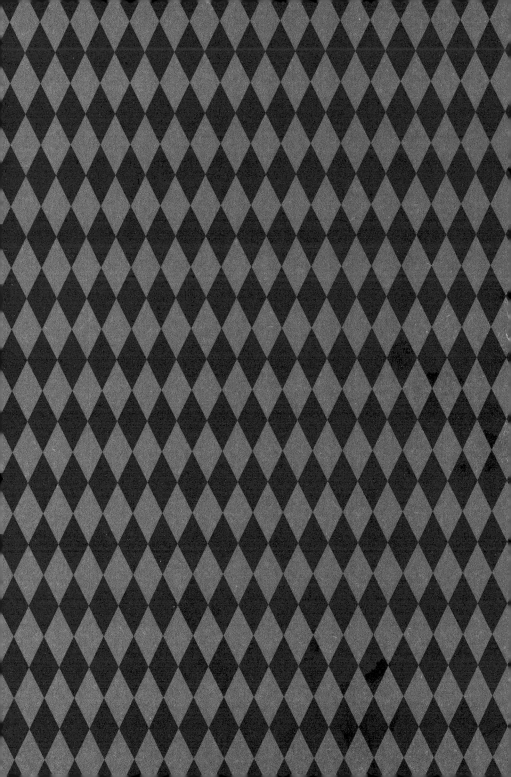

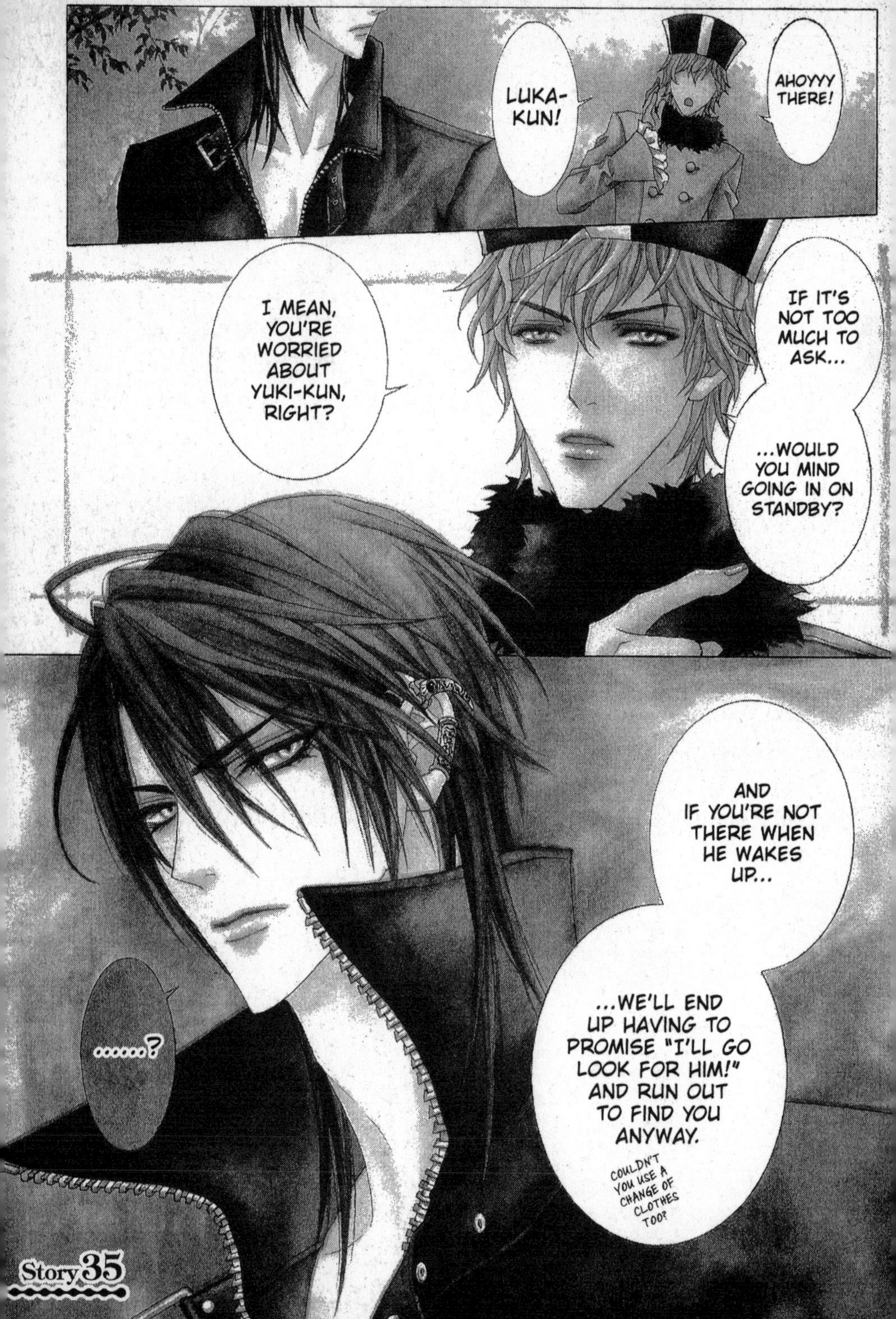
AHOYYY THERE!
LUKA-KUN!
IF IT'S NOT TOO MUCH TO ASK...
...WOULD YOU MIND GOING IN ON STANDBY?
I MEAN, YOU'RE WORRIED ABOUT YUKI-KUN, RIGHT?
AND IF YOU'RE NOT THERE WHEN HE WAKES UP...
...WE'LL END UP HAVING TO PROMISE "I'LL GO LOOK FOR HIM!" AND RUN OUT TO FIND YOU ANYWAY.
COULDN'T YOU USE A CHANGE OF CLOTHES TOO?
......?
Story 35

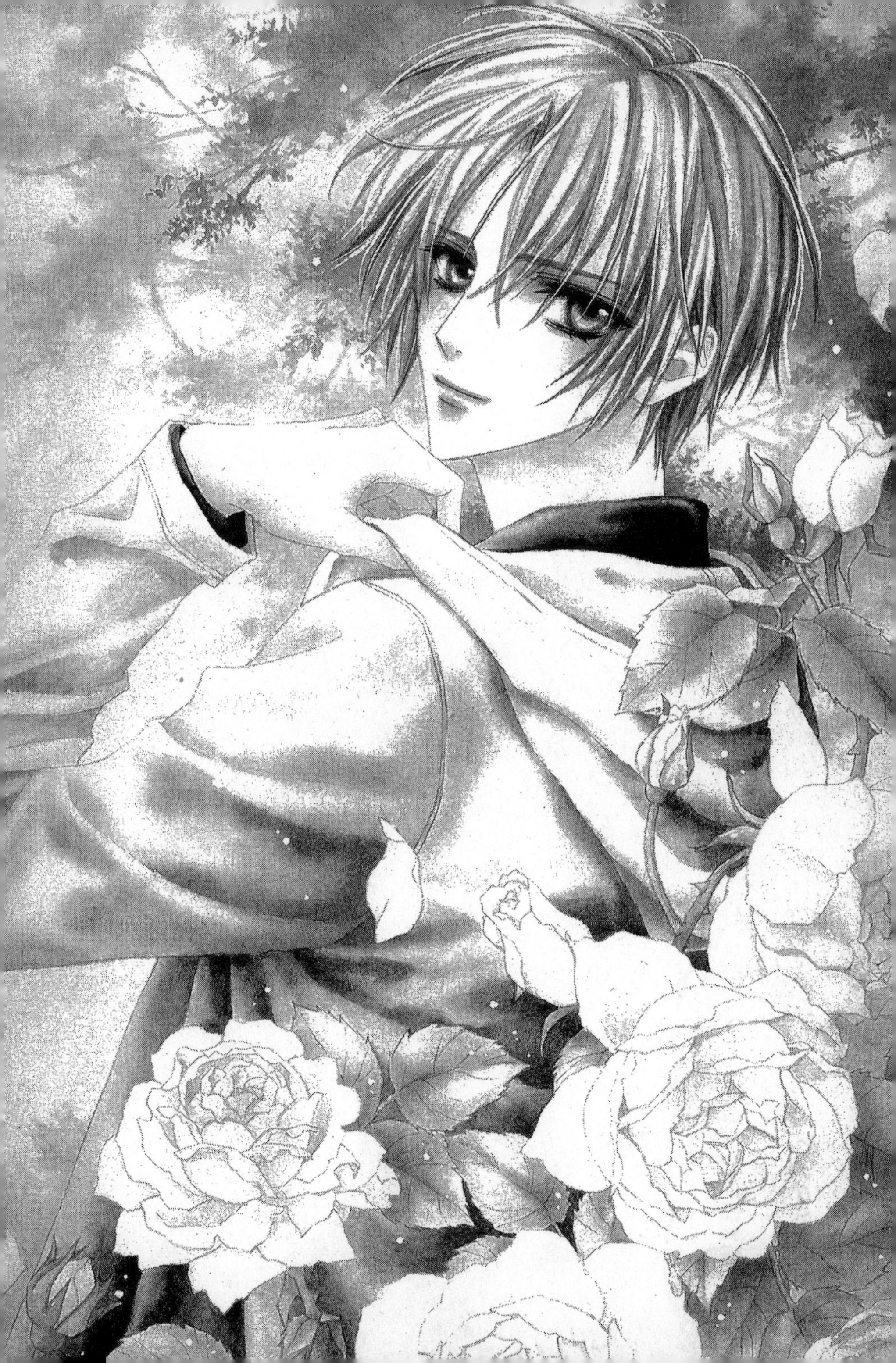

Story 35

Sleep Now, My Sorrows...

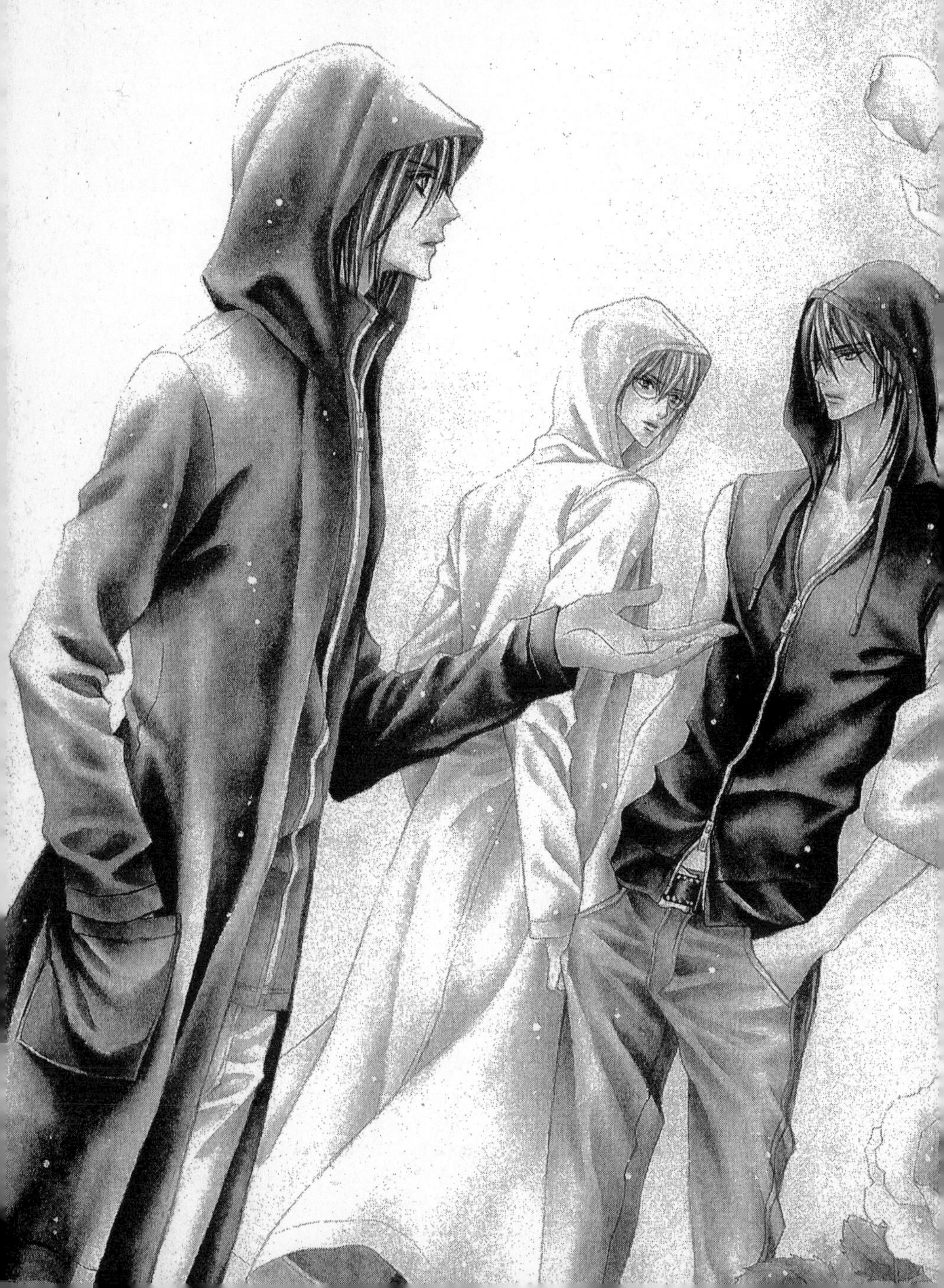

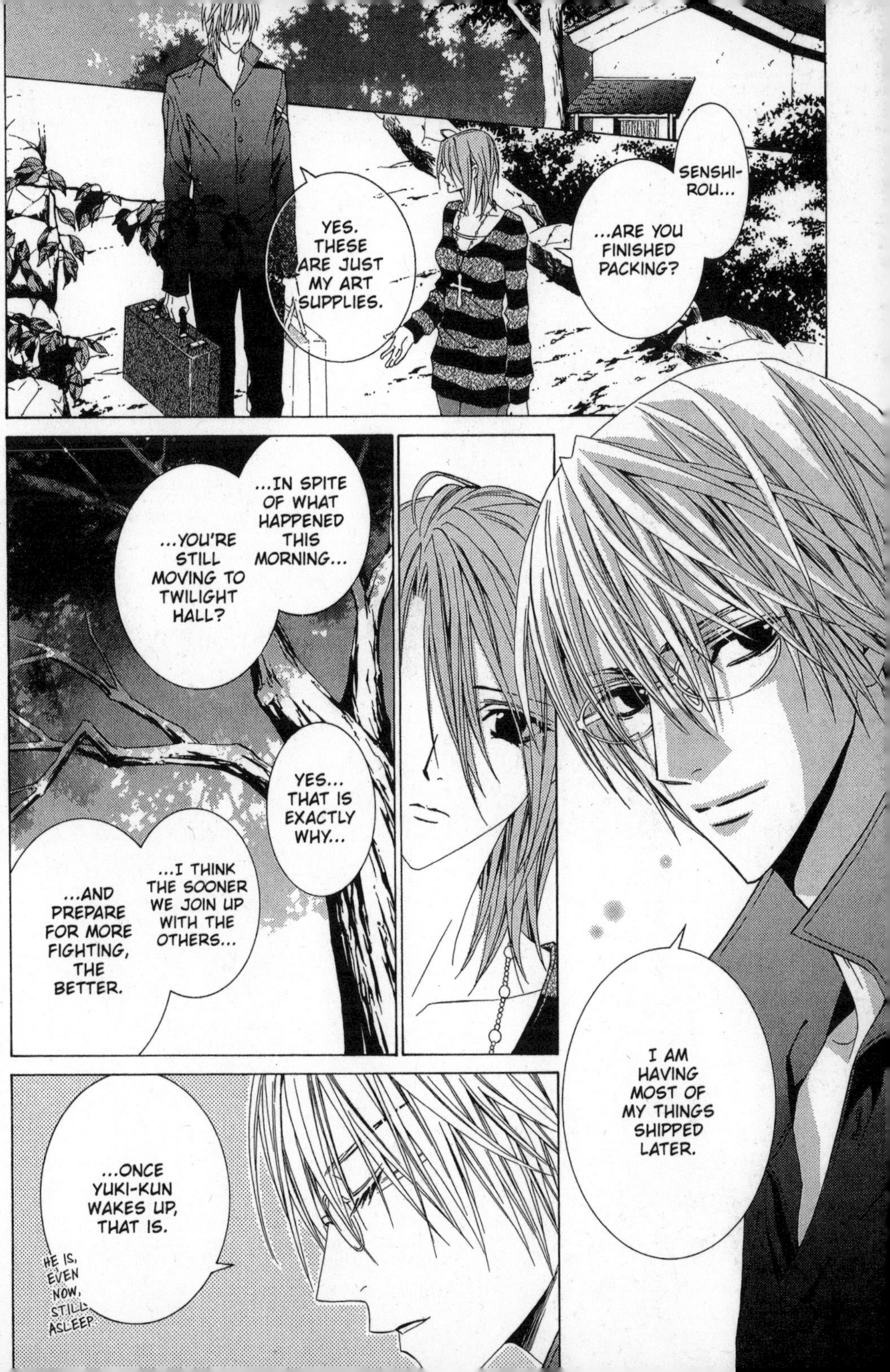
SENSHI-ROU...
...ARE YOU FINISHED PACKING?
YES. THESE ARE JUST MY ART SUPPLIES.
I AM HAVING MOST OF MY THINGS SHIPPED LATER.
...IN SPITE OF WHAT HAPPENED THIS MORNING...
...YOU'RE STILL MOVING TO TWILIGHT HALL?
YES... THAT IS EXACTLY WHY...
...I THINK THE SOONER WE JOIN UP WITH THE OTHERS...
...AND PREPARE FOR MORE FIGHTING, THE BETTER.
...ONCE YUKI-KUN WAKES UP, THAT IS.
HE IS, EVEN NOW, STILL ASLEEP.

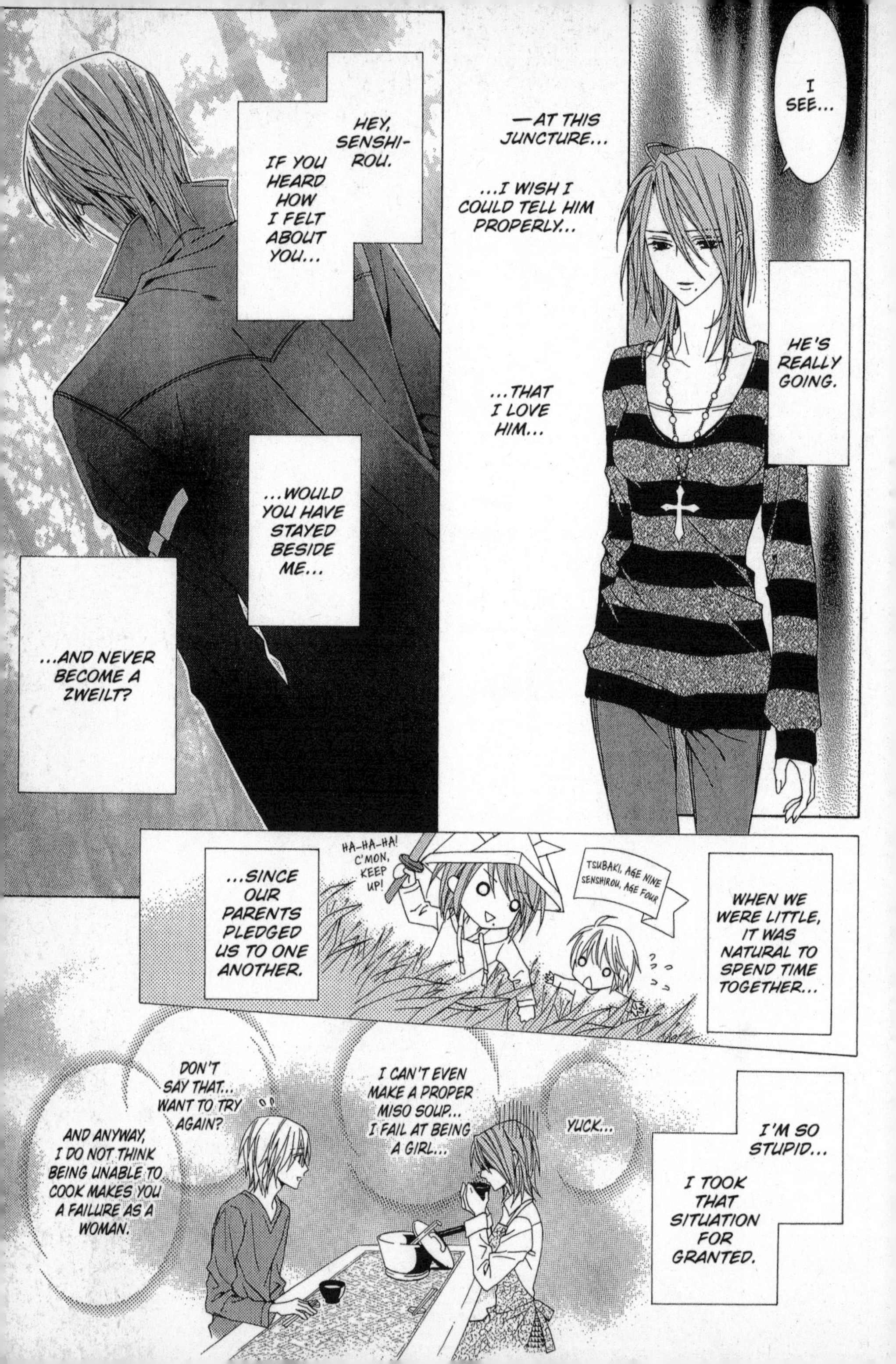
I SEE...
HE'S REALLY GOING.
—AT THIS JUNCTURE...
...I WISH I COULD TELL HIM PROPERLY...
...THAT I LOVE HIM...
HEY, SENSHIROU.
IF YOU HEARD HOW I FELT ABOUT YOU...
...WOULD YOU HAVE STAYED BESIDE ME...
...AND NEVER BECOME A ZWEILT?
WHEN WE WERE LITTLE, IT WAS NATURAL TO SPEND TIME TOGETHER...
TSUBAKI, AGE NINE SENSHIROU, AGE FOUR
HA-HA-HA! C'MON, KEEP UP!
...SINCE OUR PARENTS PLEDGED US TO ONE ANOTHER.
I'M SO STUPID...
I TOOK THAT SITUATION FOR GRANTED.
YUCK...
I CAN'T EVEN MAKE A PROPER MISO SOUP... I FAIL AT BEING A GIRL...
DON'T SAY THAT... WANT TO TRY AGAIN?
AND ANYWAY, I DO NOT THINK BEING UNABLE TO COOK MAKES YOU A FAILURE AS A WOMAN.

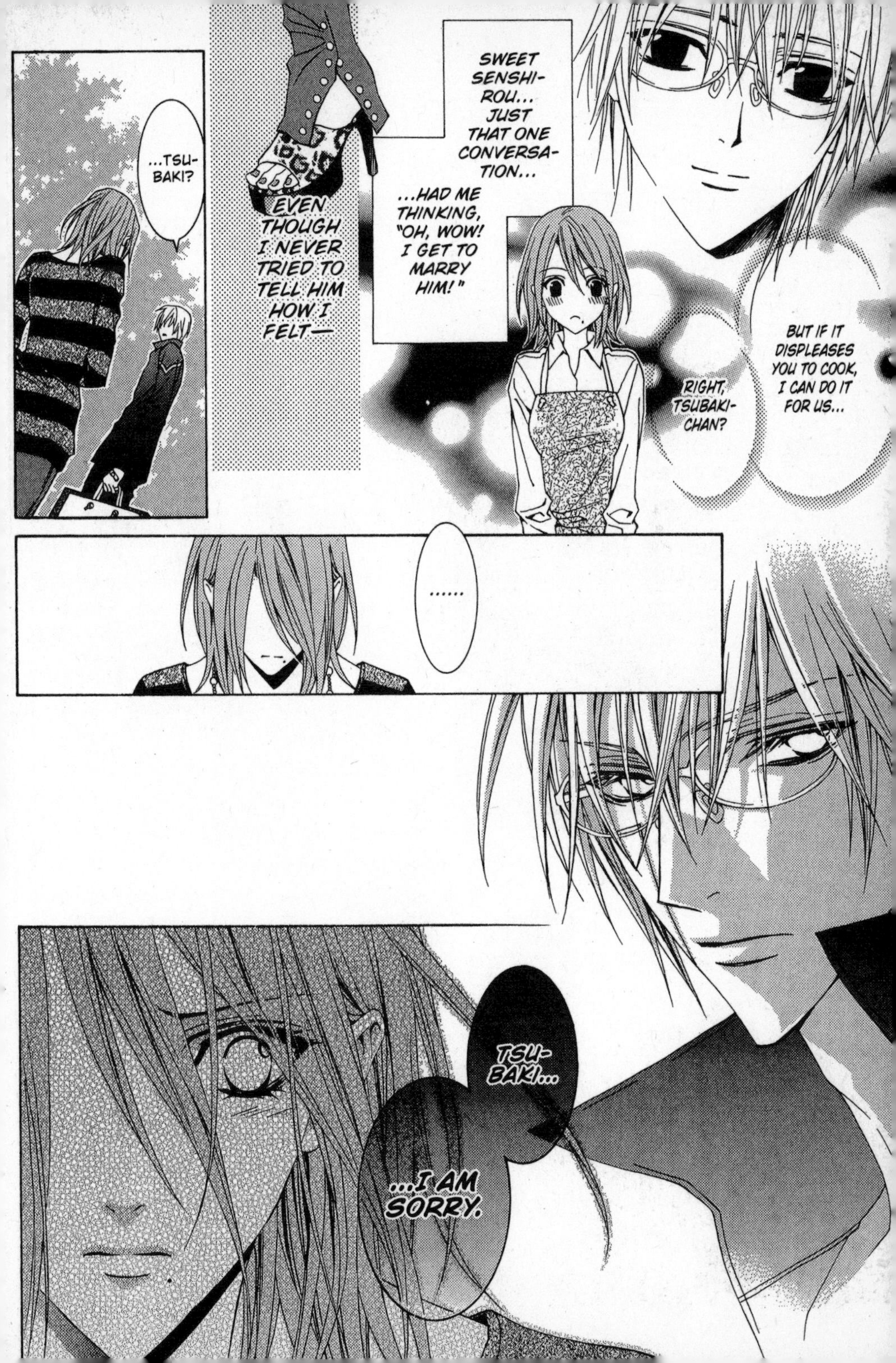
BUT IF IT DISPLEASES YOU TO COOK, I CAN DO IT FOR US...
RIGHT, TSUBAKI-CHAN?
SWEET SENSHIROU... JUST THAT ONE CONVERSATION...
...HAD ME THINKING, "OH, WOW! I GET TO MARRY HIM!"
EVEN THOUGH I NEVER TRIED TO TELL HIM HOW I FELT—
...TSUBAKI?
......
TSU-BAKI...
...I AM SORRY.

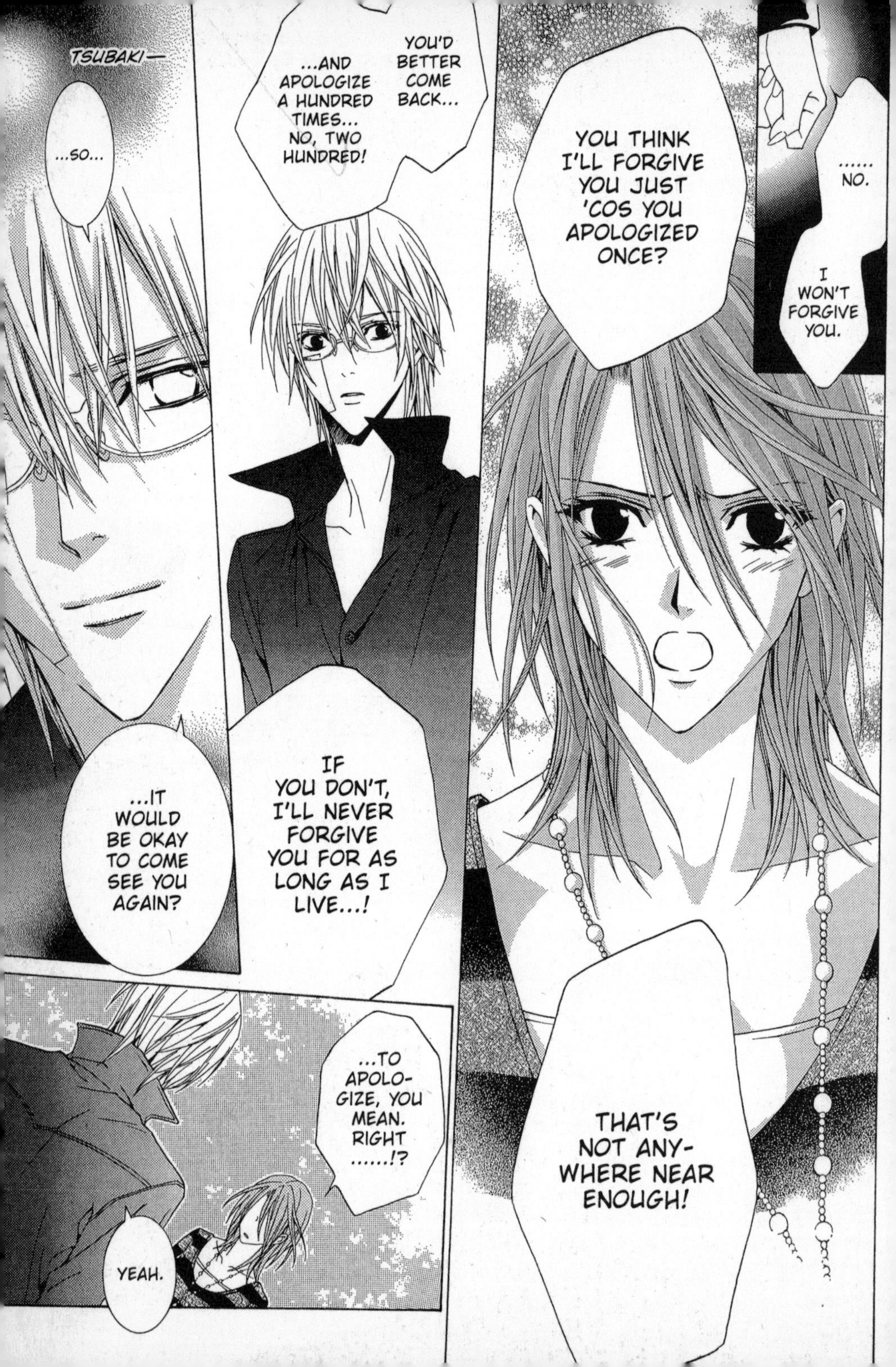
......NO.
I WON'T FORGIVE YOU.
YOU THINK I'LL FORGIVE YOU JUST 'COS YOU APOLOGIZED ONCE?
THAT'S NOT ANY-WHERE NEAR ENOUGH!
YOU'D BETTER COME BACK...
...AND APOLOGIZE A HUNDRED TIMES... NO, TWO HUNDRED!
IF YOU DON'T, I'LL NEVER FORGIVE YOU FOR AS LONG AS I LIVE...!
TSUBAKI—
...SO...
...IT WOULD BE OKAY TO COME SEE YOU AGAIN?
...TO APOLO-GIZE, YOU MEAN. RIGHT ......!?
YEAH.

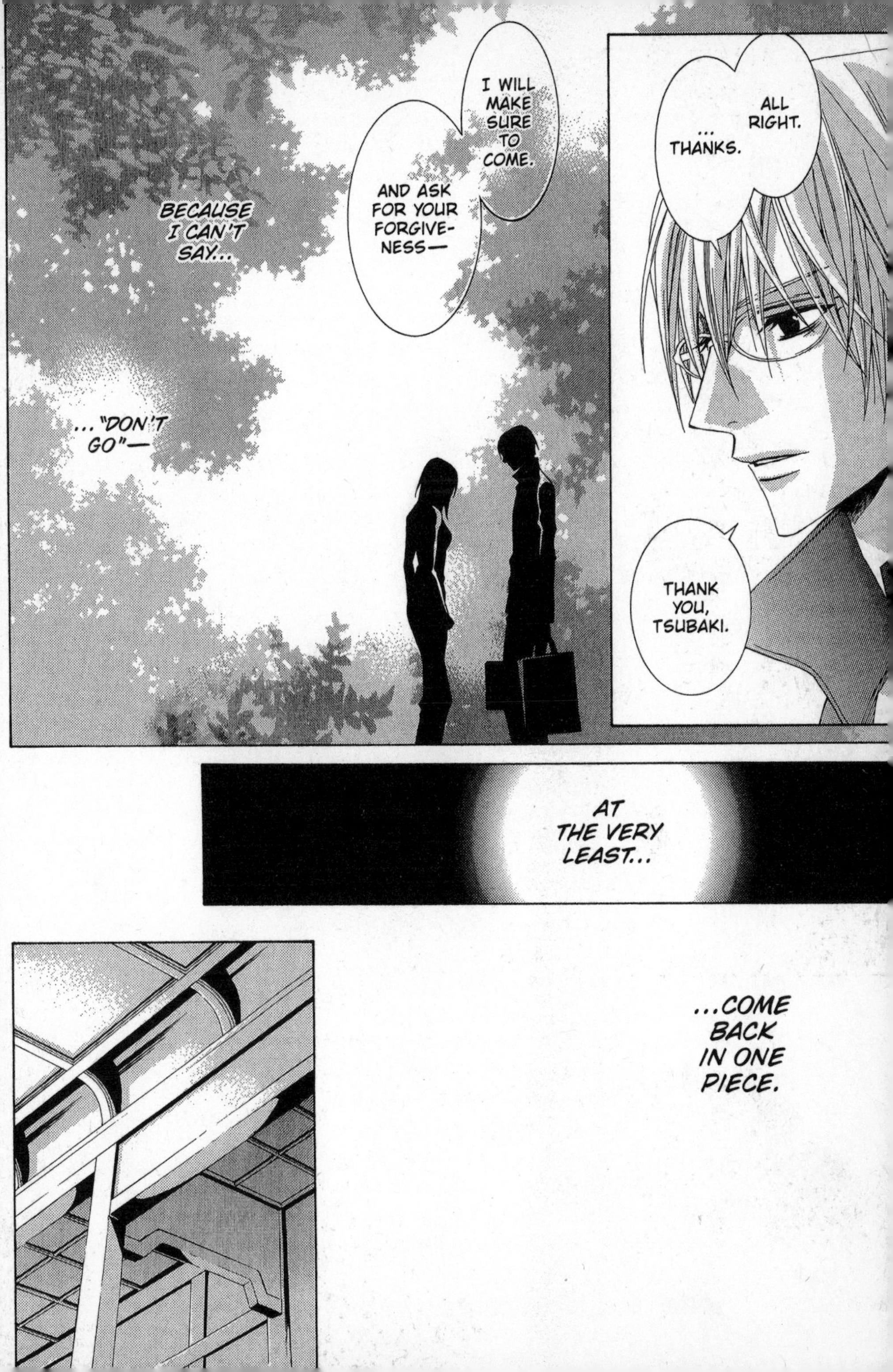
ALL RIGHT. ...THANKS.
THANK YOU, TSUBAKI.
I WILL MAKE SURE TO COME.
AND ASK FOR YOUR FORGIVE-NESS—
BECAUSE I CAN'T SAY...
..."DON'T GO"—
AT THE VERY LEAST...
...COME BACK IN ONE PIECE.

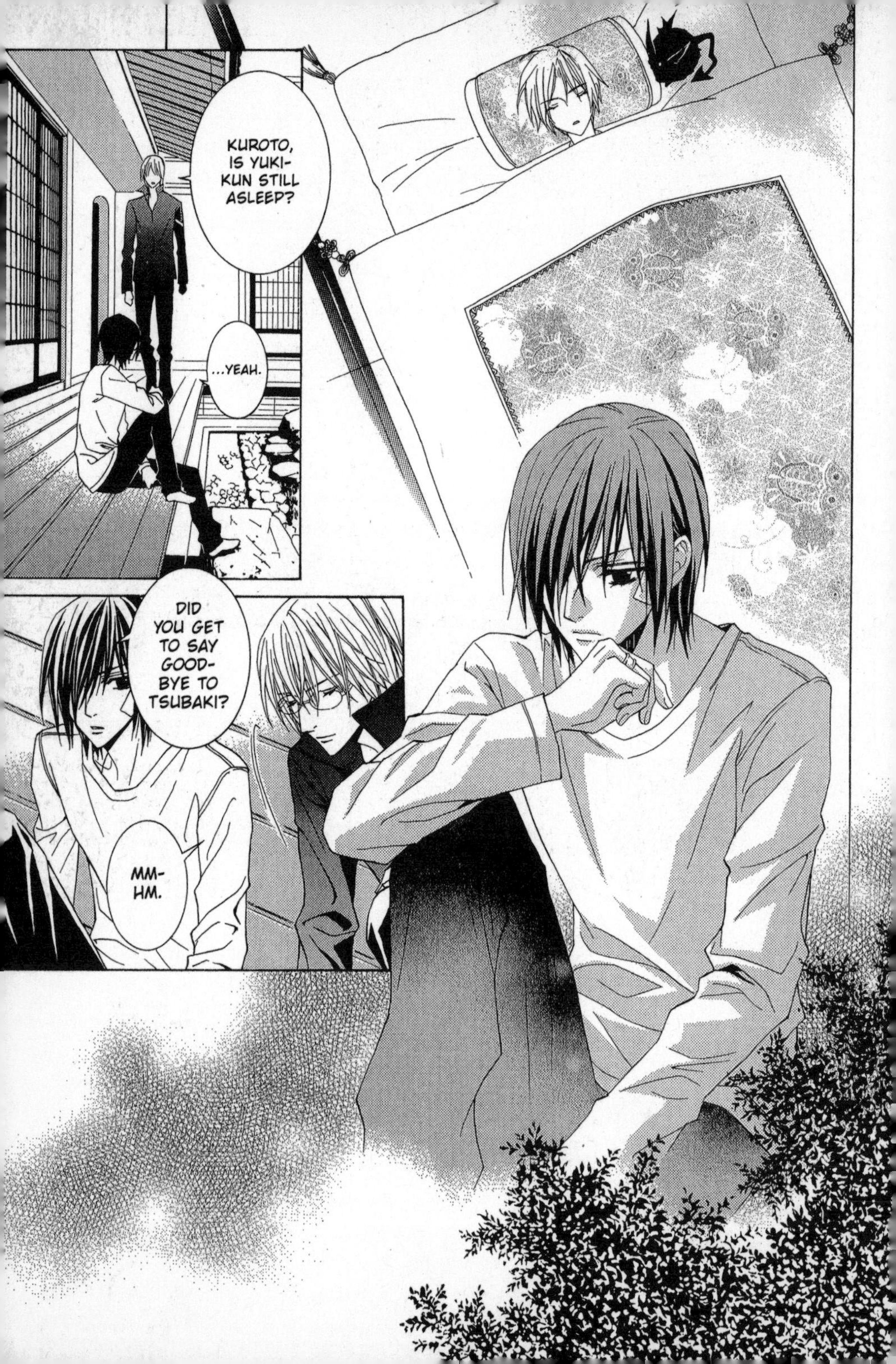
KUROTO, IS YUKI-KUN STILL ASLEEP?
...YEAH.
DID YOU GET TO SAY GOOD-BYE TO TSUBAKI?
MM-HM.

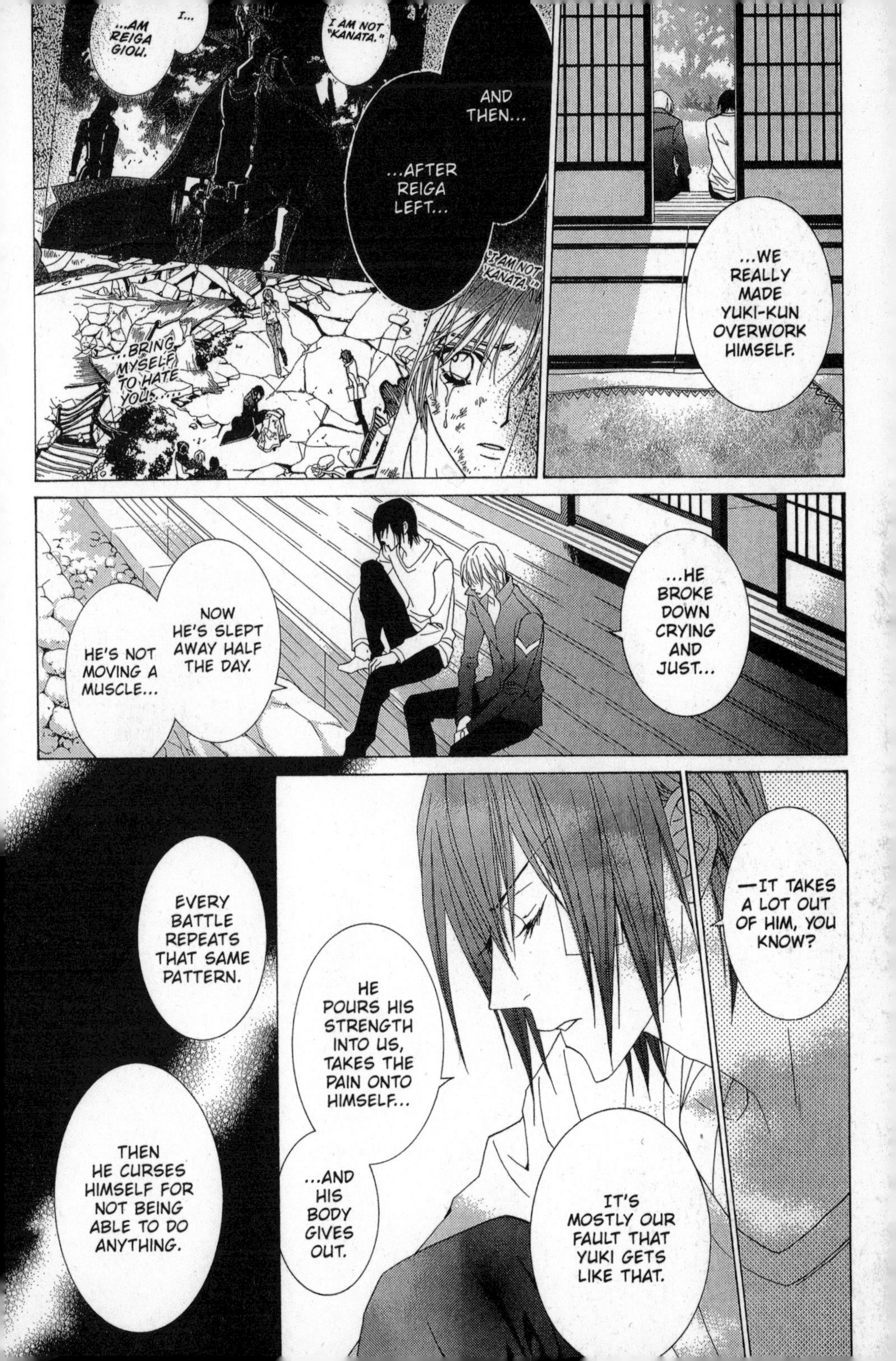
...WE REALLY MADE YUKI-KUN OVERWORK HIMSELF.
AND THEN...
...AFTER REIGA LEFT...
I AM NOT "KANATA."
I...
...AM REIGA GIOU.
"I AM NOT KANATA."
...BRING MYSELF TO HATE YOU...
...HE BROKE DOWN CRYING AND JUST...
NOW HE'S SLEPT AWAY HALF THE DAY.
HE'S NOT MOVING A MUSCLE...
—IT TAKES A LOT OUT OF HIM, YOU KNOW?
IT'S MOSTLY OUR FAULT THAT YUKI GETS LIKE THAT.
HE POURS HIS STRENGTH INTO US, TAKES THE PAIN ONTO HIMSELF...
...AND HIS BODY GIVES OUT.
EVERY BATTLE REPEATS THAT SAME PATTERN.
THEN HE CURSES HIMSELF FOR NOT BEING ABLE TO DO ANYTHING.

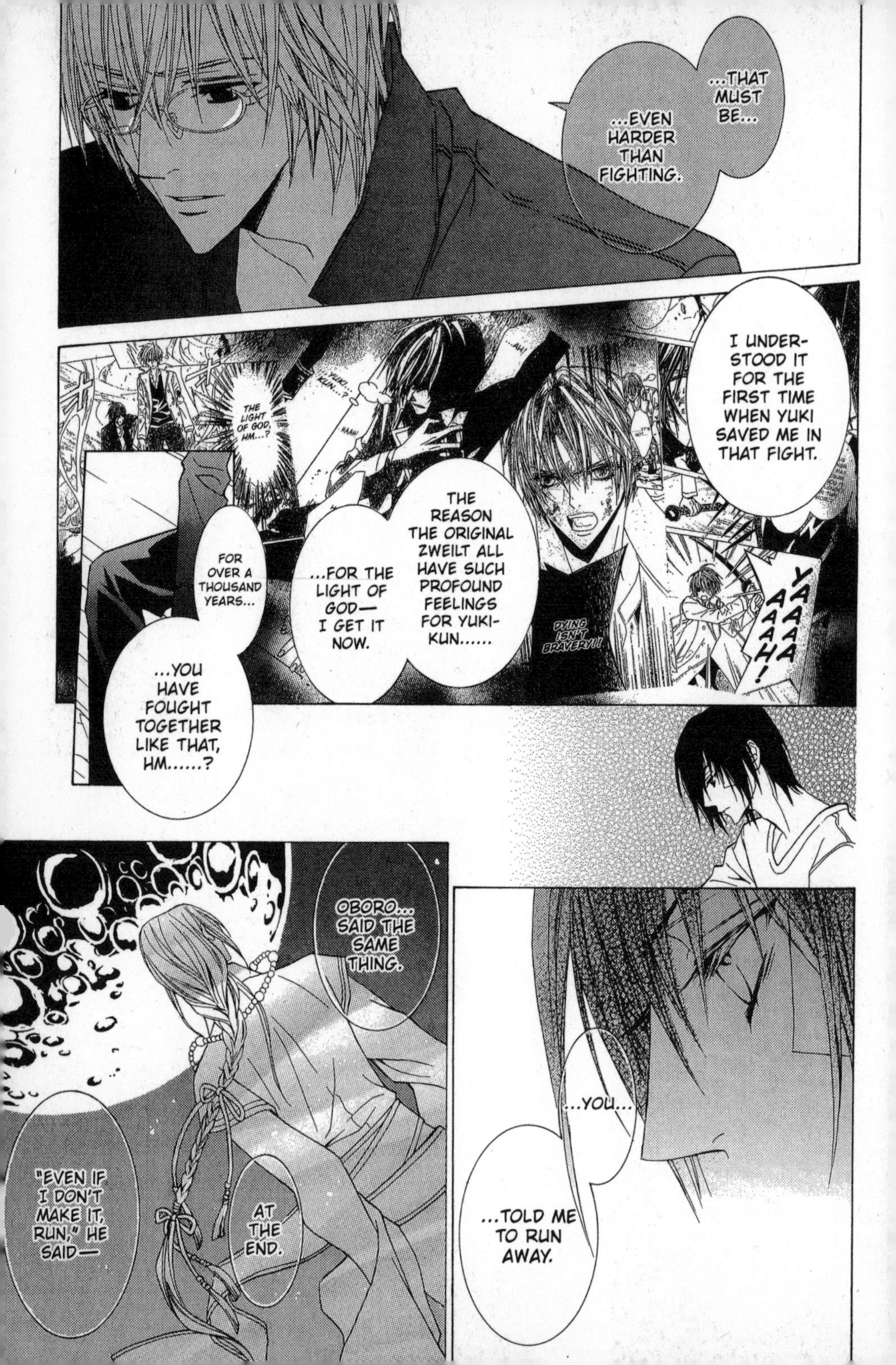
...THAT MUST BE...
...EVEN HARDER THAN FIGHTING.
I UNDERSTOOD IT FOR THE FIRST TIME WHEN YUKI SAVED ME IN THAT FIGHT.
YAAAAAAAH!
DYING ISN'T BRAVERY!!
...AH!
THE REASON THE ORIGINAL ZWEILT ALL HAVE SUCH PROFOUND FEELINGS FOR YUKI-KUN......
YUKI-KUN...?
HAAH!
...FOR THE LIGHT OF GOD— I GET IT NOW.
THE LIGHT OF GOD, HM...?
FOR OVER A THOUSAND YEARS...
...YOU HAVE FOUGHT TOGETHER LIKE THAT, HM......?
...YOU...
...TOLD ME TO RUN AWAY.
OBORO... SAID THE SAME THING.
AT THE END.
"EVEN IF I DON'T MAKE IT, RUN," HE SAID—

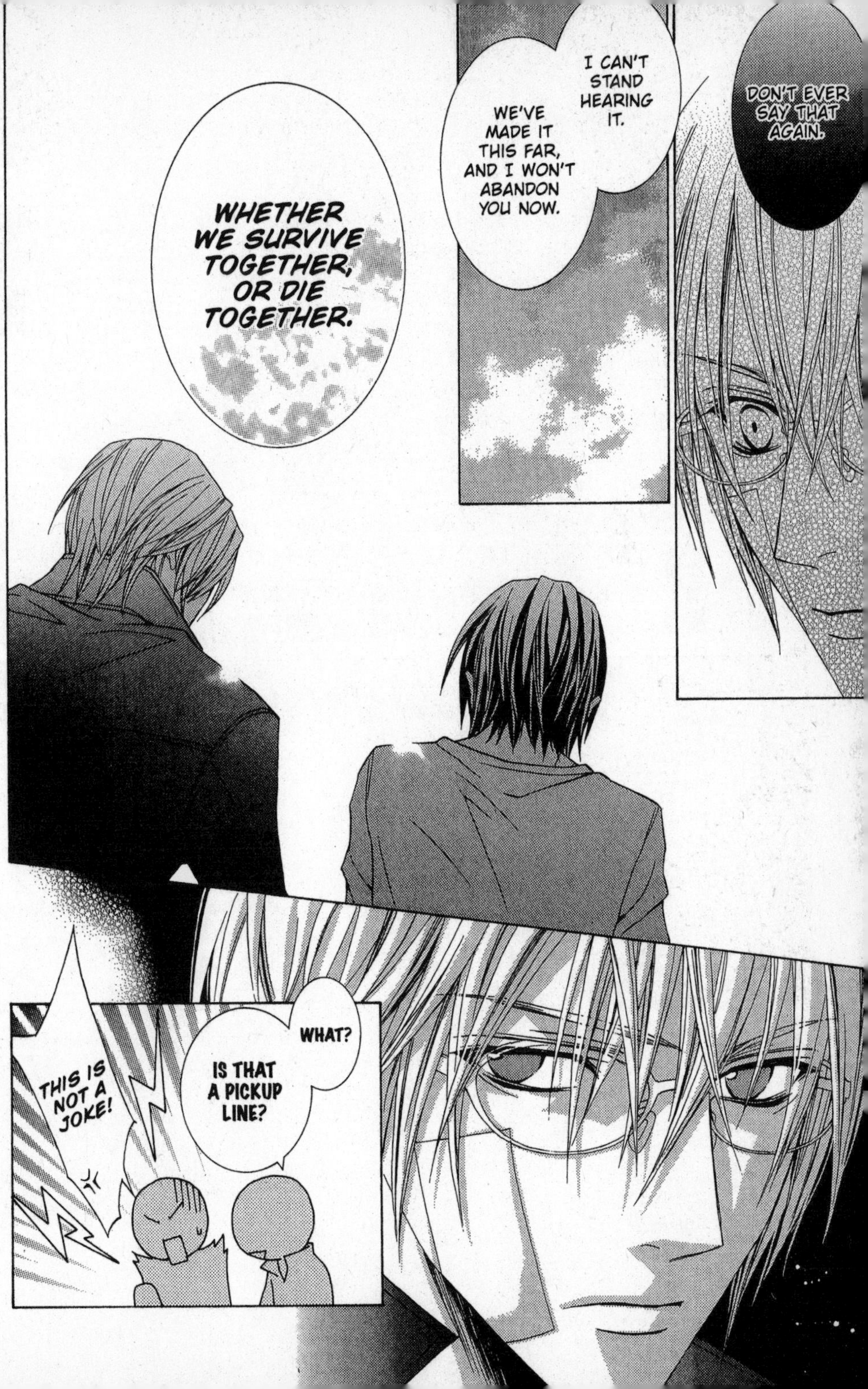
DON'T EVER SAY THAT AGAIN.
I CAN'T STAND HEARING IT.
WE'VE MADE IT THIS FAR, AND I WON'T ABANDON YOU NOW.
WHETHER WE SURVIVE TOGETHER, OR DIE TOGETHER.
WHAT?
IS THAT A PICKUP LINE?
THIS IS NOT A JOKE!

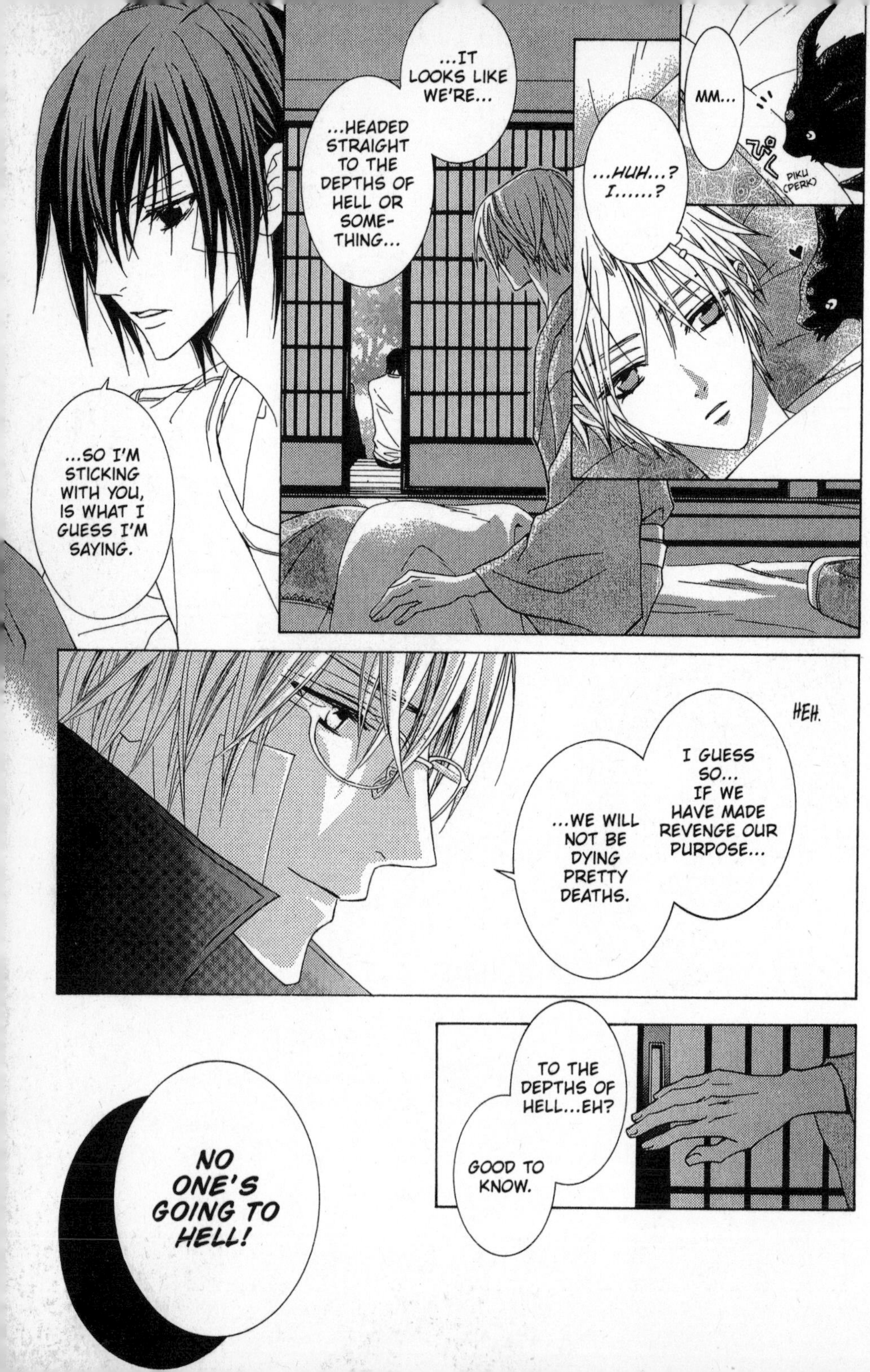
MM...
PIKU (PERK)
...HUH...? I......?
...IT LOOKS LIKE WE'RE...
...HEADED STRAIGHT TO THE DEPTHS OF HELL OR SOME-THING...
...SO I'M STICKING WITH YOU, IS WHAT I GUESS I'M SAYING.
HEH.
I GUESS SO... IF WE HAVE MADE REVENGE OUR PURPOSE...
...WE WILL NOT BE DYING PRETTY DEATHS.
TO THE DEPTHS OF HELL...EH?
GOOD TO KNOW.
NO ONE'S GOING TO HELL!

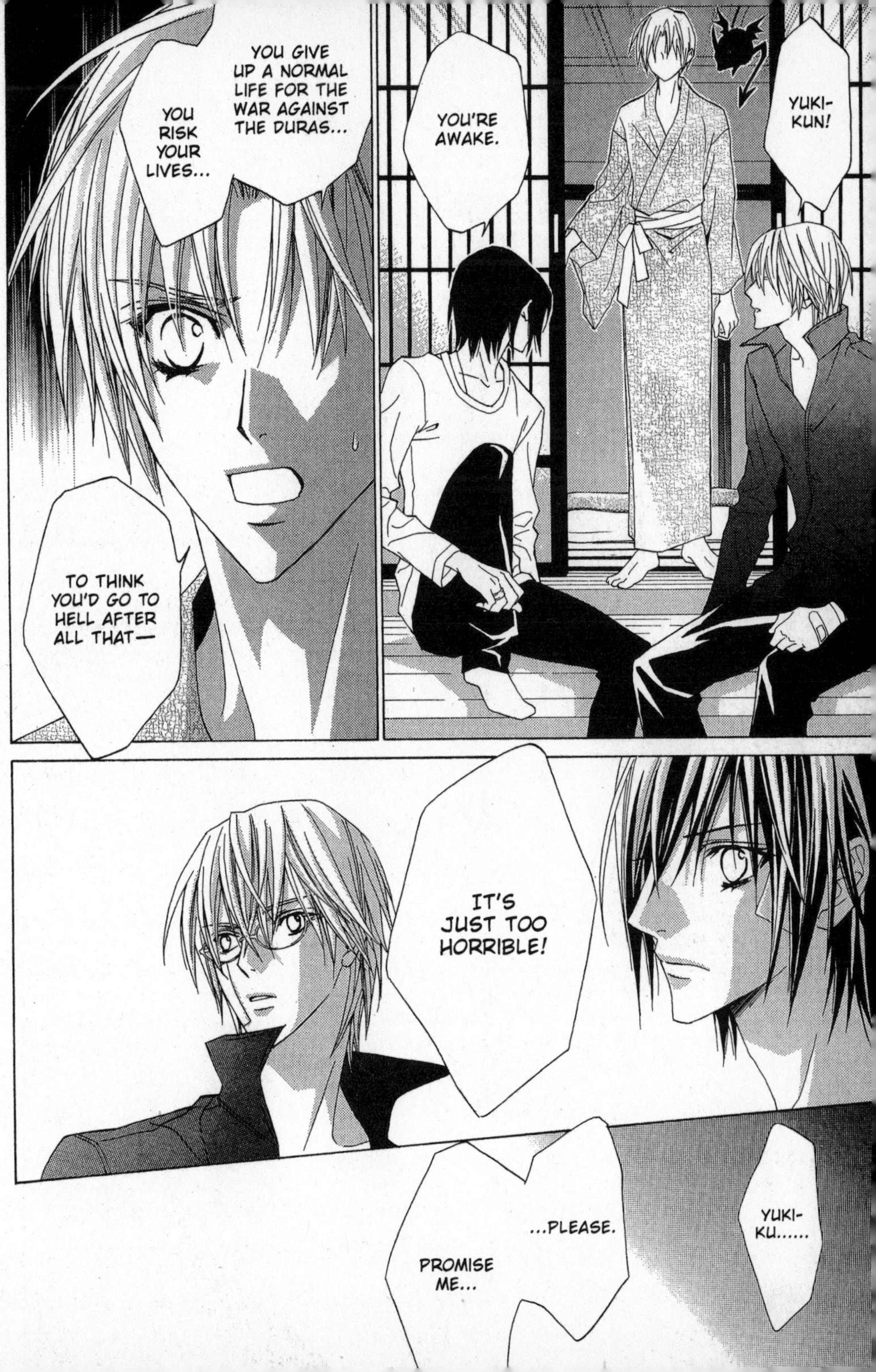
YUKI-KUN!
YOU'RE AWAKE.
YOU GIVE UP A NORMAL LIFE FOR THE WAR AGAINST THE DURAS...
YOU RISK YOUR LIVES...
TO THINK YOU'D GO TO HELL AFTER ALL THAT—
IT'S JUST TOO HORRIBLE!
YUKI-KU......
...PLEASE.
PROMISE ME...

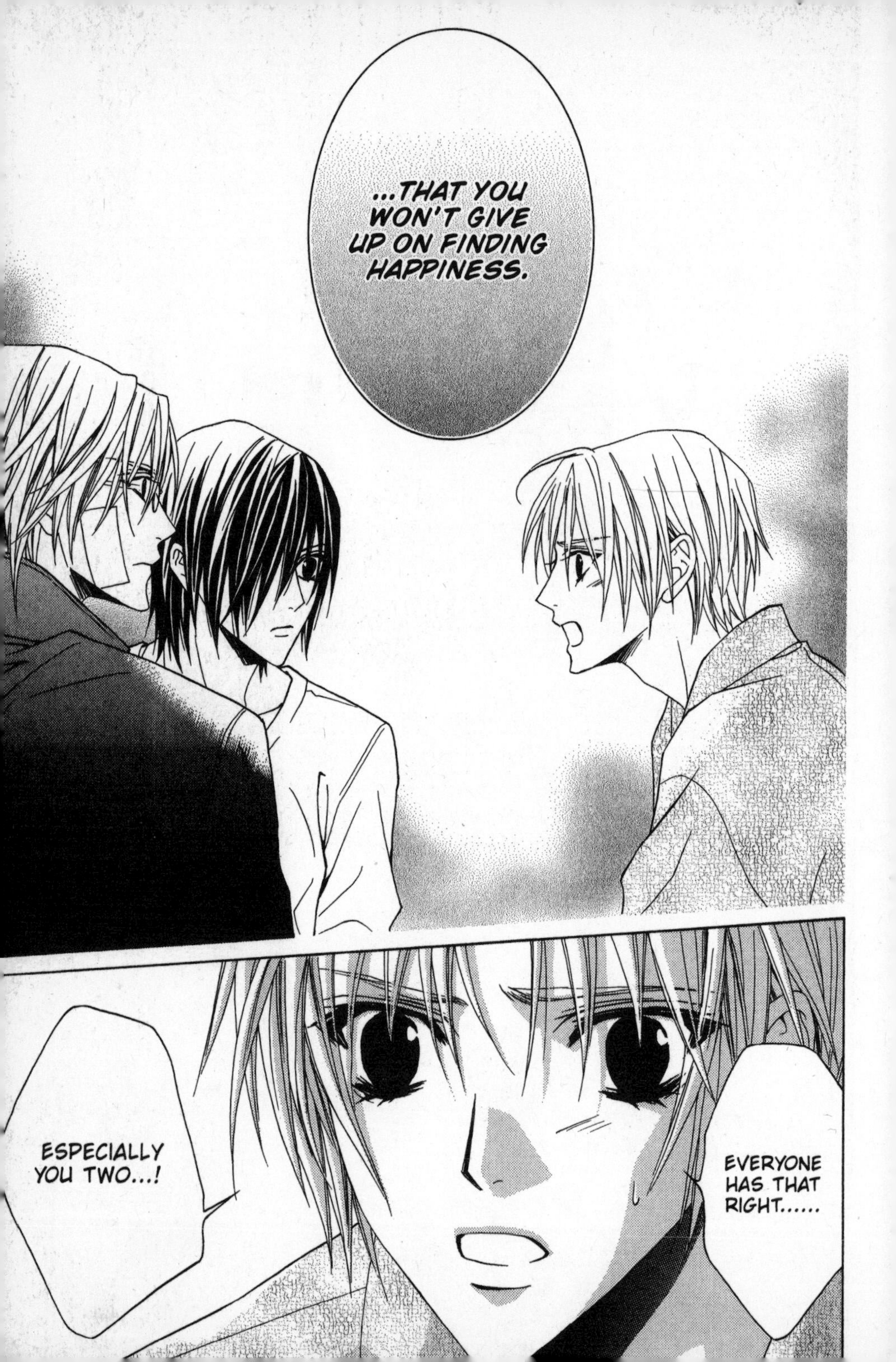
...THAT YOU WON'T GIVE UP ON FINDING HAPPINESS.
EVERYONE HAS THAT RIGHT......
ESPECIALLY YOU TWO...!

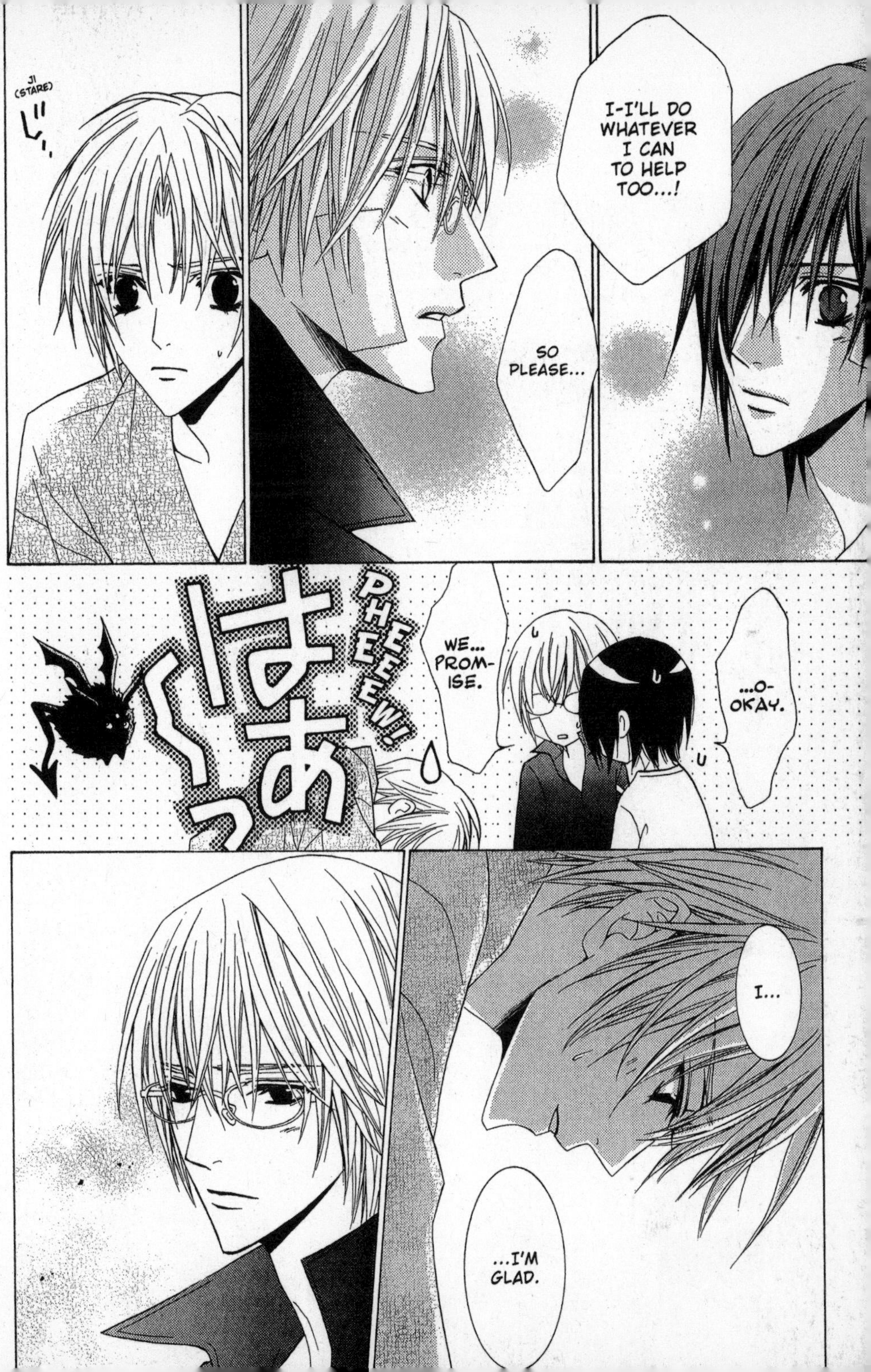

I-I'LL DO WHATEVER I CAN TO HELP TOO...!
SO PLEASE...
JI (STARE)
...O-OKAY.
WE... PROMISE.
PHEEEW!
はあっ
I...
...I'M GLAD.

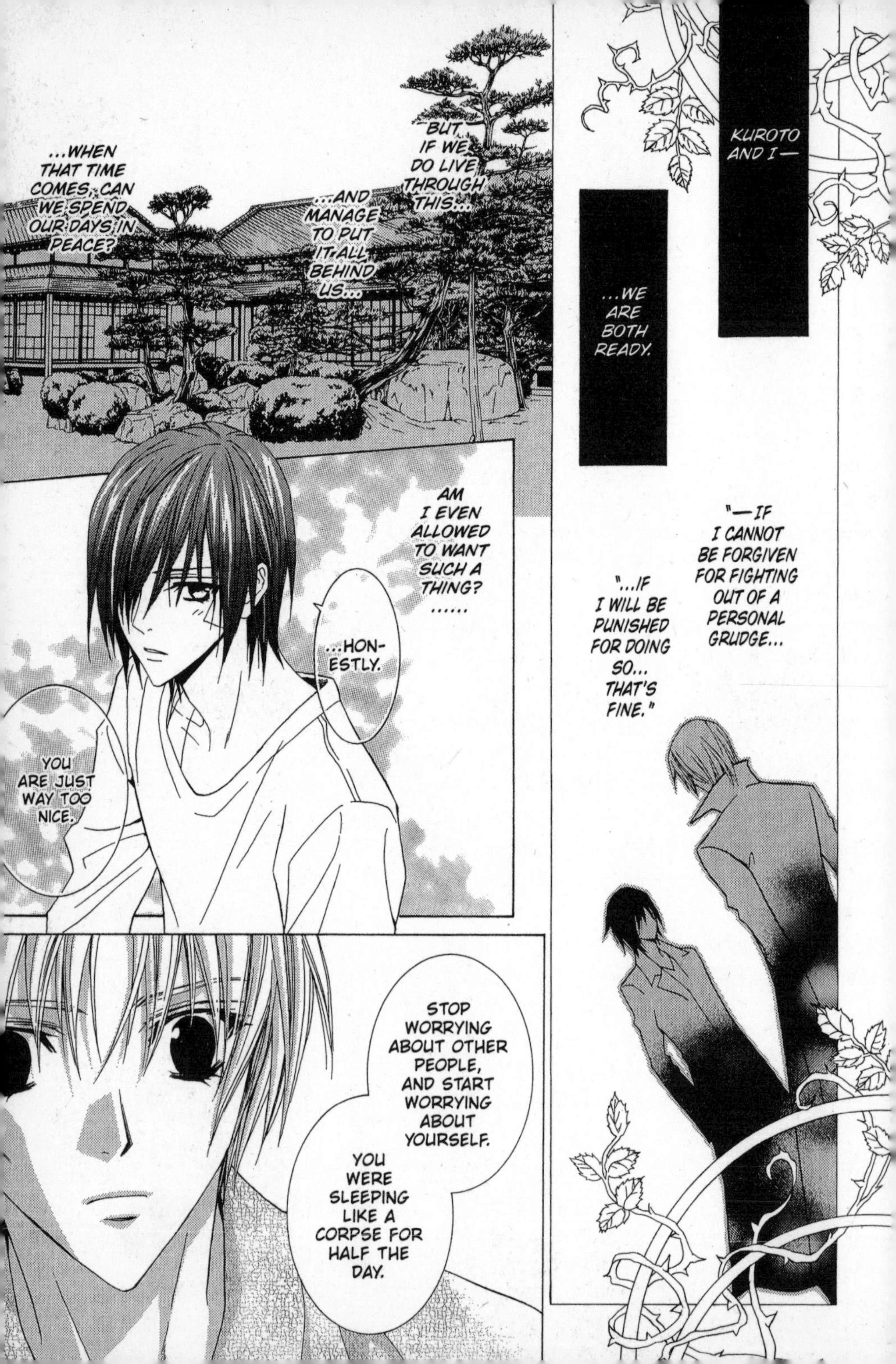
KUROTO AND I—
...WE ARE BOTH READY.
"—IF I CANNOT BE FORGIVEN FOR FIGHTING OUT OF A PERSONAL GRUDGE...
"...IF I WILL BE PUNISHED FOR DOING SO... THAT'S FINE."
BUT IF WE DO LIVE THROUGH THIS...
...AND MANAGE TO PUT IT ALL BEHIND US...
...WHEN THAT TIME COMES, CAN WE SPEND OUR DAYS IN PEACE?
AM I EVEN ALLOWED TO WANT SUCH A THING? ......
...HON-ESTLY.
YOU ARE JUST WAY TOO NICE.
STOP WORRYING ABOUT OTHER PEOPLE, AND START WORRYING ABOUT YOURSELF.
YOU WERE SLEEPING LIKE A CORPSE FOR HALF THE DAY.

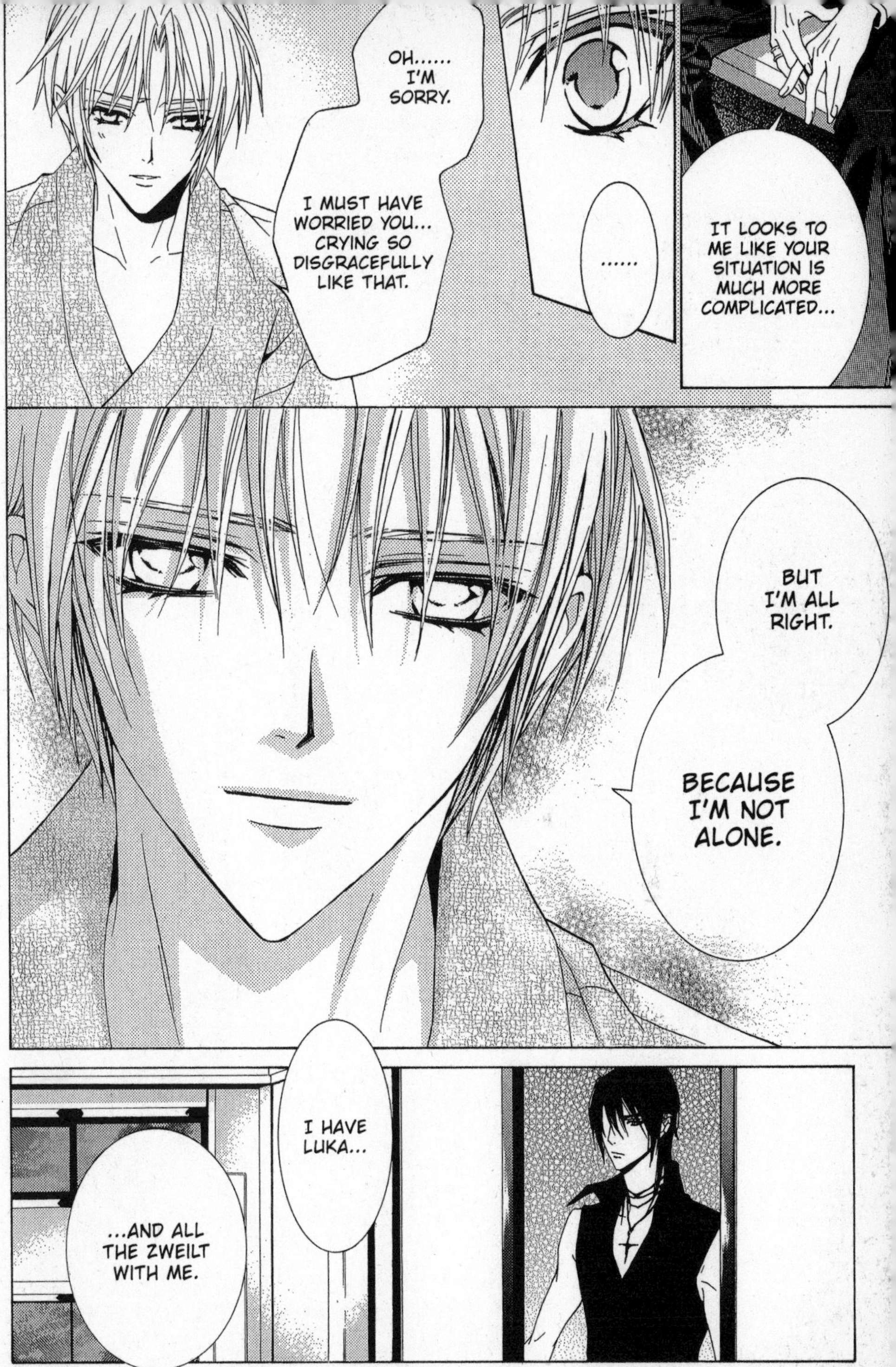
IT LOOKS TO ME LIKE YOUR SITUATION IS MUCH MORE COMPLICATED...
......
OH...... I'M SORRY.
I MUST HAVE WORRIED YOU... CRYING SO DISGRACEFULLY LIKE THAT.
BUT I'M ALL RIGHT.
BECAUSE I'M NOT ALONE.
I HAVE LUKA...
...AND ALL THE ZWEILT WITH ME.

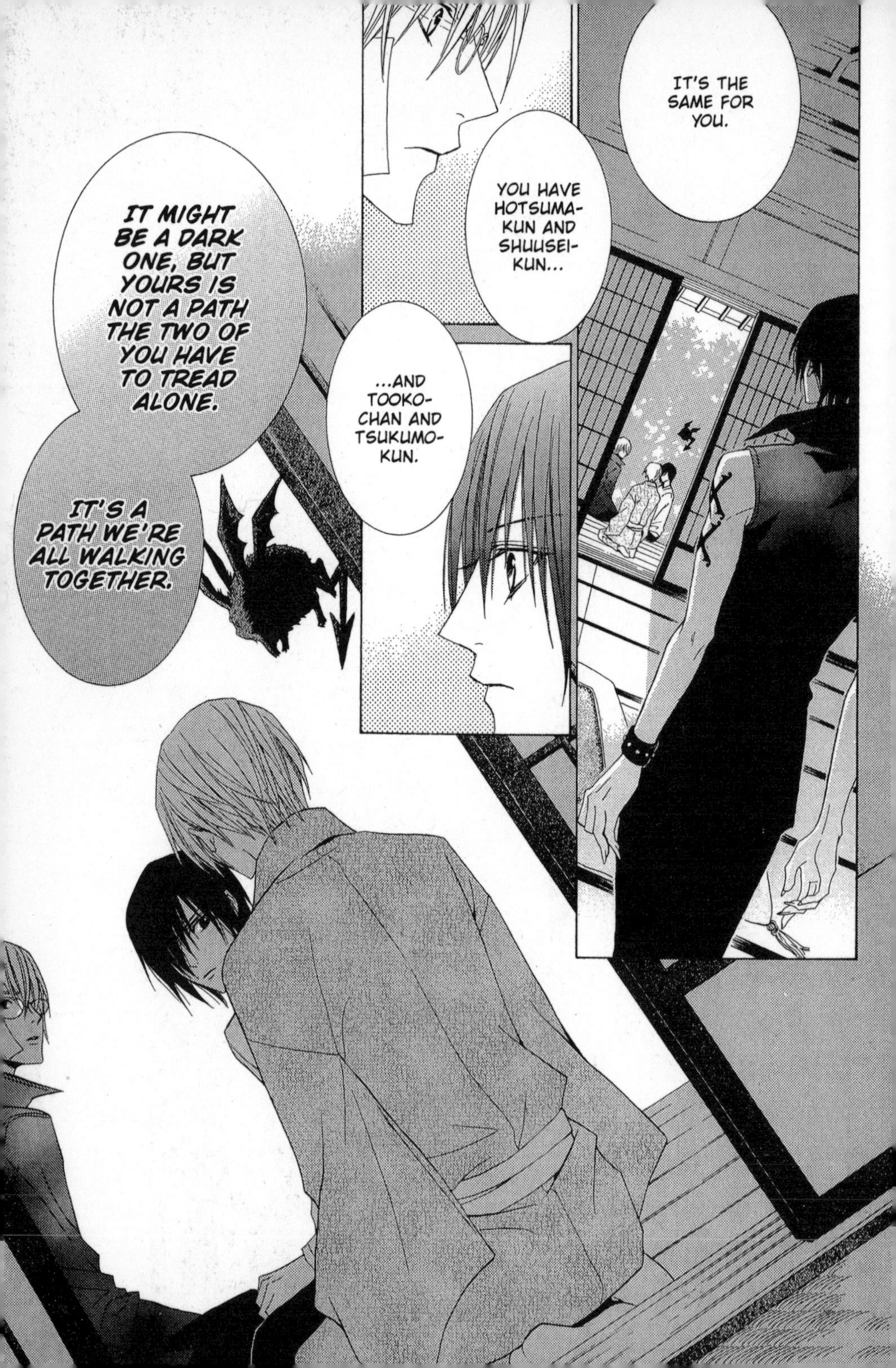
IT'S THE SAME FOR YOU.
YOU HAVE HOTSUMA-KUN AND SHUUSEI-KUN...
...AND TOOKO-CHAN AND TSUKUMO-KUN.
IT MIGHT BE A DARK ONE, BUT YOURS IS NOT A PATH THE TWO OF YOU HAVE TO TREAD ALONE.
IT'S A PATH WE'RE ALL WALKING TOGETHER.

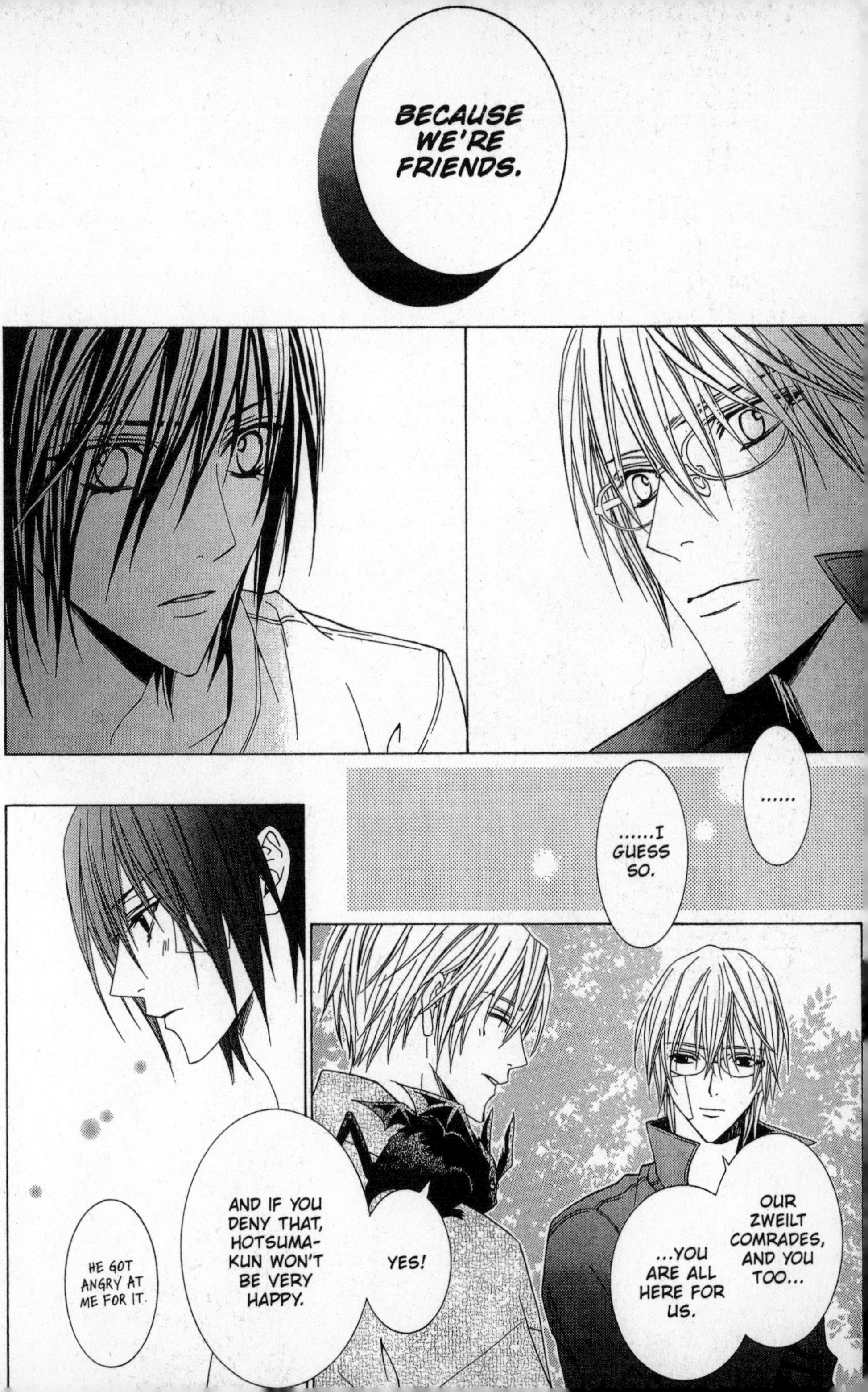
BECAUSE WE'RE FRIENDS.
......
......I GUESS SO.
OUR ZWEILT COMRADES, AND YOU TOO...
...YOU ARE ALL HERE FOR US.
YES!
AND IF YOU DENY THAT, HOTSUMA-KUN WON'T BE VERY HAPPY.
HE GOT ANGRY AT ME FOR IT.

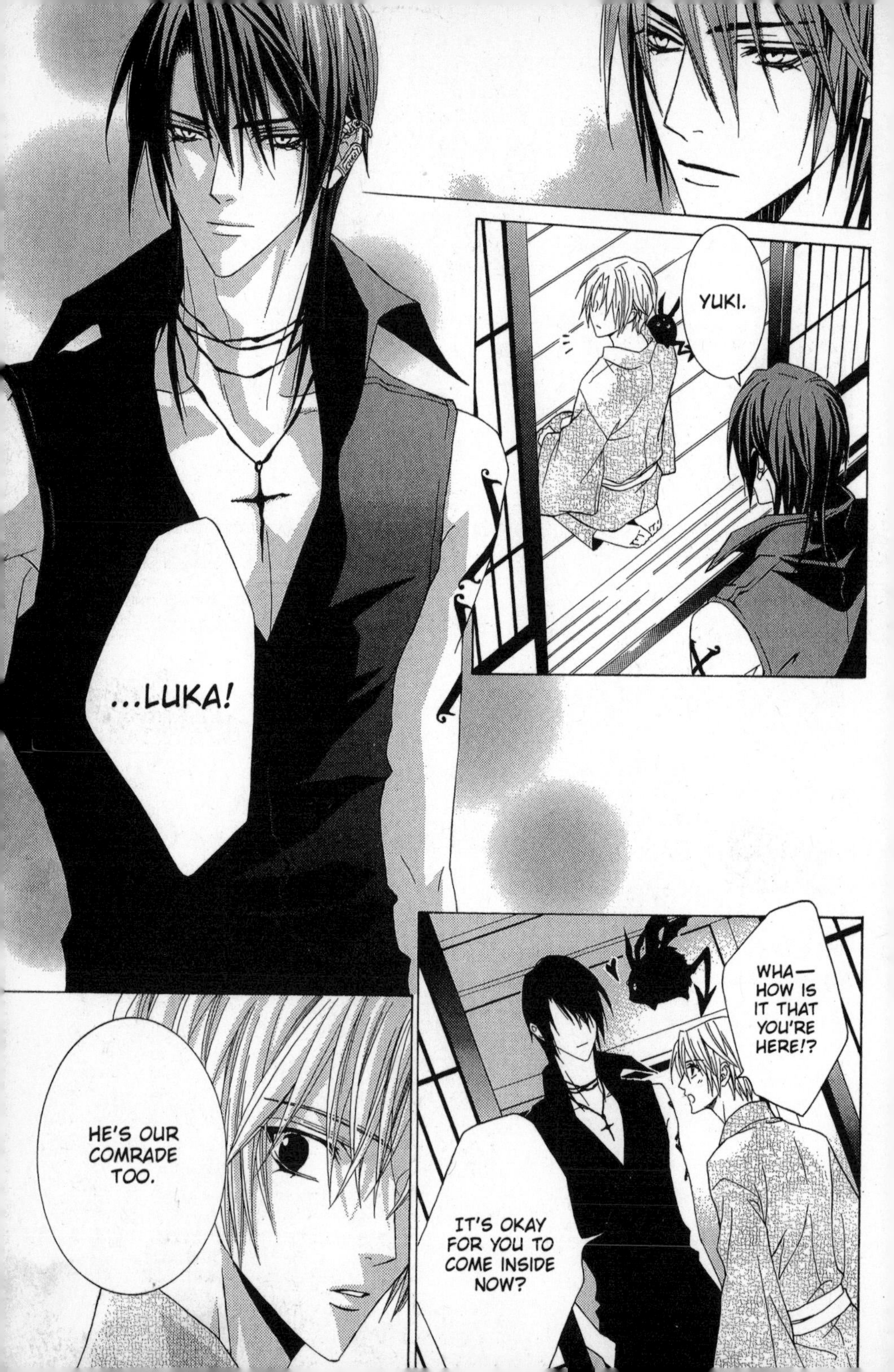
YUKI.
...LUKA!
WHA—HOW IS IT THAT YOU'RE HERE!?
IT'S OKAY FOR YOU TO COME INSIDE NOW?
HE'S OUR COMRADE TOO.

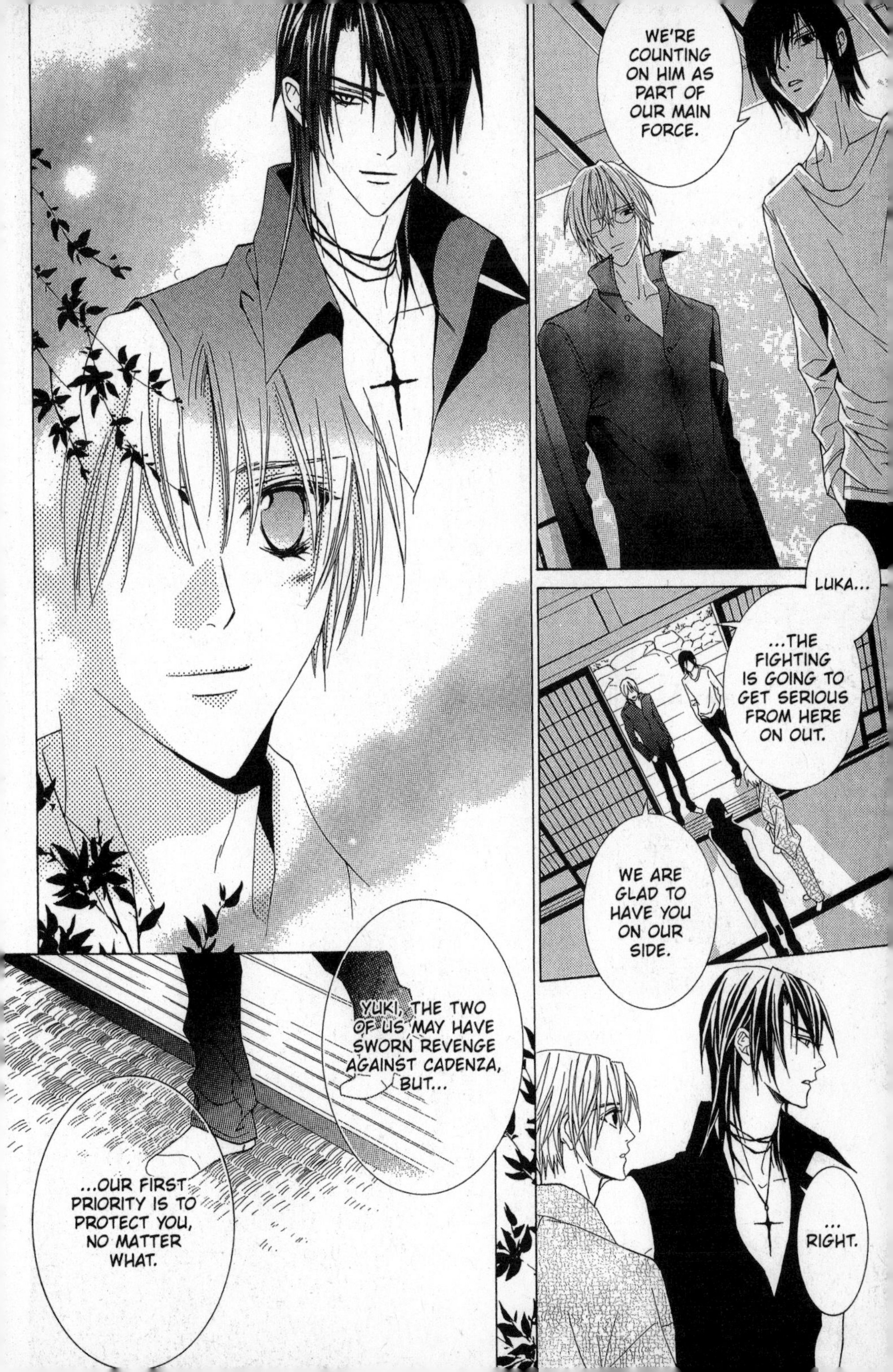
WE'RE COUNTING ON HIM AS PART OF OUR MAIN FORCE.
LUKA...
...THE FIGHTING IS GOING TO GET SERIOUS FROM HERE ON OUT.
WE ARE GLAD TO HAVE YOU ON OUR SIDE.
...RIGHT.
YUKI, THE TWO OF US MAY HAVE SWORN REVENGE AGAINST CADENZA, BUT...
...OUR FIRST PRIORITY IS TO PROTECT YOU, NO MATTER WHAT.

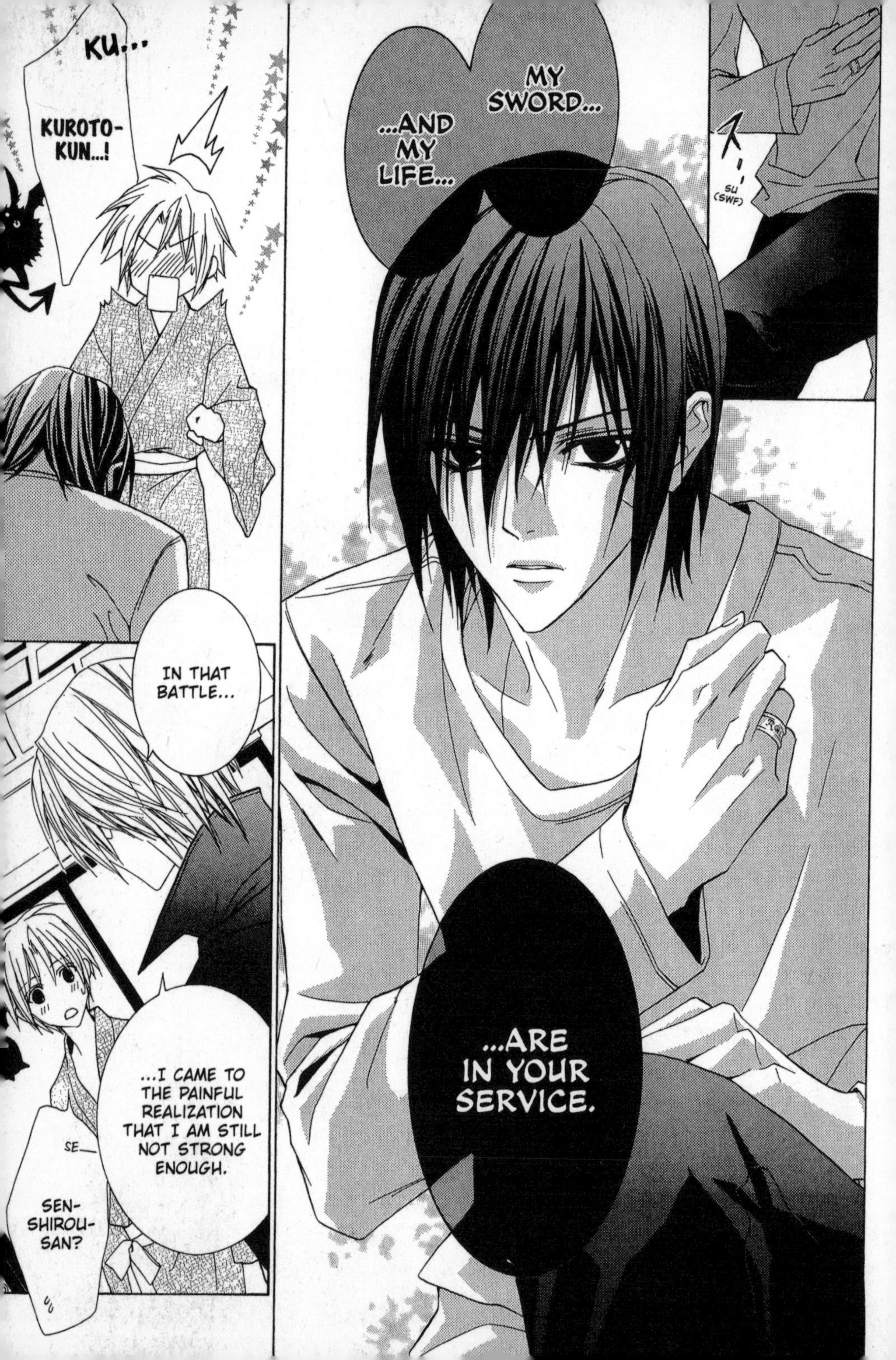
SU (SWF)
MY SWORD...
...AND MY LIFE...
...ARE IN YOUR SERVICE.
KU...
KUROTO-KUN...!
IN THAT BATTLE...
...I CAME TO THE PAINFUL REALIZATION THAT I AM STILL NOT STRONG ENOUGH.
SE—
SEN-SHIROU-SAN?
UU

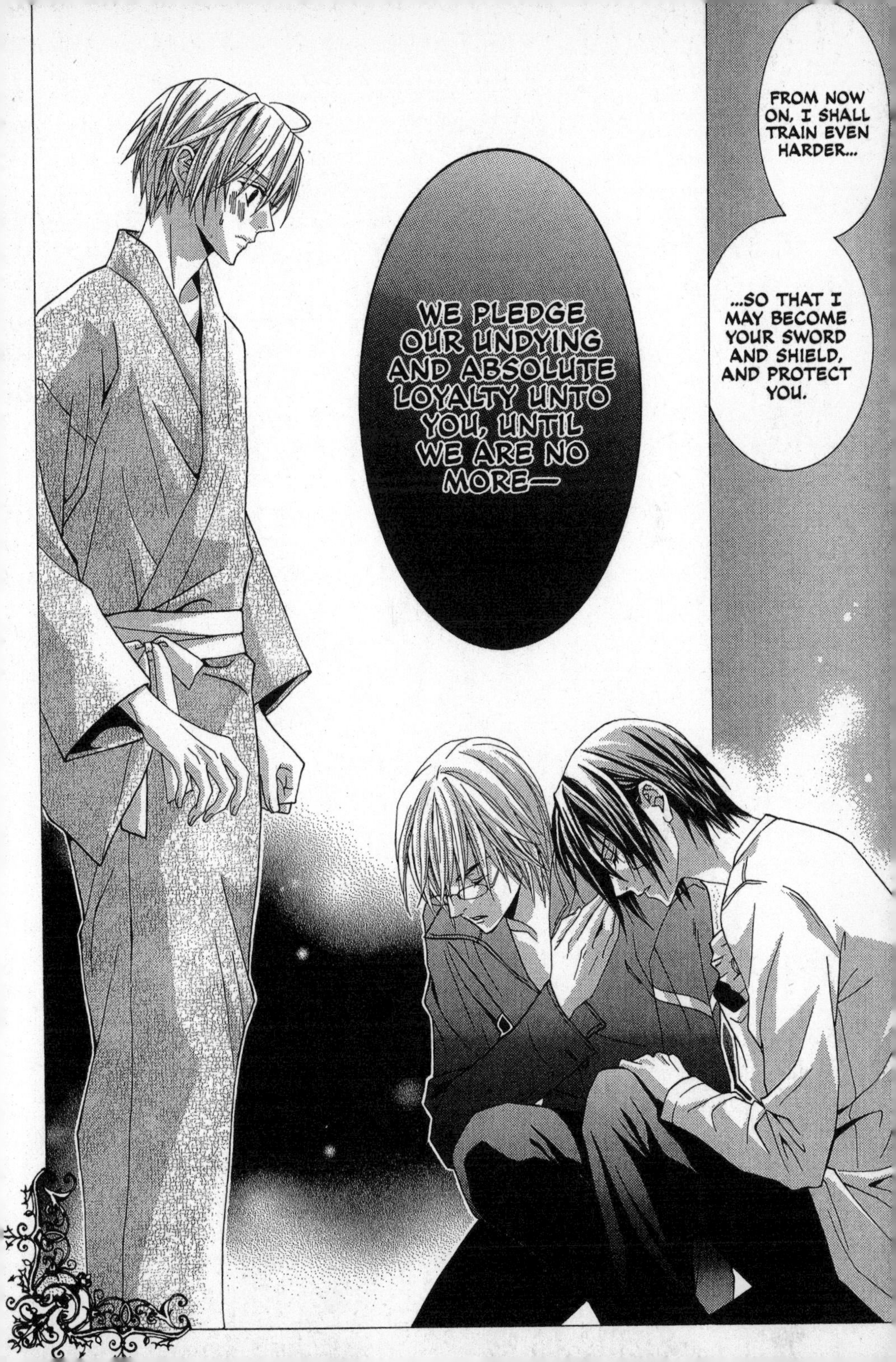
FROM NOW ON, I SHALL TRAIN EVEN HARDER...
...SO THAT I MAY BECOME YOUR SWORD AND SHIELD, AND PROTECT YOU.
WE PLEDGE OUR UNDYING AND ABSOLUTE LOYALTY UNTO YOU, UNTIL WE ARE NO MORE—

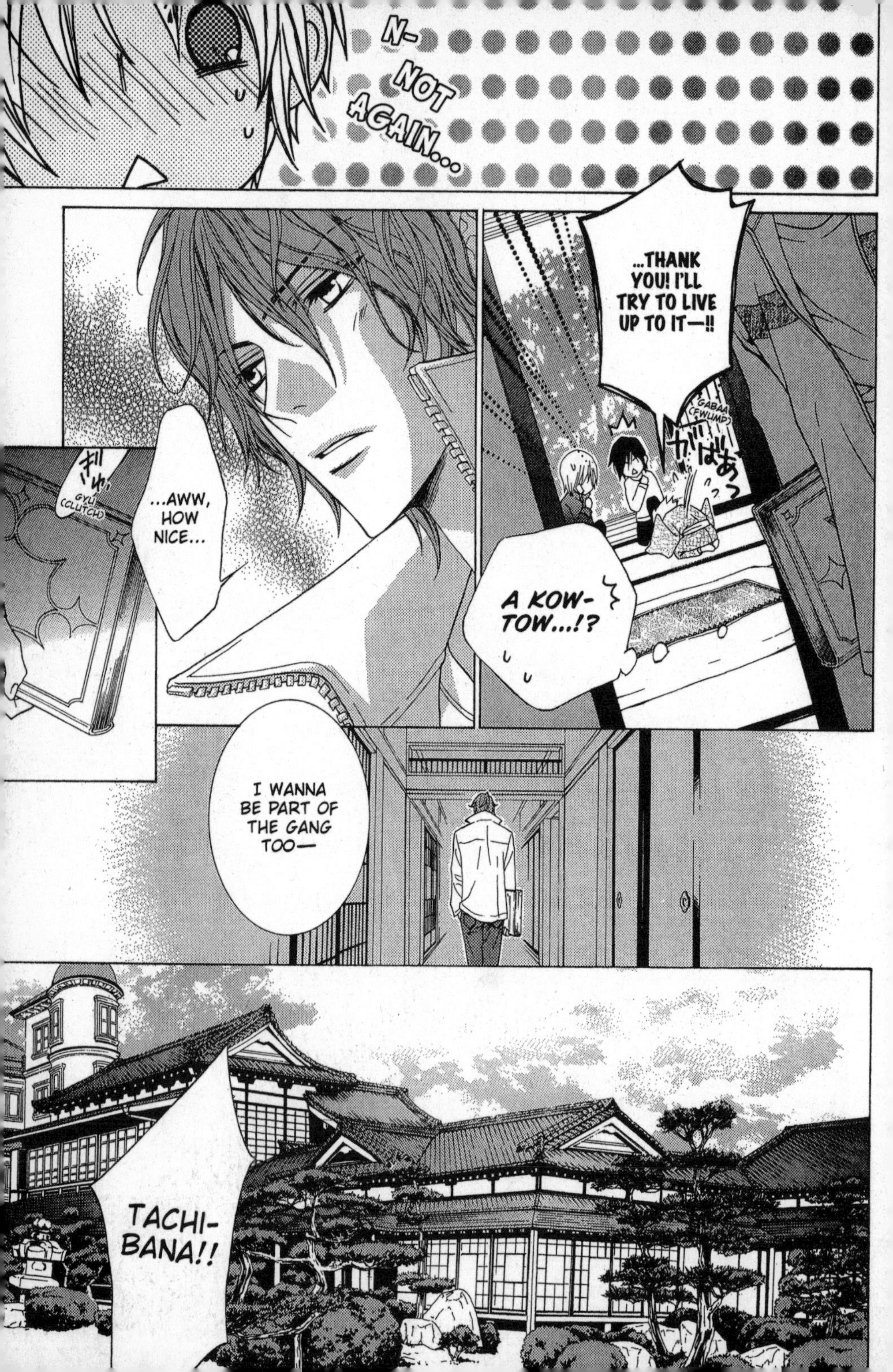
N-
NOT
AGAIN...
...THANK YOU! I'LL TRY TO LIVE UP TO IT—!!
GABAA (FWUMP)
A KOW-TOW...!?
...AWW, HOW NICE...
GYU (CLUTCH)
I WANNA BE PART OF THE GANG TOO—
TACHI-BANA!!

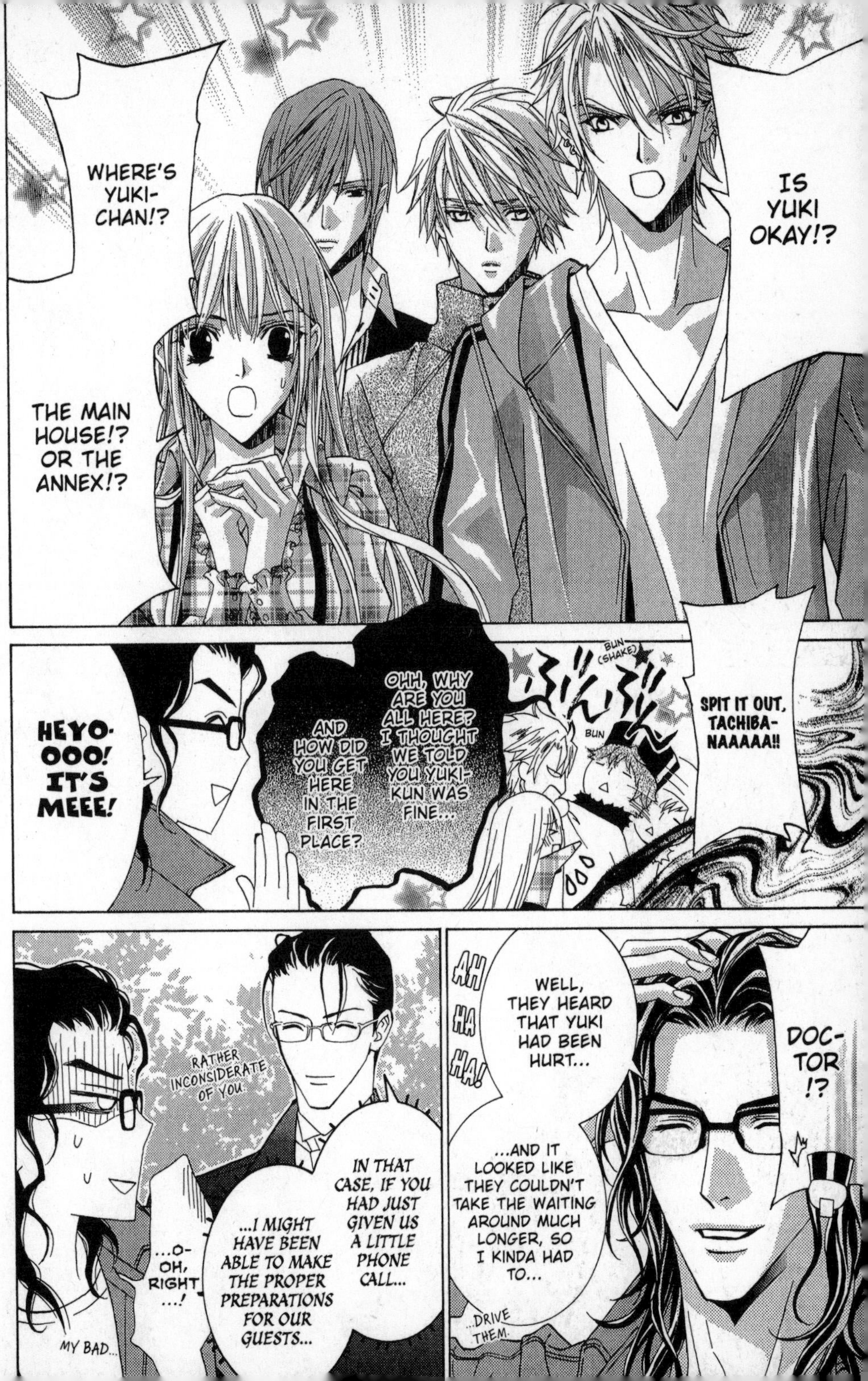
IS YUKI OKAY!?
WHERE'S YUKI-CHAN!?
THE MAIN HOUSE!? OR THE ANNEX!?
SPIT IT OUT, TACHIBA-NAAAAAA!!
BUN (SHAKE)
BUN
OHH, WHY ARE YOU ALL HERE? I THOUGHT WE TOLD YOU YUKI-KUN WAS FINE...
AND HOW DID YOU GET HERE IN THE FIRST PLACE?
HEYO-OOO! IT'S MEEE!
DOC-TOR!?
AH HA HA HA!
WELL, THEY HEARD THAT YUKI HAD BEEN HURT...
...AND IT LOOKED LIKE THEY COULDN'T TAKE THE WAITING AROUND MUCH LONGER, SO I KINDA HAD TO...
...DRIVE THEM.
IN THAT CASE, IF YOU HAD JUST GIVEN US A LITTLE PHONE CALL...
...I MIGHT HAVE BEEN ABLE TO MAKE THE PROPER PREPARATIONS FOR OUR GUESTS...
RATHER INCONSIDERATE OF YOU.
...O-OH, RIGHT...!
MY BAD...

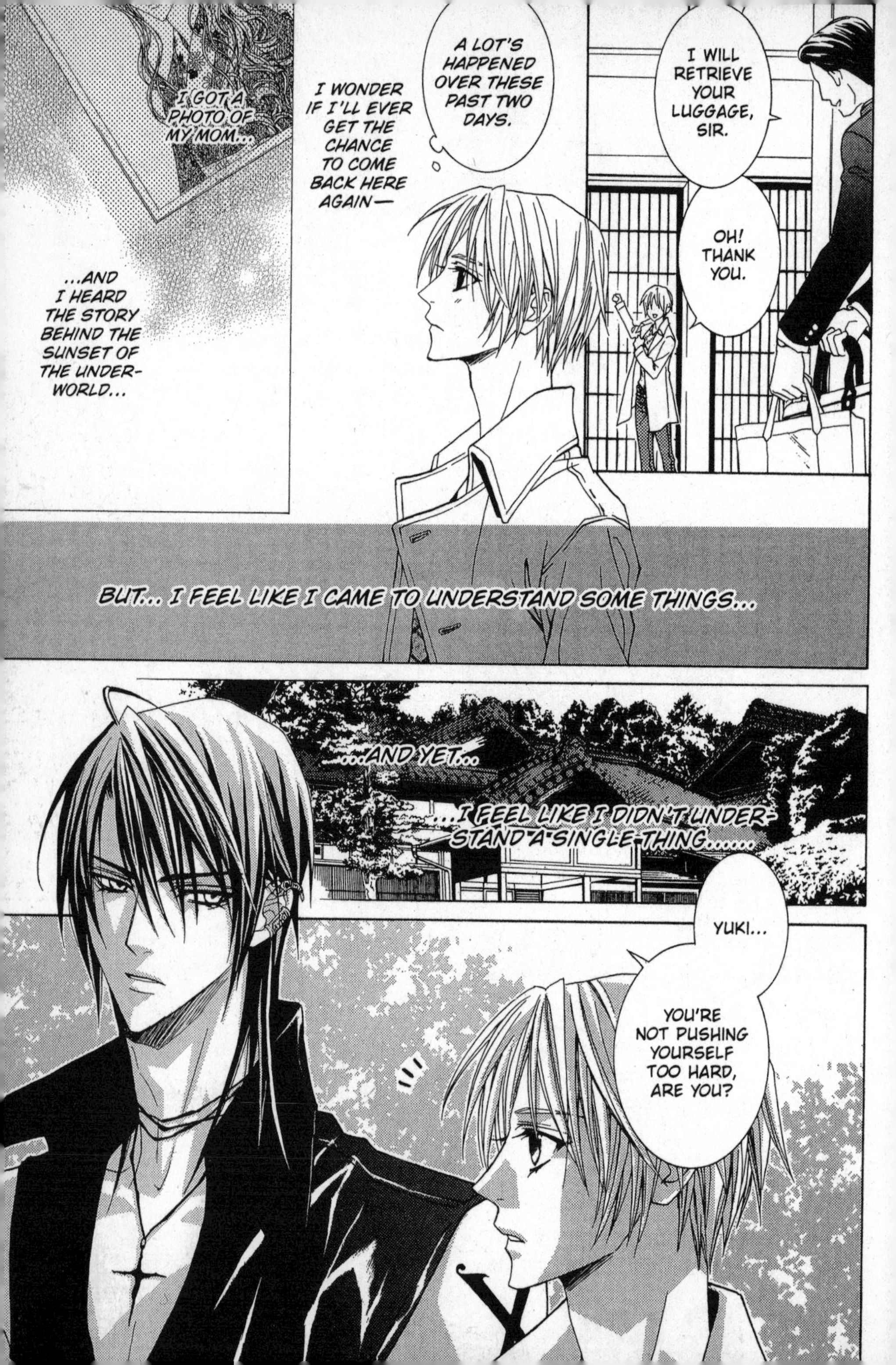
I WILL RETRIEVE YOUR LUGGAGE, SIR.
OH! THANK YOU.
A LOT'S HAPPENED OVER THESE PAST TWO DAYS.
I WONDER IF I'LL EVER GET THE CHANCE TO COME BACK HERE AGAIN—
I GOT A PHOTO OF MY MOM...
...AND I HEARD THE STORY BEHIND THE SUNSET OF THE UNDER-WORLD...
BUT... I FEEL LIKE I CAME TO UNDERSTAND SOME THINGS...
...AND YET...
...I FEEL LIKE I DIDN'T UNDER-STAND A SINGLE THING......
YUKI...
YOU'RE NOT PUSHING YOURSELF TOO HARD, ARE YOU?

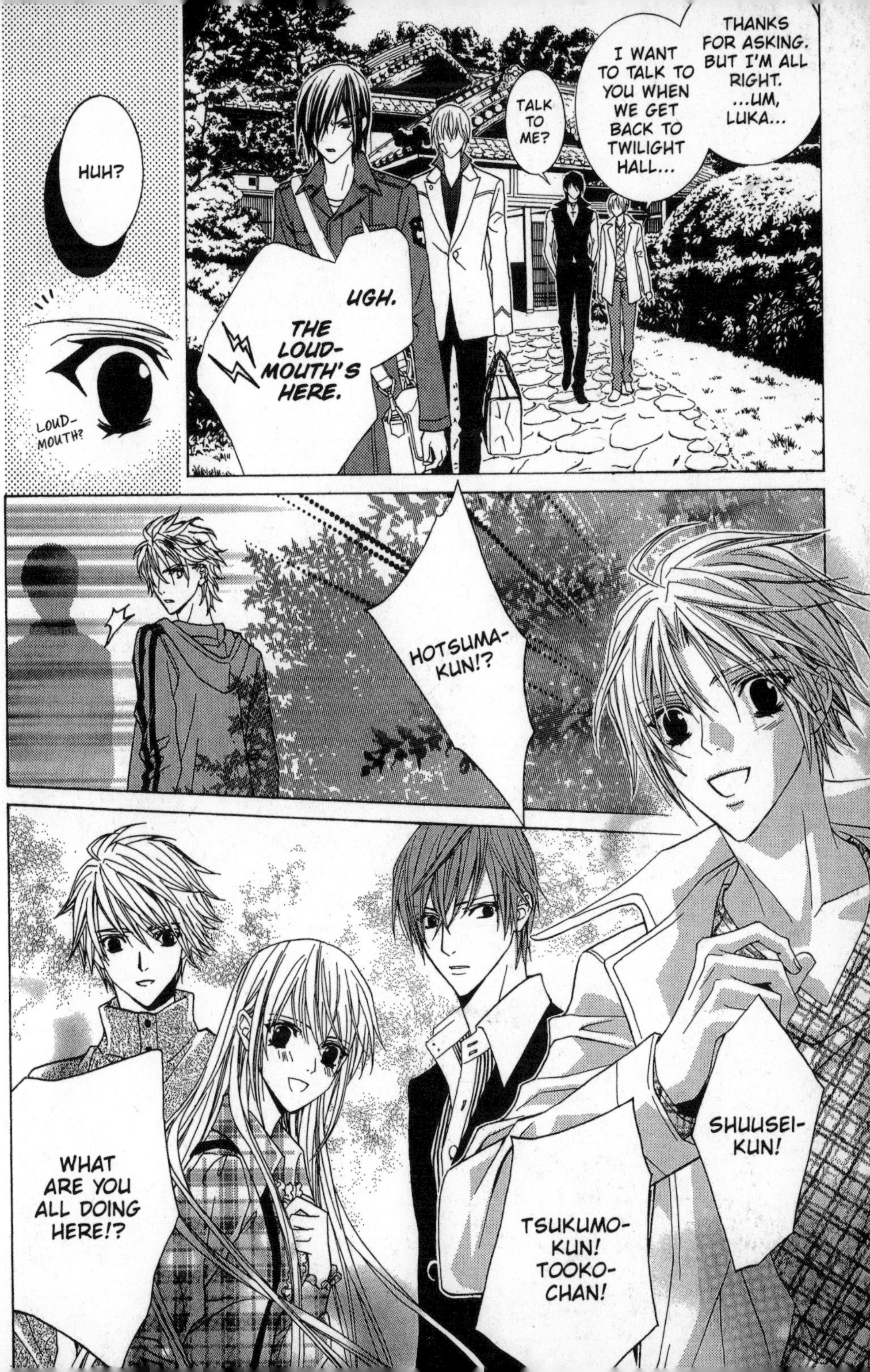
THANKS FOR ASKING. BUT I'M ALL RIGHT. ...UM, LUKA...
I WANT TO TALK TO YOU WHEN WE GET BACK TO TWILIGHT HALL...
TALK TO ME?
UGH. THE LOUD-MOUTH'S HERE.
HUH?
LOUD-MOUTH?
HOTSUMA-KUN!?
SHUUSEI-KUN!
TSUKUMO-KUN! TOOKO-CHAN!
WHAT ARE YOU ALL DOING HERE!?

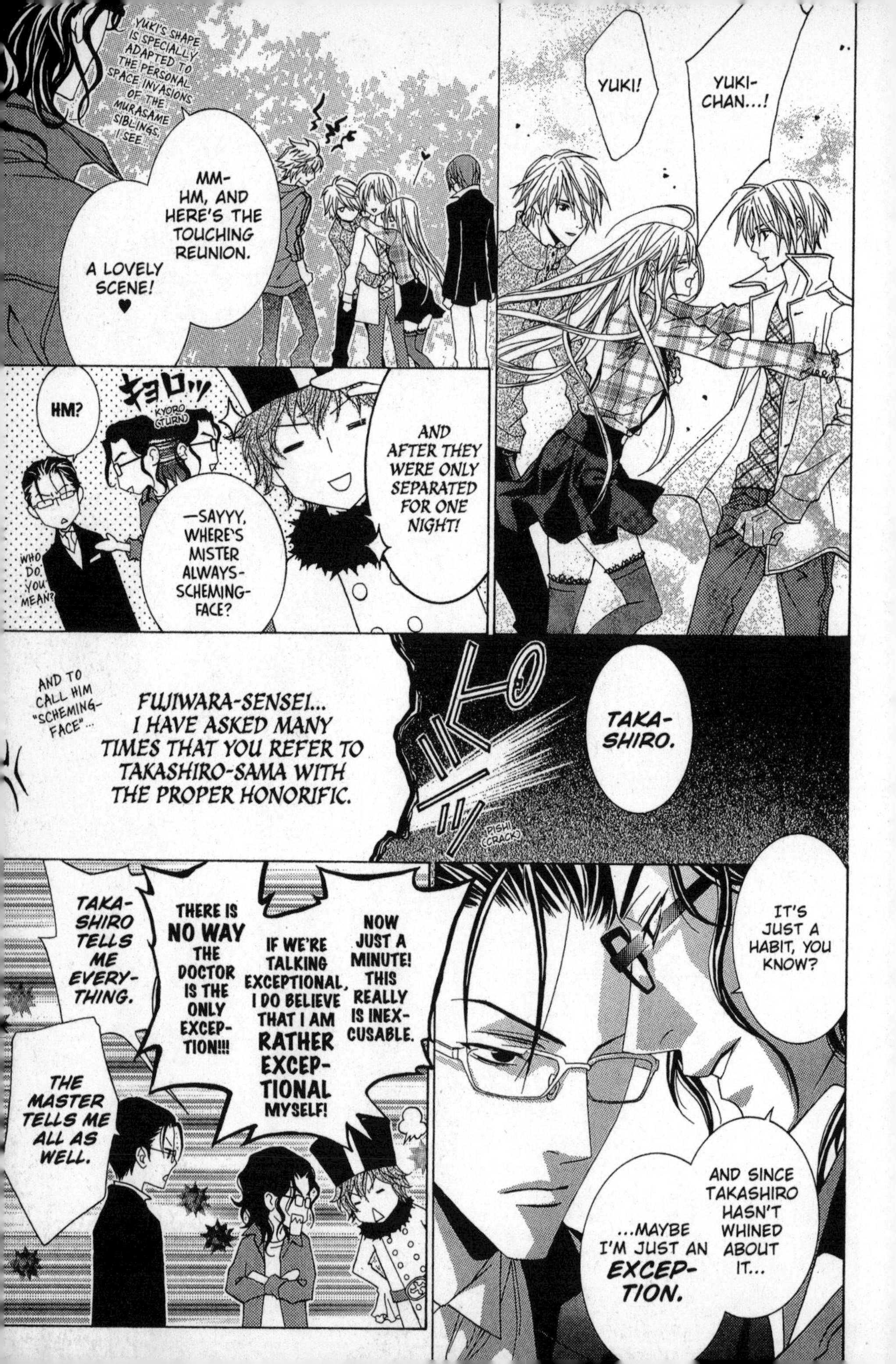
YUKI-CHAN...!
YUKI!
MM-HM, AND HERE'S THE TOUCHING REUNION.
A LOVELY SCENE! ♥
YUKI'S SHAPE IS SPECIALLY ADAPTED TO THE PERSONAL SPACE INVASIONS OF THE MURASAME SIBLINGS, I SEE.
AND AFTER THEY WERE ONLY SEPARATED FOR ONE NIGHT!
—SAYYY, WHERE'S MISTER ALWAYS-SCHEMING-FACE?
キョロッ
KYORO (TURN)
HM?
WHO DO YOU MEAN?
TAKA-SHIRO.
PISHI (CRACK)
FUJIWARA-SENSEI... I HAVE ASKED MANY TIMES THAT YOU REFER TO TAKASHIRO-SAMA WITH THE PROPER HONORIFIC.
AND TO CALL HIM "SCHEMING-FACE"...
IT'S JUST A HABIT, YOU KNOW?
AND SINCE TAKASHIRO HASN'T WHINED ABOUT IT...
...MAYBE I'M JUST AN EXCEPTION.
NOW JUST A MINUTE! THIS REALLY IS INEXCUSABLE.
IF WE'RE TALKING EXCEPTIONAL, I DO BELIEVE THAT I AM RATHER EXCEPTIONAL MYSELF!
THERE IS NO WAY THE DOCTOR IS THE ONLY EXCEPTION!!!
TAKASHIRO TELLS ME EVERYTHING.
THE MASTER TELLS ME ALL AS WELL.

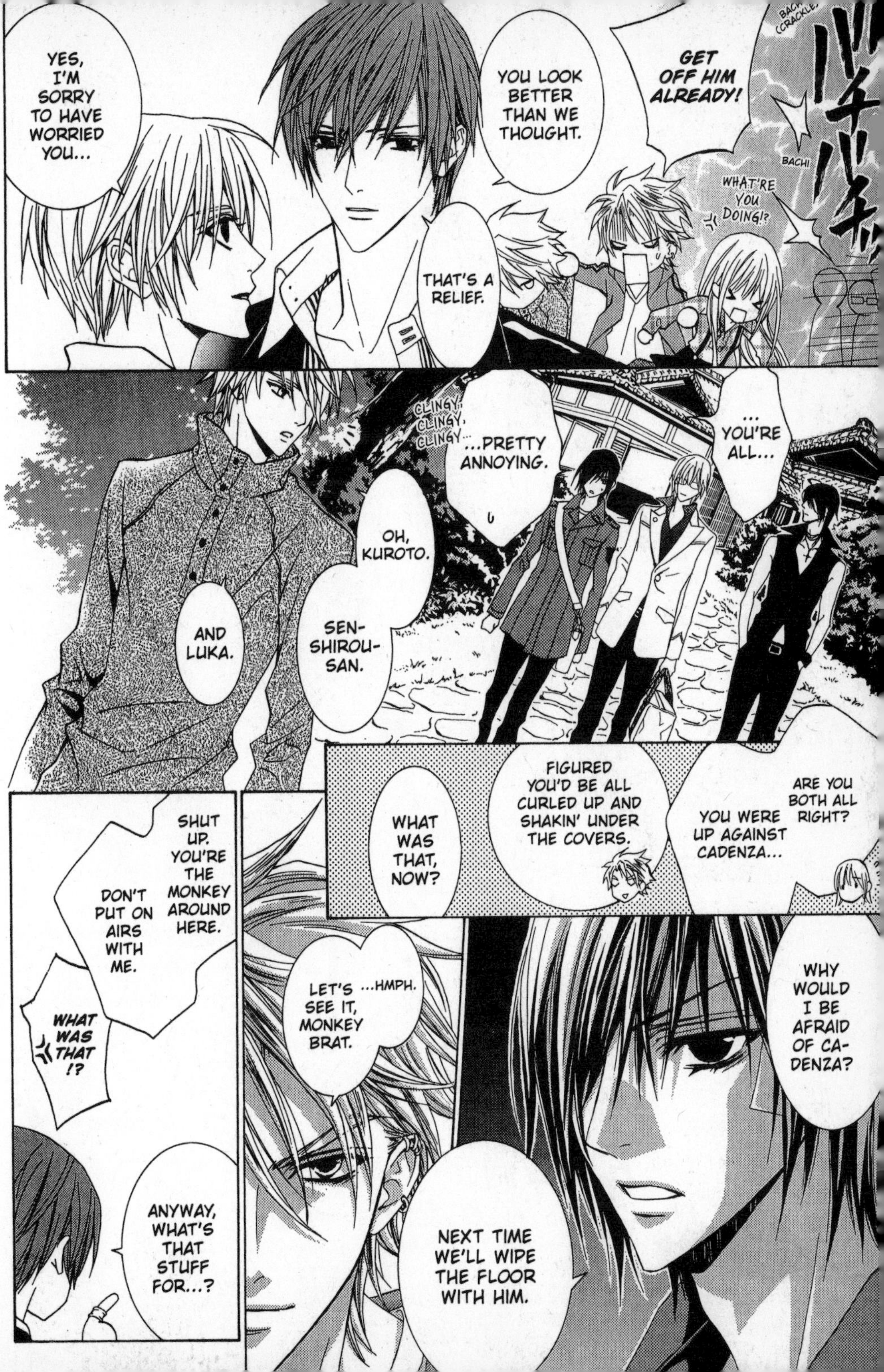

CRACKLE
GET OFF HIM ALREADY!
BACHI
WHAT'RE YOU DOING!?
YOU LOOK BETTER THAN WE THOUGHT.
THAT'S A RELIEF.
YES, I'M SORRY TO HAVE WORRIED YOU...
...YOU'RE ALL...
...PRETTY ANNOYING.
CLINGY, CLINGY, CLINGY...
OH, KUROTO.
SEN-SHIROU-SAN.
AND LUKA.
ARE YOU BOTH ALL RIGHT?
YOU WERE UP AGAINST CADENZA...
FIGURED YOU'D BE ALL CURLED UP AND SHAKIN' UNDER THE COVERS.
WHAT WAS THAT, NOW?
WHY WOULD I BE AFRAID OF CA-DENZA?
NEXT TIME WE'LL WIPE THE FLOOR WITH HIM.
...HMPH.
LET'S SEE IT, MONKEY BRAT.
SHUT UP. YOU'RE THE MONKEY AROUND HERE.
DON'T PUT ON AIRS WITH ME.
WHAT WAS THAT!?
ANYWAY, WHAT'S THAT STUFF FOR...?

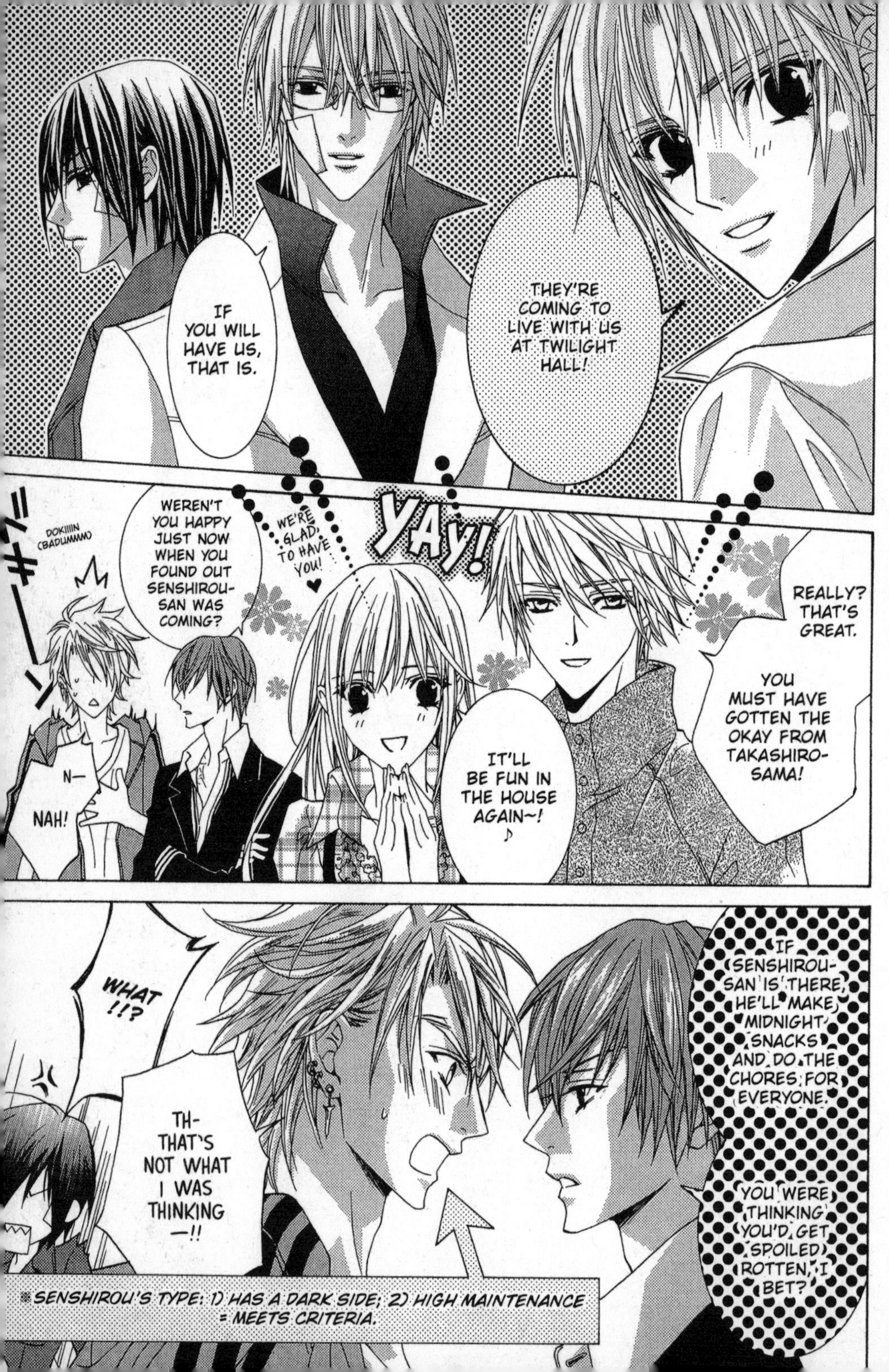
THEY'RE COMING TO LIVE WITH US AT TWILIGHT HALL!
IF YOU WILL HAVE US, THAT IS.
REALLY? THAT'S GREAT.
YOU MUST HAVE GOTTEN THE OKAY FROM TAKASHIRO-SAMA!
YAY!
IT'LL BE FUN IN THE HOUSE AGAIN~! ♪
WE'RE GLAD TO HAVE YOU! ♥
WEREN'T YOU HAPPY JUST NOW WHEN YOU FOUND OUT SENSHIROU-SAN WAS COMING?
DOKIIIIN (BADUMMM)
N—
NAH!
IF SENSHIROU-SAN IS THERE, HE'LL MAKE MIDNIGHT SNACKS AND DO THE CHORES FOR EVERYONE.
YOU WERE THINKING YOU'D GET SPOILED ROTTEN, I BET?
WHAT!!?
TH-THAT'S NOT WHAT I WAS THINKING—!!
※SENSHIROU'S TYPE: 1) HAS A DARK SIDE; 2) HIGH MAINTENANCE = MEETS CRITERIA.

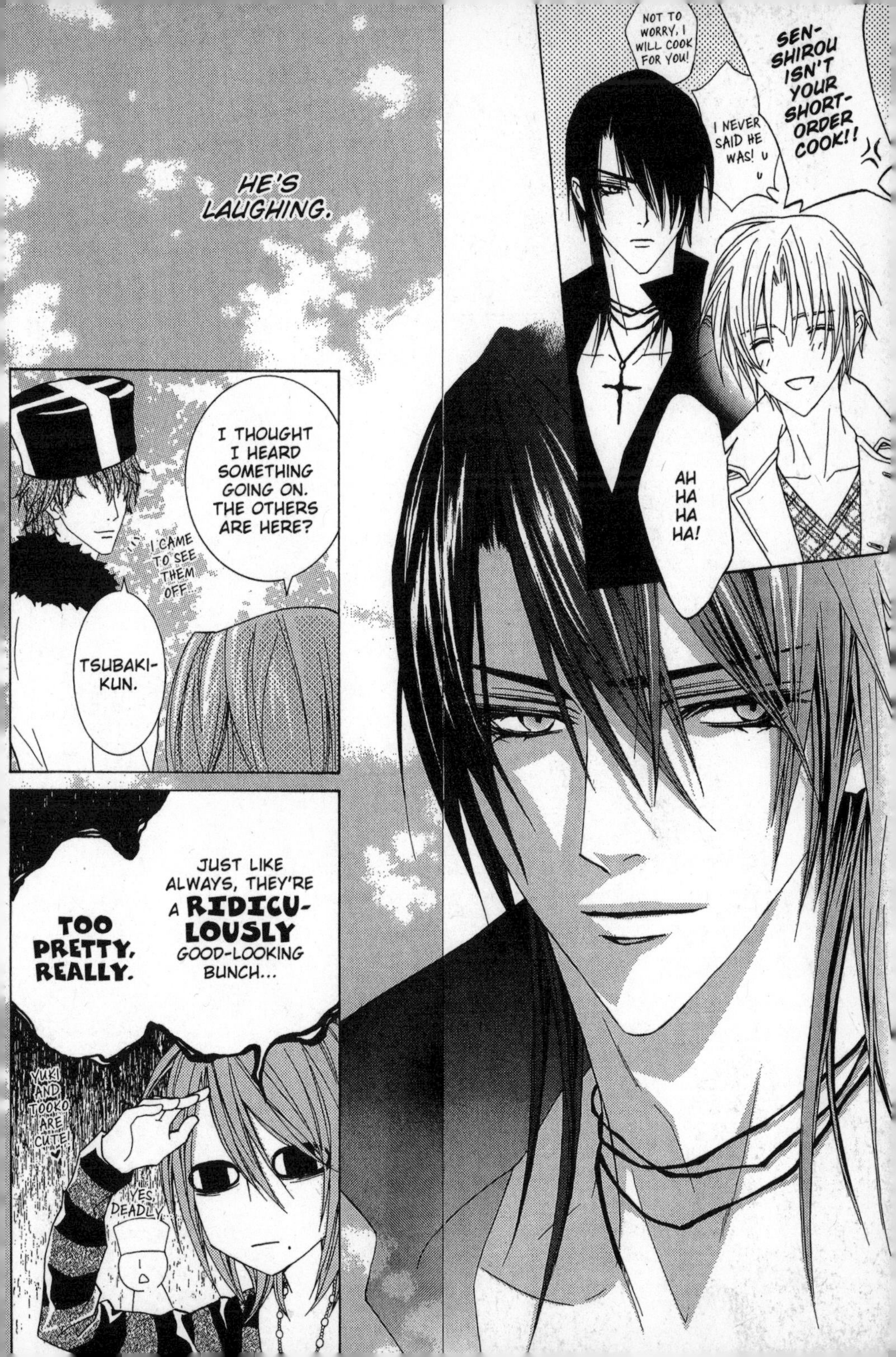
SEN-SHIROU ISN'T YOUR SHORT-ORDER COOK!!
NOT TO WORRY, I WILL COOK FOR YOU!
I NEVER SAID HE WAS!
AH HA HA HA!
HE'S LAUGHING.
I THOUGHT I HEARD SOMETHING GOING ON. THE OTHERS ARE HERE?
I CAME TO SEE THEM OFF
TSUBAKI-KUN.
JUST LIKE ALWAYS, THEY'RE A RIDICULOUSLY GOOD-LOOKING BUNCH...
TOO PRETTY, REALLY.
YUKI AND TOOKO ARE CUTE!
YES, DEADLY.

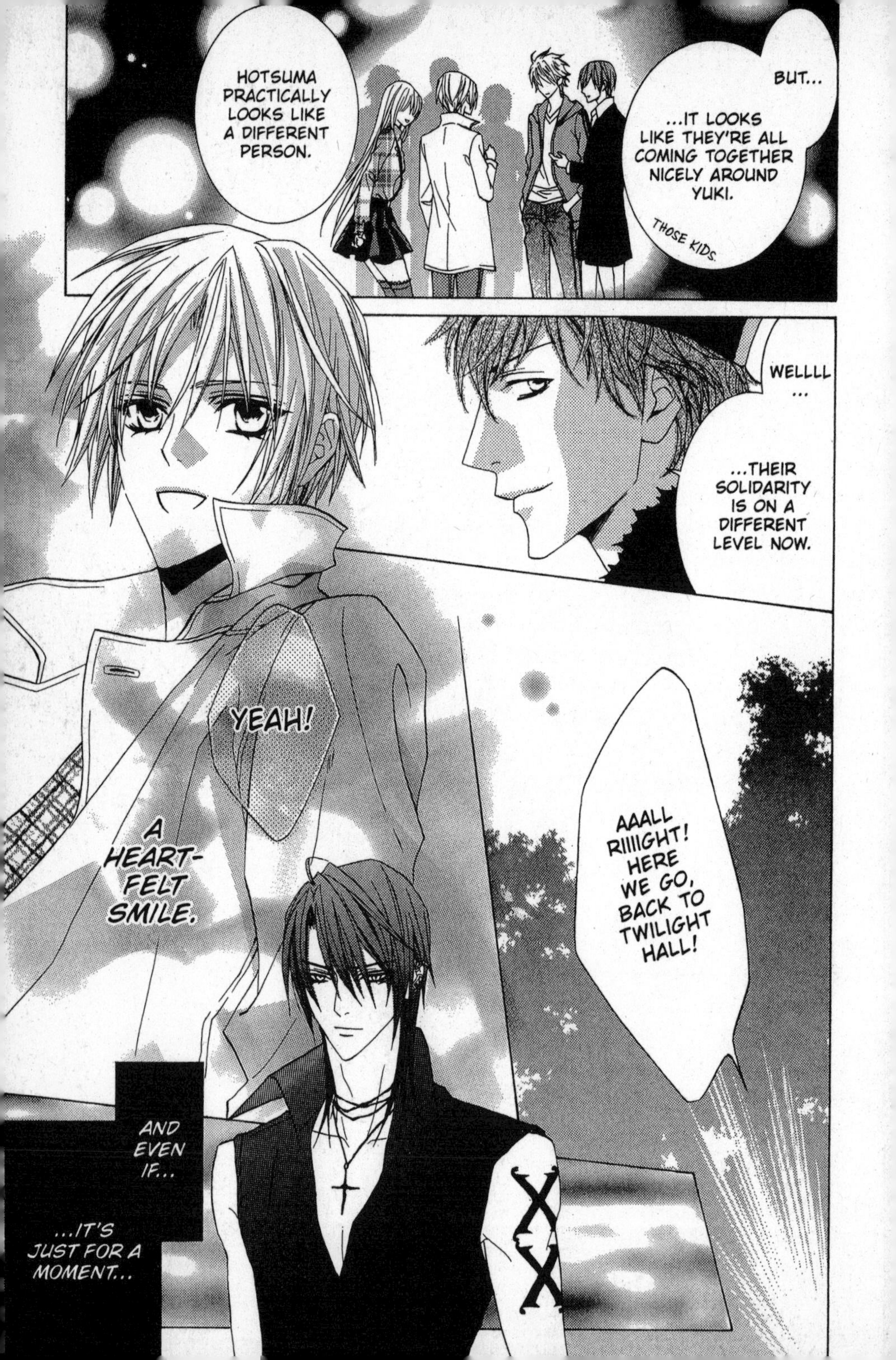
BUT...
...IT LOOKS LIKE THEY'RE ALL COMING TOGETHER NICELY AROUND YUKI.
THOSE KIDS.
HOTSUMA PRACTICALLY LOOKS LIKE A DIFFERENT PERSON.
WELLLL...
...THEIR SOLIDARITY IS ON A DIFFERENT LEVEL NOW.
AAALL RIIIIGHT! HERE WE GO, BACK TO TWILIGHT HALL!
YEAH!
A HEART-FELT SMILE.
AND EVEN IF...
...IT'S JUST FOR A MOMENT...

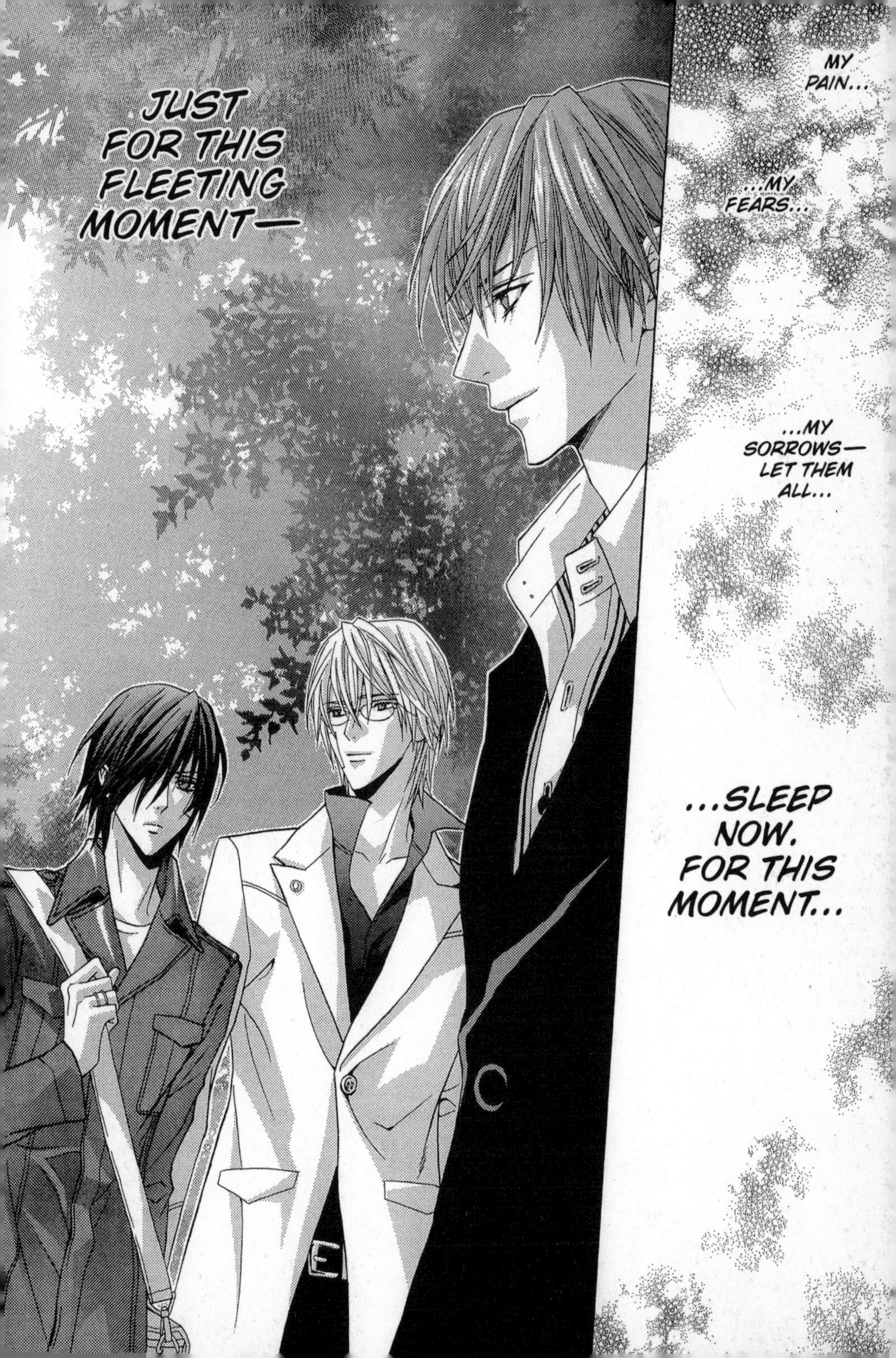
MY PAIN...
...MY FEARS...
...MY SORROWS—LET THEM ALL...
...SLEEP NOW. FOR THIS MOMENT...
JUST FOR THIS FLEETING MOMENT—

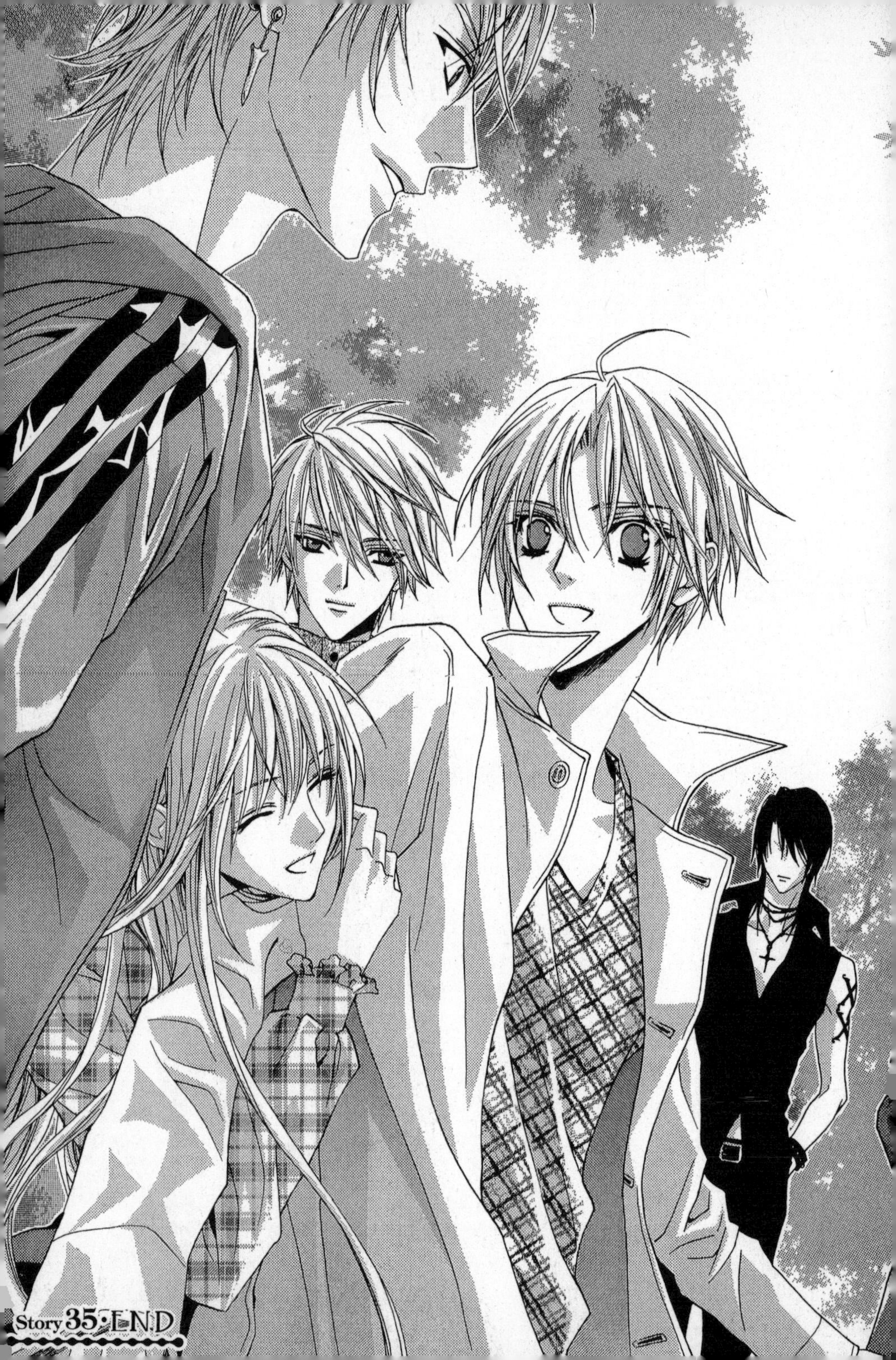
Story 35 • END

◆CHILDISH ADULTS...CONTINUED◆

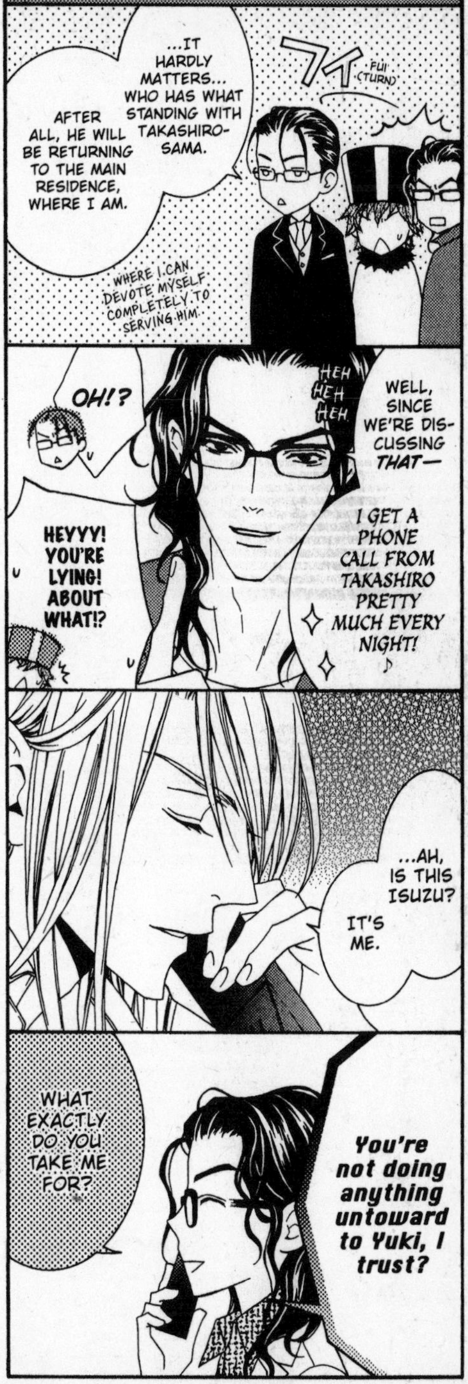
フイ
FUI (TURN)
...IT HARDLY MATTERS... WHO HAS WHAT STANDING WITH TAKASHIRO-SAMA.
AFTER ALL, HE WILL BE RETURNING TO THE MAIN RESIDENCE, WHERE I AM.
WHERE I CAN DEVOTE MYSELF COMPLETELY TO SERVING HIM.
WELL, SINCE WE'RE DIS-CUSSING *THAT*—
I GET A PHONE CALL FROM TAKASHIRO PRETTY MUCH EVERY NIGHT! ♪
HEH HEH HEH
OH!?
HEYYY! YOU'RE LYING! ABOUT WHAT!?
...AH, IS THIS ISUZU?
IT'S ME.
You're not doing anything untoward to Yuki, I trust?
WHAT EXACTLY DO YOU TAKE ME FOR?

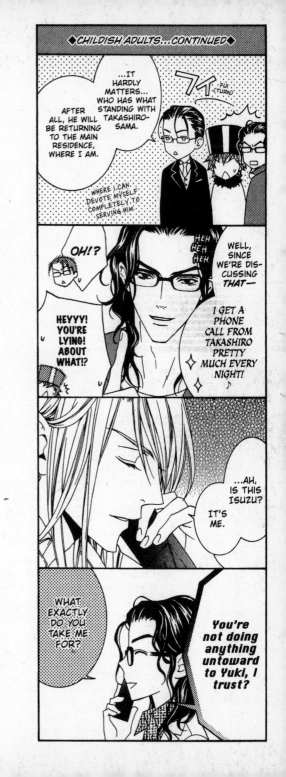

SPECIAL THANKS

✝

K-san
H.Sanbe
T.Kondo
H.Matsuo
K.Fukano
S.Y.

M.Okazaki
K.Sato
K.Okuda
E.Yamagishi

Y.Suzuki

Y.Ishii

…… and You

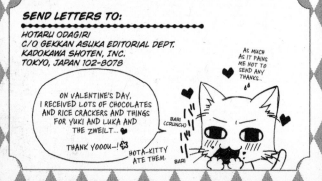

SEND LETTERS TO:

HOTARU ODAGIRI
C/O GEKKAN ASUKA EDITORIAL DEPT.
KADOKAWA SHOTEN, INC.
TOKYO, JAPAN 102-8078

AS MUCH AS IT PAINS ME NOT TO SEND ANY THANKS...

ON VALENTINE'S DAY, I RECEIVED LOTS OF CHOCOLATES AND RICE CRACKERS AND THINGS FOR YUKI AND LUKA AND THE ZWEILT...

THANK YOOOU—!

BARI CCRUNCHO

HOTA-KITTY ATE THEM.

BARI

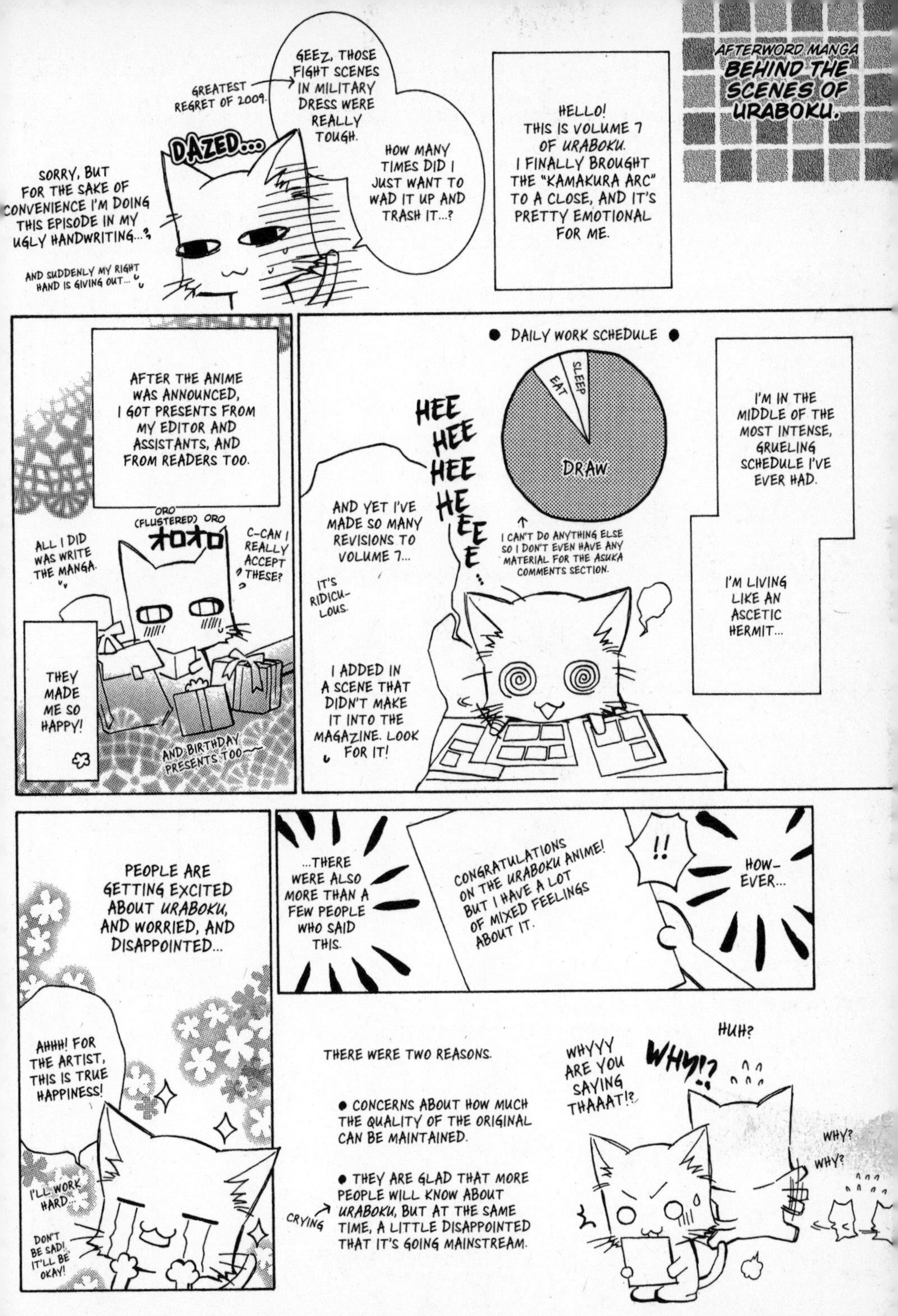
AFTERWORD MANGA
BEHIND THE SCENES OF URABOKU.
HELLO! THIS IS VOLUME 7 OF *URABOKU*. I FINALLY BROUGHT THE "KAMAKURA ARC" TO A CLOSE, AND IT'S PRETTY EMOTIONAL FOR ME.
GEEZ, THOSE FIGHT SCENES IN MILITARY DRESS WERE REALLY TOUGH.
GREATEST REGRET OF 2009.
HOW MANY TIMES DID I JUST WANT TO WAD IT UP AND TRASH IT...?
DAZED...
SORRY, BUT FOR THE SAKE OF CONVENIENCE I'M DOING THIS EPISODE IN MY UGLY HANDWRITING...
AND SUDDENLY MY RIGHT HAND IS GIVING OUT...
I'M IN THE MIDDLE OF THE MOST INTENSE, GRUELING SCHEDULE I'VE EVER HAD.
I'M LIVING LIKE AN ASCETIC HERMIT...
DAILY WORK SCHEDULE
SLEEP
EAT
DRAW
I CAN'T DO ANYTHING ELSE SO I DON'T EVEN HAVE ANY MATERIAL FOR THE ASUKA COMMENTS SECTION.
HEE HEE HEE HEEEE...
AND YET I'VE MADE SO MANY REVISIONS TO VOLUME 7...
IT'S RIDICU-LOUS.
I ADDED IN A SCENE THAT DIDN'T MAKE IT INTO THE MAGAZINE. LOOK FOR IT!
AFTER THE ANIME WAS ANNOUNCED, I GOT PRESENTS FROM MY EDITOR AND ASSISTANTS, AND FROM READERS TOO.
C-CAN I REALLY ACCEPT THESE?
ORO (FLUSTERED) ORO
オロオロ
ALL I DID WAS WRITE THE MANGA.
THEY MADE ME SO HAPPY!
AND BIRTHDAY PRESENTS TOO~~
HOW-EVER...
!!
CONGRATULATIONS ON THE URABOKU ANIME! BUT I HAVE A LOT OF MIXED FEELINGS ABOUT IT.
...THERE WERE ALSO MORE THAN A FEW PEOPLE WHO SAID THIS.
HUH?
WHY!?
WHYYY ARE YOU SAYING THAAAT!?
WHY?
WHY?
THERE WERE TWO REASONS.
● CONCERNS ABOUT HOW MUCH THE QUALITY OF THE ORIGINAL CAN BE MAINTAINED.
● THEY ARE GLAD THAT MORE PEOPLE WILL KNOW ABOUT *URABOKU*, BUT AT THE SAME TIME, A LITTLE DISAPPOINTED THAT IT'S GOING MAINSTREAM.
CRYING
PEOPLE ARE GETTING EXCITED ABOUT *URABOKU*, AND WORRIED, AND DISAPPOINTED...
AHHH! FOR THE ARTIST, THIS IS TRUE HAPPINESS!
I'LL WORK HARD...
DON'T BE SAD! IT'LL BE OKAY!

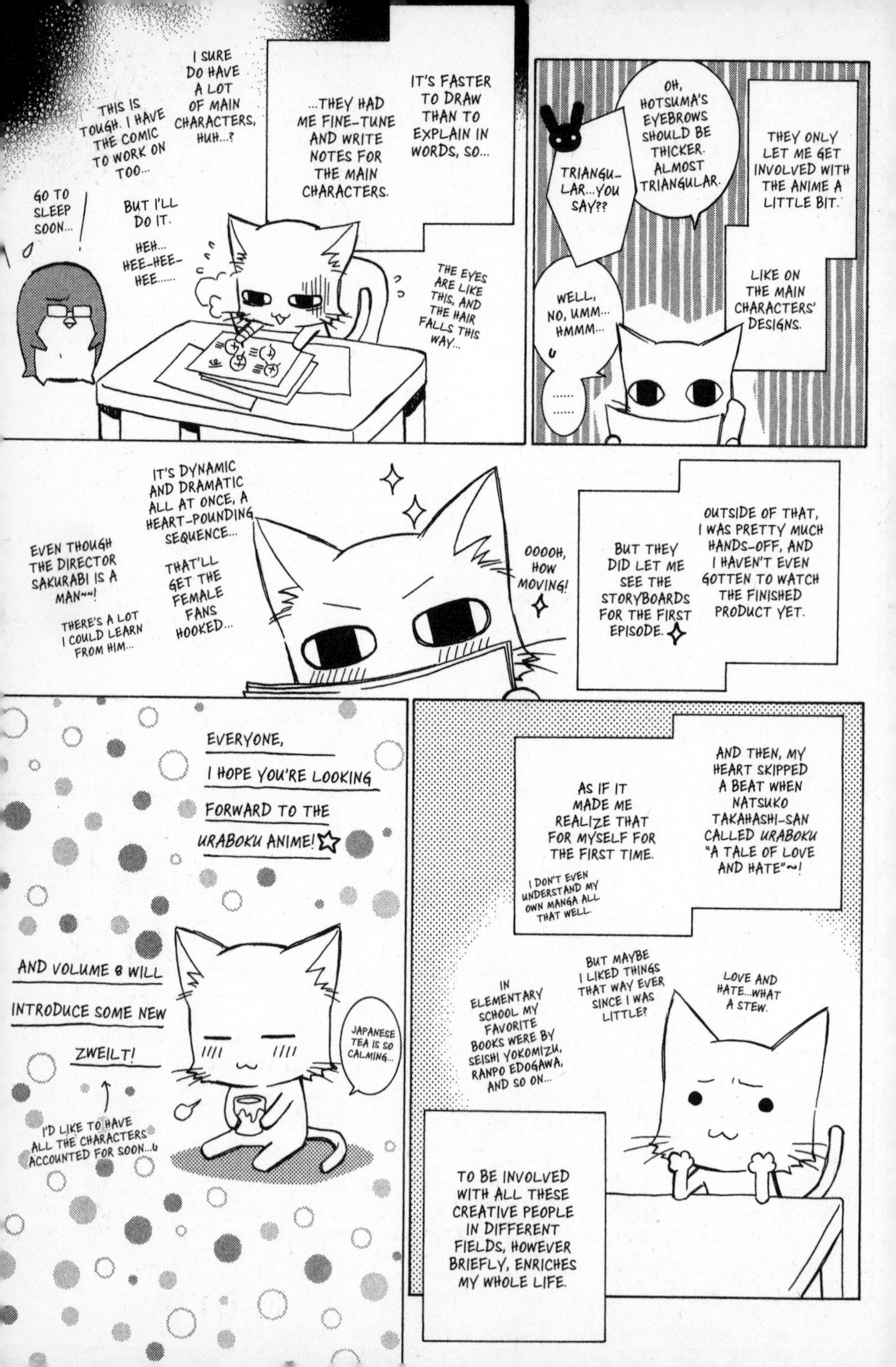
THEY ONLY LET ME GET INVOLVED WITH THE ANIME A LITTLE BIT.
LIKE ON THE MAIN CHARACTERS' DESIGNS.
OH, HOTSUMA'S EYEBROWS SHOULD BE THICKER. ALMOST TRIANGULAR.
TRIANGU-LAR...YOU SAY??
WELL, NO, UMM... HMMM...
......
......
IT'S FASTER TO DRAW THAN TO EXPLAIN IN WORDS, SO...
...THEY HAD ME FINE-TUNE AND WRITE NOTES FOR THE MAIN CHARACTERS.
I SURE DO HAVE A LOT OF MAIN CHARACTERS, HUH...?
THIS IS TOUGH. I HAVE THE COMIC TO WORK ON TOO...
BUT I'LL DO IT.
HEH... HEE-HEE-HEE......
THE EYES ARE LIKE THIS, AND THE HAIR FALLS THIS WAY...
GO TO SLEEP SOON...
OUTSIDE OF THAT, I WAS PRETTY MUCH HANDS-OFF, AND I HAVEN'T EVEN GOTTEN TO WATCH THE FINISHED PRODUCT YET.
BUT THEY DID LET ME SEE THE STORYBOARDS FOR THE FIRST EPISODE.
OOOOH, HOW MOVING!
IT'S DYNAMIC AND DRAMATIC ALL AT ONCE, A HEART-POUNDING SEQUENCE...
THAT'LL GET THE FEMALE FANS HOOKED...
EVEN THOUGH THE DIRECTOR SAKURABI IS A MAN~~!
THERE'S A LOT I COULD LEARN FROM HIM...
AND THEN, MY HEART SKIPPED A BEAT WHEN NATSUKO TAKAHASHI-SAN CALLED *URABOKU* "A TALE OF LOVE AND HATE"~!
AS IF IT MADE ME REALIZE THAT FOR MYSELF FOR THE FIRST TIME.
I DON'T EVEN UNDERSTAND MY OWN MANGA ALL THAT WELL.
LOVE AND HATE...WHAT A STEW.
BUT MAYBE I LIKED THINGS THAT WAY EVER SINCE I WAS LITTLE?
IN ELEMENTARY SCHOOL MY FAVORITE BOOKS WERE BY SEISHI YOKOMIZU, RANPO EDOGAWA, AND SO ON...
TO BE INVOLVED WITH ALL THESE CREATIVE PEOPLE IN DIFFERENT FIELDS, HOWEVER BRIEFLY, ENRICHES MY WHOLE LIFE.
EVERYONE, I HOPE YOU'RE LOOKING FORWARD TO THE URABOKU ANIME! ☆
JAPANESE TEA IS SO CALMING...
AND VOLUME 8 WILL INTRODUCE SOME NEW ZWEILT!
I'D LIKE TO HAVE ALL THE CHARACTERS ACCOUNTED FOR SOON...

Story 36

SEARCHING FOR YOU

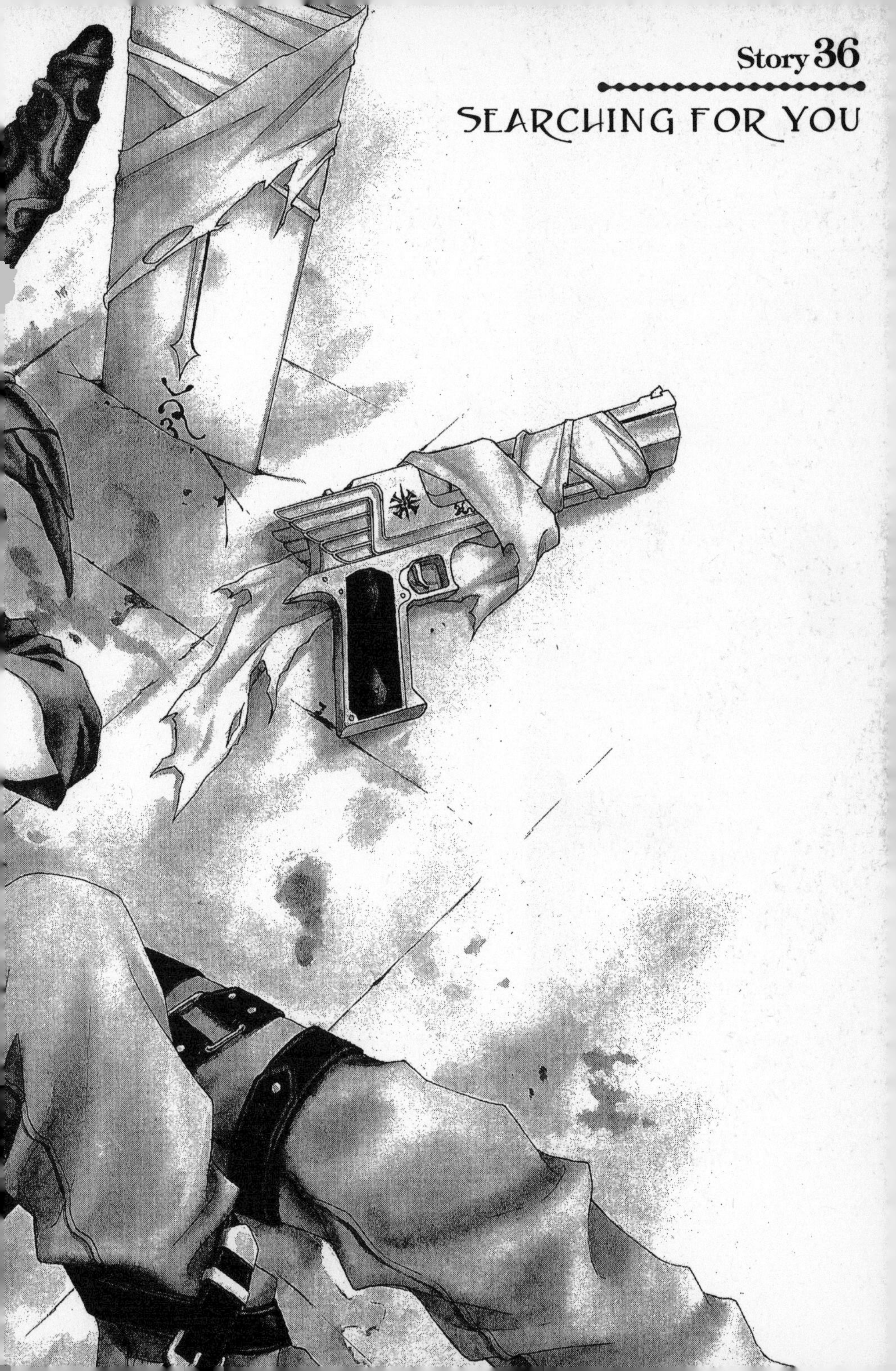

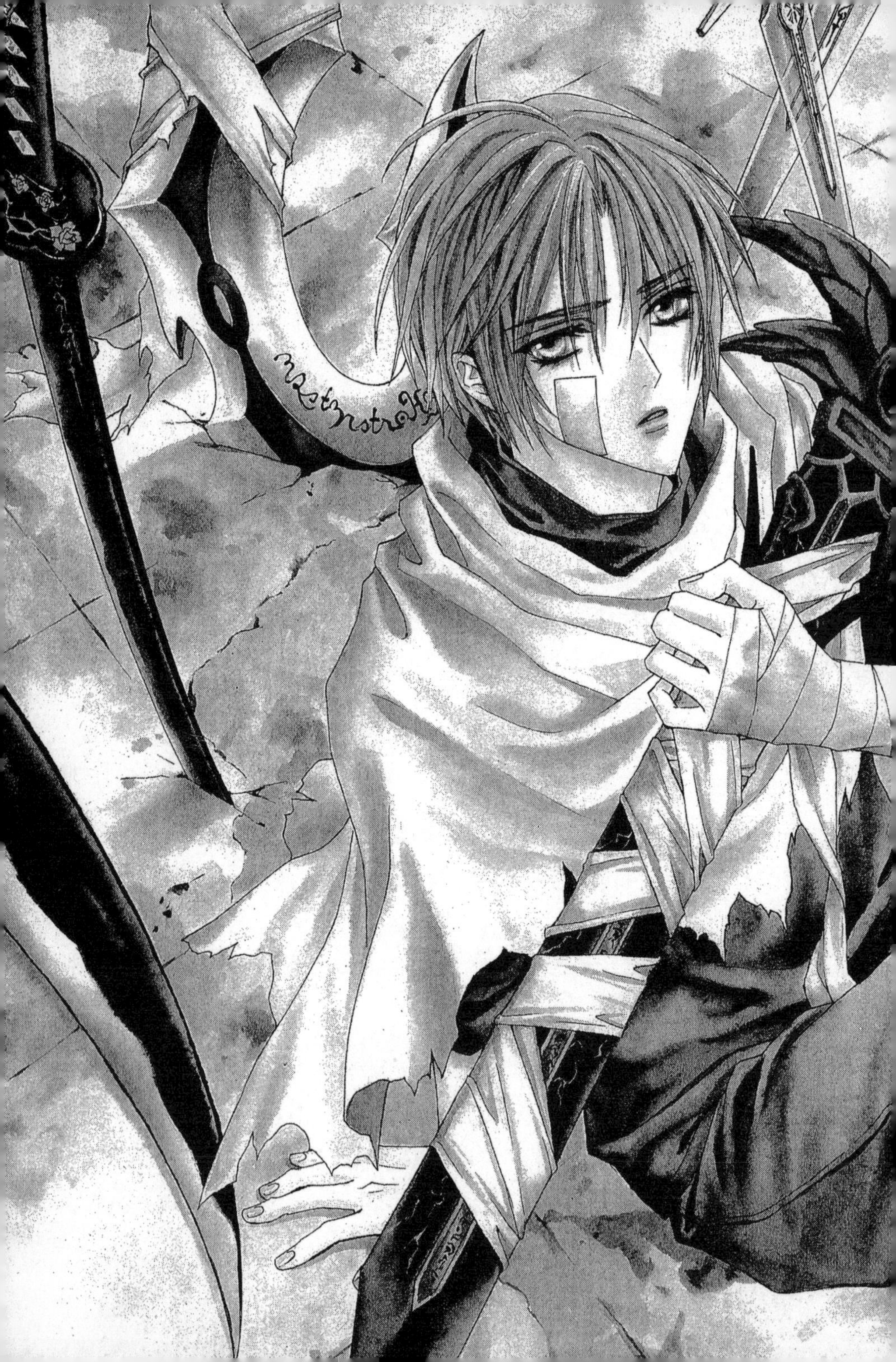

THE BETRAYAL KNOWS MY NAME

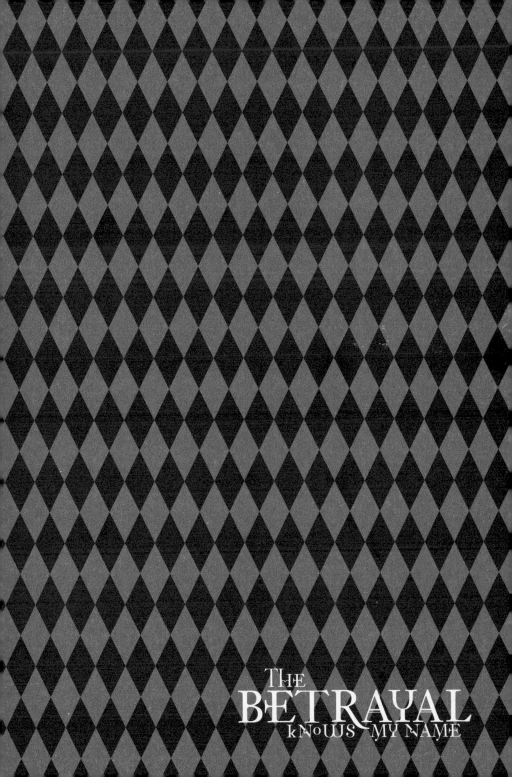

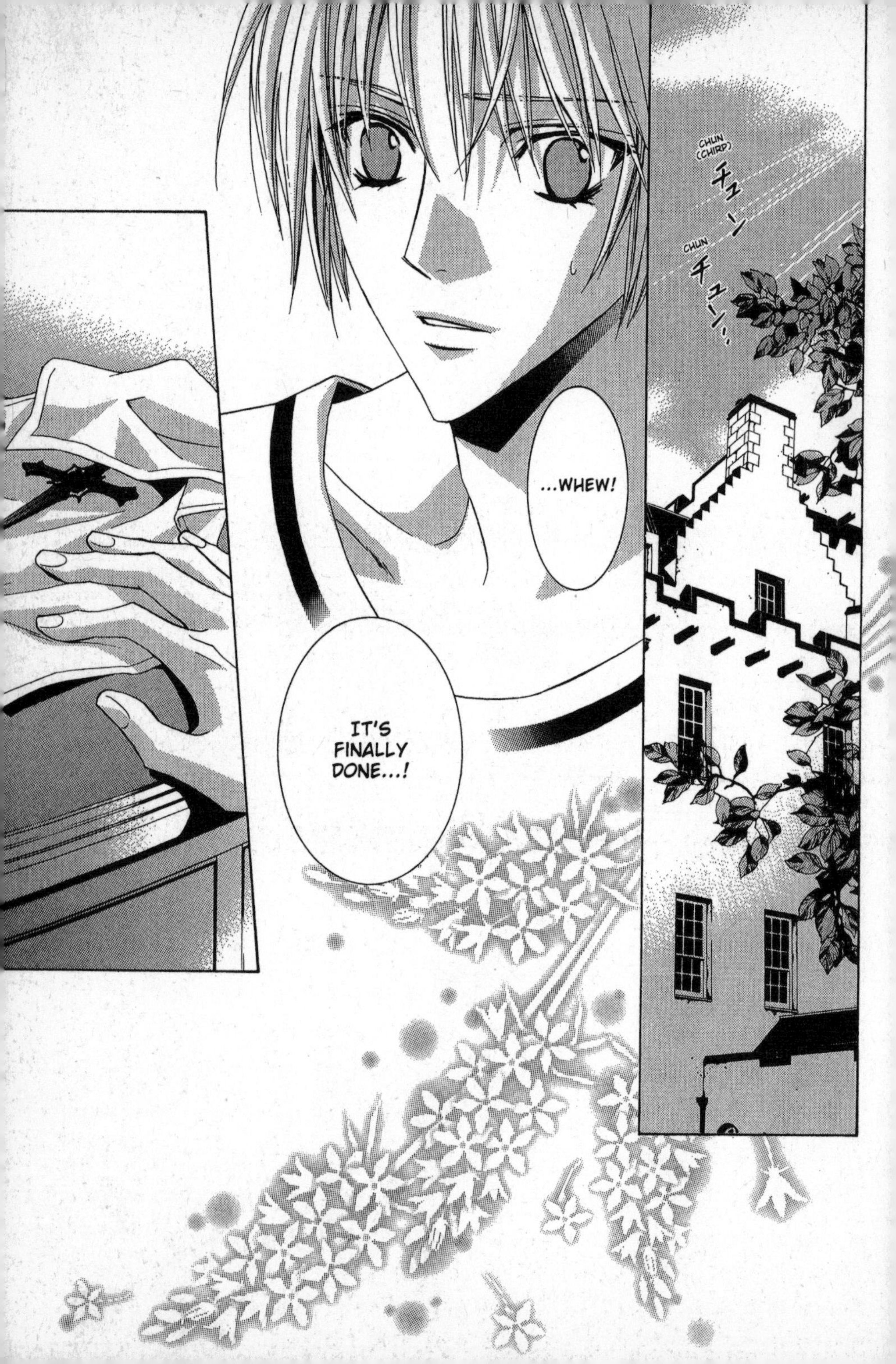
CHUN (CHIRP)
チュン
CHUN
チュン…
...WHEW!
IT'S FINALLY DONE...!

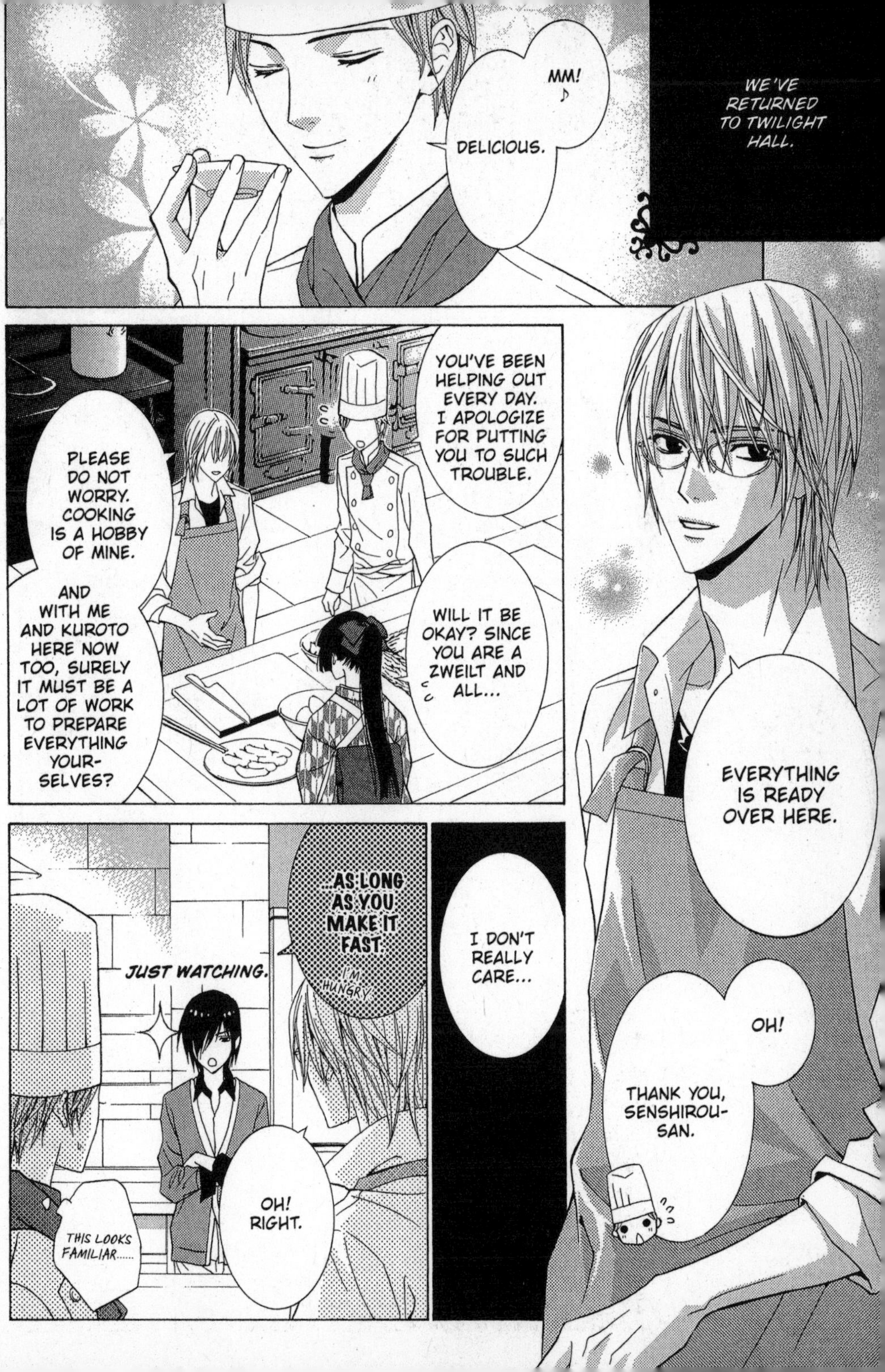
WE'VE RETURNED TO TWILIGHT HALL.
MM! ♪
DELICIOUS.
EVERYTHING IS READY OVER HERE.
OH!
THANK YOU, SENSHIROU-SAN.
YOU'VE BEEN HELPING OUT EVERY DAY. I APOLOGIZE FOR PUTTING YOU TO SUCH TROUBLE.
PLEASE DO NOT WORRY. COOKING IS A HOBBY OF MINE.
AND WITH ME AND KUROTO HERE NOW TOO, SURELY IT MUST BE A LOT OF WORK TO PREPARE EVERYTHING YOURSELVES?
WILL IT BE OKAY? SINCE YOU ARE A ZWEILT AND ALL...
I DON'T REALLY CARE...
...AS LONG AS YOU MAKE IT FAST.
I'M HUNGRY.
JUST WATCHING.
OH! RIGHT.
THIS LOOKS FAMILIAR......

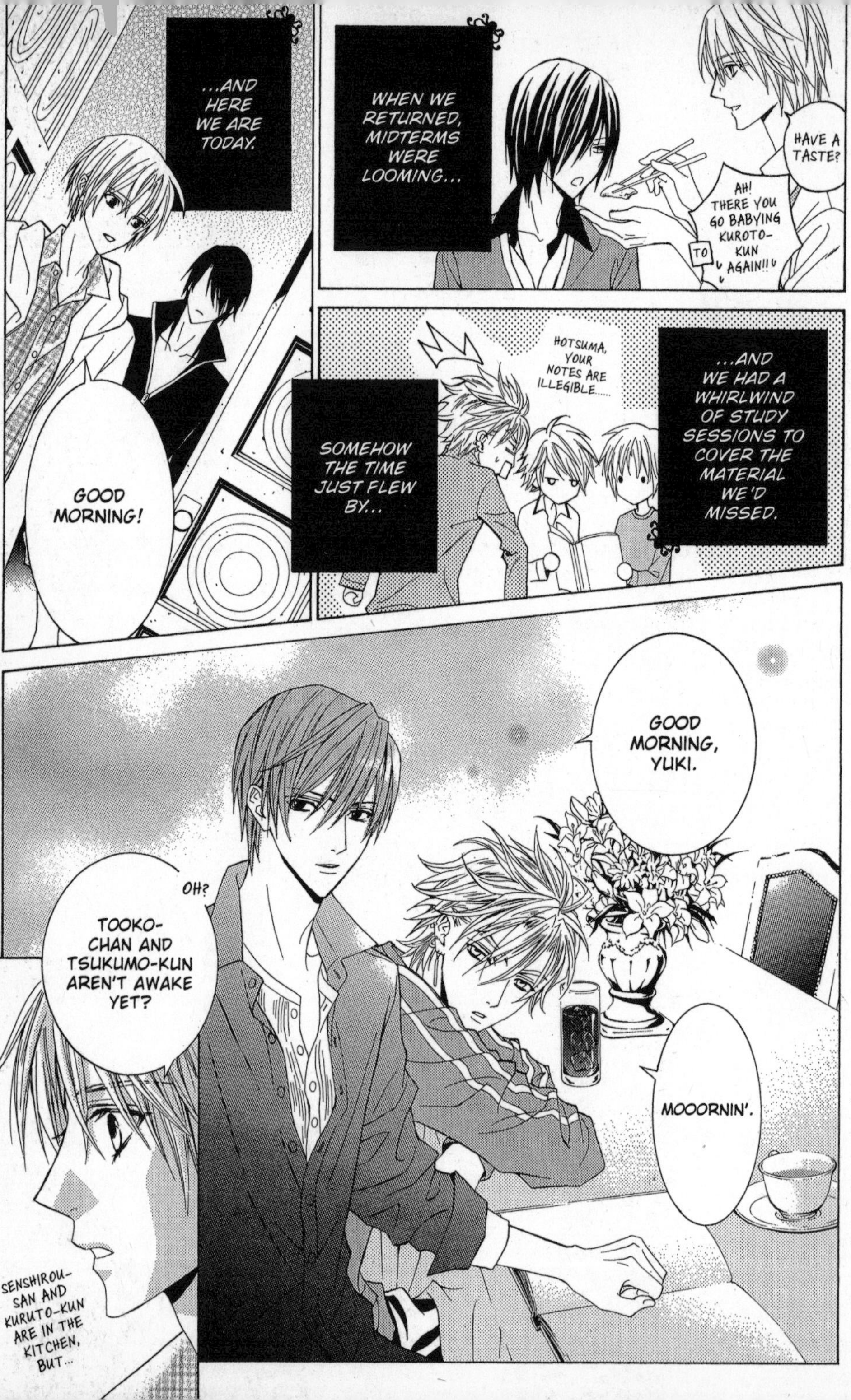
WHEN WE RETURNED, MIDTERMS WERE LOOMING...
HAVE A TASTE?
AH! THERE YOU GO BABYING KUROTO-KUN AGAIN!!
TO
...AND WE HAD A WHIRLWIND OF STUDY SESSIONS TO COVER THE MATERIAL WE'D MISSED.
HOTSUMA, YOUR NOTES ARE ILLEGIBLE.....
SOMEHOW THE TIME JUST FLEW BY...
...AND HERE WE ARE TODAY.
GOOD MORNING!
GOOD MORNING, YUKI.
MOOORNIN'.
OH?
TOOKO-CHAN AND TSUKUMO-KUN AREN'T AWAKE YET?
SENSHIROU-SAN AND KURUTO-KUN ARE IN THE KITCHEN, BUT...

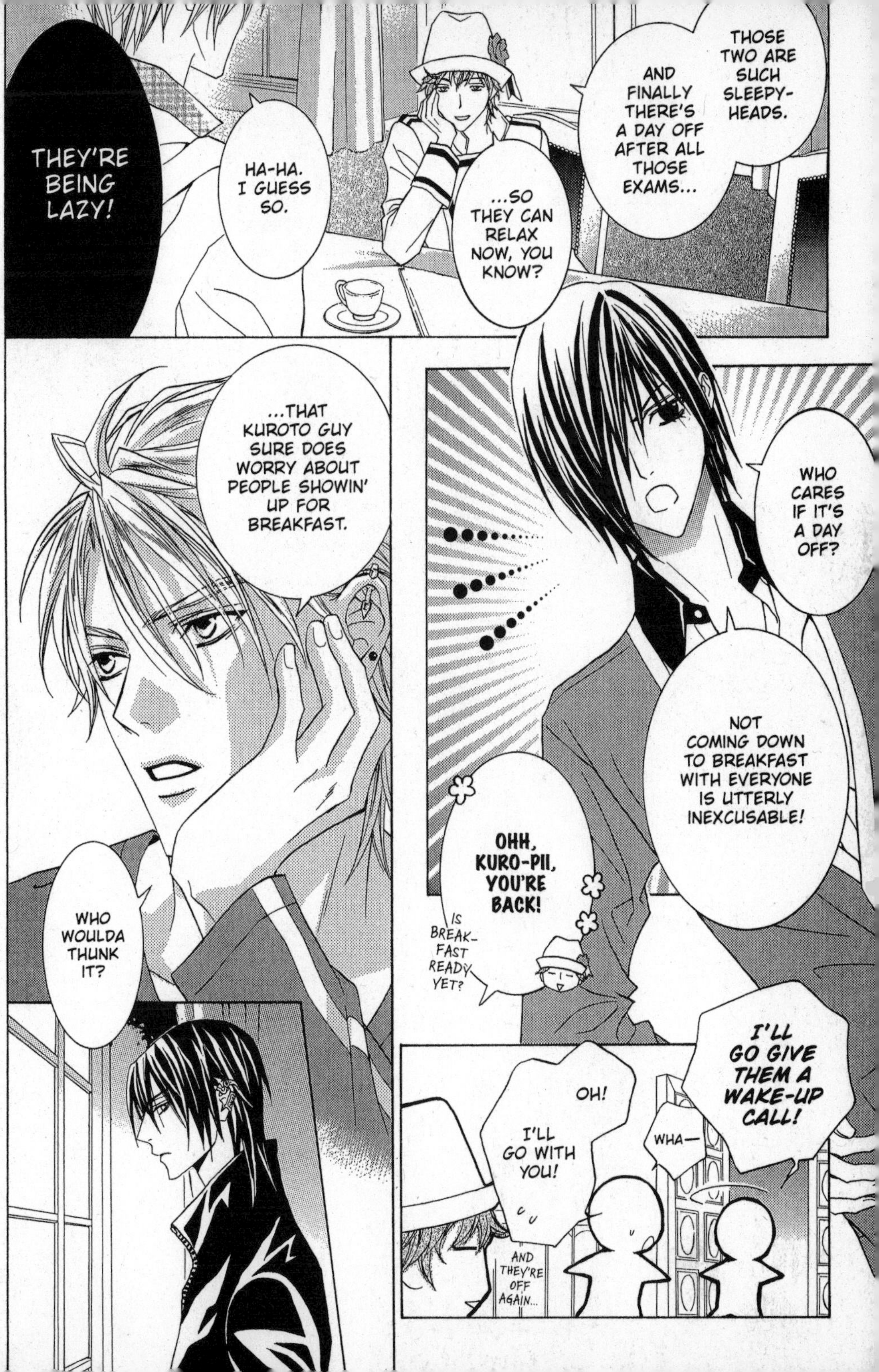

THOSE TWO ARE SUCH SLEEPY-HEADS.
AND FINALLY THERE'S A DAY OFF AFTER ALL THOSE EXAMS...
...SO THEY CAN RELAX NOW, YOU KNOW?
HA-HA. I GUESS SO.
THEY'RE BEING LAZY!
WHO CARES IF IT'S A DAY OFF?
NOT COMING DOWN TO BREAKFAST WITH EVERYONE IS UTTERLY INEXCUSABLE!
OHH, KURO-PII, YOU'RE BACK!
IS BREAK-FAST READY YET?
I'LL GO GIVE THEM A WAKE-UP CALL!
WHA—
OH!
I'LL GO WITH YOU!
AND THEY'RE OFF AGAIN...
...THAT KUROTO GUY SURE DOES WORRY ABOUT PEOPLE SHOWIN' UP FOR BREAKFAST.
WHO WOULDA THUNK IT?

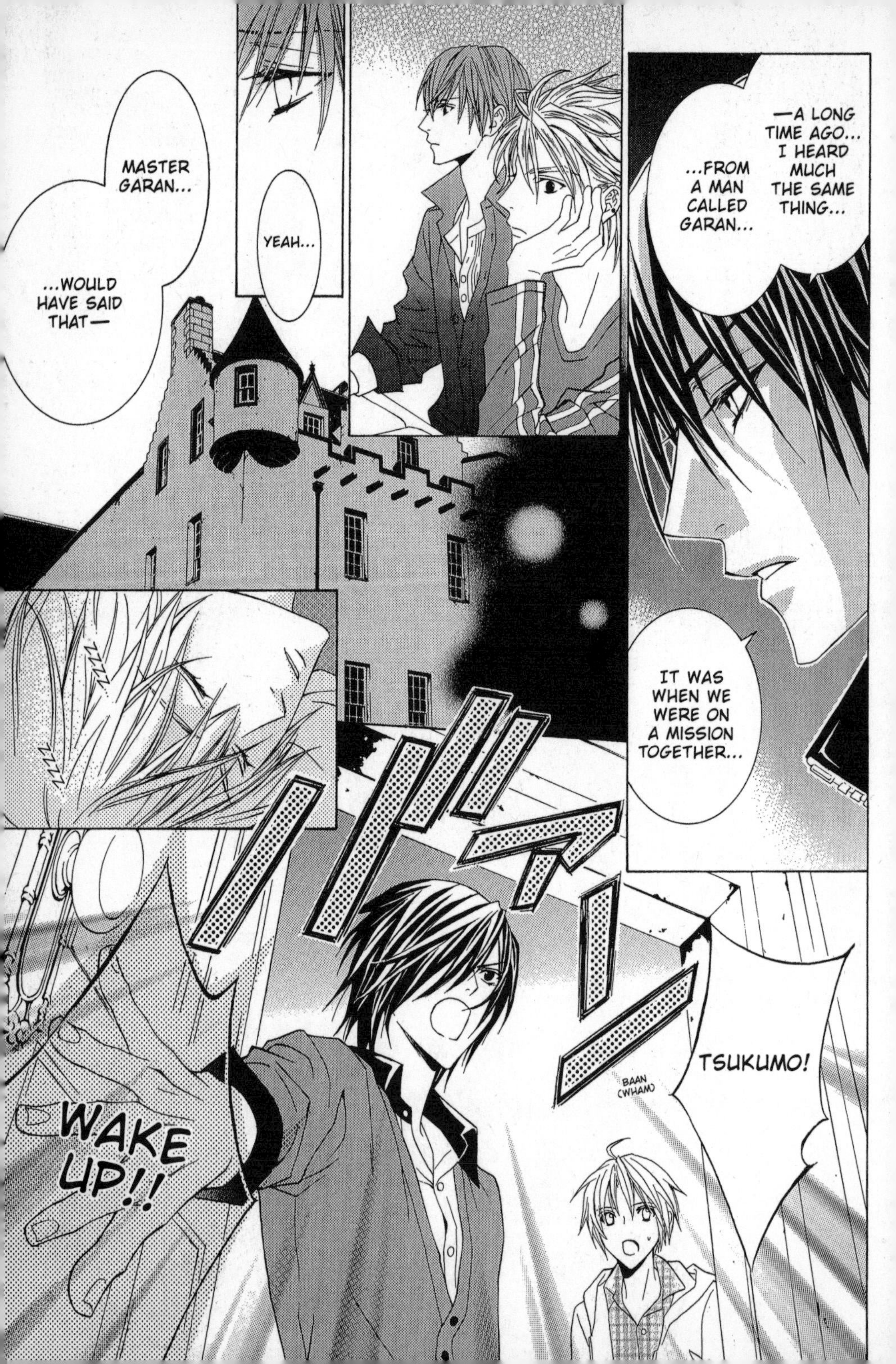
—A LONG TIME AGO... I HEARD MUCH THE SAME THING...
...FROM A MAN CALLED GARAN...
IT WAS WHEN WE WERE ON A MISSION TOGETHER...
YEAH...
MASTER GARAN...
...WOULD HAVE SAID THAT—
TSUKUMO!
BAAN (WHAM)
WAKE UP!!

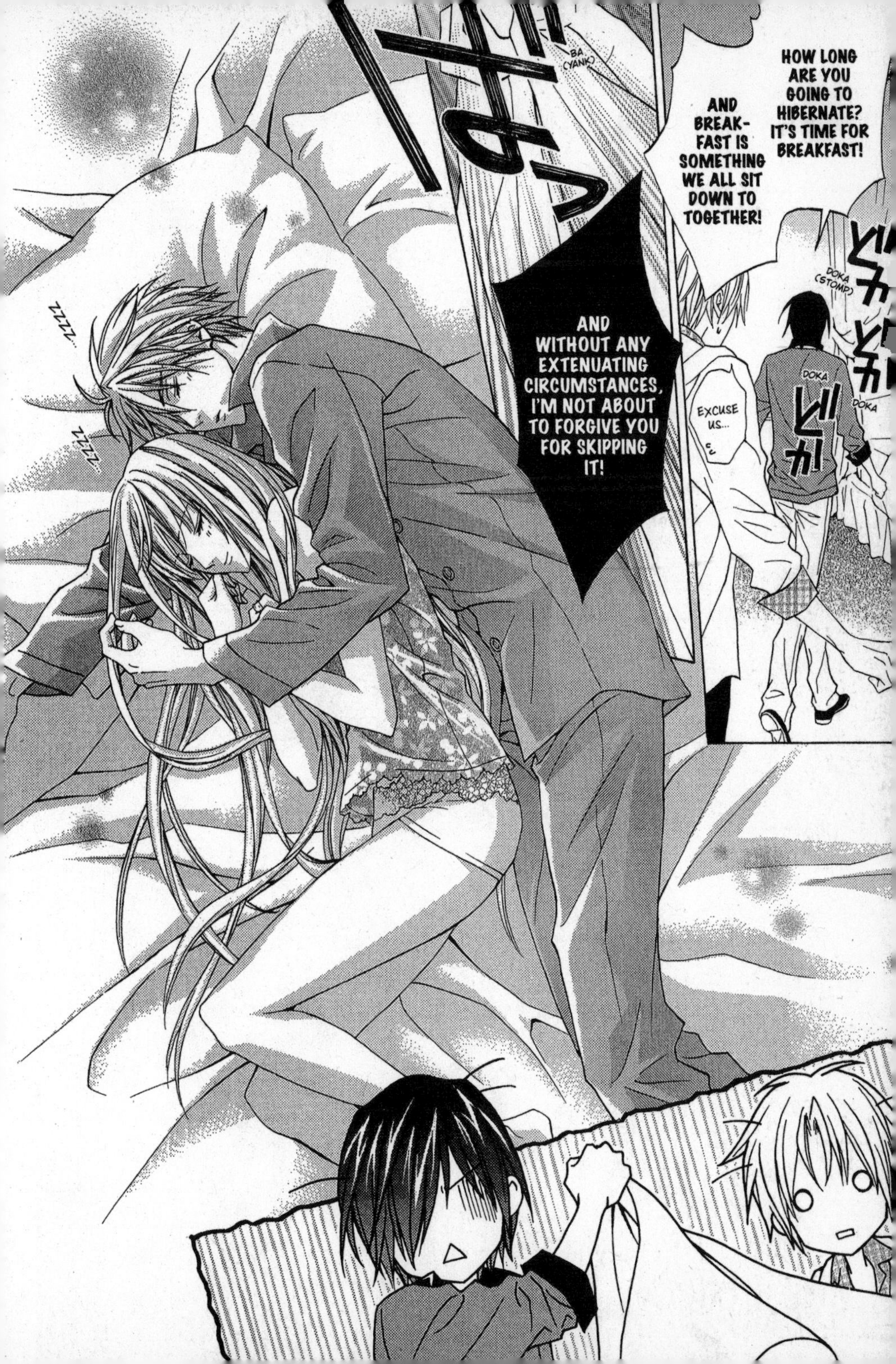

HOW LONG ARE YOU GOING TO HIBERNATE? IT'S TIME FOR BREAKFAST!
AND BREAK-FAST IS SOMETHING WE ALL SIT DOWN TO TOGETHER!
DOKA (STOMP)
DOKA
DOKA
EXCUSE US...
BA (YANK)
AND WITHOUT ANY EXTENUATING CIRCUMSTANCES, I'M NOT ABOUT TO FORGIVE YOU FOR SKIPPING IT!
ZZZZ
ZZZZ

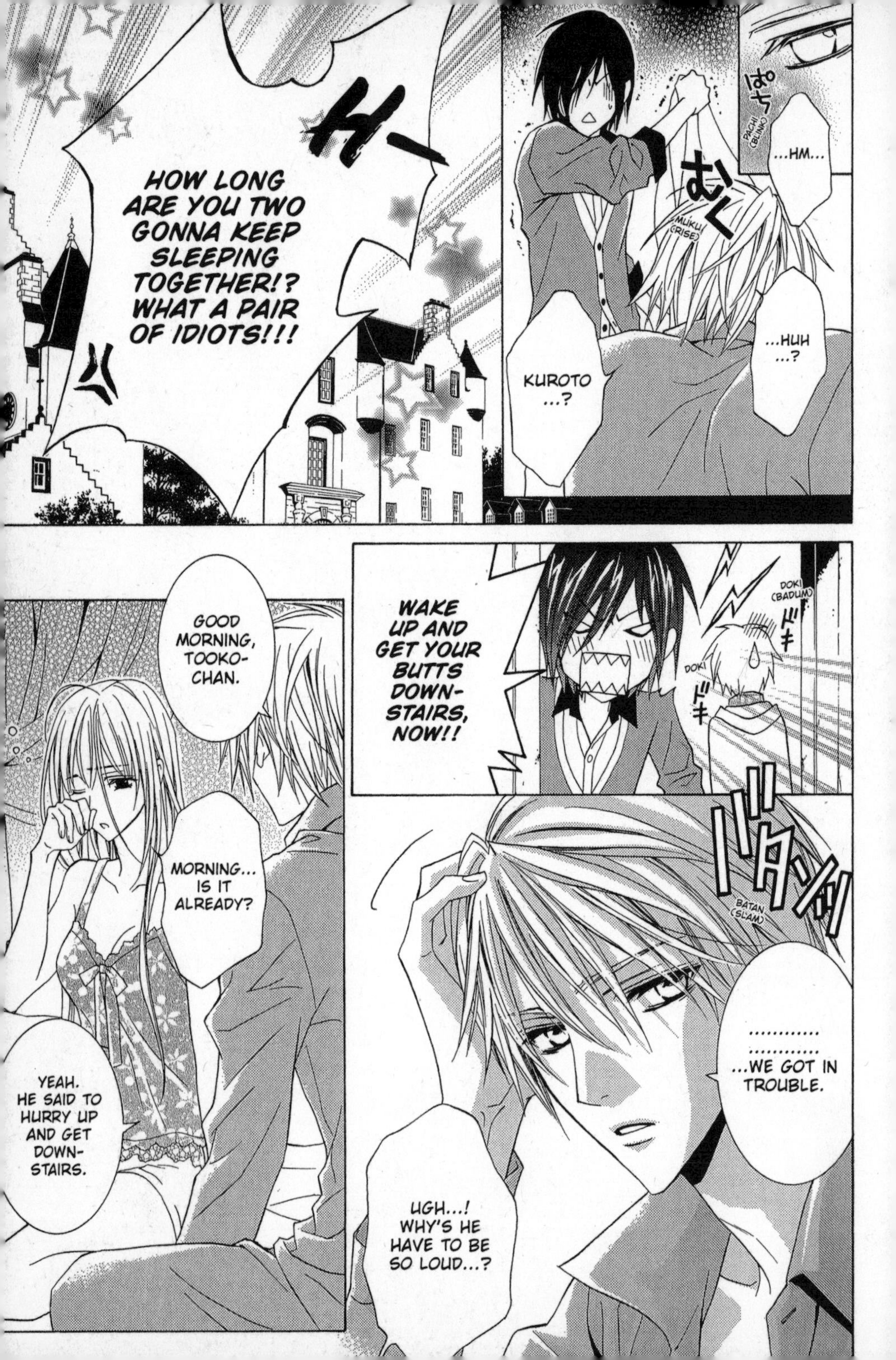

ぱち
PACHI (BLINK)
...HM...
むく
MUKU (RISE)
...HUH ...?
KUROTO ...?
H—
HOW LONG ARE YOU TWO GONNA KEEP SLEEPING TOGETHER!? WHAT A PAIR OF IDIOTS!!!
WAKE UP AND GET YOUR BUTTS DOWN-STAIRS, NOW!!
ドキ
DOKI (BADUM)
ドキ
DOKI
バタン
BATAN (SLAM)
....WE GOT IN TROUBLE.
UGH...! WHY'S HE HAVE TO BE SO LOUD...?
GOOD MORNING, TOOKO-CHAN.
MORNING... IS IT ALREADY?
YEAH. HE SAID TO HURRY UP AND GET DOWN-STAIRS.

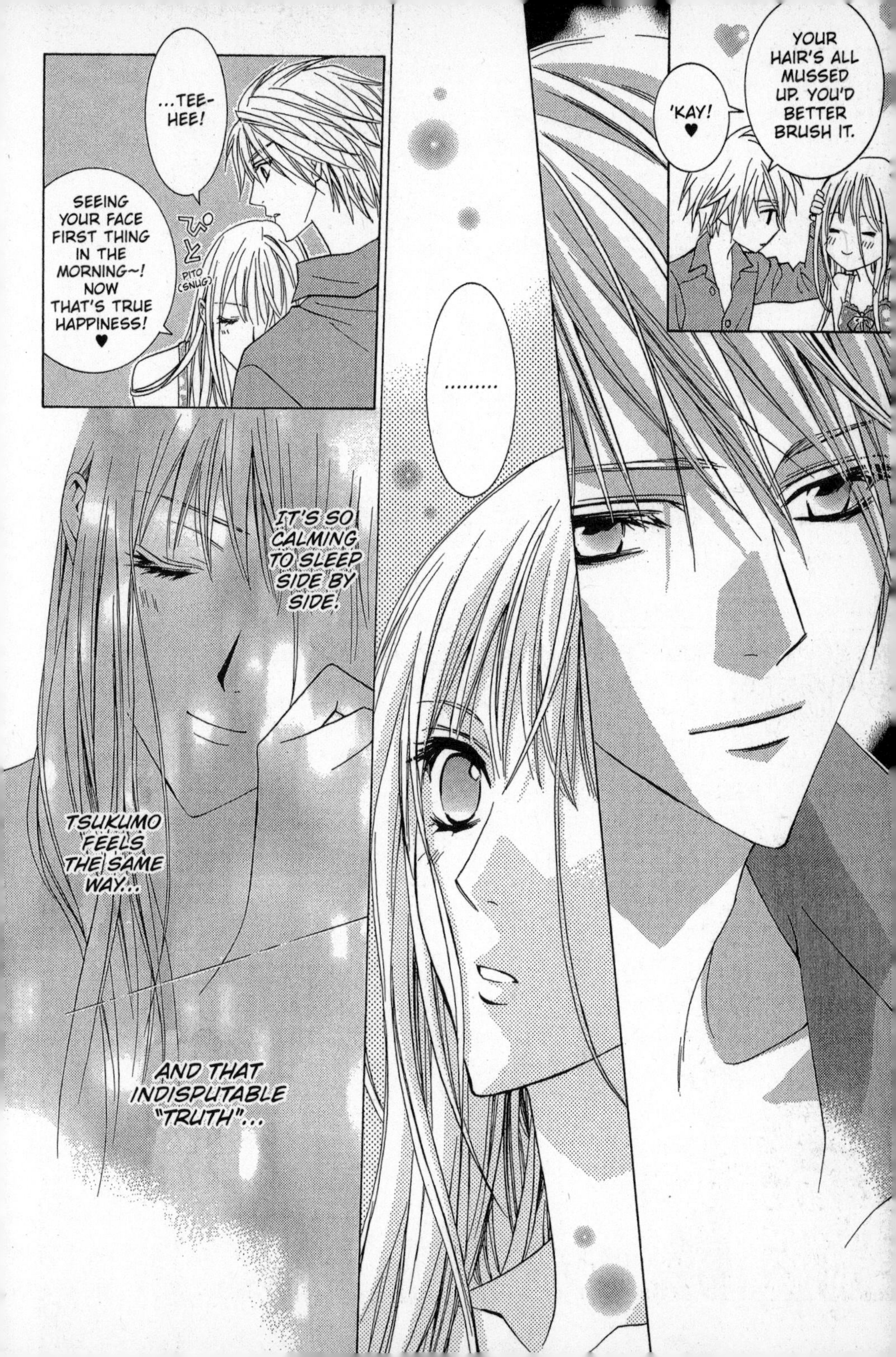
YOUR HAIR'S ALL MUSSED UP. YOU'D BETTER BRUSH IT.
'KAY! ♥
...TEE-HEE!
SEEING YOUR FACE FIRST THING IN THE MORNING~! NOW THAT'S TRUE HAPPINESS! ♥
PITO (SNUG)
....
IT'S SO CALMING TO SLEEP SIDE BY SIDE.
TSUKUMO FEELS THE SAME WAY...
AND THAT INDISPUTABLE "TRUTH"...

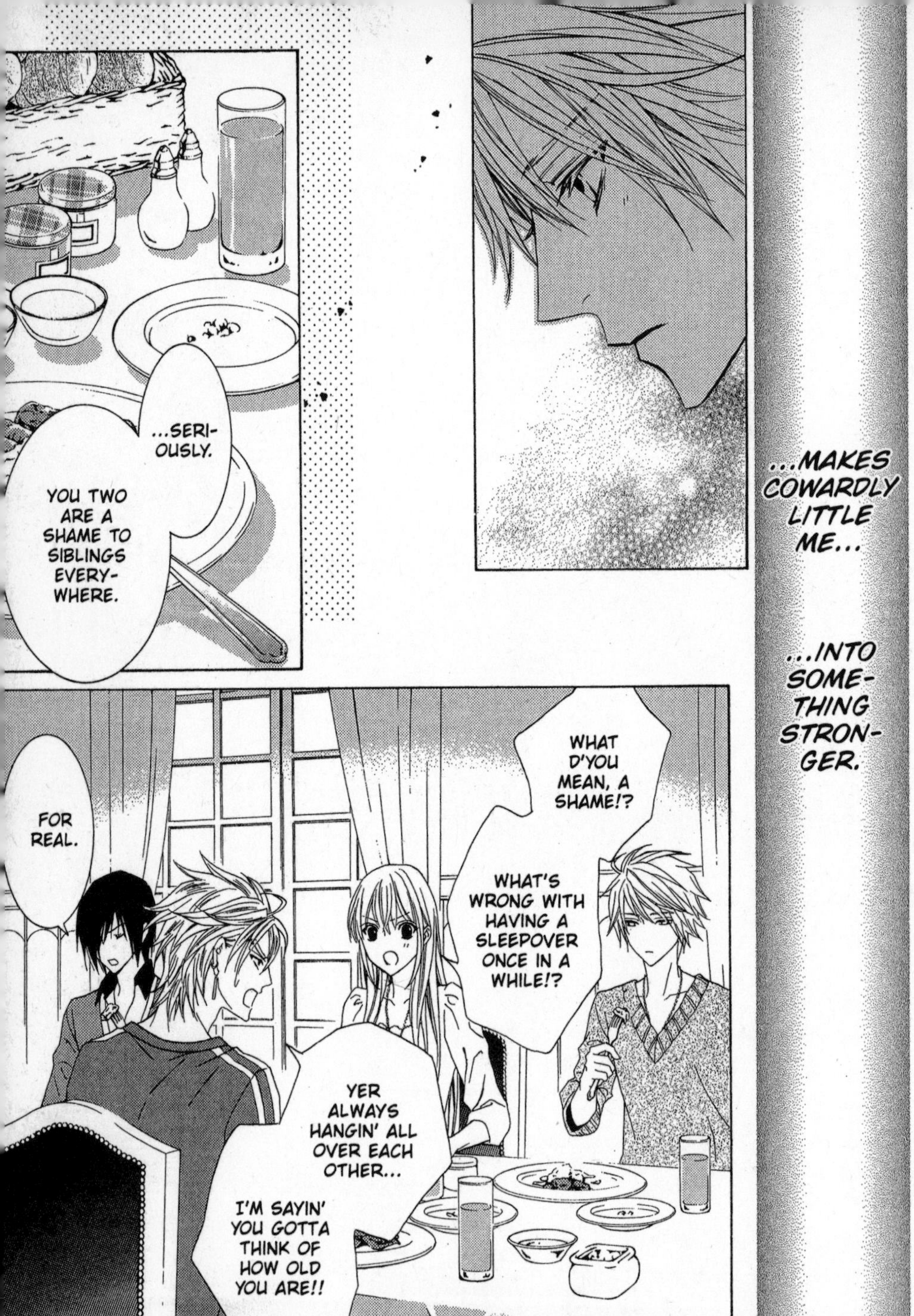
...MAKES COWARDLY LITTLE ME...
...INTO SOMETHING STRONGER.
...SERIOUSLY.
YOU TWO ARE A SHAME TO SIBLINGS EVERYWHERE.
WHAT D'YOU MEAN, A SHAME!?
WHAT'S WRONG WITH HAVING A SLEEPOVER ONCE IN A WHILE!?
YER ALWAYS HANGIN' ALL OVER EACH OTHER...
I'M SAYIN' YOU GOTTA THINK OF HOW OLD YOU ARE!!
FOR REAL.

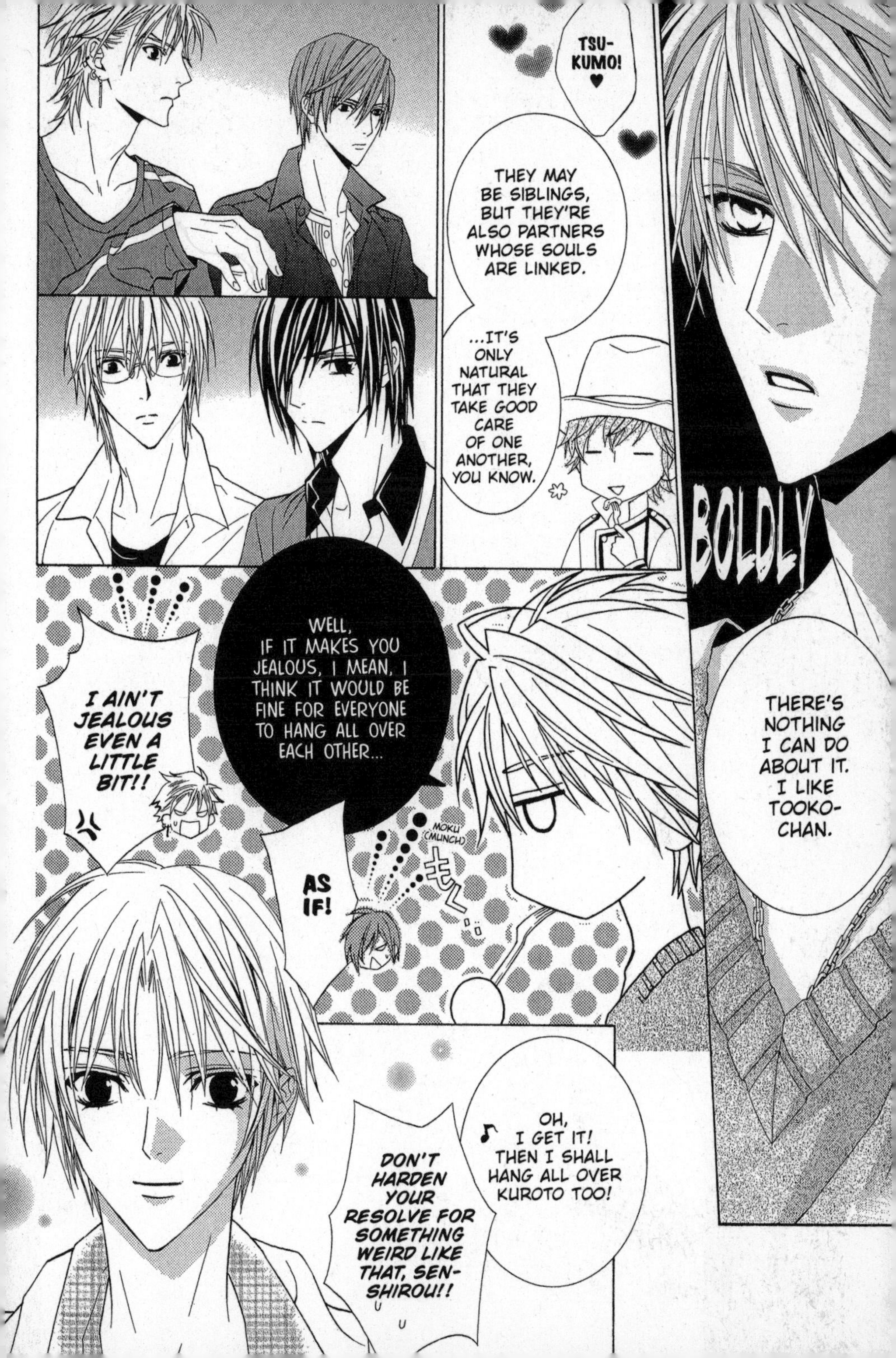
BOLDLY
THERE'S NOTHING I CAN DO ABOUT IT. I LIKE TOOKO-CHAN.
TSU-KUMO! ♥
THEY MAY BE SIBLINGS, BUT THEY'RE ALSO PARTNERS WHOSE SOULS ARE LINKED.
...IT'S ONLY NATURAL THAT THEY TAKE GOOD CARE OF ONE ANOTHER, YOU KNOW.
WELL, IF IT MAKES YOU JEALOUS, I MEAN, I THINK IT WOULD BE FINE FOR EVERYONE TO HANG ALL OVER EACH OTHER...
MOKU (MUNCH)
AS IF!
I AIN'T JEALOUS EVEN A LITTLE BIT!!
OH, I GET IT! THEN I SHALL HANG ALL OVER KUROTO TOO!
DON'T HARDEN YOUR RESOLVE FOR SOMETHING WEIRD LIKE THAT, SEN-SHIROU!!

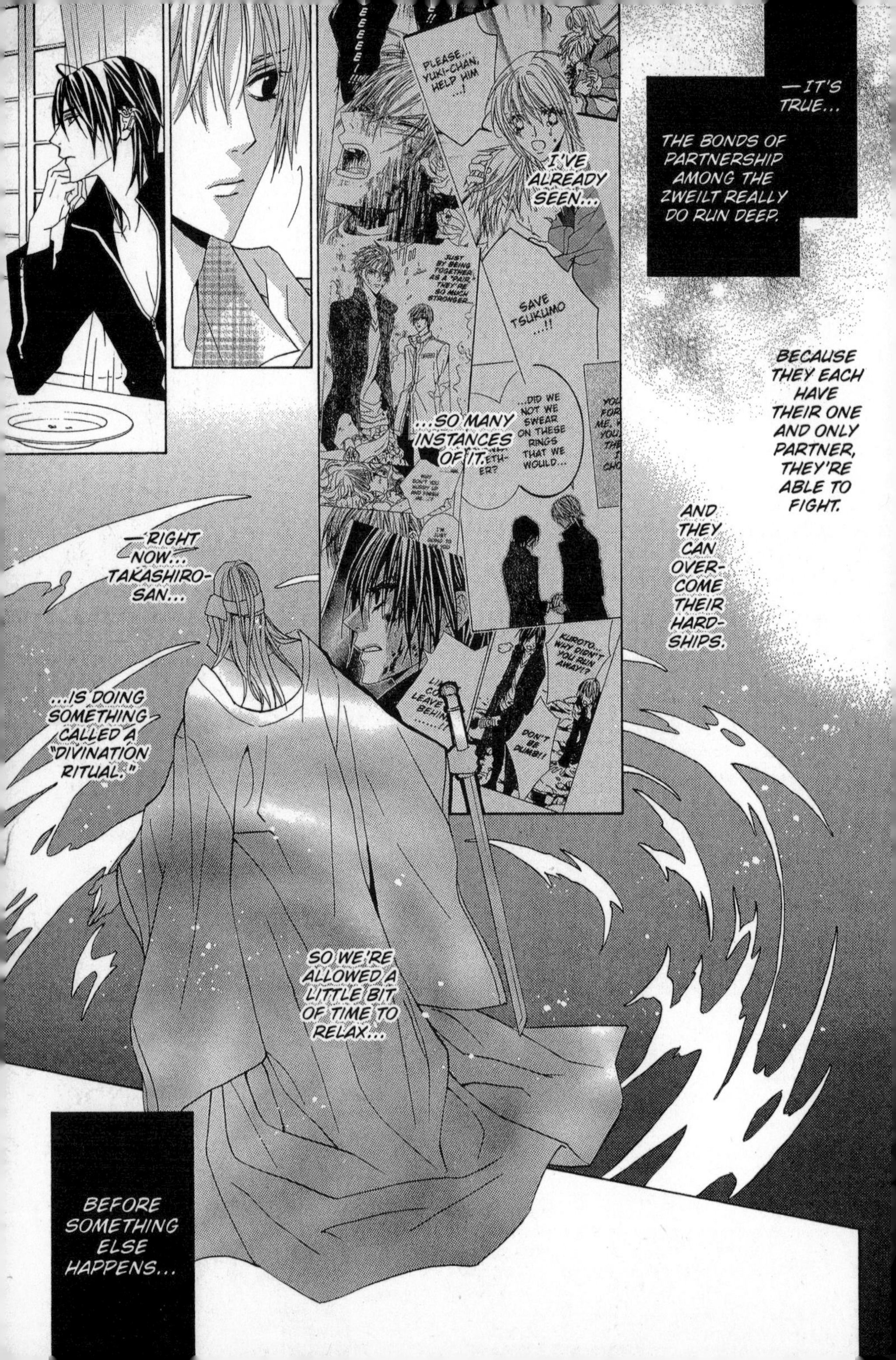
—IT'S TRUE…
THE BONDS OF PARTNERSHIP AMONG THE ZWEILT REALLY DO RUN DEEP.
BECAUSE THEY EACH HAVE THEIR ONE AND ONLY PARTNER, THEY'RE ABLE TO FIGHT.
AND THEY CAN OVERCOME THEIR HARDSHIPS.
PLEASE… YUKI-CHAN, HELP HIM …!
I'VE ALREADY SEEN…
SAVE TSUKUMO …!!
JUST BY BEING TOGETHER AS A "PAIR," THEY'RE SO MUCH STRONGER…
…DID WE NOT WE SWEAR ON THESE RINGS THAT WE WOULD…
…SO MANY INSTANCES OF IT.
KUROTO… WHY DIDN'T YOU RUN AWAY!?
DON'T BE DUMB!!
—RIGHT NOW… TAKASHIRO-SAN…
…IS DOING SOMETHING CALLED A "DIVINATION RITUAL."
SO WE'RE ALLOWED A LITTLE BIT OF TIME TO RELAX…
BEFORE SOMETHING ELSE HAPPENS…

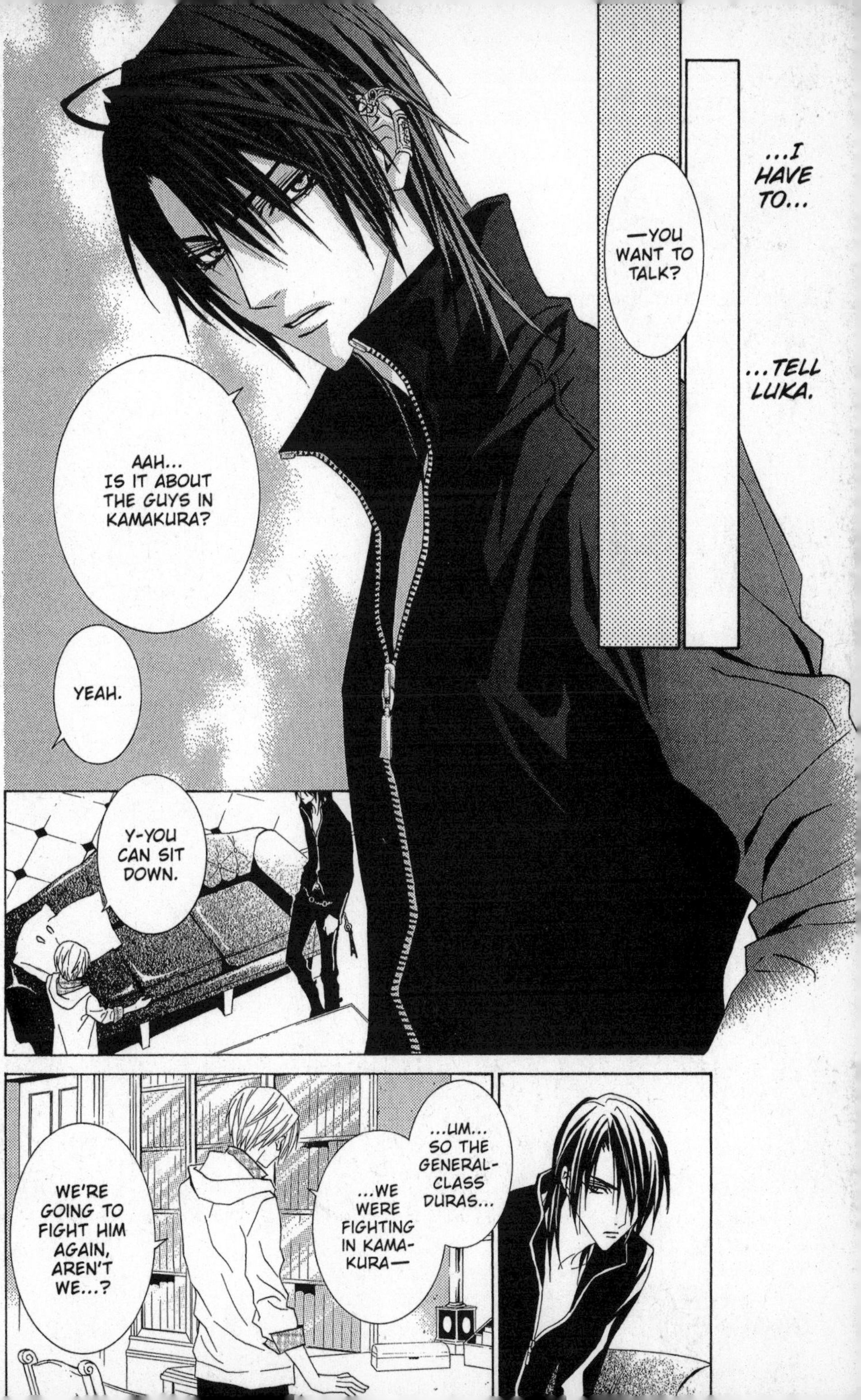
...I HAVE TO...
...TELL LUKA.
—YOU WANT TO TALK?
AAH... IS IT ABOUT THE GUYS IN KAMAKURA?
YEAH.
Y-YOU CAN SIT DOWN.
...UM... SO THE GENERAL-CLASS DURAS...
...WE WERE FIGHTING IN KAMA-KURA—
WE'RE GOING TO FIGHT HIM AGAIN, AREN'T WE...?

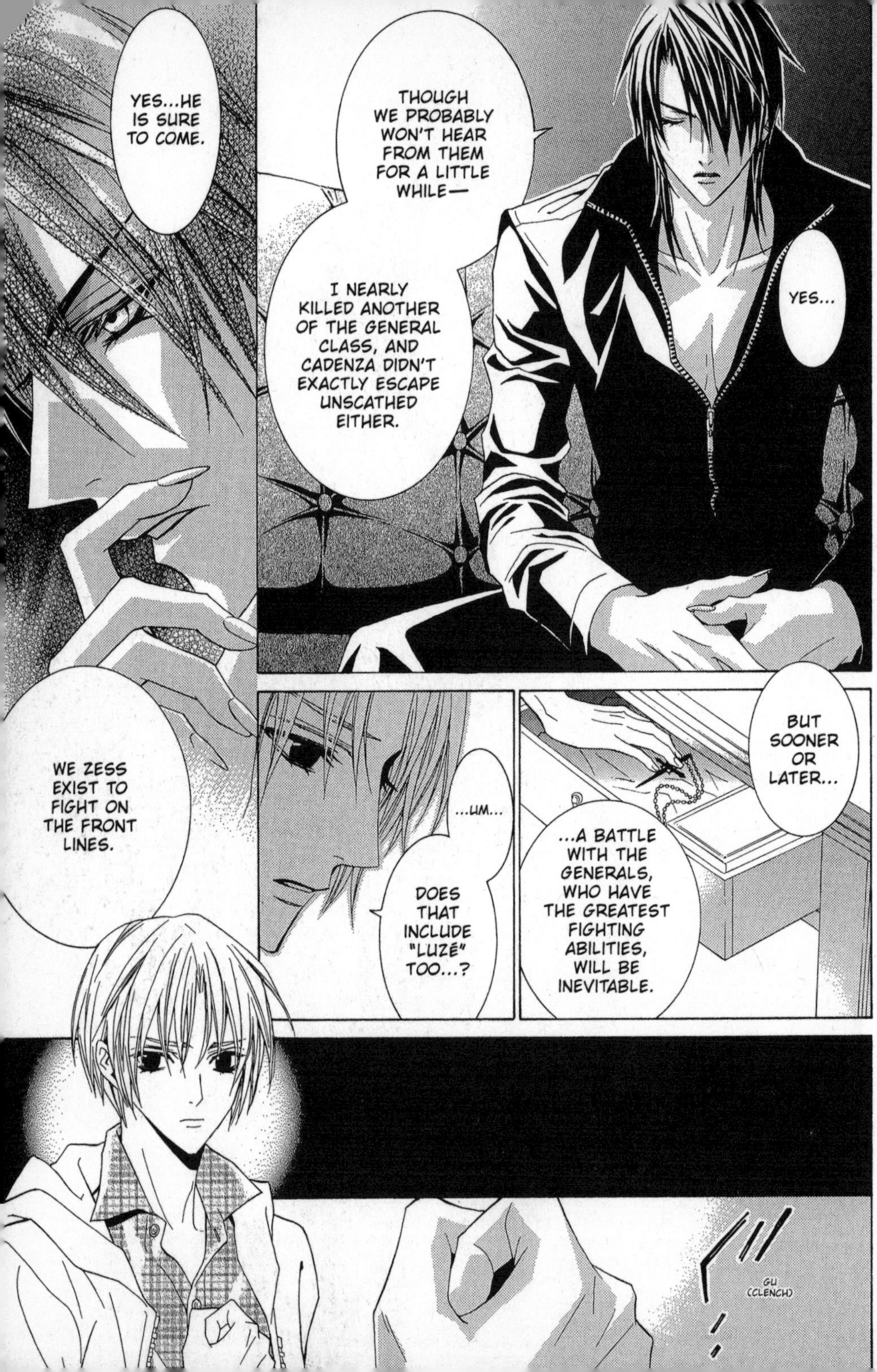
THOUGH WE PROBABLY WON'T HEAR FROM THEM FOR A LITTLE WHILE—
I NEARLY KILLED ANOTHER OF THE GENERAL CLASS, AND CADENZA DIDN'T EXACTLY ESCAPE UNSCATHED EITHER.
YES...
BUT SOONER OR LATER...
...A BATTLE WITH THE GENERALS, WHO HAVE THE GREATEST FIGHTING ABILITIES, WILL BE INEVITABLE.
...UM...
DOES THAT INCLUDE "LUZÉ" TOO...?
YES...HE IS SURE TO COME.
WE ZESS EXIST TO FIGHT ON THE FRONT LINES.
GU (CLENCH)

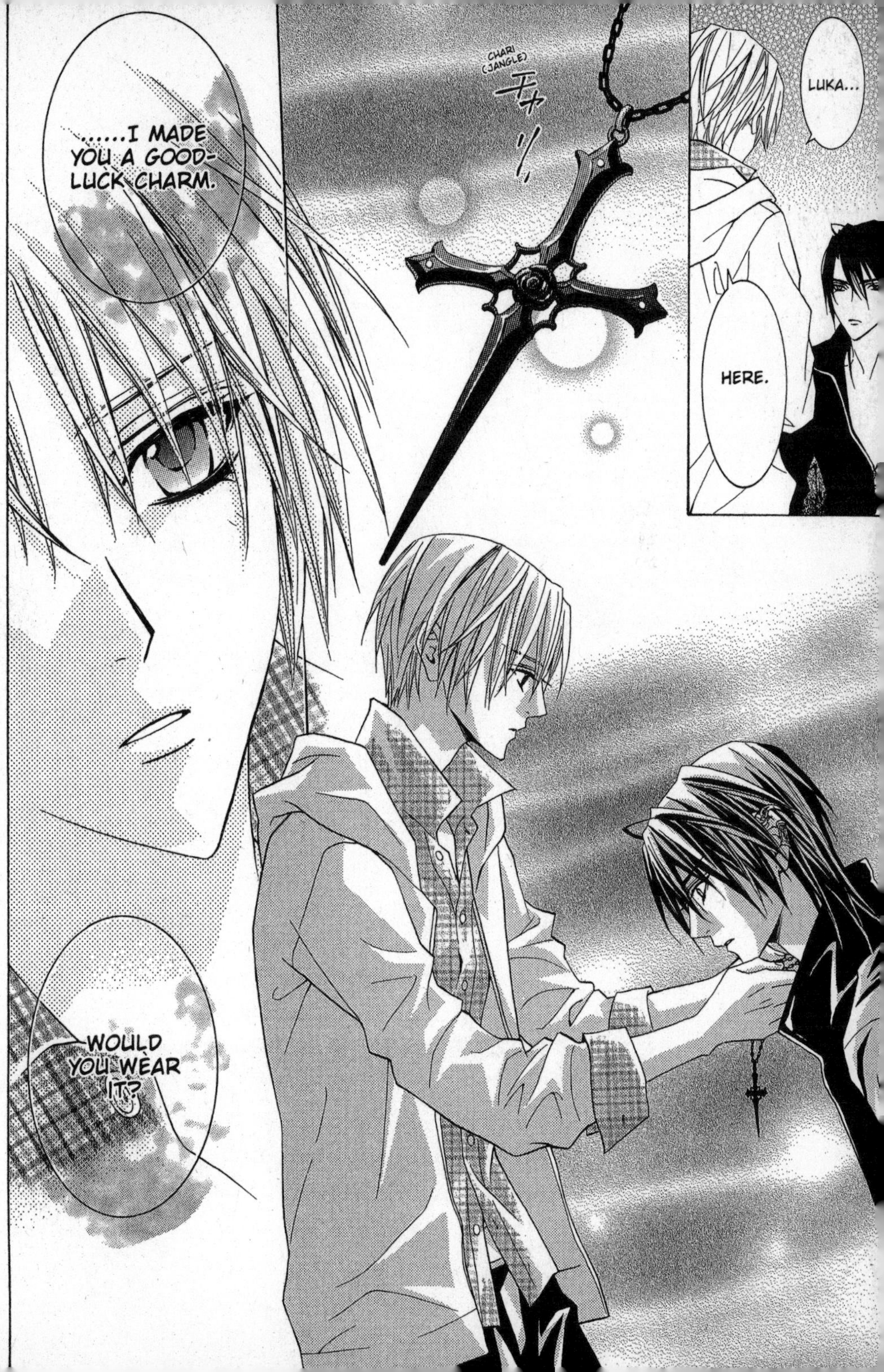
LUKA...
HERE.
CHARI (JANGLE)
チャリ
......I MADE YOU A GOOD-LUCK CHARM.
WOULD YOU WEAR IT?

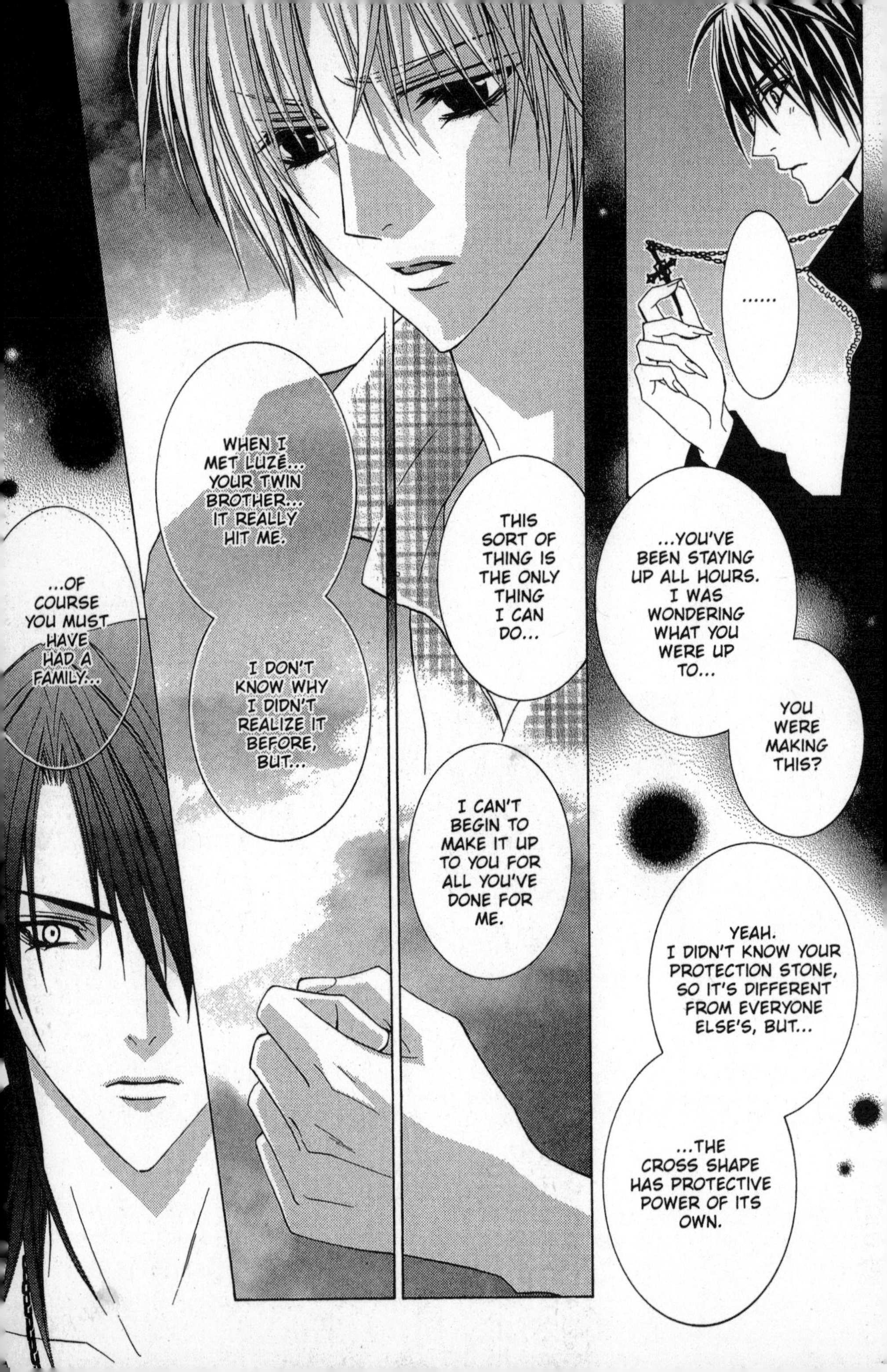
......
...YOU'VE BEEN STAYING UP ALL HOURS. I WAS WONDERING WHAT YOU WERE UP TO...
YOU WERE MAKING THIS?
YEAH. I DIDN'T KNOW YOUR PROTECTION STONE, SO IT'S DIFFERENT FROM EVERYONE ELSE'S, BUT...
...THE CROSS SHAPE HAS PROTECTIVE POWER OF ITS OWN.
THIS SORT OF THING IS THE ONLY THING I CAN DO...
I CAN'T BEGIN TO MAKE IT UP TO YOU FOR ALL YOU'VE DONE FOR ME.
WHEN I MET LUZÉ... YOUR TWIN BROTHER... IT REALLY HIT ME.
I DON'T KNOW WHY I DIDN'T REALIZE IT BEFORE, BUT...
...OF COURSE YOU MUST HAVE HAD A FAMILY...

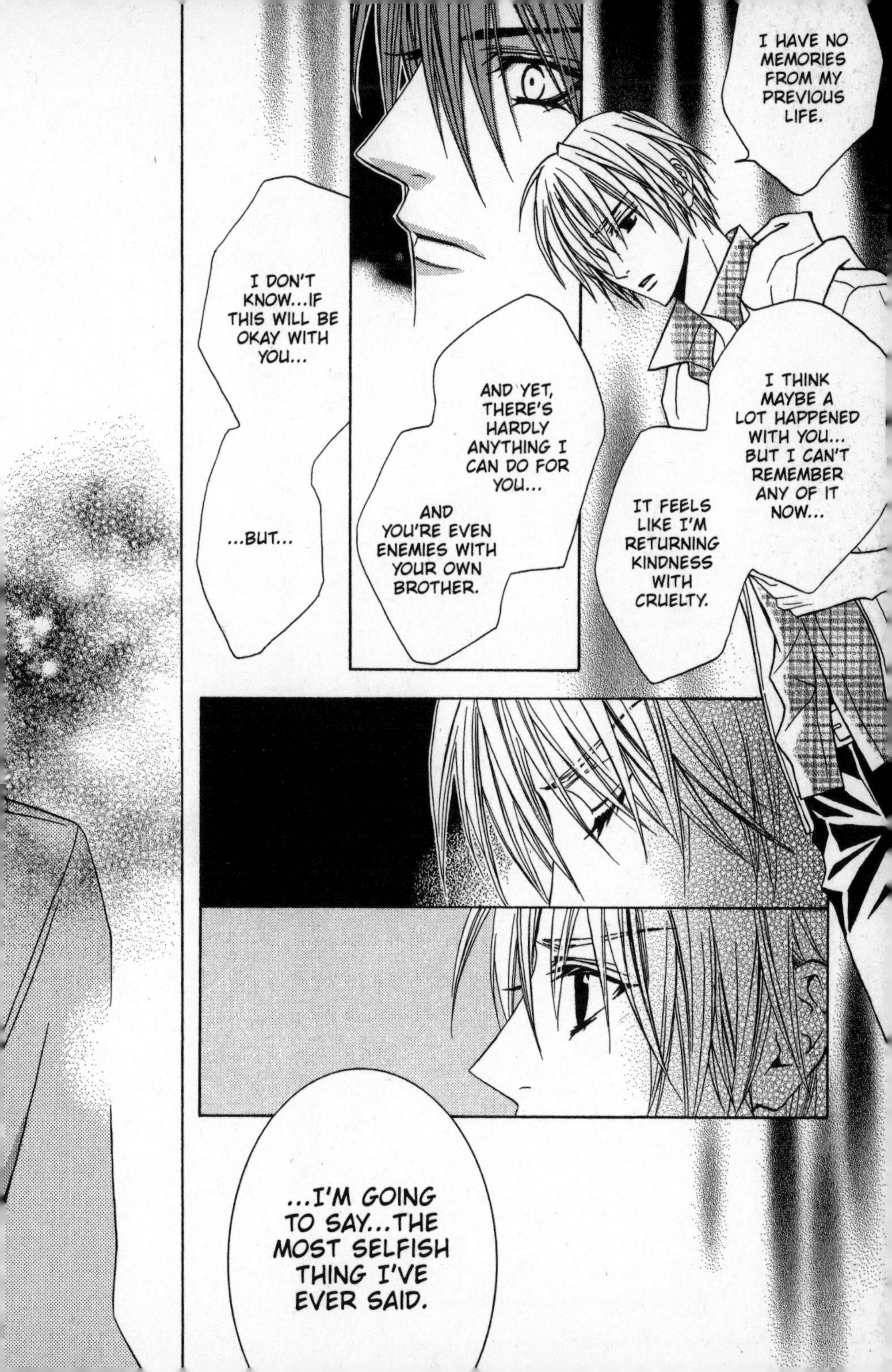
I HAVE NO MEMORIES FROM MY PREVIOUS LIFE.
I THINK MAYBE A LOT HAPPENED WITH YOU... BUT I CAN'T REMEMBER ANY OF IT NOW...
IT FEELS LIKE I'M RETURNING KINDNESS WITH CRUELTY.
AND YET, THERE'S HARDLY ANYTHING I CAN DO FOR YOU...
AND YOU'RE EVEN ENEMIES WITH YOUR OWN BROTHER.
I DON'T KNOW...IF THIS WILL BE OKAY WITH YOU...
...BUT...
...I'M GOING TO SAY...THE MOST SELFISH THING I'VE EVER SAID.

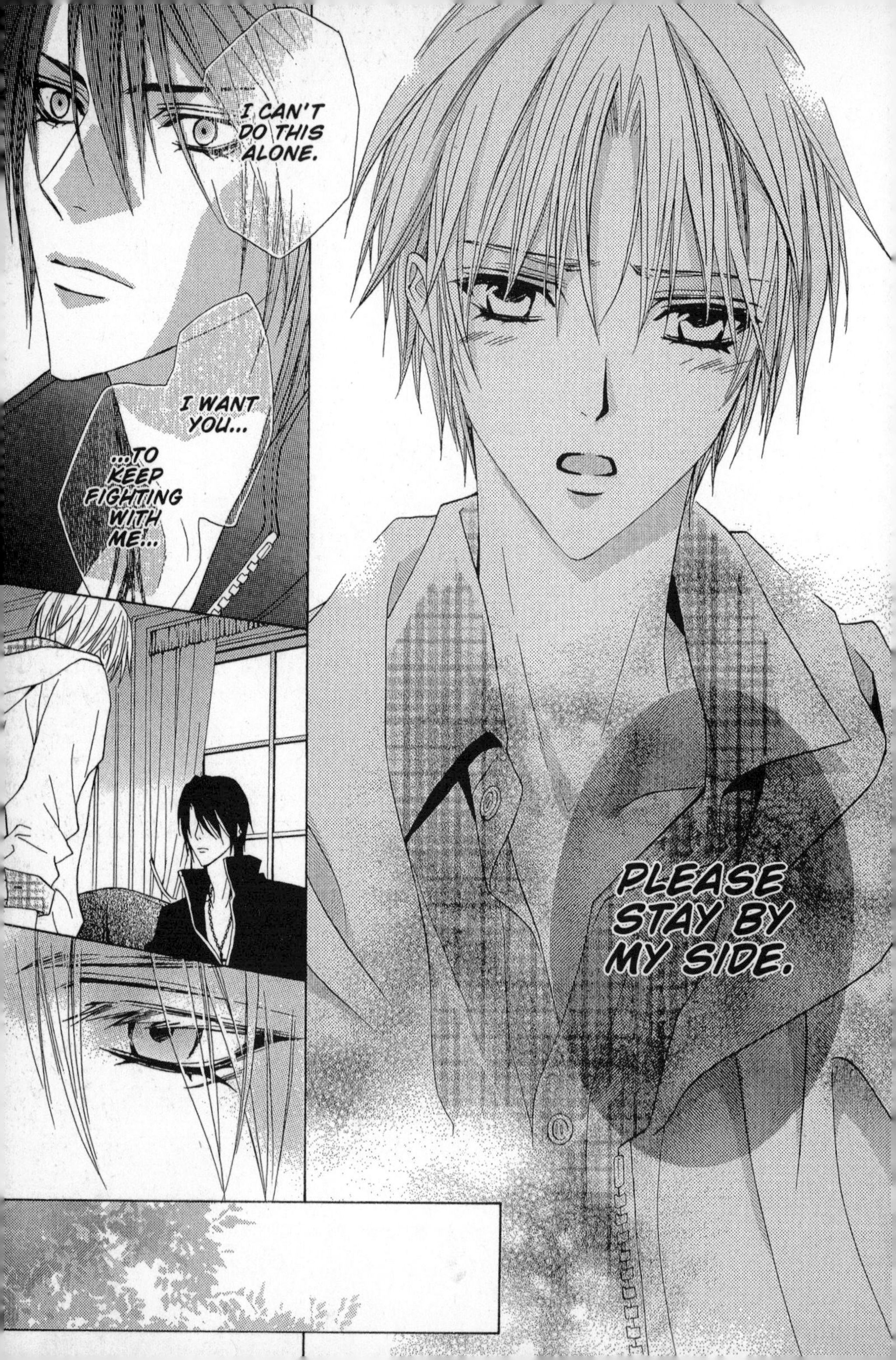
PLEASE STAY BY MY SIDE.
I CAN'T DO THIS ALONE.
I WANT YOU...
...TO KEEP FIGHTING WITH ME...

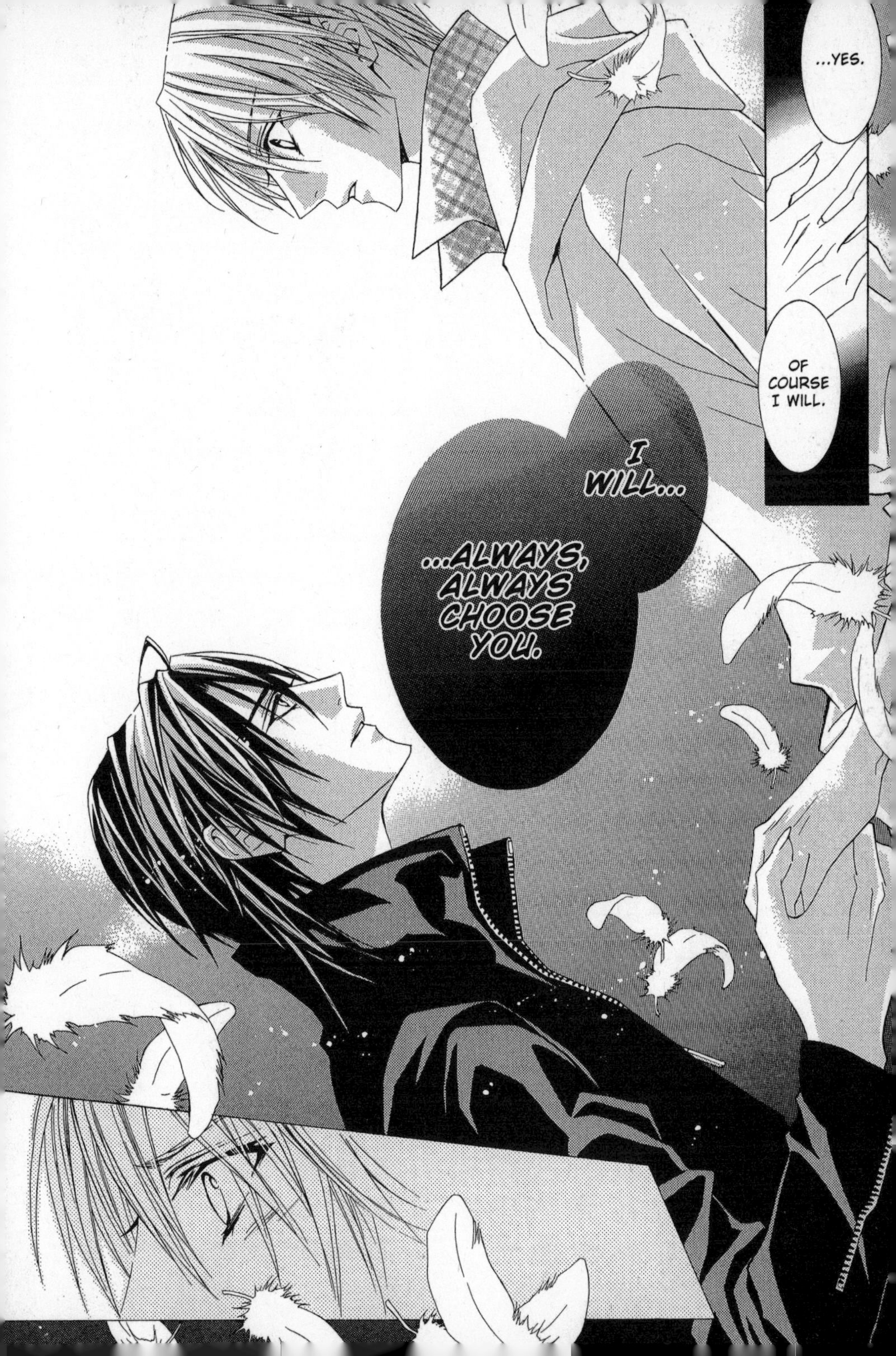
...YES.
OF COURSE I WILL.
I WILL...
...ALWAYS, ALWAYS CHOOSE YOU.

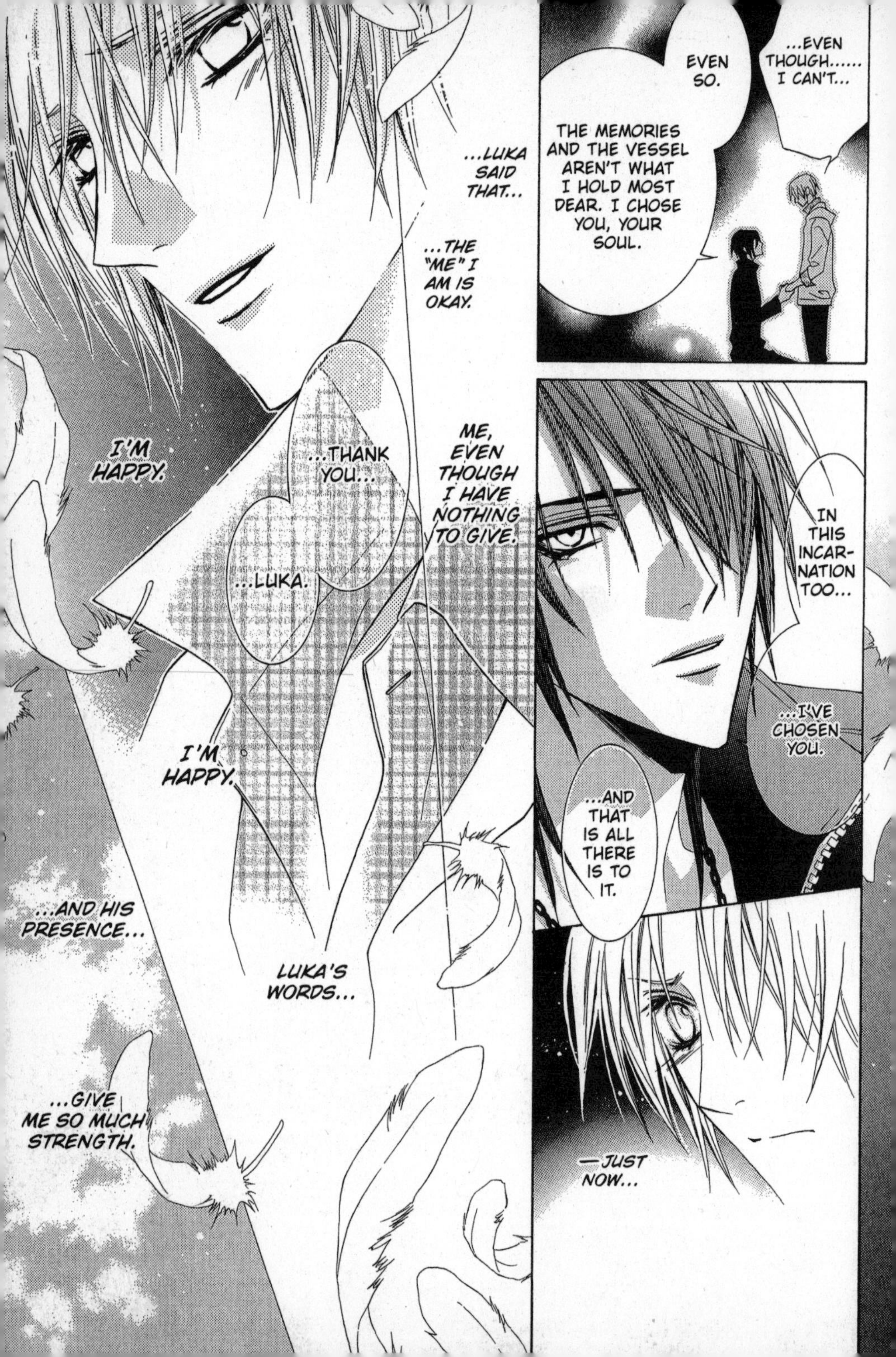
...EVEN THOUGH...... I CAN'T...
EVEN SO.
THE MEMORIES AND THE VESSEL AREN'T WHAT I HOLD MOST DEAR. I CHOSE YOU, YOUR SOUL.
IN THIS INCARNATION TOO...
...I'VE CHOSEN YOU.
...AND THAT IS ALL THERE IS TO IT.
—JUST NOW...
...LUKA SAID THAT...
...THE "ME" I AM IS OKAY.
ME, EVEN THOUGH I HAVE NOTHING TO GIVE.
...THANK YOU...
...LUKA.
I'M HAPPY.
I'M HAPPY.
LUKA'S WORDS...
...AND HIS PRESENCE...
...GIVE ME SO MUCH STRENGTH.

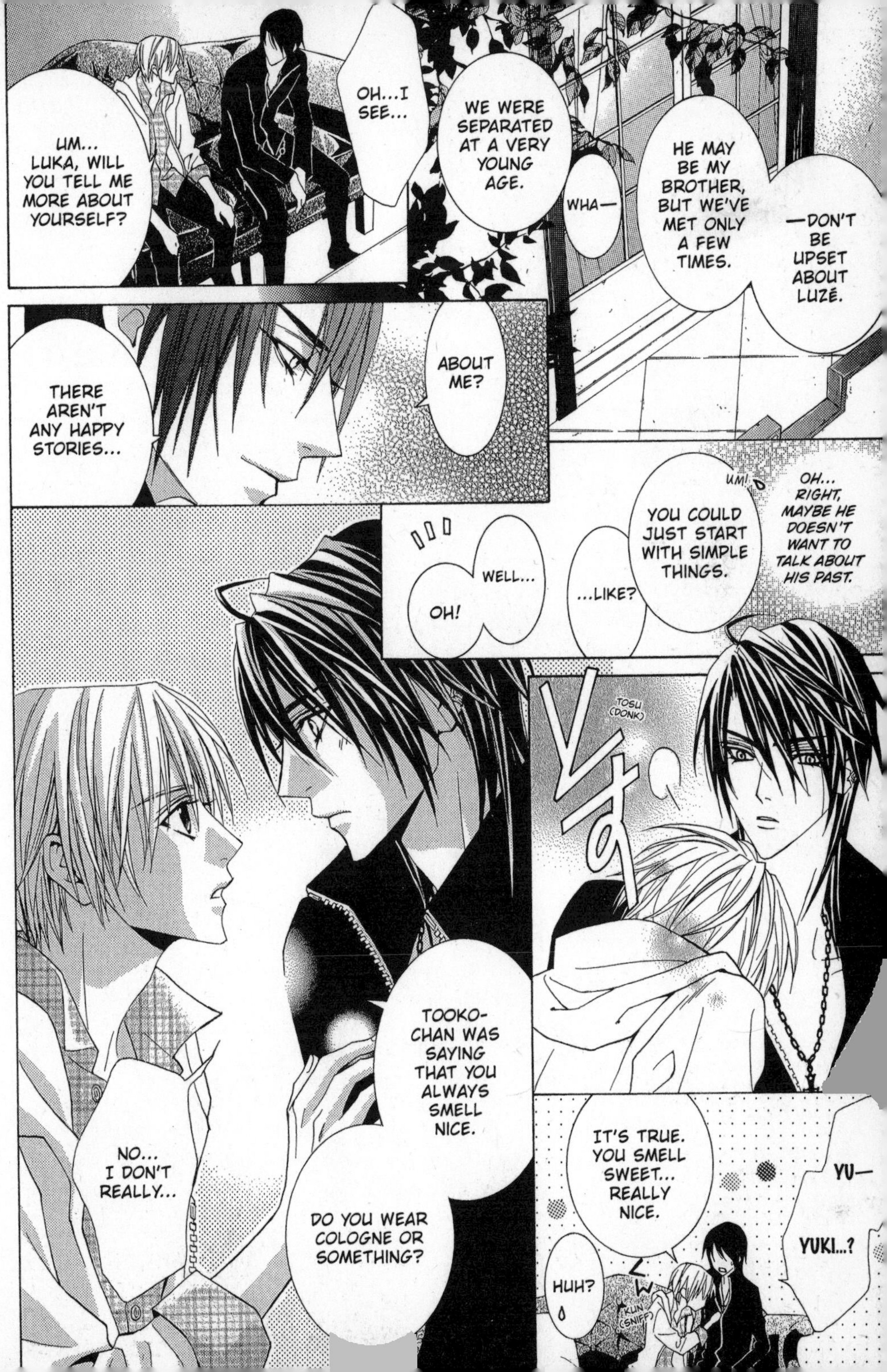
HE MAY BE MY BROTHER, BUT WE'VE MET ONLY A FEW TIMES.
—DON'T BE UPSET ABOUT LUZÉ.
WHA—
WE WERE SEPARATED AT A VERY YOUNG AGE.
OH...I SEE...
UM... LUKA, WILL YOU TELL ME MORE ABOUT YOURSELF?
ABOUT ME?
THERE AREN'T ANY HAPPY STORIES...
OH... RIGHT, MAYBE HE DOESN'T WANT TO TALK ABOUT HIS PAST.
UM!
YOU COULD JUST START WITH SIMPLE THINGS.
...LIKE?
WELL...
OH!
TOOKO-CHAN WAS SAYING THAT YOU ALWAYS SMELL NICE.
DO YOU WEAR COLOGNE OR SOMETHING?
NO... I DON'T REALLY...
TOSU (DONK)
YU—
YUKI...?
IT'S TRUE. YOU SMELL SWEET... REALLY NICE.
HUH?
KUN (SNIFF)

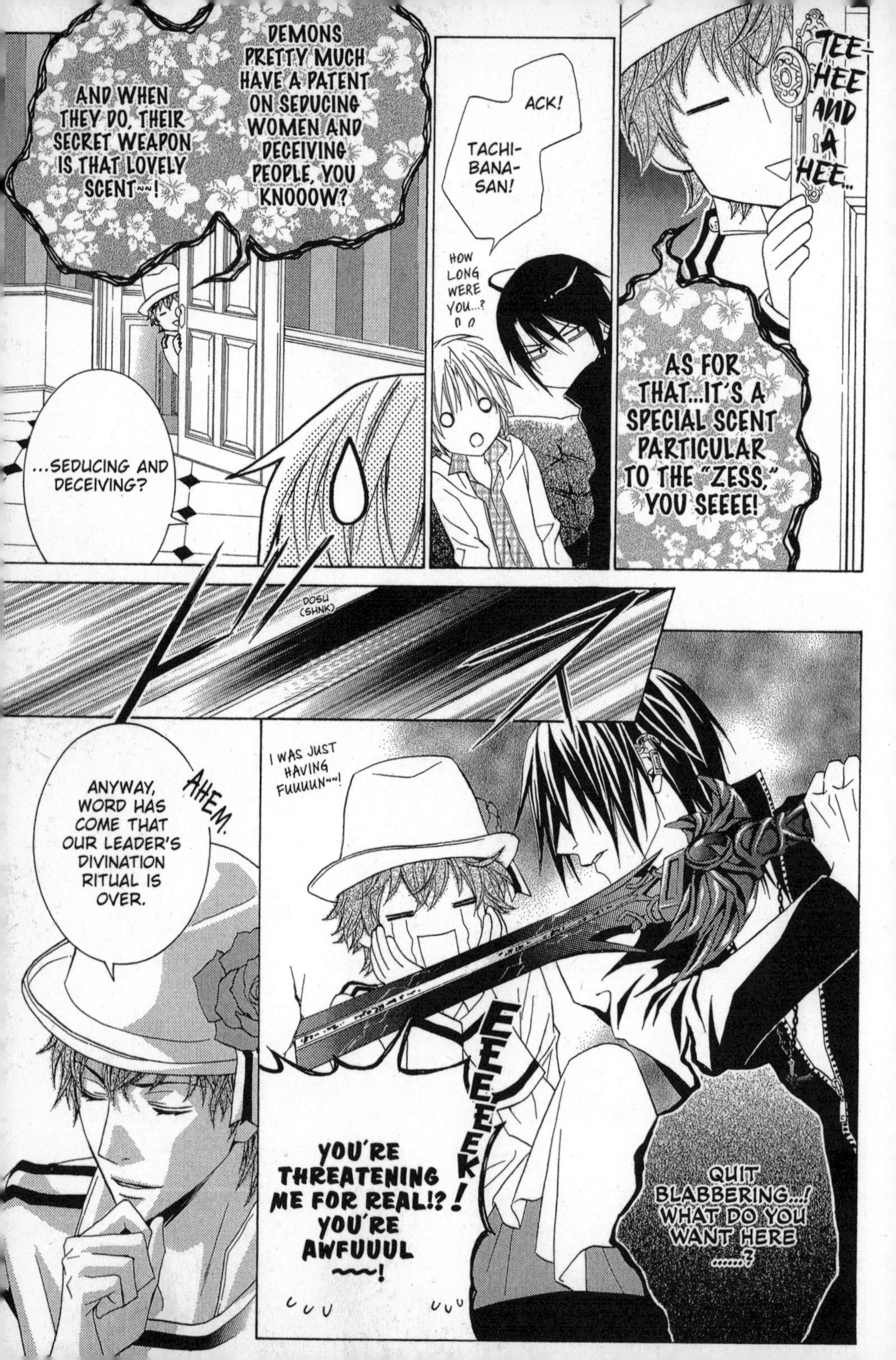
TEE-HEE AND A HEE...
AS FOR THAT...IT'S A SPECIAL SCENT PARTICULAR TO THE "ZESS," YOU SEEEE!
ACK!
TACHI-BANA-SAN!
HOW LONG WERE YOU...?
DEMONS PRETTY MUCH HAVE A PATENT ON SEDUCING WOMEN AND DECEIVING PEOPLE, YOU KNOOOW?
AND WHEN THEY DO, THEIR SECRET WEAPON IS THAT LOVELY SCENT~~!
...SEDUCING AND DECEIVING?
DOSU (SHNK)
QUIT BLABBERING...! WHAT DO YOU WANT HERE ......?
I WAS JUST HAVING FUUUUN~~!
EEEEEEK!
YOU'RE THREATENING ME FOR REAL!? YOU'RE AWFUUUL ~~~!
AHEM.
ANYWAY, WORD HAS COME THAT OUR LEADER'S DIVINATION RITUAL IS OVER.

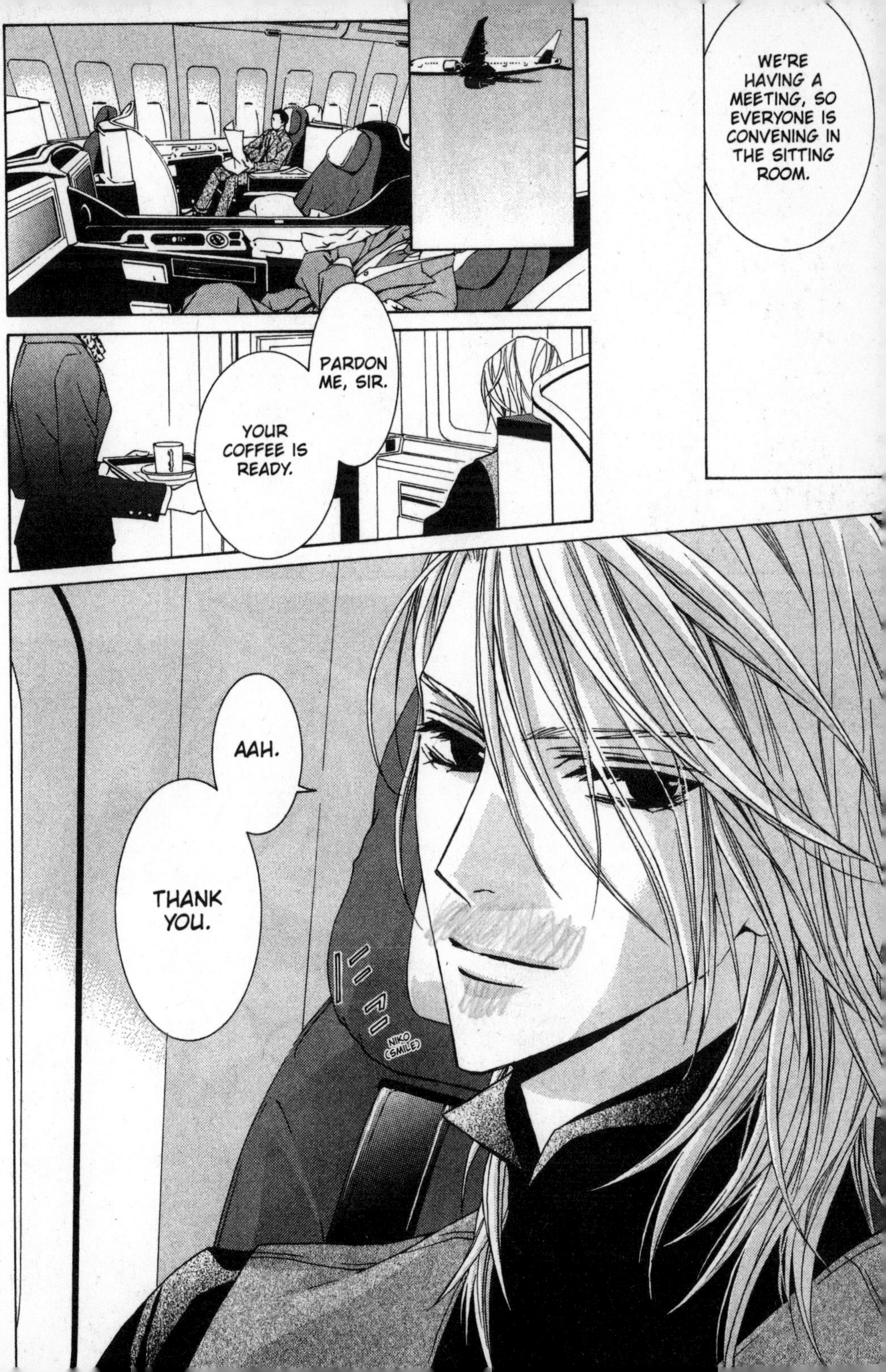
WE'RE HAVING A MEETING, SO EVERYONE IS CONVENING IN THE SITTING ROOM.
PARDON ME, SIR.
YOUR COFFEE IS READY.
AAH.
THANK YOU.
NIKO (SMILE)

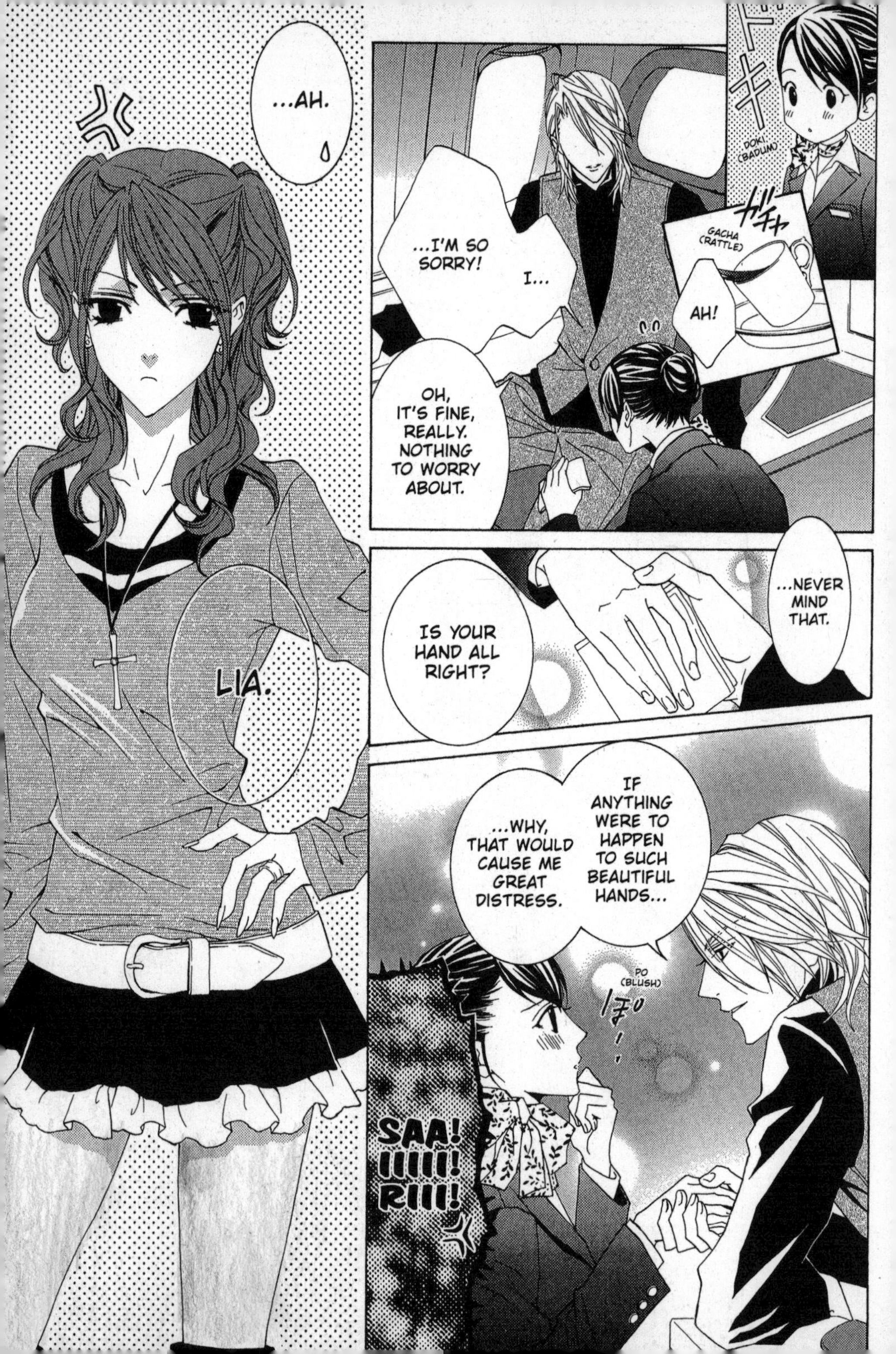
DOKI (BADUM)
GACHA (RATTLE)
AH!
...I'M SO SORRY!
I...
OH, IT'S FINE, REALLY. NOTHING TO WORRY ABOUT.
...NEVER MIND THAT.
IS YOUR HAND ALL RIGHT?
IF ANYTHING WERE TO HAPPEN TO SUCH BEAUTIFUL HANDS...
...WHY, THAT WOULD CAUSE ME GREAT DISTRESS.
PO (BLUSH)
SAA! IIIII! RIII!
...AH.
LIA.

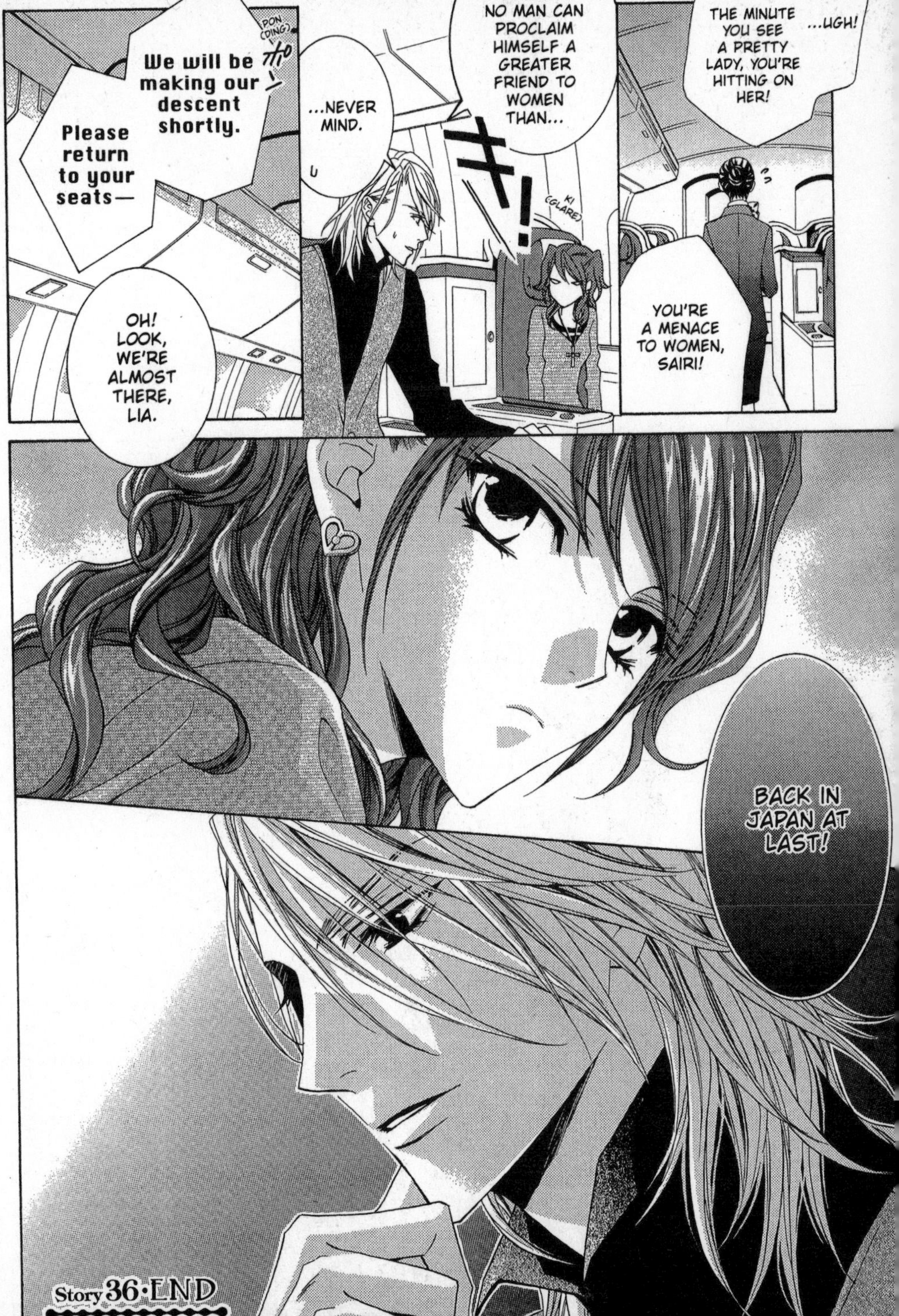
...UGH!
THE MINUTE YOU SEE A PRETTY LADY, YOU'RE HITTING ON HER!
YOU'RE A MENACE TO WOMEN, SAIRI!
THAT'S RIDICULOUS. NO MAN CAN PROCLAIM HIMSELF A GREATER FRIEND TO WOMEN THAN...
KI (GLARE)
...NEVER MIND.
PON (DING)
We will be making our descent shortly.
Please return to your seats—
OH! LOOK, WE'RE ALMOST THERE, LIA.
BACK IN JAPAN AT LAST!

Story 36・END

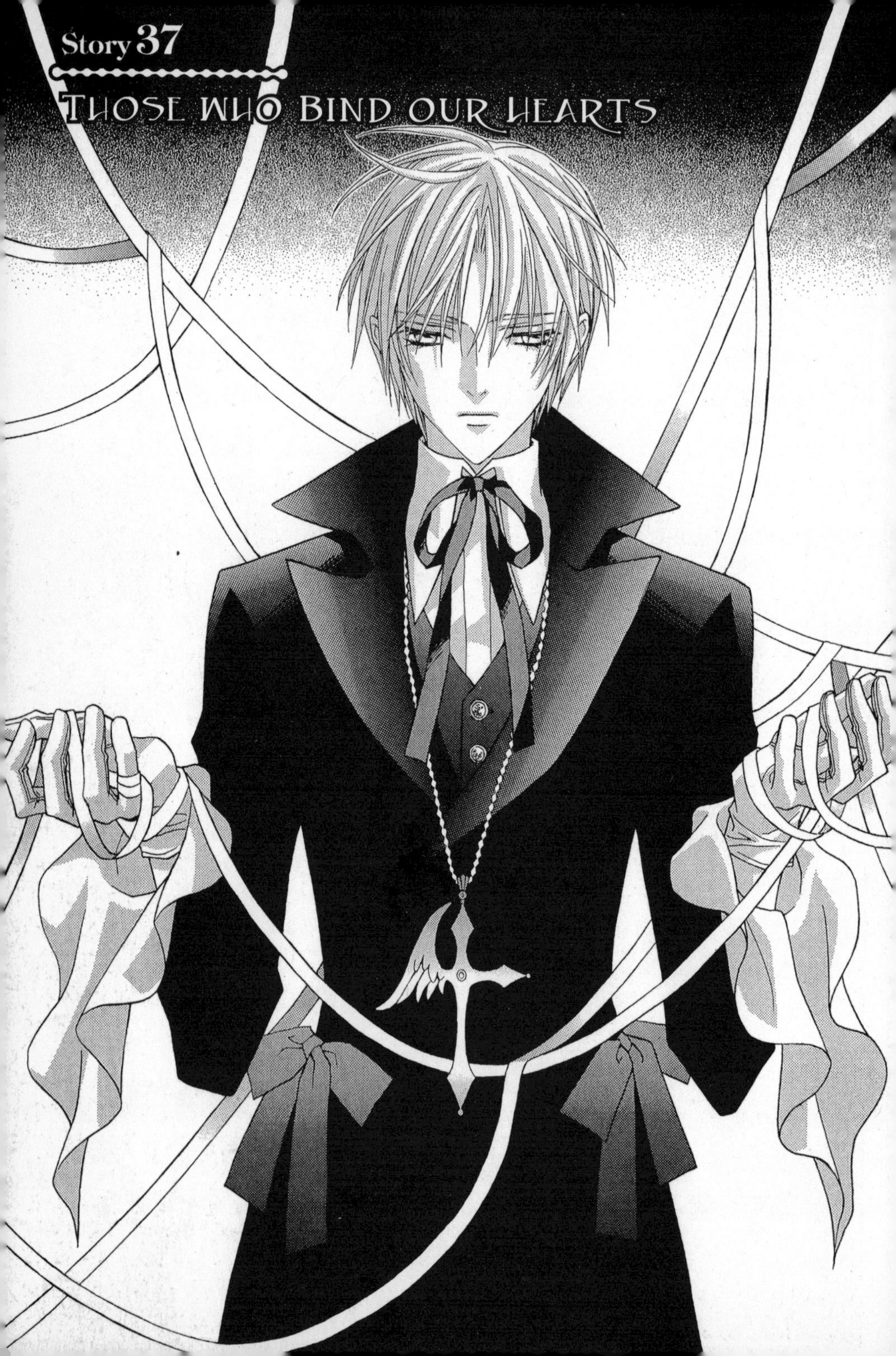
Story 37
Those Who Bind Our Hearts

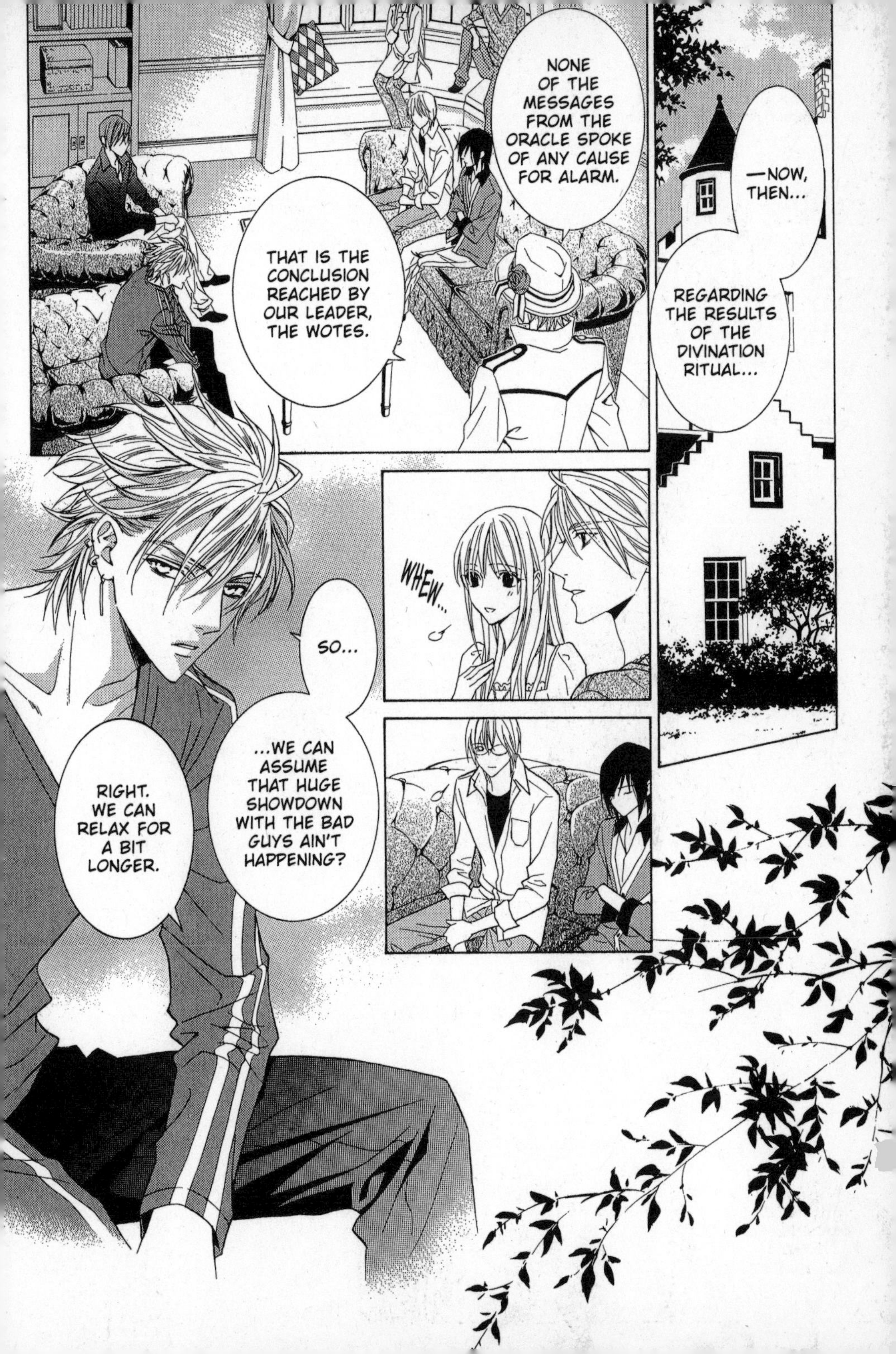

—NOW, THEN...
REGARDING THE RESULTS OF THE DIVINATION RITUAL...
NONE OF THE MESSAGES FROM THE ORACLE SPOKE OF ANY CAUSE FOR ALARM.
THAT IS THE CONCLUSION REACHED BY OUR LEADER, THE WOTES.
WHEW...
SO...
...WE CAN ASSUME THAT HUGE SHOWDOWN WITH THE BAD GUYS AIN'T HAPPENING?
RIGHT. WE CAN RELAX FOR A BIT LONGER.

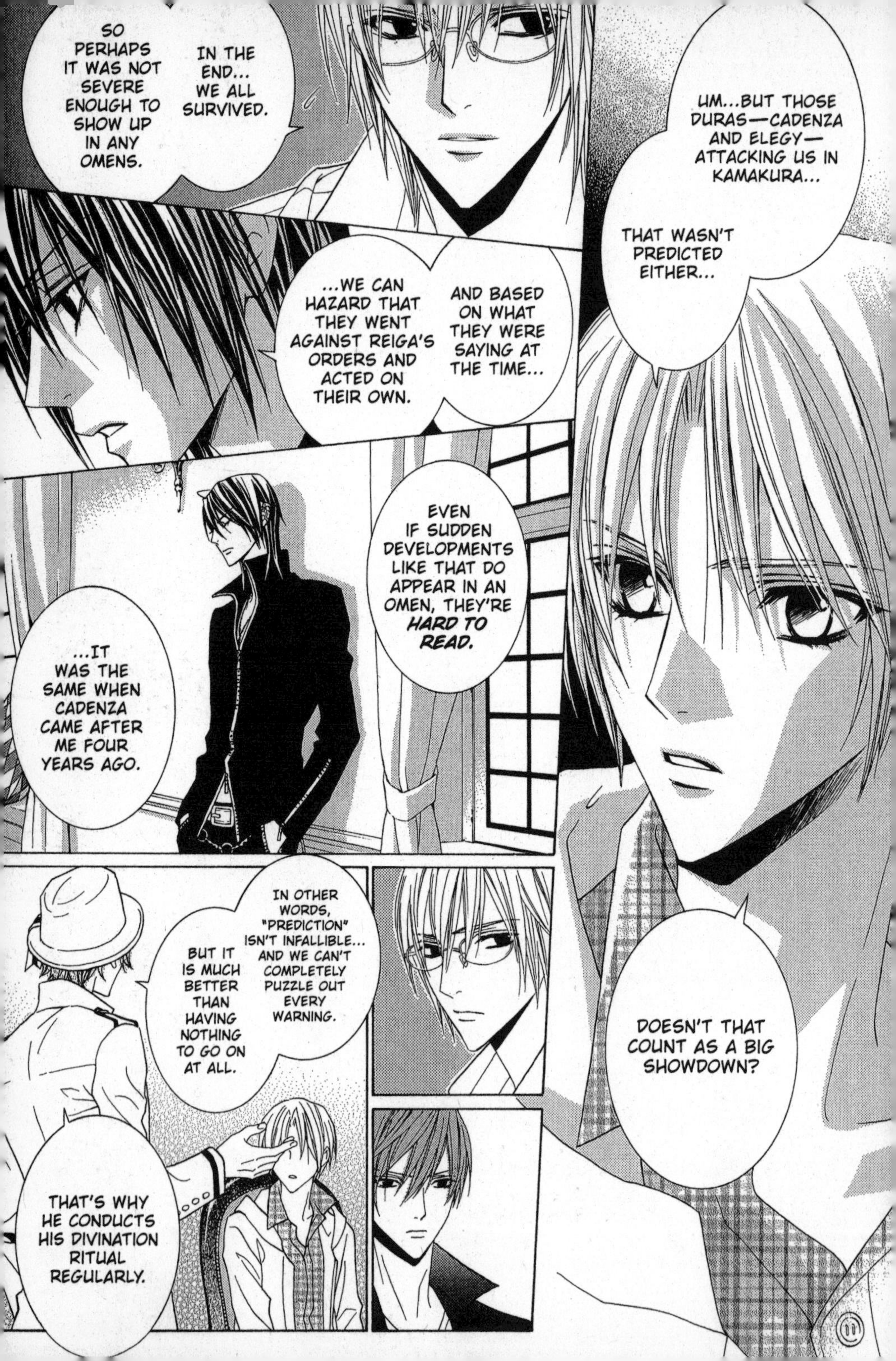
UM...BUT THOSE DURAS—CADENZA AND ELEGY—ATTACKING US IN KAMAKURA...
THAT WASN'T PREDICTED EITHER...
DOESN'T THAT COUNT AS A BIG SHOWDOWN?
IN THE END... WE ALL SURVIVED.
SO PERHAPS IT WAS NOT SEVERE ENOUGH TO SHOW UP IN ANY OMENS.
AND BASED ON WHAT THEY WERE SAYING AT THE TIME...
...WE CAN HAZARD THAT THEY WENT AGAINST REIGA'S ORDERS AND ACTED ON THEIR OWN.
EVEN IF SUDDEN DEVELOPMENTS LIKE THAT DO APPEAR IN AN OMEN, THEY'RE *HARD TO READ.*
...IT WAS THE SAME WHEN CADENZA CAME AFTER ME FOUR YEARS AGO.
IN OTHER WORDS, "PREDICTION" ISN'T INFALLIBLE... AND WE CAN'T COMPLETELY PUZZLE OUT EVERY WARNING.
BUT IT IS MUCH BETTER THAN HAVING NOTHING TO GO ON AT ALL.
THAT'S WHY HE CONDUCTS HIS DIVINATION RITUAL REGULARLY.

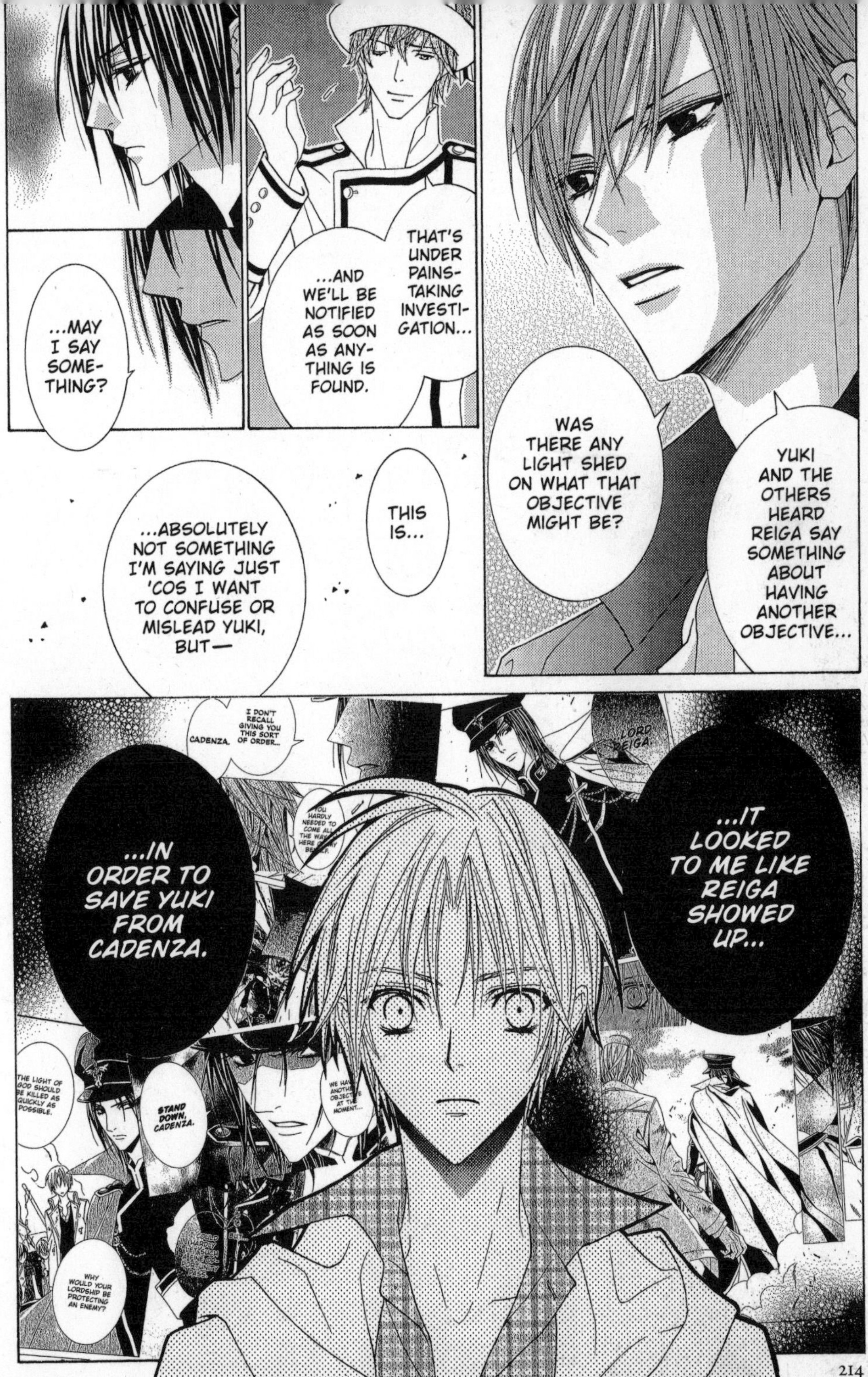
YUKI AND THE OTHERS HEARD REIGA SAY SOMETHING ABOUT HAVING ANOTHER OBJECTIVE...
WAS THERE ANY LIGHT SHED ON WHAT THAT OBJECTIVE MIGHT BE?
THAT'S UNDER PAINS-TAKING INVESTI-GATION...
...AND WE'LL BE NOTIFIED AS SOON AS ANY-THING IS FOUND.
...MAY I SAY SOME-THING?
THIS IS...
...ABSOLUTELY NOT SOMETHING I'M SAYING JUST 'COS I WANT TO CONFUSE OR MISLEAD YUKI, BUT—
...IT LOOKED TO ME LIKE REIGA SHOWED UP...
LORD REIGA.
I DON'T RECALL GIVING YOU THIS SORT OF ORDER...
CADENZA.
...IN ORDER TO SAVE YUKI FROM CADENZA.
STAND DOWN, CADENZA.
THE LIGHT OF GOD SHOULD BE KILLED AS QUICKLY AS POSSIBLE.
BUT...
I COULD HARDLY LET SUCH A FINE OP-PORTUNITY PASS.
WHY WOULD YOUR LORDSHIP BE PROTECTING AN ENEMY?

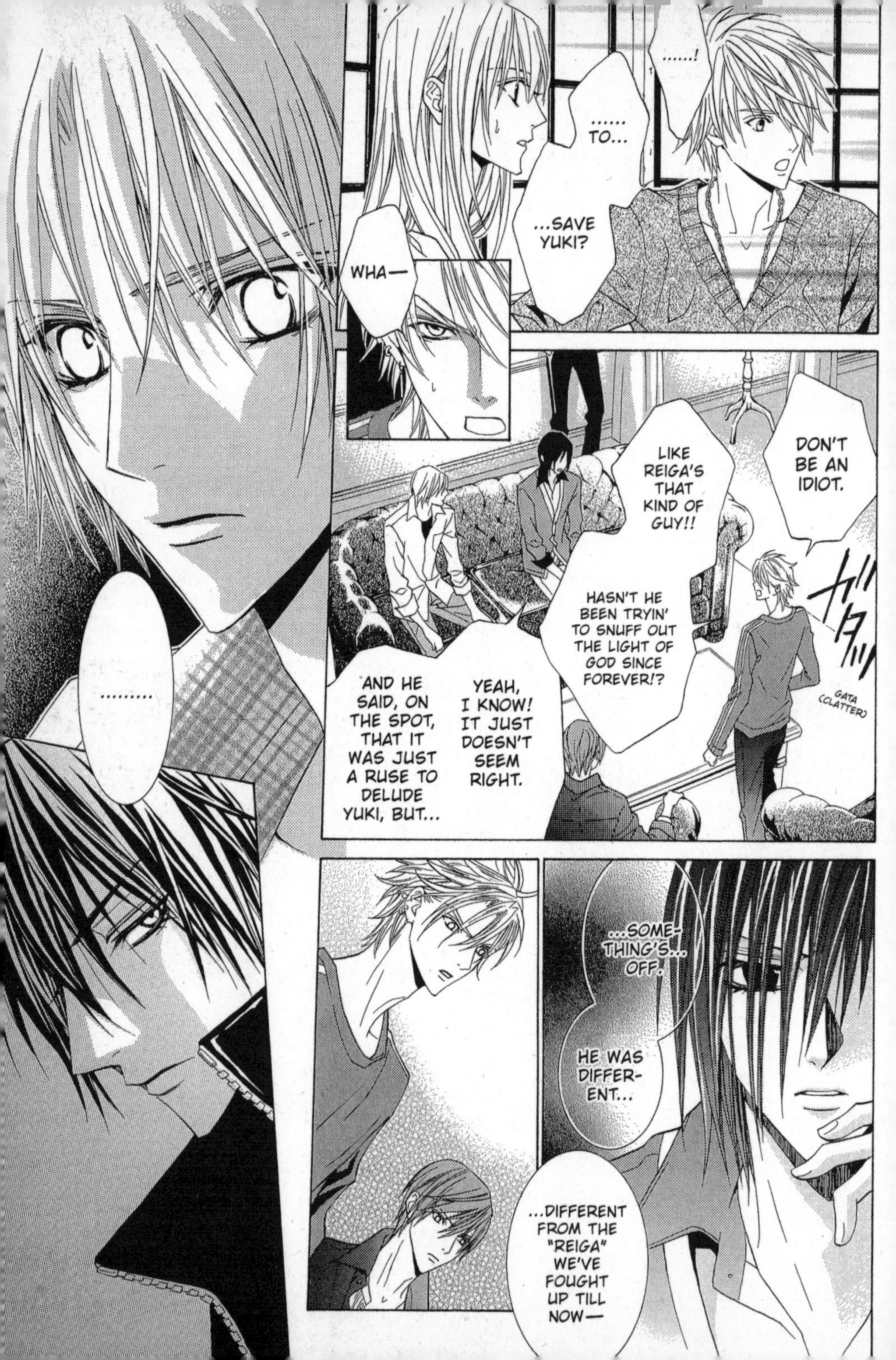
.......!
...... TO...
...SAVE YUKI?
WHA—
DON'T BE AN IDIOT.
LIKE REIGA'S THAT KIND OF GUY!!
HASN'T HE BEEN TRYIN' TO SNUFF OUT THE LIGHT OF GOD SINCE FOREVER!?
GATA (CLATTER)
YEAH, I KNOW! IT JUST DOESN'T SEEM RIGHT.
AND HE SAID, ON THE SPOT, THAT IT WAS JUST A RUSE TO DELUDE YUKI, BUT...
...SOME-THING'S... OFF.
HE WAS DIFFER-ENT...
...DIFFERENT FROM THE "REIGA" WE'VE FOUGHT UP TILL NOW—
....

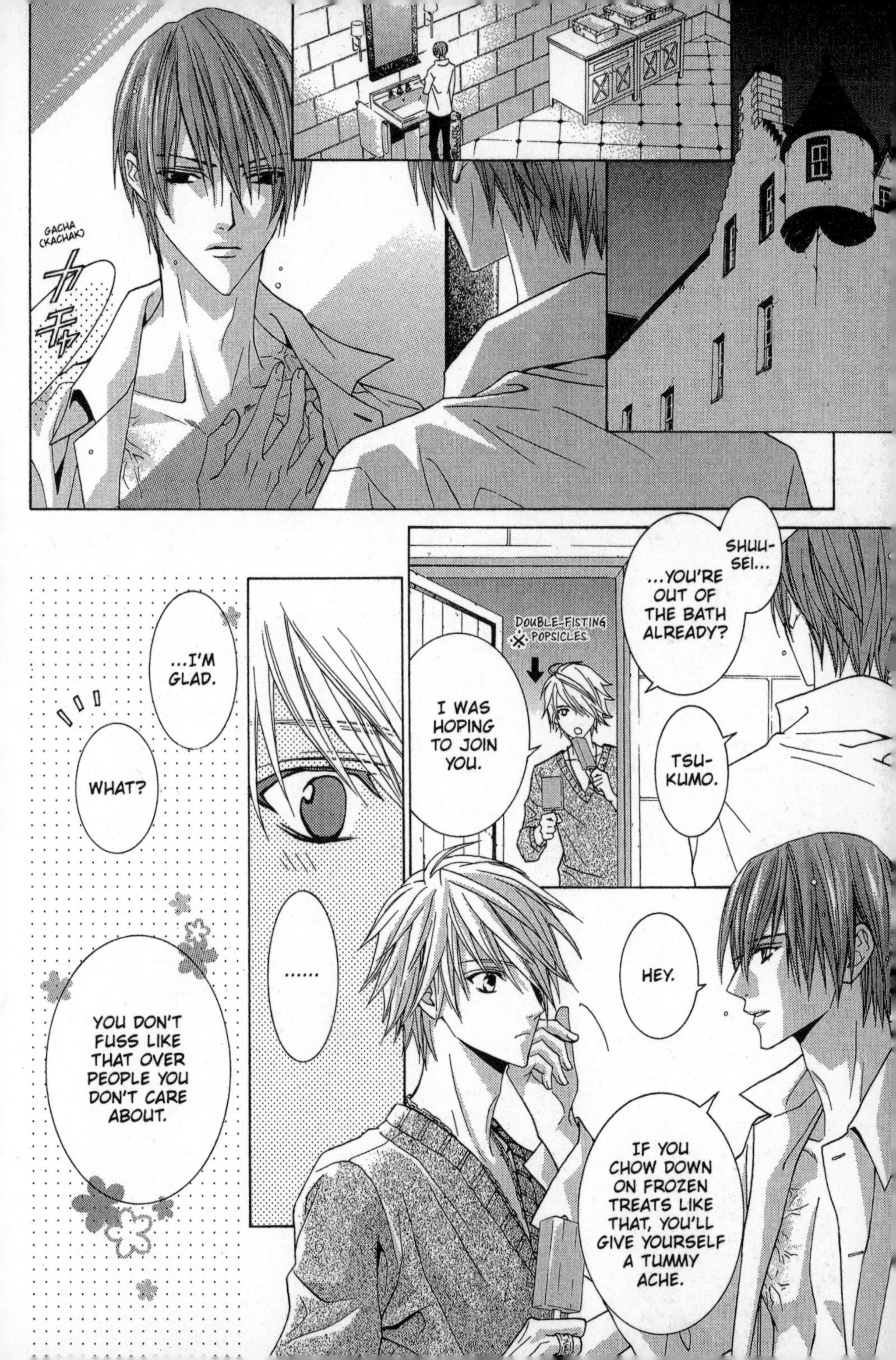

GACHA (KACHAK)
カチャ
SHUU-SEI...
...YOU'RE OUT OF THE BATH ALREADY?
TSU-KUMO.
DOUBLE-FISTING ※ POPSICLES
I WAS HOPING TO JOIN YOU.
HEY.
IF YOU CHOW DOWN ON FROZEN TREATS LIKE THAT, YOU'LL GIVE YOURSELF A TUMMY ACHE.
......
...I'M GLAD.
WHAT?
YOU DON'T FUSS LIKE THAT OVER PEOPLE YOU DON'T CARE ABOUT.

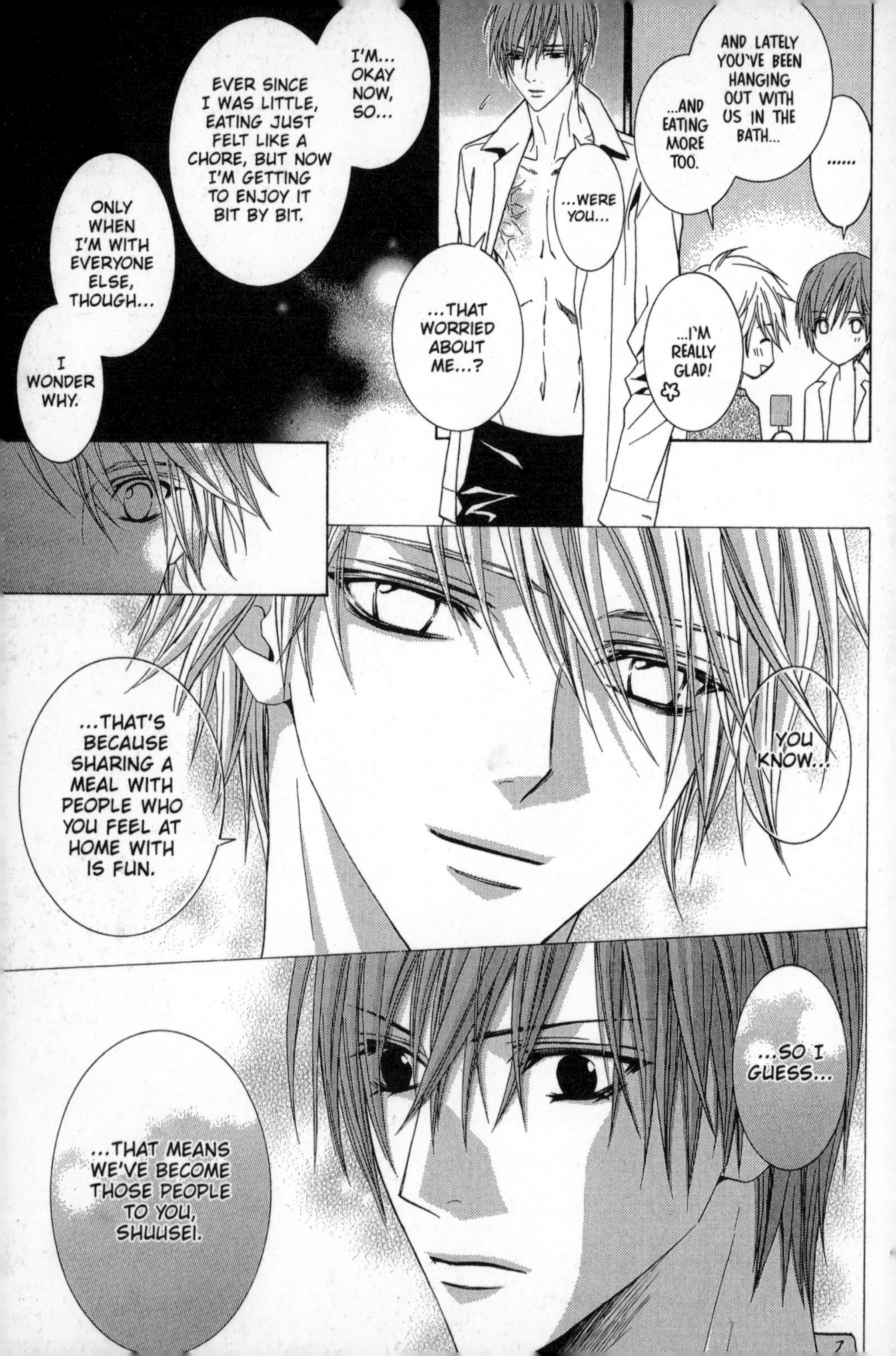
AND LATELY YOU'VE BEEN HANGING OUT WITH US IN THE BATH...
...AND EATING MORE TOO.
......
...WERE YOU...
...THAT WORRIED ABOUT ME...?
...I'M REALLY GLAD!
I'M... OKAY NOW, SO...
EVER SINCE I WAS LITTLE, EATING JUST FELT LIKE A CHORE, BUT NOW I'M GETTING TO ENJOY IT BIT BY BIT.
ONLY WHEN I'M WITH EVERYONE ELSE, THOUGH...
I WONDER WHY.
YOU KNOW...
...THAT'S BECAUSE SHARING A MEAL WITH PEOPLE WHO YOU FEEL AT HOME WITH IS FUN.
...SO I GUESS...
...THAT MEANS WE'VE BECOME THOSE PEOPLE TO YOU, SHUUSEI.

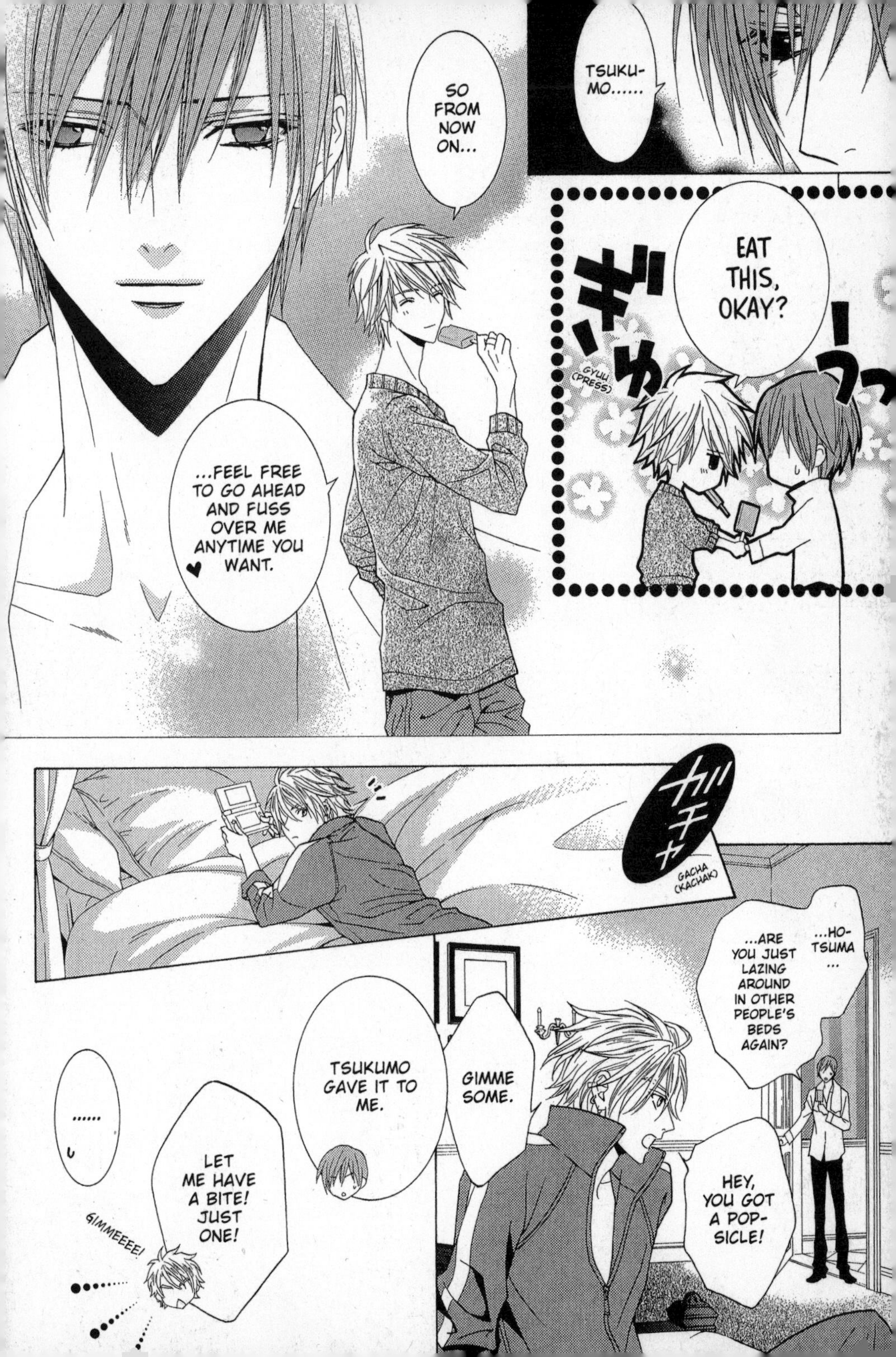
TSUKU-MO......
EAT THIS, OKAY?
ぎゅっ
GYUU (PRESS)
SO FROM NOW ON...
...FEEL FREE TO GO AHEAD AND FUSS OVER ME ANYTIME YOU WANT. ♥
カチャ
GACHA (KACHAK)
...HO-TSUMA...
...ARE YOU JUST LAZING AROUND IN OTHER PEOPLE'S BEDS AGAIN?
HEY, YOU GOT A POP-SICLE!
GIMME SOME.
TSUKUMO GAVE IT TO ME.
LET ME HAVE A BITE! JUST ONE!
GIMMEEEE!
......

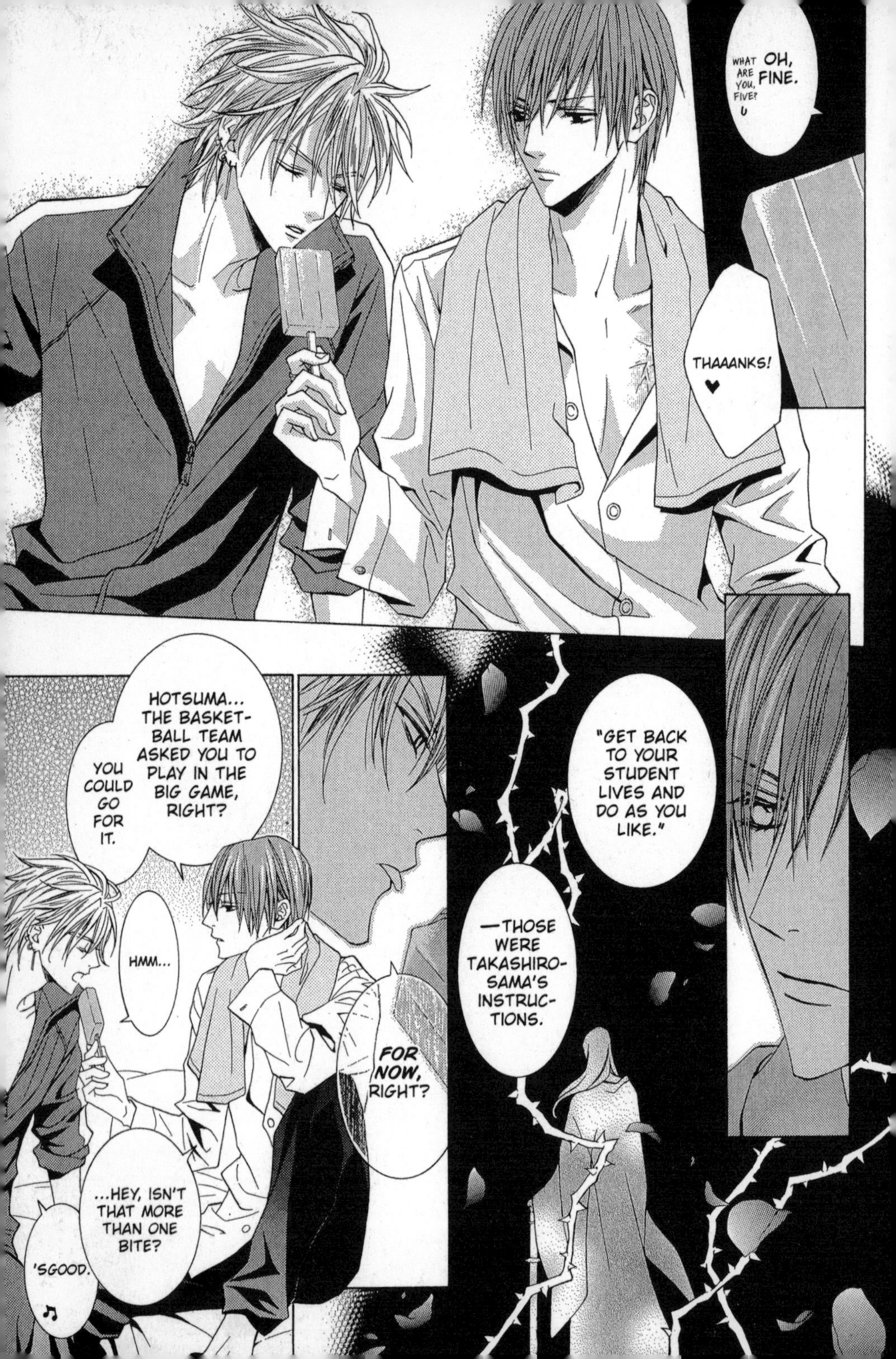
OH, FINE.
WHAT ARE YOU, FIVE?
THAAANKS! ♥
"GET BACK TO YOUR STUDENT LIVES AND DO AS YOU LIKE."
—THOSE WERE TAKASHIRO-SAMA'S INSTRUCTIONS.
FOR NOW, RIGHT?
HOTSUMA... THE BASKET-BALL TEAM ASKED YOU TO PLAY IN THE BIG GAME, RIGHT?
YOU COULD GO FOR IT.
HMM...
...HEY, ISN'T THAT MORE THAN ONE BITE?
'SGOOD. ♫

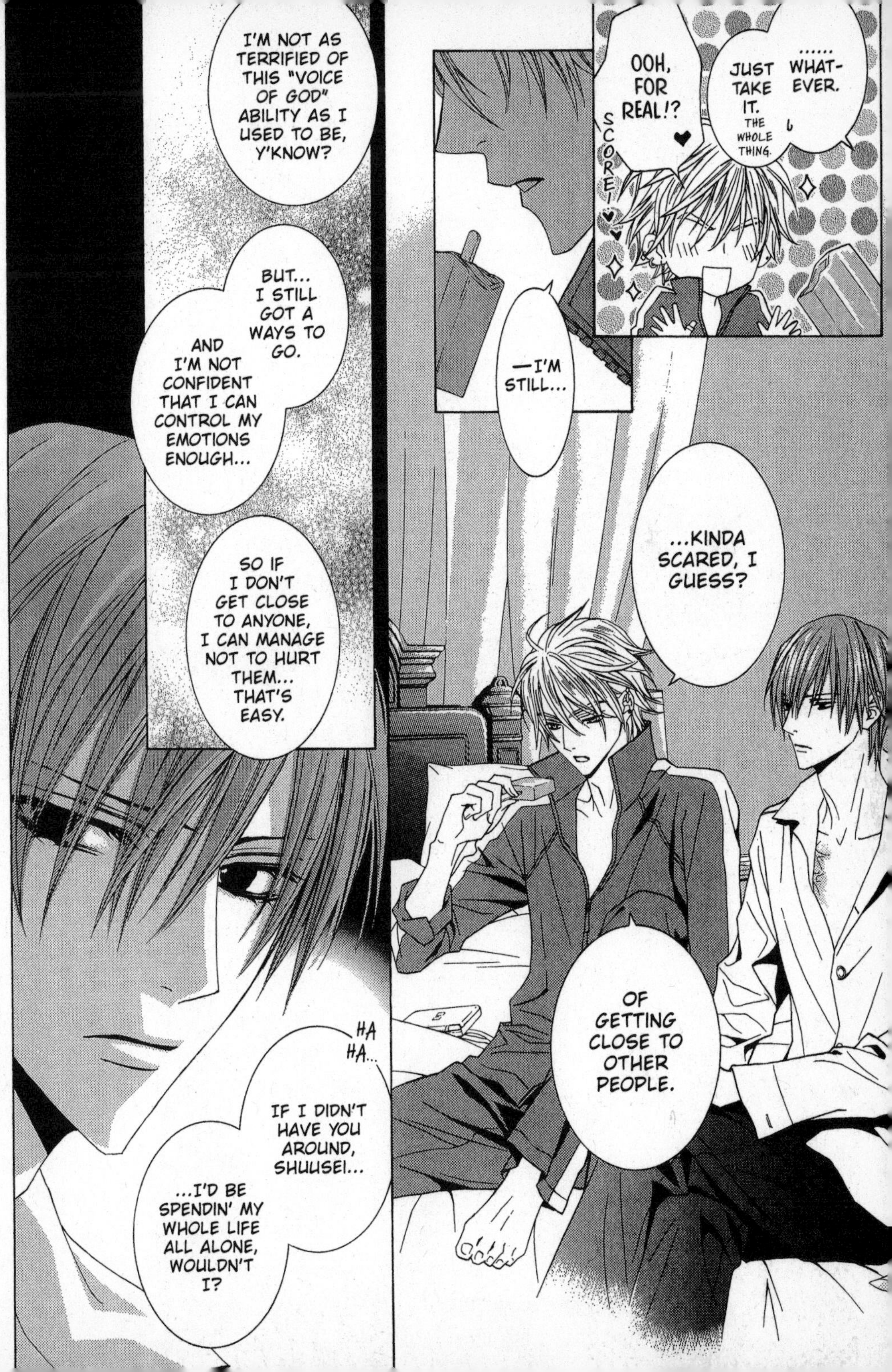

......WHAT-EVER.
JUST TAKE IT. THE WHOLE THING.
OOH, FOR REAL!?
SCORE!
—I'M STILL...
...KINDA SCARED, I GUESS?
OF GETTING CLOSE TO OTHER PEOPLE.
I'M NOT AS TERRIFIED OF THIS "VOICE OF GOD" ABILITY AS I USED TO BE, Y'KNOW?
BUT... I STILL GOT A WAYS TO GO.
AND I'M NOT CONFIDENT THAT I CAN CONTROL MY EMOTIONS ENOUGH...
SO IF I DON'T GET CLOSE TO ANYONE, I CAN MANAGE NOT TO HURT THEM... THAT'S EASY.
HA HA...
IF I DIDN'T HAVE YOU AROUND, SHUUSEI...
...I'D BE SPENDIN' MY WHOLE LIFE ALL ALONE, WOULDN'T I?

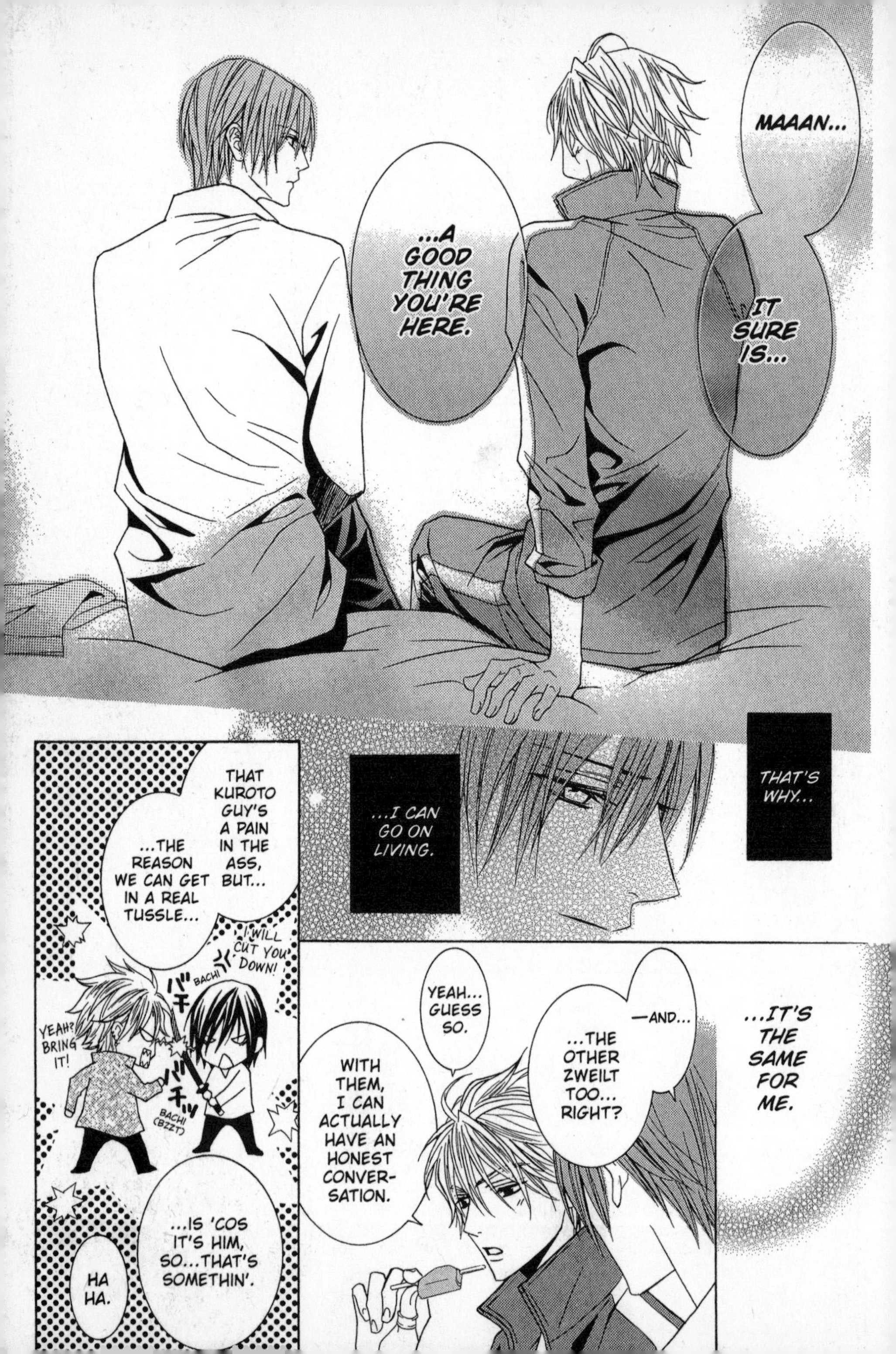
MAAAN...
IT SURE IS...
...A GOOD THING YOU'RE HERE.
THAT'S WHY...
...I CAN GO ON LIVING.
...IT'S THE SAME FOR ME.
—AND...
...THE OTHER ZWEILT TOO... RIGHT?
YEAH... GUESS SO.
WITH THEM, I CAN ACTUALLY HAVE AN HONEST CONVER-SATION.
THAT KUROTO GUY'S A PAIN IN THE ASS, BUT...
...THE REASON WE CAN GET IN A REAL TUSSLE...
I WILL CUT YOU DOWN!
バチ
BACHI
YEAH? BRING IT!
バチッ
BACHI (BZZT)
...IS 'COS IT'S HIM, SO...THAT'S SOMETHIN'.
HA HA.

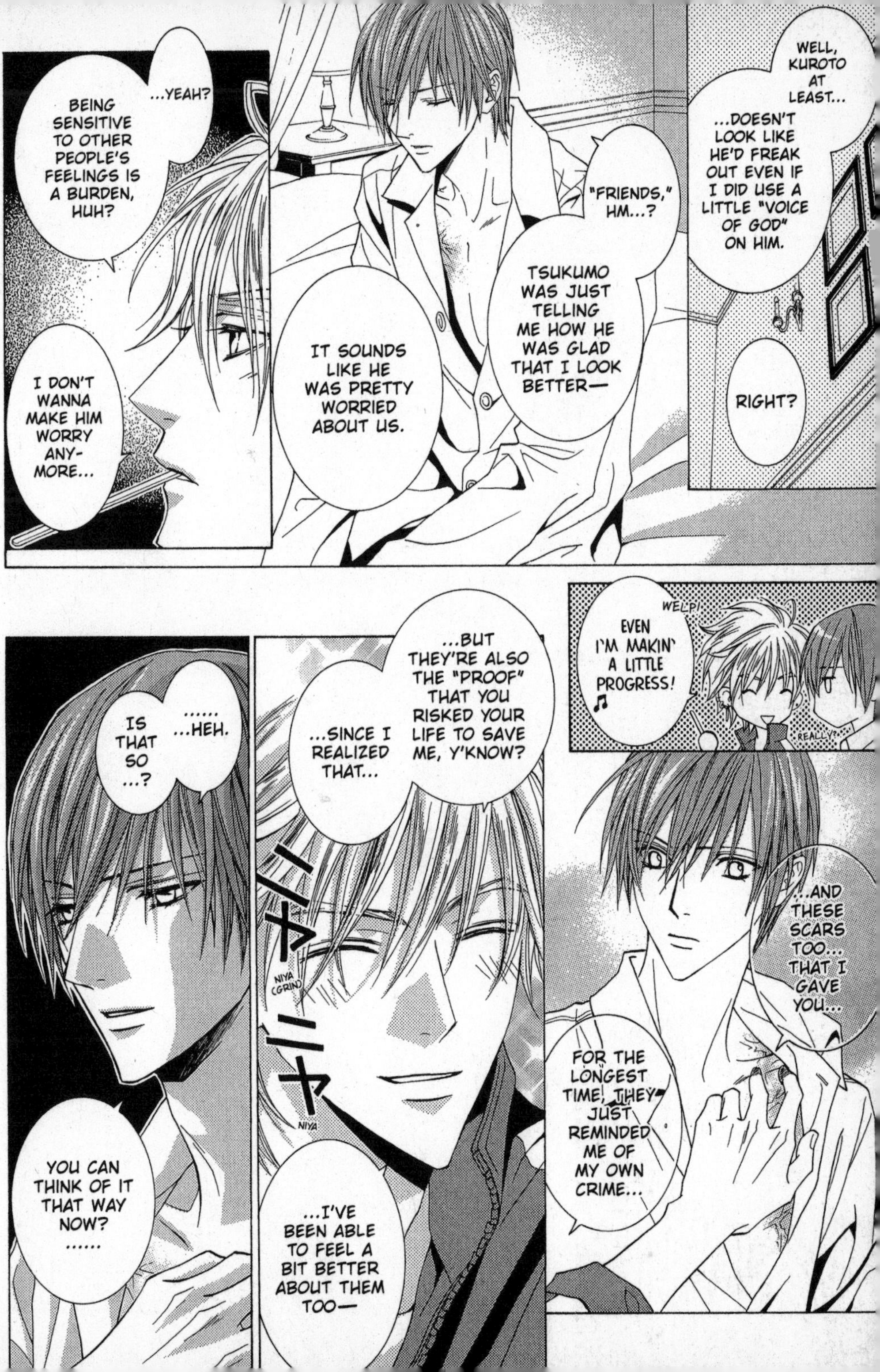
WELL, KUROTO AT LEAST...
...DOESN'T LOOK LIKE HE'D FREAK OUT EVEN IF I DID USE A LITTLE "VOICE OF GOD" ON HIM.
RIGHT?
"FRIENDS," HM...?
TSUKUMO WAS JUST TELLING ME HOW HE WAS GLAD THAT I LOOK BETTER—
IT SOUNDS LIKE HE WAS PRETTY WORRIED ABOUT US.
...YEAH?
BEING SENSITIVE TO OTHER PEOPLE'S FEELINGS IS A BURDEN, HUH?
I DON'T WANNA MAKE HIM WORRY ANY-MORE...
WELP!
EVEN I'M MAKIN' A LITTLE PROGRESS! ♫
REALLY?
...AND THESE SCARS TOO... THAT I GAVE YOU...
FOR THE LONGEST TIME, THEY JUST REMINDED ME OF MY OWN CRIME...
...BUT THEY'RE ALSO THE "PROOF" THAT YOU RISKED YOUR LIFE TO SAVE ME, Y'KNOW?
...SINCE I REALIZED THAT...
NIYA (GRIN)
NIYA
...I'VE BEEN ABLE TO FEEL A BIT BETTER ABOUT THEM TOO—
....HEH.
IS THAT SO ...?
YOU CAN THINK OF IT THAT WAY NOW? ......

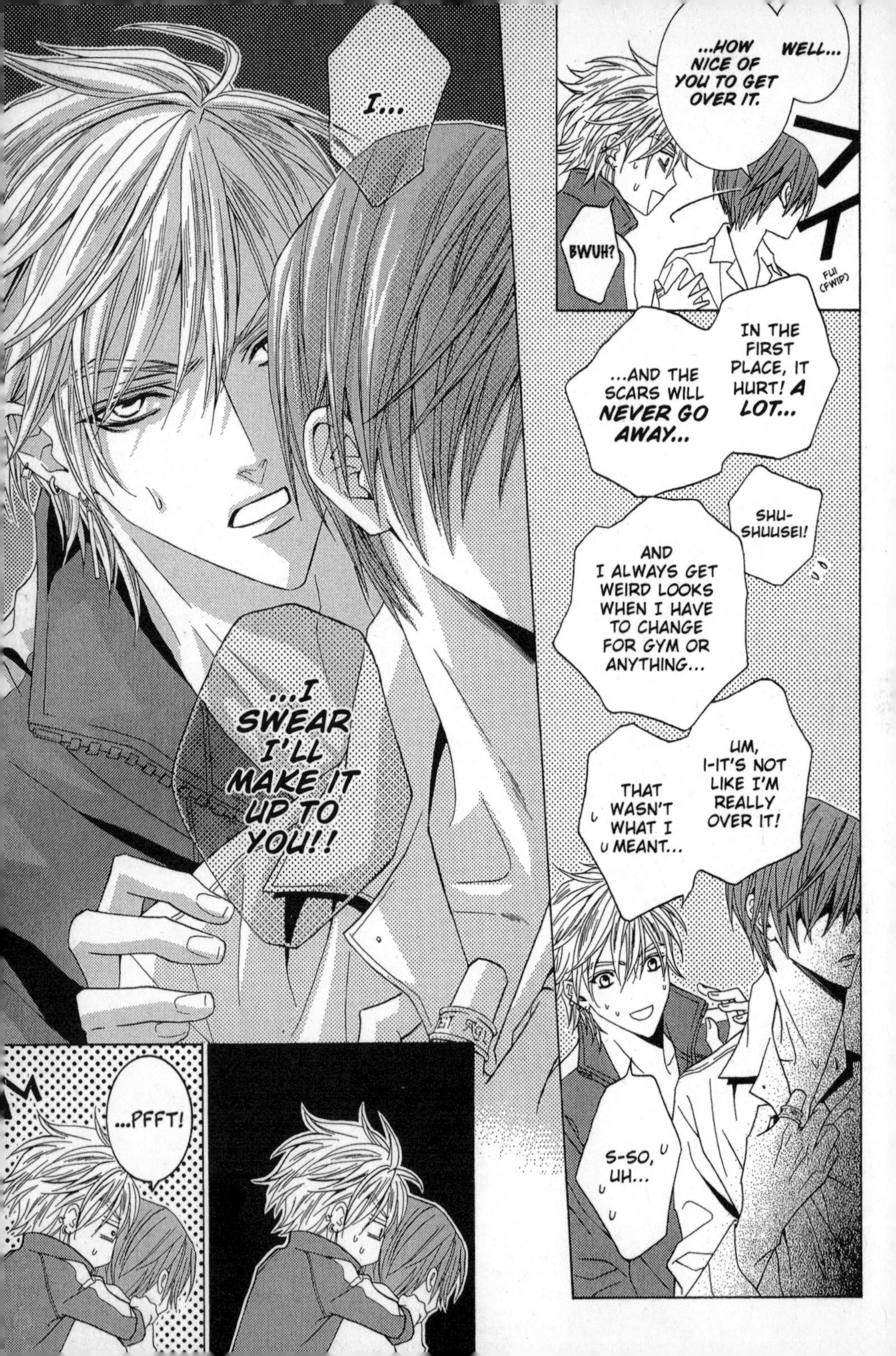
WELL...
...HOW NICE OF YOU TO GET OVER IT.
BWUH?
FUI (FWIP)
IN THE FIRST PLACE, IT HURT! A LOT...
...AND THE SCARS WILL NEVER GO AWAY...
SHU-SHUUSEI!
AND I ALWAYS GET WEIRD LOOKS WHEN I HAVE TO CHANGE FOR GYM OR ANYTHING...
UM, I-IT'S NOT LIKE I'M REALLY OVER IT!
THAT WASN'T WHAT I MEANT...
S-SO, UH...
I...
...I SWEAR I'LL MAKE IT UP TO YOU!!
...PFFT!

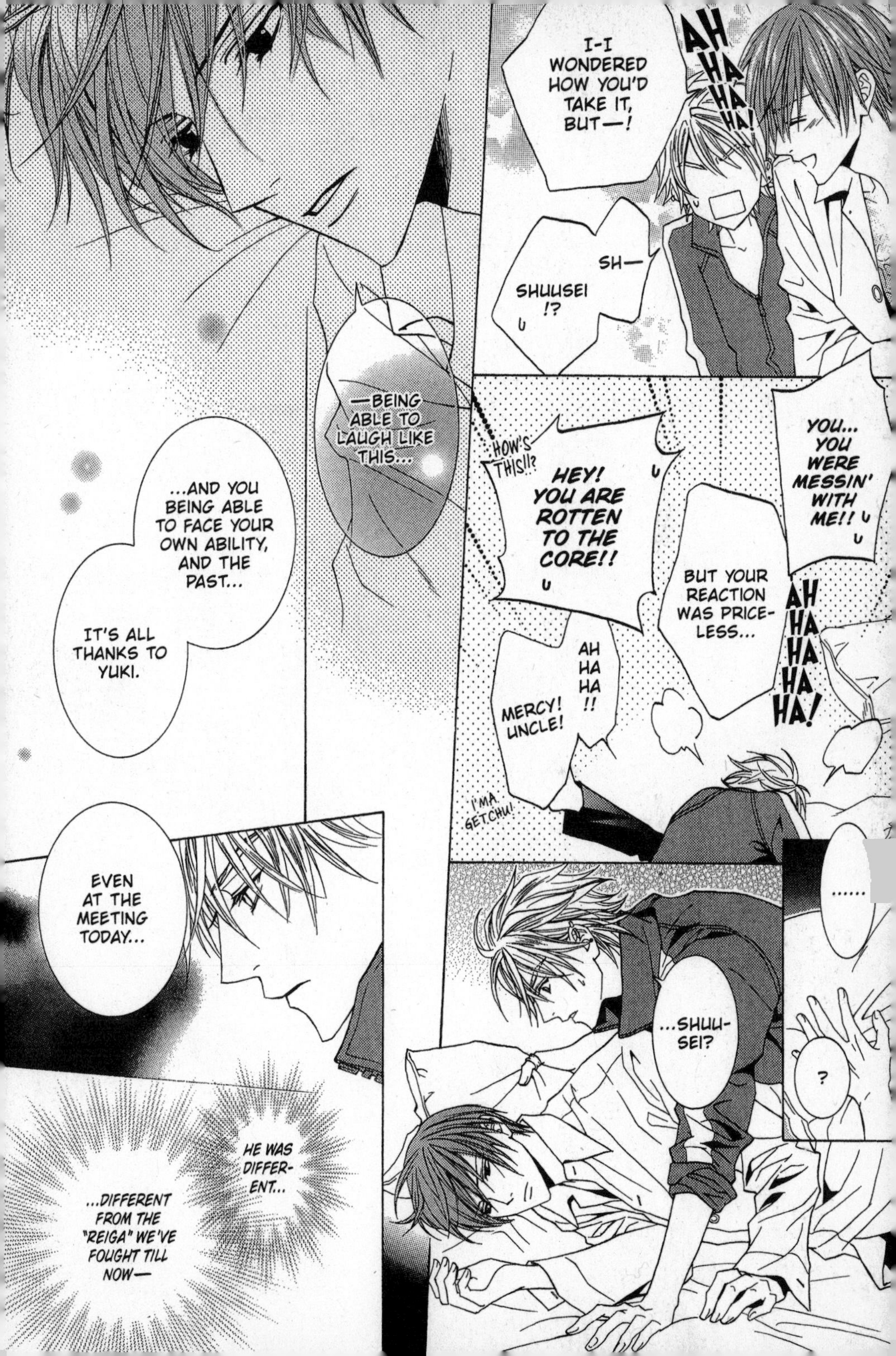
AHAHAHA!
I-I WONDERED HOW YOU'D TAKE IT, BUT—!
SH— SHUUSEI!?
YOU... YOU WERE MESSIN' WITH ME!!
BUT YOUR REACTION WAS PRICE-LESS...
AHAHAHAHA!
HOW'S THIS!!?
HEY! YOU ARE ROTTEN TO THE CORE!!
AH HA HA!!
MERCY! UNCLE!
I'MA GETCHU!
......
?
...SHUU-SEI?
—BEING ABLE TO LAUGH LIKE THIS...
...AND YOU BEING ABLE TO FACE YOUR OWN ABILITY, AND THE PAST...
IT'S ALL THANKS TO YUKI.
EVEN AT THE MEETING TODAY...
HE WAS DIFFER-ENT...
...DIFFERENT FROM THE "REIGA" WE'VE FOUGHT TILL NOW—

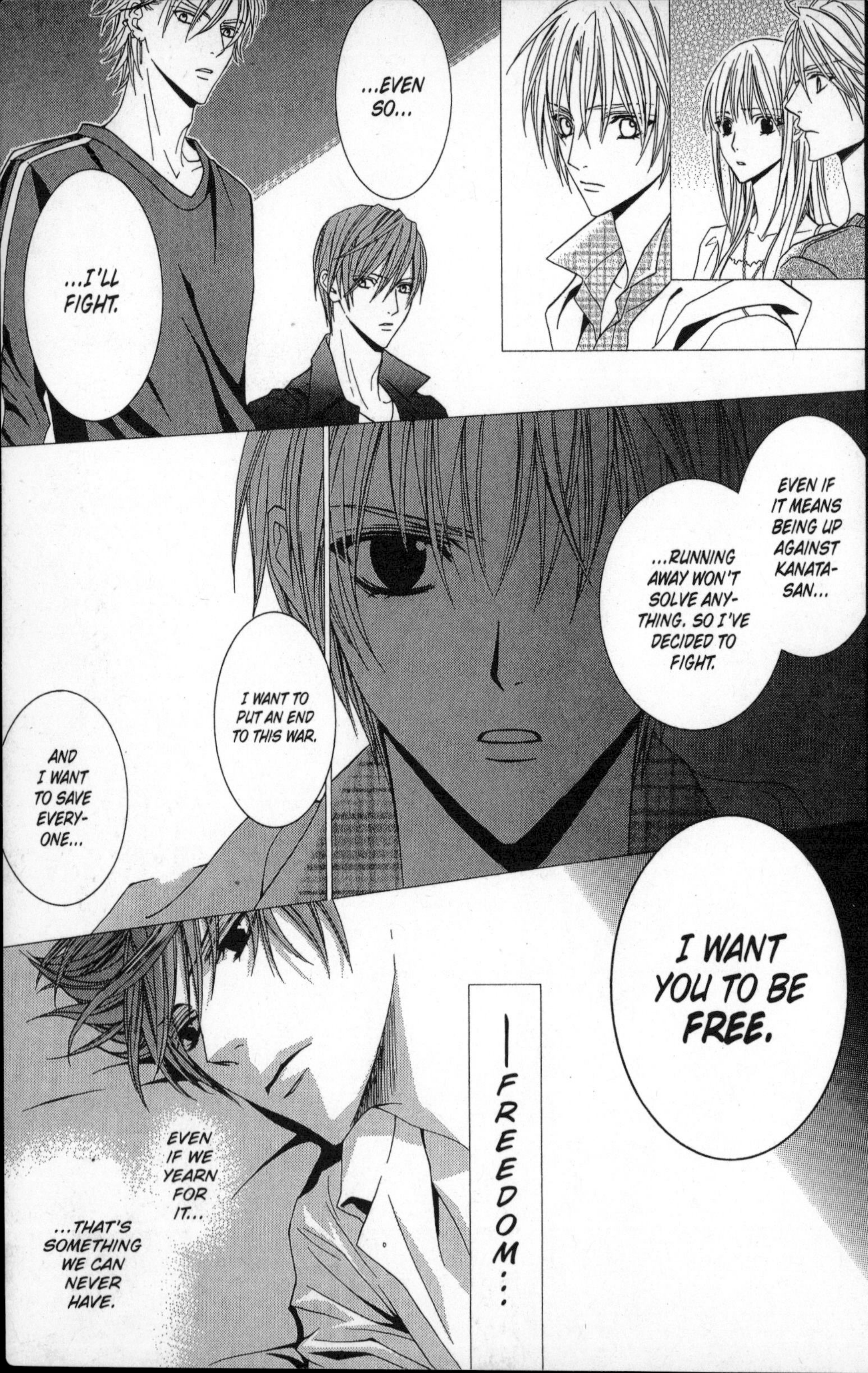
...EVEN SO...
...I'LL FIGHT.
EVEN IF IT MEANS BEING UP AGAINST KANATA-SAN...
...RUNNING AWAY WON'T SOLVE ANY-THING. SO I'VE DECIDED TO FIGHT.
I WANT TO PUT AN END TO THIS WAR.
AND I WANT TO SAVE EVERY-ONE...
I WANT YOU TO BE FREE.
FREEDOM...
EVEN IF WE YEARN FOR IT...
...THAT'S SOMETHING WE CAN NEVER HAVE.

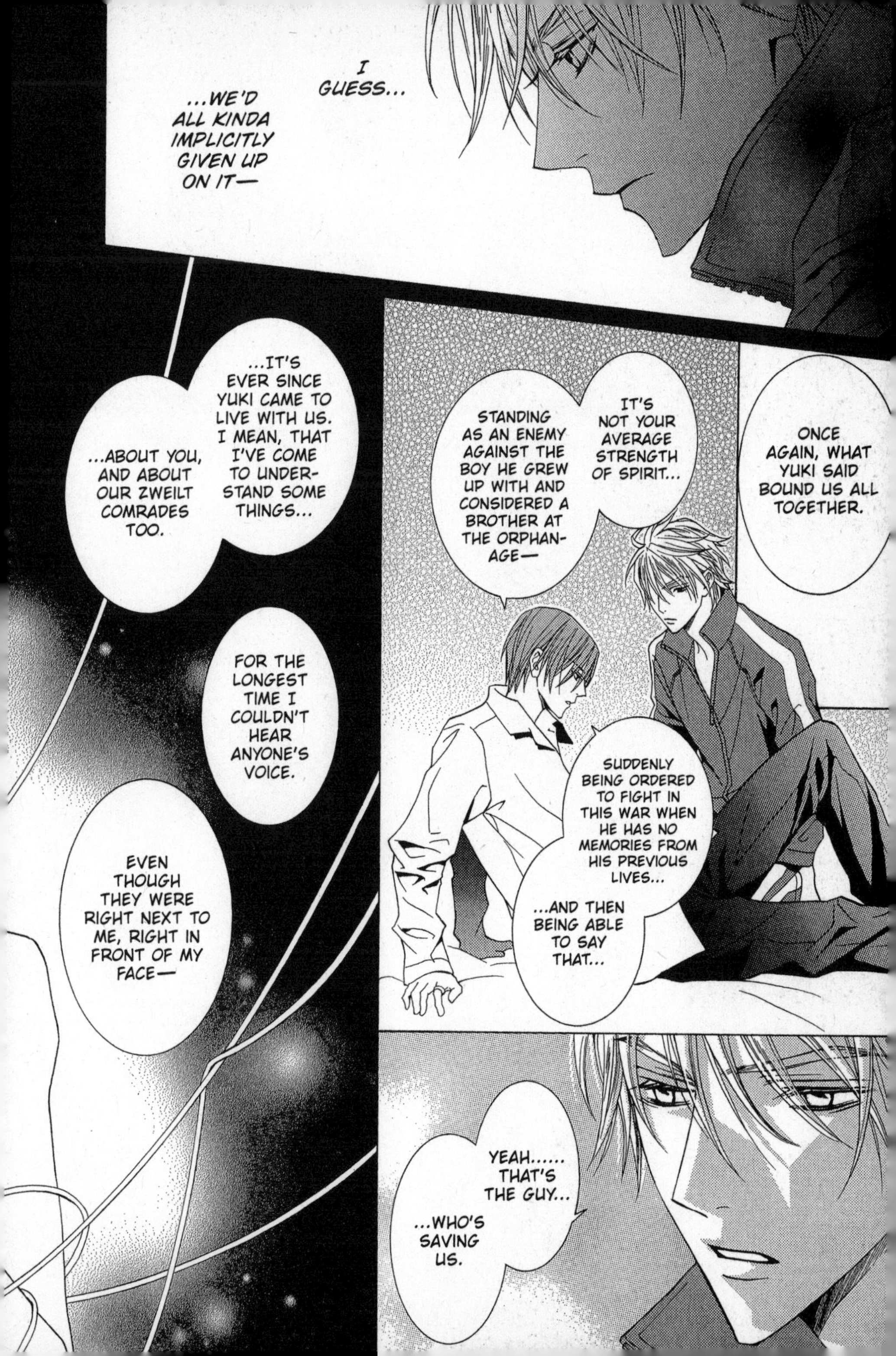
I GUESS...
...WE'D ALL KINDA IMPLICITLY GIVEN UP ON IT—
ONCE AGAIN, WHAT YUKI SAID BOUND US ALL TOGETHER.
IT'S NOT YOUR AVERAGE STRENGTH OF SPIRIT...
STANDING AS AN ENEMY AGAINST THE BOY HE GREW UP WITH AND CONSIDERED A BROTHER AT THE ORPHAN-AGE—
SUDDENLY BEING ORDERED TO FIGHT IN THIS WAR WHEN HE HAS NO MEMORIES FROM HIS PREVIOUS LIVES...
...AND THEN BEING ABLE TO SAY THAT...
YEAH...... THAT'S THE GUY...
...WHO'S SAVING US.
...IT'S EVER SINCE YUKI CAME TO LIVE WITH US. I MEAN, THAT I'VE COME TO UNDER-STAND SOME THINGS...
...ABOUT YOU, AND ABOUT OUR ZWEILT COMRADES TOO.
FOR THE LONGEST TIME I COULDN'T HEAR ANYONE'S VOICE.
EVEN THOUGH THEY WERE RIGHT NEXT TO ME, RIGHT IN FRONT OF MY FACE—

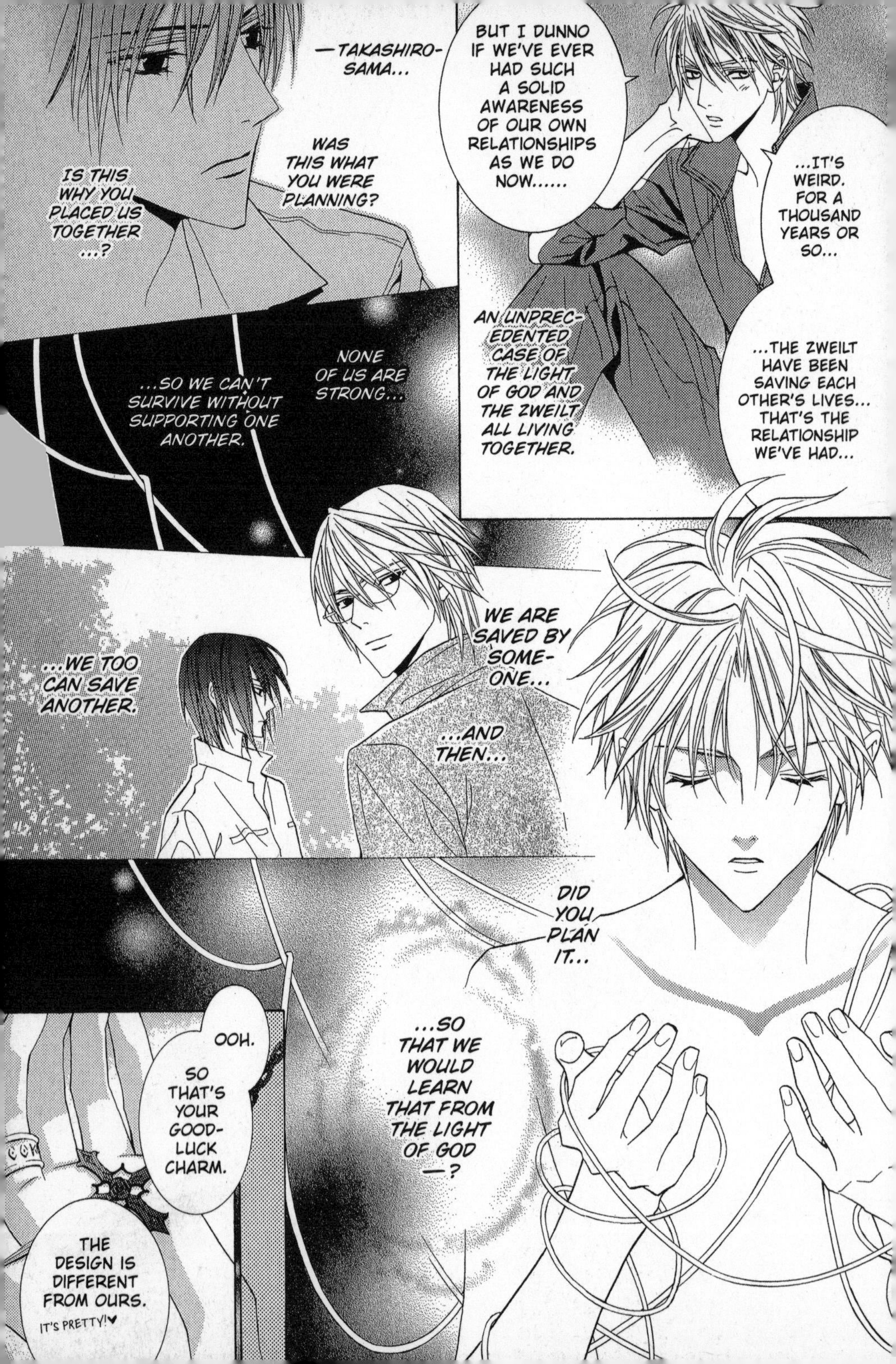
...IT'S WEIRD. FOR A THOUSAND YEARS OR SO...
...THE ZWEILT HAVE BEEN SAVING EACH OTHER'S LIVES... THAT'S THE RELATIONSHIP WE'VE HAD...
BUT I DUNNO IF WE'VE EVER HAD SUCH A SOLID AWARENESS OF OUR OWN RELATIONSHIPS AS WE DO NOW......
AN UNPRECEDENTED CASE OF THE LIGHT OF GOD AND THE ZWEILT ALL LIVING TOGETHER.
—TAKASHIRO-SAMA...
WAS THIS WHAT YOU WERE PLANNING?
IS THIS WHY YOU PLACED US TOGETHER ...?
NONE OF US ARE STRONG...
...SO WE CAN'T SURVIVE WITHOUT SUPPORTING ONE ANOTHER.
WE ARE SAVED BY SOME-ONE...
...AND THEN...
...WE TOO CAN SAVE ANOTHER.
DID YOU PLAN IT...
...SO THAT WE WOULD LEARN THAT FROM THE LIGHT OF GOD —?
OOH.
SO THAT'S YOUR GOOD-LUCK CHARM.
THE DESIGN IS DIFFERENT FROM OURS.
IT'S PRETTY!♥

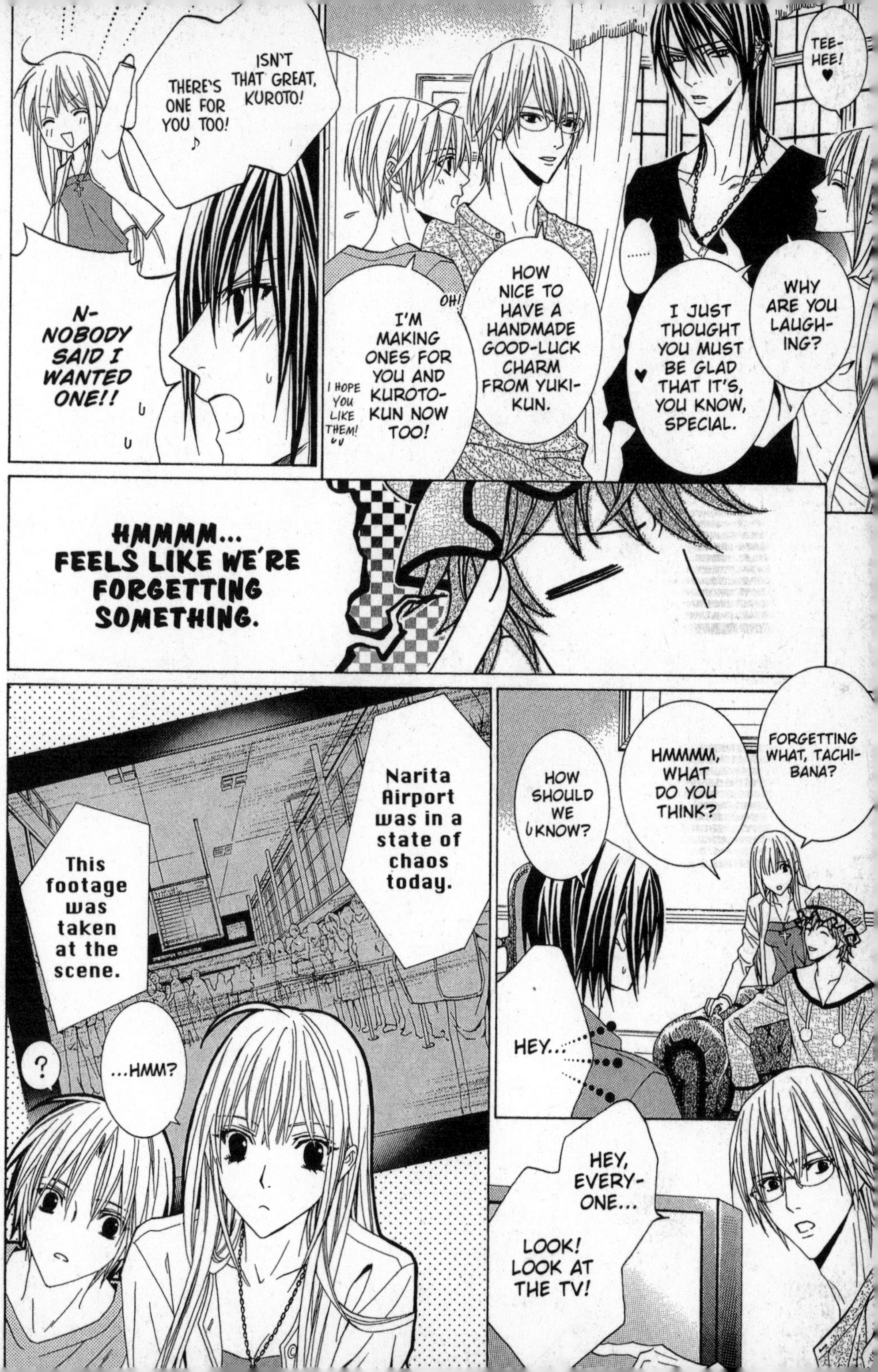
TEE-HEE! ♥
......
WHY ARE YOU LAUGHING?
I JUST THOUGHT YOU MUST BE GLAD THAT IT'S, YOU KNOW, SPECIAL.
HOW NICE TO HAVE A HANDMADE GOOD-LUCK CHARM FROM YUKI-KUN.
OH!
I'M MAKING ONES FOR YOU AND KUROTO-KUN NOW TOO!
I HOPE YOU LIKE THEM!
ISN'T THAT GREAT, KUROTO!
THERE'S ONE FOR YOU TOO! ♪
N-NOBODY SAID I WANTED ONE!!
HMMMM... FEELS LIKE WE'RE FORGETTING SOMETHING.
FORGETTING WHAT, TACHIBANA?
HMMMM, WHAT DO YOU THINK?
HOW SHOULD WE KNOW?
HEY...
HEY, EVERY-ONE...
LOOK! LOOK AT THE TV!
Narita Airport was in a state of chaos today.
This footage was taken at the scene.
...HMM?
?

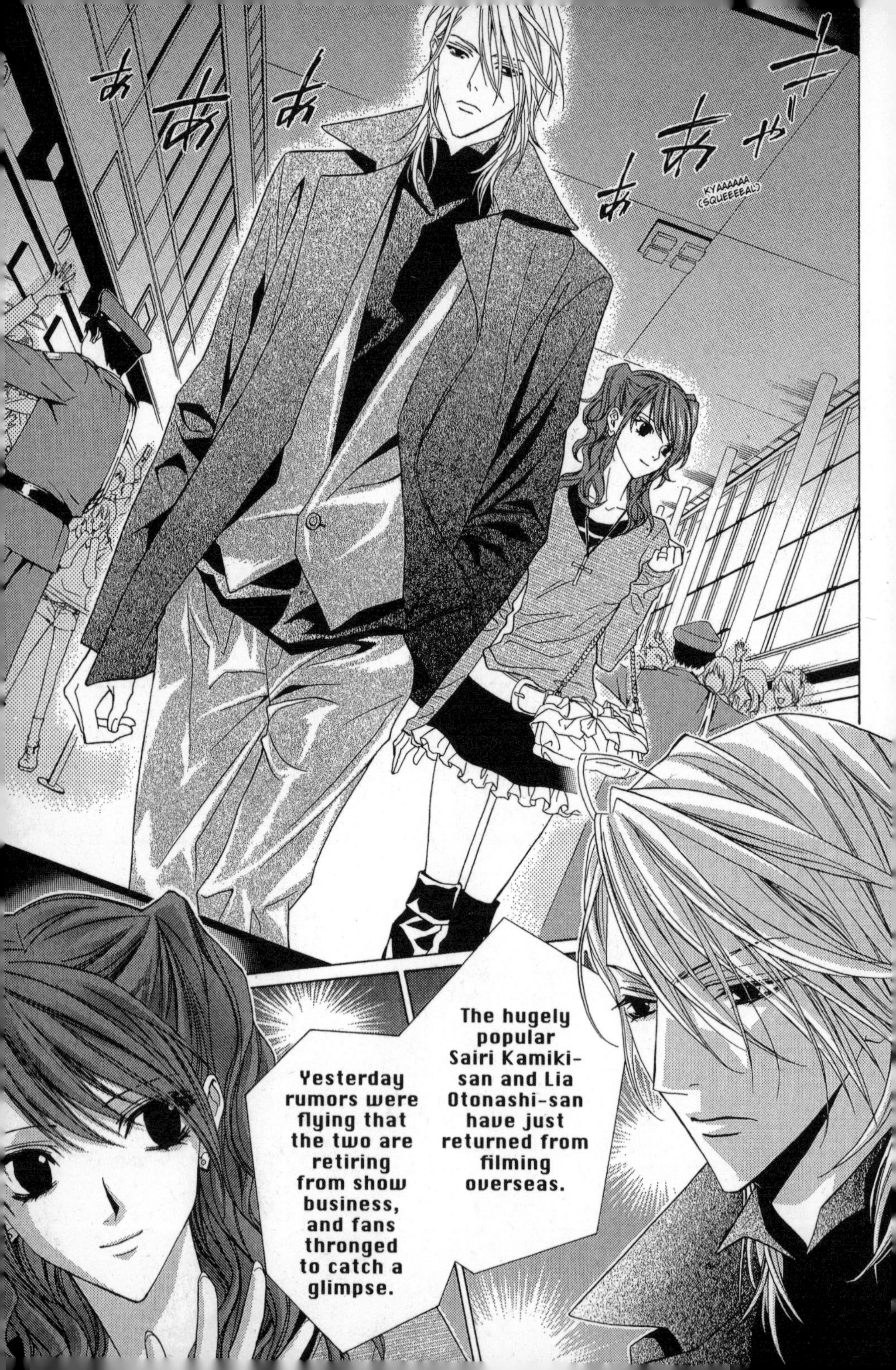
KYAAAAAA (SQUEEEEAL)
The hugely popular Sairi Kamiki-san and Lia Otonashi-san have just returned from filming overseas.
Yesterday rumors were flying that the two are retiring from show business, and fans thronged to catch a glimpse.

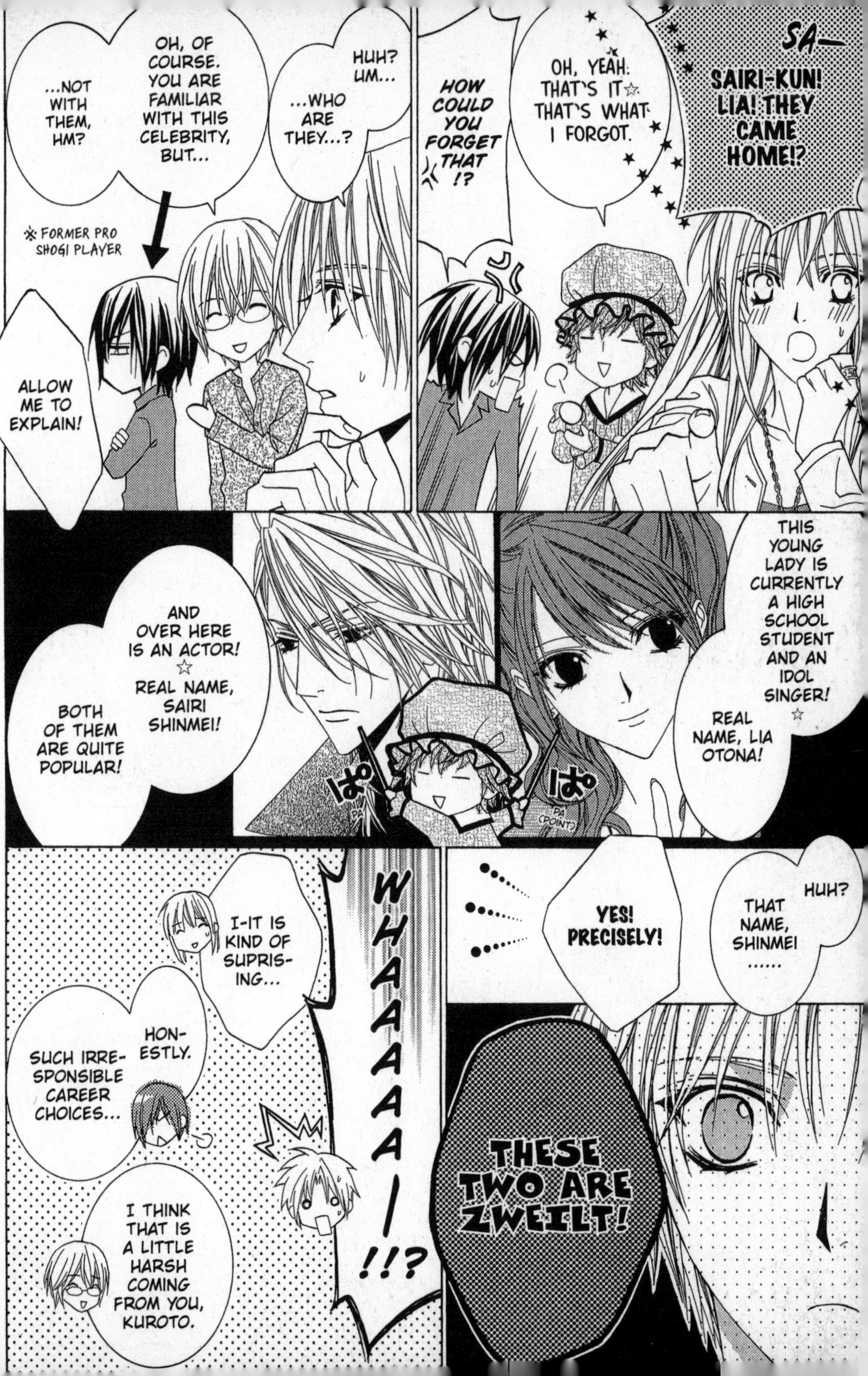
SA—
SAIRI-KUN! LIA! THEY CAME HOME!?
OH, YEAH. THAT'S IT☆ THAT'S WHAT I FORGOT.
HOW COULD YOU FORGET THAT!?
HUH? UM...
...WHO ARE THEY...?
OH, OF COURSE. YOU ARE FAMILIAR WITH THIS CELEBRITY, BUT...
...NOT WITH THEM, HM?
※FORMER PRO SHOGI PLAYER
ALLOW ME TO EXPLAIN!
THIS YOUNG LADY IS CURRENTLY A HIGH SCHOOL STUDENT AND AN IDOL SINGER! ☆
REAL NAME, LIA OTONA!
ぱ PA (POINT)
ぱ PA
AND OVER HERE IS AN ACTOR! ☆
REAL NAME, SAIRI SHINMEI!
BOTH OF THEM ARE QUITE POPULAR!
HUH?
THAT NAME, SHINMEI ......
YES! PRECISELY!
THESE TWO ARE ZWEILT!
WHAAAAAA—!!?
I-IT IS KIND OF SUPRIS-ING...
HON-ESTLY.
SUCH IRRE-SPONSIBLE CAREER CHOICES...
I THINK THAT IS A LITTLE HARSH COMING FROM YOU, KUROTO.

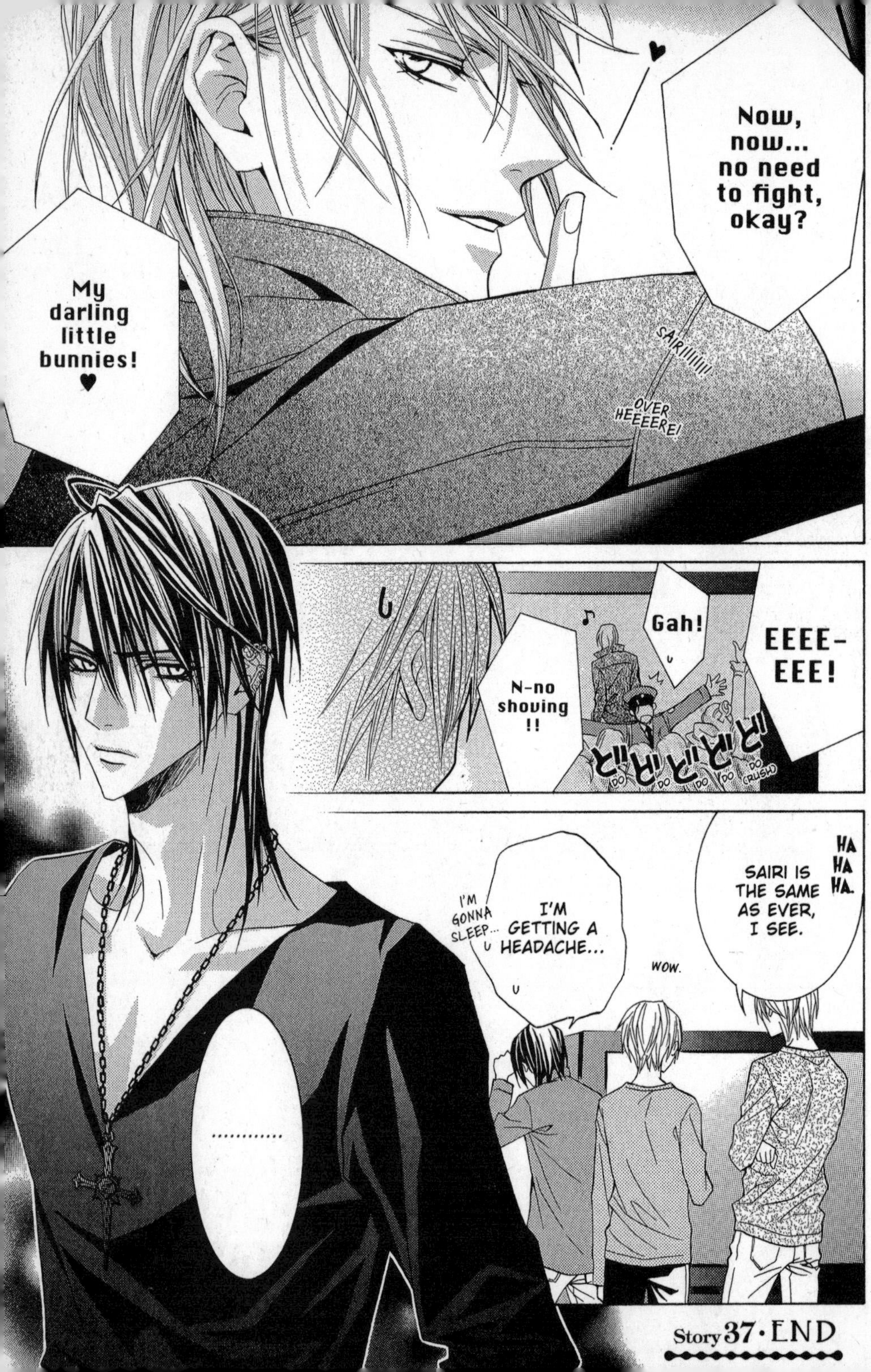
Now, now... no need to fight, okay?
My darling little bunnies! ♥
SAIRIIIIIIII!
OVER HEEEERE!
EEEE-EEE!
Gah!
N-no shoving!!
DO DO DO DO DO (CRUSH)
HA HA HA.
SAIRI IS THE SAME AS EVER, I SEE.
WOW.
I'M GETTING A HEADACHE...
I'M GONNA SLEEP...
....
Story 37 • END

THE
BETRAYAL
KNOWS MY NAME

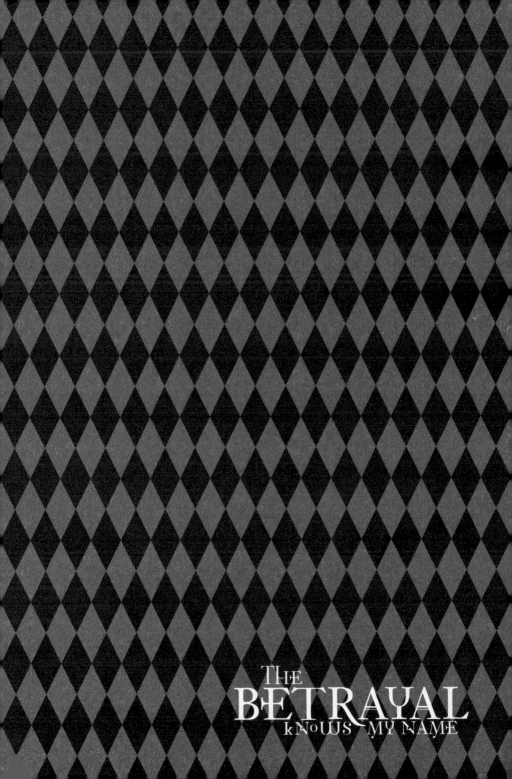

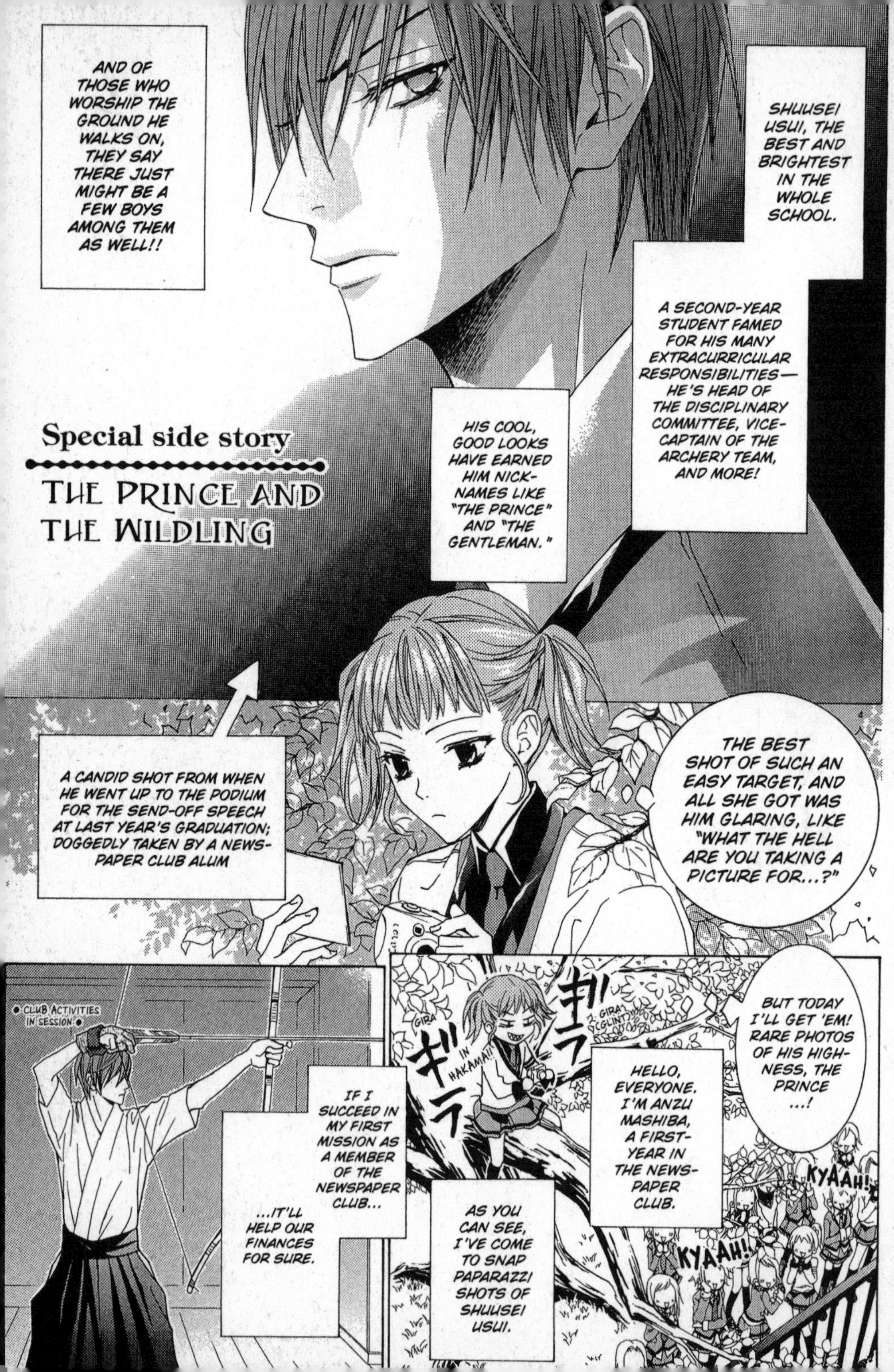
SHUUSEI USUI, THE BEST AND BRIGHTEST IN THE WHOLE SCHOOL.
A SECOND-YEAR STUDENT FAMED FOR HIS MANY EXTRACURRICULAR RESPONSIBILITIES—HE'S HEAD OF THE DISCIPLINARY COMMITTEE, VICE-CAPTAIN OF THE ARCHERY TEAM, AND MORE!
HIS COOL, GOOD LOOKS HAVE EARNED HIM NICK-NAMES LIKE "THE PRINCE" AND "THE GENTLEMAN."
AND OF THOSE WHO WORSHIP THE GROUND HE WALKS ON, THEY SAY THERE JUST MIGHT BE A FEW BOYS AMONG THEM AS WELL!!
Special side story
THE PRINCE AND THE WILDLING
THE BEST SHOT OF SUCH AN EASY TARGET, AND ALL SHE GOT WAS HIM GLARING, LIKE "WHAT THE HELL ARE YOU TAKING A PICTURE FOR...?"
A CANDID SHOT FROM WHEN HE WENT UP TO THE PODIUM FOR THE SEND-OFF SPEECH AT LAST YEAR'S GRADUATION; DOGGEDLY TAKEN BY A NEWS-PAPER CLUB ALUM
BUT TODAY I'LL GET 'EM! RARE PHOTOS OF HIS HIGH-NESS, THE PRINCE ...!
ギラ
1. GIRA (GLINT)
ギラ
GIRA
IN HAKAMA!!
HELLO, EVERYONE. I'M ANZU MASHIBA, A FIRST-YEAR IN THE NEWS-PAPER CLUB.
AS YOU CAN SEE, I'VE COME TO SNAP PAPARAZZI SHOTS OF SHUUSEI USUI.
KYAAH!!
KYAAH!!
CLUB ACTIVITIES IN SESSION
IF I SUCCEED IN MY FIRST MISSION AS A MEMBER OF THE NEWSPAPER CLUB...
...IT'LL HELP OUR FINANCES FOR SURE.

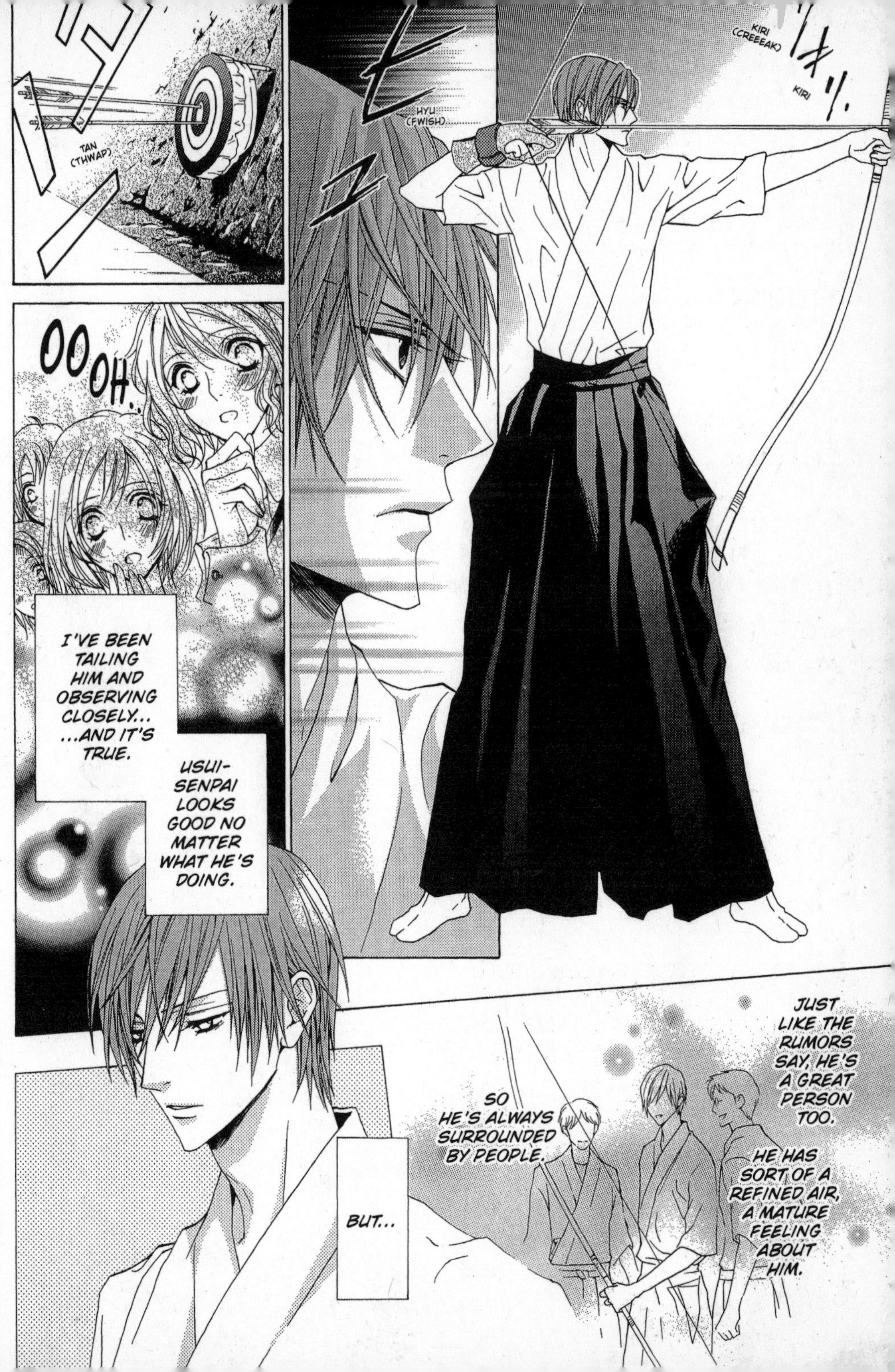
KIRI (CREEEAK)
KIRI
HYU (FWISH)
TAN (THWAP)
OOOH...
I'VE BEEN TAILING HIM AND OBSERVING CLOSELY... ...AND IT'S TRUE.
USUI-SENPAI LOOKS GOOD NO MATTER WHAT HE'S DOING.
JUST LIKE THE RUMORS SAY, HE'S A GREAT PERSON TOO.
HE HAS SORT OF A REFINED AIR, A MATURE FEELING ABOUT HIM.
SO HE'S ALWAYS SURROUNDED BY PEOPLE.
BUT...

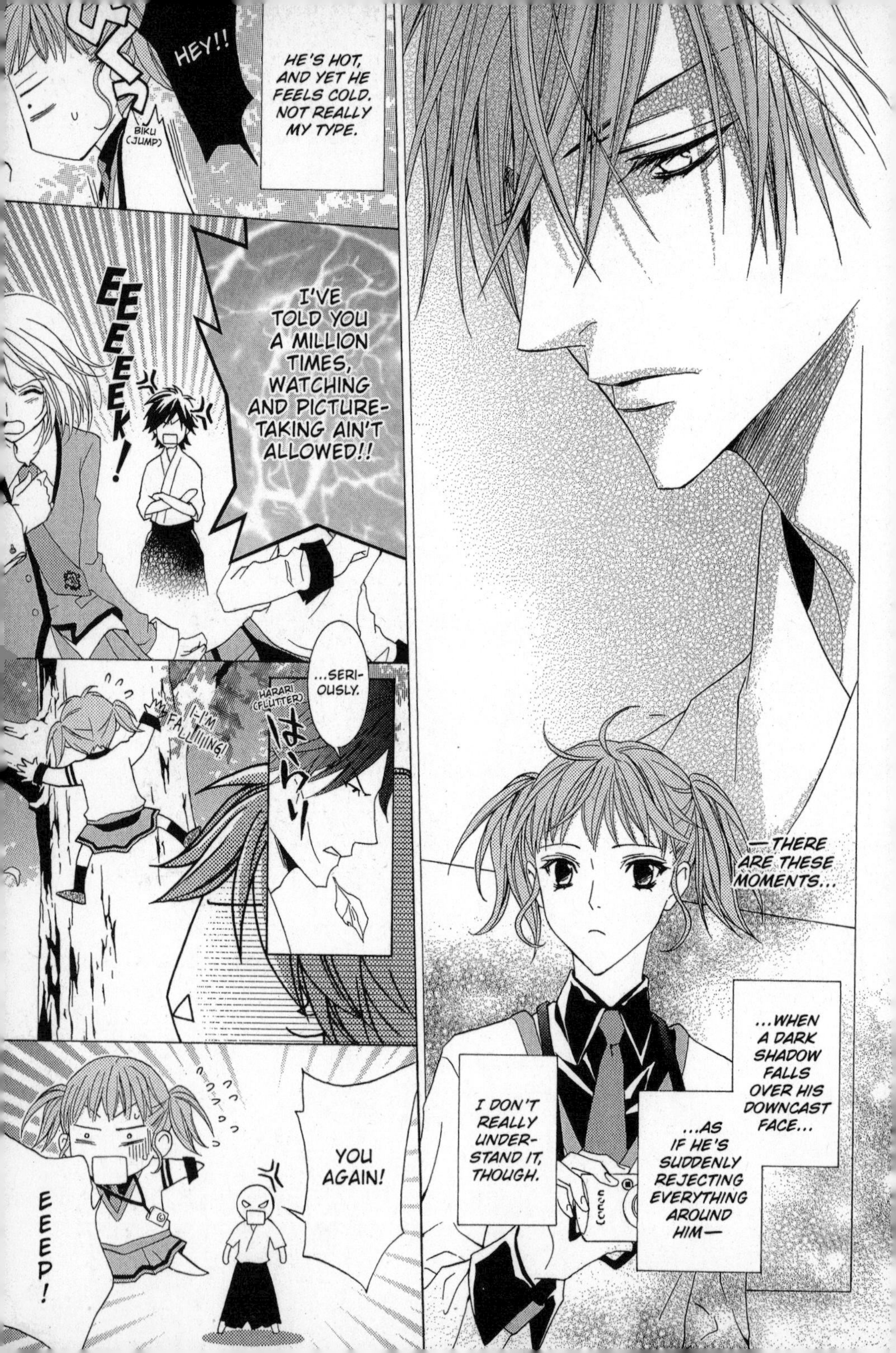
—THERE ARE THESE MOMENTS...
...WHEN A DARK SHADOW FALLS OVER HIS DOWNCAST FACE...
...AS IF HE'S SUDDENLY REJECTING EVERYTHING AROUND HIM—
I DON'T REALLY UNDERSTAND IT, THOUGH.
HE'S HOT, AND YET HE FEELS COLD. NOT REALLY MY TYPE.
HEY!!
BIKU (JUMP)
I'VE TOLD YOU A MILLION TIMES, WATCHING AND PICTURE-TAKING AIN'T ALLOWED!!
EEEEEK!
...SERIOUSLY.
HARARI (FLUTTER)
I-I'M FALLIIIING!
YOU AGAIN!
EEEP!

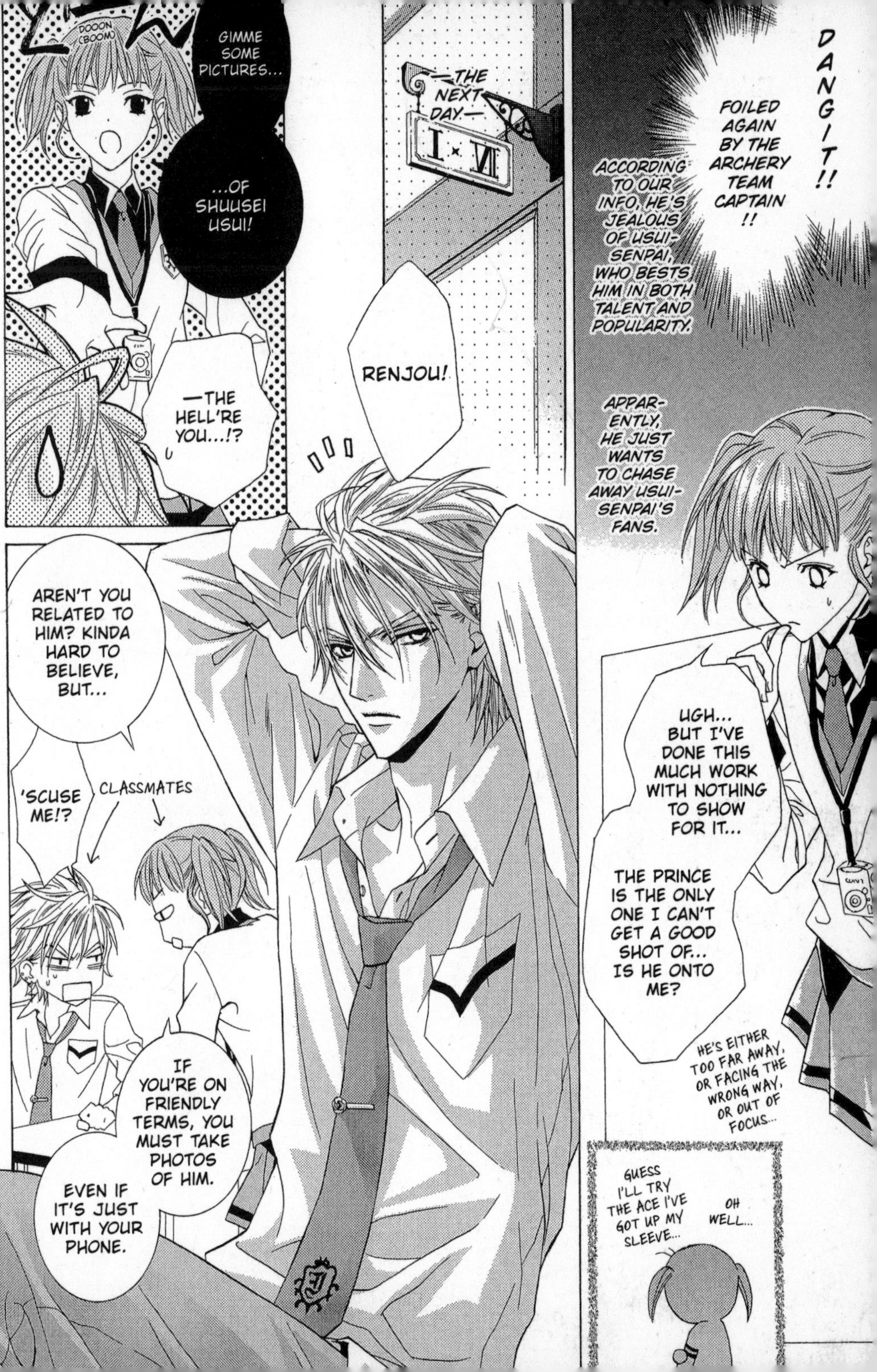
DANGIT!!
FOILED AGAIN BY THE ARCHERY TEAM CAPTAIN !!
ACCORDING TO OUR INFO, HE'S JEALOUS OF USUI-SENPAI, WHO BESTS HIM IN BOTH TALENT AND POPULARITY.
APPARENTLY, HE JUST WANTS TO CHASE AWAY USUI-SENPAI'S FANS.
UGH... BUT I'VE DONE THIS MUCH WORK WITH NOTHING TO SHOW FOR IT...
THE PRINCE IS THE ONLY ONE I CAN'T GET A GOOD SHOT OF... IS HE ONTO ME?
HE'S EITHER TOO FAR AWAY, OR FACING THE WRONG WAY, OR OUT OF FOCUS...
OH WELL...
GUESS I'LL TRY THE ACE I'VE GOT UP MY SLEEVE...
—THE NEXT DAY—
RENJOU!
GIMME SOME PICTURES...
...OF SHUUSEI USUI!
DOOON (BOOM)
—THE HELL'RE YOU...!?
AREN'T YOU RELATED TO HIM? KINDA HARD TO BELIEVE, BUT...
'SCUSE ME!?
CLASSMATES
IF YOU'RE ON FRIENDLY TERMS, YOU MUST TAKE PHOTOS OF HIM.
EVEN IF IT'S JUST WITH YOUR PHONE.

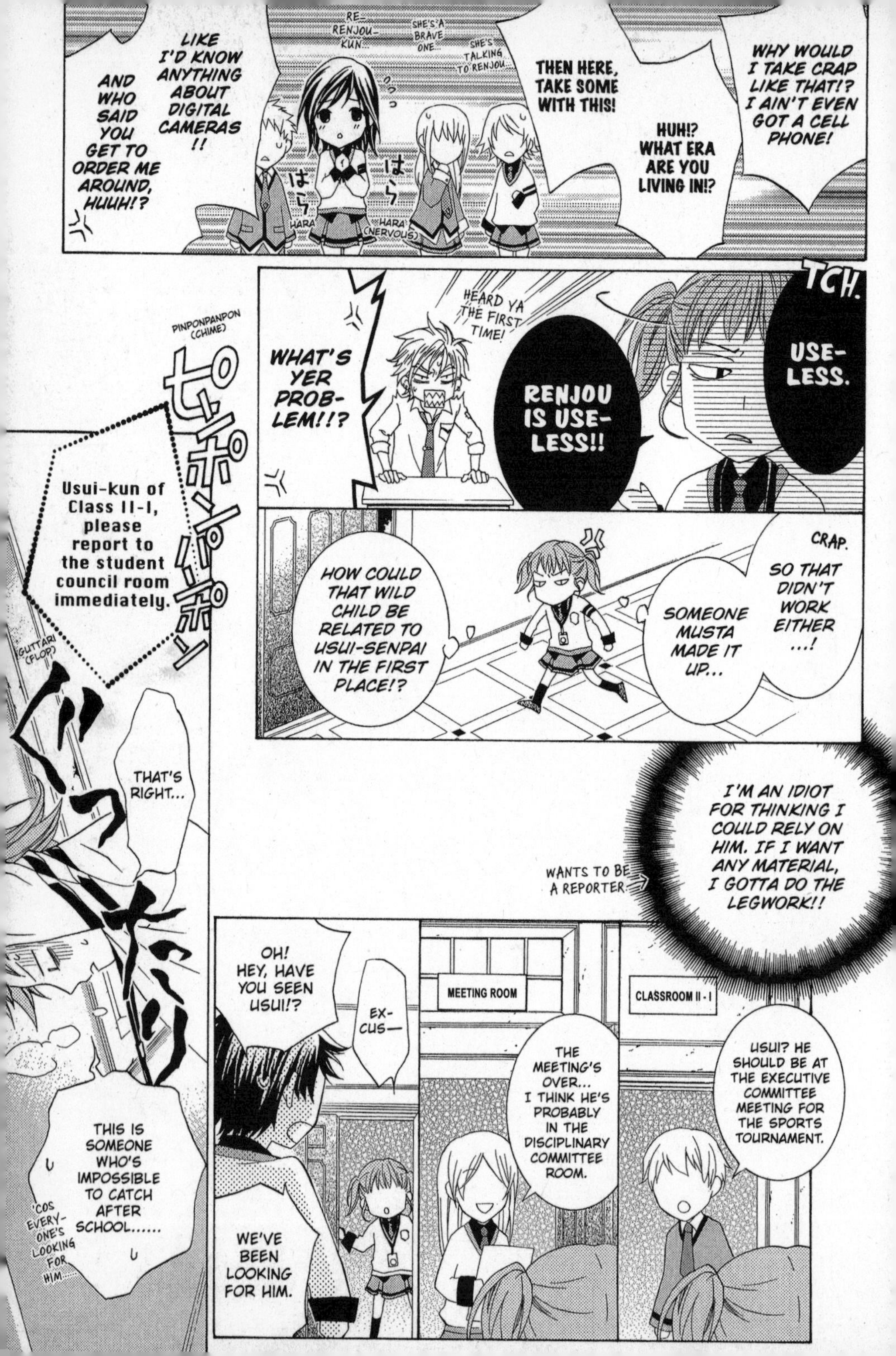
WHY WOULD I TAKE CRAP LIKE THAT!? I AIN'T EVEN GOT A CELL PHONE!
HUH!? WHAT ERA ARE YOU LIVING IN!?
THEN HERE, TAKE SOME WITH THIS!
SHE'S TALKING TO RENJOU...
SHE'S A BRAVE ONE...
RE-RENJOU-KUN...
はら HARA (NERVOUS)
はら HARA
LIKE I'D KNOW ANYTHING ABOUT DIGITAL CAMERAS!!
AND WHO SAID YOU GET TO ORDER ME AROUND, HUUH!?
TCH.
USE-LESS.
RENJOU IS USE-LESS!!
HEARD YA THE FIRST TIME!
WHAT'S YER PROB-LEM!!?
CRAP.
SO THAT DIDN'T WORK EITHER...!
SOMEONE MUSTA MADE IT UP...
HOW COULD THAT WILD CHILD BE RELATED TO USUI-SENPAI IN THE FIRST PLACE!?
I'M AN IDIOT FOR THINKING I COULD RELY ON HIM. IF I WANT ANY MATERIAL, I GOTTA DO THE LEGWORK!!
WANTS TO BE A REPORTER
CLASSROOM II - I
USUI? HE SHOULD BE AT THE EXECUTIVE COMMITTEE MEETING FOR THE SPORTS TOURNAMENT.
MEETING ROOM
THE MEETING'S OVER... I THINK HE'S PROBABLY IN THE DISCIPLINARY COMMITTEE ROOM.
EX-CUS—
OH! HEY, HAVE YOU SEEN USUI!?
WE'VE BEEN LOOKING FOR HIM.
ピンポンパンポン
PINPONPANPON (CHIME)
Usui-kun of Class II-I, please report to the student council room immediately.
GUTTARI (FLOP)
THAT'S RIGHT...
THIS IS SOMEONE WHO'S IMPOSSIBLE TO CATCH AFTER SCHOOL......
'COS EVERY-ONE'S LOOKING FOR HIM...

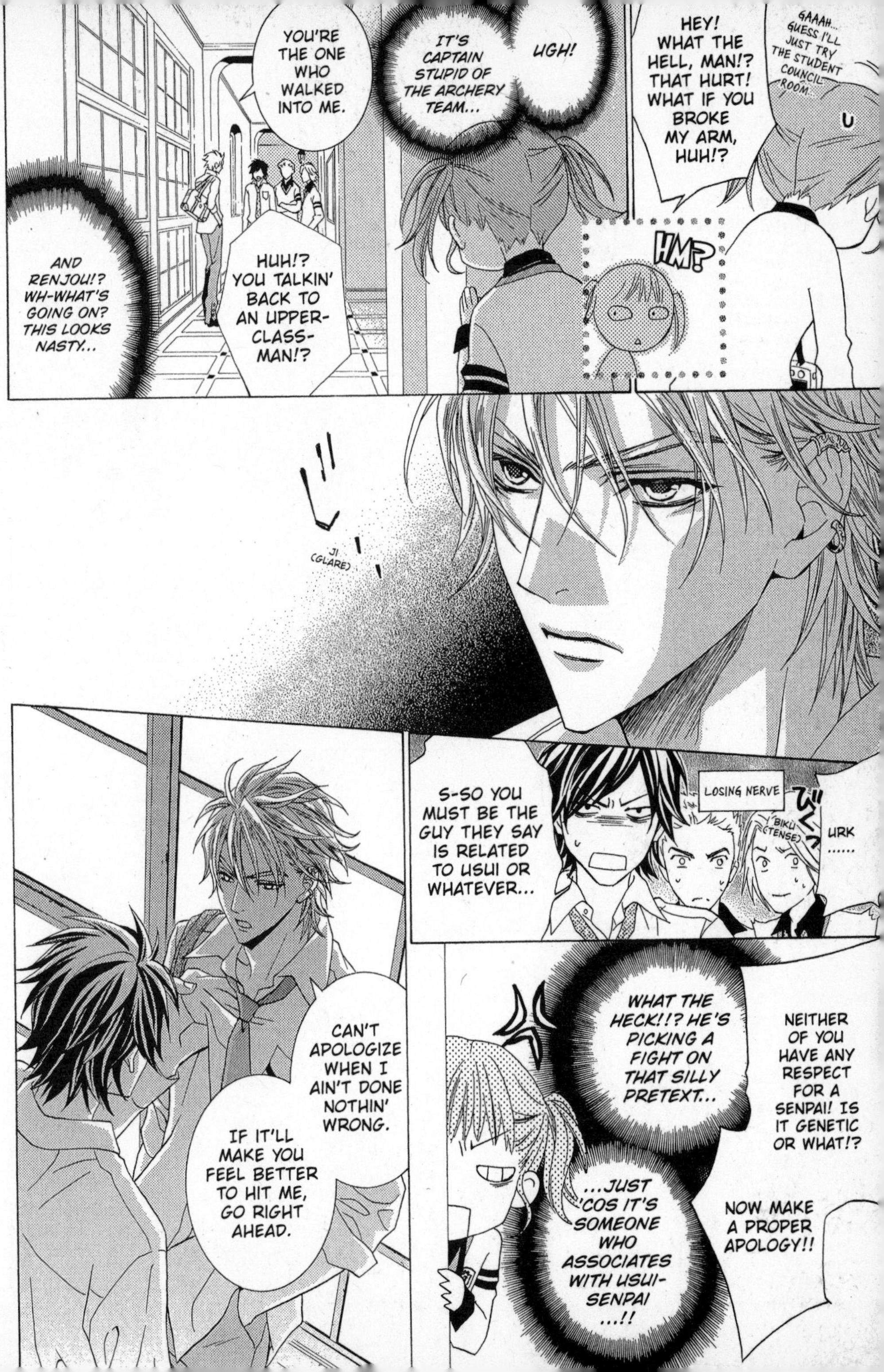
GAAAH... GUESS I'LL JUST TRY THE STUDENT COUNCIL ROOM...
HEY! WHAT THE HELL, MAN!? THAT HURT! WHAT IF YOU BROKE MY ARM, HUH!?
U
HM?
UGH!
IT'S CAPTAIN STUPID OF THE ARCHERY TEAM...
YOU'RE THE ONE WHO WALKED INTO ME.
HUH!? YOU TALKIN' BACK TO AN UPPER-CLASSMAN!?
AND RENJOU!? WH-WHAT'S GOING ON? THIS LOOKS NASTY...
JI (GLARE)
URK ......
LOSING NERVE
BIKU (TENSE)
S-SO YOU MUST BE THE GUY THEY SAY IS RELATED TO USUI OR WHATEVER...
NEITHER OF YOU HAVE ANY RESPECT FOR A SENPAI! IS IT GENETIC OR WHAT!?
WHAT THE HECK!!? HE'S PICKING A FIGHT ON THAT SILLY PRETEXT...
NOW MAKE A PROPER APOLOGY!!
...JUST 'COS IT'S SOMEONE WHO ASSOCIATES WITH USUI-SENPAI ...!!
CAN'T APOLOGIZE WHEN I AIN'T DONE NOTHIN' WRONG.
IF IT'LL MAKE YOU FEEL BETTER TO HIT ME, GO RIGHT AHEAD.

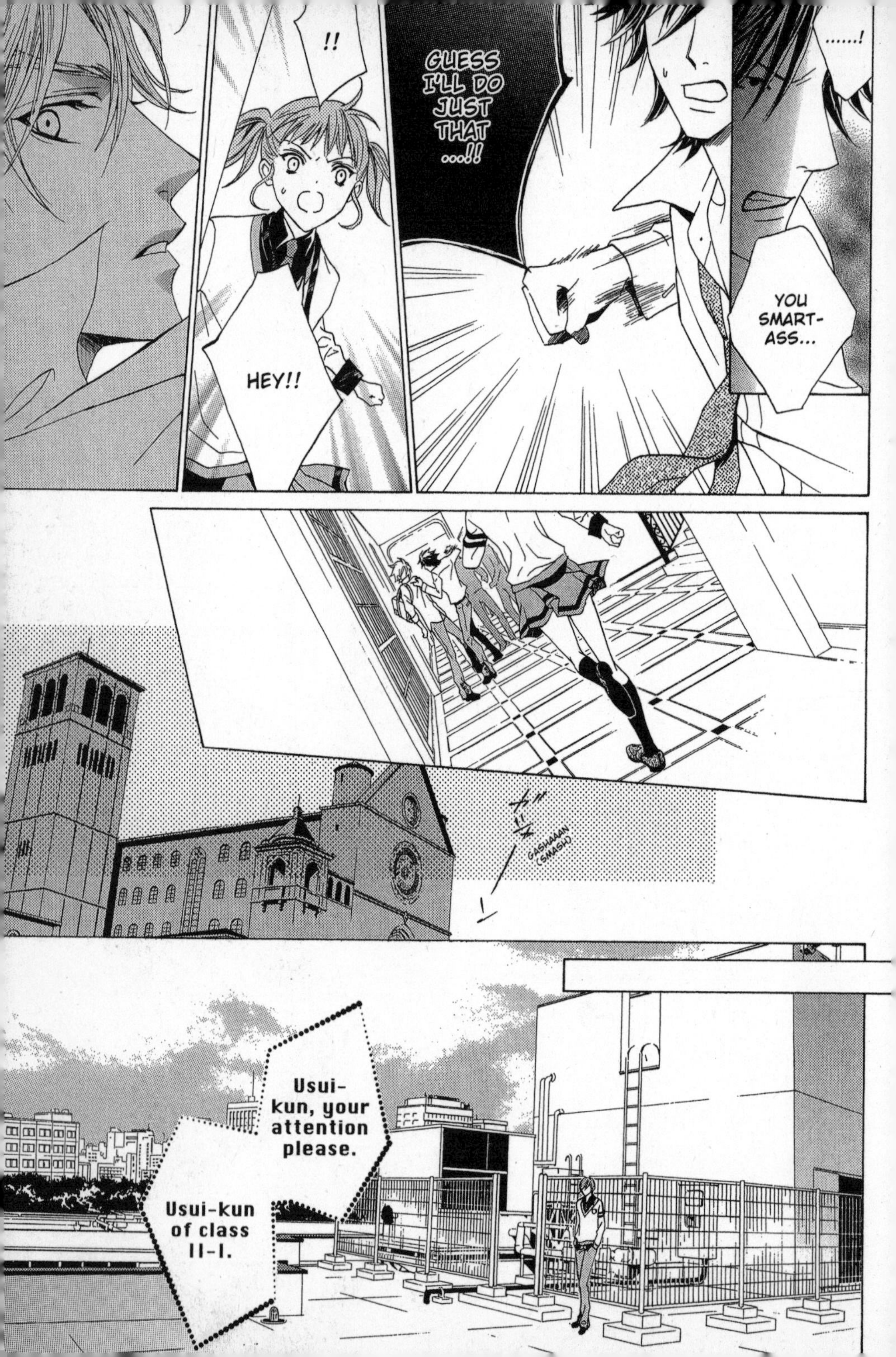

......!
YOU SMART-ASS...
GUESS I'LL DO JUST THAT ...!!
!!
HEY!!
GASHAAAN (SMASH)
!
Usui-kun, your attention please.
Usui-kun of class II-1.

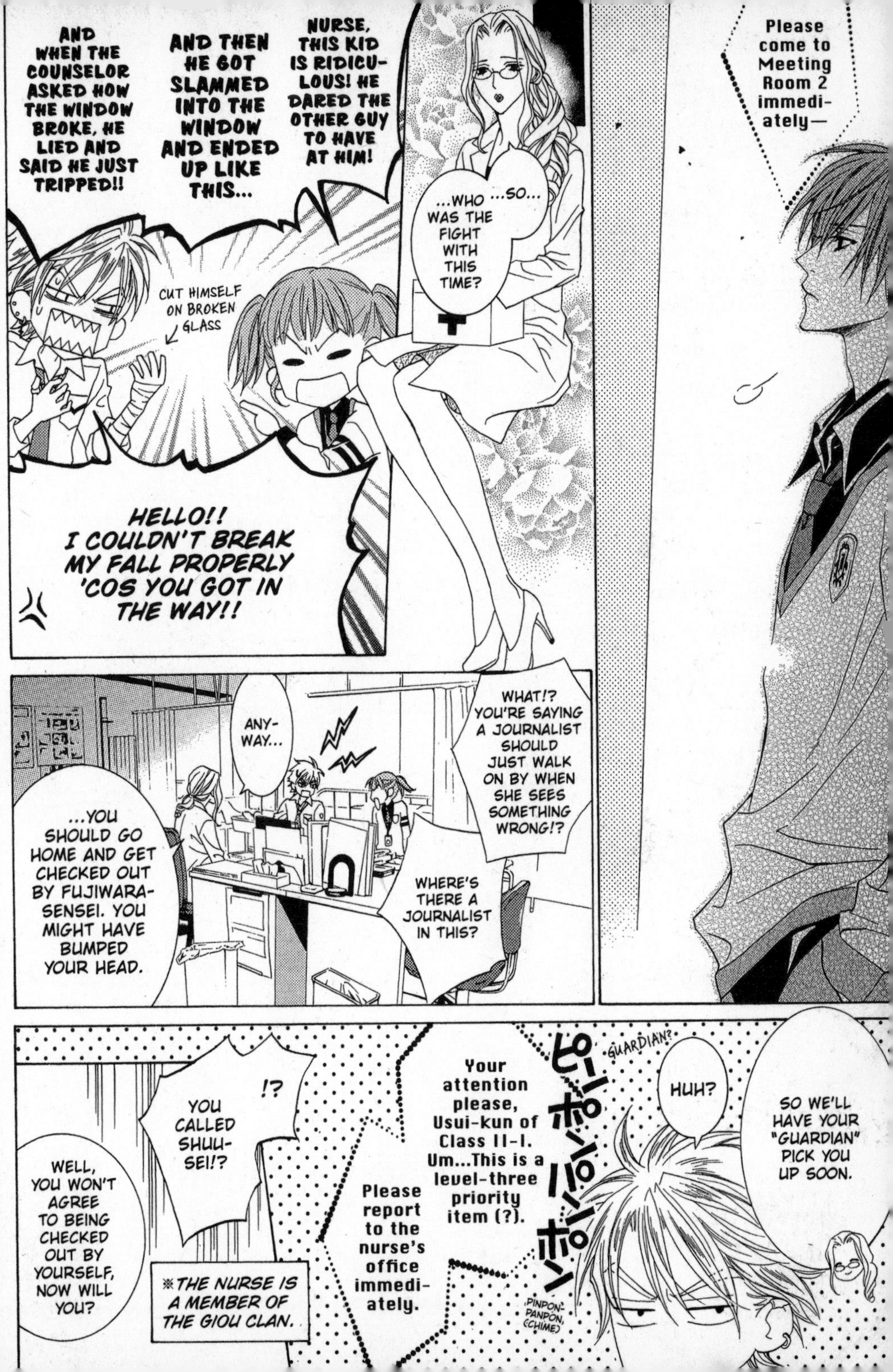
Please come to Meeting Room 2 immedi-ately—
...SO...
...WHO WAS THE FIGHT WITH THIS TIME?
NURSE, THIS KID IS RIDICU-LOUS! HE DARED THE OTHER GUY TO HAVE AT HIM!
AND THEN HE GOT SLAMMED INTO THE WINDOW AND ENDED UP LIKE THIS...
AND WHEN THE COUNSELOR ASKED HOW THE WINDOW BROKE, HE LIED AND SAID HE JUST TRIPPED!!
CUT HIMSELF ON BROKEN GLASS
HELLO!! I COULDN'T BREAK MY FALL PROPERLY 'COS YOU GOT IN THE WAY!!
WHAT!? YOU'RE SAYING A JOURNALIST SHOULD JUST WALK ON BY WHEN SHE SEES SOMETHING WRONG!?
WHERE'S THERE A JOURNALIST IN THIS?
ANY-WAY...
...YOU SHOULD GO HOME AND GET CHECKED OUT BY FUJIWARA-SENSEI. YOU MIGHT HAVE BUMPED YOUR HEAD.
SO WE'LL HAVE YOUR "GUARDIAN" PICK YOU UP SOON.
HUH?
GUARDIAN?
ピーンポーンパーンポーン
PINPON-PANPON (CHIME)
Your attention please, Usui-kun of Class II-1. Um...This is a level-three priority item (?).
Please report to the nurse's office immedi-ately.
!?
YOU CALLED SHUU-SEI!?
WELL, YOU WON'T AGREE TO BEING CHECKED OUT BY YOURSELF, NOW WILL YOU?
※THE NURSE IS A MEMBER OF THE GIOU CLAN.

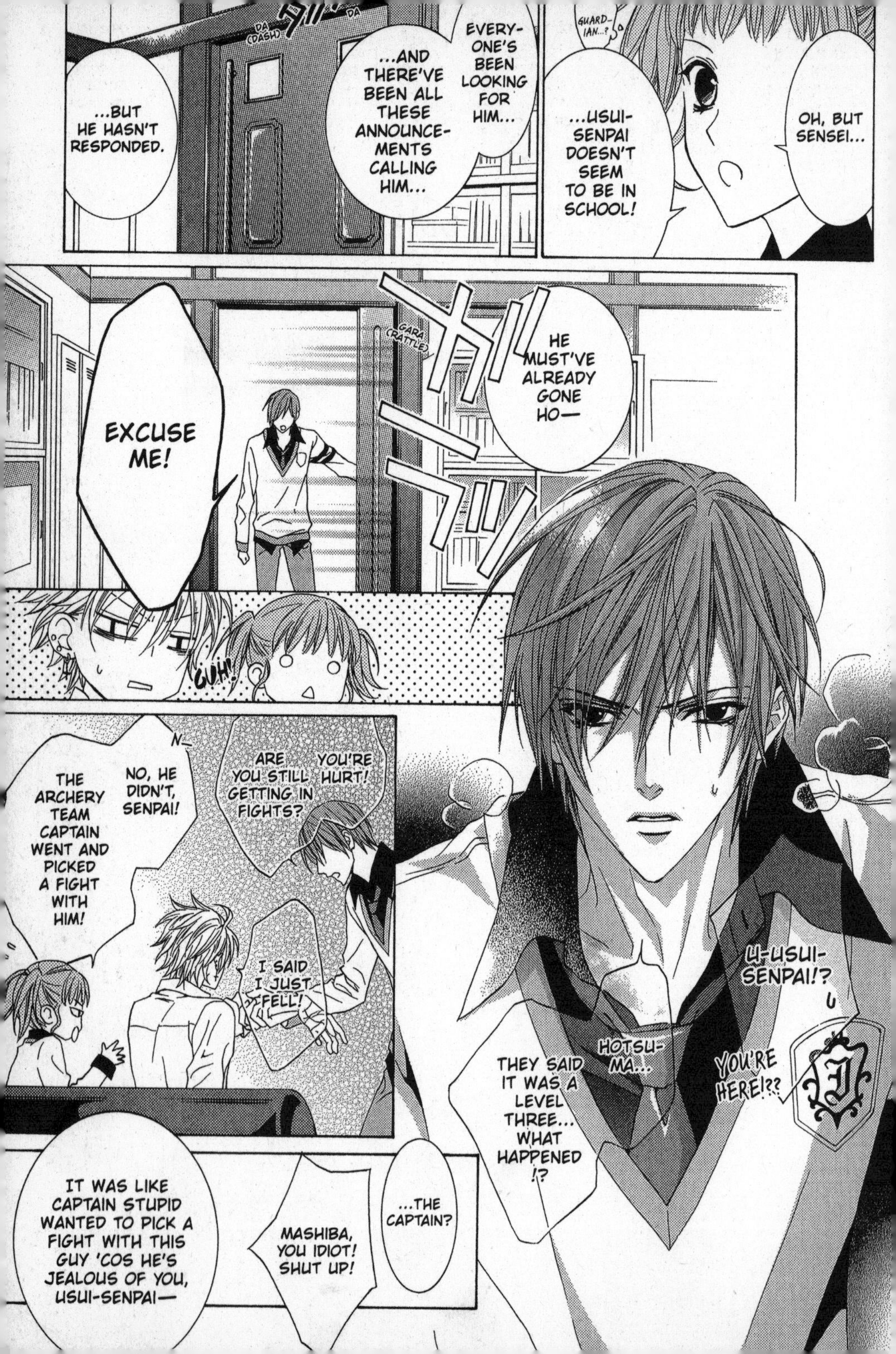
GUARDIAN...?
OH, BUT SENSEI...
...USUI-SENPAI DOESN'T SEEM TO BE IN SCHOOL!
DA (DASH) DA
EVERYONE'S BEEN LOOKING FOR HIM...
...AND THERE'VE BEEN ALL THESE ANNOUNCEMENTS CALLING HIM...
...BUT HE HASN'T RESPONDED.
HE MUST'VE ALREADY GONE HO—
GARA (RATTLE)
EXCUSE ME!
GUH!
U-USUI-SENPAI!? YOU'RE HERE!??
HOTSUMA...
THEY SAID IT WAS A LEVEL THREE... WHAT HAPPENED!?
YOU'RE HURT!
ARE YOU STILL GETTING IN FIGHTS?
I SAID I JUST FELL!
N—
NO, HE DIDN'T, SENPAI!
THE ARCHERY TEAM CAPTAIN WENT AND PICKED A FIGHT WITH HIM!
...THE CAPTAIN?
MASHIBA, YOU IDIOT! SHUT UP!
IT WAS LIKE CAPTAIN STUPID WANTED TO PICK A FIGHT WITH THIS GUY 'COS HE'S JEALOUS OF YOU, USUI-SENPAI—

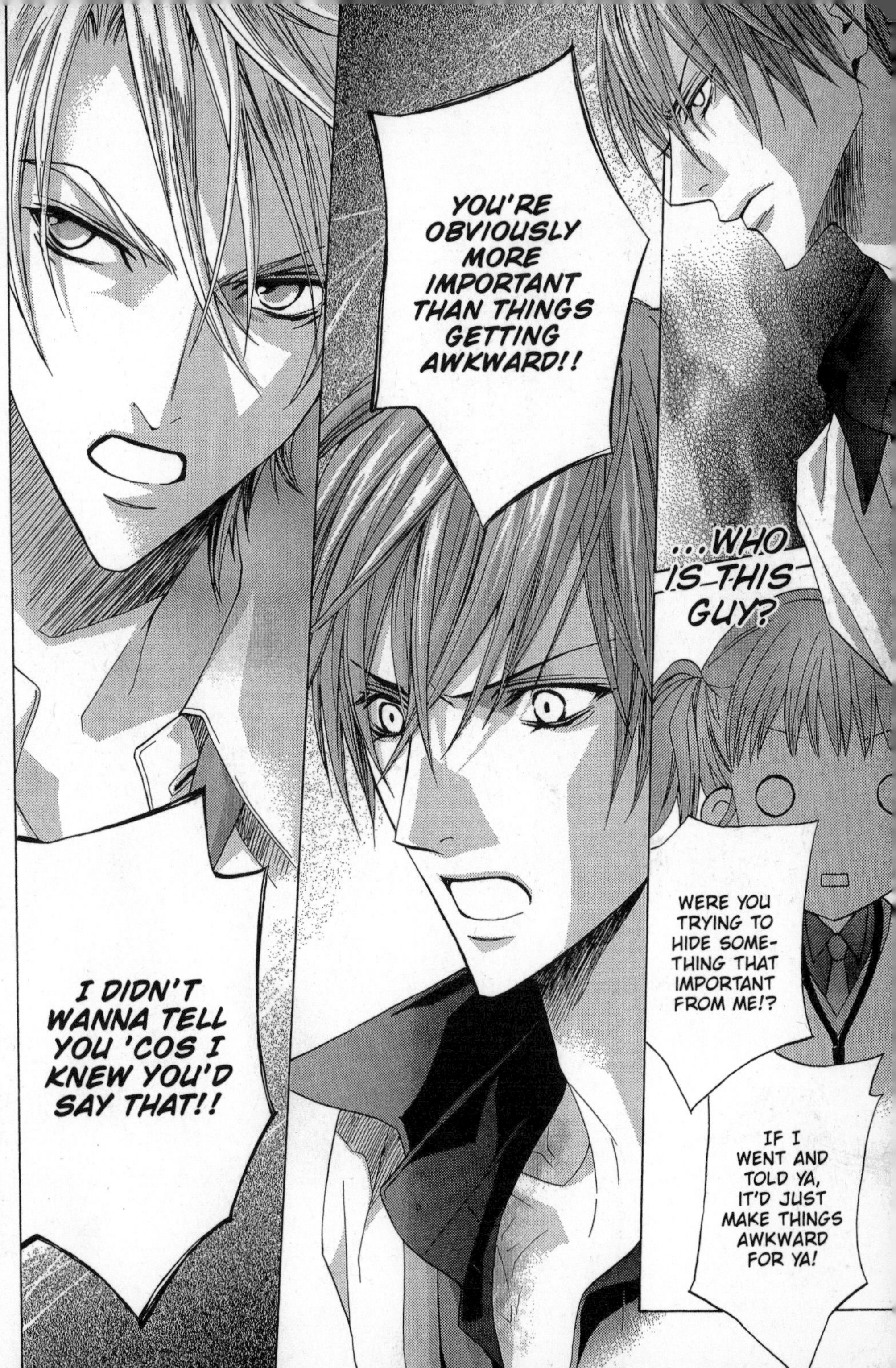
...WHO IS THIS GUY?
WERE YOU TRYING TO HIDE SOME-THING THAT IMPORTANT FROM ME!?
IF I WENT AND TOLD YA, IT'D JUST MAKE THINGS AWKWARD FOR YA!
YOU'RE OBVIOUSLY MORE IMPORTANT THAN THINGS GETTING AWKWARD!!
I DIDN'T WANNA TELL YOU 'COS I KNEW YOU'D SAY THAT!!

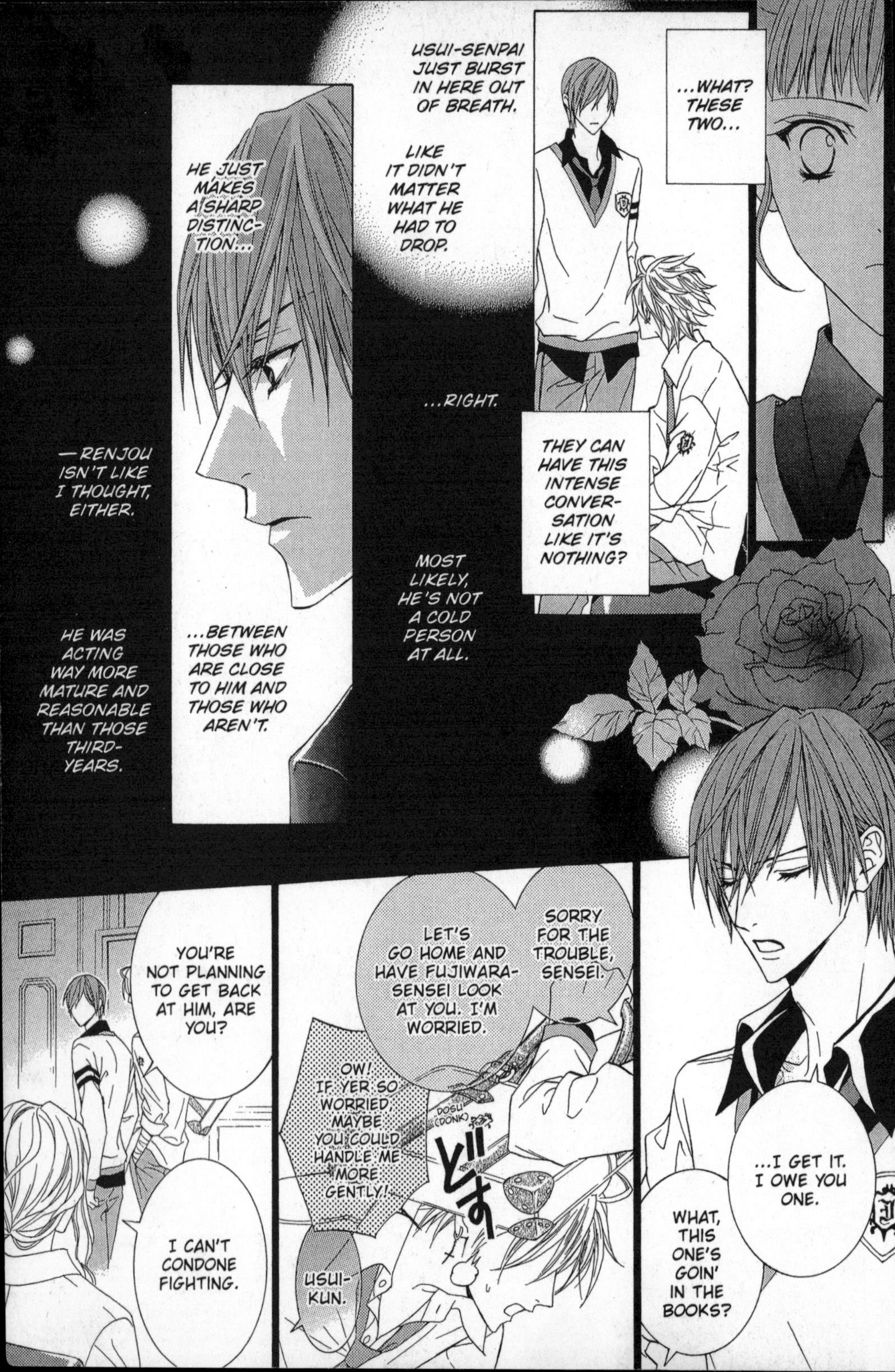
...WHAT? THESE TWO...
THEY CAN HAVE THIS INTENSE CONVERSATION LIKE IT'S NOTHING?
USUI-SENPAI JUST BURST IN HERE OUT OF BREATH.
LIKE IT DIDN'T MATTER WHAT HE HAD TO DROP.
...RIGHT.
MOST LIKELY, HE'S NOT A COLD PERSON AT ALL.
HE JUST MAKES A SHARP DISTINCTION...
...BETWEEN THOSE WHO ARE CLOSE TO HIM AND THOSE WHO AREN'T.
—RENJOU ISN'T LIKE I THOUGHT, EITHER.
HE WAS ACTING WAY MORE MATURE AND REASONABLE THAN THOSE THIRD-YEARS.
...I GET IT. I OWE YOU ONE.
WHAT, THIS ONE'S GOIN' IN THE BOOKS?
SORRY FOR THE TROUBLE, SENSEI.
LET'S GO HOME AND HAVE FUJIWARA-SENSEI LOOK AT YOU. I'M WORRIED.
OW! IF YER SO WORRIED, MAYBE YOU COULD HANDLE ME MORE GENTLY!
DOSU (DONK)
USUI-KUN.
YOU'RE NOT PLANNING TO GET BACK AT HIM, ARE YOU?
I CAN'T CONDONE FIGHTING.

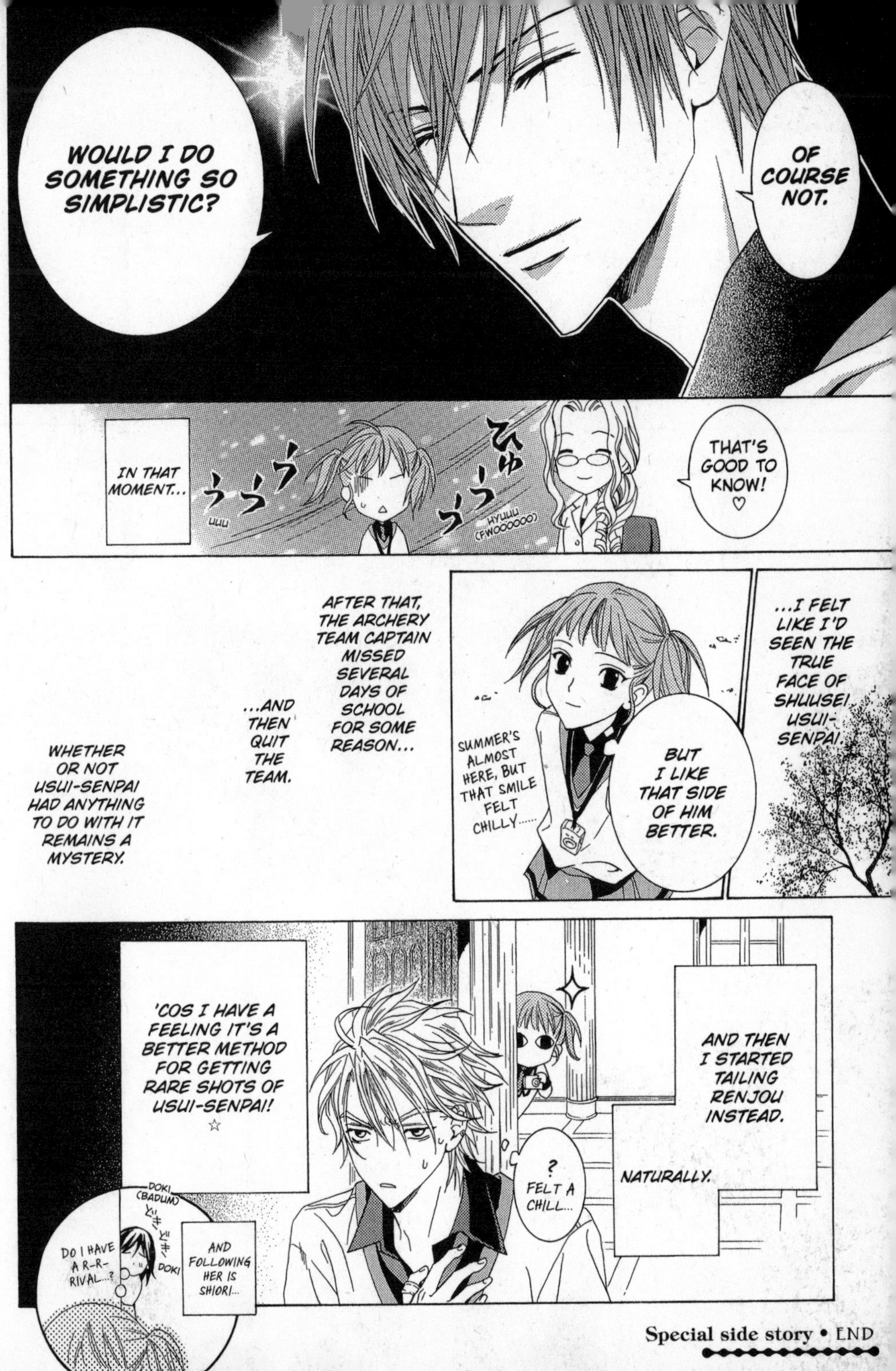
OF COURSE NOT.
WOULD I DO SOMETHING SO SIMPLISTIC?
THAT'S GOOD TO KNOW! ♡
HYUUU (FWOOOOOO)
UUU
IN THAT MOMENT...
...I FELT LIKE I'D SEEN THE TRUE FACE OF SHUUSEI USUI-SENPAI.
BUT I LIKE THAT SIDE OF HIM BETTER.
SUMMER'S ALMOST HERE, BUT THAT SMILE FELT CHILLY......
AFTER THAT, THE ARCHERY TEAM CAPTAIN MISSED SEVERAL DAYS OF SCHOOL FOR SOME REASON...
...AND THEN QUIT THE TEAM.
WHETHER OR NOT USUI-SENPAI HAD ANYTHING TO DO WITH IT REMAINS A MYSTERY.
AND THEN I STARTED TAILING RENJOU INSTEAD.
NATURALLY.
? FELT A CHILL...
'COS I HAVE A FEELING IT'S A BETTER METHOD FOR GETTING RARE SHOTS OF USUI-SENPAI! ☆
AND FOLLOWING HER IS SHIORI...
DOKI (BADUM)
DOKI
DO I HAVE A R-R-RIVAL...?

Special side story • END

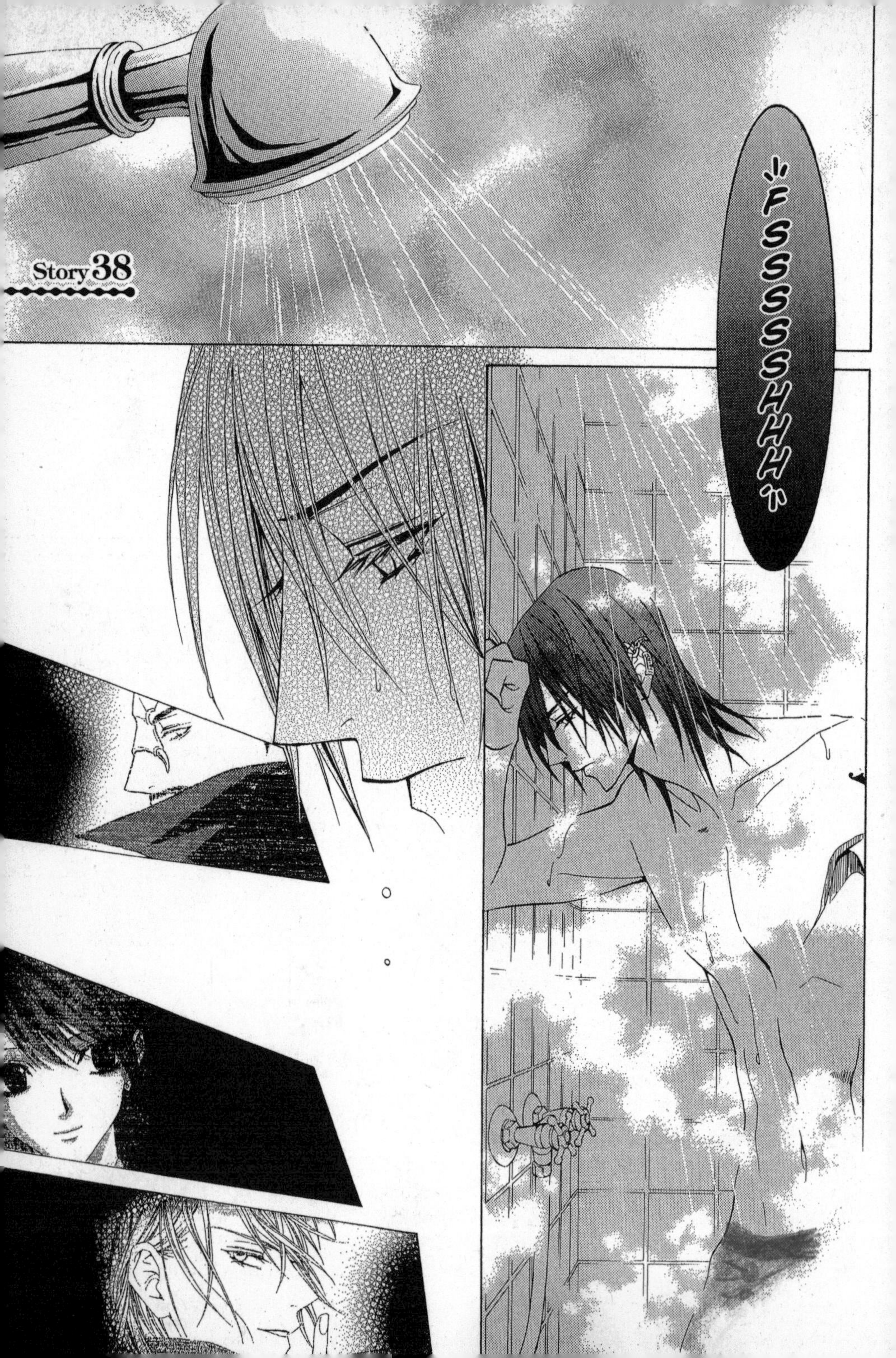
Story 38
FSSSSSHHH

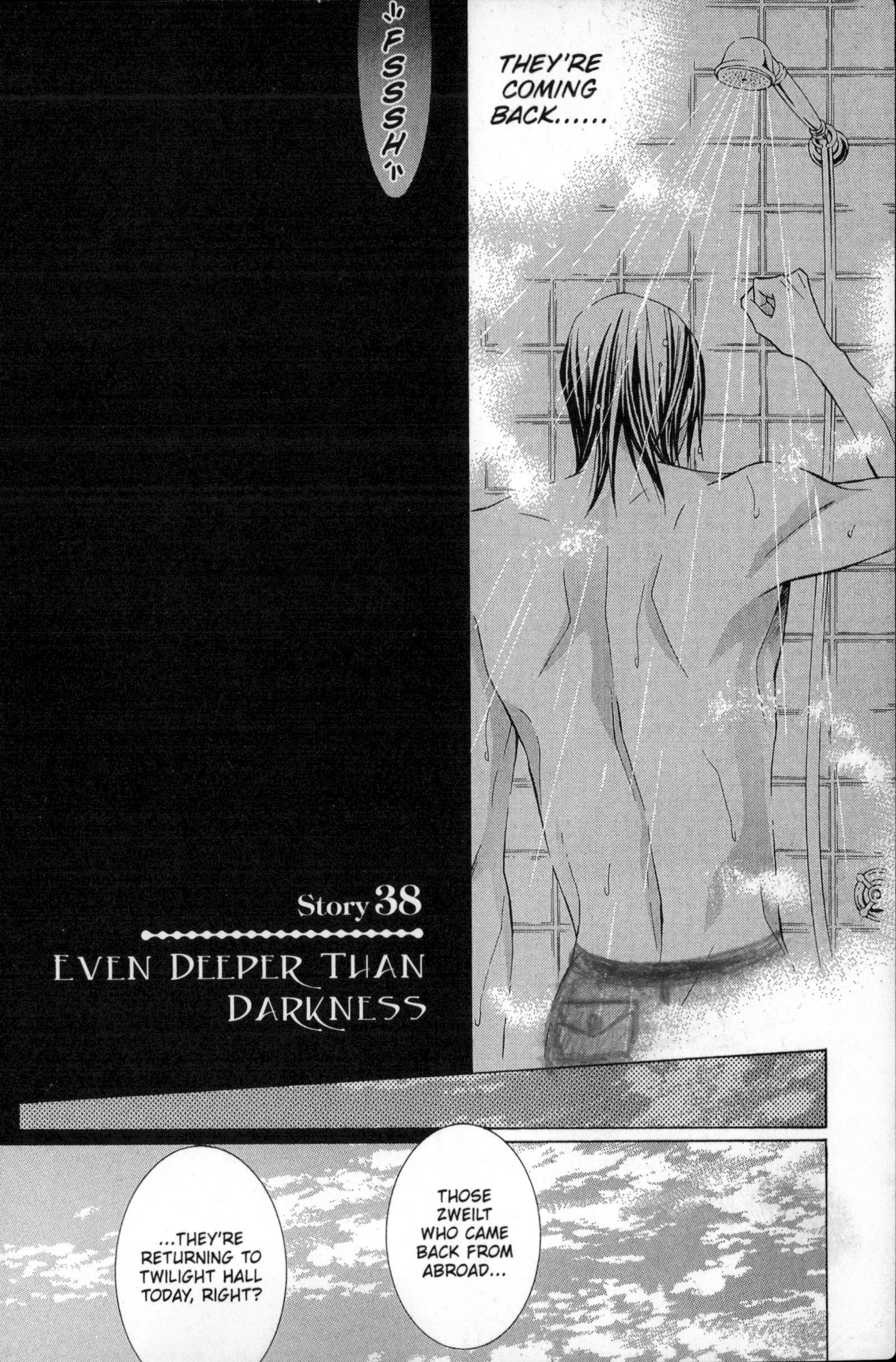
THEY'RE COMING BACK......
FSSSH
Story 38
EVEN DEEPER THAN DARKNESS
THOSE ZWEILT WHO CAME BACK FROM ABROAD...
...THEY'RE RETURNING TO TWILIGHT HALL TODAY, RIGHT?

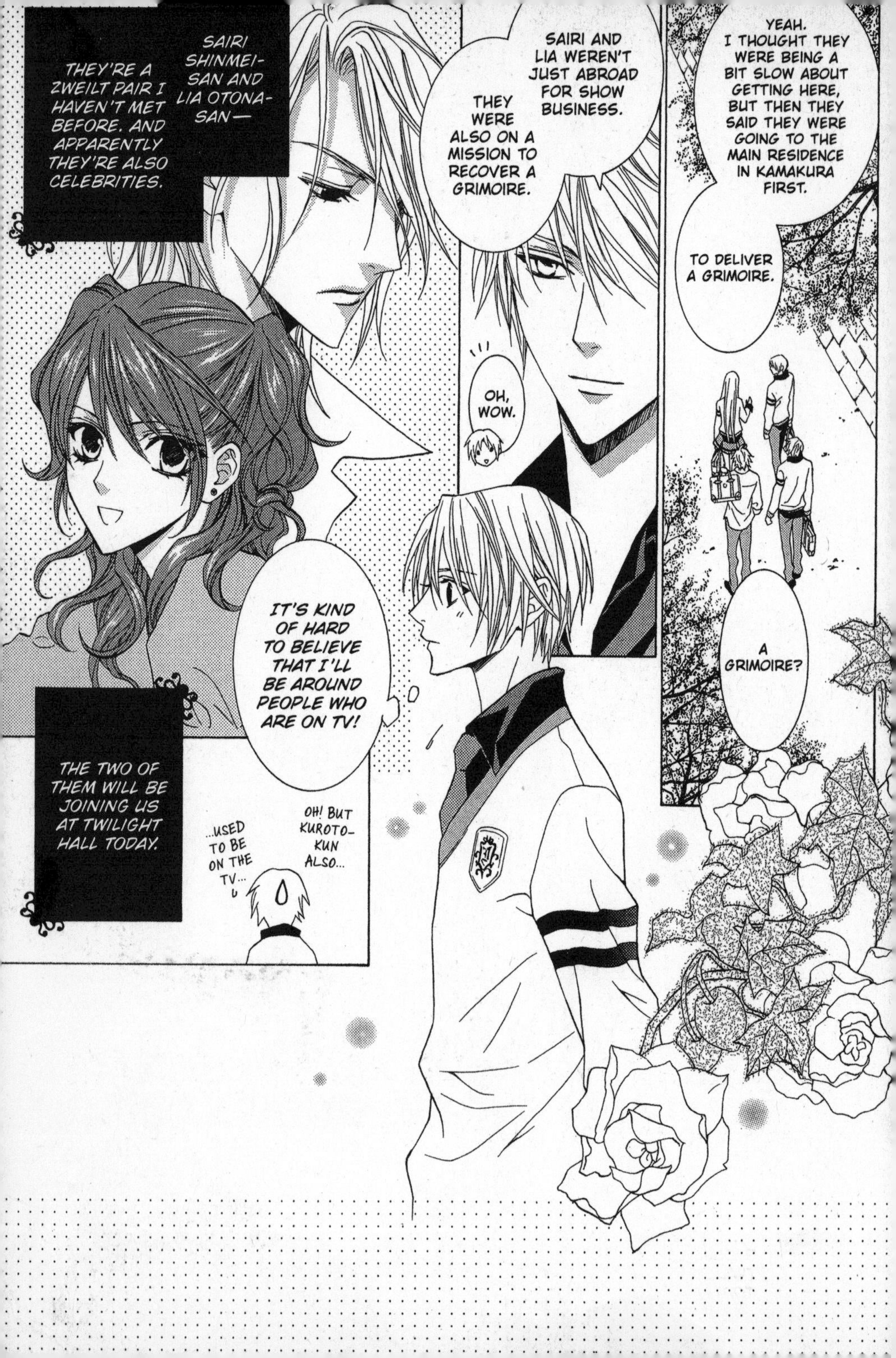
YEAH. I THOUGHT THEY WERE BEING A BIT SLOW ABOUT GETTING HERE, BUT THEN THEY SAID THEY WERE GOING TO THE MAIN RESIDENCE IN KAMAKURA FIRST.
TO DELIVER A GRIMOIRE.
A GRIMOIRE?
SAIRI AND LIA WEREN'T JUST ABROAD FOR SHOW BUSINESS.
THEY WERE ALSO ON A MISSION TO RECOVER A GRIMOIRE.
OH, WOW.
SAIRI SHINMEI-SAN AND LIA OTONA-SAN—
THEY'RE A ZWEILT PAIR I HAVEN'T MET BEFORE. AND APPARENTLY THEY'RE ALSO CELEBRITIES.
IT'S KIND OF HARD TO BELIEVE THAT I'LL BE AROUND PEOPLE WHO ARE ON TV!
THE TWO OF THEM WILL BE JOINING US AT TWILIGHT HALL TODAY.
OH! BUT KUROTO-KUN ALSO...
...USED TO BE ON THE TV...

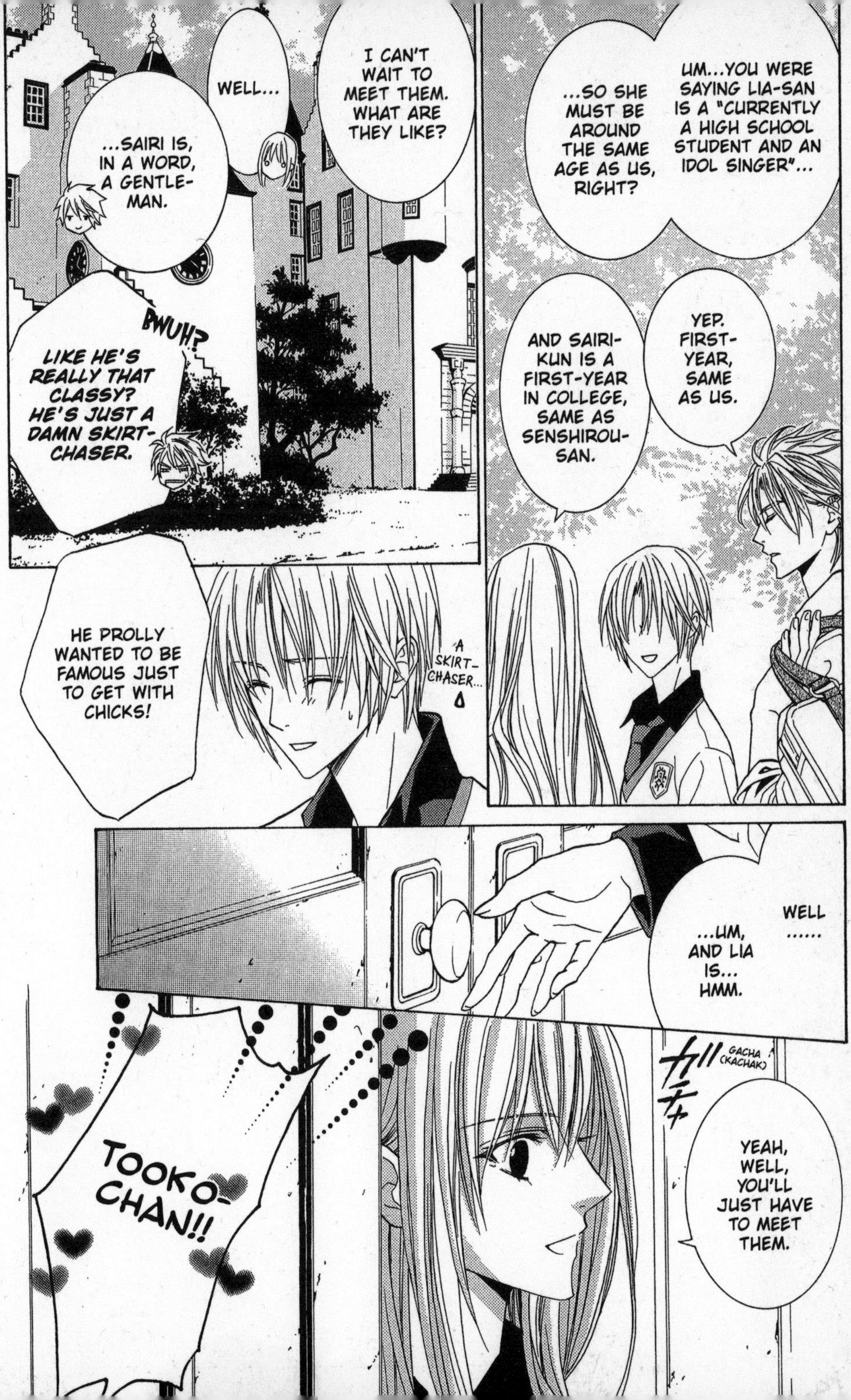
UM...YOU WERE SAYING LIA-SAN IS A "CURRENTLY A HIGH SCHOOL STUDENT AND AN IDOL SINGER"...
...SO SHE MUST BE AROUND THE SAME AGE AS US, RIGHT?
YEP. FIRST-YEAR, SAME AS US.
AND SAIRI-KUN IS A FIRST-YEAR IN COLLEGE, SAME AS SENSHIROU-SAN.
I CAN'T WAIT TO MEET THEM. WHAT ARE THEY LIKE?
WELL...
...SAIRI IS, IN A WORD, A GENTLE-MAN.
BWUH?
LIKE HE'S REALLY THAT CLASSY? HE'S JUST A DAMN SKIRT-CHASER.
A SKIRT-CHASER...
HE PROLLY WANTED TO BE FAMOUS JUST TO GET WITH CHICKS!
WELL ......
...UM, AND LIA IS... HMM.
GACHA (KACHAK)
YEAH, WELL, YOU'LL JUST HAVE TO MEET THEM.
TOOKO-CHAN!!

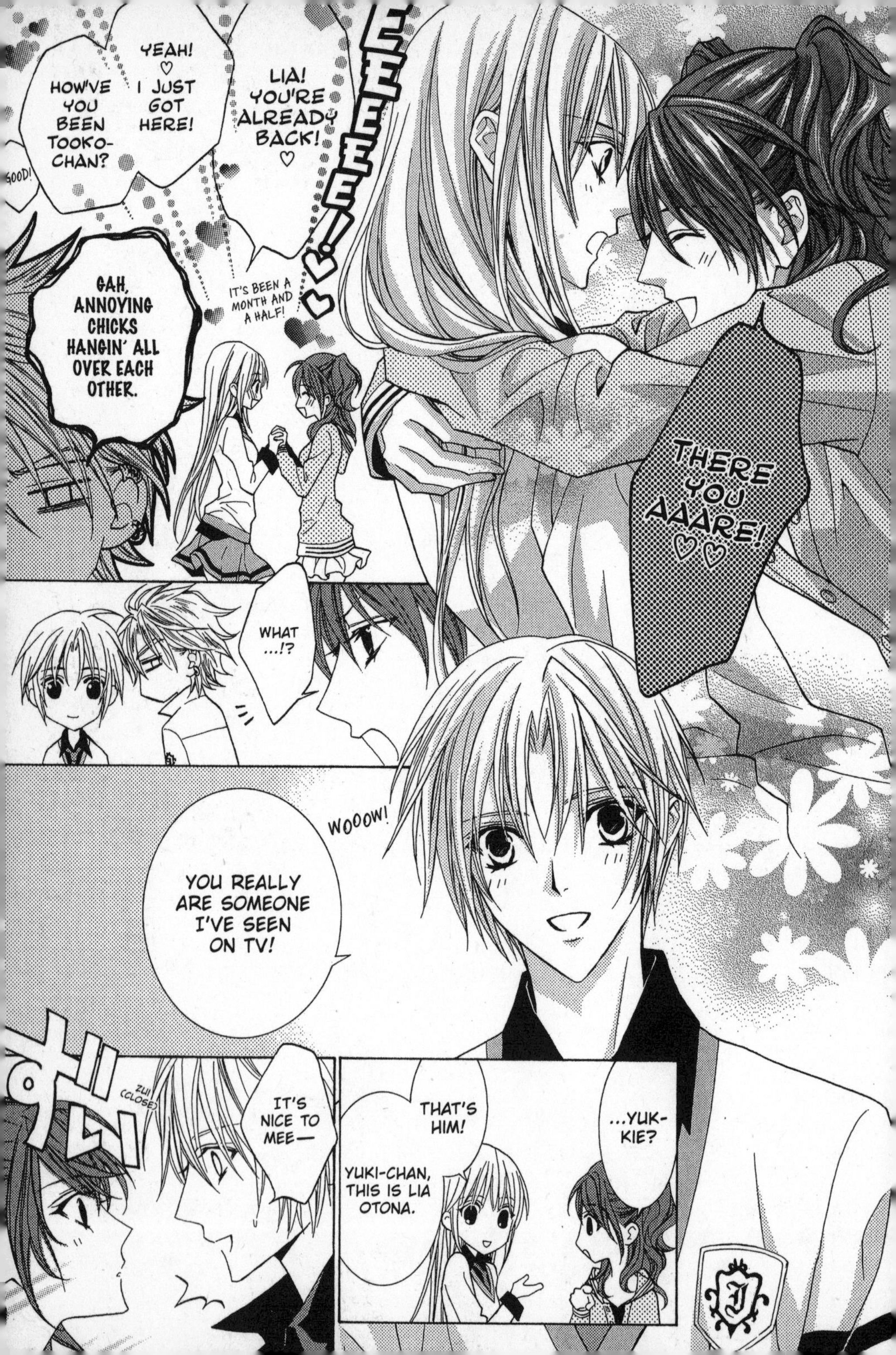
THERE YOU AAARE! ♡♡
EEEEEE!!
LIA! YOU'RE ALREADY BACK! ♡
YEAH! ♡ I JUST GOT HERE!
HOW'VE YOU BEEN TOOKO-CHAN?
GOOD!
IT'S BEEN A MONTH AND A HALF!
GAH, ANNOYING CHICKS HANGIN' ALL OVER EACH OTHER.
WHAT ...!?
WOOOW!
YOU REALLY ARE SOMEONE I'VE SEEN ON TV!
...YUK-KIE?
THAT'S HIM!
YUKI-CHAN, THIS IS LIA OTONA.
IT'S NICE TO MEE—
ZUI (CLOSE)

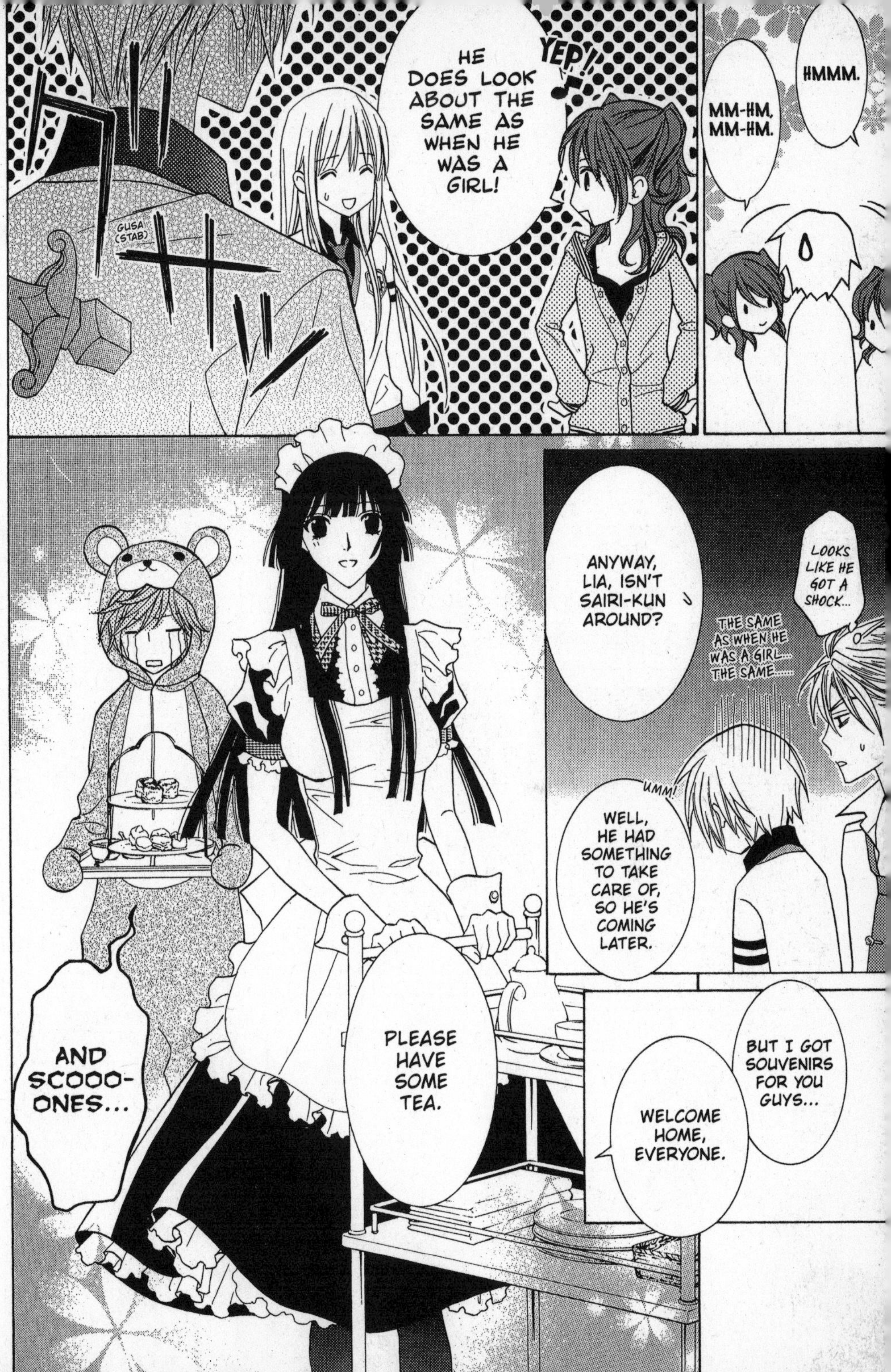
HMMM.
MM-HM, MM-HM.
YEP!!
HE DOES LOOK ABOUT THE SAME AS WHEN HE WAS A GIRL!
GUSA (STAB)
LOOKS LIKE HE GOT A SHOCK...
THE SAME AS WHEN HE WAS A GIRL... THE SAME......
ANYWAY, LIA, ISN'T SAIRI-KUN AROUND?
UMM!
WELL, HE HAD SOMETHING TO TAKE CARE OF, SO HE'S COMING LATER.
BUT I GOT SOUVENIRS FOR YOU GUYS...
WELCOME HOME, EVERYONE.
PLEASE HAVE SOME TEA.
AND SCOOOO-ONES...

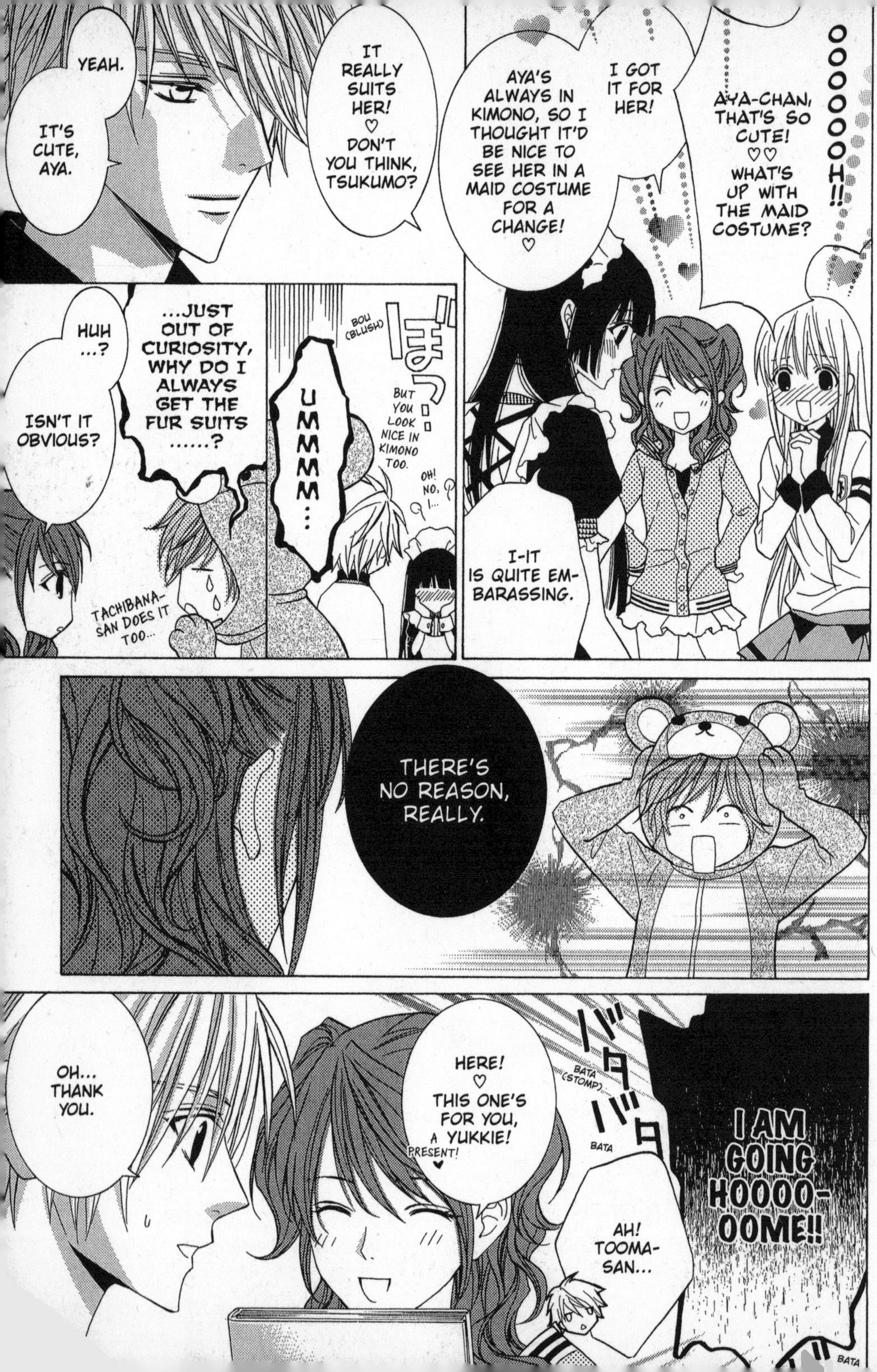
OOOOOOOH!!
AYA-CHAN, THAT'S SO CUTE! ♡♡ WHAT'S UP WITH THE MAID COSTUME?
I GOT IT FOR HER!
AYA'S ALWAYS IN KIMONO, SO I THOUGHT IT'D BE NICE TO SEE HER IN A MAID COSTUME FOR A CHANGE! ♡
I-IT IS QUITE EM-BARASSING.
IT REALLY SUITS HER! ♡ DON'T YOU THINK, TSUKUMO?
YEAH.
IT'S CUTE, AYA.
BOU (BLUSH)
UMMMM...
BUT YOU LOOK NICE IN KIMONO TOO.
OH! NO, I...
...JUST OUT OF CURIOSITY, WHY DO I ALWAYS GET THE FUR SUITS ......?
HUH ...?
ISN'T IT OBVIOUS?
TACHIBANA-SAN DOES IT TOO...
THERE'S NO REASON, REALLY.
I AM GOING HOOOO-OOME!!
BATA (STOMP)
BATA
BATA
AH! TOOMA-SAN...
HERE! ♡ THIS ONE'S FOR YOU, YUKKIE!
A PRESENT! ♥
OH... THANK YOU.

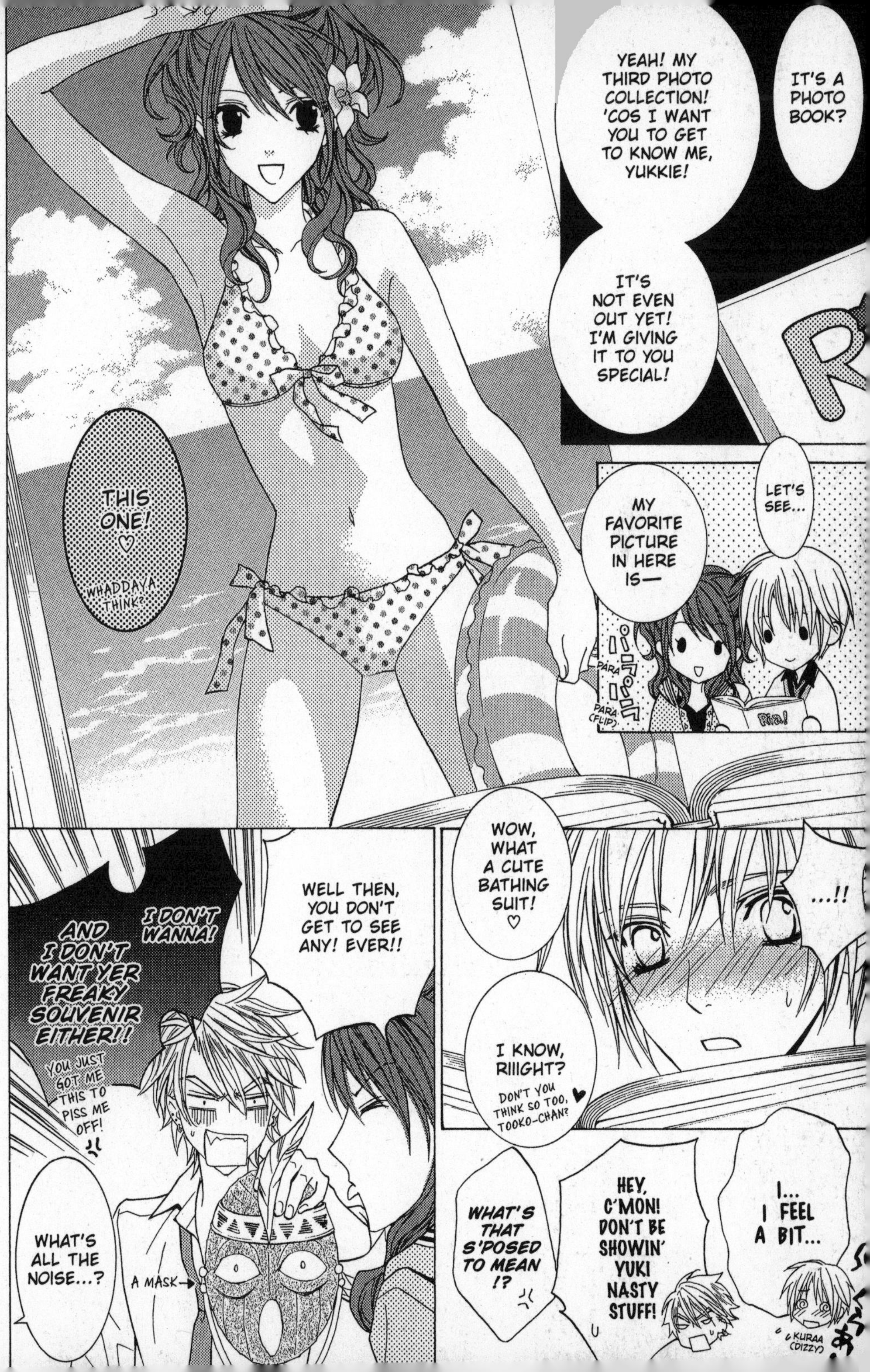
IT'S A PHOTO BOOK?
YEAH! MY THIRD PHOTO COLLECTION! 'COS I WANT YOU TO GET TO KNOW ME, YUKKIE!
IT'S NOT EVEN OUT YET! I'M GIVING IT TO YOU SPECIAL!
LET'S SEE...
MY FAVORITE PICTURE IN HERE IS—
PARA
PARA (FLIP)
Ria!
THIS ONE! ♡
WHADDAYA THINK?
...!!
WOW, WHAT A CUTE BATHING SUIT! ♡
I KNOW, RIIIGHT?
DON'T YOU THINK SO TOO, TOOKO-CHAN? ♥
WELL THEN, YOU DON'T GET TO SEE ANY! EVER!!
I DON'T WANNA!
AND I DON'T WANT YER FREAKY SOUVENIR EITHER!!
YOU JUST GOT ME THIS TO PISS ME OFF!
I... I FEEL A BIT...
KURAA (DIZZY)
HEY, C'MON! DON'T BE SHOWIN' YUKI NASTY STUFF!
WHAT'S THAT S'POSED TO MEAN!?
WHAT'S ALL THE NOISE...?
A MASK

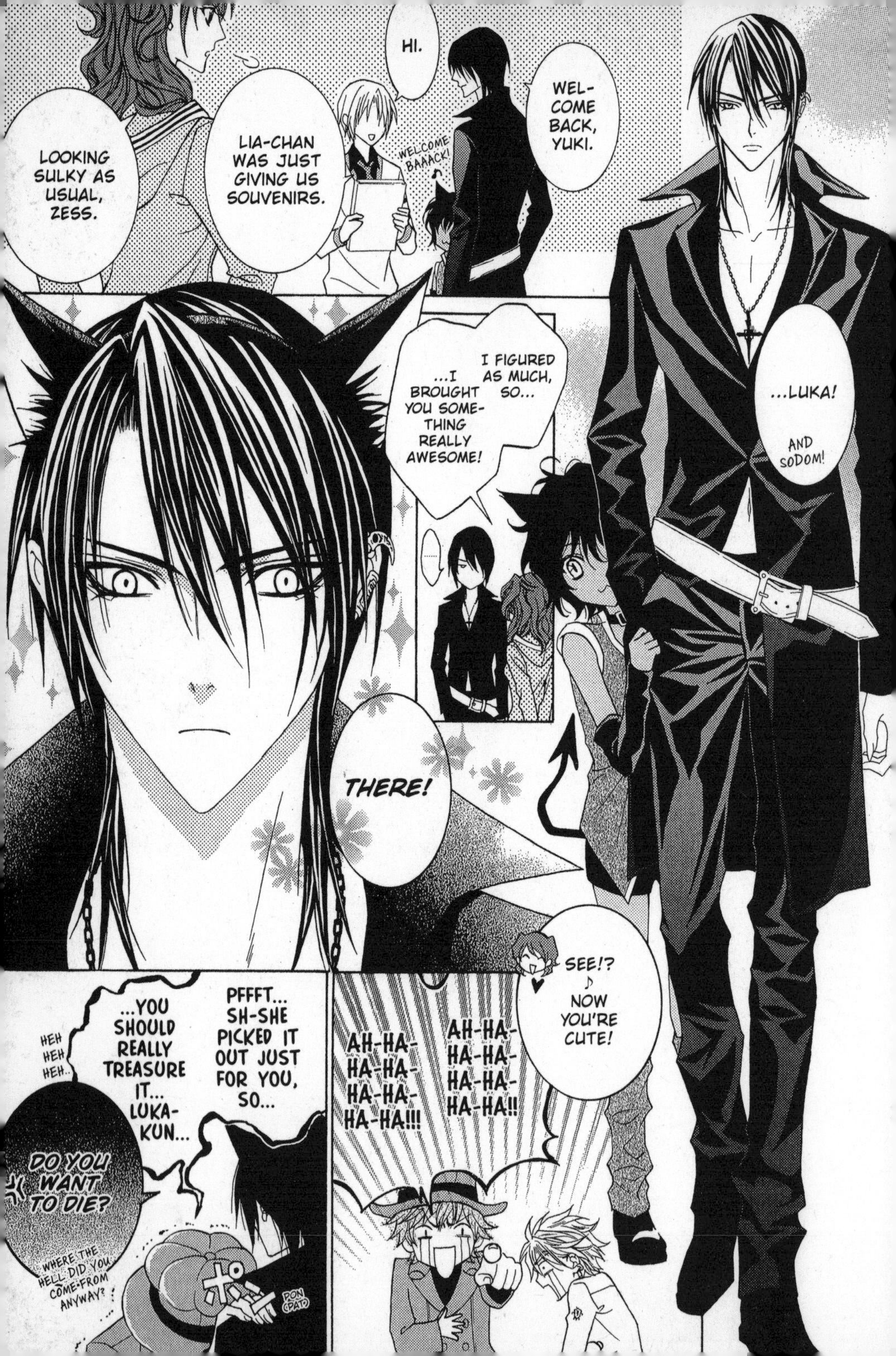
WEL-COME BACK, YUKI.
HI.
WELCOME BAAACK! ♪
LIA-CHAN WAS JUST GIVING US SOUVENIRS.
LOOKING SULKY AS USUAL, ZESS.
...LUKA!
AND SODOM!
I FIGURED AS MUCH, SO...
...I BROUGHT YOU SOME-THING REALLY AWESOME!
......
THERE!
SEE!? ♪ NOW YOU'RE CUTE!
AH-HA-HA-HA-HA-HA-HA-HA!!
AH-HA-HA-HA-HA-HA-HA-HA!!!
PFFFT... SH-SHE PICKED IT OUT JUST FOR YOU, SO...
...YOU SHOULD REALLY TREASURE IT... LUKA-KUN...
HEH HEH HEH...
DO YOU WANT TO DIE?
WHERE THE HELL DID YOU COME FROM ANYWAY?
PON (PAT)

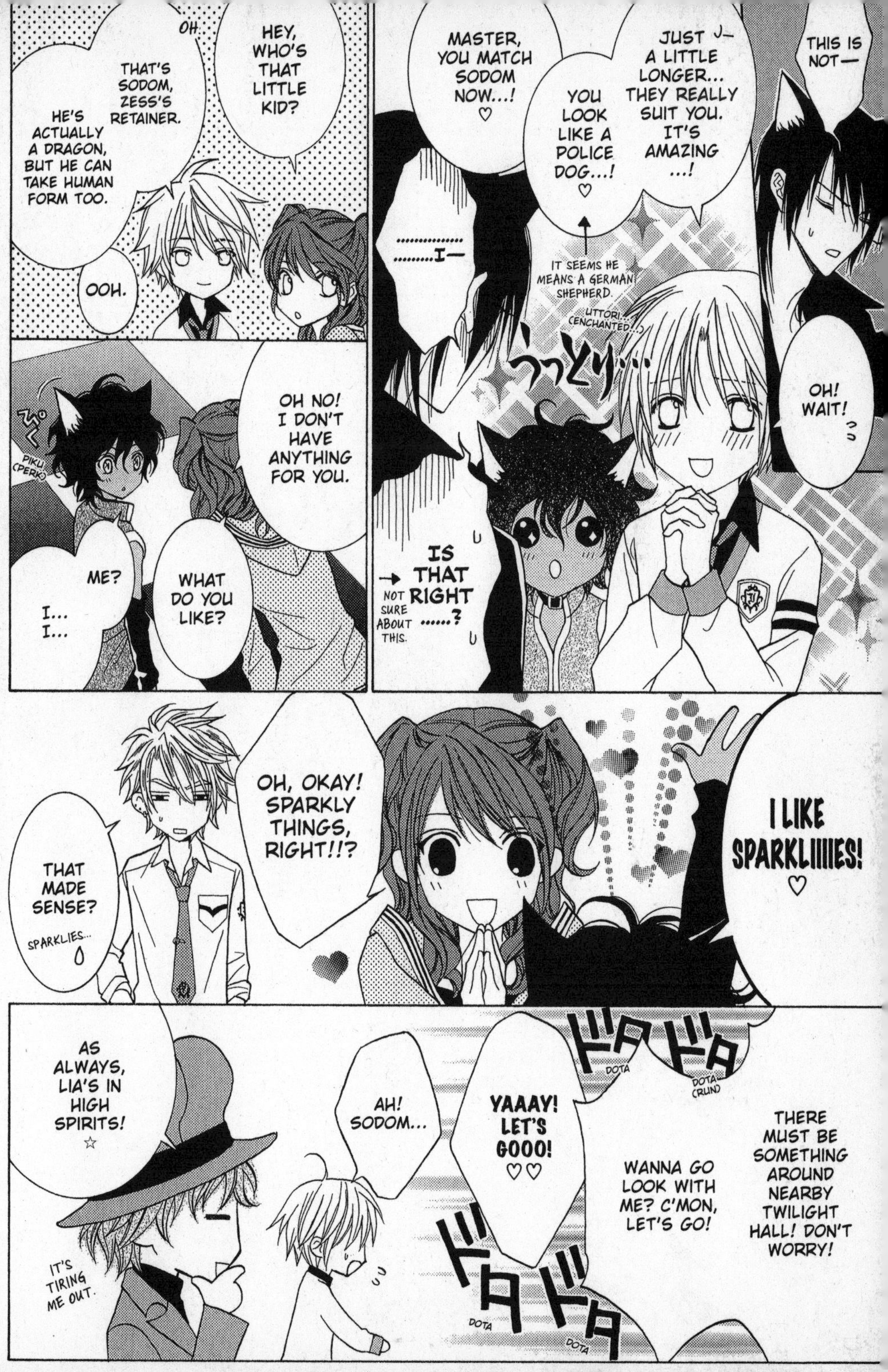
THIS IS NOT—
JUST A LITTLE LONGER... THEY REALLY SUIT YOU. IT'S AMAZING...!
MASTER, YOU MATCH SODOM NOW...! ♡
YOU LOOK LIKE A POLICE DOG...! ♡
IT SEEMS HE MEANS A GERMAN SHEPHERD.
....I—
OH! WAIT!
うっとり…
UTTORI (ENCHANTED...)
IS THAT RIGHT ......?
NOT SURE ABOUT THIS.
HEY, WHO'S THAT LITTLE KID?
OH.
THAT'S SODOM, ZESS'S RETAINER.
HE'S ACTUALLY A DRAGON, BUT HE CAN TAKE HUMAN FORM TOO.
OOH.
OH NO! I DON'T HAVE ANYTHING FOR YOU.
WHAT DO YOU LIKE?
PIKU (PERK)
ME?
I... I...
I LIKE SPARKLIIIIES! ♡
OH, OKAY! SPARKLY THINGS, RIGHT!!?
THAT MADE SENSE?
SPARKLIES...
ドタドタ
DOTA DOTA (RUN)
THERE MUST BE SOMETHING AROUND NEARBY TWILIGHT HALL! DON'T WORRY!
WANNA GO LOOK WITH ME? C'MON, LET'S GO!
YAAAY! LET'S GOOO! ♡♡
AH! SODOM...
ドタドタ
DOTA DOTA
AS ALWAYS, LIA'S IN HIGH SPIRITS! ☆
IT'S TIRING ME OUT.

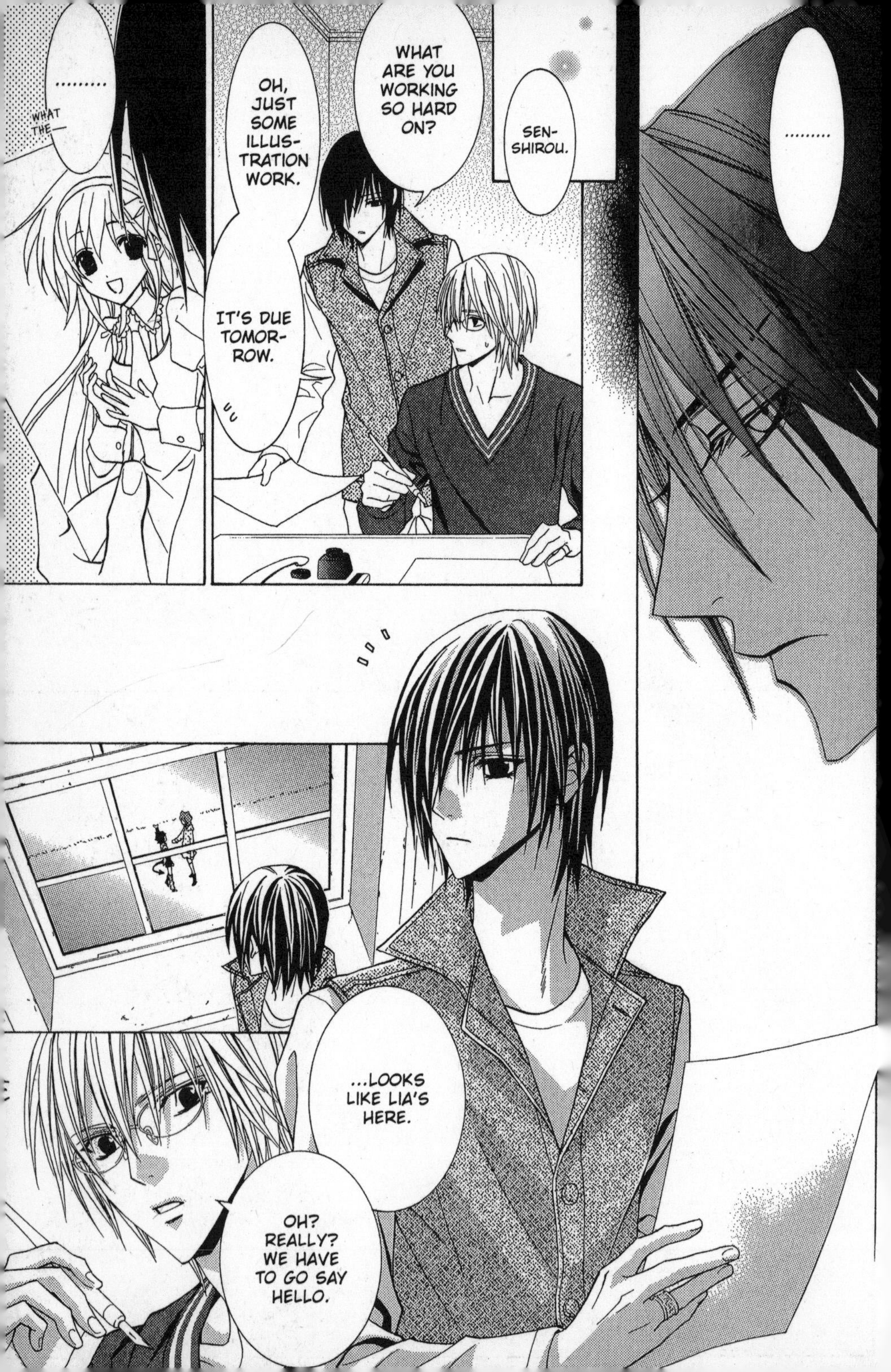
....
SEN-SHIROU.
WHAT ARE YOU WORKING SO HARD ON?
OH, JUST SOME ILLUSTRATION WORK.
IT'S DUE TOMORROW.
....
WHAT THE—
...LOOKS LIKE LIA'S HERE.
OH? REALLY? WE HAVE TO GO SAY HELLO.

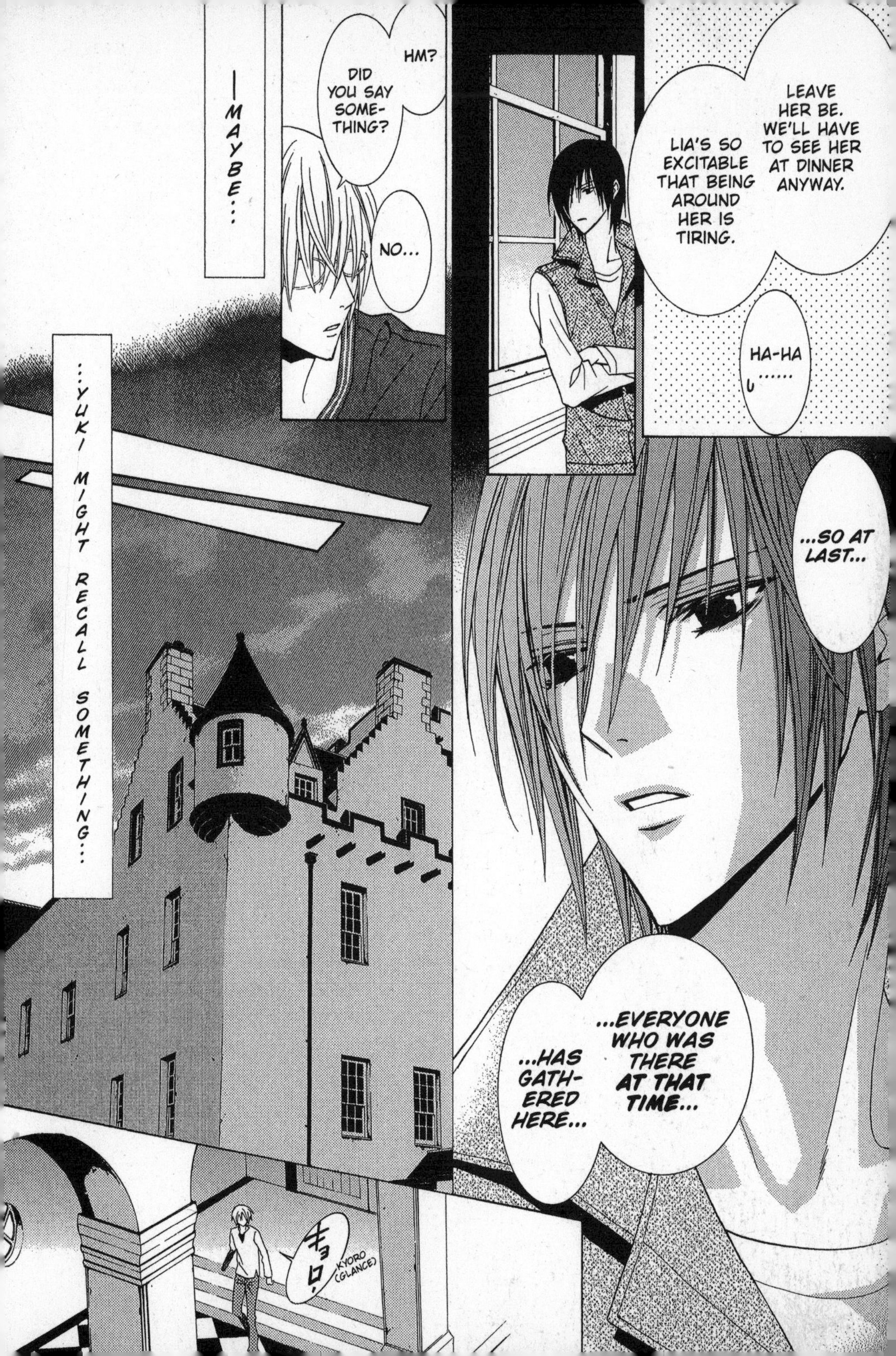
LIA'S SO EXCITABLE THAT BEING AROUND HER IS TIRING.
LEAVE HER BE. WE'LL HAVE TO SEE HER AT DINNER ANYWAY.
HA-HA ......
...SO AT LAST...
...EVERYONE WHO WAS THERE AT THAT TIME...
...HAS GATHERED HERE...
HM?
DID YOU SAY SOMETHING?
NO...
MAYBE...
...YUKI MIGHT RECALL SOMETHING...
キョロ
KYORO (GLANCE)

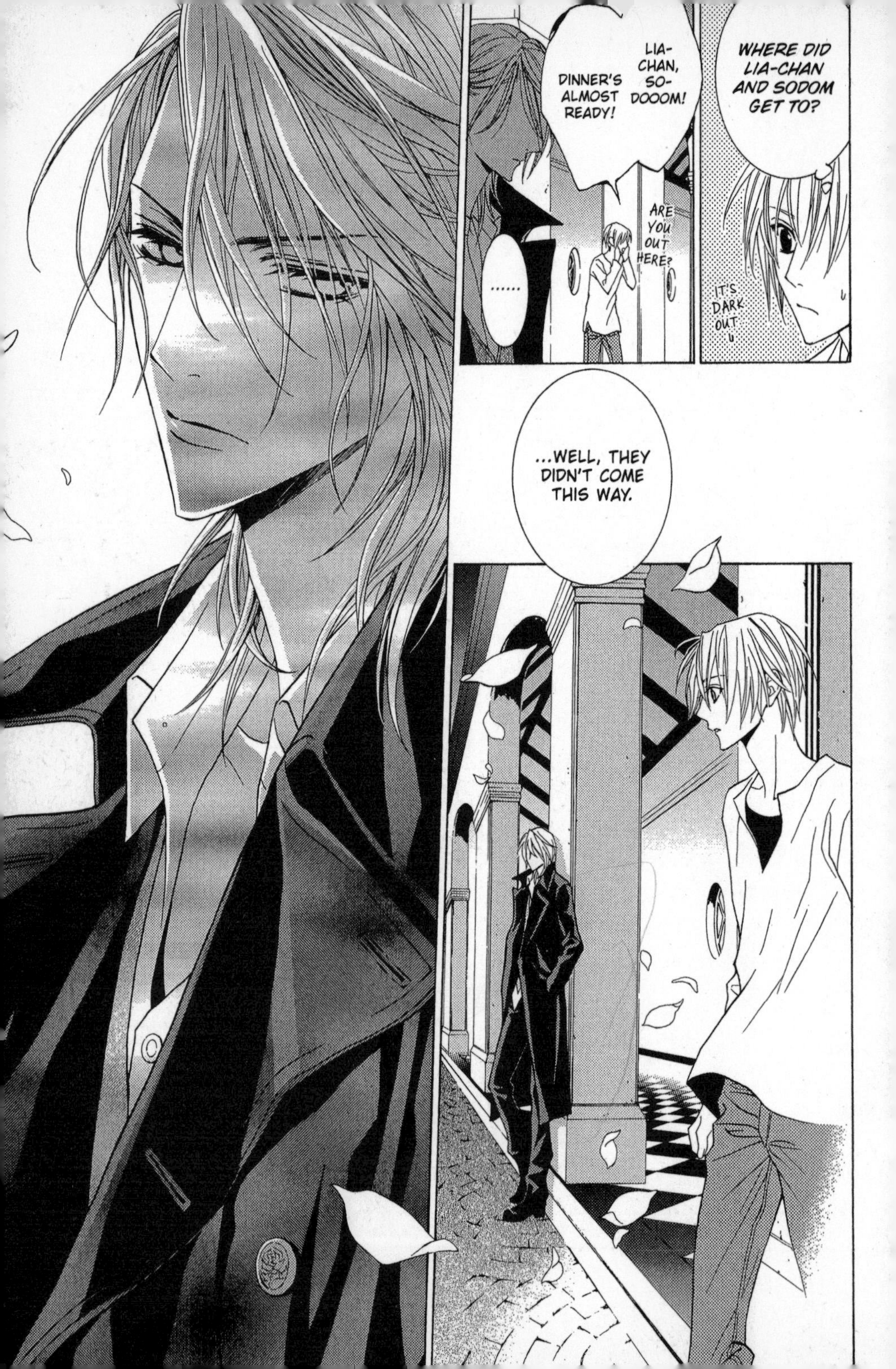
WHERE DID LIA-CHAN AND SODOM GET TO?
IT'S DARK OUT
LIA-CHAN, SO-DOOOM!
DINNER'S ALMOST READY!
ARE YOU OUT HERE?
......
...WELL, THEY DIDN'T COME THIS WAY.

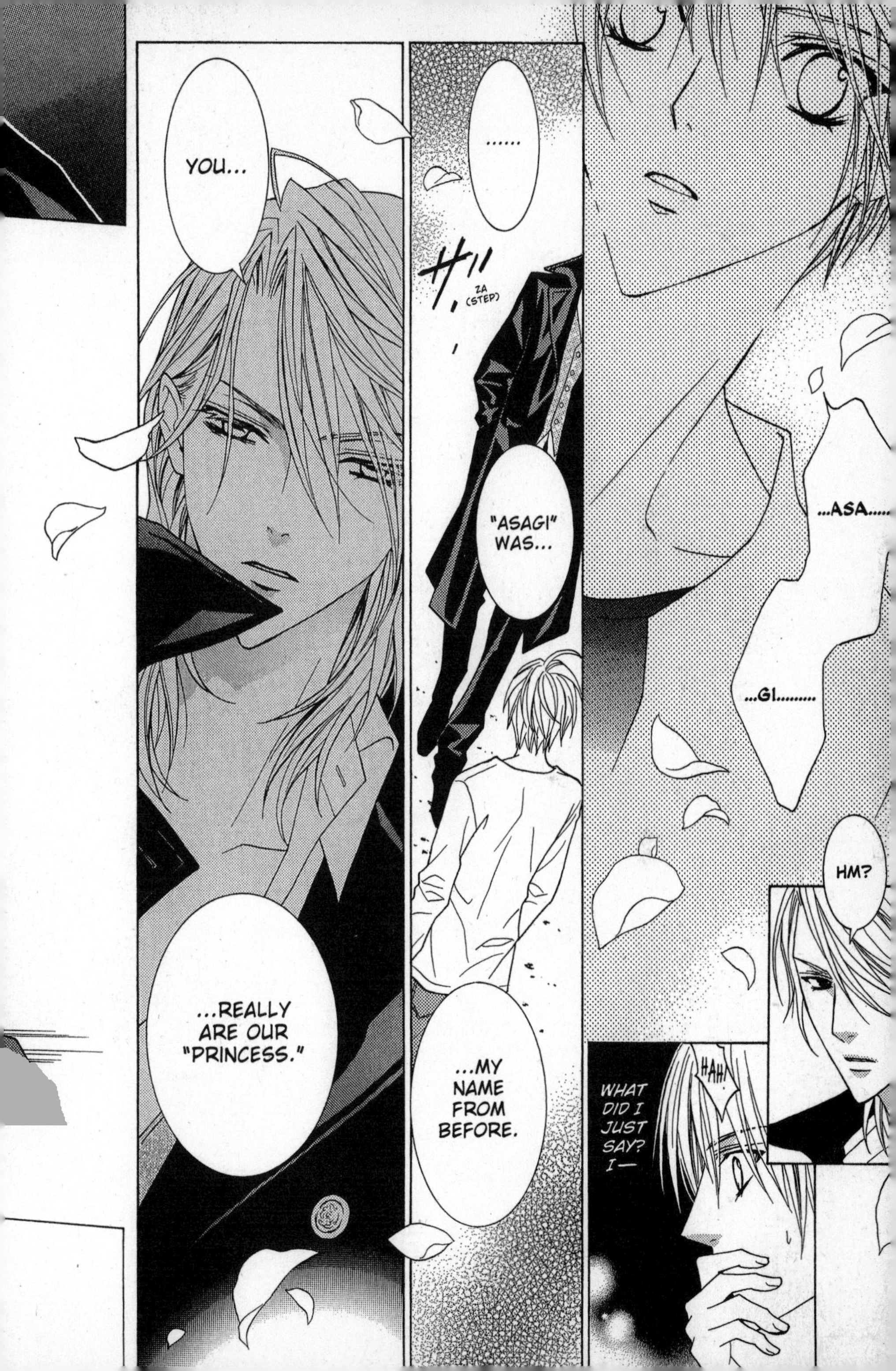
...ASA.....
...GI.........
HM?
HAH!
WHAT DID I JUST SAY? I—
......
ZA (STEP)
"ASAGI" WAS...
...MY NAME FROM BEFORE.
YOU...
...REALLY ARE OUR "PRINCESS."

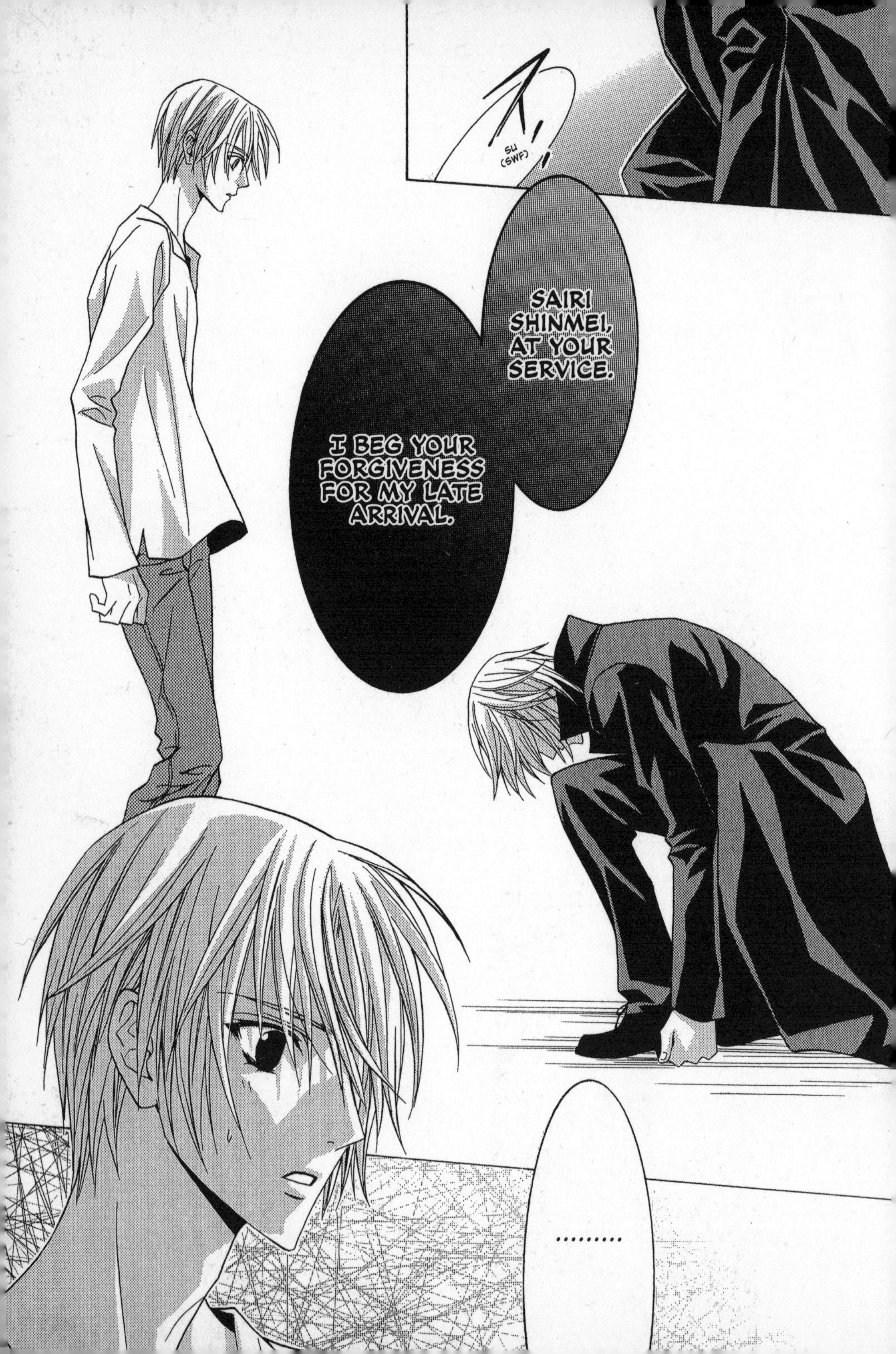
SU (SWF)
SAIRI SHINMEI, AT YOUR SERVICE.
I BEG YOUR FORGIVENESS FOR MY LATE ARRIVAL.
....

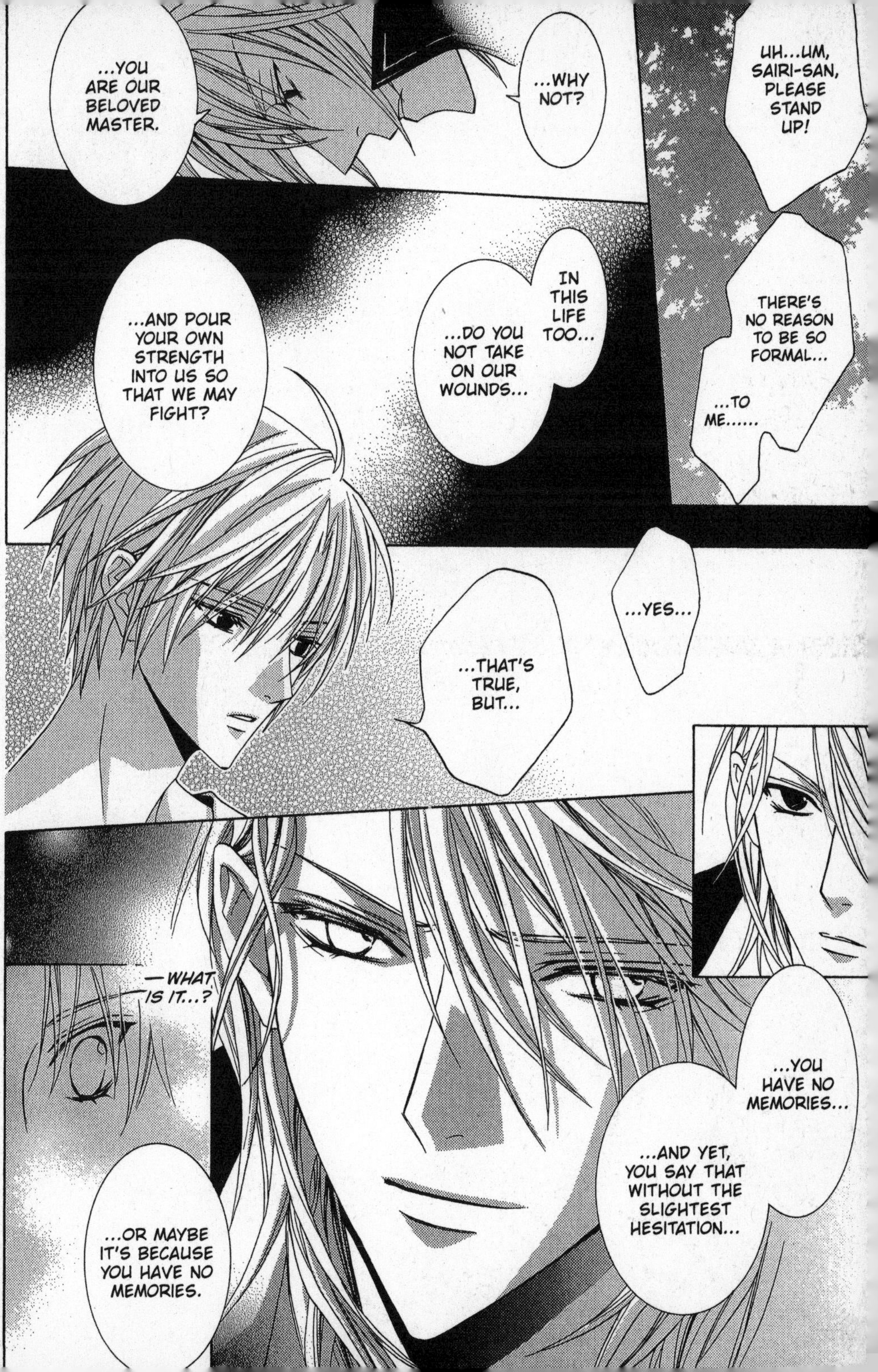

UH...UM, SAIRI-SAN, PLEASE STAND UP!
THERE'S NO REASON TO BE SO FORMAL...
...TO ME......
...WHY NOT?
...YOU ARE OUR BELOVED MASTER.
IN THIS LIFE TOO...
...DO YOU NOT TAKE ON OUR WOUNDS...
...AND POUR YOUR OWN STRENGTH INTO US SO THAT WE MAY FIGHT?
...YES...
...THAT'S TRUE, BUT...
...YOU HAVE NO MEMORIES...
...AND YET, YOU SAY THAT WITHOUT THE SLIGHTEST HESITATION...
—WHAT IS IT...?
...OR MAYBE IT'S BECAUSE YOU HAVE NO MEMORIES.

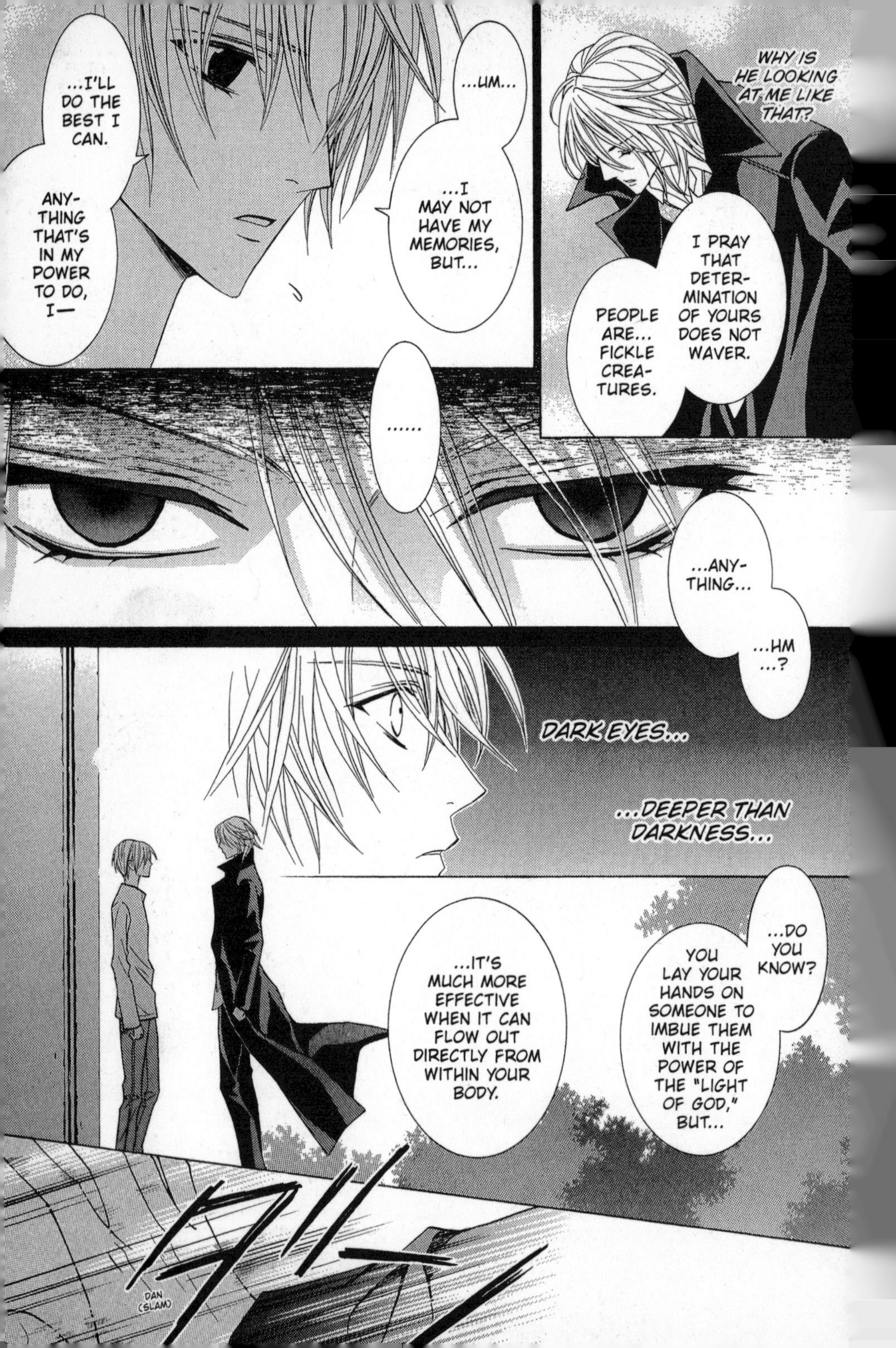
WHY IS HE LOOKING AT ME LIKE THAT?
I PRAY THAT DETER-MINATION OF YOURS DOES NOT WAVER.
PEOPLE ARE... FICKLE CREA-TURES.
...UM...
...I MAY NOT HAVE MY MEMORIES, BUT...
...I'LL DO THE BEST I CAN.
ANY-THING THAT'S IN MY POWER TO DO, I—
......
...ANY-THING...
...HM ...?
DARK EYES...
...DEEPER THAN DARKNESS...
...DO YOU KNOW?
YOU LAY YOUR HANDS ON SOMEONE TO IMBUE THEM WITH THE POWER OF THE "LIGHT OF GOD," BUT...
...IT'S MUCH MORE EFFECTIVE WHEN IT CAN FLOW OUT DIRECTLY FROM WITHIN YOUR BODY.
DAN (SLAM)

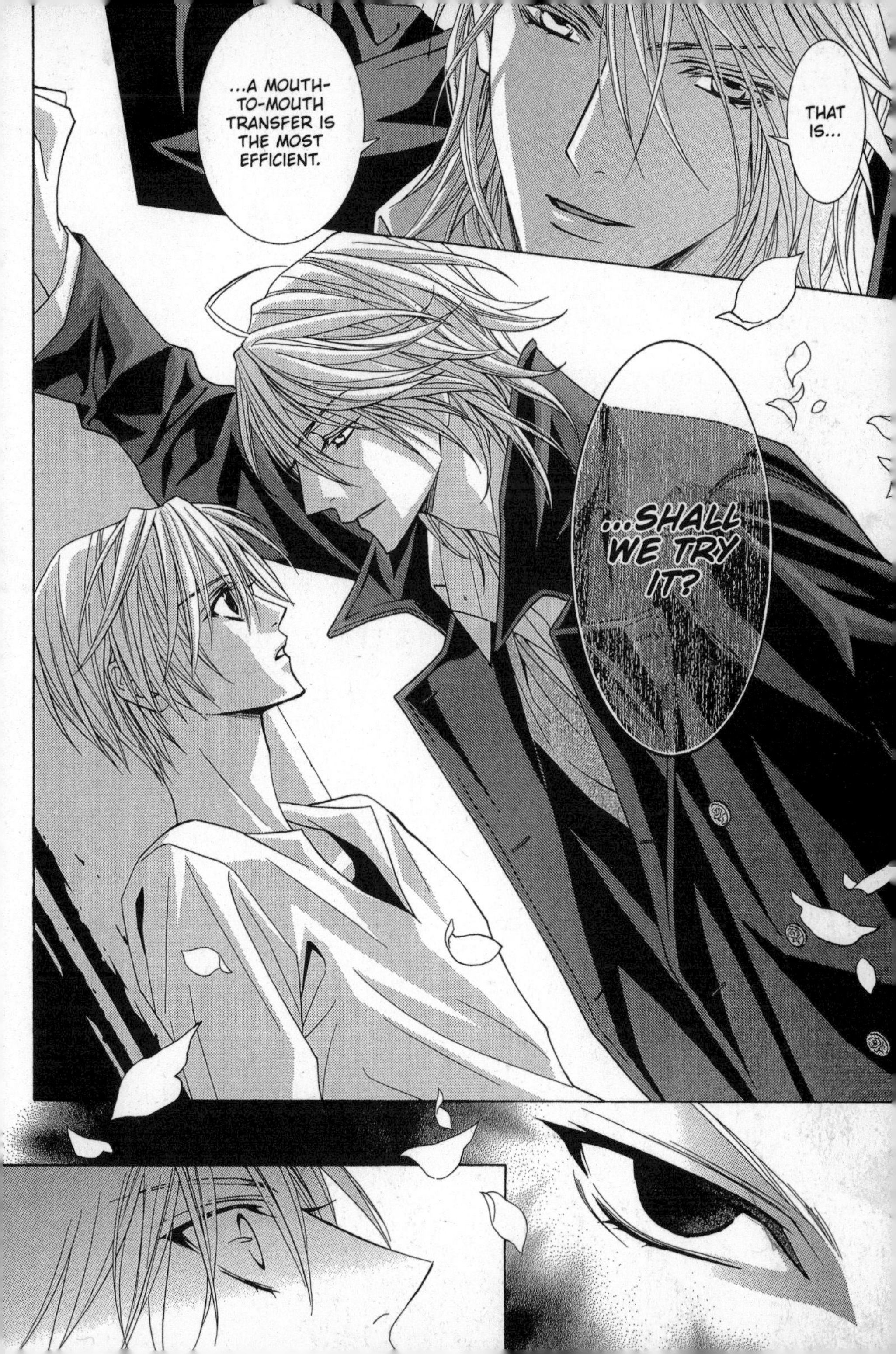
THAT IS...
...A MOUTH-TO-MOUTH TRANSFER IS THE MOST EFFICIENT.
...SHALL WE TRY IT?

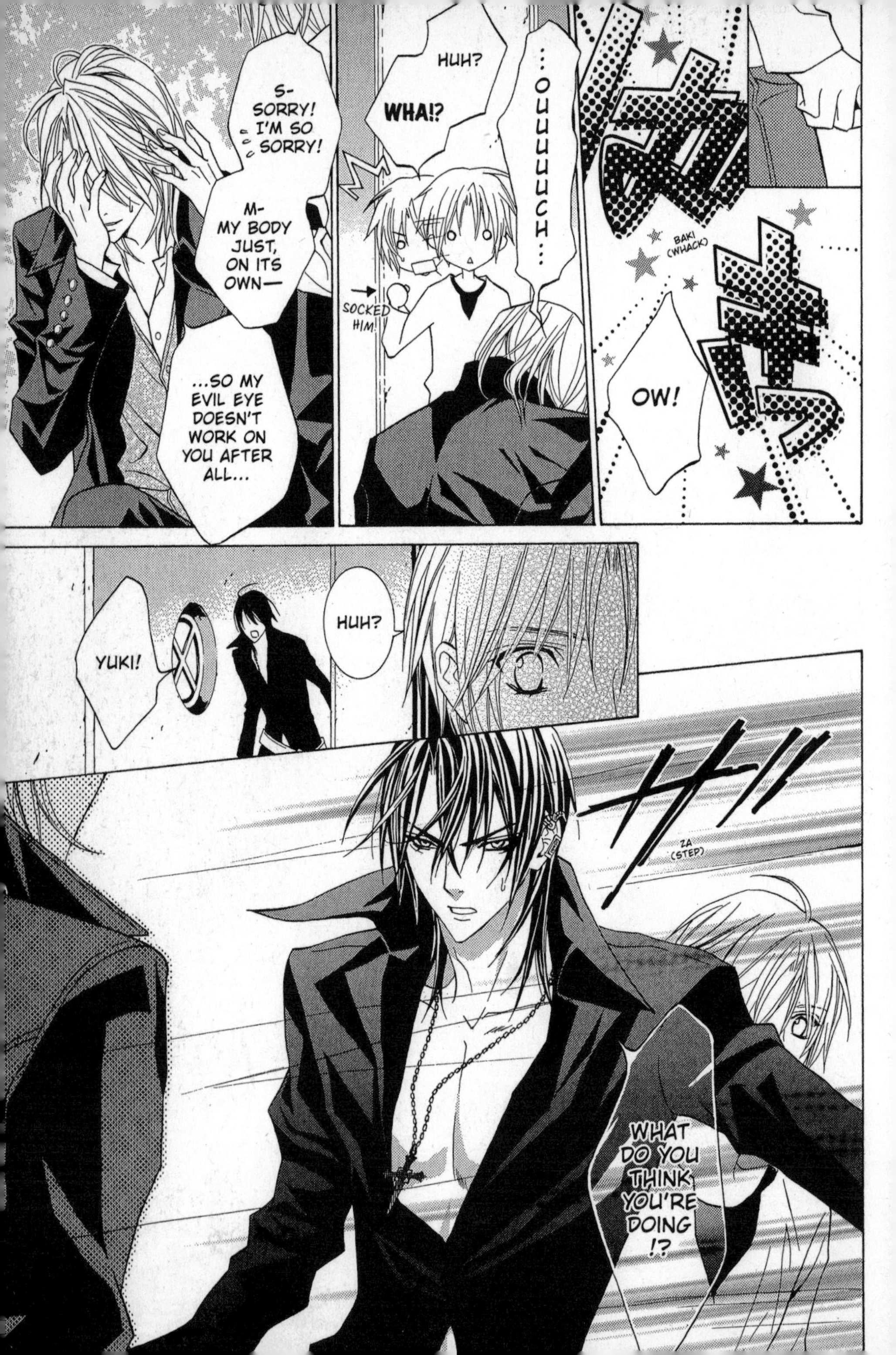
BAKI (WHACK)
OW!
...OUUUUUCH...
HUH?
WHA!?
SOCKED HIM!
S-SORRY! I'M SO SORRY!
M-MY BODY JUST, ON ITS OWN—
...SO MY EVIL EYE DOESN'T WORK ON YOU AFTER ALL...
HUH?
YUKI!
ZA (STEP)
WHAT DO YOU THINK YOU'RE DOING!?

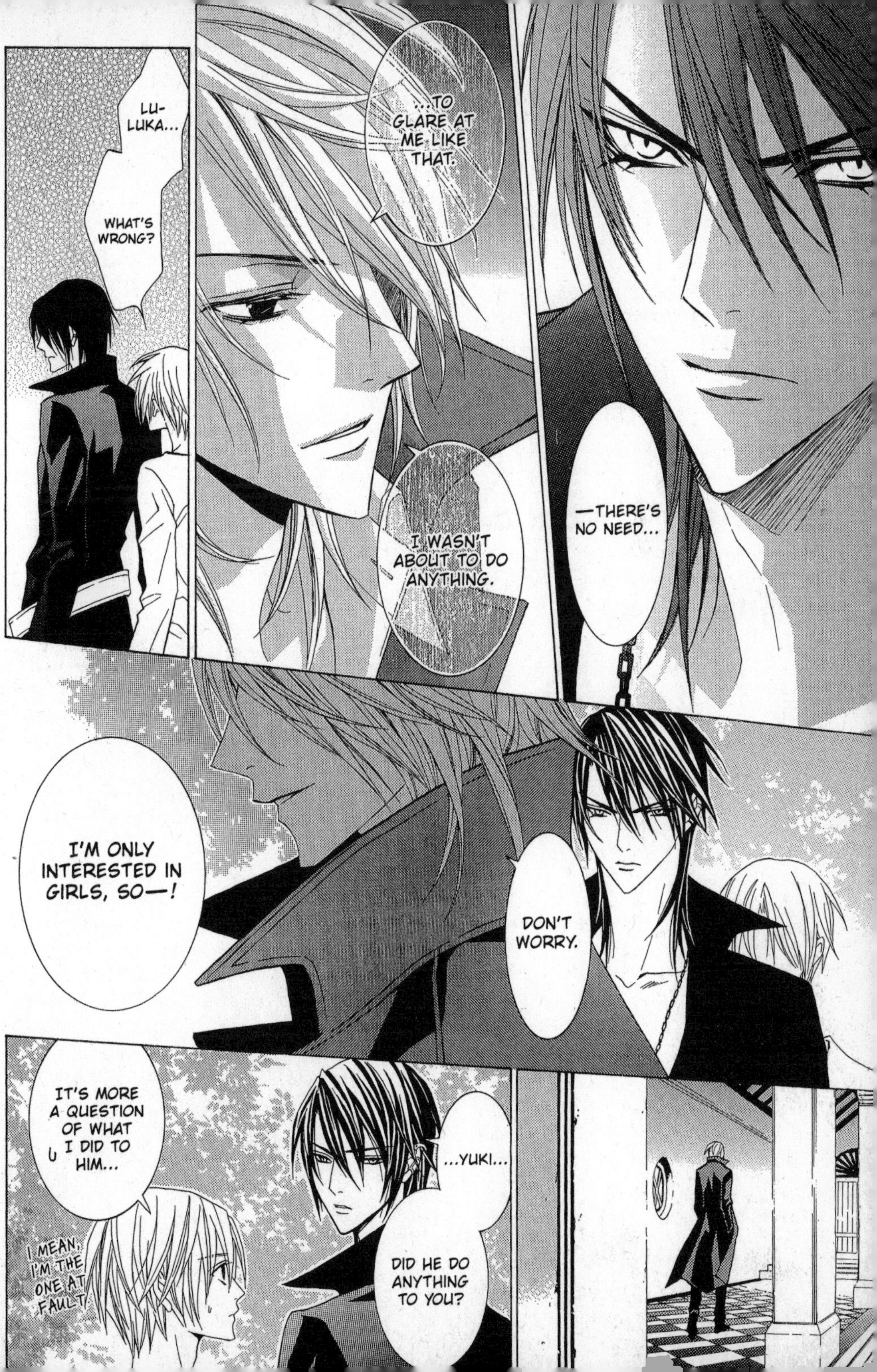
—THERE'S NO NEED...
...TO GLARE AT ME LIKE THAT.
I WASN'T ABOUT TO DO ANYTHING.
LU-LUKA...
WHAT'S WRONG?
DON'T WORRY.
I'M ONLY INTERESTED IN GIRLS, SO—!
...YUKI...
DID HE DO ANYTHING TO YOU?
IT'S MORE A QUESTION OF WHAT I DID TO HIM...
I MEAN, I'M THE ONE AT FAULT.

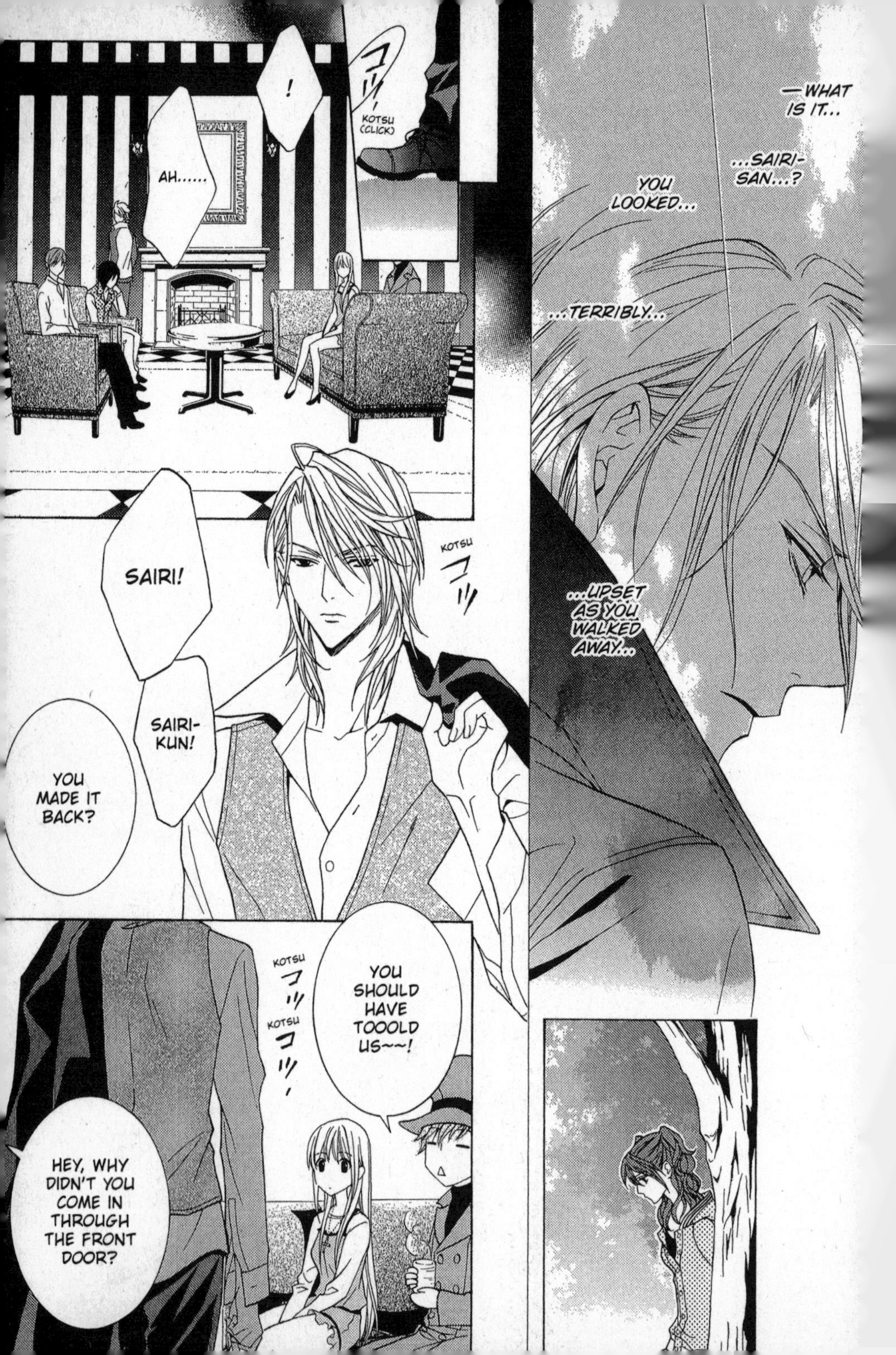
—WHAT IS IT...
...SAIRI-SAN...?
YOU LOOKED...
...TERRIBLY...
...UPSET AS YOU WALKED AWAY...
KOTSU (CLICK)
!
AH......
SAIRI!
KOTSU
SAIRI-KUN!
YOU MADE IT BACK?
YOU SHOULD HAVE TOOOLD US~~!
KOTSU
KOTSU
HEY, WHY DIDN'T YOU COME IN THROUGH THE FRONT DOOR?

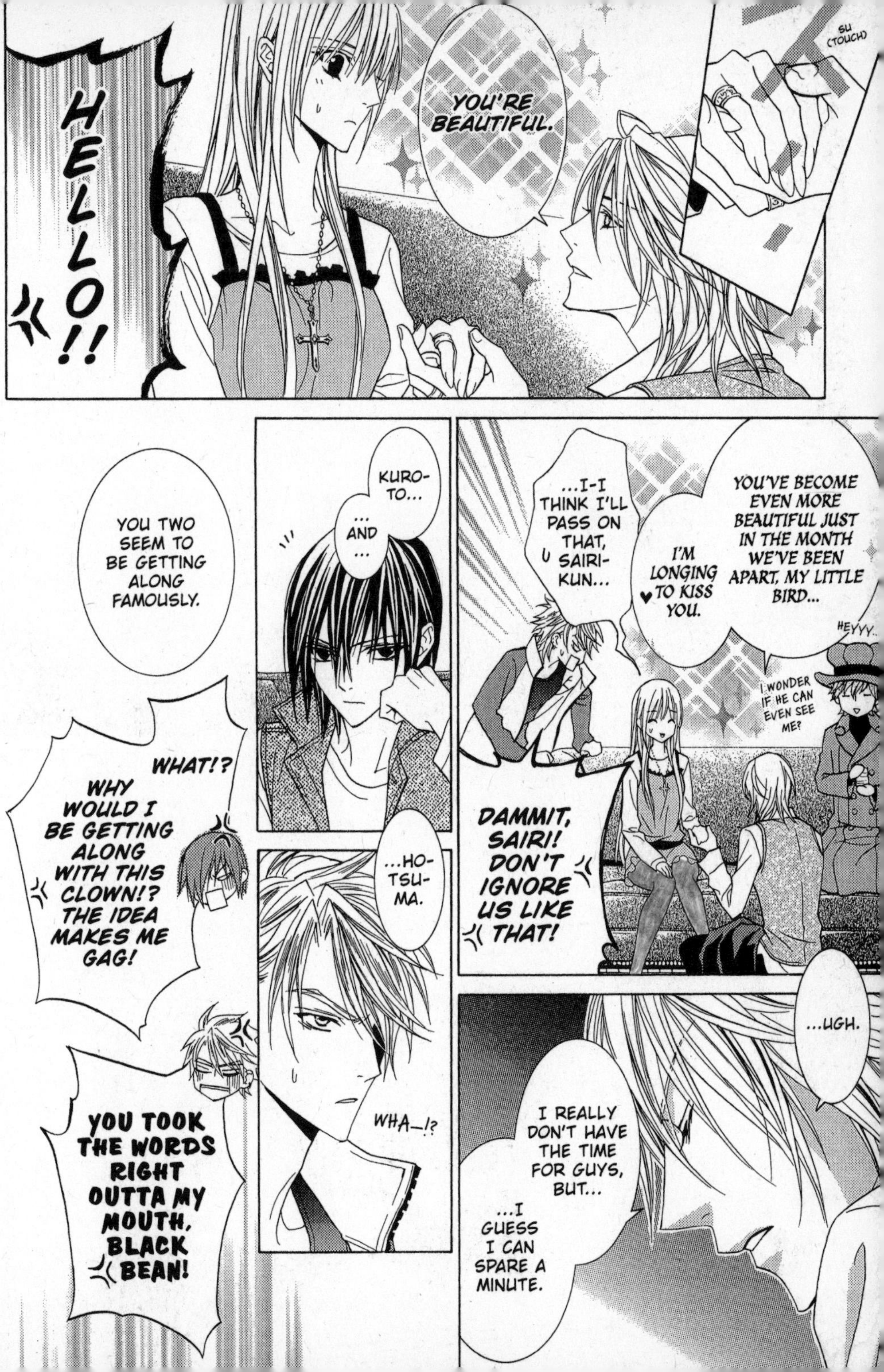
SU (TOUCH)
YOU'RE BEAUTIFUL.
HELLO!!
YOU'VE BECOME EVEN MORE BEAUTIFUL JUST IN THE MONTH WE'VE BEEN APART, MY LITTLE BIRD...
I'M LONGING TO KISS YOU.
...I-I THINK I'LL PASS ON THAT, SAIRI-KUN...
HEYYY..
I WONDER IF HE CAN EVEN SEE ME?
DAMMIT, SAIRI! DON'T IGNORE US LIKE THAT!
...UGH.
I REALLY DON'T HAVE THE TIME FOR GUYS, BUT...
...I GUESS I CAN SPARE A MINUTE.
KURO-TO...
...AND...
...HO-TSU-MA.
WHA-!?
YOU TWO SEEM TO BE GETTING ALONG FAMOUSLY.
WHAT!? WHY WOULD I BE GETTING ALONG WITH THIS CLOWN!? THE IDEA MAKES ME GAG!
YOU TOOK THE WORDS RIGHT OUTTA MY MOUTH, BLACK BEAN!

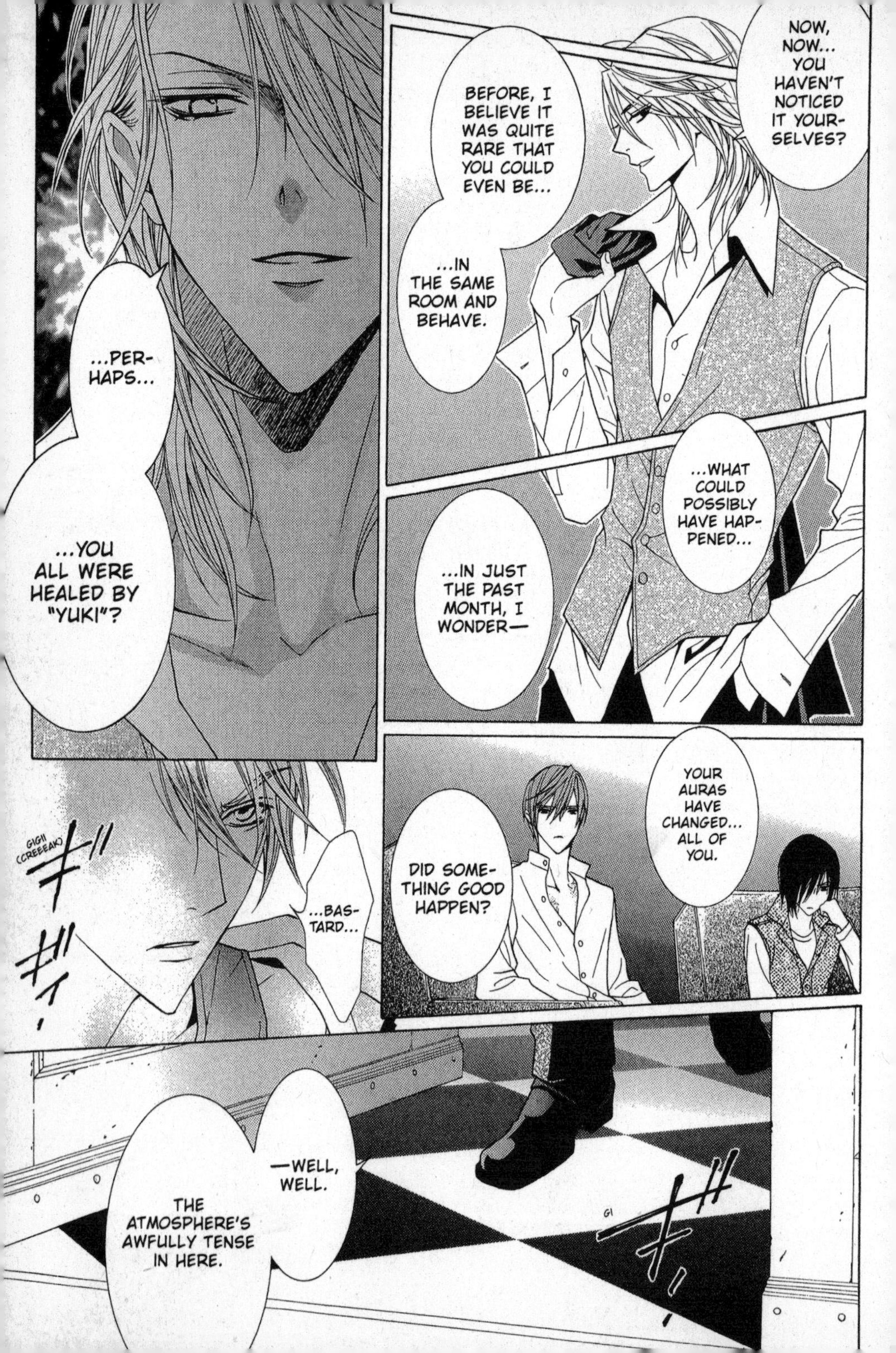
NOW, NOW... YOU HAVEN'T NOTICED IT YOURSELVES?
BEFORE, I BELIEVE IT WAS QUITE RARE THAT YOU COULD EVEN BE...
...IN THE SAME ROOM AND BEHAVE.
...WHAT COULD POSSIBLY HAVE HAPPENED...
...IN JUST THE PAST MONTH, I WONDER—
...PERHAPS...
...YOU ALL WERE HEALED BY "YUKI"?
YOUR AURAS HAVE CHANGED... ALL OF YOU.
DID SOMETHING GOOD HAPPEN?
...BASTARD...
GIGII (CREEEAK)
GI
—WELL, WELL.
THE ATMOSPHERE'S AWFULLY TENSE IN HERE.

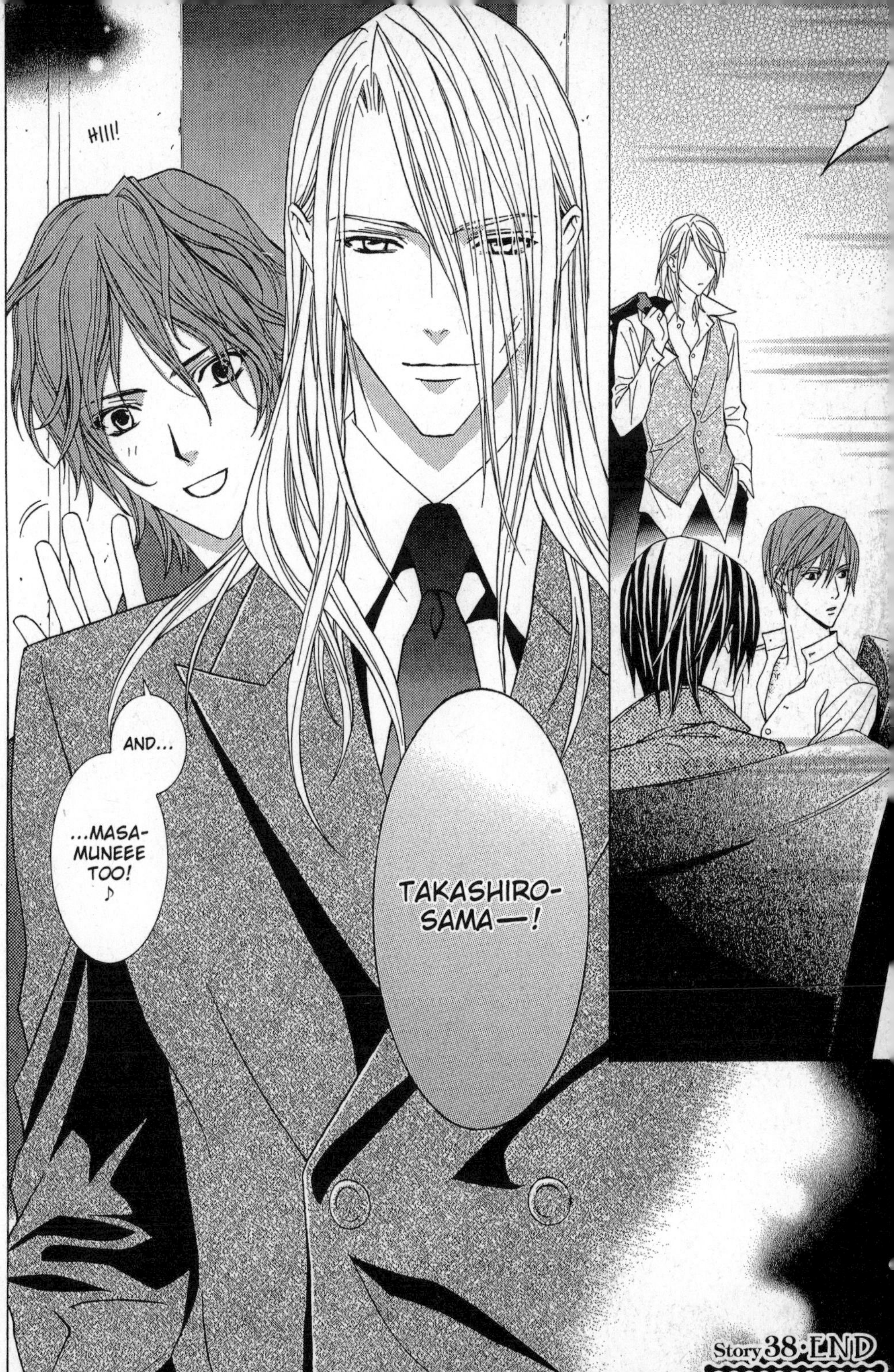
HIII!
TAKASHIRO-SAMA—!
AND...
...MASA-MUNEEE TOO! ♪

Story 38 • END

THE BETRAYAL KNOWS MY NAME

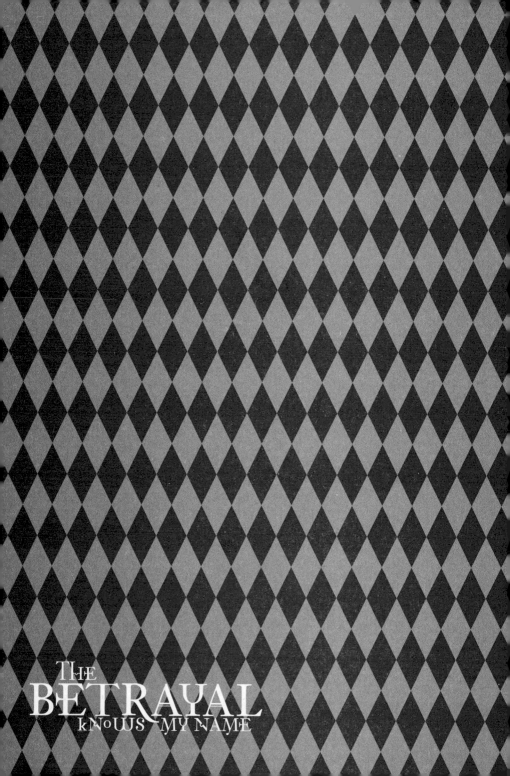

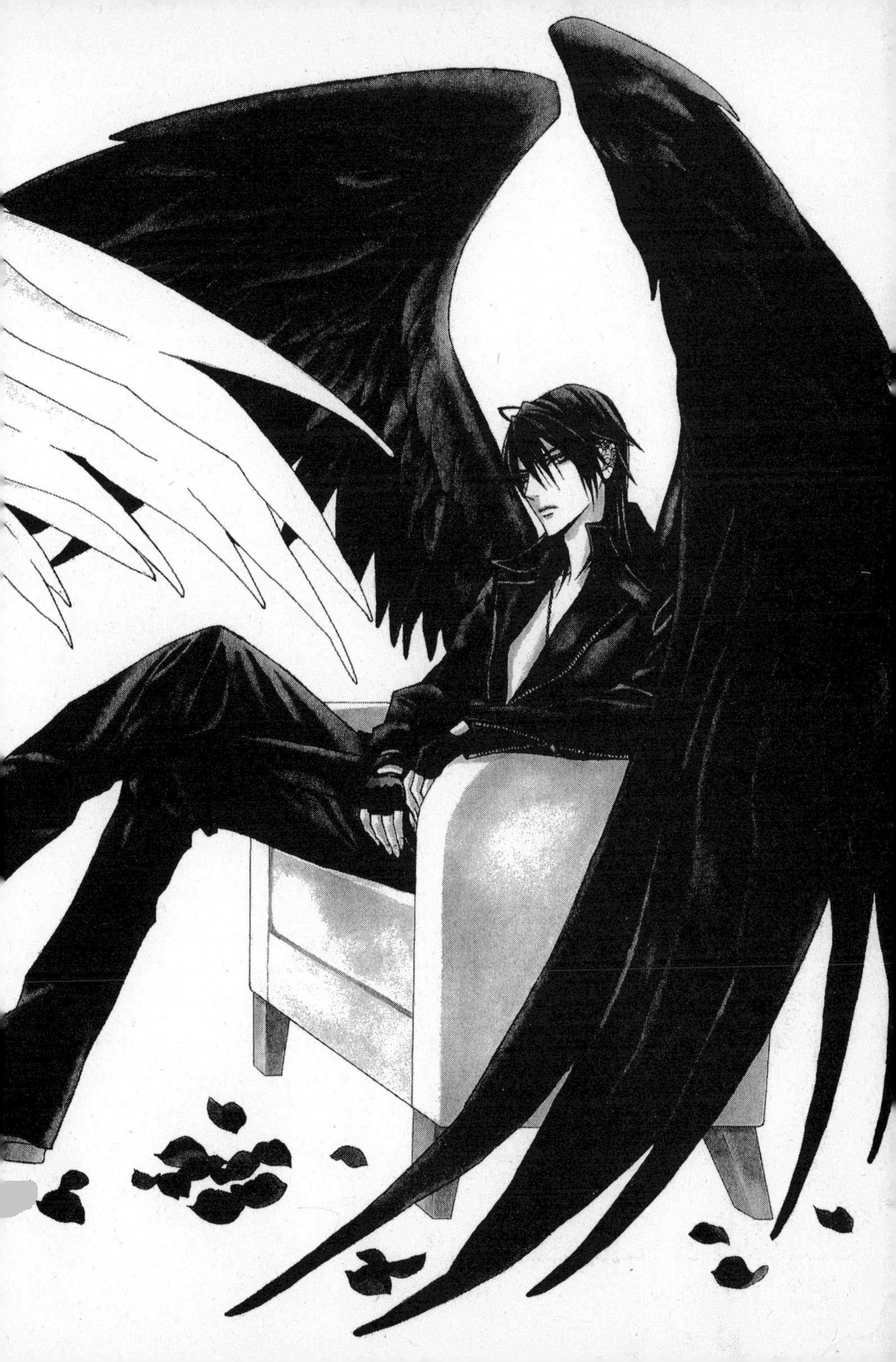

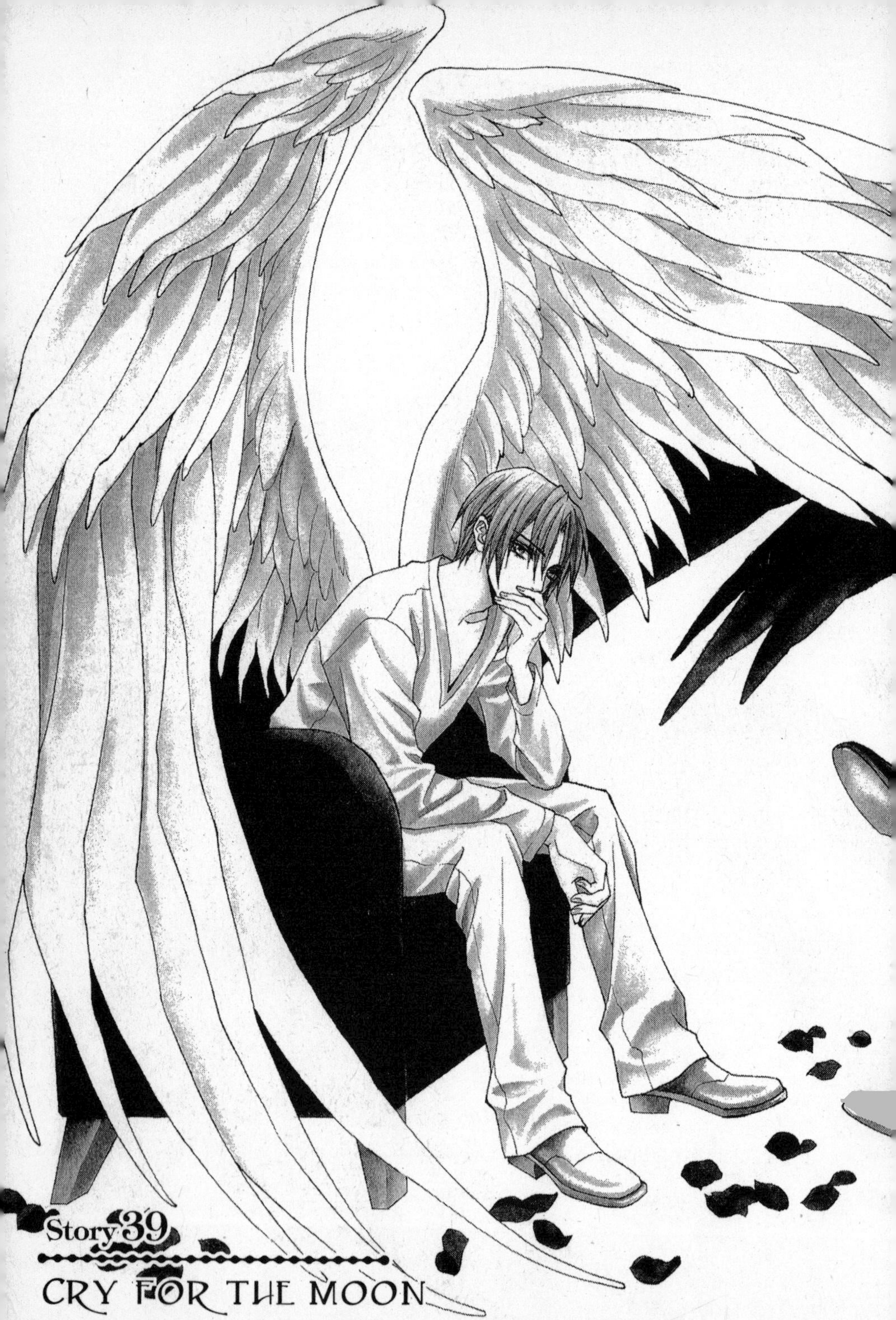

Story 39

CRY FOR THE MOON

The
BETRAYAL
knows my name

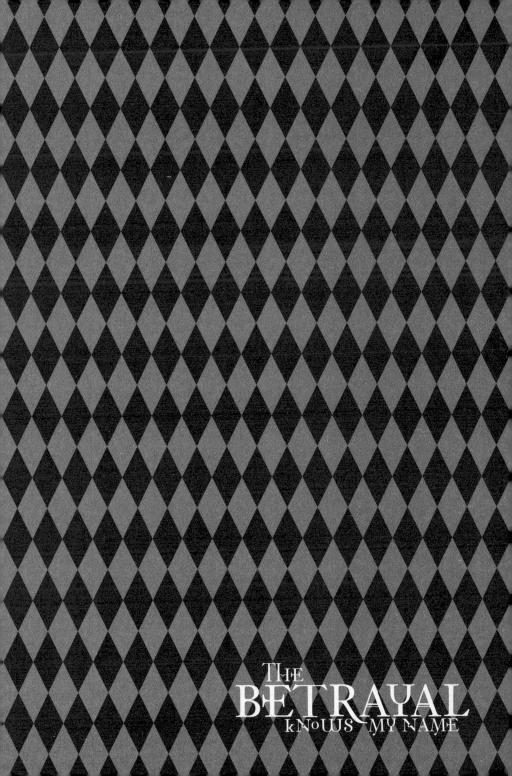

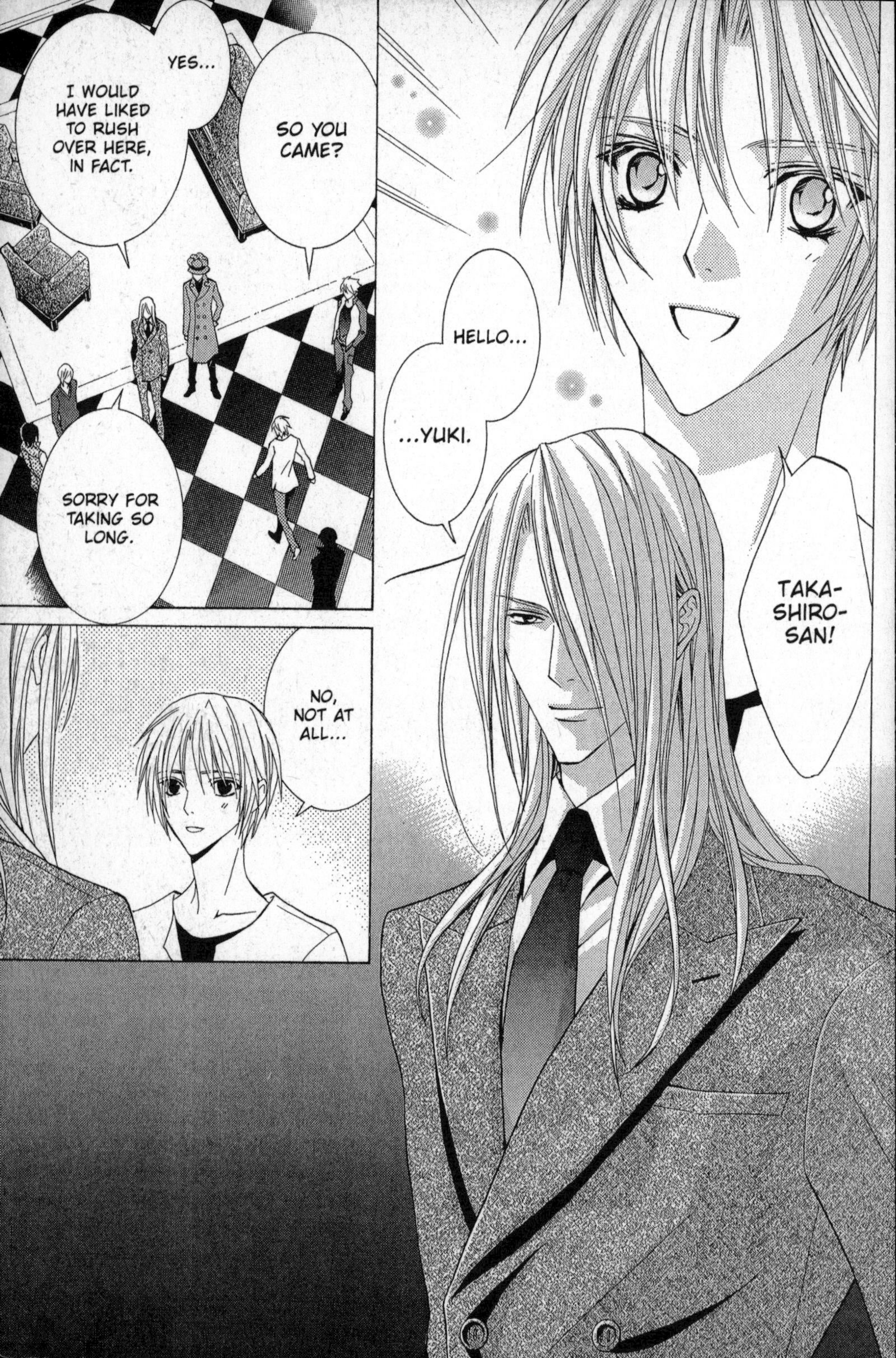
TAKA-SHIRO-SAN!
HELLO... ...YUKI.
SO YOU CAME?
YES... I WOULD HAVE LIKED TO RUSH OVER HERE, IN FACT.
SORRY FOR TAKING SO LONG.
NO, NOT AT ALL...

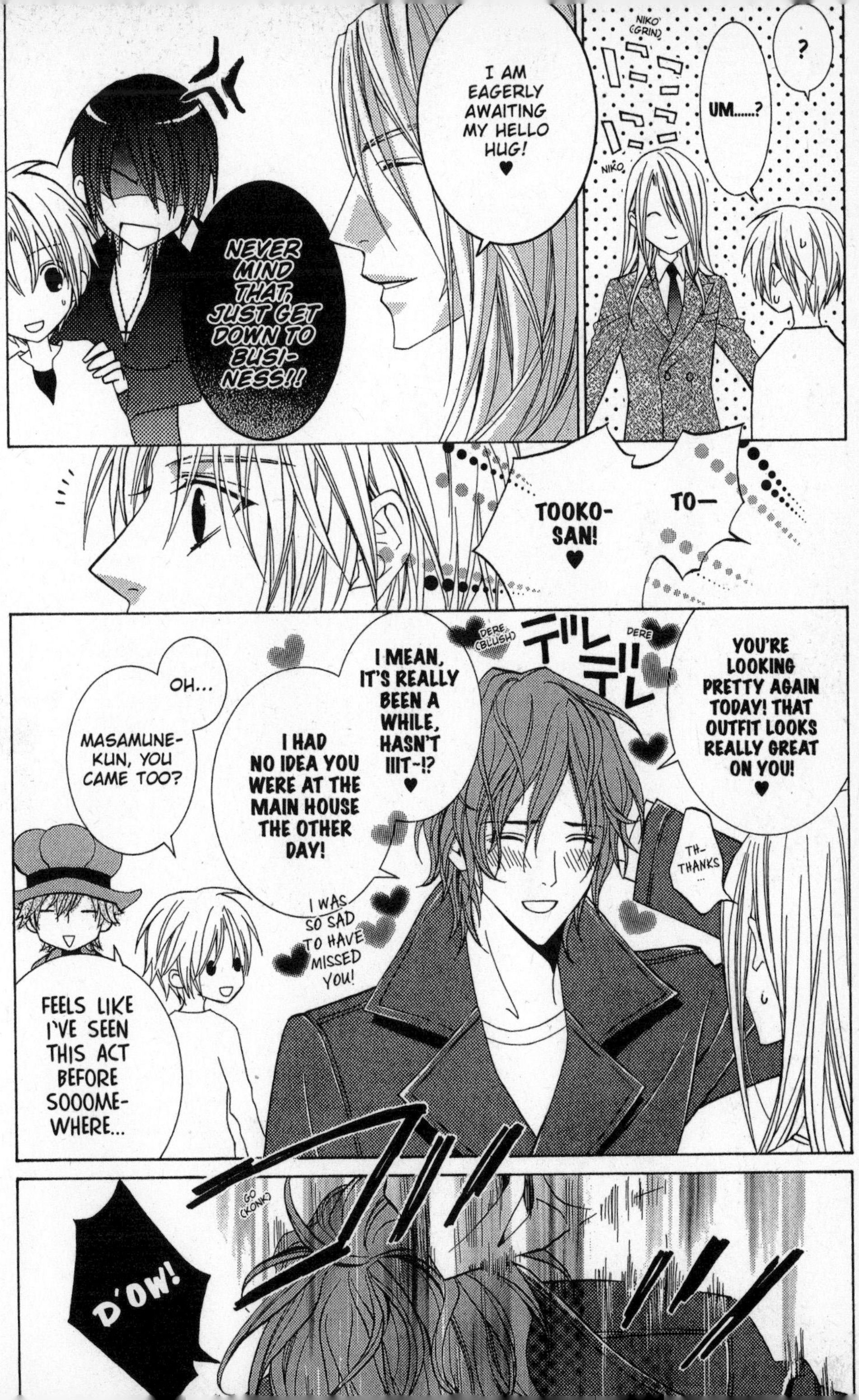
?
UM......?
NIKO' (GRIN)
NIKO
I AM EAGERLY AWAITING MY HELLO HUG! ♥
NEVER MIND THAT, JUST GET DOWN TO BUSI-NESS!!
TO—
TOOKO-SAN! ♥
YOU'RE LOOKING PRETTY AGAIN TODAY! THAT OUTFIT LOOKS REALLY GREAT ON YOU! ♥
DERE
デレデレ
DERE (BLUSH)
TH-THANKS...
I MEAN, IT'S REALLY BEEN A WHILE, HASN'T IIIT~!? ♥
I HAD NO IDEA YOU WERE AT THE MAIN HOUSE THE OTHER DAY!
I WAS SO SAD TO HAVE MISSED YOU!
OH...
MASAMUNE-KUN, YOU CAME TOO?
FEELS LIKE I'VE SEEN THIS ACT BEFORE SOOOME-WHERE...
GO (KONK)
D'OW!

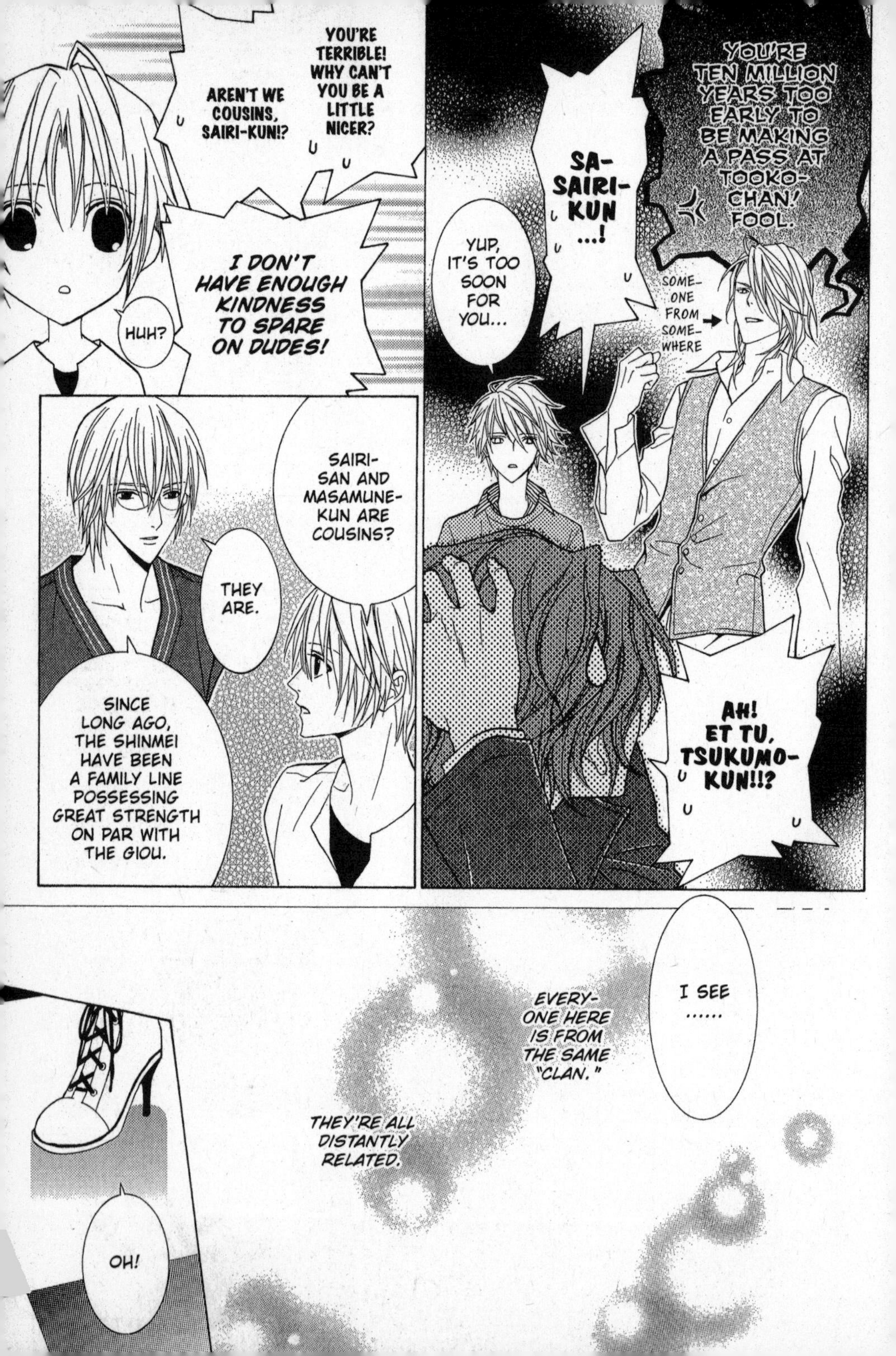
YOU'RE TEN MILLION YEARS TOO EARLY TO BE MAKING A PASS AT TOOKO-CHAN! FOOL.
SOME-ONE FROM SOME-WHERE
SA-SAIRI-KUN ...!
YUP, IT'S TOO SOON FOR YOU...
AH! ET TU, TSUKUMO-KUN!!?
YOU'RE TERRIBLE! WHY CAN'T YOU BE A LITTLE NICER?
AREN'T WE COUSINS, SAIRI-KUN!?
I DON'T HAVE ENOUGH KINDNESS TO SPARE ON DUDES!
HUH?
SAIRI-SAN AND MASAMUNE-KUN ARE COUSINS?
THEY ARE.
SINCE LONG AGO, THE SHINMEI HAVE BEEN A FAMILY LINE POSSESSING GREAT STRENGTH ON PAR WITH THE GIOU.
I SEE ......
EVERY-ONE HERE IS FROM THE SAME "CLAN."
THEY'RE ALL DISTANTLY RELATED.
OH!

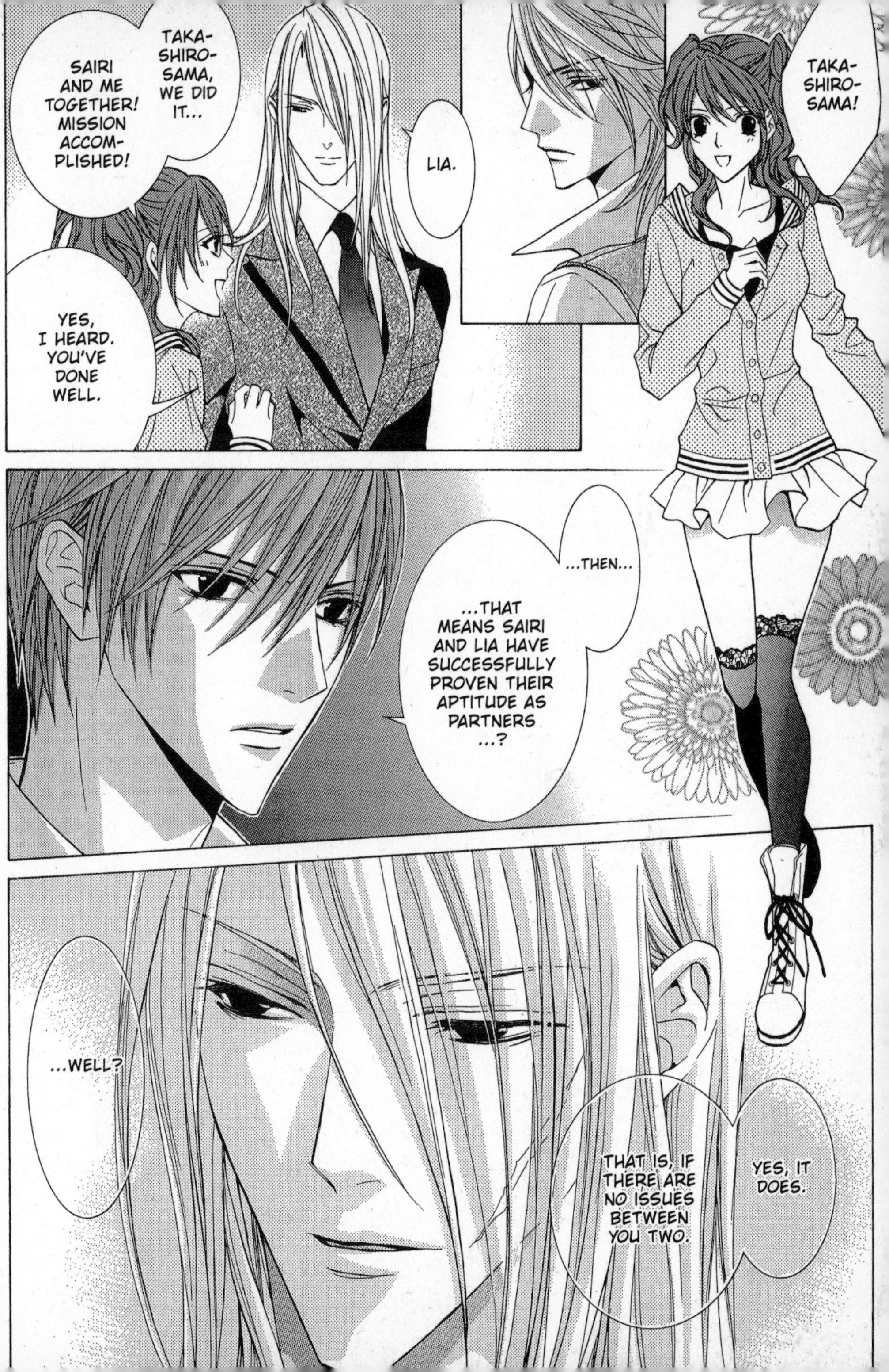
TAKA-SHIRO-SAMA!
LIA.
TAKA-SHIRO-SAMA, WE DID IT...
SAIRI AND ME TOGETHER! MISSION ACCOM-PLISHED!
YES, I HEARD. YOU'VE DONE WELL.
...THEN...
...THAT MEANS SAIRI AND LIA HAVE SUCCESSFULLY PROVEN THEIR APTITUDE AS PARTNERS ...?
YES, IT DOES.
THAT IS, IF THERE ARE NO ISSUES BETWEEN YOU TWO.
...WELL?

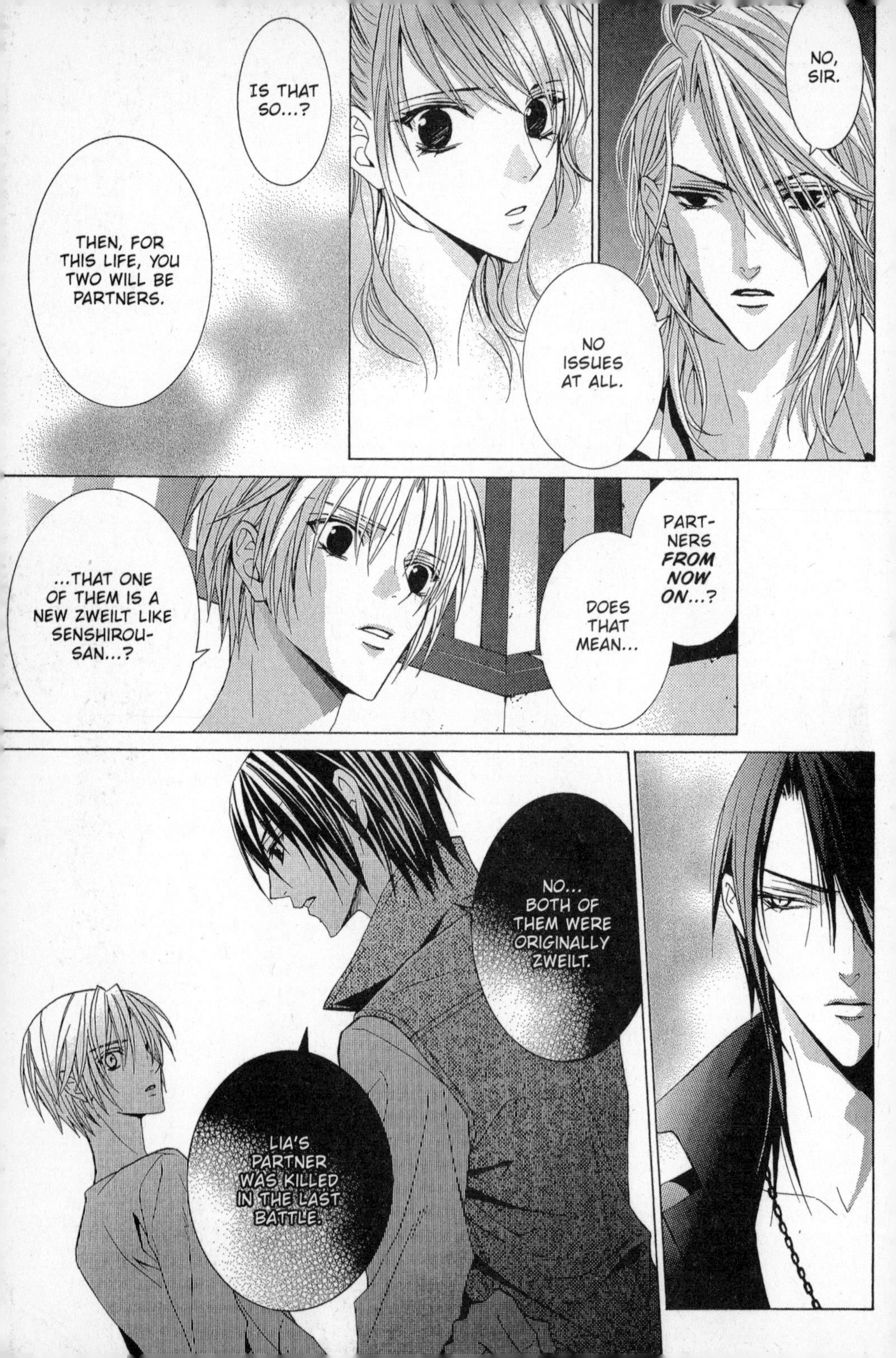

NO, SIR.
NO ISSUES AT ALL.
IS THAT SO...?
THEN, FOR THIS LIFE, YOU TWO WILL BE PARTNERS.
PART-NERS *FROM NOW ON*...?
DOES THAT MEAN...
...THAT ONE OF THEM IS A NEW ZWEILT LIKE SENSHIROU-SAN...?
NO... BOTH OF THEM WERE ORIGINALLY ZWEILT.
LIA'S PARTNER WAS KILLED IN THE LAST BATTLE.

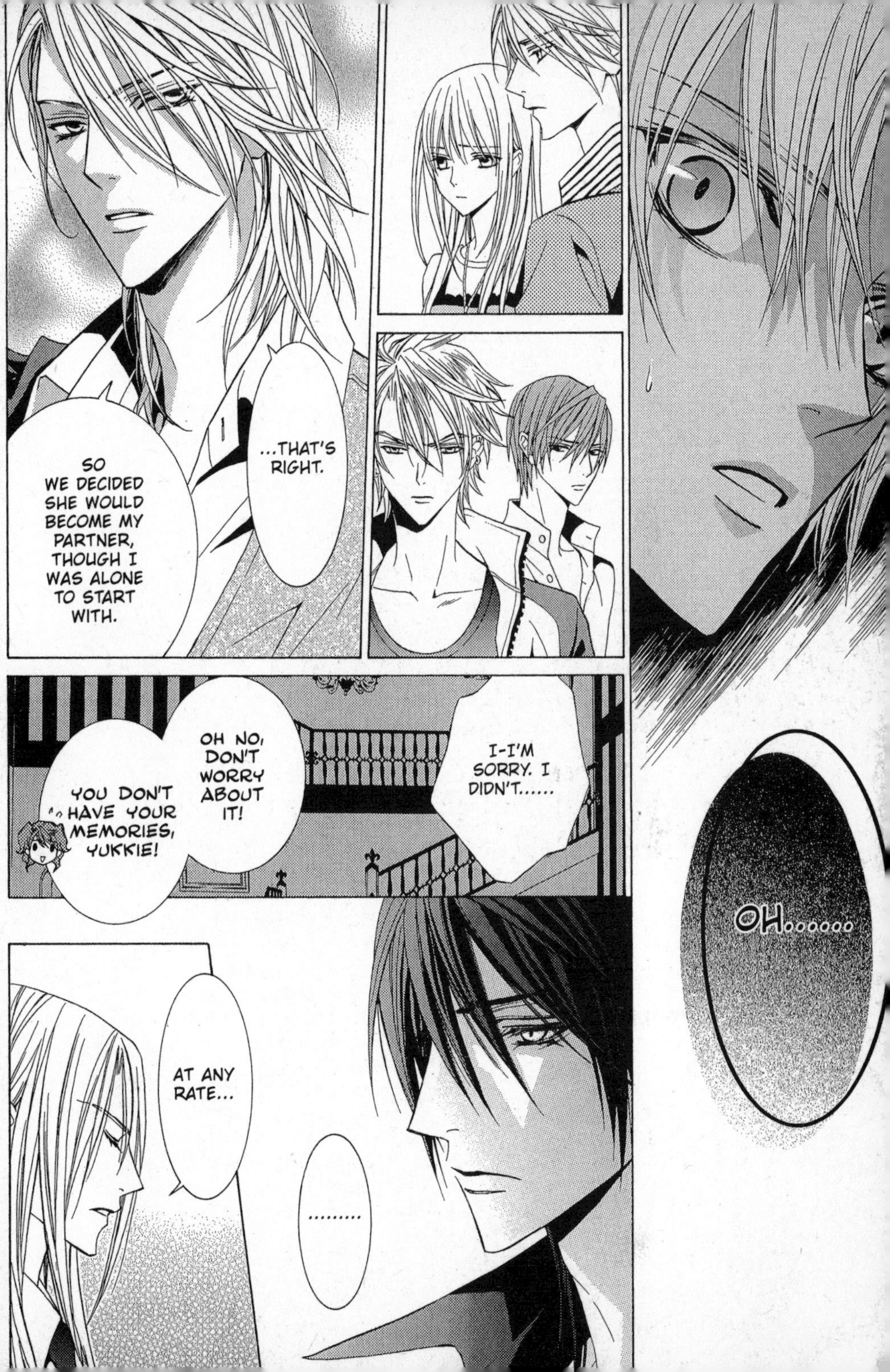
OH......
...THAT'S RIGHT.
SO WE DECIDED SHE WOULD BECOME MY PARTNER, THOUGH I WAS ALONE TO START WITH.
I-I'M SORRY. I DIDN'T......
OH NO, DON'T WORRY ABOUT IT!
YOU DON'T HAVE YOUR MEMORIES, YUKKIE!
....
AT ANY RATE...

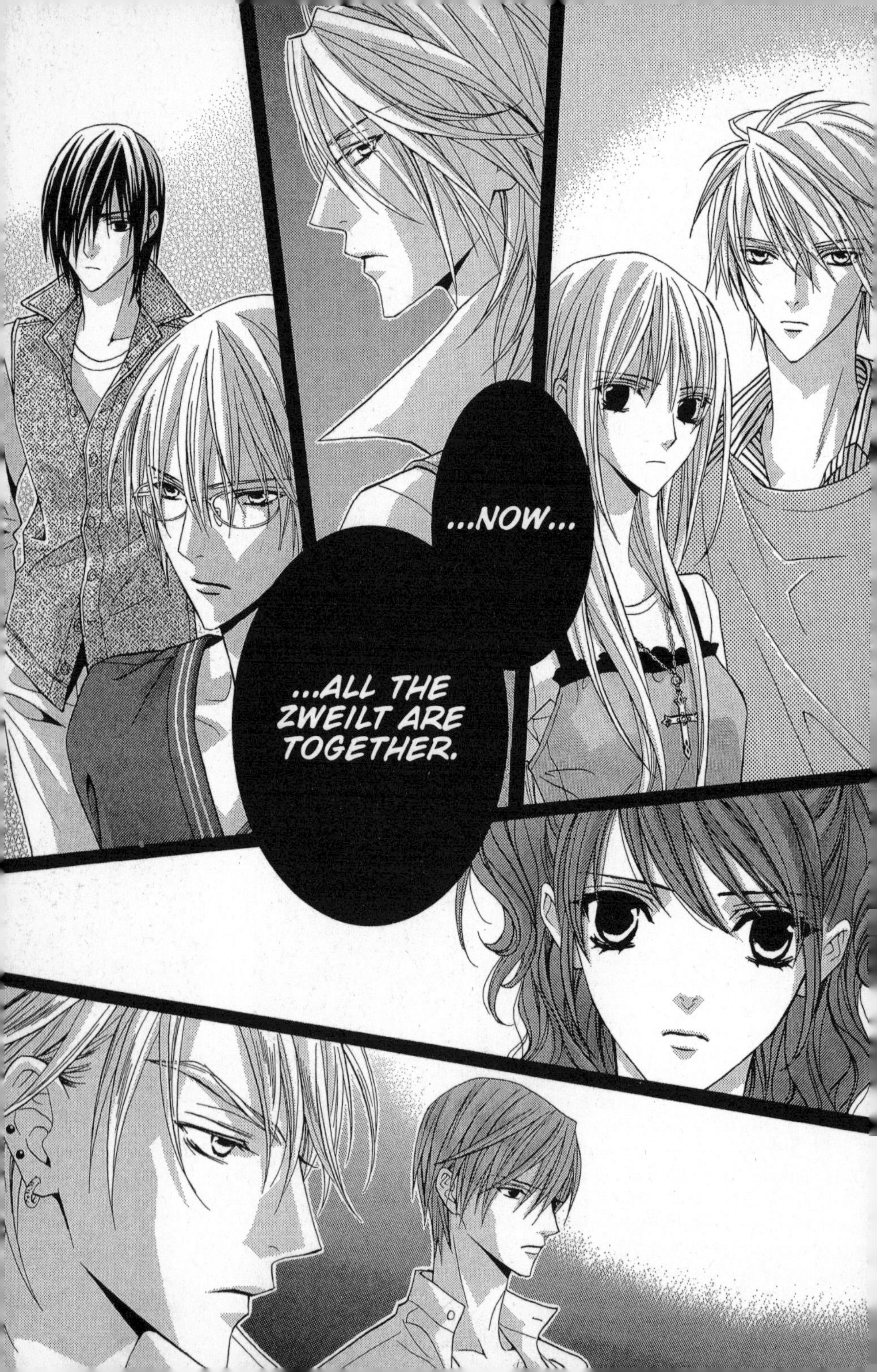
...NOW...
...ALL THE ZWEILT ARE TOGETHER.

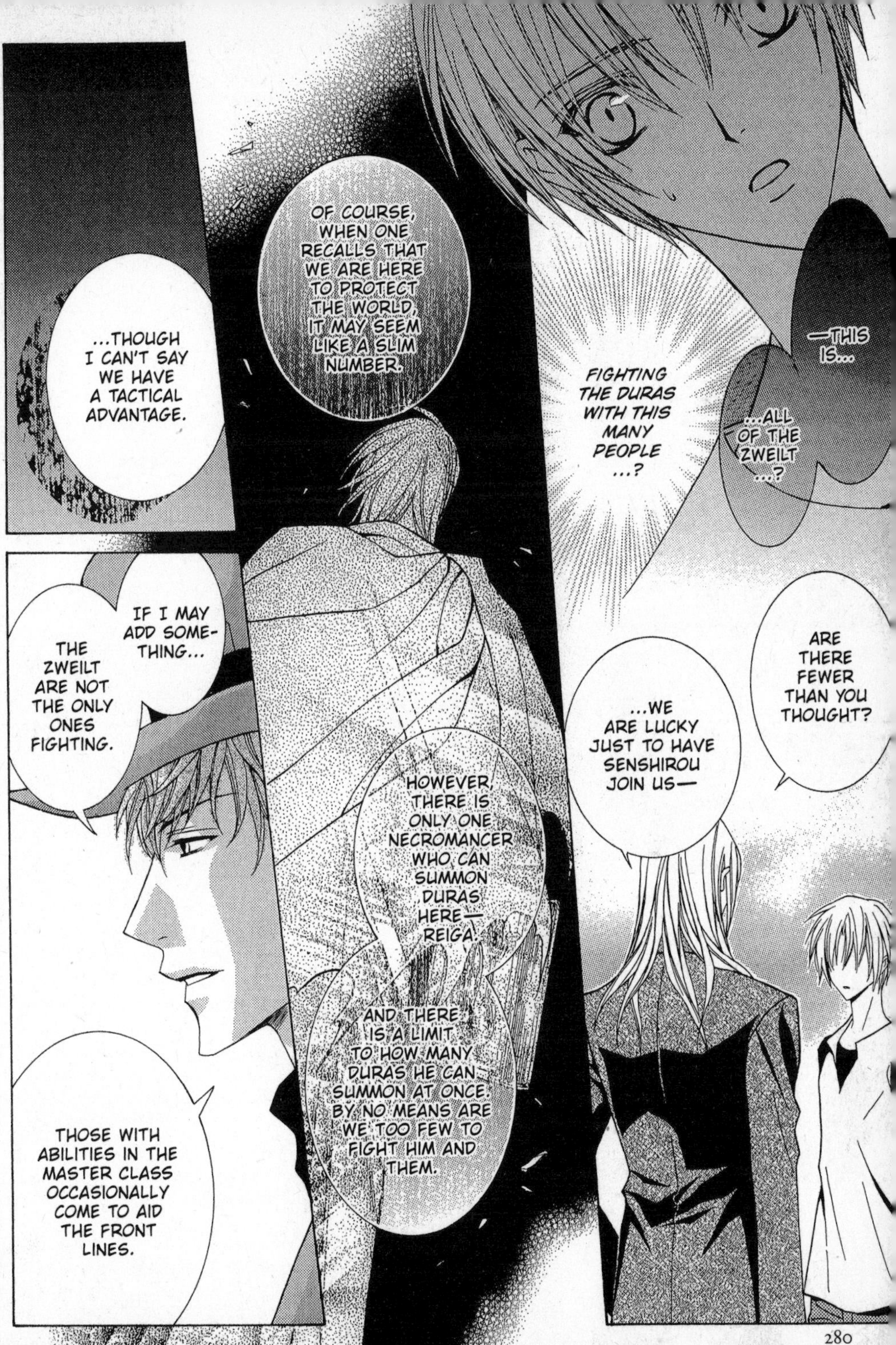
—THIS IS...
...ALL OF THE ZWEILT ...?
FIGHTING THE DURAS WITH THIS MANY PEOPLE ...?
ARE THERE FEWER THAN YOU THOUGHT?
...WE ARE LUCKY JUST TO HAVE SENSHIROU JOIN US—
OF COURSE, WHEN ONE RECALLS THAT WE ARE HERE TO PROTECT THE WORLD, IT MAY SEEM LIKE A SLIM NUMBER.
...THOUGH I CAN'T SAY WE HAVE A TACTICAL ADVANTAGE.
HOWEVER, THERE IS ONLY ONE NECROMANCER WHO CAN SUMMON DURAS HERE—REIGA.
AND THERE IS A LIMIT TO HOW MANY DURAS HE CAN SUMMON AT ONCE. BY NO MEANS ARE WE TOO FEW TO FIGHT HIM AND THEM.
IF I MAY ADD SOMETHING...
THE ZWEILT ARE NOT THE ONLY ONES FIGHTING.
THOSE WITH ABILITIES IN THE MASTER CLASS OCCASIONALLY COME TO AID THE FRONT LINES.

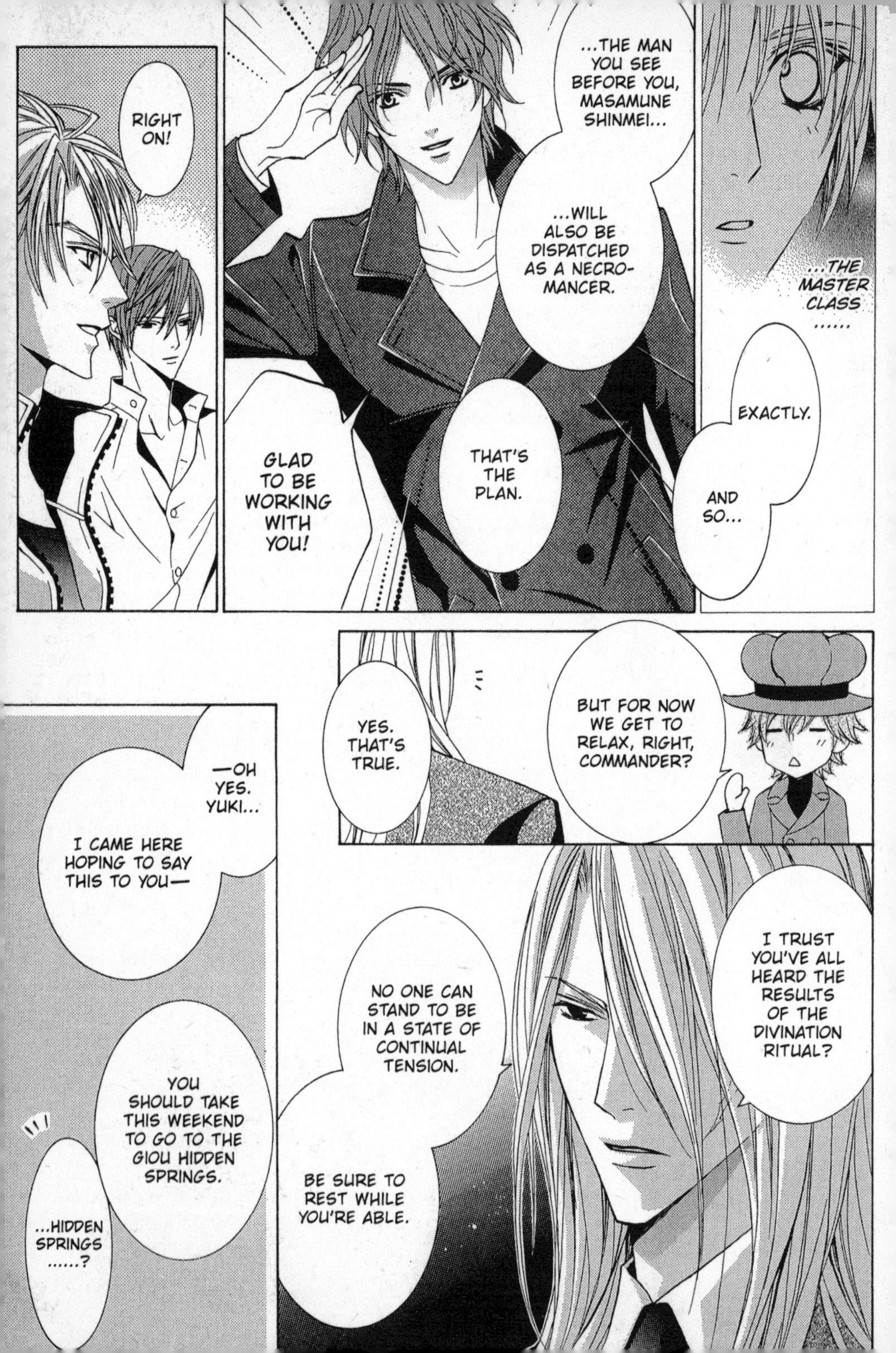
...THE MASTER CLASS ......
EXACTLY.
AND SO...
...THE MAN YOU SEE BEFORE YOU, MASAMUNE SHINMEI...
...WILL ALSO BE DISPATCHED AS A NECRO-MANCER.
THAT'S THE PLAN.
GLAD TO BE WORKING WITH YOU!
RIGHT ON!
BUT FOR NOW WE GET TO RELAX, RIGHT, COMMANDER?
YES. THAT'S TRUE.
I TRUST YOU'VE ALL HEARD THE RESULTS OF THE DIVINATION RITUAL?
NO ONE CAN STAND TO BE IN A STATE OF CONTINUAL TENSION.
BE SURE TO REST WHILE YOU'RE ABLE.
—OH YES. YUKI...
I CAME HERE HOPING TO SAY THIS TO YOU—
YOU SHOULD TAKE THIS WEEKEND TO GO TO THE GIOU HIDDEN SPRINGS.
!!!
...HIDDEN SPRINGS ......?

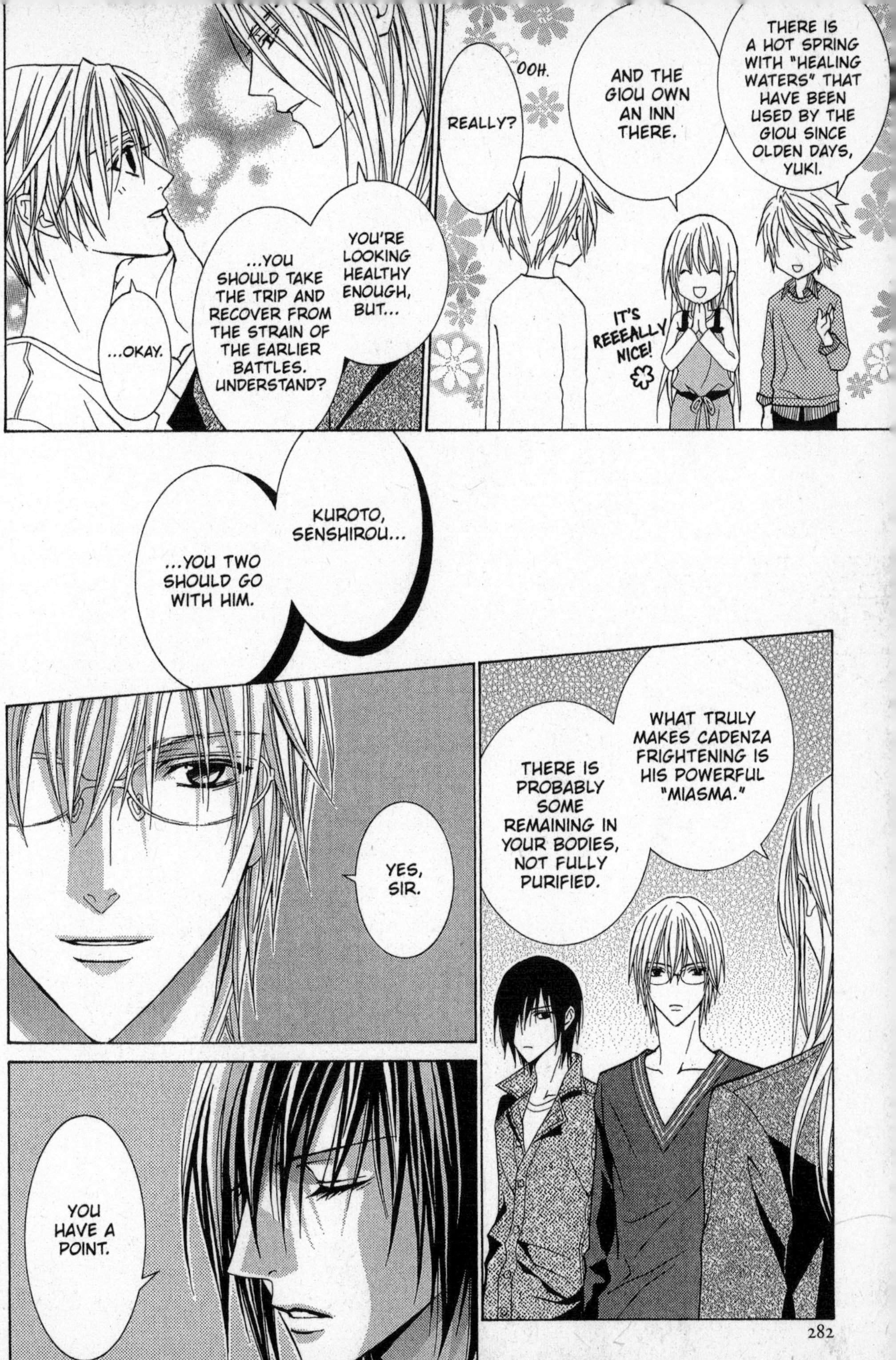
THERE IS A HOT SPRING WITH "HEALING WATERS" THAT HAVE BEEN USED BY THE GIOU SINCE OLDEN DAYS, YUKI.
AND THE GIOU OWN AN INN THERE.
OOH.
REALLY?
IT'S REEEALLY NICE!
YOU'RE LOOKING HEALTHY ENOUGH, BUT...
...YOU SHOULD TAKE THE TRIP AND RECOVER FROM THE STRAIN OF THE EARLIER BATTLES. UNDERSTAND?
...OKAY.
KUROTO, SENSHIROU...
...YOU TWO SHOULD GO WITH HIM.
WHAT TRULY MAKES CADENZA FRIGHTENING IS HIS POWERFUL "MIASMA."
THERE IS PROBABLY SOME REMAINING IN YOUR BODIES, NOT FULLY PURIFIED.
YES, SIR.
YOU HAVE A POINT.

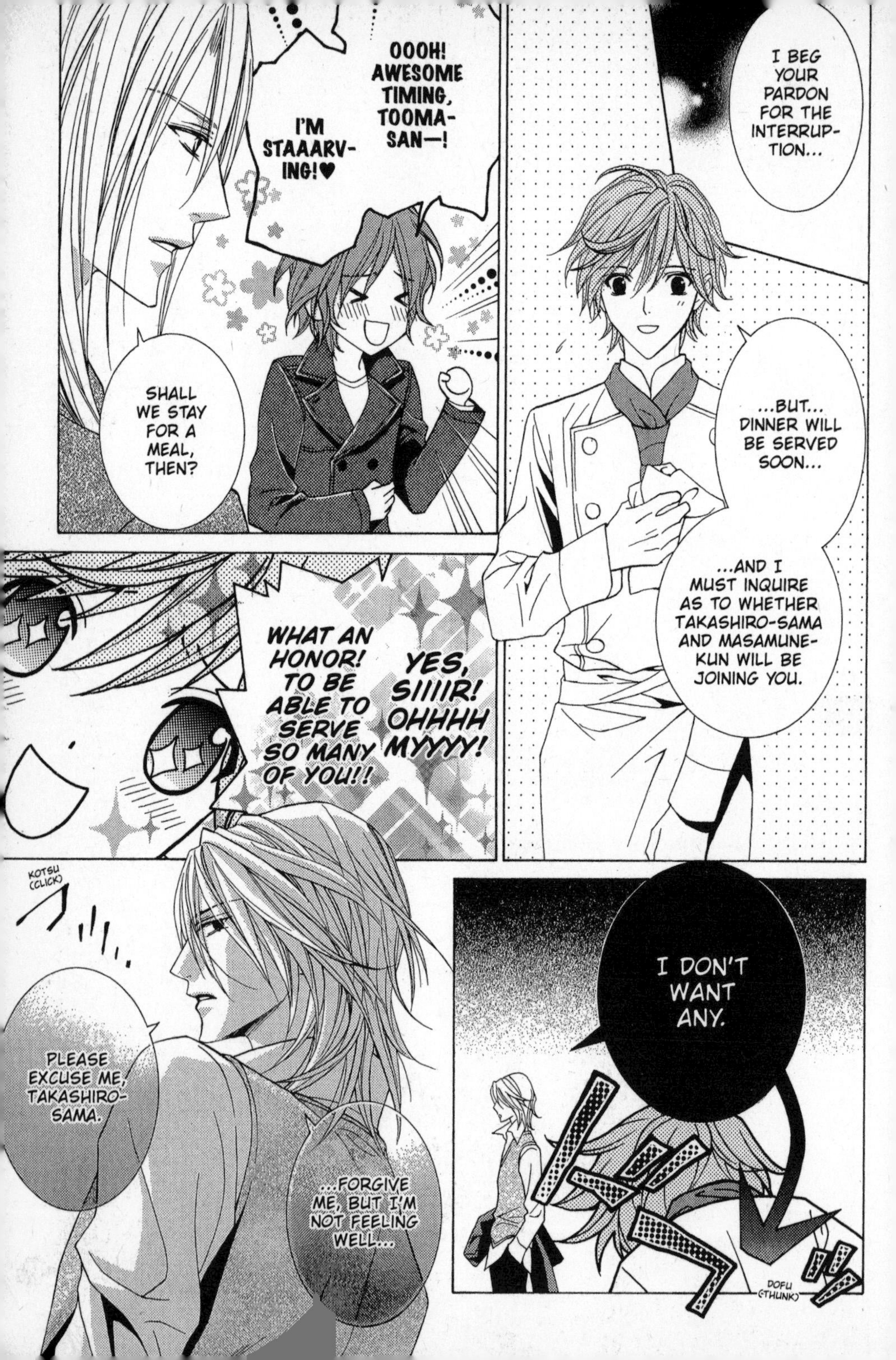
I BEG YOUR PARDON FOR THE INTERRUPTION...
...BUT... DINNER WILL BE SERVED SOON...
...AND I MUST INQUIRE AS TO WHETHER TAKASHIRO-SAMA AND MASAMUNE-KUN WILL BE JOINING YOU.
OOOH! AWESOME TIMING, TOOMA-SAN—!
I'M STAAARVING!♥
SHALL WE STAY FOR A MEAL, THEN?
YES, SIIIIR! OHHHH MYYYY!
WHAT AN HONOR! TO BE ABLE TO SERVE SO MANY OF YOU!!
I DON'T WANT ANY.
DOFU (THUNK)
KOTSU (CLICK)
PLEASE EXCUSE ME, TAKASHIRO-SAMA.
...FORGIVE ME, BUT I'M NOT FEELING WELL...

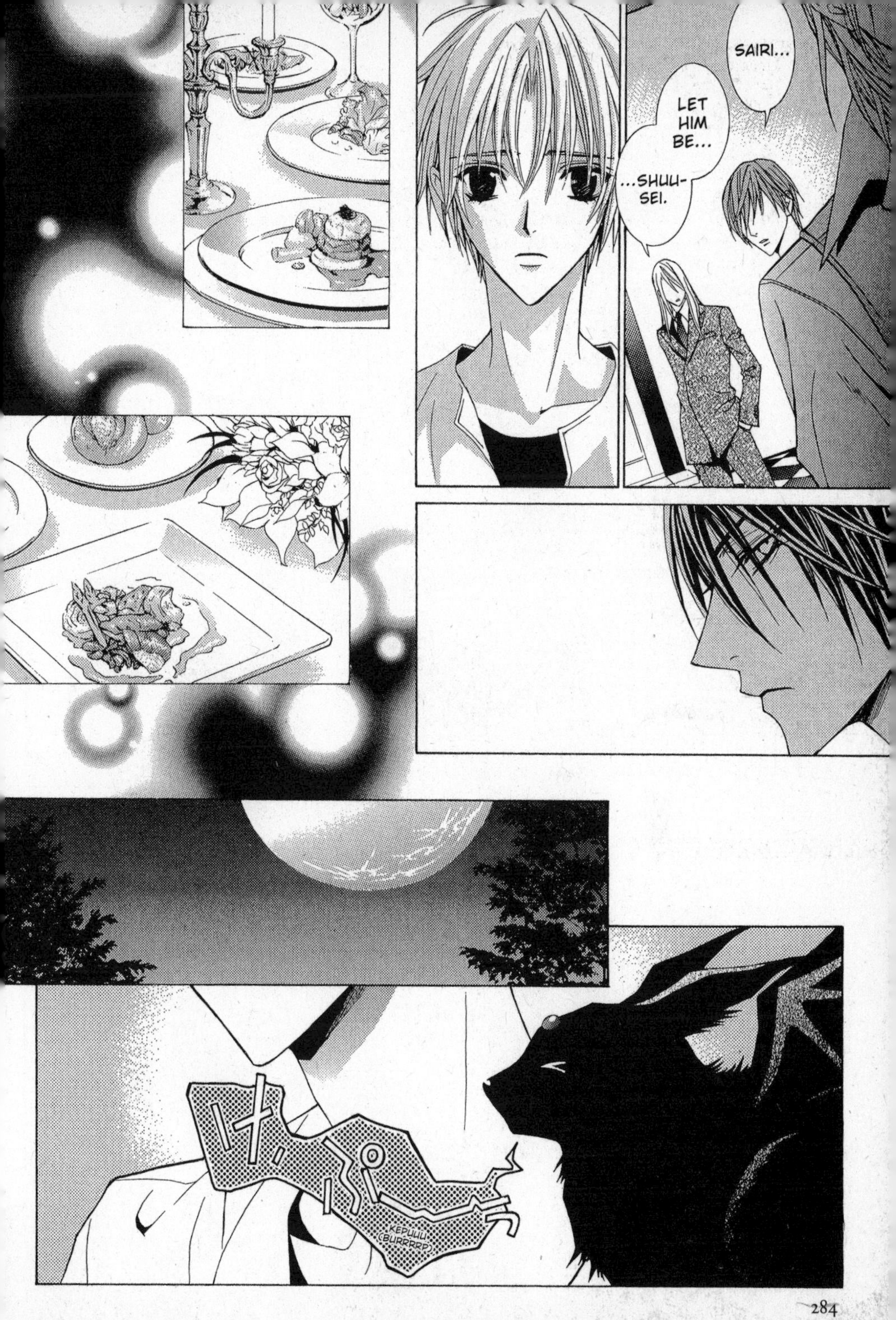
SAIRI...
LET HIM BE...
...SHUU-SEI.
KEPUUU (BURRRRP)

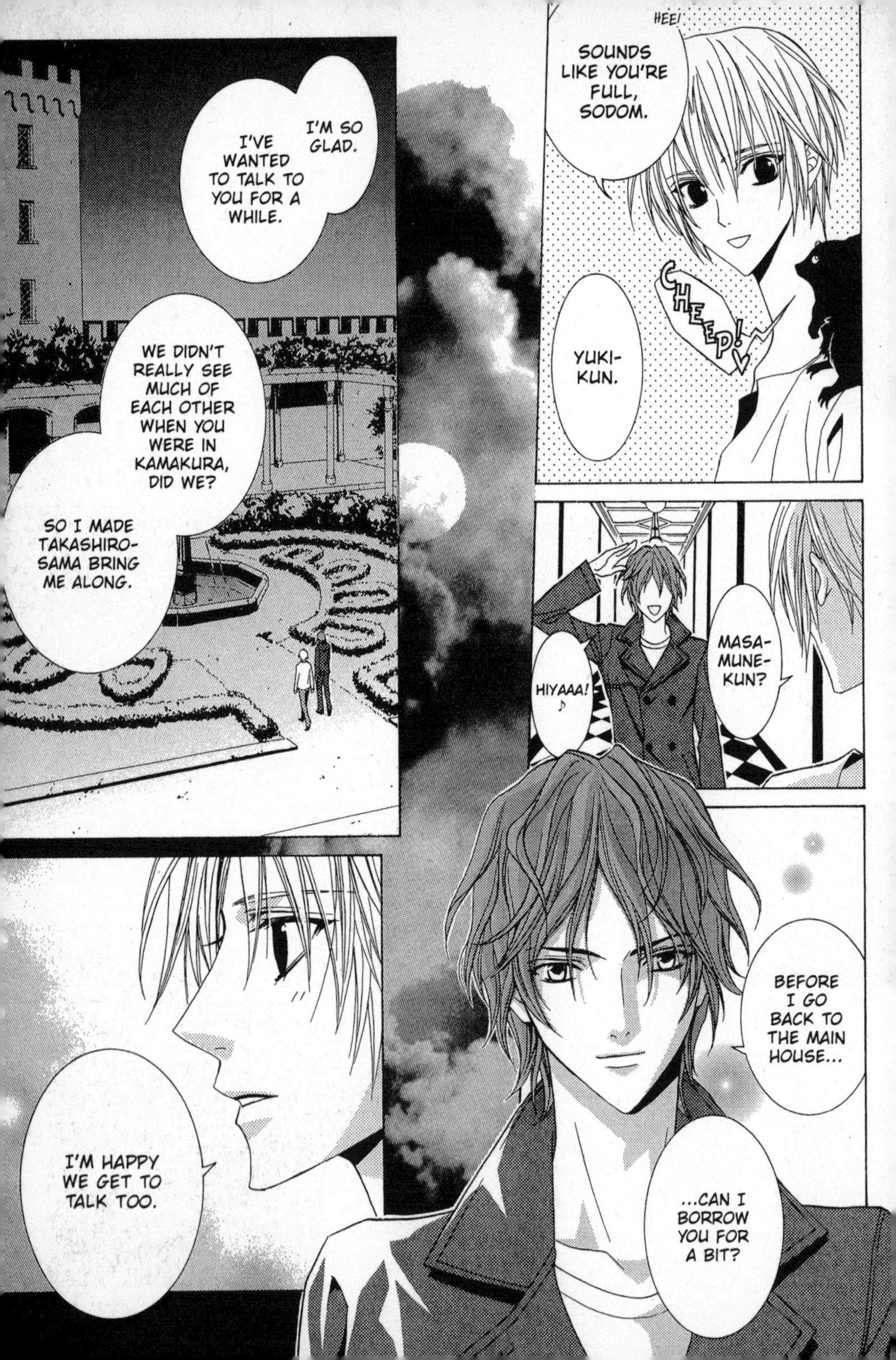
HEE!
SOUNDS LIKE YOU'RE FULL, SODOM.
CHEEP! ♥
YUKI-KUN.
MASA-MUNE-KUN?
HIYAAA! ♪
BEFORE I GO BACK TO THE MAIN HOUSE...
...CAN I BORROW YOU FOR A BIT?
I'M SO GLAD.
I'VE WANTED TO TALK TO YOU FOR A WHILE.
WE DIDN'T REALLY SEE MUCH OF EACH OTHER WHEN YOU WERE IN KAMAKURA, DID WE?
SO I MADE TAKASHIRO-SAMA BRING ME ALONG.
I'M HAPPY WE GET TO TALK TOO.

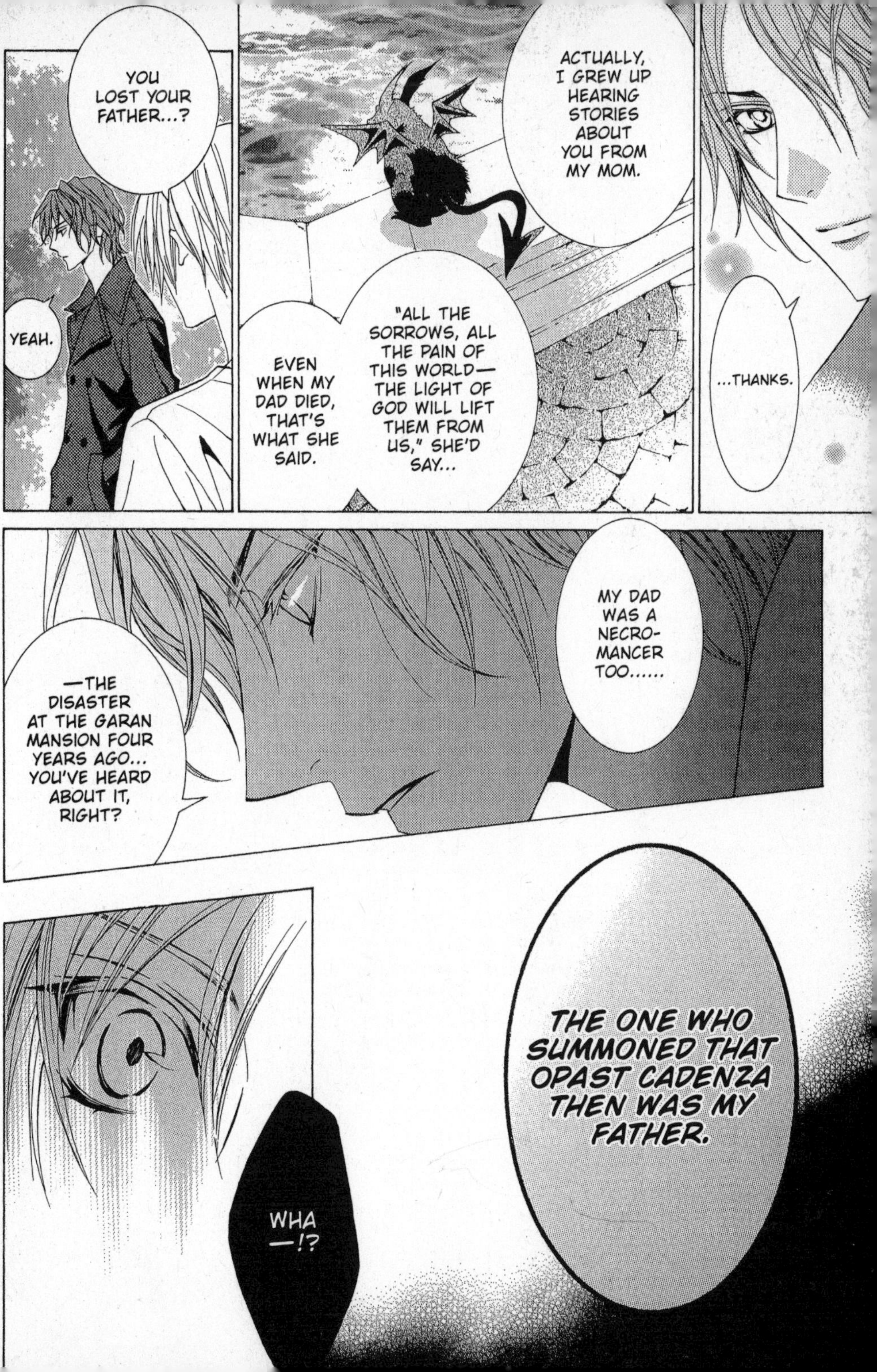
...THANKS.
ACTUALLY, I GREW UP HEARING STORIES ABOUT YOU FROM MY MOM.
"ALL THE SORROWS, ALL THE PAIN OF THIS WORLD—THE LIGHT OF GOD WILL LIFT THEM FROM US," SHE'D SAY...
EVEN WHEN MY DAD DIED, THAT'S WHAT SHE SAID.
YOU LOST YOUR FATHER...?
YEAH.
MY DAD WAS A NECRO-MANCER TOO......
—THE DISASTER AT THE GARAN MANSION FOUR YEARS AGO... YOU'VE HEARD ABOUT IT, RIGHT?
THE ONE WHO SUMMONED THAT OPAST CADENZA THEN WAS MY FATHER.
WHA—!?

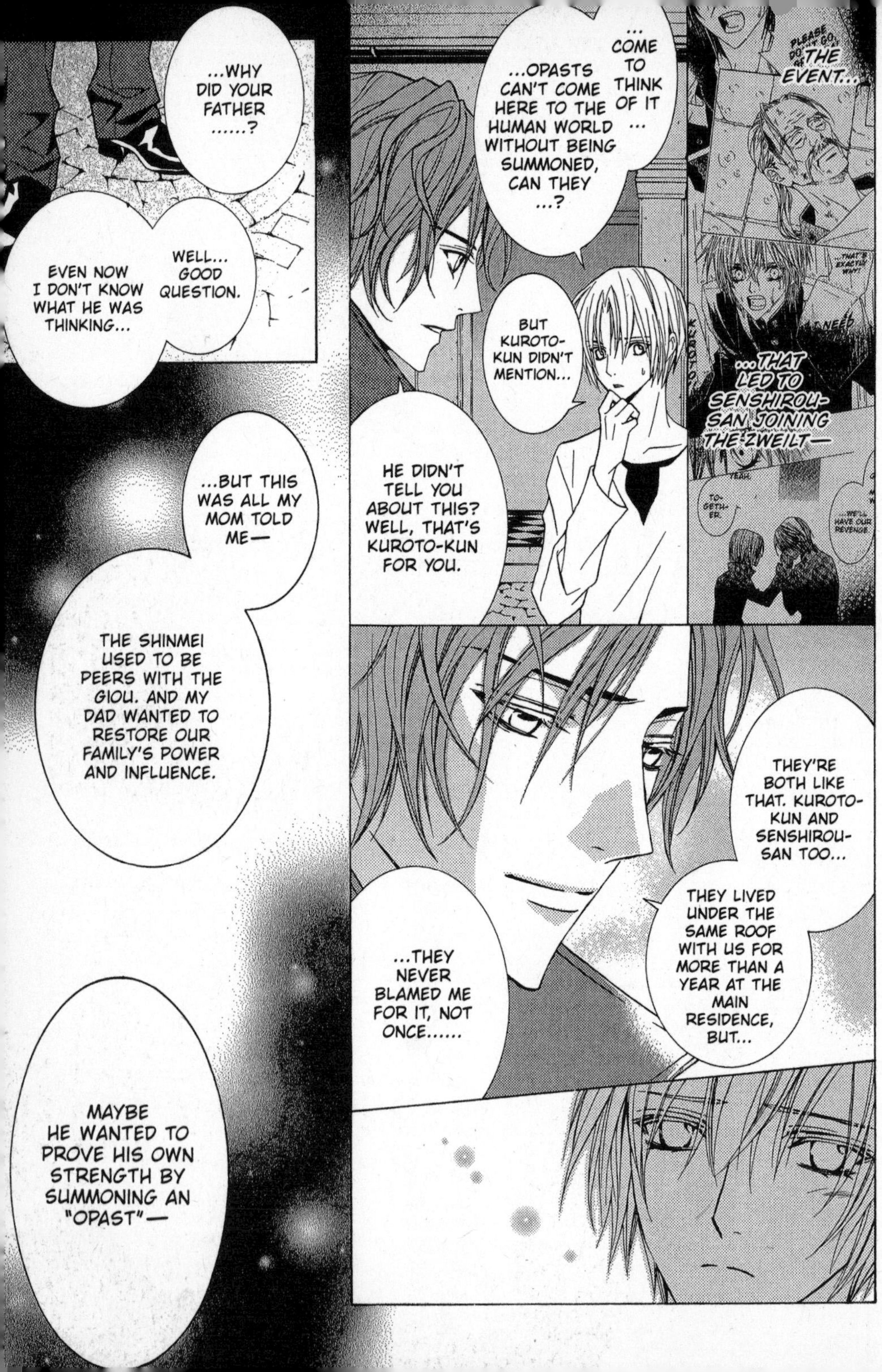
PLEASE DON'T GO
...THE EVENT...
...THAT'S EXACTLY WHY!
I NEED
...THAT LED TO SENSHIROU-SAN JOINING THE ZWEILT—
YEAH.
...WE'LL HAVE OUR REVENGE.
TO-GETH-ER.
...COME TO THINK OF IT...
...OPASTS CAN'T COME HERE TO THE HUMAN WORLD WITHOUT BEING SUMMONED, CAN THEY...?
BUT KUROTO-KUN DIDN'T MENTION...
HE DIDN'T TELL YOU ABOUT THIS? WELL, THAT'S KUROTO-KUN FOR YOU.
THEY'RE BOTH LIKE THAT. KUROTO-KUN AND SENSHIROU-SAN TOO...
THEY LIVED UNDER THE SAME ROOF WITH US FOR MORE THAN A YEAR AT THE MAIN RESIDENCE, BUT...
...THEY NEVER BLAMED ME FOR IT, NOT ONCE......
...WHY DID YOUR FATHER......?
WELL... GOOD QUESTION.
EVEN NOW I DON'T KNOW WHAT HE WAS THINKING...
...BUT THIS WAS ALL MY MOM TOLD ME—
THE SHINMEI USED TO BE PEERS WITH THE GIOU. AND MY DAD WANTED TO RESTORE OUR FAMILY'S POWER AND INFLUENCE.
MAYBE HE WANTED TO PROVE HIS OWN STRENGTH BY SUMMONING AN "OPAST"—

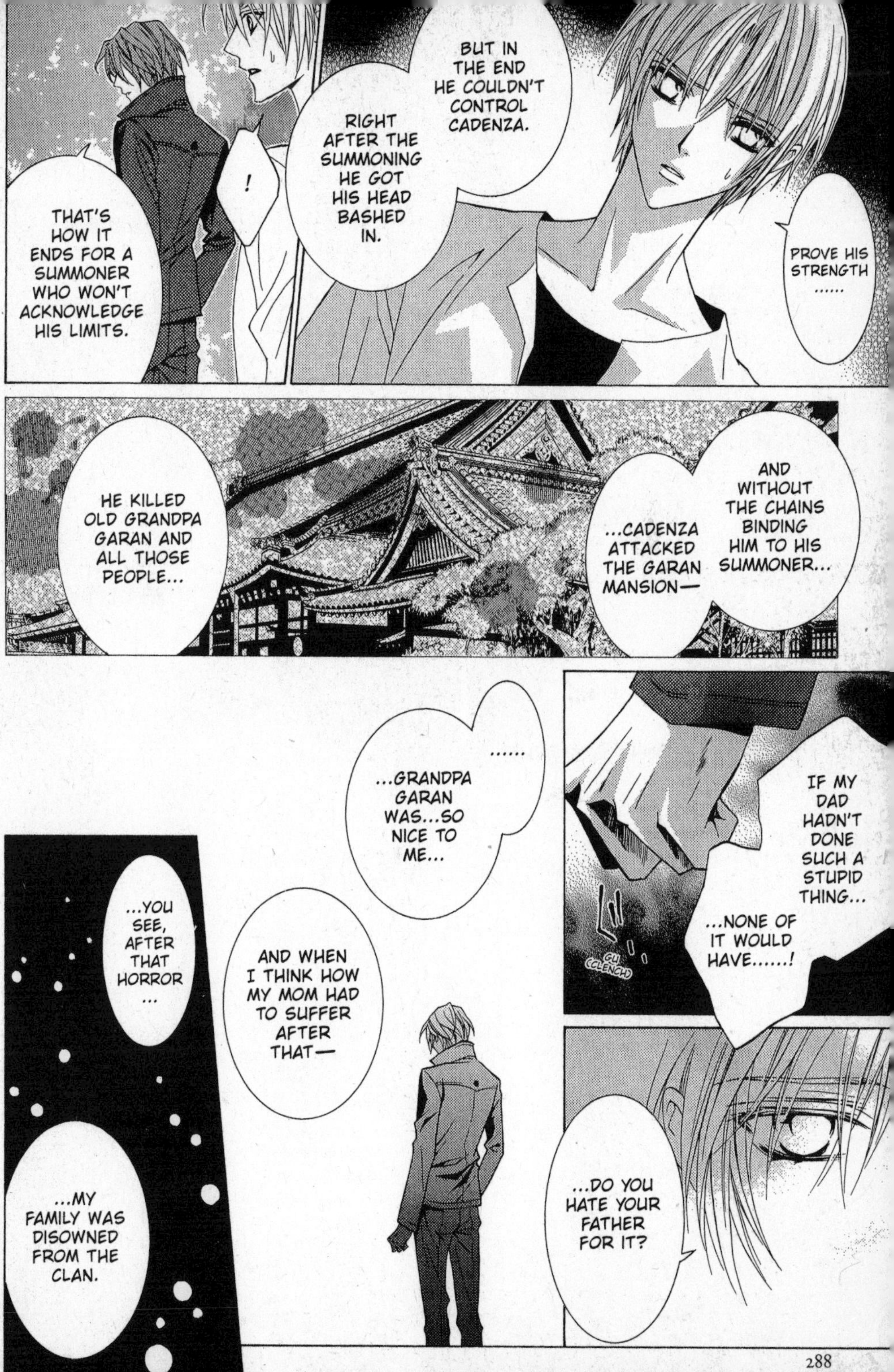
PROVE HIS STRENGTH ......
BUT IN THE END HE COULDN'T CONTROL CADENZA.
RIGHT AFTER THE SUMMONING HE GOT HIS HEAD BASHED IN.
!
THAT'S HOW IT ENDS FOR A SUMMONER WHO WON'T ACKNOWLEDGE HIS LIMITS.
AND WITHOUT THE CHAINS BINDING HIM TO HIS SUMMONER...
...CADENZA ATTACKED THE GARAN MANSION—
HE KILLED OLD GRANDPA GARAN AND ALL THOSE PEOPLE...
IF MY DAD HADN'T DONE SUCH A STUPID THING...
...NONE OF IT WOULD HAVE......!
GU (CLENCH)
...DO YOU HATE YOUR FATHER FOR IT?
......
...GRANDPA GARAN WAS...SO NICE TO ME...
AND WHEN I THINK HOW MY MOM HAD TO SUFFER AFTER THAT—
...YOU SEE, AFTER THAT HORROR ...
...MY FAMILY WAS DISOWNED FROM THE CLAN.

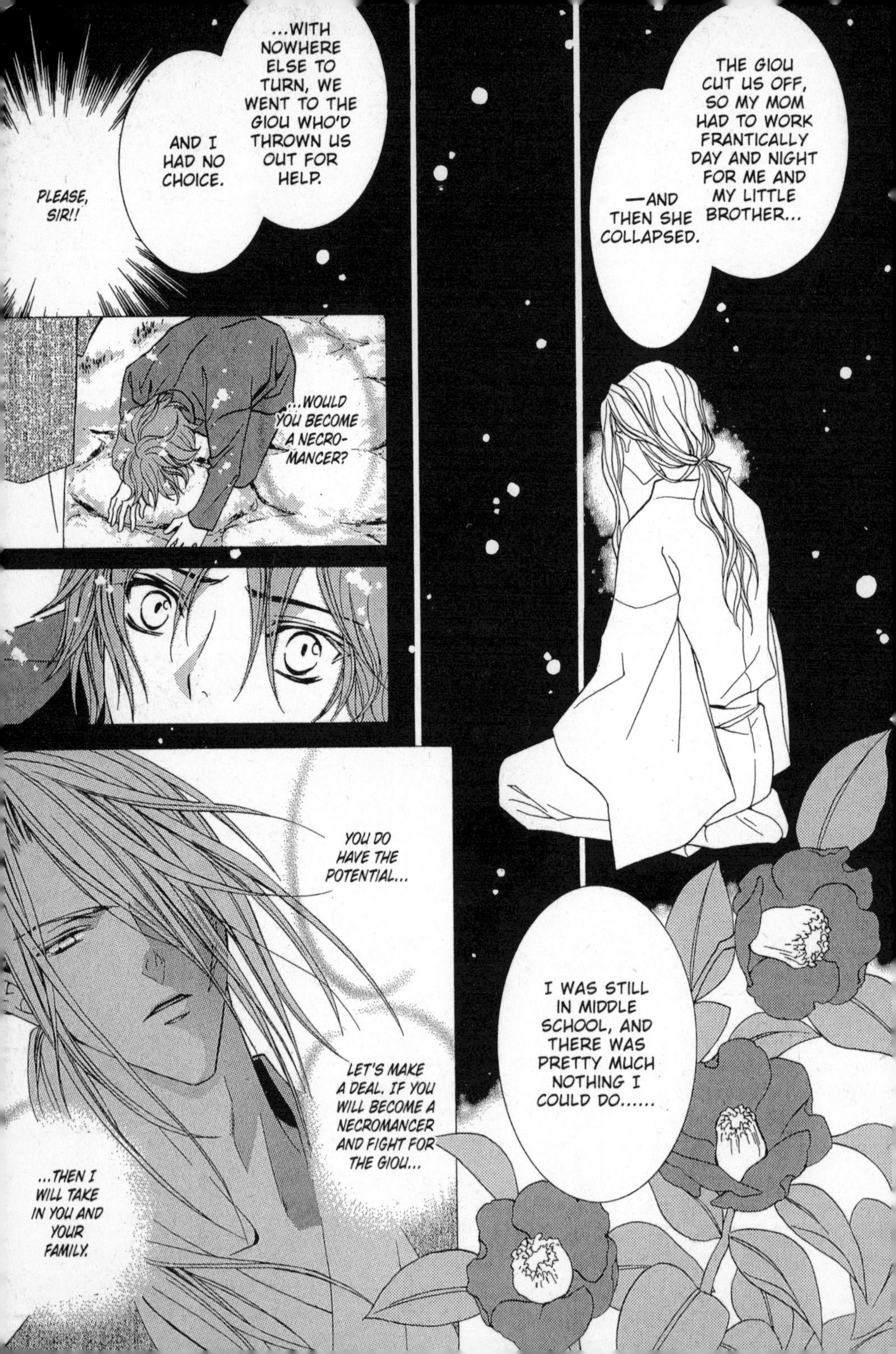
THE GIOU CUT US OFF, SO MY MOM HAD TO WORK FRANTICALLY DAY AND NIGHT FOR ME AND MY LITTLE BROTHER...
—AND THEN SHE COLLAPSED.
I WAS STILL IN MIDDLE SCHOOL, AND THERE WAS PRETTY MUCH NOTHING I COULD DO......
...WITH NOWHERE ELSE TO TURN, WE WENT TO THE GIOU WHO'D THROWN US OUT FOR HELP.
AND I HAD NO CHOICE.
PLEASE, SIR!!
...WOULD YOU BECOME A NECRO-MANCER?
YOU DO HAVE THE POTENTIAL...
LET'S MAKE A DEAL. IF YOU WILL BECOME A NECROMANCER AND FIGHT FOR THE GIOU...
...THEN I WILL TAKE IN YOU AND YOUR FAMILY.

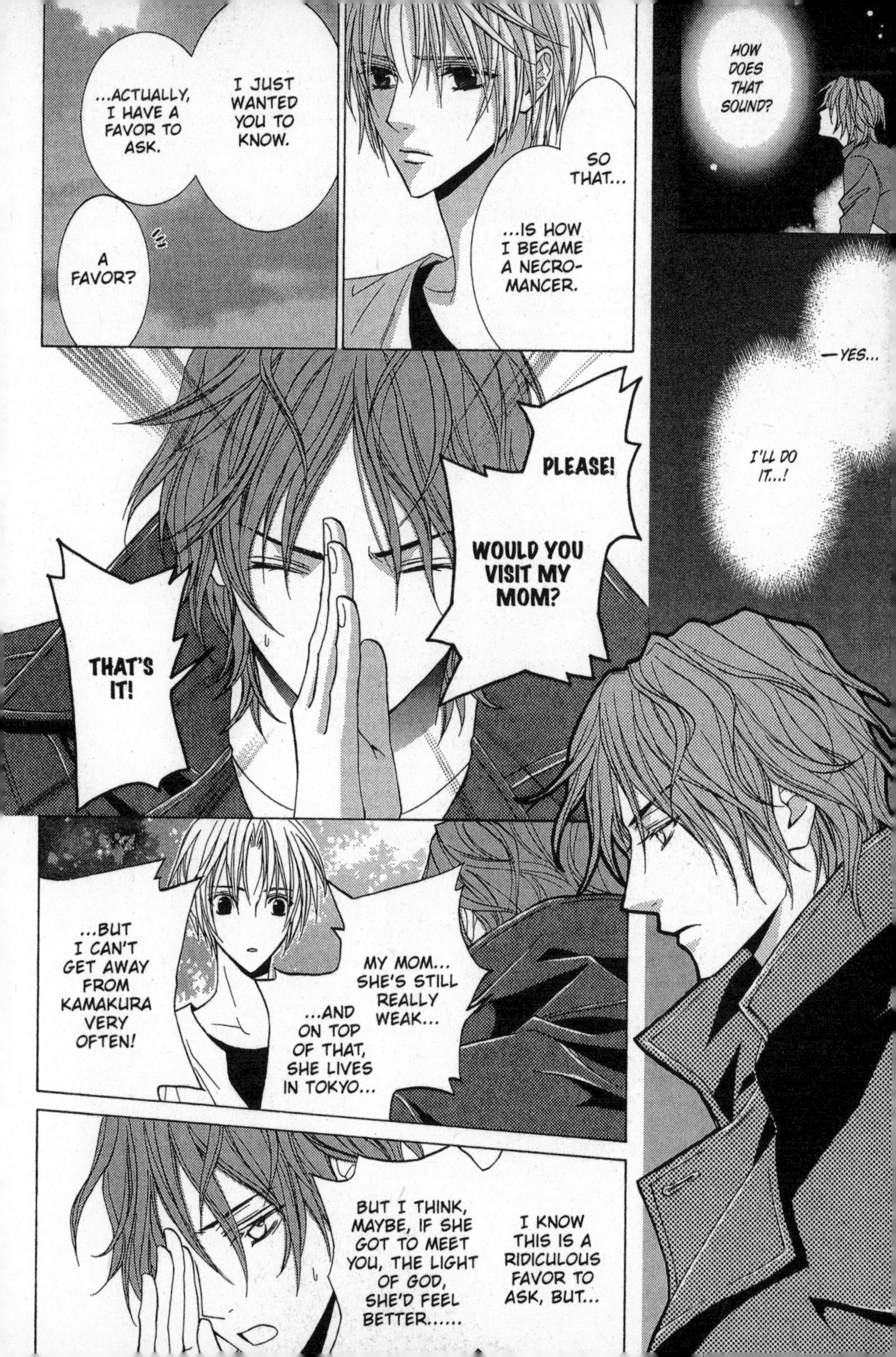
HOW DOES THAT SOUND?
—YES...
I'LL DO IT...!
SO THAT...
...IS HOW I BECAME A NECROMANCER.
I JUST WANTED YOU TO KNOW.
...ACTUALLY, I HAVE A FAVOR TO ASK.
A FAVOR?
PLEASE!
WOULD YOU VISIT MY MOM?
THAT'S IT!
MY MOM... SHE'S STILL REALLY WEAK...
...AND ON TOP OF THAT, SHE LIVES IN TOKYO...
...BUT I CAN'T GET AWAY FROM KAMAKURA VERY OFTEN!
I KNOW THIS IS A RIDICULOUS FAVOR TO ASK, BUT...
BUT I THINK, MAYBE, IF SHE GOT TO MEET YOU, THE LIGHT OF GOD, SHE'D FEEL BETTER......

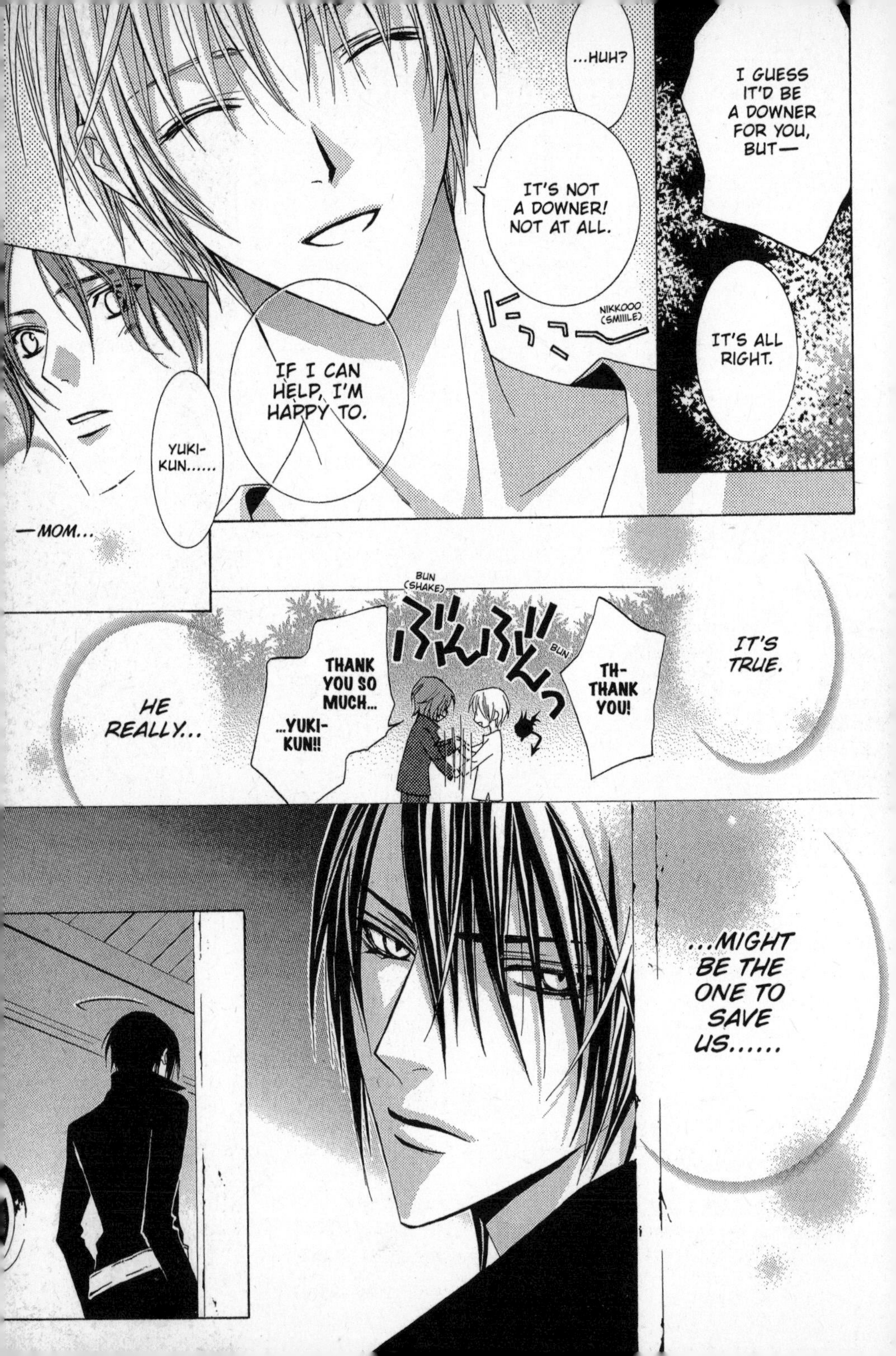
I GUESS IT'D BE A DOWNER FOR YOU, BUT—
IT'S ALL RIGHT.
...HUH?
IT'S NOT A DOWNER! NOT AT ALL.
NIKKOOO (SMIIILE)
IF I CAN HELP, I'M HAPPY TO.
YUKI-KUN......
—MOM...
IT'S TRUE.
TH-THANK YOU!
BUN
BUN (SHAKE)
THANK YOU SO MUCH...
...YUKI-KUN!!
HE REALLY...
...MIGHT BE THE ONE TO SAVE US......

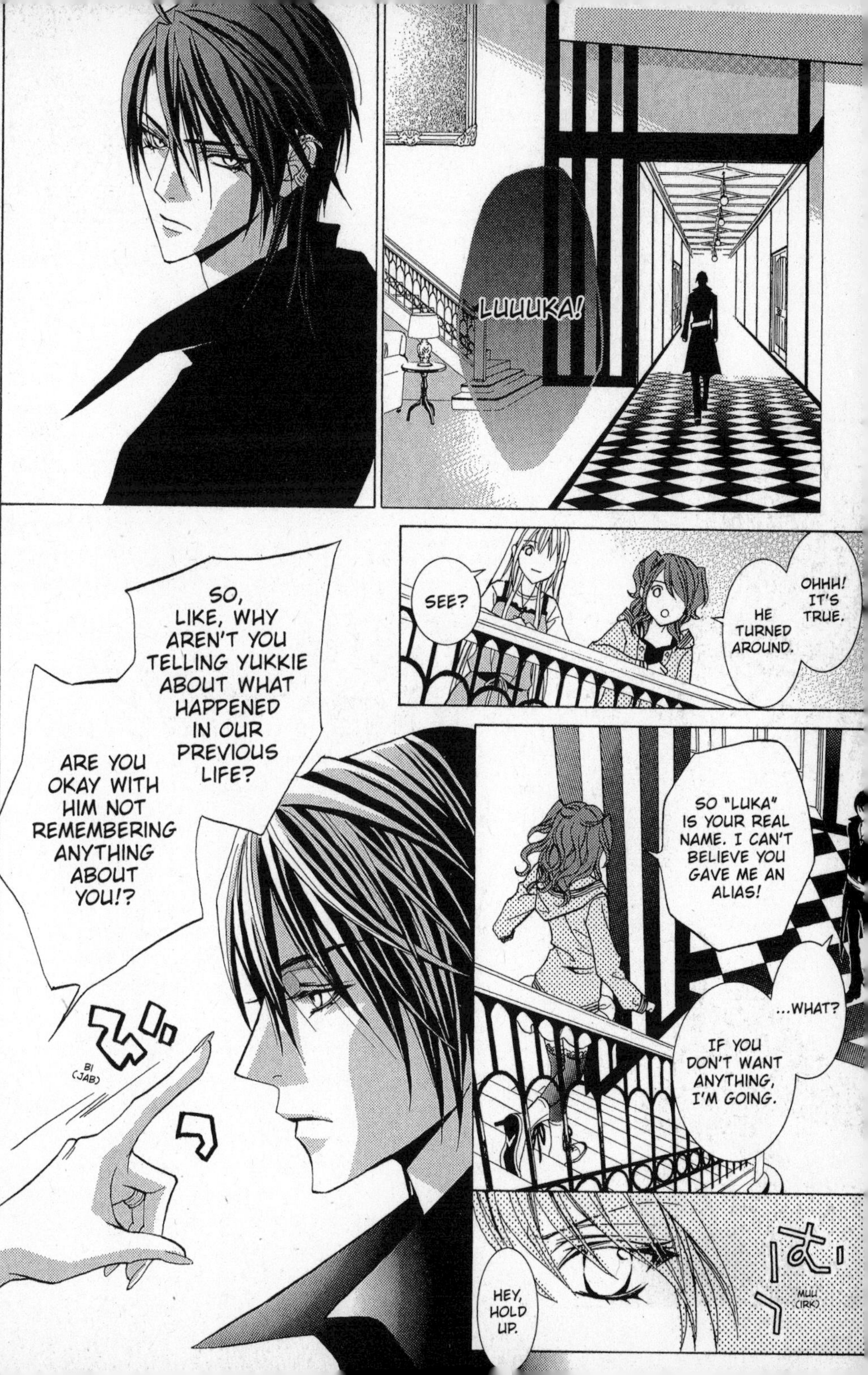
LUUUKA!
OHHH! IT'S TRUE.
HE TURNED AROUND.
SEE?
SO "LUKA" IS YOUR REAL NAME. I CAN'T BELIEVE YOU GAVE ME AN ALIAS!
...WHAT?
IF YOU DON'T WANT ANYTHING, I'M GOING.
MUU (IRK)
HEY, HOLD UP.
SO, LIKE, WHY AREN'T YOU TELLING YUKKIE ABOUT WHAT HAPPENED IN OUR PREVIOUS LIFE?
ARE YOU OKAY WITH HIM NOT REMEMBERING ANYTHING ABOUT YOU!?
BI (JAB)

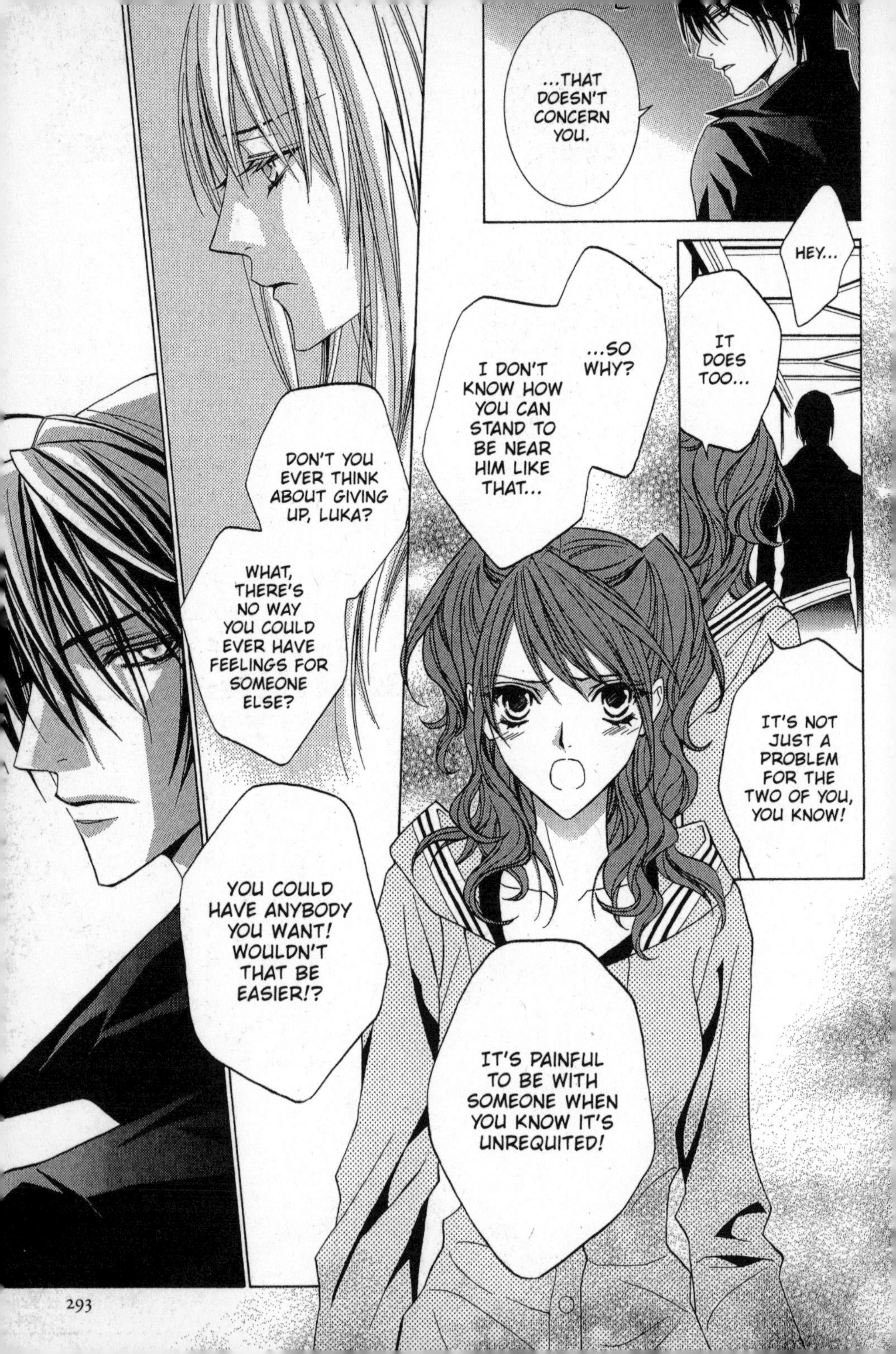
...THAT DOESN'T CONCERN YOU.
HEY...
IT DOES TOO...
IT'S NOT JUST A PROBLEM FOR THE TWO OF YOU, YOU KNOW!
...SO WHY?
I DON'T KNOW HOW YOU CAN STAND TO BE NEAR HIM LIKE THAT...
IT'S PAINFUL TO BE WITH SOMEONE WHEN YOU KNOW IT'S UNREQUITED!
DON'T YOU EVER THINK ABOUT GIVING UP, LUKA?
WHAT, THERE'S NO WAY YOU COULD EVER HAVE FEELINGS FOR SOMEONE ELSE?
YOU COULD HAVE ANYBODY YOU WANT! WOULDN'T THAT BE EASIER!?

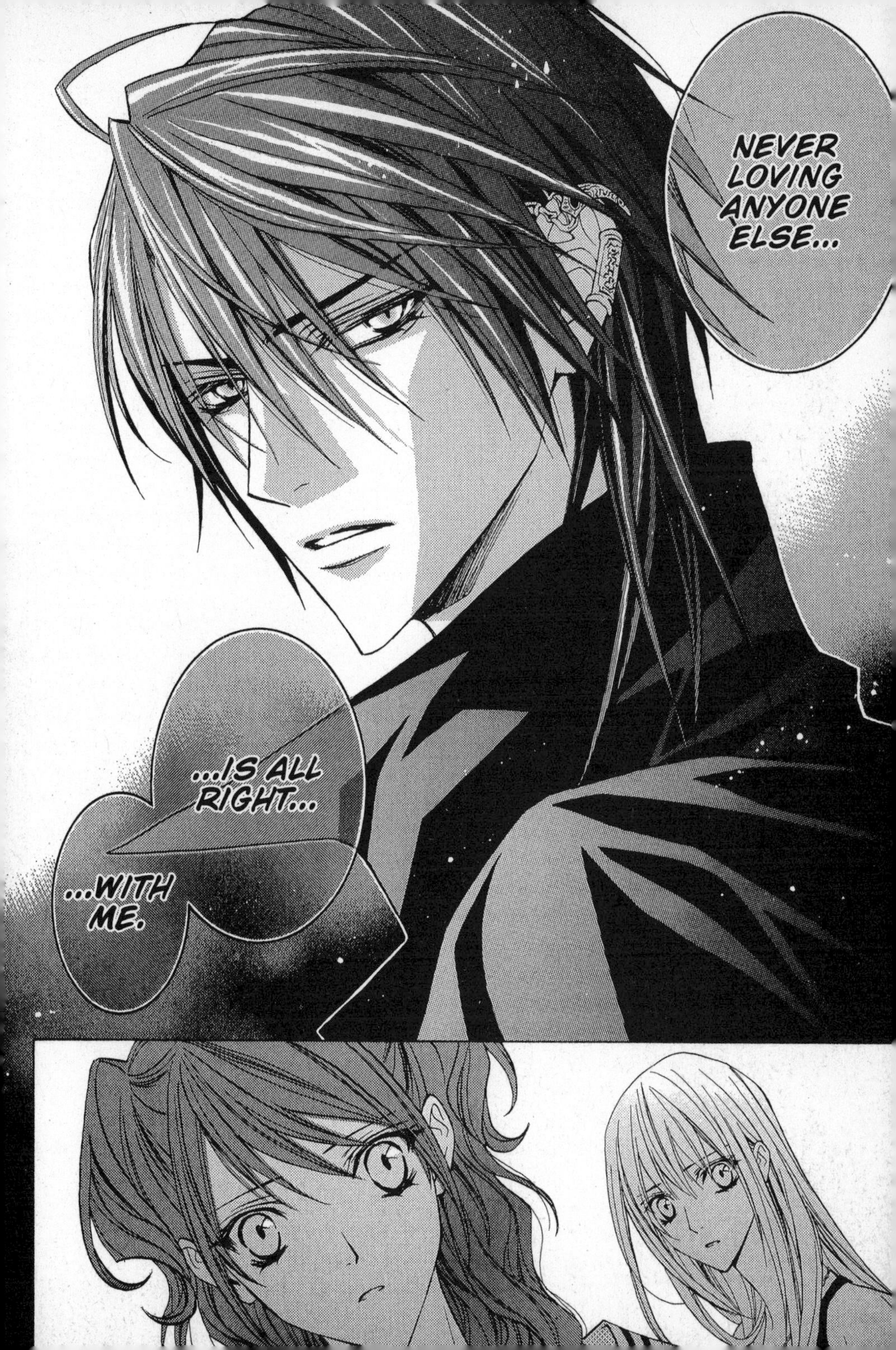
NEVER LOVING ANYONE ELSE...
...IS ALL RIGHT...
...WITH ME.

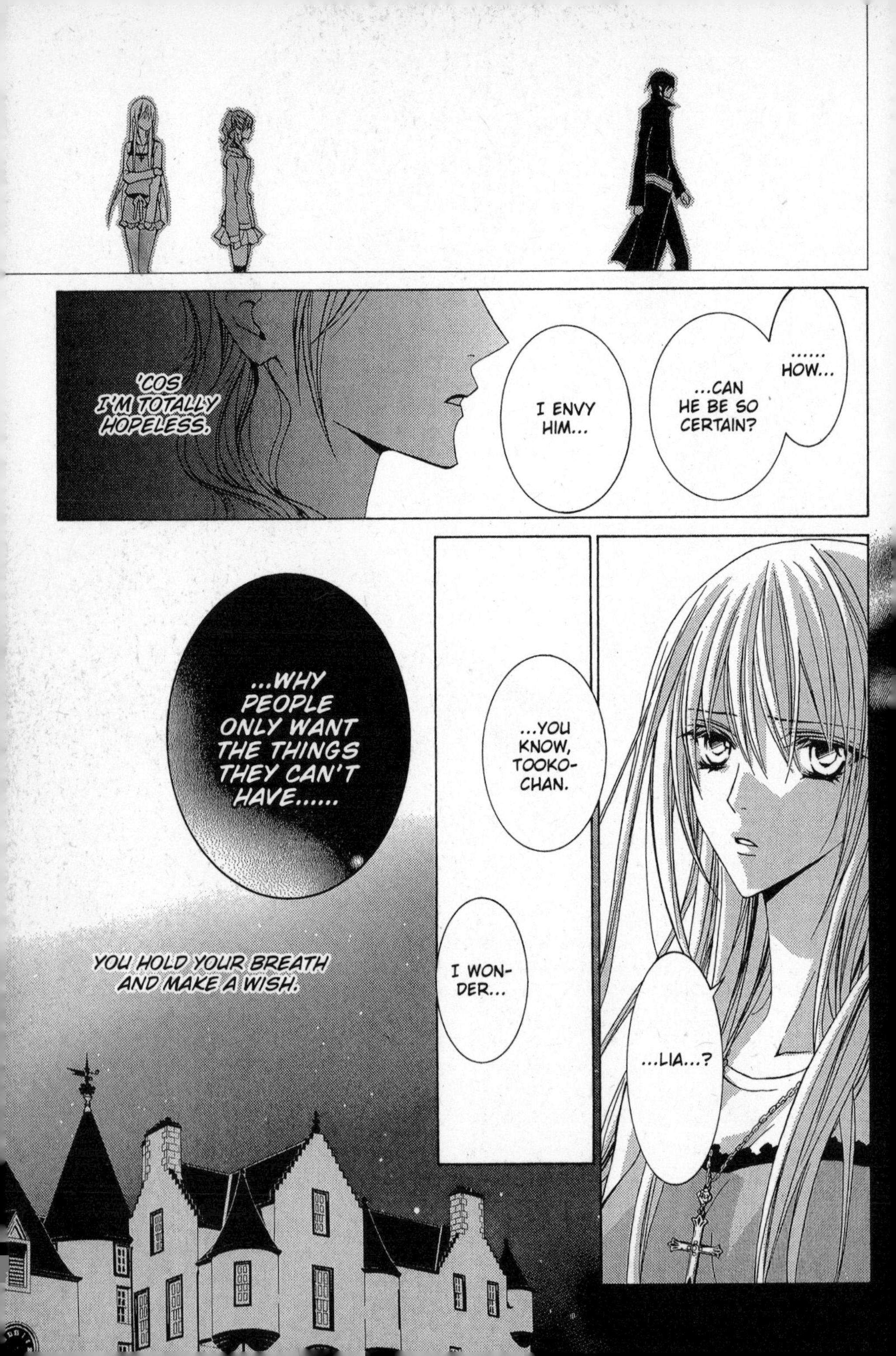
......HOW...
...CAN HE BE SO CERTAIN?
I ENVY HIM...
'COS I'M TOTALLY HOPELESS.
...LIA...?
...YOU KNOW, TOOKO-CHAN.
I WON-DER...
...WHY PEOPLE ONLY WANT THE THINGS THEY CAN'T HAVE......
YOU HOLD YOUR BREATH AND MAKE A WISH.

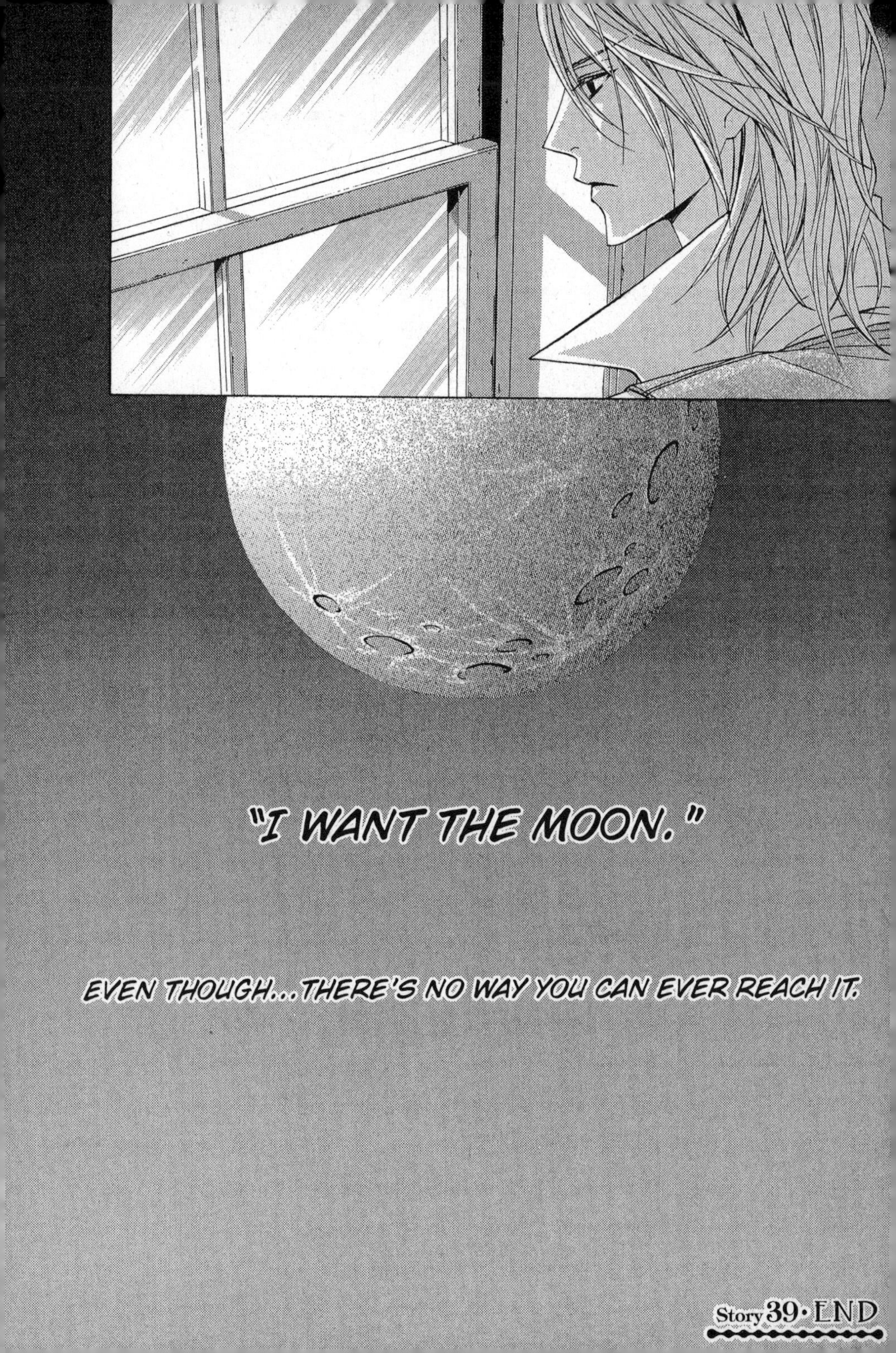
"I WANT THE MOON."
EVEN THOUGH...THERE'S NO WAY YOU CAN EVER REACH IT.
Story 39 • END

The
BETRAYAL
knows my name

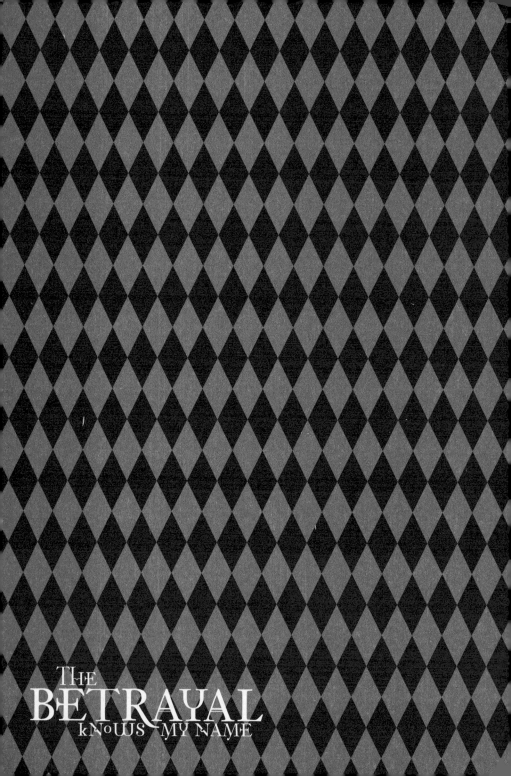

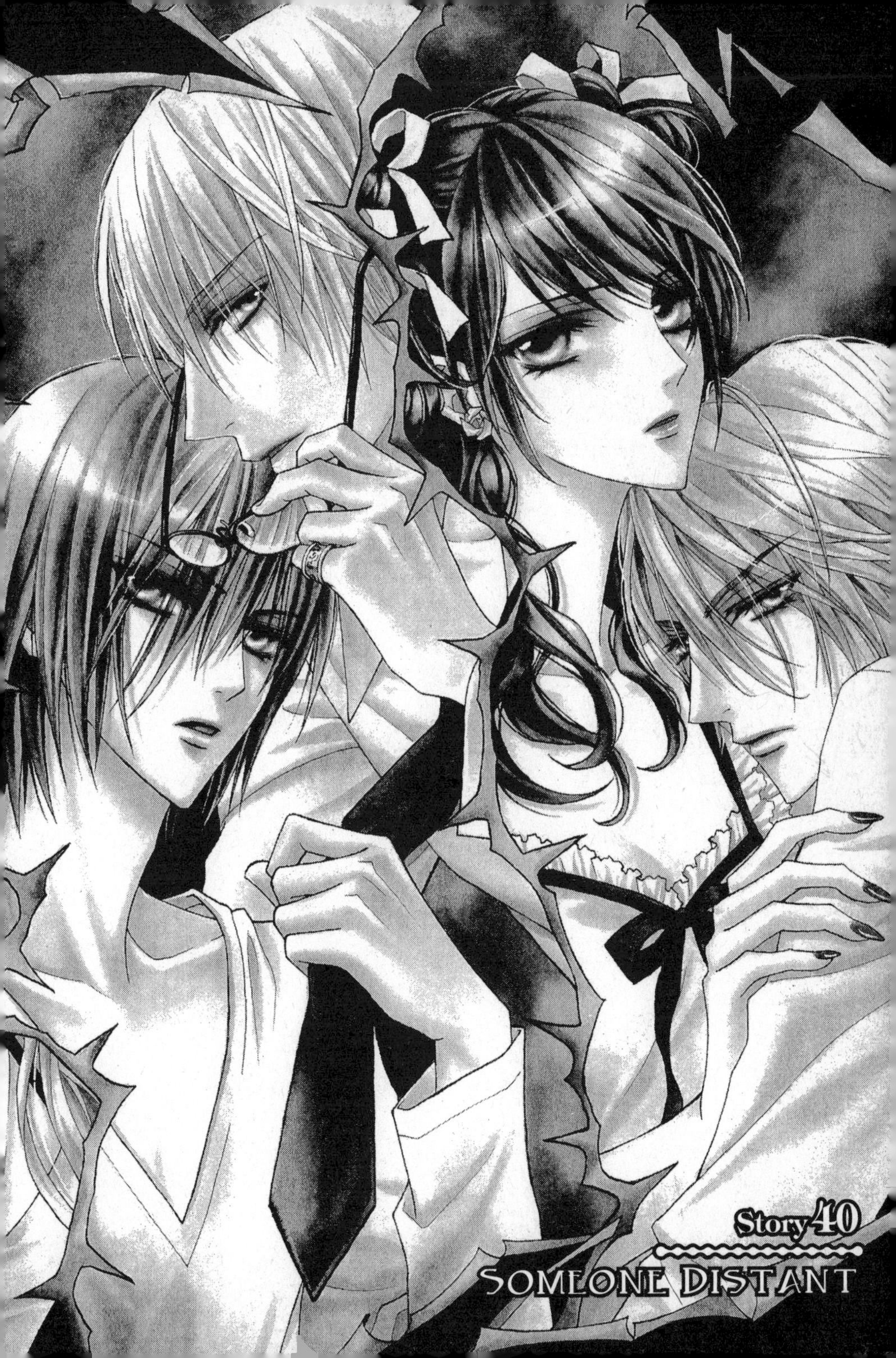
Story 40
SOMEONE DISTANT

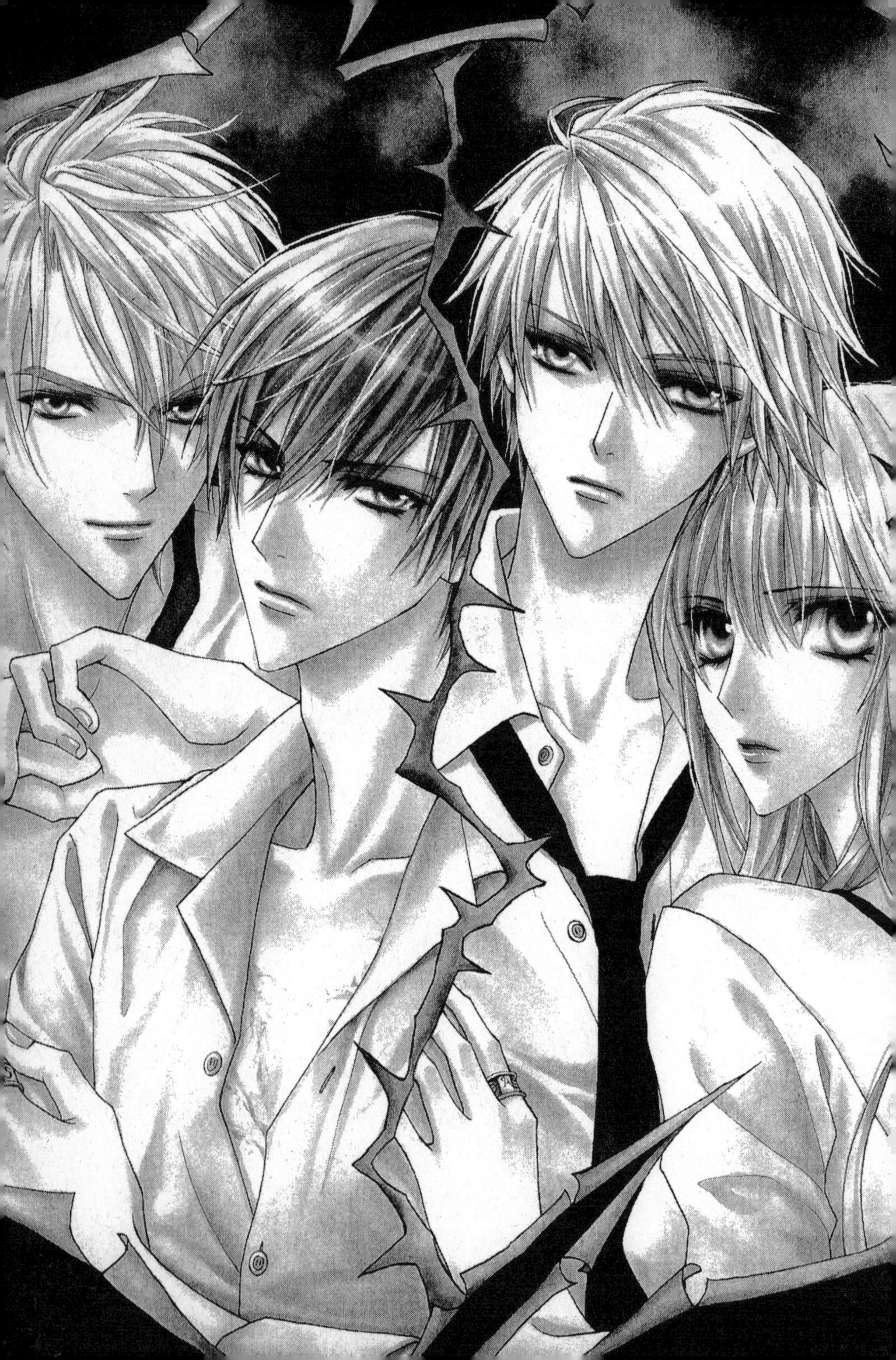

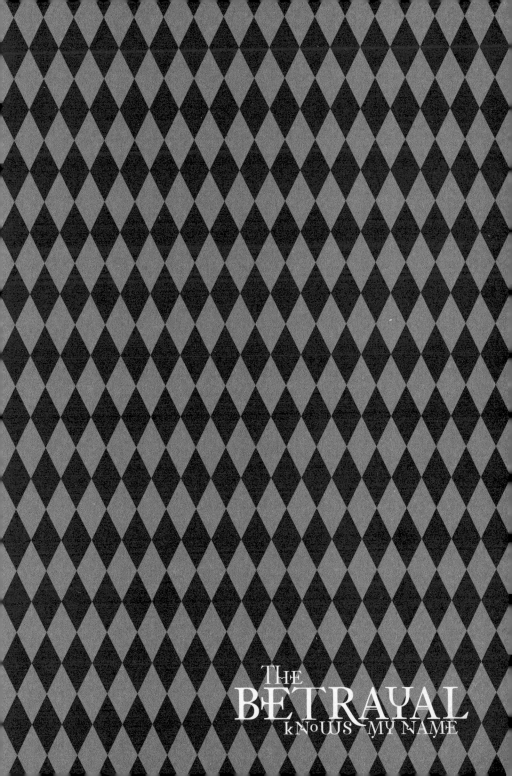

THE
BETRAYAL
kNoWS MY NAME

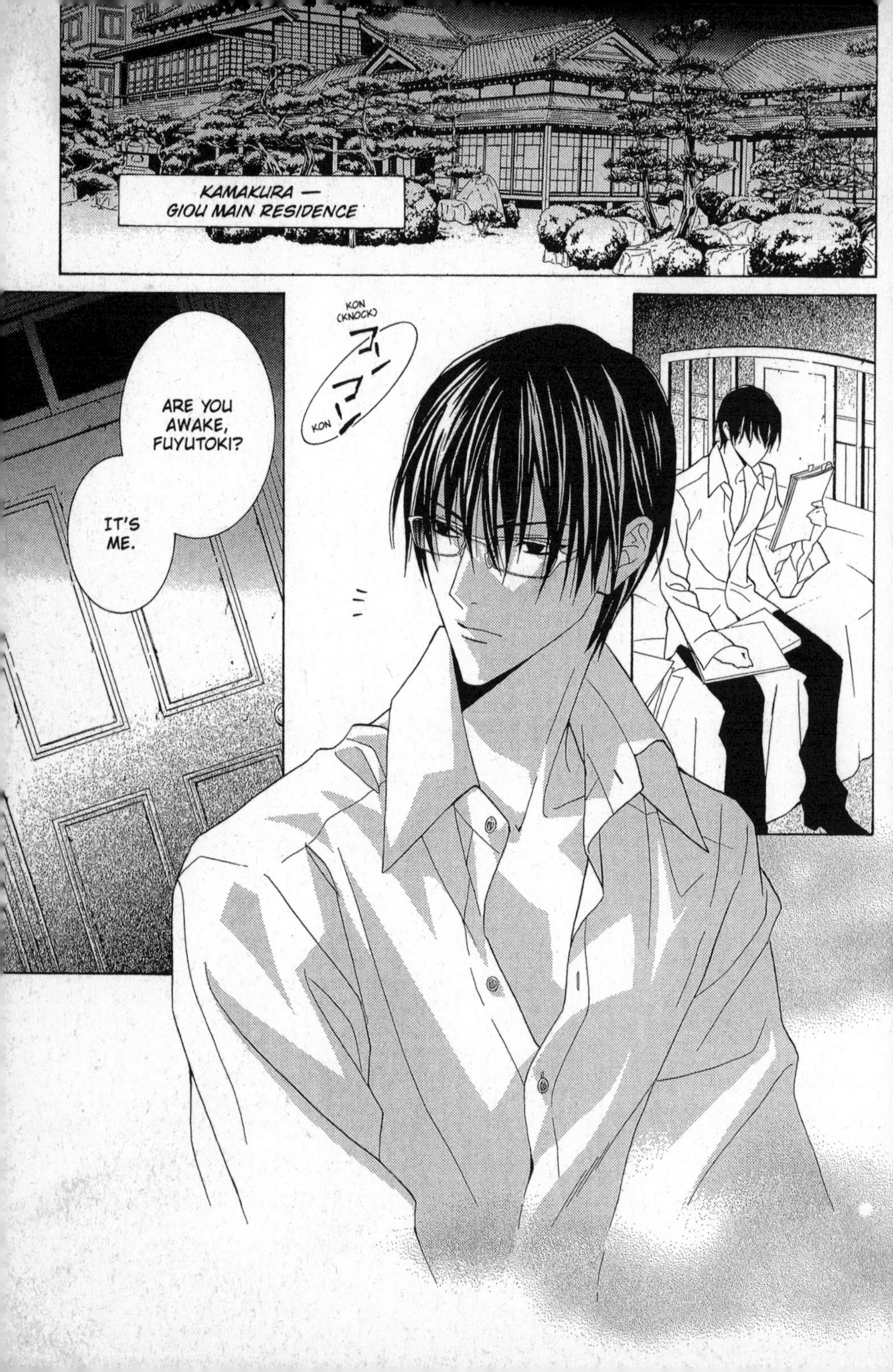
KAMAKURA —
GIOU MAIN RESIDENCE
KON (KNOCK)
KON
ARE YOU AWAKE, FUYUTOKI?
IT'S ME.

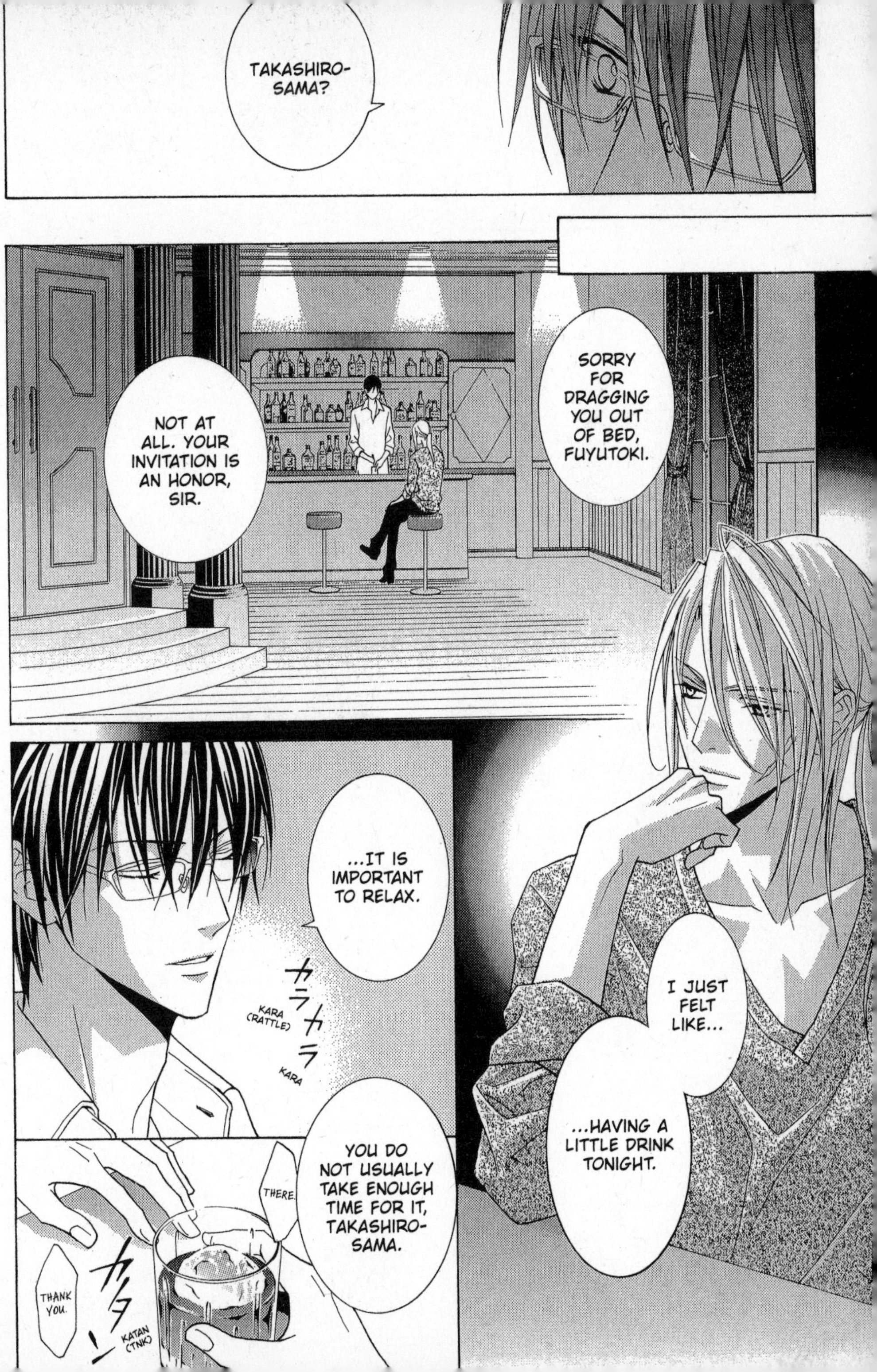
TAKASHIRO-SAMA?
SORRY FOR DRAGGING YOU OUT OF BED, FUYUTOKI.
NOT AT ALL. YOUR INVITATION IS AN HONOR, SIR.
I JUST FELT LIKE...
...HAVING A LITTLE DRINK TONIGHT.
...IT IS IMPORTANT TO RELAX.
KARA (RATTLE)
KARA
YOU DO NOT USUALLY TAKE ENOUGH TIME FOR IT, TAKASHIRO-SAMA.
THERE.
THANK YOU.
KATAN (TNK)

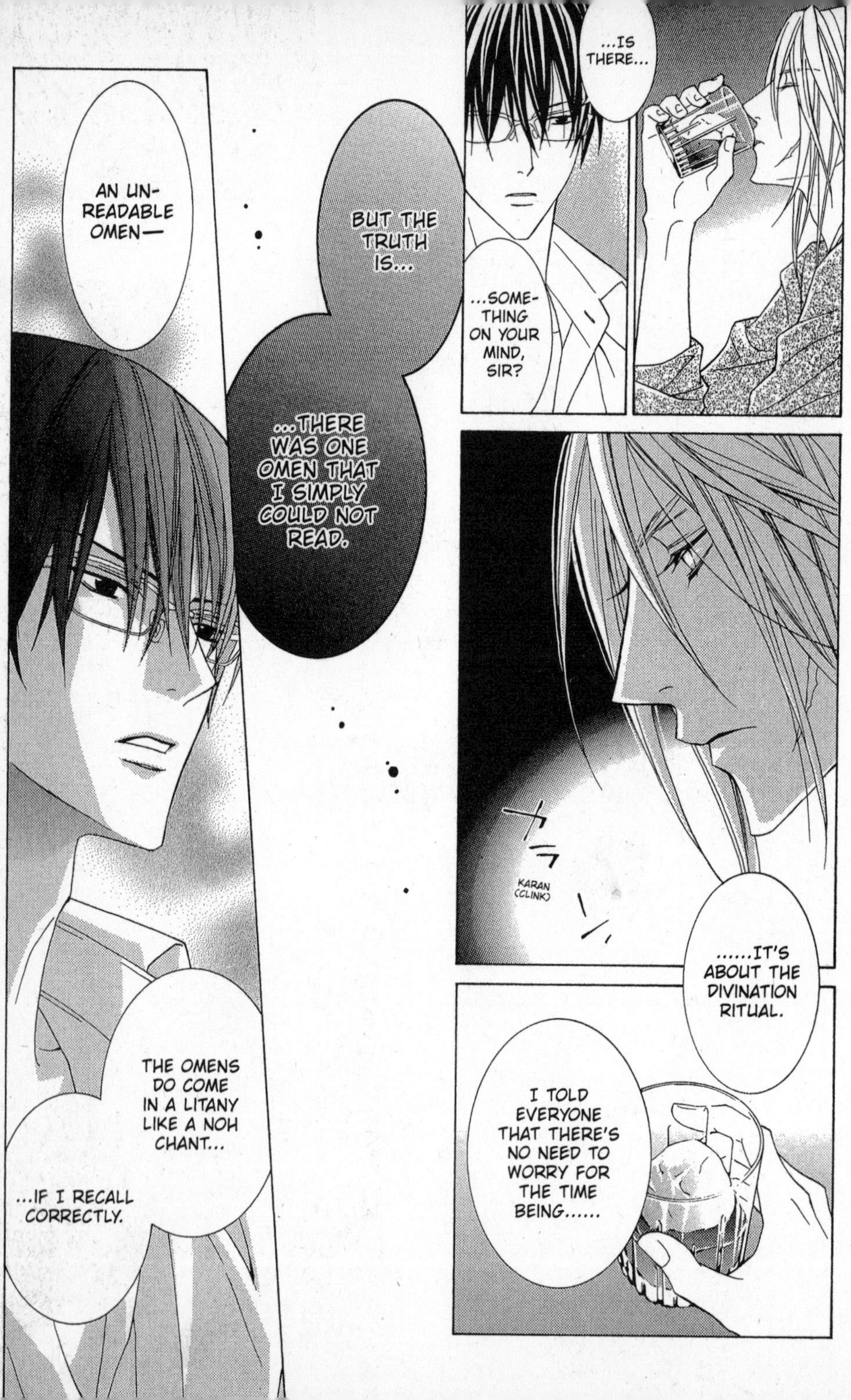
...IS THERE...
...SOMETHING ON YOUR MIND, SIR?
KARAN (CLINK)
......IT'S ABOUT THE DIVINATION RITUAL.
I TOLD EVERYONE THAT THERE'S NO NEED TO WORRY FOR THE TIME BEING......
BUT THE TRUTH IS...
...THERE WAS ONE OMEN THAT I SIMPLY COULD NOT READ.
AN UN-READABLE OMEN—
THE OMENS DO COME IN A LITANY LIKE A NOH CHANT...
...IF I RECALL CORRECTLY.

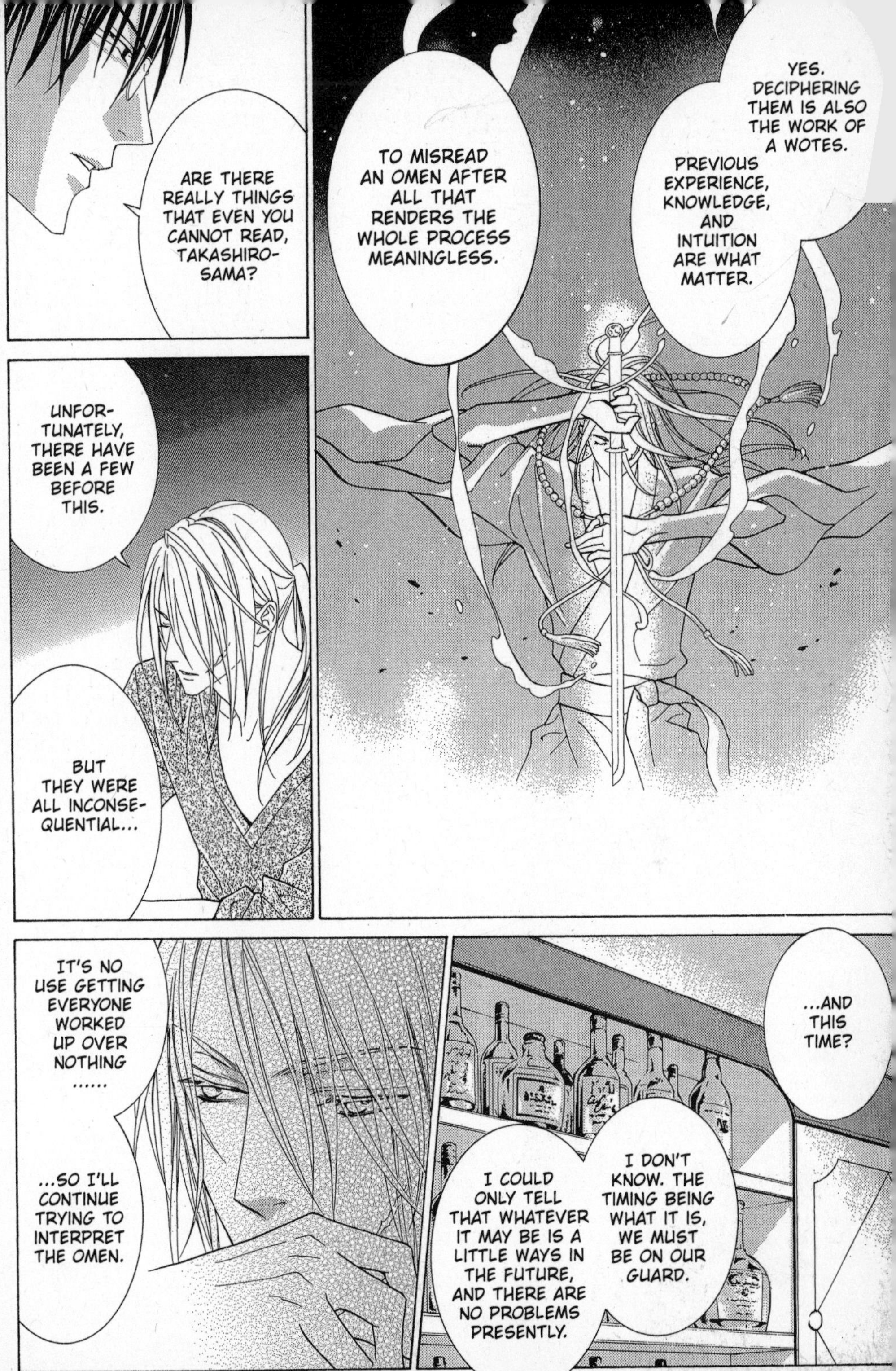
YES. DECIPHERING THEM IS ALSO THE WORK OF A WOTES.
PREVIOUS EXPERIENCE, KNOWLEDGE, AND INTUITION ARE WHAT MATTER.
TO MISREAD AN OMEN AFTER ALL THAT RENDERS THE WHOLE PROCESS MEANINGLESS.
ARE THERE REALLY THINGS THAT EVEN YOU CANNOT READ, TAKASHIRO-SAMA?
UNFOR-TUNATELY, THERE HAVE BEEN A FEW BEFORE THIS.
BUT THEY WERE ALL INCONSE-QUENTIAL...
...AND THIS TIME?
I DON'T KNOW. THE TIMING BEING WHAT IT IS, WE MUST BE ON OUR GUARD.
I COULD ONLY TELL THAT WHATEVER IT MAY BE IS A LITTLE WAYS IN THE FUTURE, AND THERE ARE NO PROBLEMS PRESENTLY.
IT'S NO USE GETTING EVERYONE WORKED UP OVER NOTHING ......
...SO I'LL CONTINUE TRYING TO INTERPRET THE OMEN.

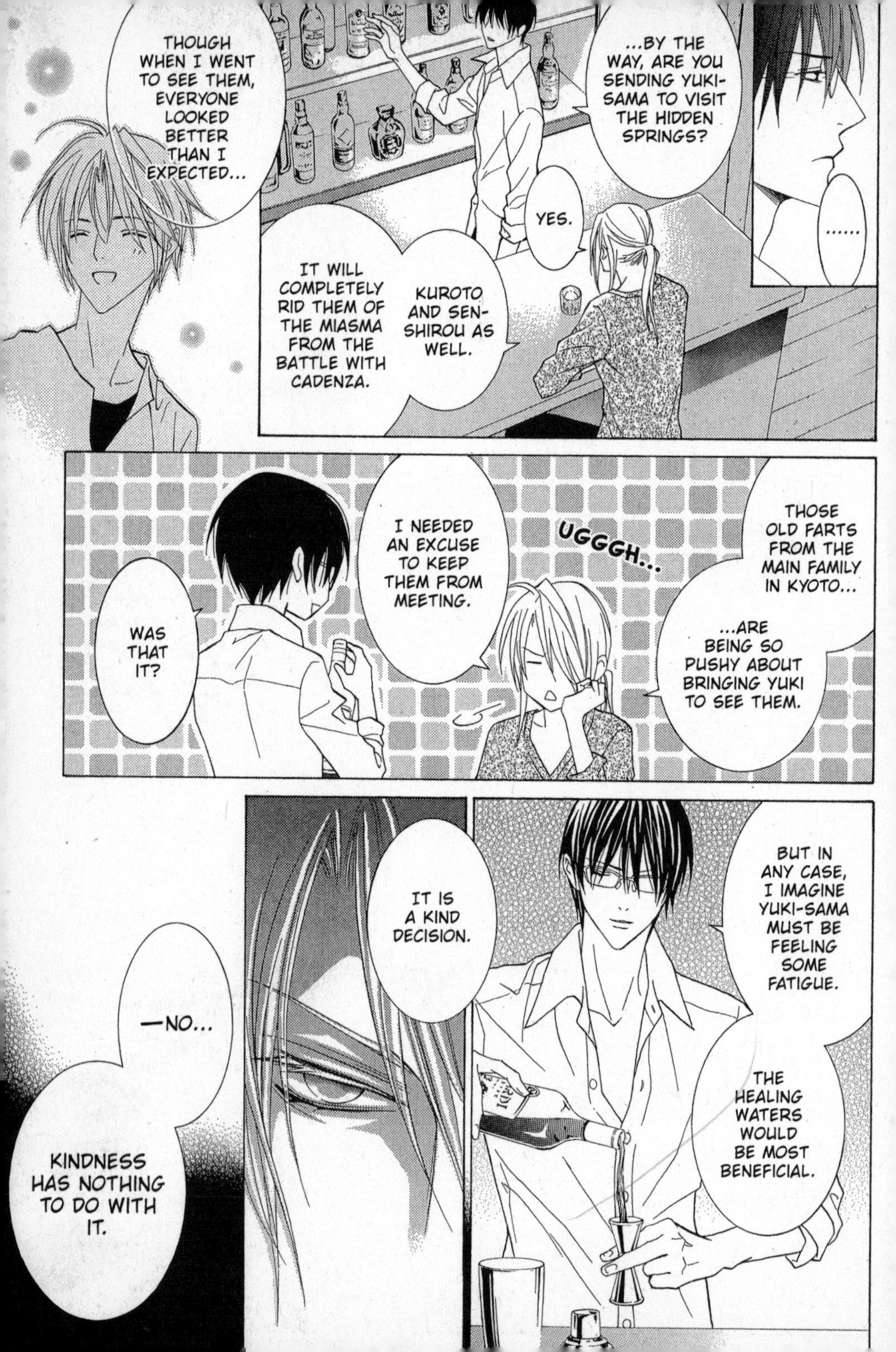
......
...BY THE WAY, ARE YOU SENDING YUKI-SAMA TO VISIT THE HIDDEN SPRINGS?
YES.
KUROTO AND SEN-SHIROU AS WELL.
IT WILL COMPLETELY RID THEM OF THE MIASMA FROM THE BATTLE WITH CADENZA.
THOUGH WHEN I WENT TO SEE THEM, EVERYONE LOOKED BETTER THAN I EXPECTED...
THOSE OLD FARTS FROM THE MAIN FAMILY IN KYOTO...
...ARE BEING SO PUSHY ABOUT BRINGING YUKI TO SEE THEM.
UGGGH...
I NEEDED AN EXCUSE TO KEEP THEM FROM MEETING.
WAS THAT IT?
BUT IN ANY CASE, I IMAGINE YUKI-SAMA MUST BE FEELING SOME FATIGUE.
THE HEALING WATERS WOULD BE MOST BENEFICIAL.
IT IS A KIND DECISION.
—NO...
KINDNESS HAS NOTHING TO DO WITH IT.

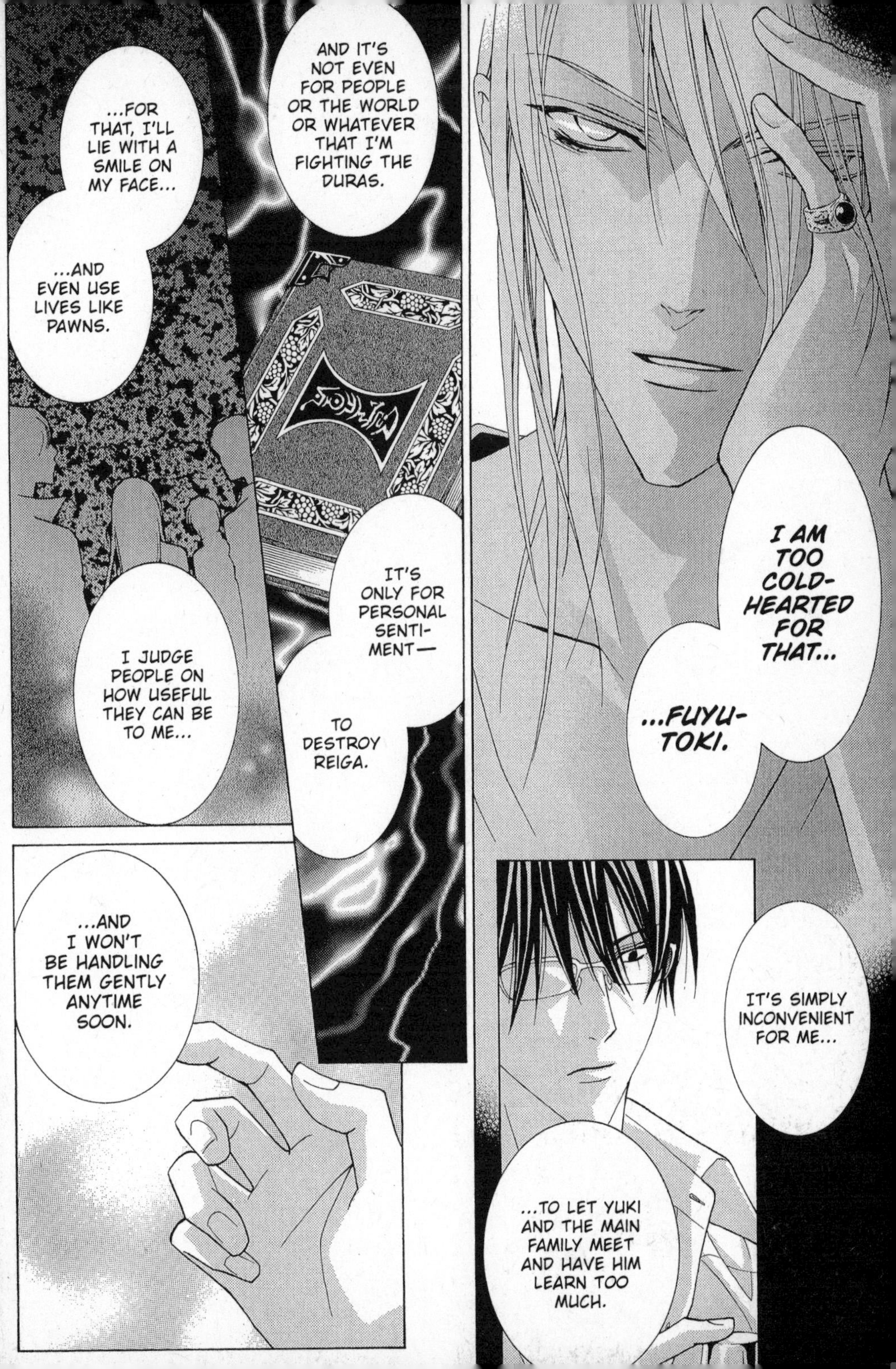
I AM TOO COLD-HEARTED FOR THAT...
...FUYUTOKI.
AND IT'S NOT EVEN FOR PEOPLE OR THE WORLD OR WHATEVER THAT I'M FIGHTING THE DURAS.
IT'S ONLY FOR PERSONAL SENTIMENT—
TO DESTROY REIGA.
...FOR THAT, I'LL LIE WITH A SMILE ON MY FACE...
...AND EVEN USE LIVES LIKE PAWNS.
I JUDGE PEOPLE ON HOW USEFUL THEY CAN BE TO ME...
IT'S SIMPLY INCONVENIENT FOR ME...
...TO LET YUKI AND THE MAIN FAMILY MEET AND HAVE HIM LEARN TOO MUCH.
...AND I WON'T BE HANDLING THEM GENTLY ANYTIME SOON.

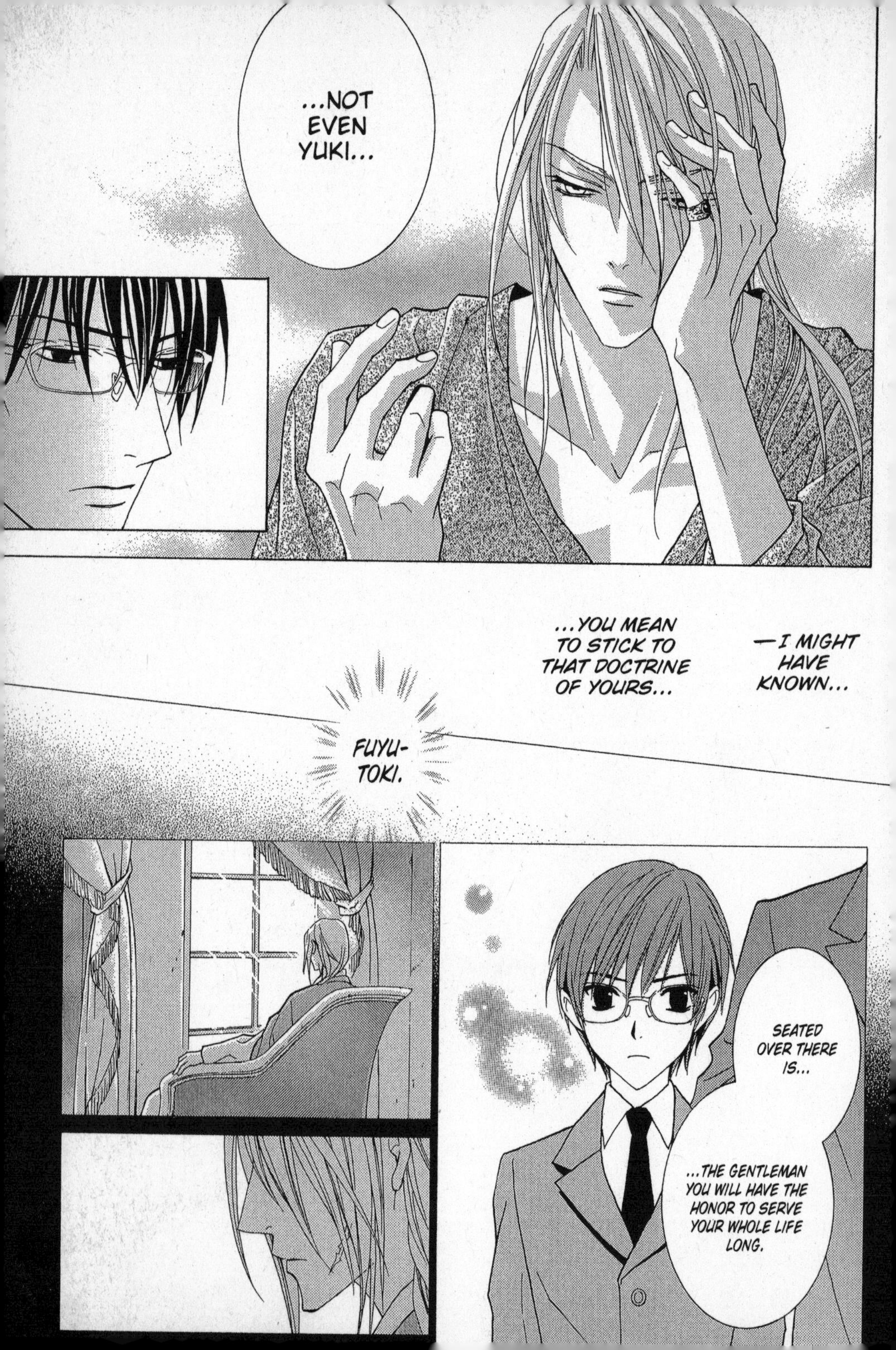
...NOT EVEN YUKI...
—I MIGHT HAVE KNOWN...
...YOU MEAN TO STICK TO THAT DOCTRINE OF YOURS...
FUYU-TOKI.
SEATED OVER THERE IS...
...THE GENTLEMAN YOU WILL HAVE THE HONOR TO SERVE YOUR WHOLE LIFE LONG.

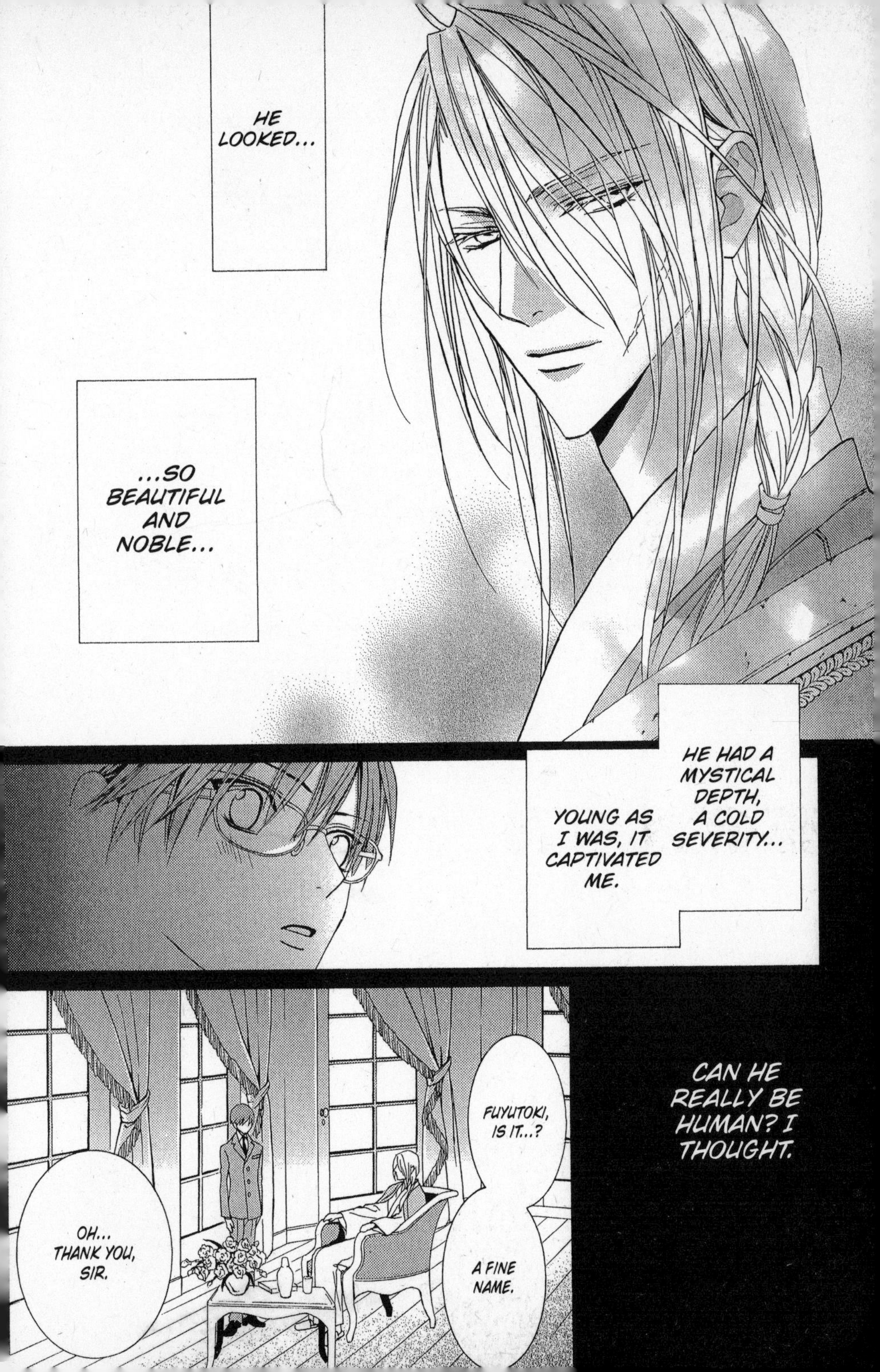
HE LOOKED...
...SO BEAUTIFUL AND NOBLE...
HE HAD A MYSTICAL DEPTH, A COLD SEVERITY...
YOUNG AS I WAS, IT CAPTIVATED ME.
CAN HE REALLY BE HUMAN? I THOUGHT.
FUYUTOKI, IS IT...?
A FINE NAME.
OH... THANK YOU, SIR.

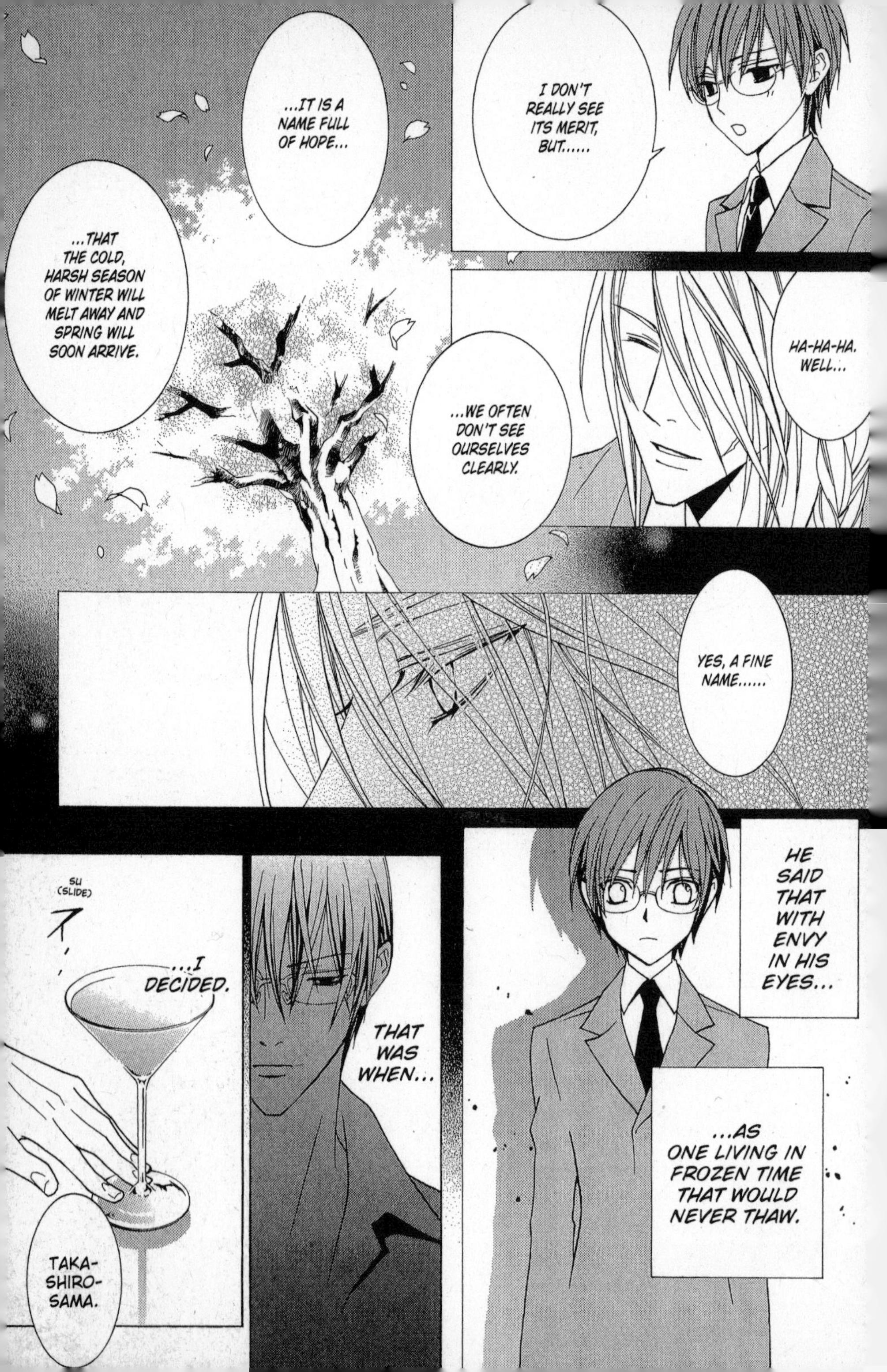
I DON'T REALLY SEE ITS MERIT, BUT......
HA-HA-HA. WELL...
...WE OFTEN DON'T SEE OURSELVES CLEARLY.
...IT IS A NAME FULL OF HOPE...
...THAT THE COLD, HARSH SEASON OF WINTER WILL MELT AWAY AND SPRING WILL SOON ARRIVE.
YES, A FINE NAME......
HE SAID THAT WITH ENVY IN HIS EYES...
...AS ONE LIVING IN FROZEN TIME THAT WOULD NEVER THAW.
THAT WAS WHEN...
SU (SLIDE)
...I DECIDED.
TAKA-SHIRO-SAMA.

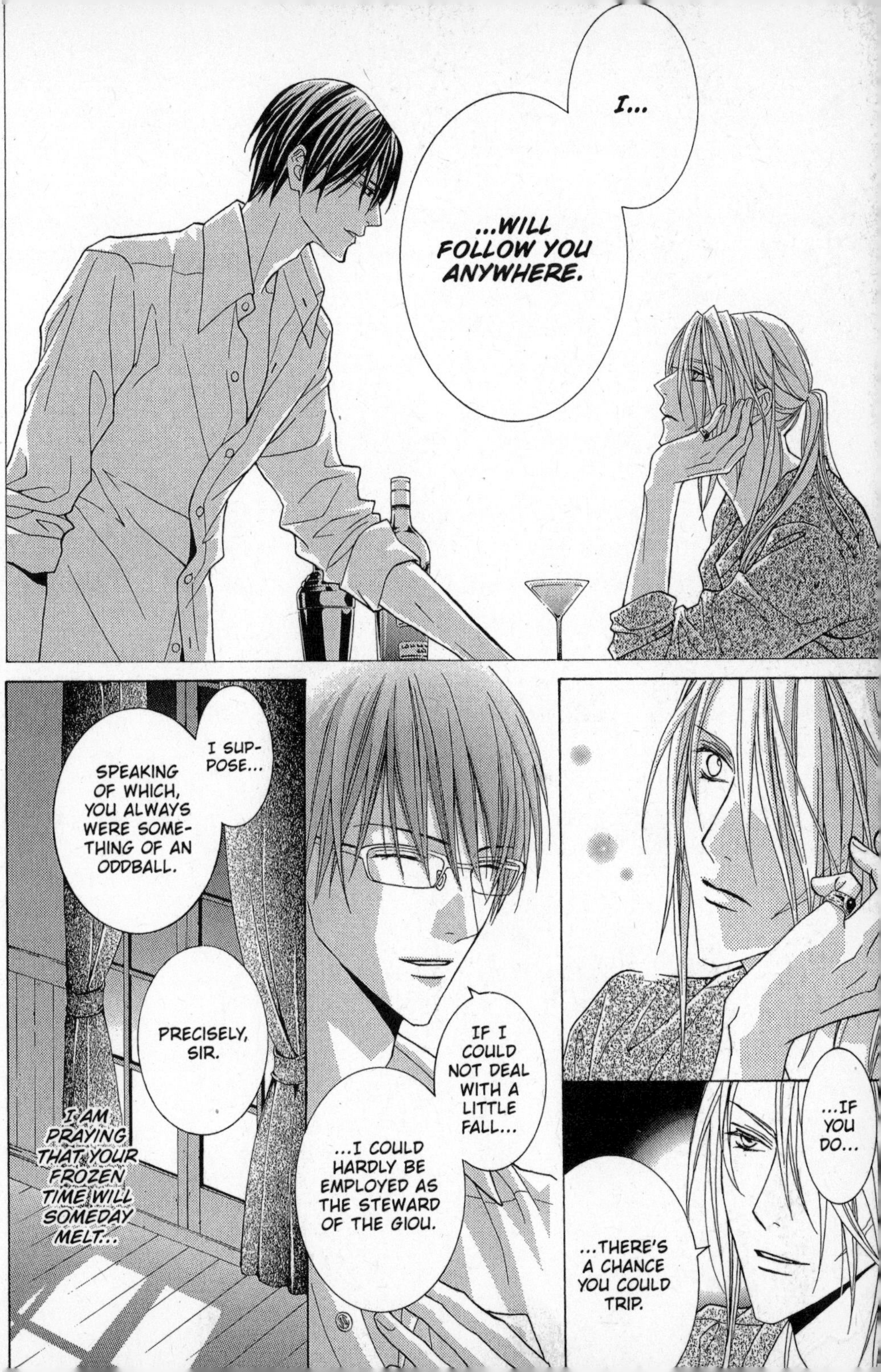
I...
...WILL FOLLOW YOU ANYWHERE.
...IF YOU DO...
...THERE'S A CHANCE YOU COULD TRIP.
IF I COULD NOT DEAL WITH A LITTLE FALL...
...I COULD HARDLY BE EMPLOYED AS THE STEWARD OF THE GIOU.
I SUP-POSE...
SPEAKING OF WHICH, YOU ALWAYS WERE SOME-THING OF AN ODDBALL.
PRECISELY, SIR.
I AM PRAYING THAT YOUR FROZEN TIME WILL SOMEDAY MELT...

...BUT IF ONLY...

...THERE WAS SOMETHING MORE I COULD DO.

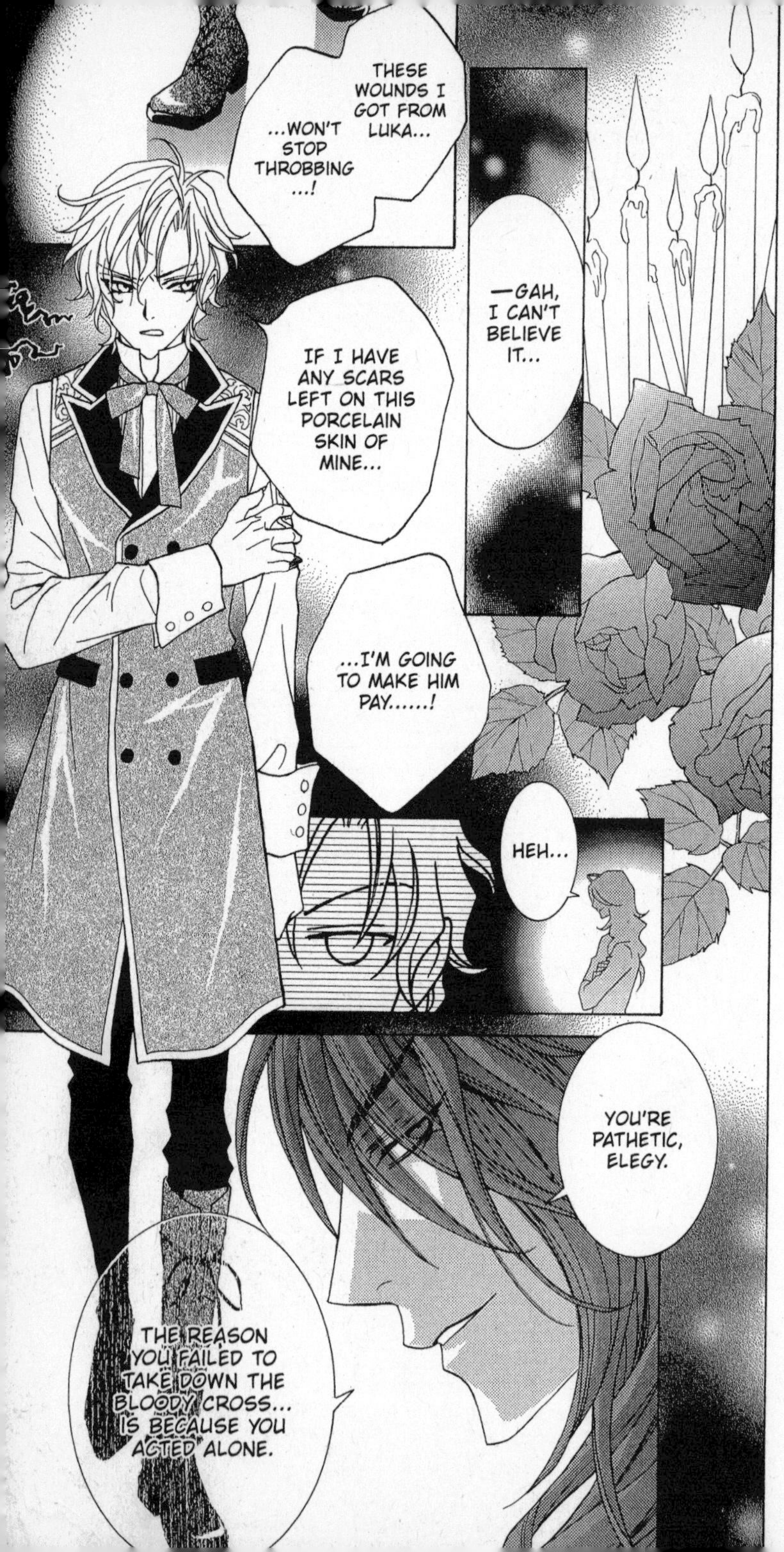
THESE WOUNDS I GOT FROM LUKA...
...WON'T STOP THROBBING...!
—GAH, I CAN'T BELIEVE IT...
IF I HAVE ANY SCARS LEFT ON THIS PORCELAIN SKIN OF MINE...
...I'M GOING TO MAKE HIM PAY......!
HEH...
YOU'RE PATHETIC, ELEGY.
THE REASON YOU FAILED TO TAKE DOWN THE BLOODY CROSS... IS BECAUSE YOU ACTED ALONE.

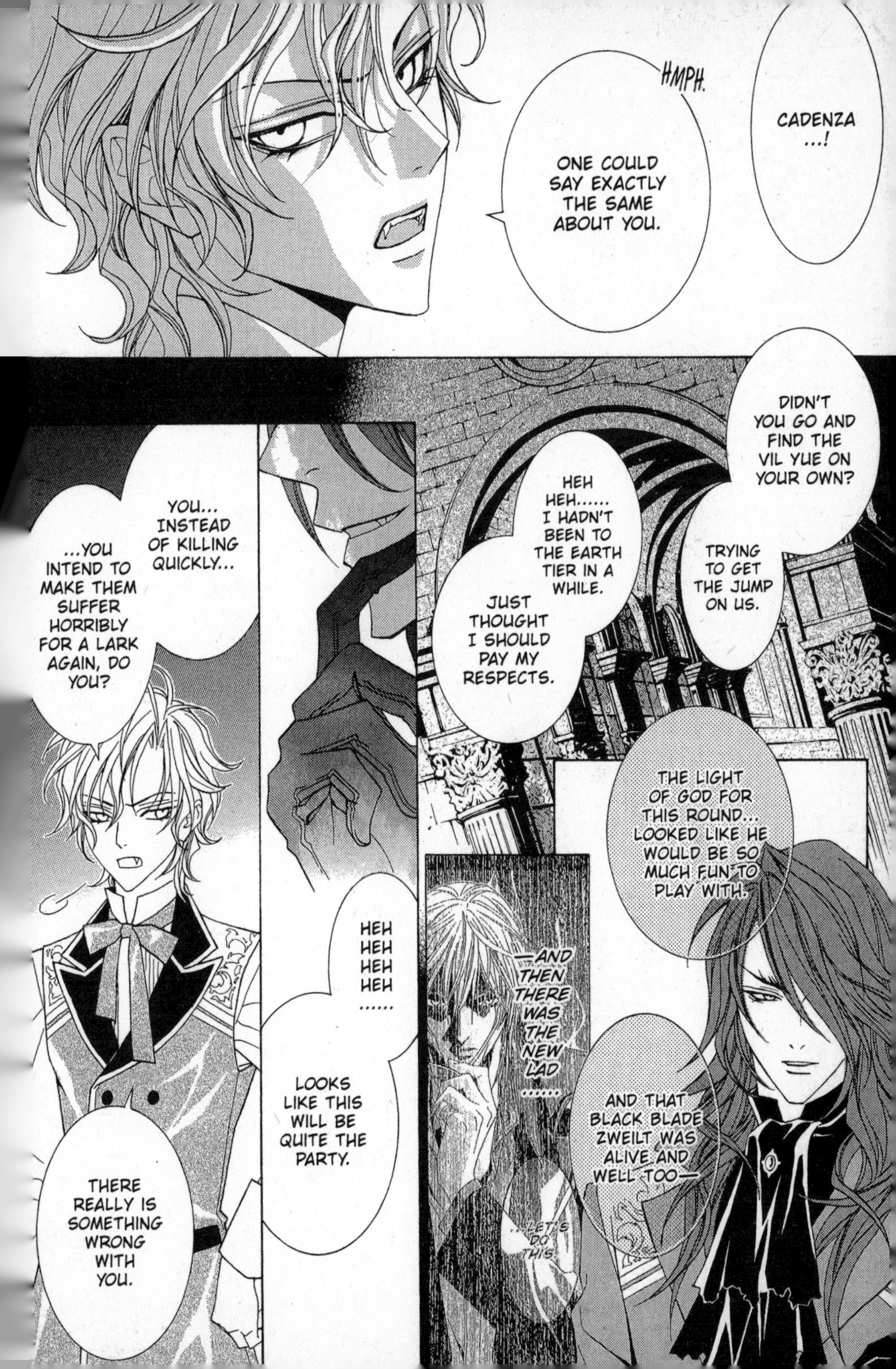
CADENZA ...!
HMPH.
ONE COULD SAY EXACTLY THE SAME ABOUT YOU.
DIDN'T YOU GO AND FIND THE VIL YUE ON YOUR OWN?
TRYING TO GET THE JUMP ON US.
HEH HEH...... I HADN'T BEEN TO THE EARTH TIER IN A WHILE.
JUST THOUGHT I SHOULD PAY MY RESPECTS.
THE LIGHT OF GOD FOR THIS ROUND... LOOKED LIKE HE WOULD BE SO MUCH FUN TO PLAY WITH.
—AND THEN THERE WAS THE NEW LAD ......
AND THAT BLACK BLADE ZWEILT WAS ALIVE AND WELL TOO—
...LET'S DO THIS.
HEH HEH HEH HEH ......
LOOKS LIKE THIS WILL BE QUITE THE PARTY.
YOU... INSTEAD OF KILLING QUICKLY...
...YOU INTEND TO MAKE THEM SUFFER HORRIBLY FOR A LARK AGAIN, DO YOU?
THERE REALLY IS SOMETHING WRONG WITH YOU.

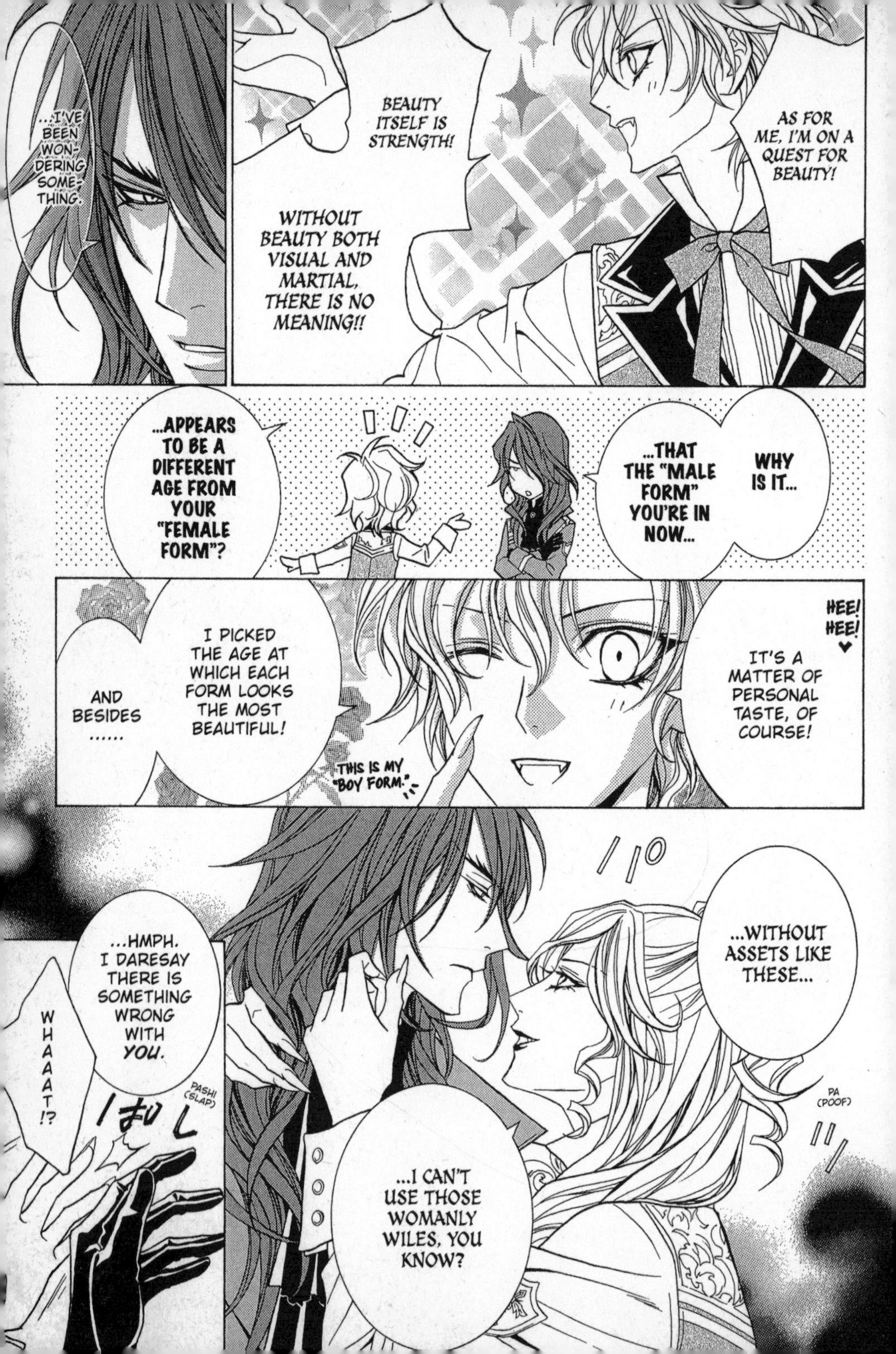
AS FOR ME, I'M ON A QUEST FOR BEAUTY!
BEAUTY ITSELF IS STRENGTH!
WITHOUT BEAUTY BOTH VISUAL AND MARTIAL, THERE IS NO MEANING!!
...I'VE BEEN WON-DERING SOME-THING.
WHY IS IT...
...THAT THE "MALE FORM" YOU'RE IN NOW...
...APPEARS TO BE A DIFFERENT AGE FROM YOUR "FEMALE FORM"?
HEE! HEE! ♥
IT'S A MATTER OF PERSONAL TASTE, OF COURSE!
THIS IS MY "BOY FORM."
I PICKED THE AGE AT WHICH EACH FORM LOOKS THE MOST BEAUTIFUL!
AND BESIDES ......
PA (POOF)
...WITHOUT ASSETS LIKE THESE...
...I CAN'T USE THOSE WOMANLY WILES, YOU KNOW?
PASHI (SLAP)
...HMPH. I DARESAY THERE IS SOMETHING WRONG WITH *YOU*.
WHAAAAT!?

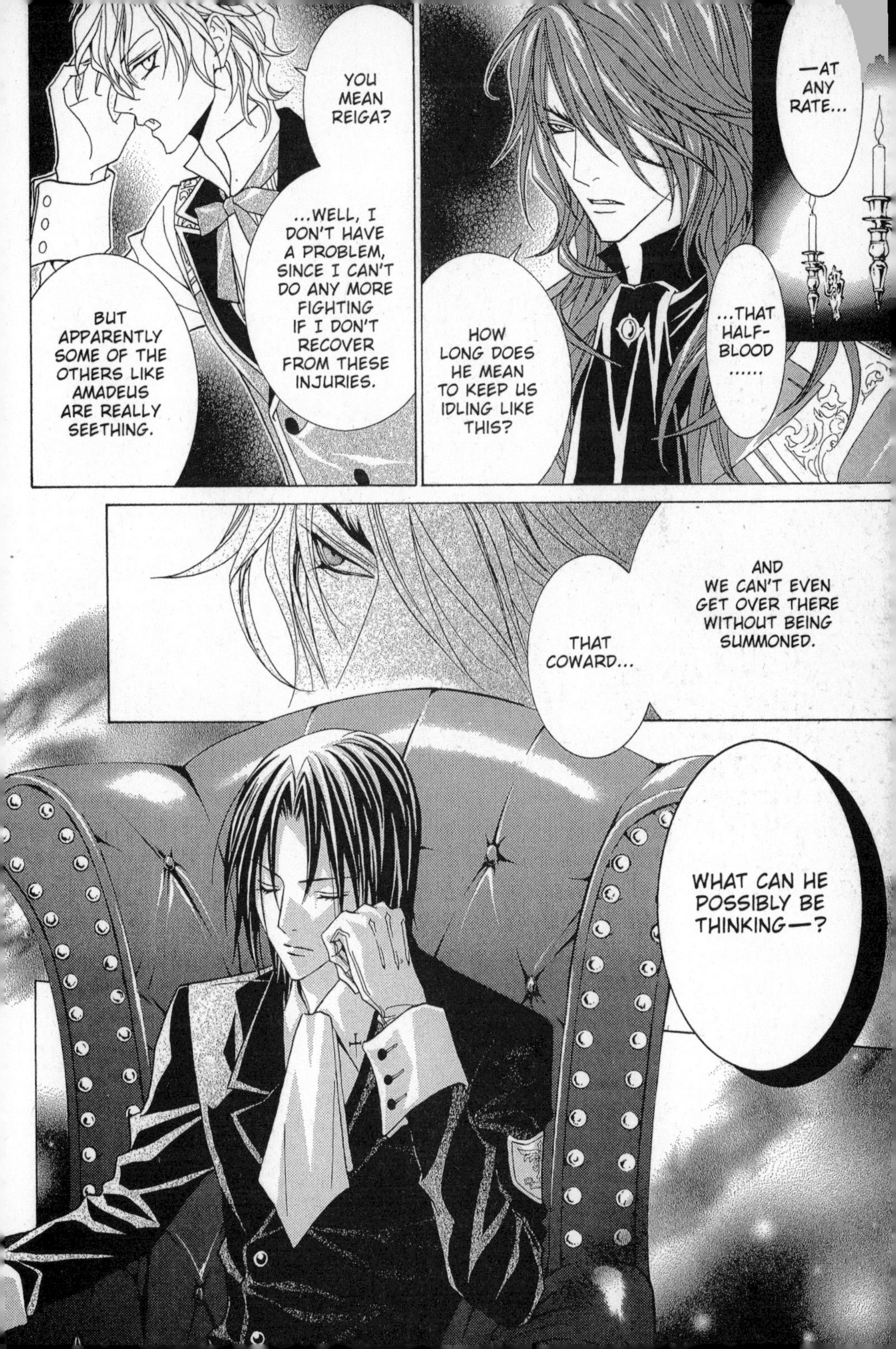
—AT ANY RATE...
...THAT HALF-BLOOD ......
HOW LONG DOES HE MEAN TO KEEP US IDLING LIKE THIS?
YOU MEAN REIGA?
...WELL, I DON'T HAVE A PROBLEM, SINCE I CAN'T DO ANY MORE FIGHTING IF I DON'T RECOVER FROM THESE INJURIES.
BUT APPARENTLY SOME OF THE OTHERS LIKE AMADEUS ARE REALLY SEETHING.
AND WE CAN'T EVEN GET OVER THERE WITHOUT BEING SUMMONED.
THAT COWARD...
WHAT CAN HE POSSIBLY BE THINKING—?

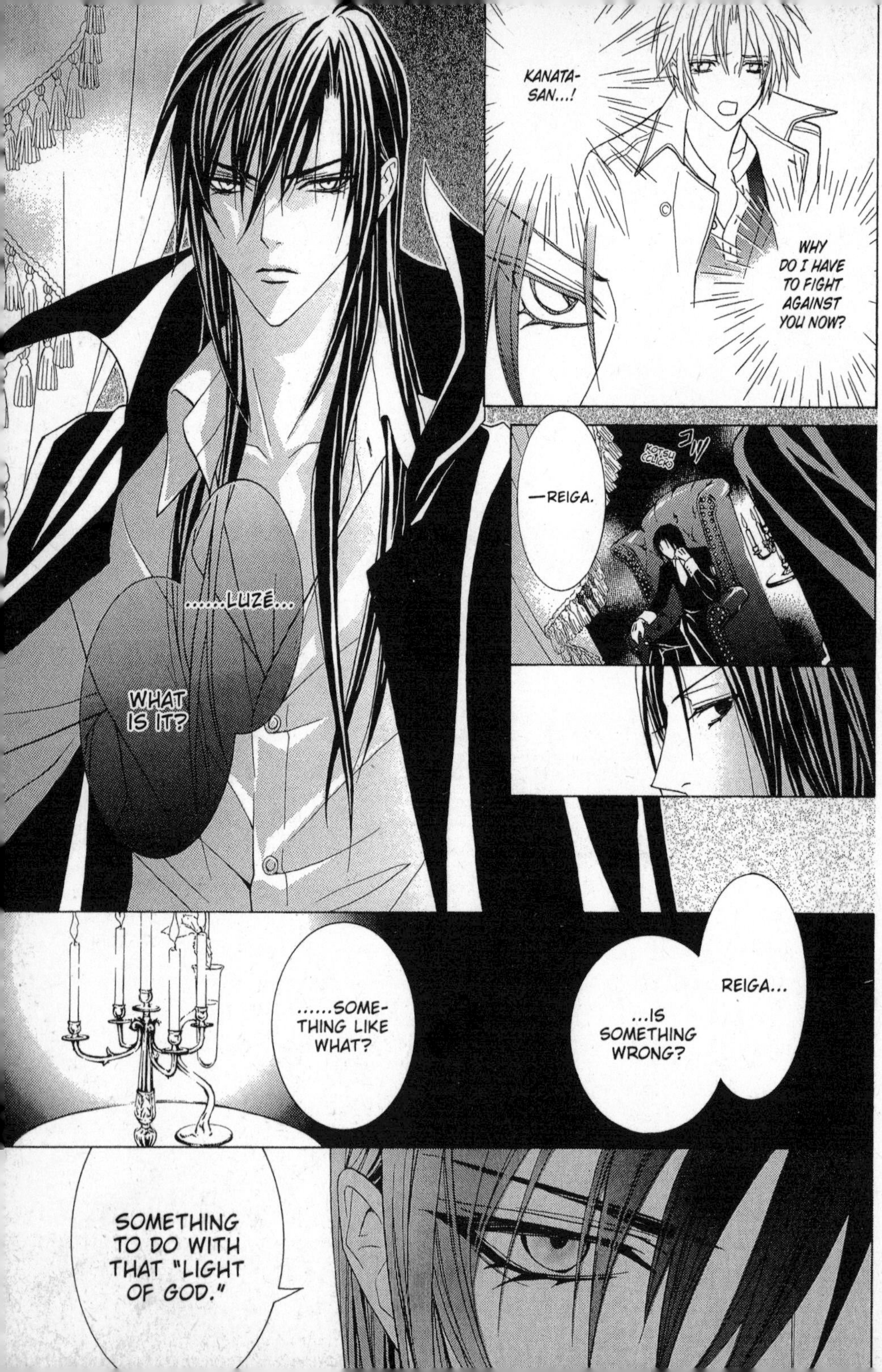
KANATA-SAN...!
WHY DO I HAVE TO FIGHT AGAINST YOU NOW?
KOTSU (CLICK)
—REIGA.
......LUZÉ...
WHAT IS IT?
REIGA...
...IS SOMETHING WRONG?
......SOME-THING LIKE WHAT?
SOMETHING TO DO WITH THAT "LIGHT OF GOD."

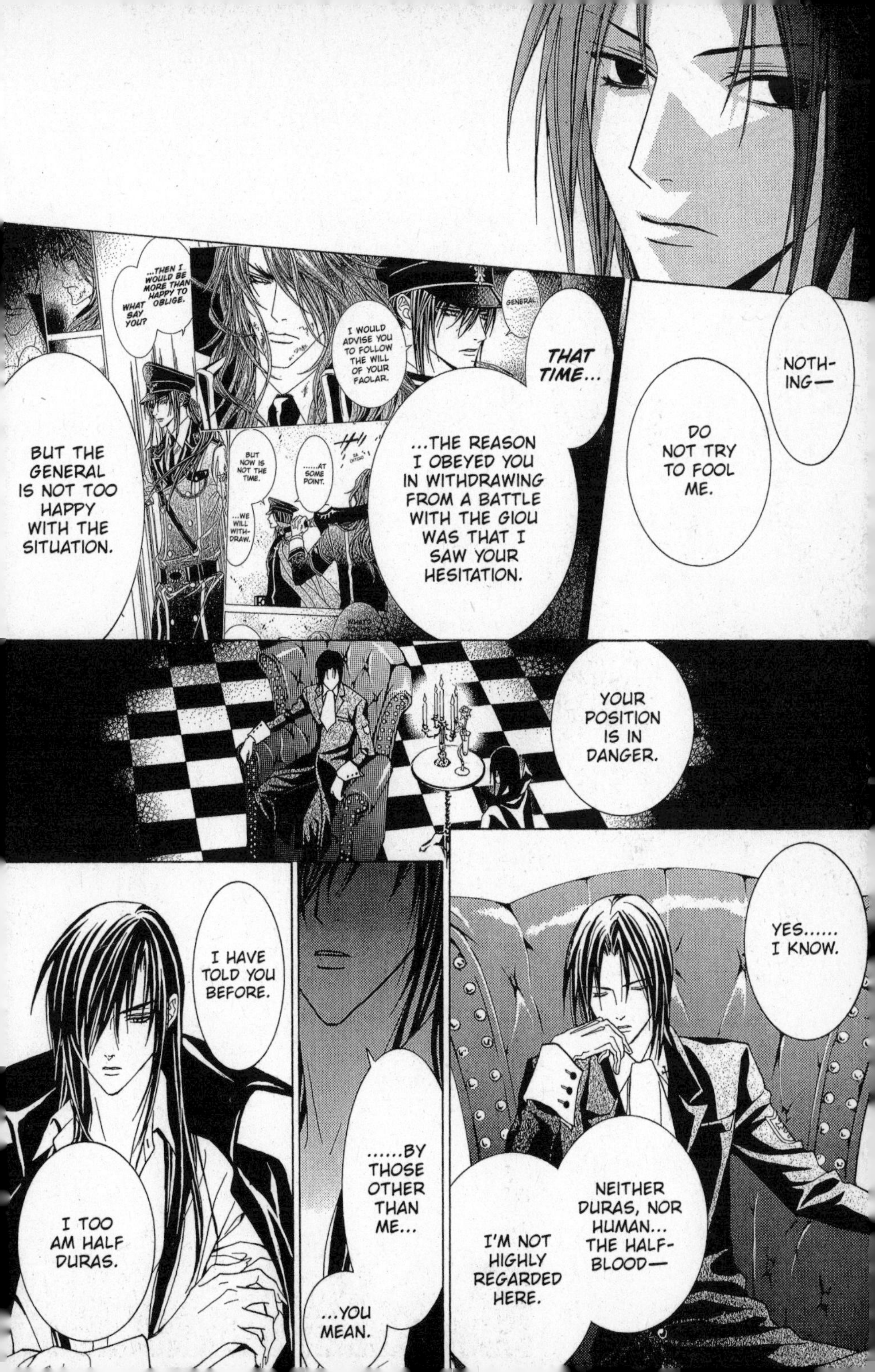
NOTHING—
DO NOT TRY TO FOOL ME.
THAT TIME...
...THE REASON I OBEYED YOU IN WITHDRAWING FROM A BATTLE WITH THE GIOU WAS THAT I SAW YOUR HESITATION.
GENERAL
I WOULD ADVISE YOU TO FOLLOW THE WILL OF YOUR FAOLAR.
...THEN I WOULD BE MORE THAN HAPPY TO OBLIGE.
WHAT SAY YOU?
......AT SOME POINT.
BUT NOW IS NOT THE TIME.
...WE WILL WITHDRAW.
BUT THE GENERAL IS NOT TOO HAPPY WITH THE SITUATION.
YOUR POSITION IS IN DANGER.
YES...... I KNOW.
NEITHER DURAS, NOR HUMAN... THE HALF-BLOOD—
I'M NOT HIGHLY REGARDED HERE.
......BY THOSE OTHER THAN ME...
...YOU MEAN.
I HAVE TOLD YOU BEFORE.
I TOO AM HALF DURAS.

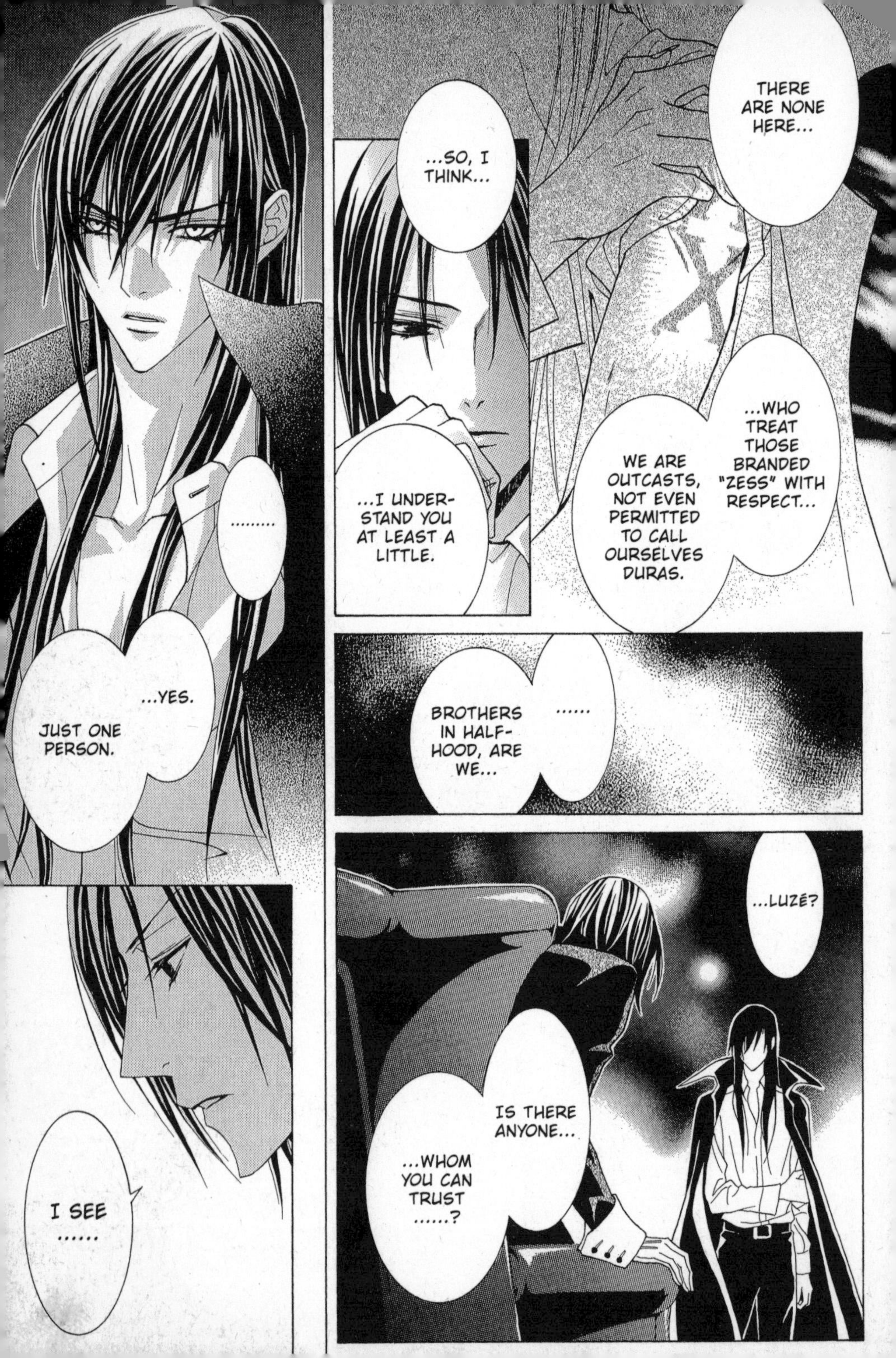
THERE ARE NONE HERE...
...WHO TREAT THOSE BRANDED "ZESS" WITH RESPECT...
WE ARE OUTCASTS, NOT EVEN PERMITTED TO CALL OURSELVES DURAS.
...SO, I THINK...
...I UNDER-STAND YOU AT LEAST A LITTLE.
......
BROTHERS IN HALF-HOOD, ARE WE...
...LUZÉ?
IS THERE ANYONE...
...WHOM YOU CAN TRUST ......?
....
...YES.
JUST ONE PERSON.
I SEE ......

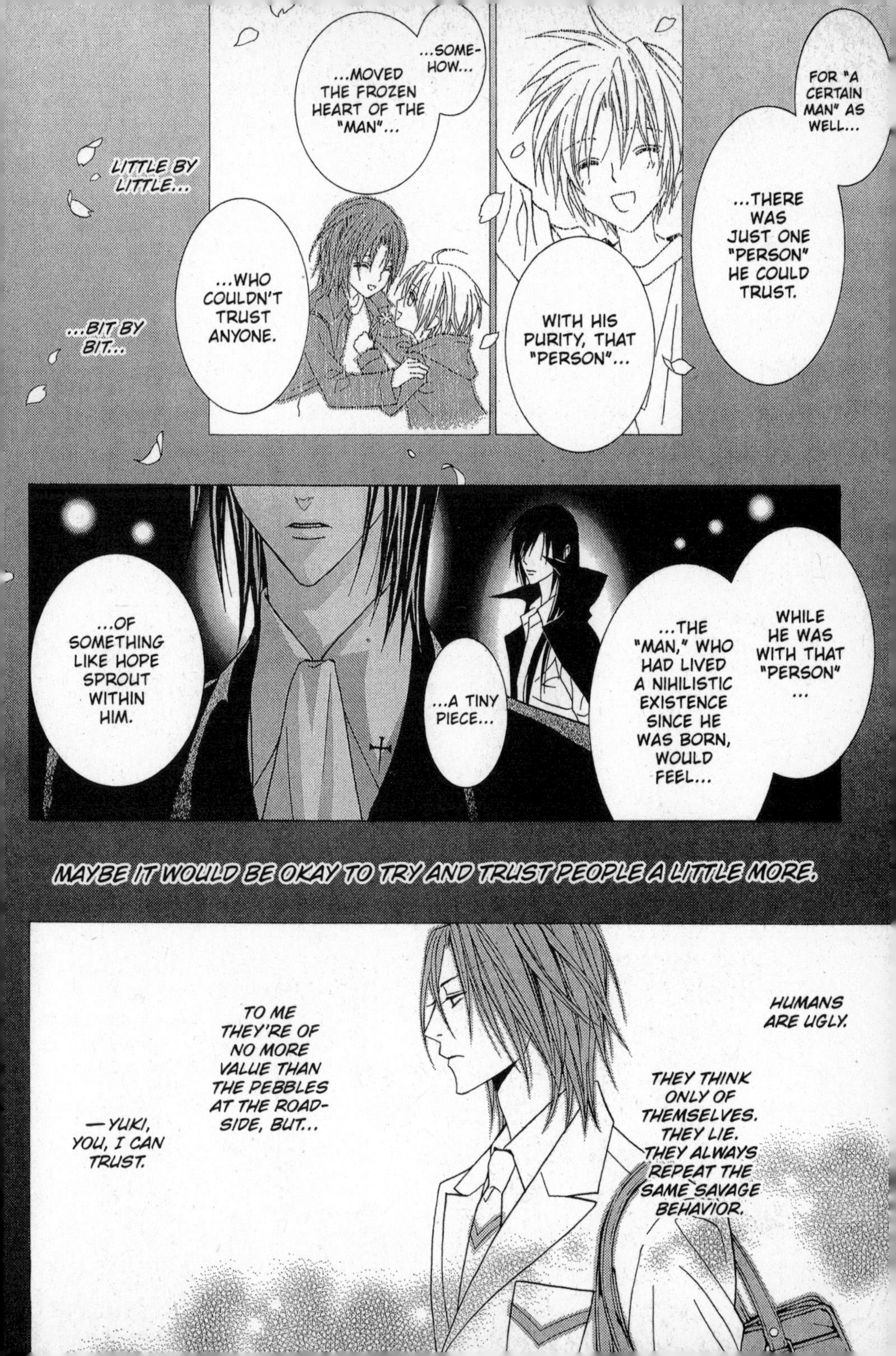
FOR "A CERTAIN MAN" AS WELL...
...THERE WAS JUST ONE "PERSON" HE COULD TRUST.
WITH HIS PURITY, THAT "PERSON"...
...SOME-HOW...
...MOVED THE FROZEN HEART OF THE "MAN"...
...WHO COULDN'T TRUST ANYONE.
LITTLE BY LITTLE...
...BIT BY BIT...
WHILE HE WAS WITH THAT "PERSON"...
...THE "MAN," WHO HAD LIVED A NIHILISTIC EXISTENCE SINCE HE WAS BORN, WOULD FEEL...
...A TINY PIECE...
...OF SOMETHING LIKE HOPE SPROUT WITHIN HIM.
MAYBE IT WOULD BE OKAY TO TRY AND TRUST PEOPLE A LITTLE MORE.
HUMANS ARE UGLY.
THEY THINK ONLY OF THEMSELVES. THEY LIE. THEY ALWAYS REPEAT THE SAME SAVAGE BEHAVIOR.
TO ME THEY'RE OF NO MORE VALUE THAN THE PEBBLES AT THE ROAD-SIDE, BUT...
—YUKI, YOU, I CAN TRUST.

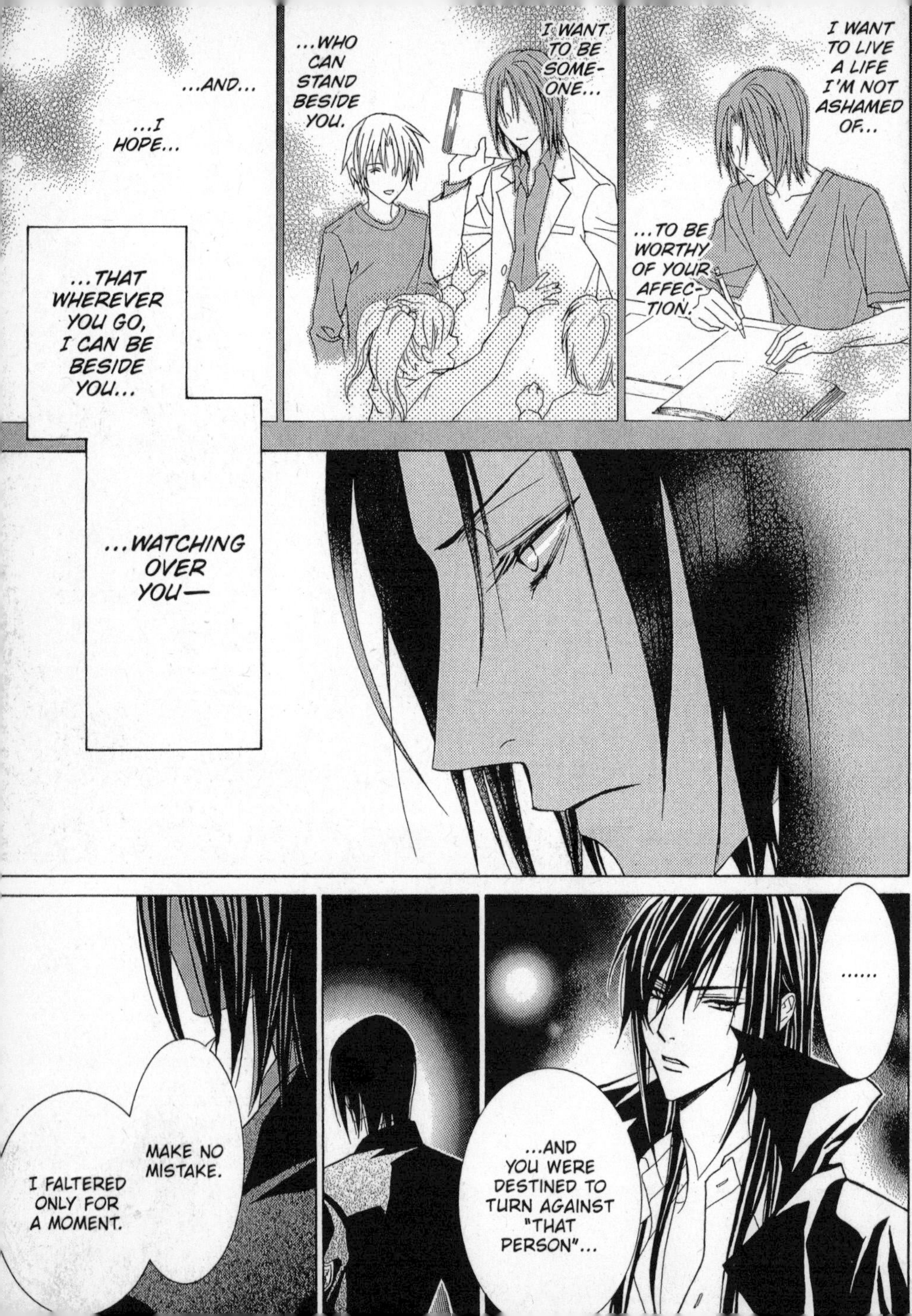
I WANT TO LIVE A LIFE I'M NOT ASHAMED OF...
...TO BE WORTHY OF YOUR AFFECTION.
I WANT TO BE SOMEONE...
...WHO CAN STAND BESIDE YOU.
...AND...
...I HOPE...
...THAT WHEREVER YOU GO, I CAN BE BESIDE YOU...
...WATCHING OVER YOU—
......
...AND YOU WERE DESTINED TO TURN AGAINST "THAT PERSON"...
MAKE NO MISTAKE.
I FALTERED ONLY FOR A MOMENT.

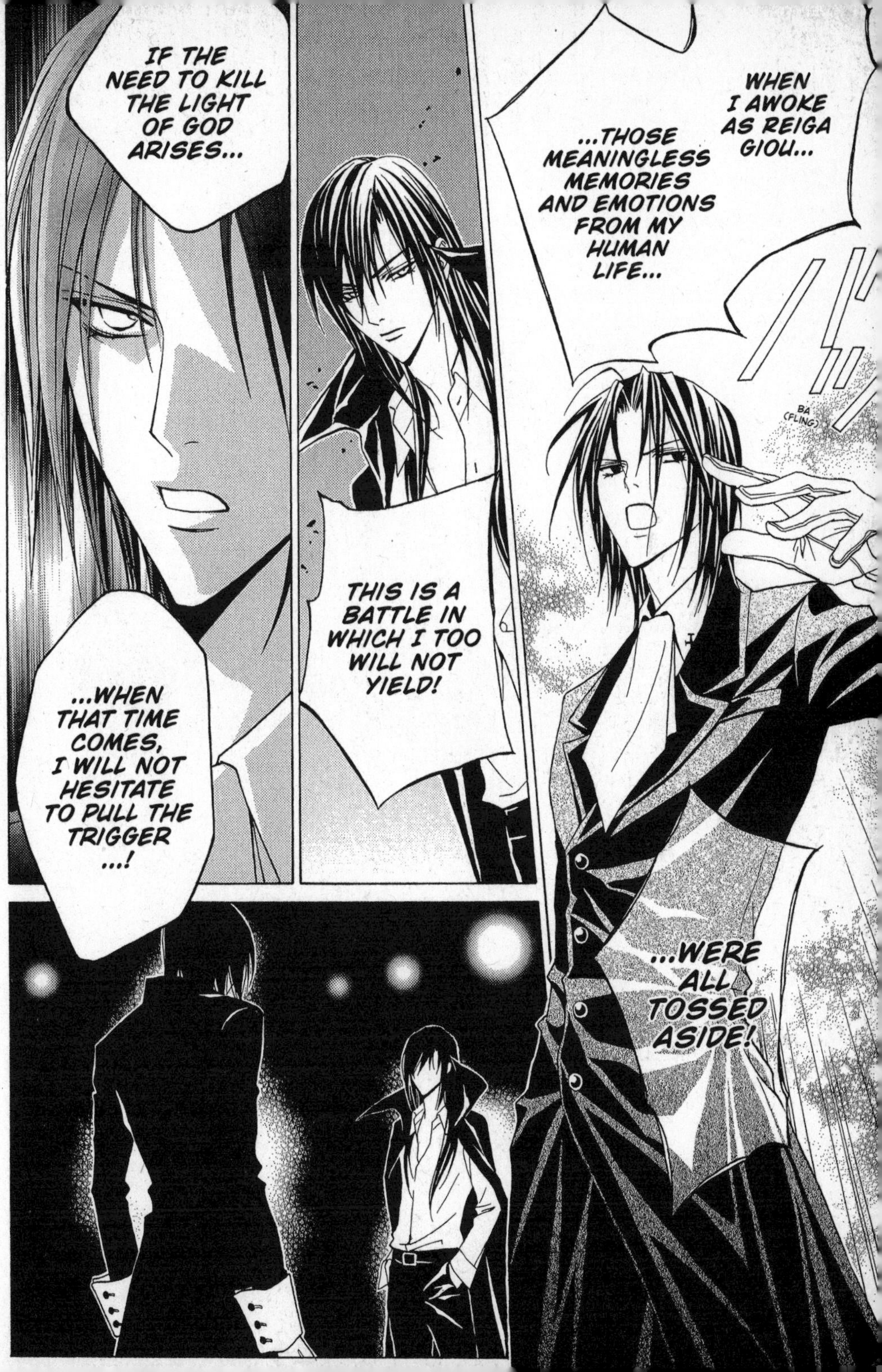
WHEN I AWOKE AS REIGA GIOU...
...THOSE MEANINGLESS MEMORIES AND EMOTIONS FROM MY HUMAN LIFE...
BA (FLING)
...WERE ALL TOSSED ASIDE!
THIS IS A BATTLE IN WHICH I TOO WILL NOT YIELD!
IF THE NEED TO KILL THE LIGHT OF GOD ARISES...
...WHEN THAT TIME COMES, I WILL NOT HESITATE TO PULL THE TRIGGER ...!

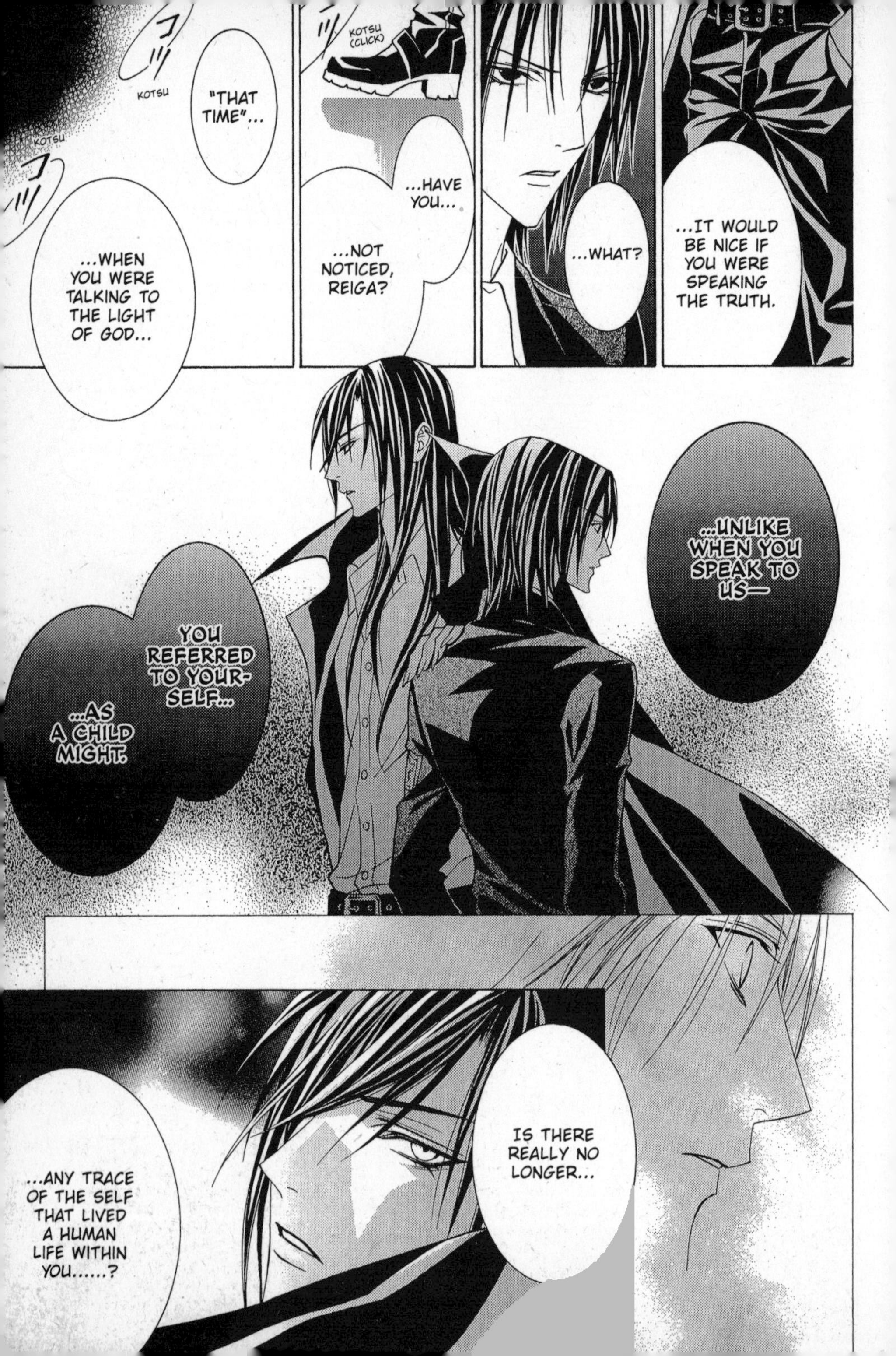
...IT WOULD BE NICE IF YOU WERE SPEAKING THE TRUTH.
...WHAT?
KOTSU (CLICK)
...HAVE YOU...
...NOT NOTICED, REIGA?
"THAT TIME"...
KOTSU
KOTSU
...WHEN YOU WERE TALKING TO THE LIGHT OF GOD...
...UNLIKE WHEN YOU SPEAK TO US—
YOU REFERRED TO YOUR-SELF...
...AS A CHILD MIGHT.
IS THERE REALLY NO LONGER...
...ANY TRACE OF THE SELF THAT LIVED A HUMAN LIFE WITHIN YOU......?

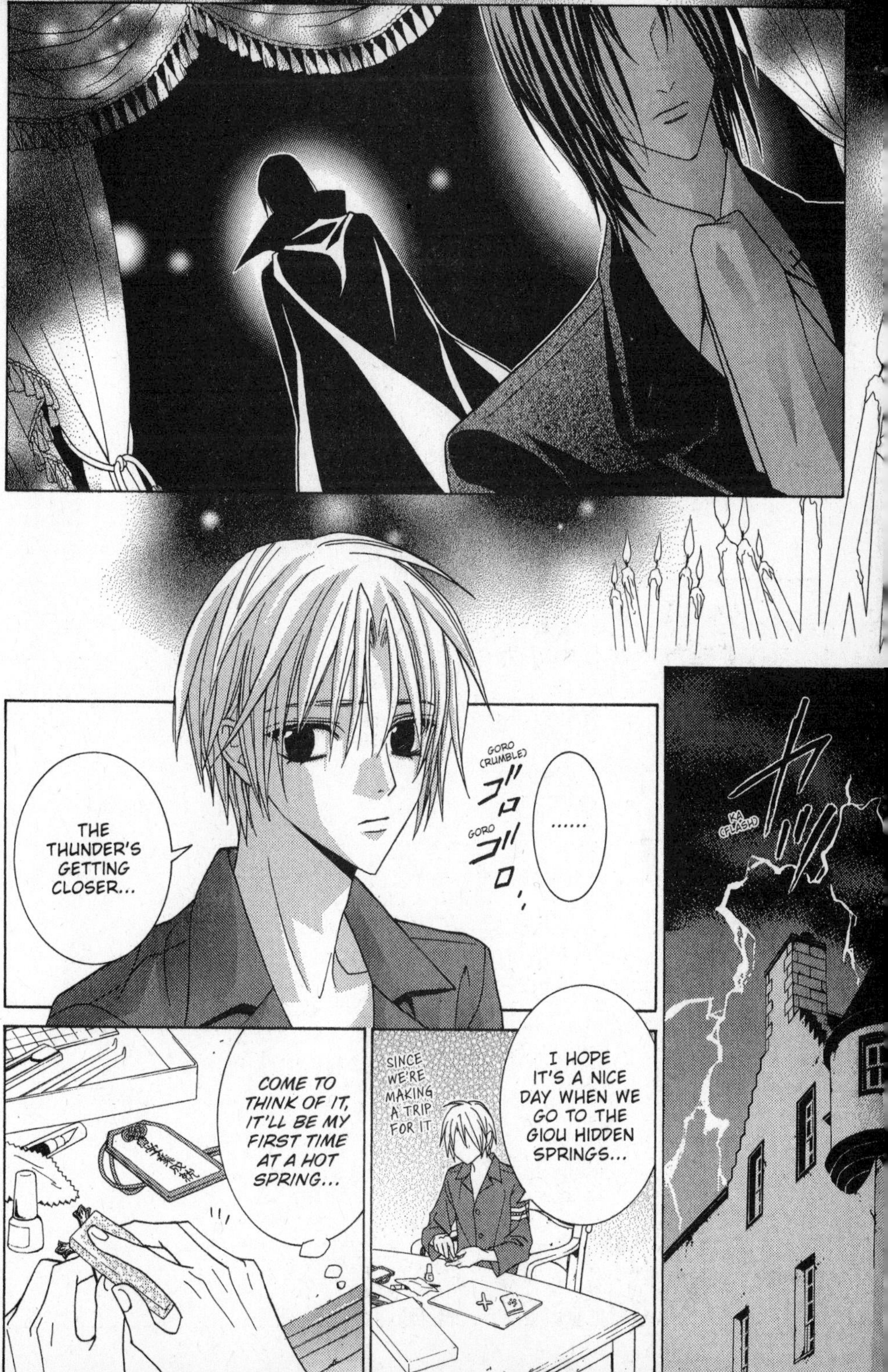
KA (FLASH)
カッ
......
GORO (RUMBLE)
ゴロ
GORO
ゴロ
THE THUNDER'S GETTING CLOSER...
I HOPE IT'S A NICE DAY WHEN WE GO TO THE GIOU HIDDEN SPRINGS...
SINCE WE'RE MAKING A TRIP FOR IT
COME TO THINK OF IT, IT'LL BE MY FIRST TIME AT A HOT SPRING...

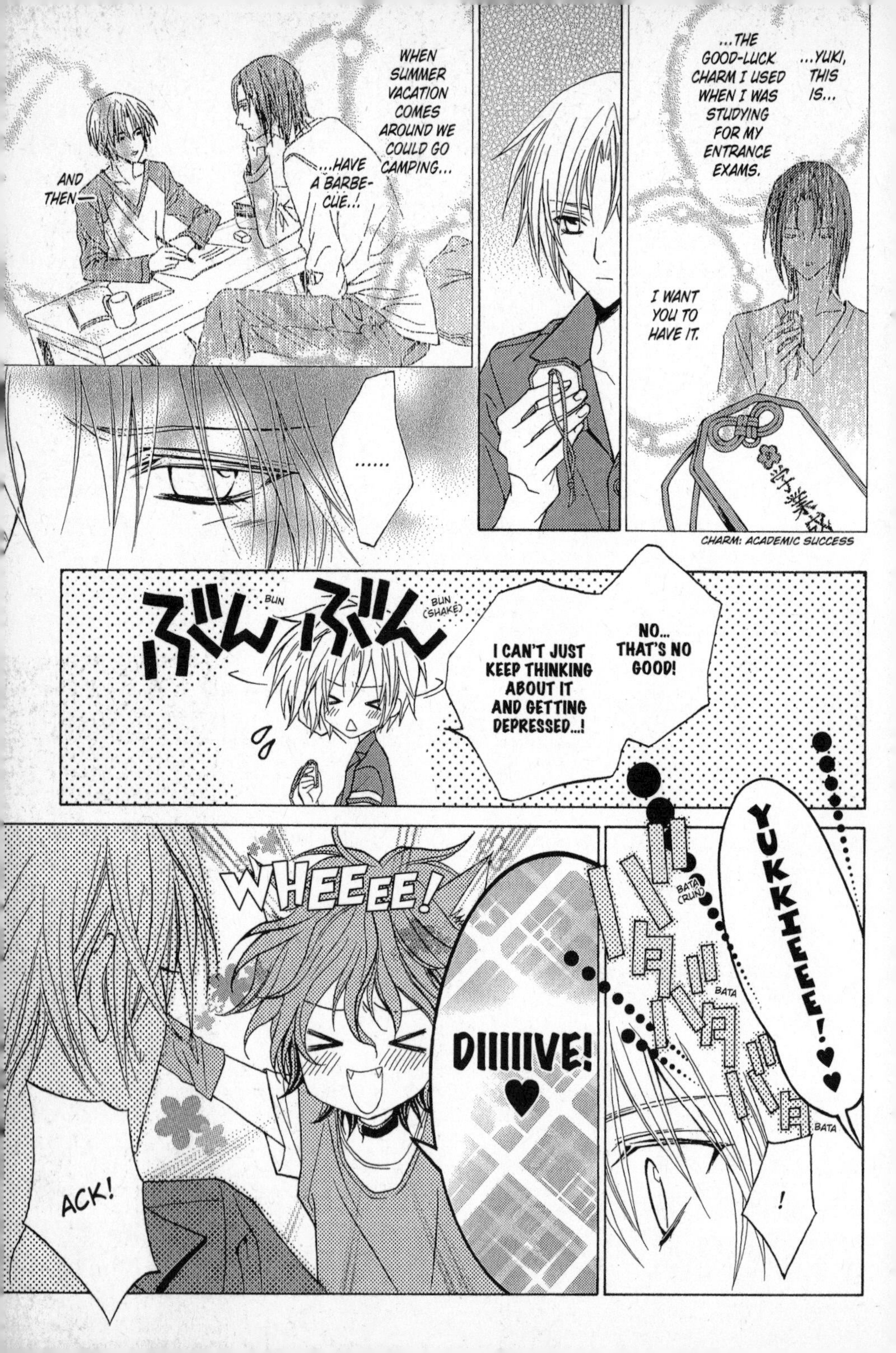
...YUKI, THIS IS...
...THE GOOD-LUCK CHARM I USED WHEN I WAS STUDYING FOR MY ENTRANCE EXAMS.
I WANT YOU TO HAVE IT.
CHARM: ACADEMIC SUCCESS
WHEN SUMMER VACATION COMES AROUND WE COULD GO CAMPING...
...HAVE A BARBE-CUE..!
AND THEN—
......
NO... THAT'S NO GOOD!
I CAN'T JUST KEEP THINKING ABOUT IT AND GETTING DEPRESSED...!
ぶんぶん
BUN BUN (SHAKE)
YUKKIEEE!♥
BATA (RUN) BATA BATA
!
WHEEEEE!
DIIIIIVE!♥
ACK!

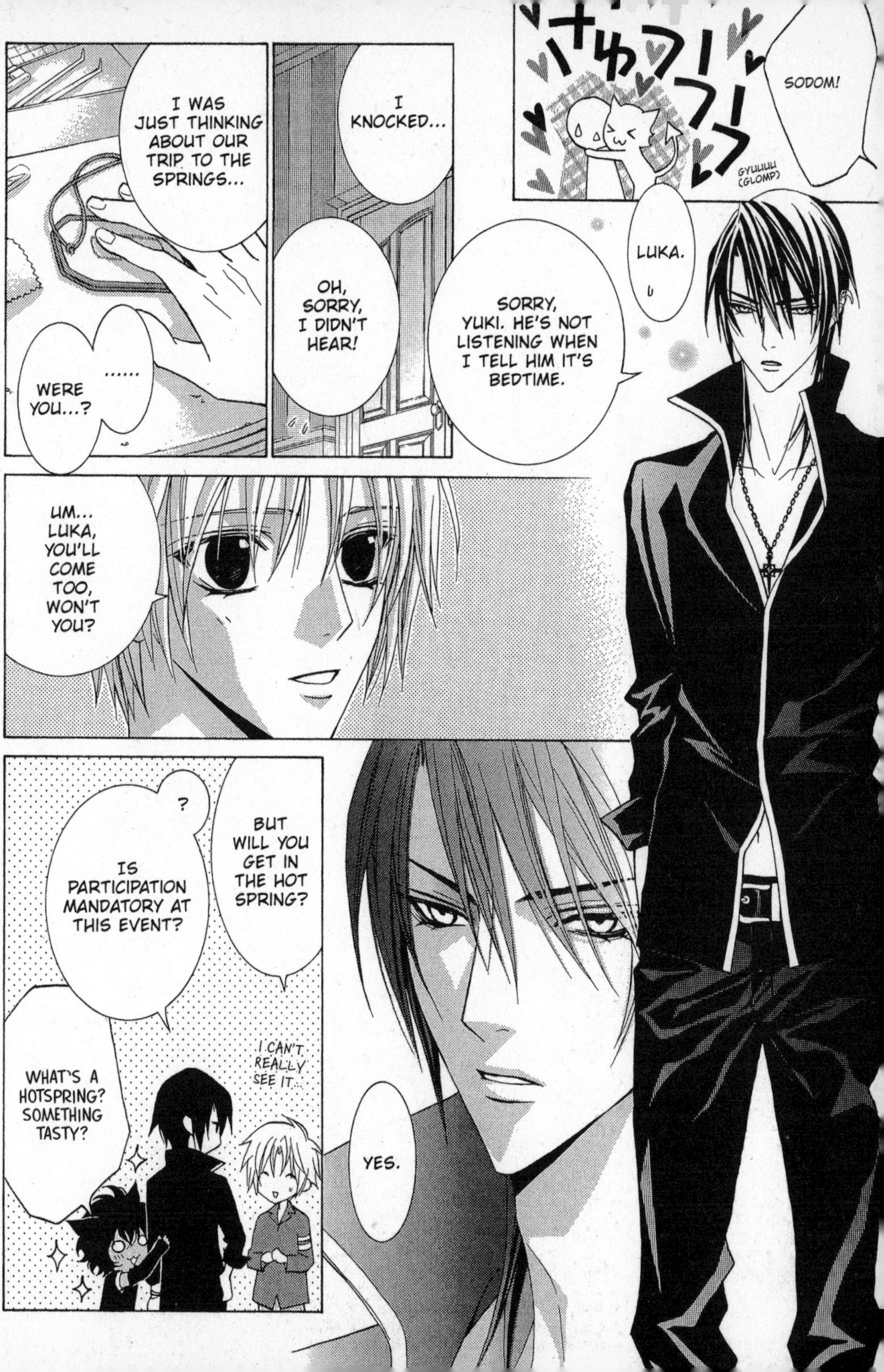
SODOM!
GYUUUU (GLOMP)
LUKA.
SORRY, YUKI. HE'S NOT LISTENING WHEN I TELL HIM IT'S BEDTIME.
I KNOCKED...
OH, SORRY, I DIDN'T HEAR!
I WAS JUST THINKING ABOUT OUR TRIP TO THE SPRINGS...
......
WERE YOU...?
UM... LUKA, YOU'LL COME TOO, WON'T YOU?
BUT WILL YOU GET IN THE HOT SPRING?
YES.
?
IS PARTICIPATION MANDATORY AT THIS EVENT?
I CAN'T REALLY SEE IT...
WHAT'S A HOTSPRING? SOMETHING TASTY?

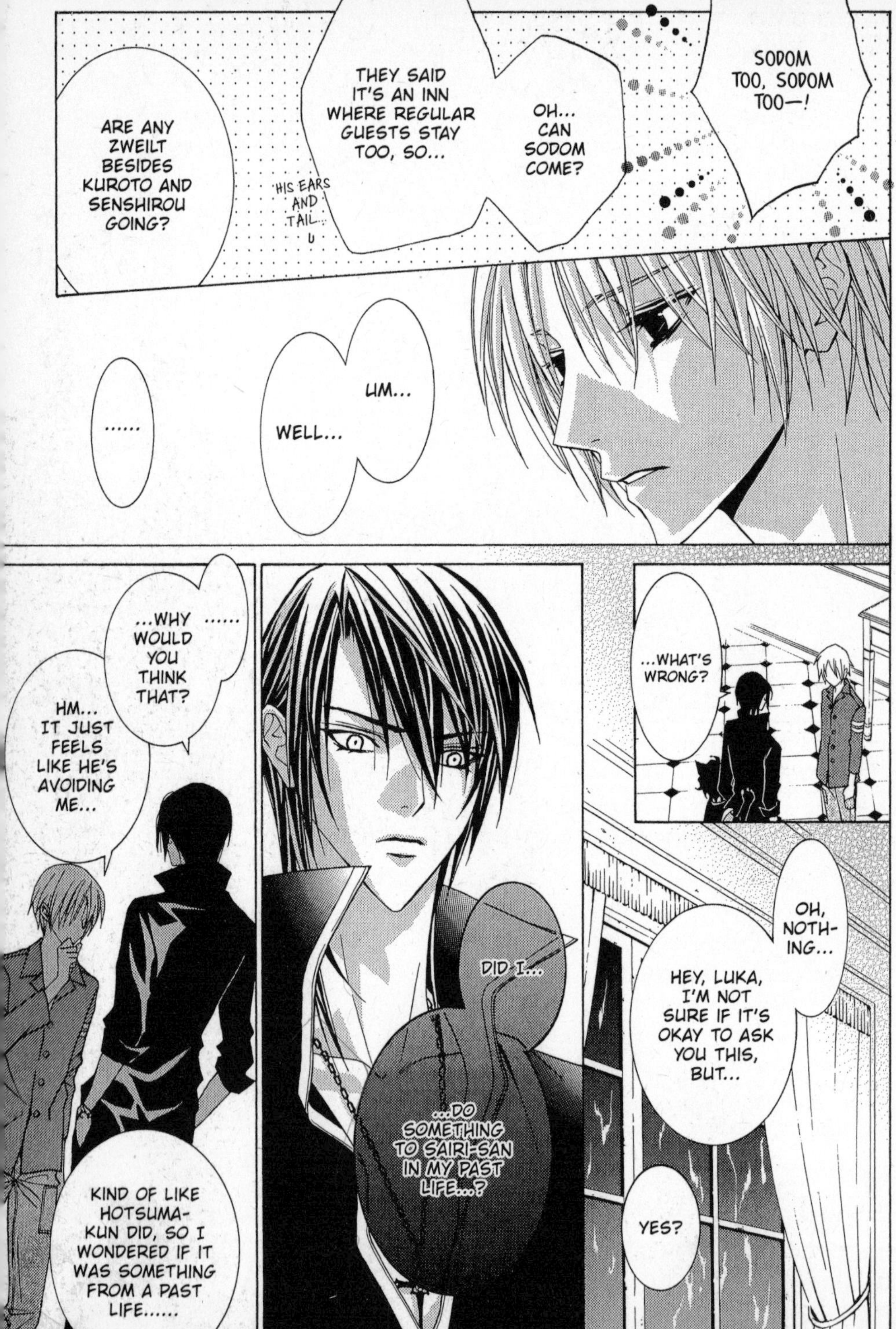
SODOM TOO, SODOM TOO—!
OH... CAN SODOM COME?
THEY SAID IT'S AN INN WHERE REGULAR GUESTS STAY TOO, SO...
HIS EARS AND TAIL...
ARE ANY ZWEILT BESIDES KUROTO AND SENSHIROU GOING?
UM...
WELL...
......
...WHAT'S WRONG?
OH, NOTHING...
HEY, LUKA, I'M NOT SURE IF IT'S OKAY TO ASK YOU THIS, BUT...
YES?
DID I...
...DO SOMETHING TO SAIRI-SAN IN MY PAST LIFE...?
......
...WHY WOULD YOU THINK THAT?
HM... IT JUST FEELS LIKE HE'S AVOIDING ME...
KIND OF LIKE HOTSUMA-KUN DID, SO I WONDERED IF IT WAS SOMETHING FROM A PAST LIFE......

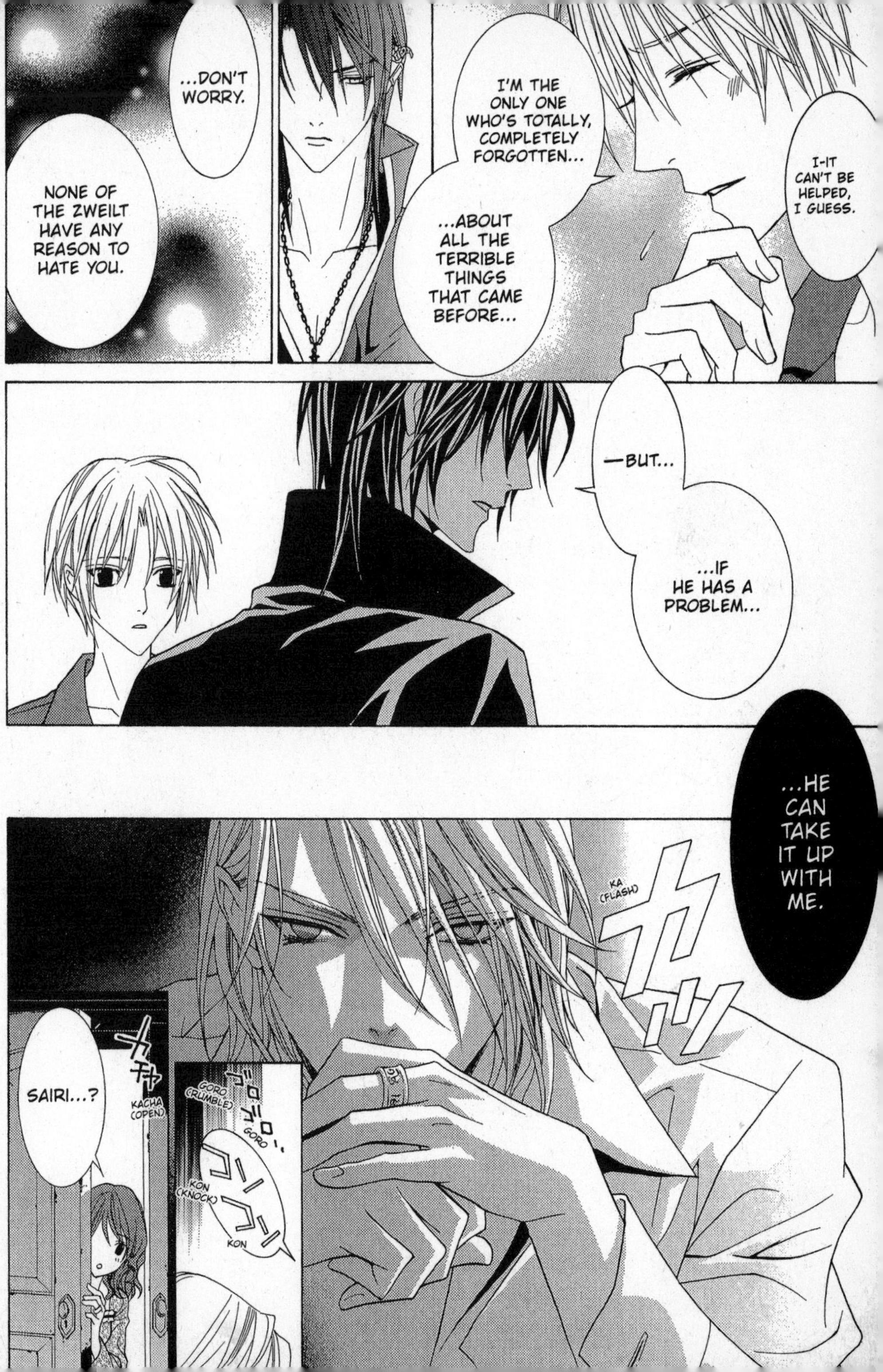
I-IT CAN'T BE HELPED, I GUESS.
I'M THE ONLY ONE WHO'S TOTALLY, COMPLETELY FORGOTTEN...
...ABOUT ALL THE TERRIBLE THINGS THAT CAME BEFORE...
...DON'T WORRY.
NONE OF THE ZWEILT HAVE ANY REASON TO HATE YOU.
—BUT...
...IF HE HAS A PROBLEM...
...HE CAN TAKE IT UP WITH ME.
KA (FLASH)
GORO (RUMBLE) GORO
KON (KNOCK) KON
KACHA (OPEN)
SAIRI...?

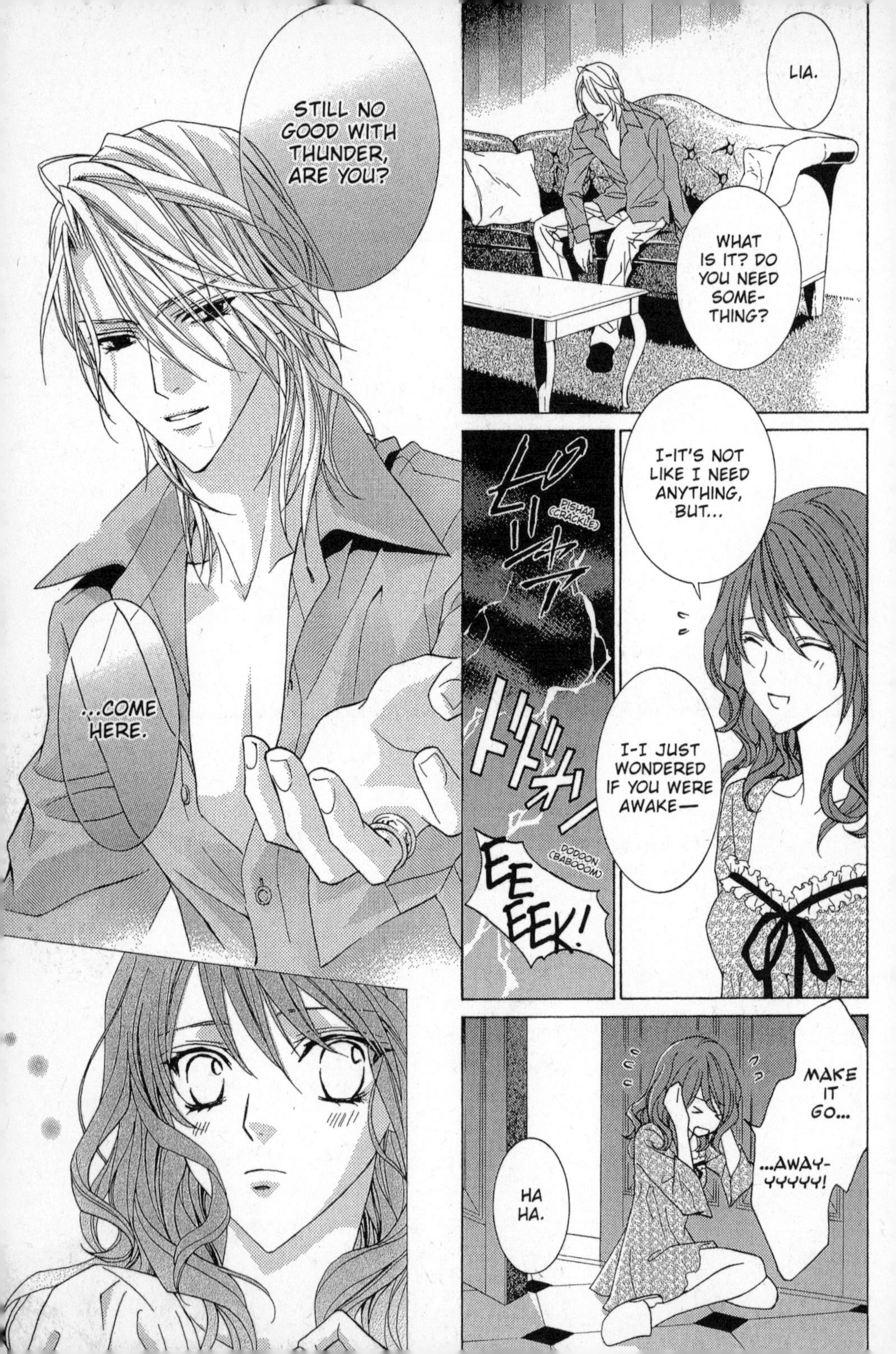
LIA.
WHAT IS IT? DO YOU NEED SOME-THING?
I-IT'S NOT LIKE I NEED ANYTHING, BUT...
I-I JUST WONDERED IF YOU WERE AWAKE—
PISHAA (CRACKLE)
DODOON (BABOOOM)
EEEEK!
MAKE IT GO...
...AWAY-YYYYY!
HA HA.
STILL NO GOOD WITH THUNDER, ARE YOU?
...COME HERE.

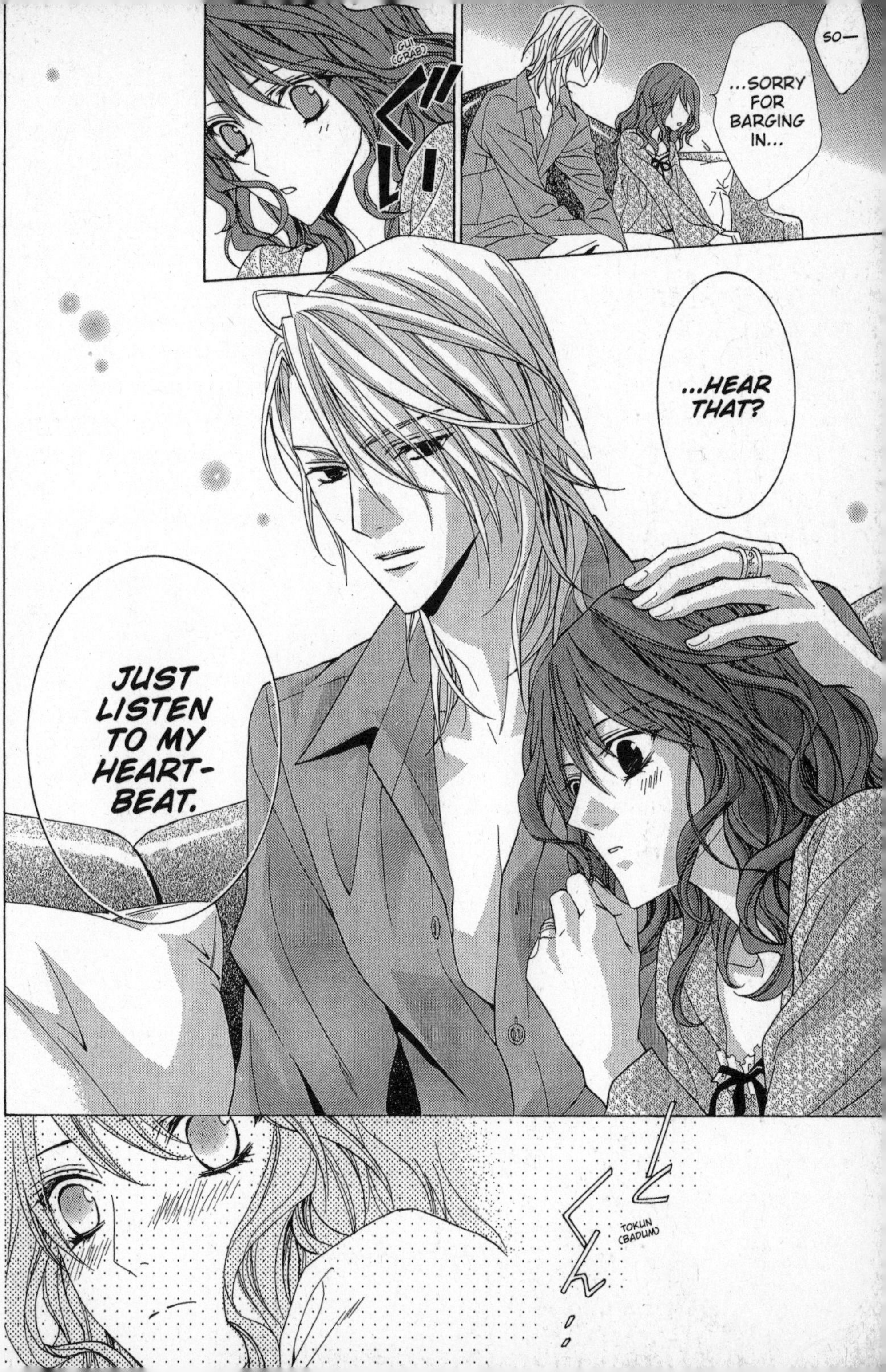
SO—
...SORRY FOR BARGING IN...
GUI (GRAB)
...HEAR THAT?
JUST LISTEN TO MY HEART-BEAT.
TOKUN (BADUM)

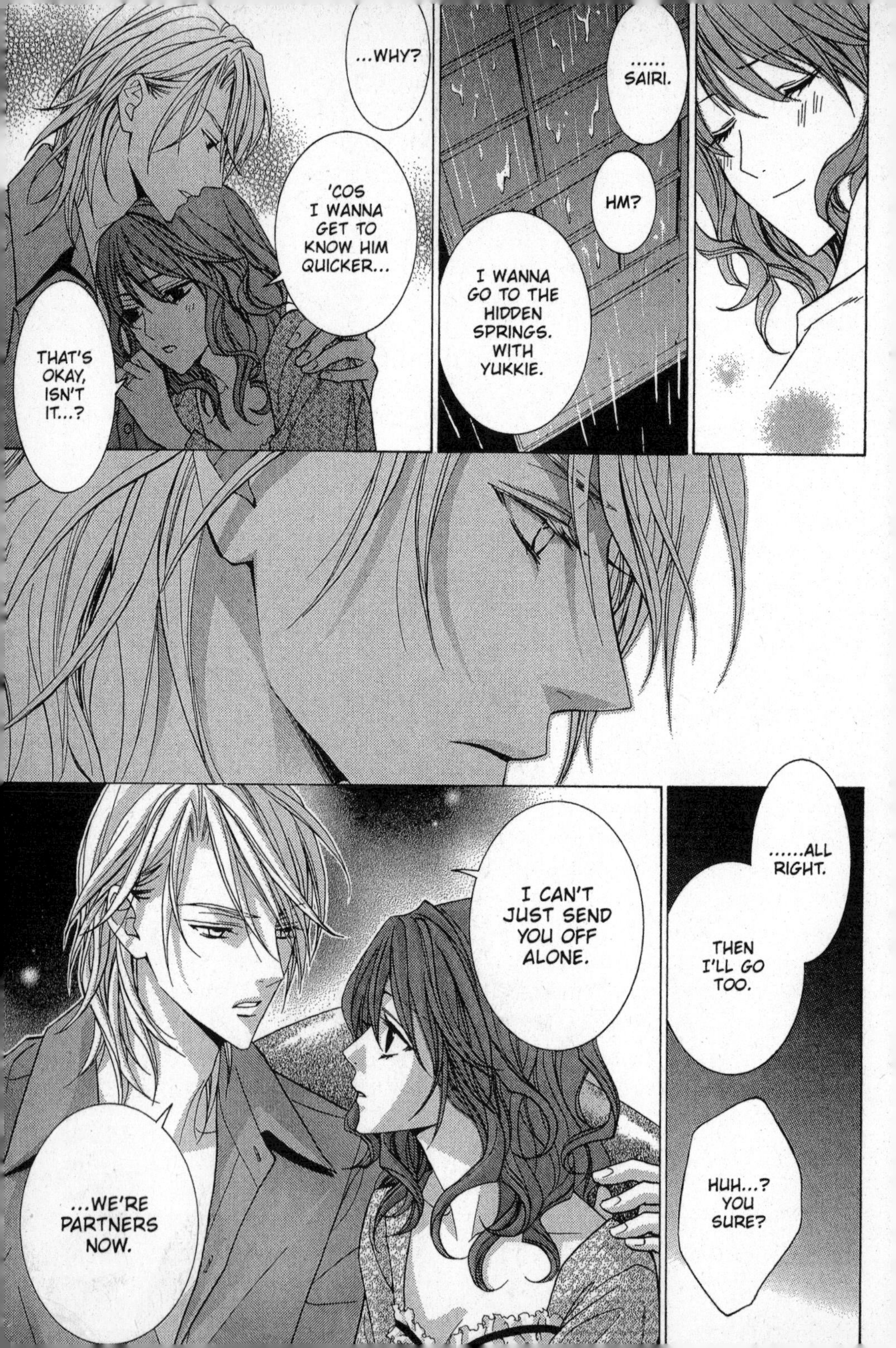
......SAIRI.
HM?
I WANNA GO TO THE HIDDEN SPRINGS. WITH YUKKIE.
...WHY?
'COS I WANNA GET TO KNOW HIM QUICKER...
THAT'S OKAY, ISN'T IT...?
......ALL RIGHT.
THEN I'LL GO TOO.
HUH...? YOU SURE?
I CAN'T JUST SEND YOU OFF ALONE.
...WE'RE PARTNERS NOW.

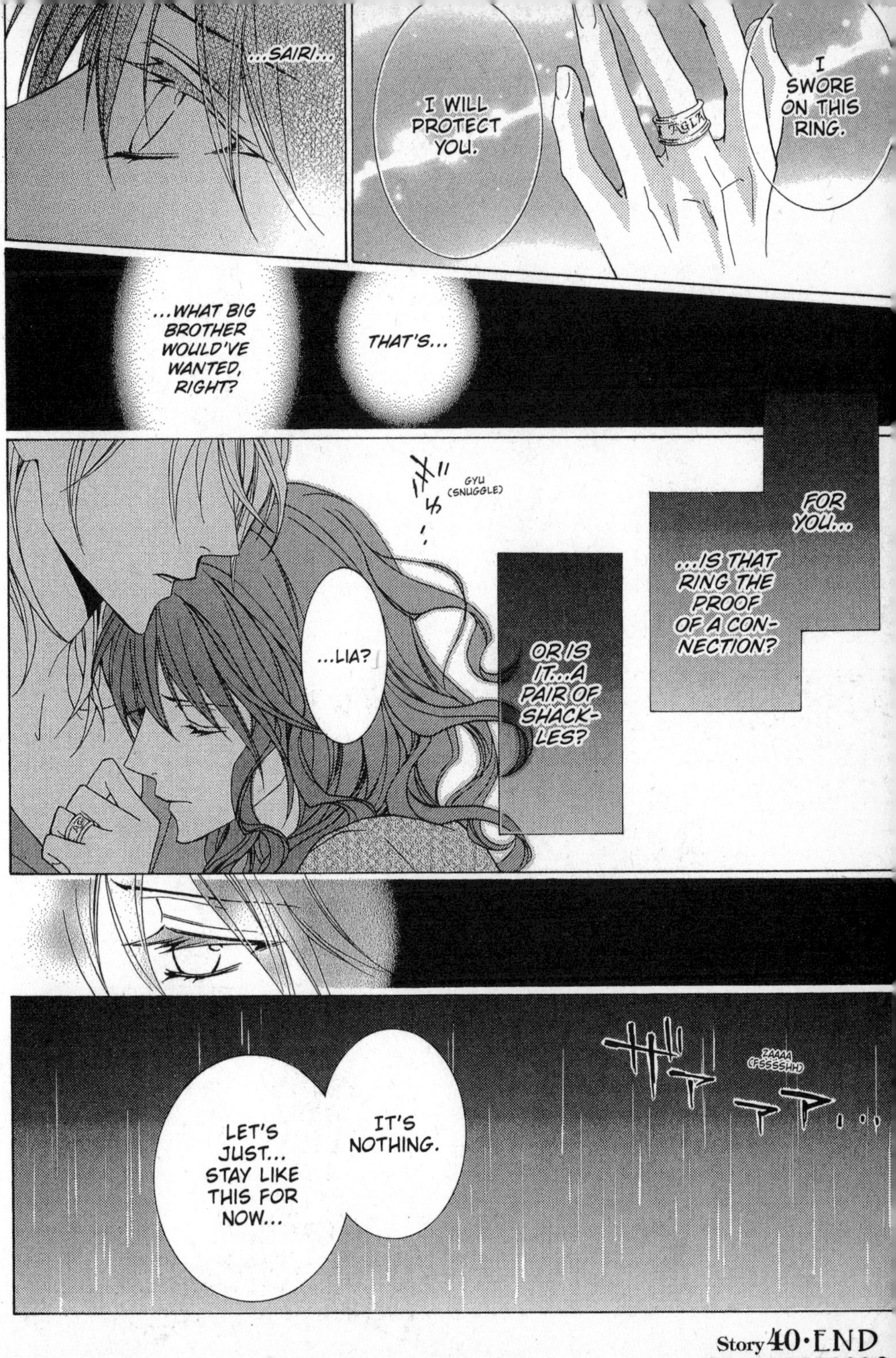
I SWORE ON THIS RING.
I WILL PROTECT YOU.
...SAIRI...
THAT'S...
...WHAT BIG BROTHER WOULD'VE WANTED, RIGHT?
FOR YOU...
...IS THAT RING THE PROOF OF A CON-NECTION?
OR IS IT...A PAIR OF SHACK-LES?
GYU (SNUGGLE)
...LIA?
ZAAAA (FSSSSHH)
IT'S NOTHING.
LET'S JUST... STAY LIKE THIS FOR NOW...

Story 40 • END

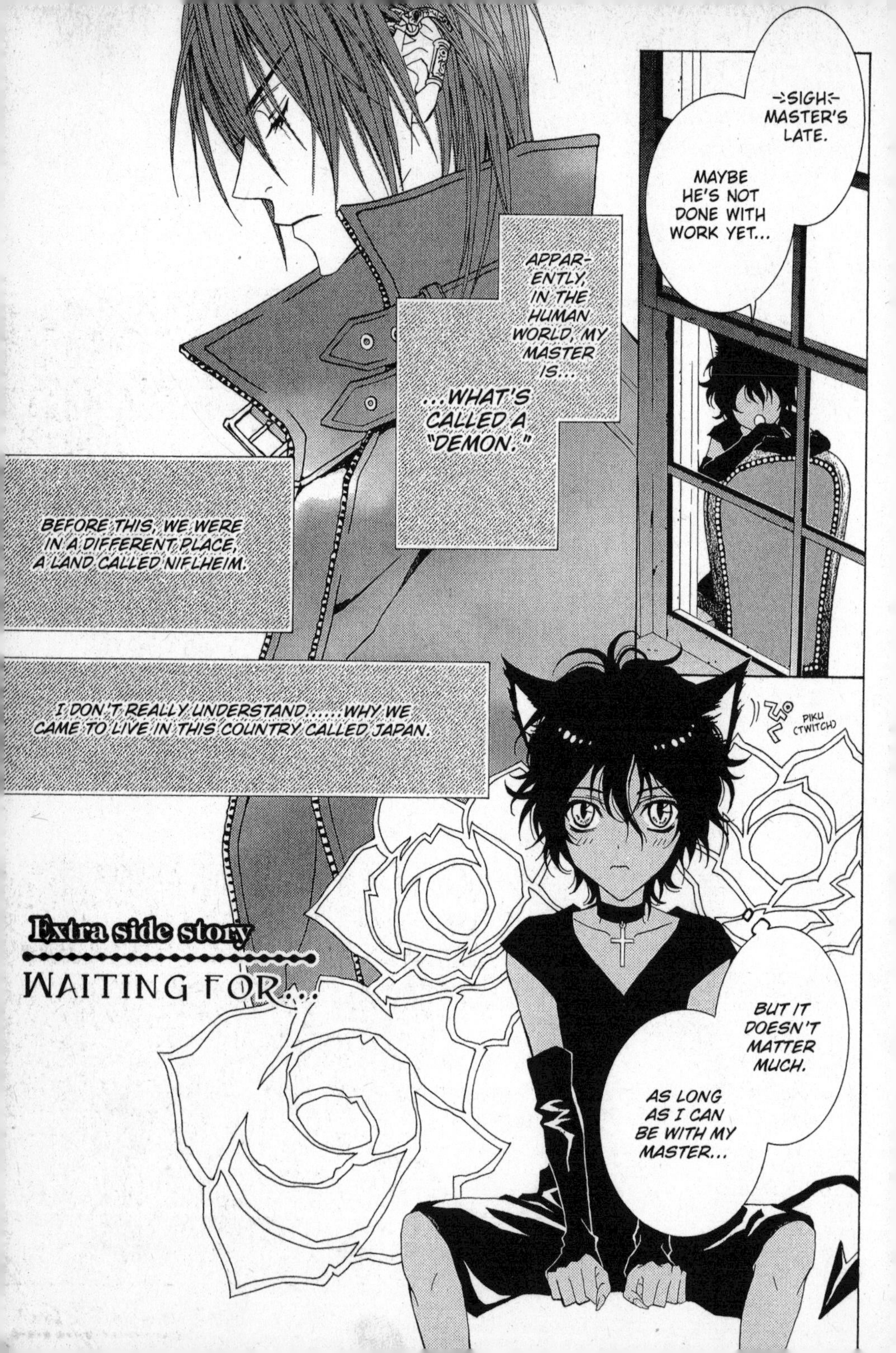

–SIGH– MASTER'S LATE.
MAYBE HE'S NOT DONE WITH WORK YET...
APPARENTLY, IN THE HUMAN WORLD, MY MASTER IS...
...WHAT'S CALLED A "DEMON."
BEFORE THIS, WE WERE IN A DIFFERENT PLACE, A LAND CALLED NIFLHEIM.
I DON'T REALLY UNDERSTAND.....WHY WE CAME TO LIVE IN THIS COUNTRY CALLED JAPAN.
PIKU (TWITCH)
Extra side story
WAITING FOR...
BUT IT DOESN'T MATTER MUCH.
AS LONG AS I CAN BE WITH MY MASTER...

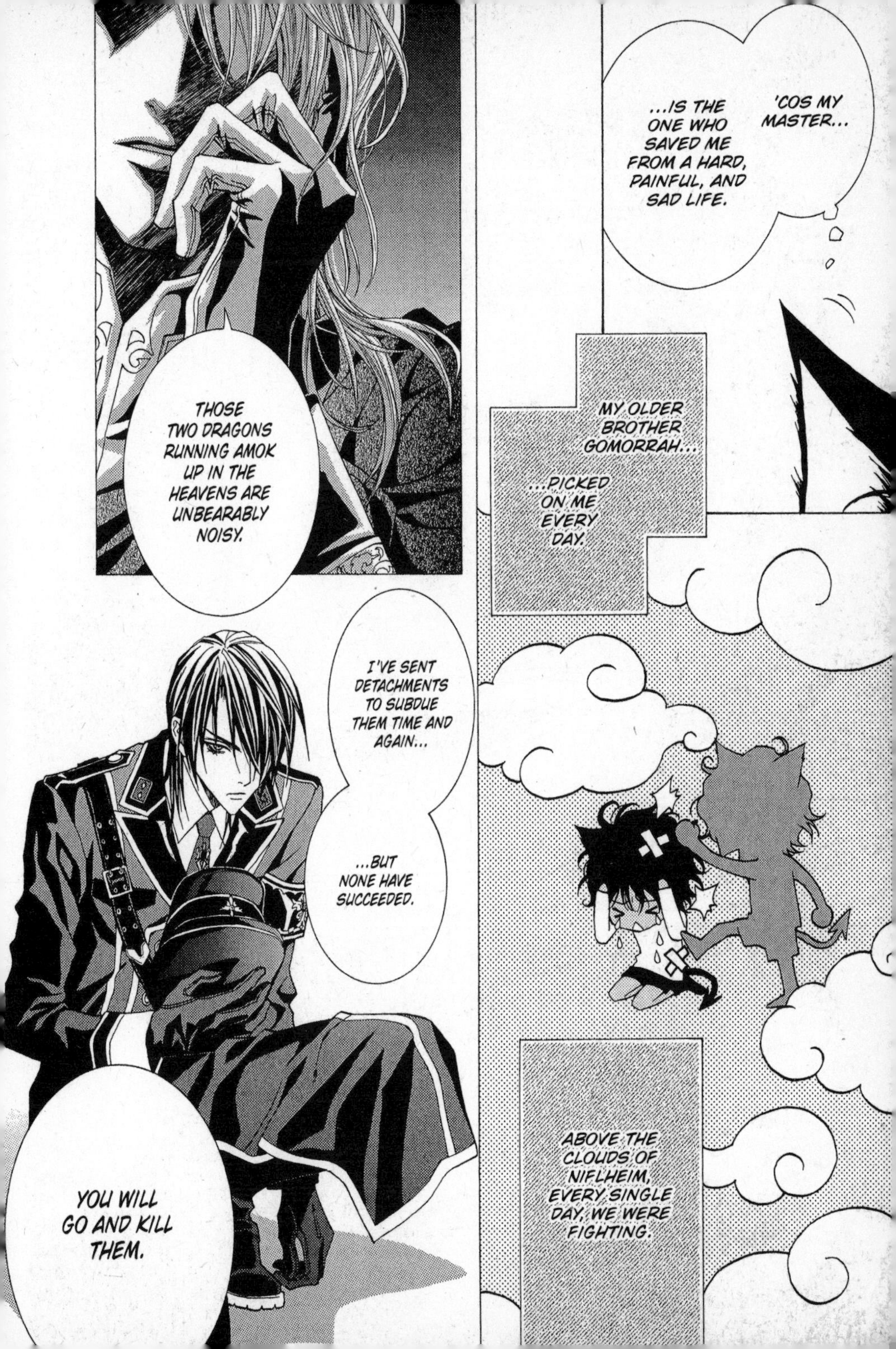
'COS MY MASTER...
...IS THE ONE WHO SAVED ME FROM A HARD, PAINFUL, AND SAD LIFE.
MY OLDER BROTHER GOMORRAH...
...PICKED ON ME EVERY DAY.
ABOVE THE CLOUDS OF NIFLHEIM, EVERY SINGLE DAY, WE WERE FIGHTING.
THOSE TWO DRAGONS RUNNING AMOK UP IN THE HEAVENS ARE UNBEARABLY NOISY.
I'VE SENT DETACHMENTS TO SUBDUE THEM TIME AND AGAIN...
...BUT NONE HAVE SUCCEEDED.
YOU WILL GO AND KILL THEM.

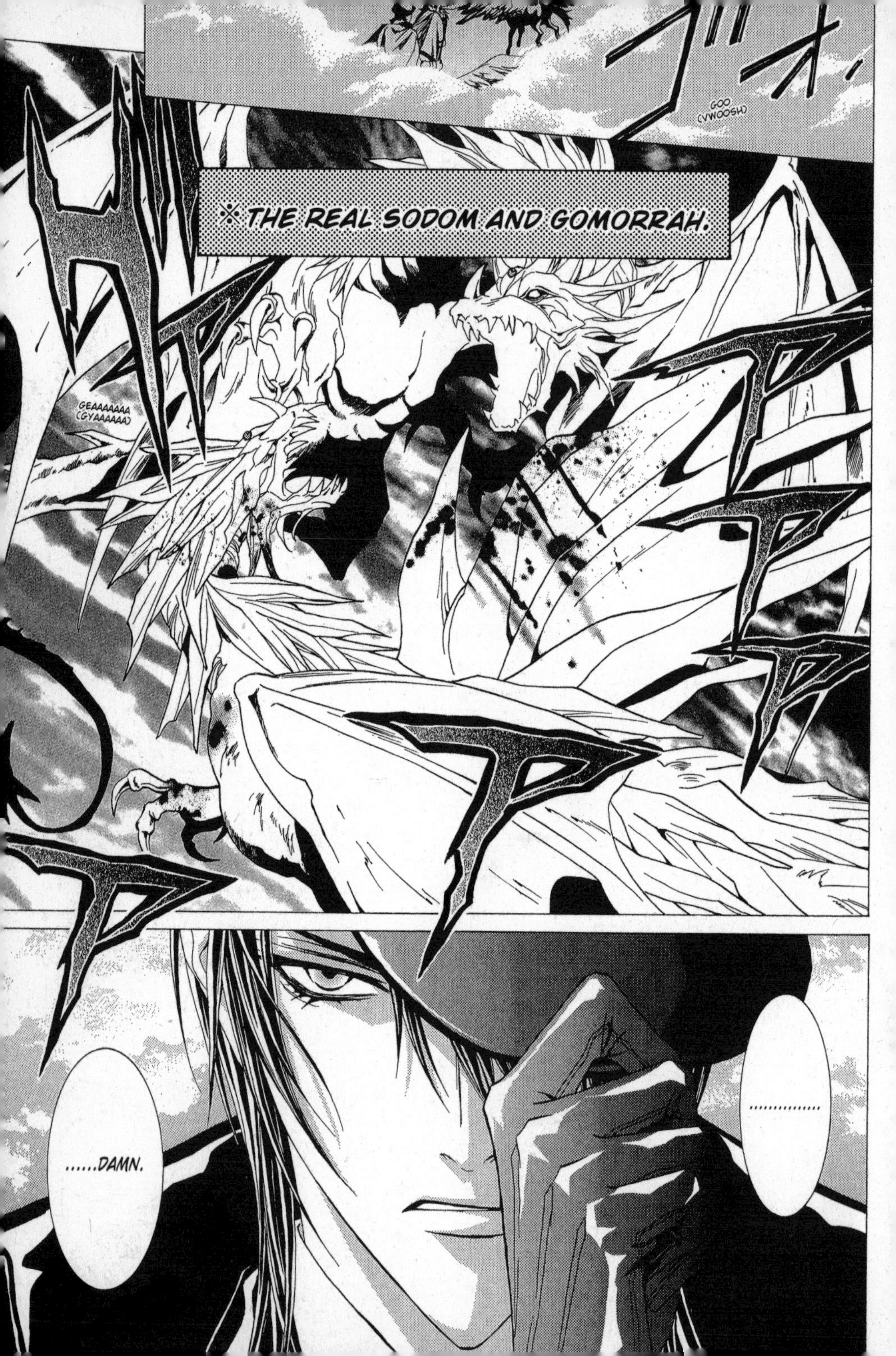

GOO (VWOOSH)
※THE REAL SODOM AND GOMORRAH.
GEAAAAAAA (GYAAAAAA)
....
......DAMN.

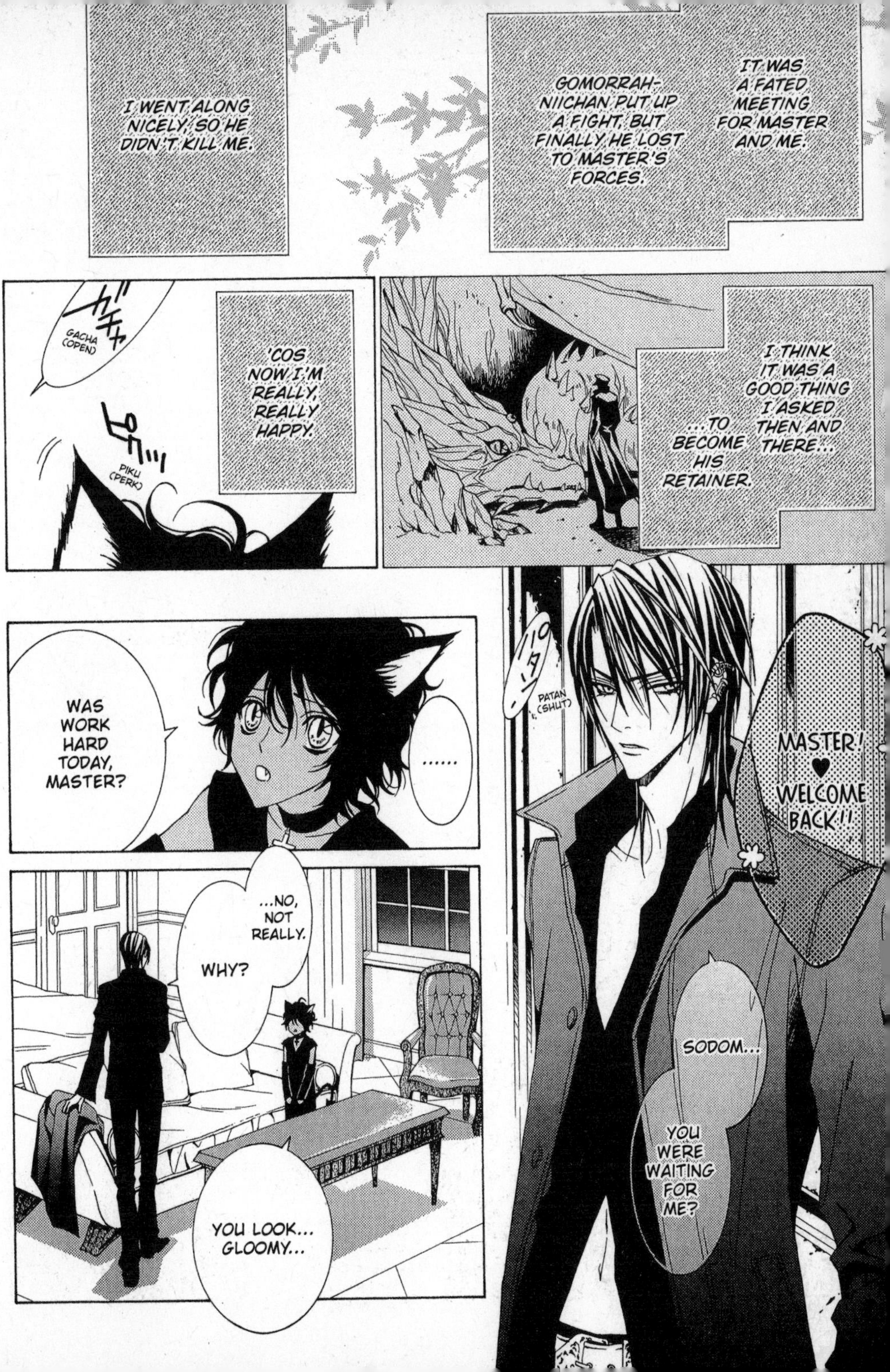
IT WAS A FATED MEETING FOR MASTER AND ME.
GOMORRAH-NIICHAN PUT UP A FIGHT, BUT FINALLY HE LOST TO MASTER'S FORCES.
I WENT ALONG NICELY, SO HE DIDN'T KILL ME.
I THINK IT WAS A GOOD THING I ASKED THEN AND THERE...
...TO BECOME HIS RETAINER.
'COS NOW I'M REALLY, REALLY HAPPY.
GACHA (OPEN)
PIKU (PERK)
PATAN (SHUT)
MASTER! ♥ WELCOME BACK!!
SODOM...
YOU WERE WAITING FOR ME?
WAS WORK HARD TODAY, MASTER?
......
...NO, NOT REALLY.
WHY?
YOU LOOK... GLOOMY...

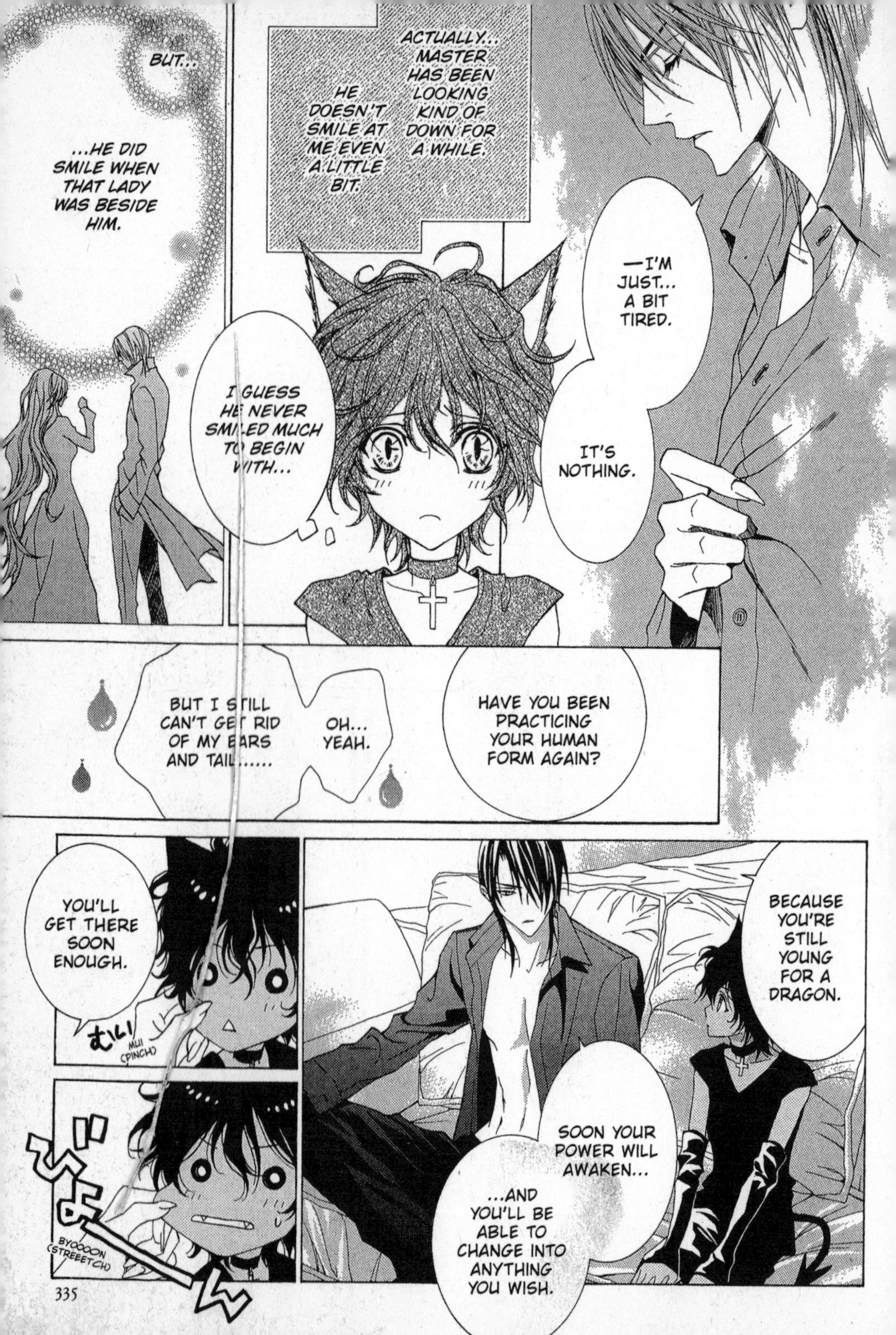
—I'M JUST... A BIT TIRED.
IT'S NOTHING.
ACTUALLY... MASTER HAS BEEN LOOKING KIND OF DOWN FOR A WHILE.
HE DOESN'T SMILE AT ME EVEN A LITTLE BIT.
I GUESS HE NEVER SMILED MUCH TO BEGIN WITH...
BUT...
...HE DID SMILE WHEN THAT LADY WAS BESIDE HIM.
HAVE YOU BEEN PRACTICING YOUR HUMAN FORM AGAIN?
OH... YEAH.
BUT I STILL CAN'T GET RID OF MY EARS AND TAIL......
BECAUSE YOU'RE STILL YOUNG FOR A DRAGON.
SOON YOUR POWER WILL AWAKEN...
...AND YOU'LL BE ABLE TO CHANGE INTO ANYTHING YOU WISH.
YOU'LL GET THERE SOON ENOUGH.
むい
MUI (PINCH)
BYOOOON (STREEETCH)

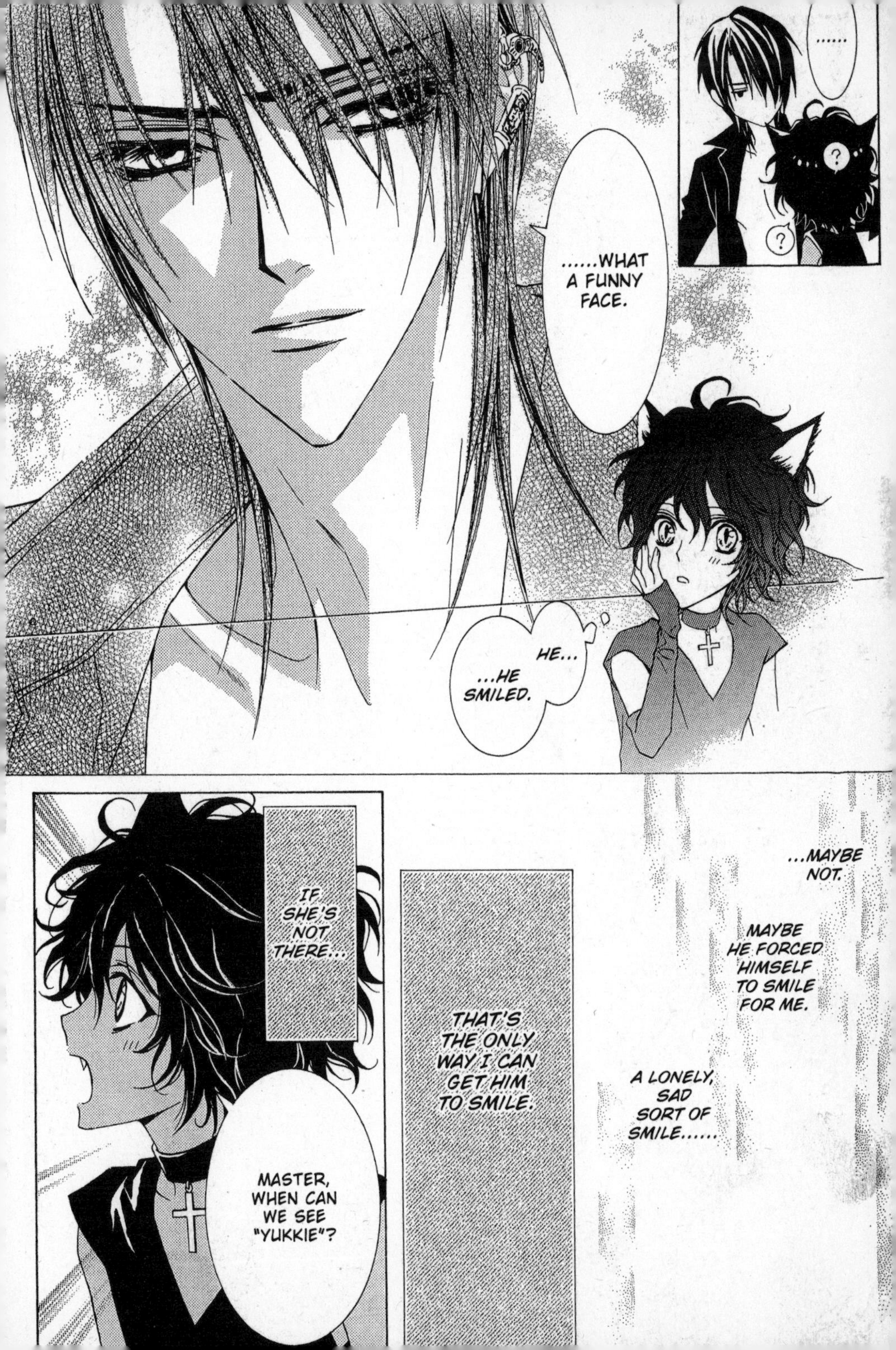
......
?
?
......WHAT A FUNNY FACE.
HE... ...HE SMILED.
...MAYBE NOT.
MAYBE HE FORCED HIMSELF TO SMILE FOR ME.
A LONELY, SAD SORT OF SMILE......
THAT'S THE ONLY WAY I CAN GET HIM TO SMILE.
IF SHE'S NOT THERE...
MASTER, WHEN CAN WE SEE "YUKKIE"?

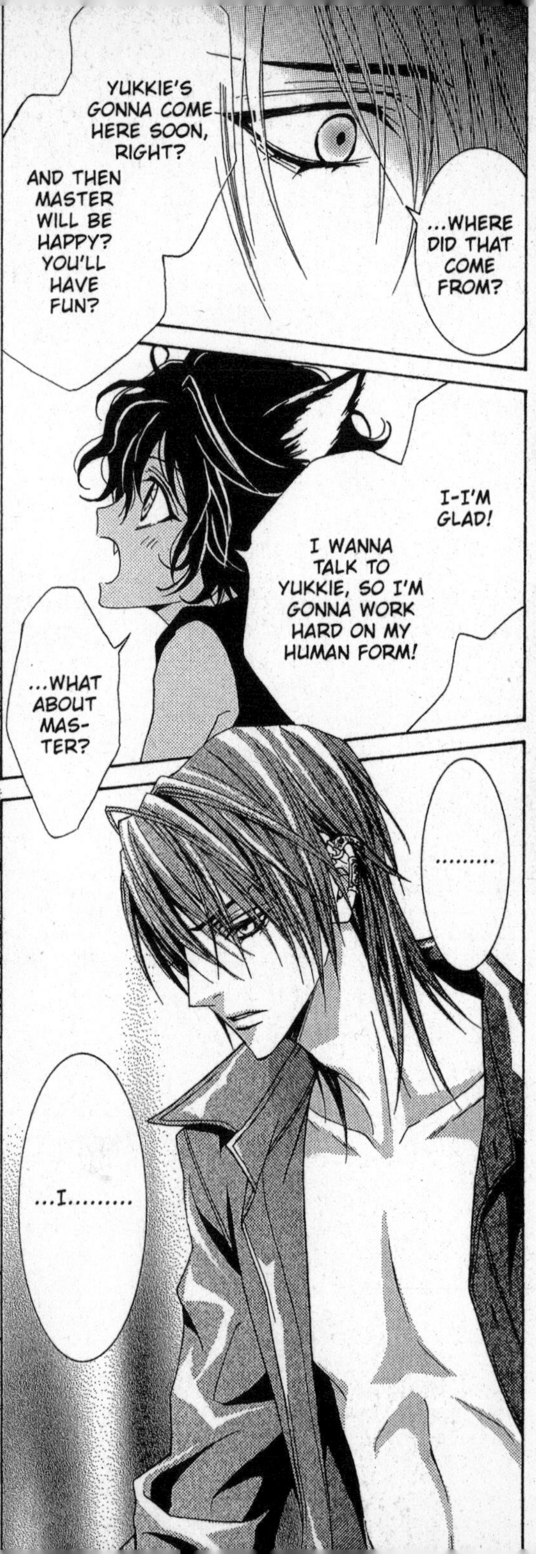
YUKKIE'S GONNA COME HERE SOON, RIGHT?
AND THEN MASTER WILL BE HAPPY? YOU'LL HAVE FUN?
...WHERE DID THAT COME FROM?
I-I'M GLAD!
I WANNA TALK TO YUKKIE, SO I'M GONNA WORK HARD ON MY HUMAN FORM!
...WHAT ABOUT MAS-TER?
....
...I........

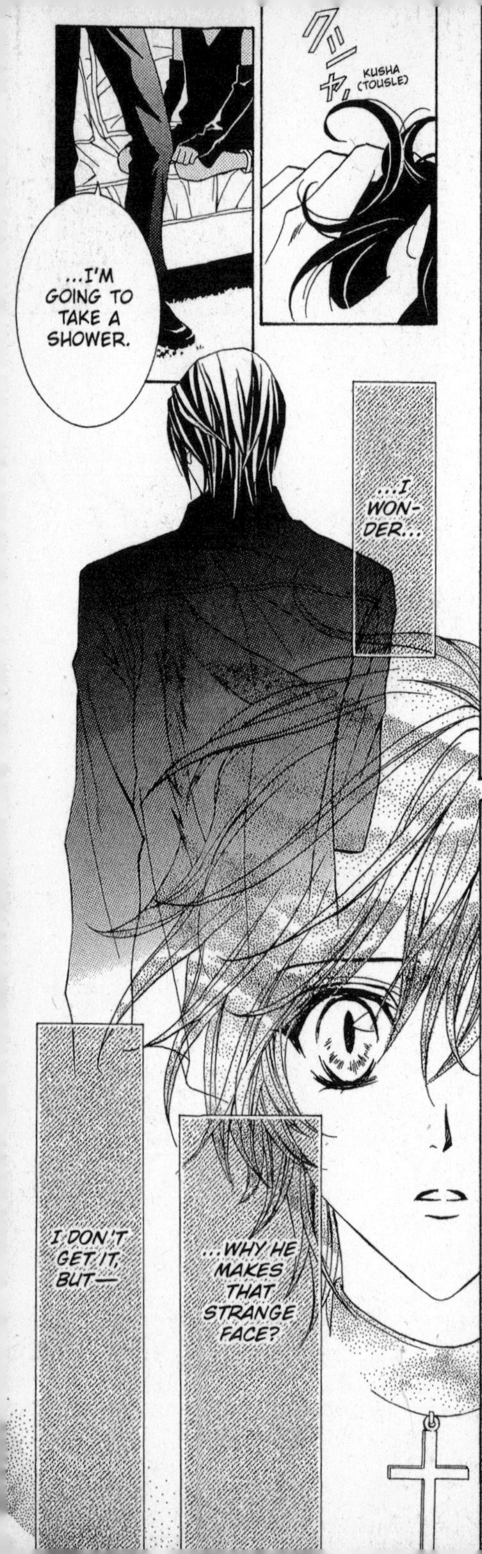
KUSHA (TOUSLE)
...I'M GOING TO TAKE A SHOWER.
...I WON-DER...
...WHY HE MAKES THAT STRANGE FACE?
I DON'T GET IT, BUT—

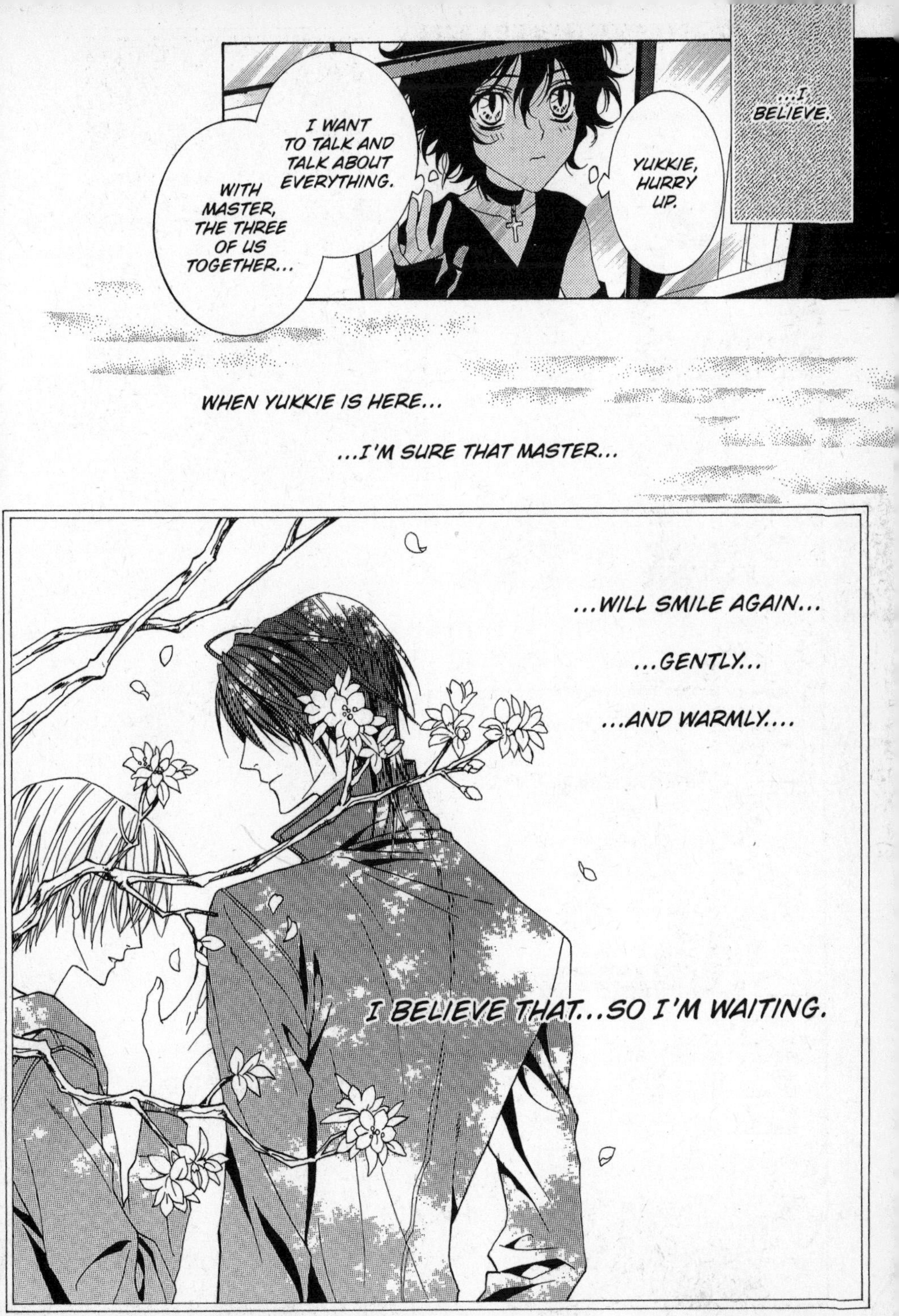
...I BELIEVE.
YUKKIE, HURRY UP.
I WANT TO TALK AND TALK ABOUT EVERYTHING.
WITH MASTER, THE THREE OF US TOGETHER...
WHEN YUKKIE IS HERE...
...I'M SURE THAT MASTER...
...WILL SMILE AGAIN...
...GENTLY...
...AND WARMLY....
I BELIEVE THAT...SO I'M WAITING.

Extra side story • END

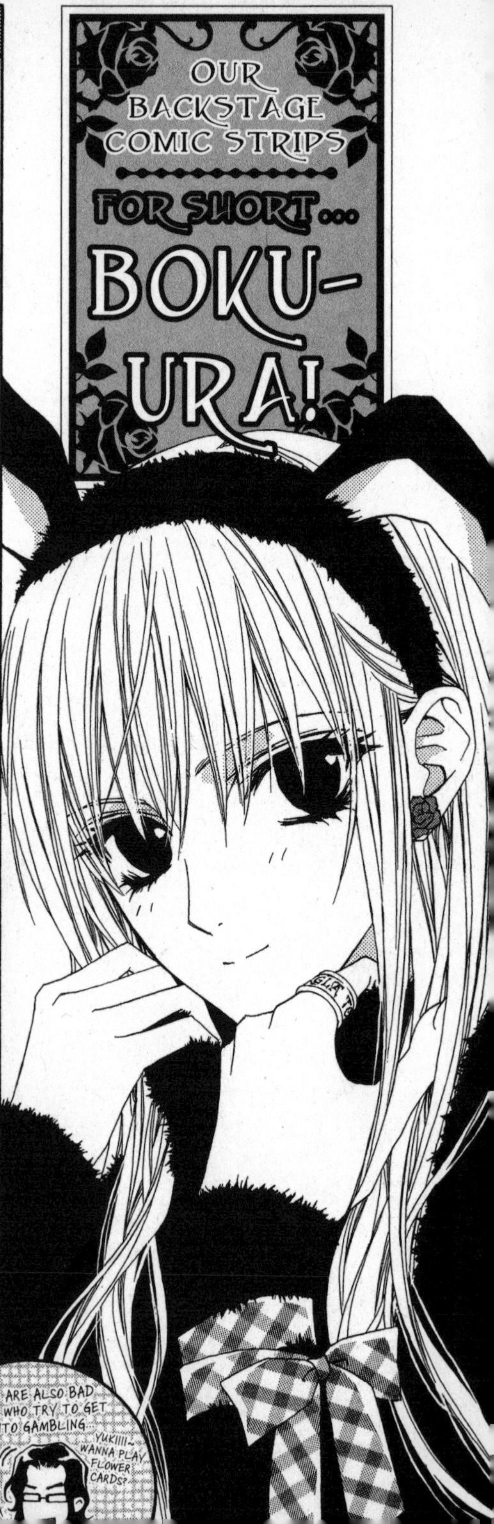
OUR BACKSTAGE COMIC STRIPS
FOR SHORT...
BOKU-URA!
THERE ARE ALSO BAD ADULTS WHO TRY TO GET HIM INTO GAMBLING...
YUKIIII~ WANNA PLAY FLOWER CARDS?

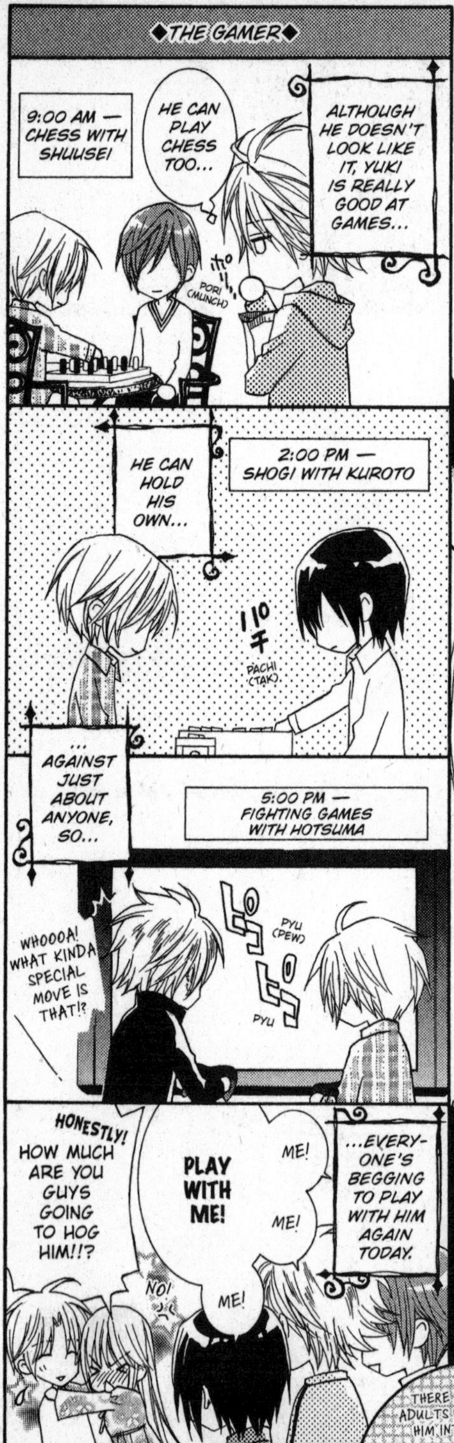
◆THE GAMER◆
ALTHOUGH HE DOESN'T LOOK LIKE IT, YUKI IS REALLY GOOD AT GAMES...
HE CAN PLAY CHESS TOO...
9:00 AM — CHESS WITH SHUUSEI
PORI (MUNCH)
2:00 PM — SHOGI WITH KUROTO
HE CAN HOLD HIS OWN...
PACHI (TAK)
...AGAINST JUST ABOUT ANYONE, SO...
5:00 PM — FIGHTING GAMES WITH HOTSUMA
PYU (PEW)
PYU
WHOOOA! WHAT KINDA SPECIAL MOVE IS THAT!?
...EVERYONE'S BEGGING TO PLAY WITH HIM AGAIN TODAY.
ME!
PLAY WITH ME!
ME!
HONESTLY! HOW MUCH ARE YOU GUYS GOING TO HOG HIM!!?
NO!
ME!

◆COOKING◆

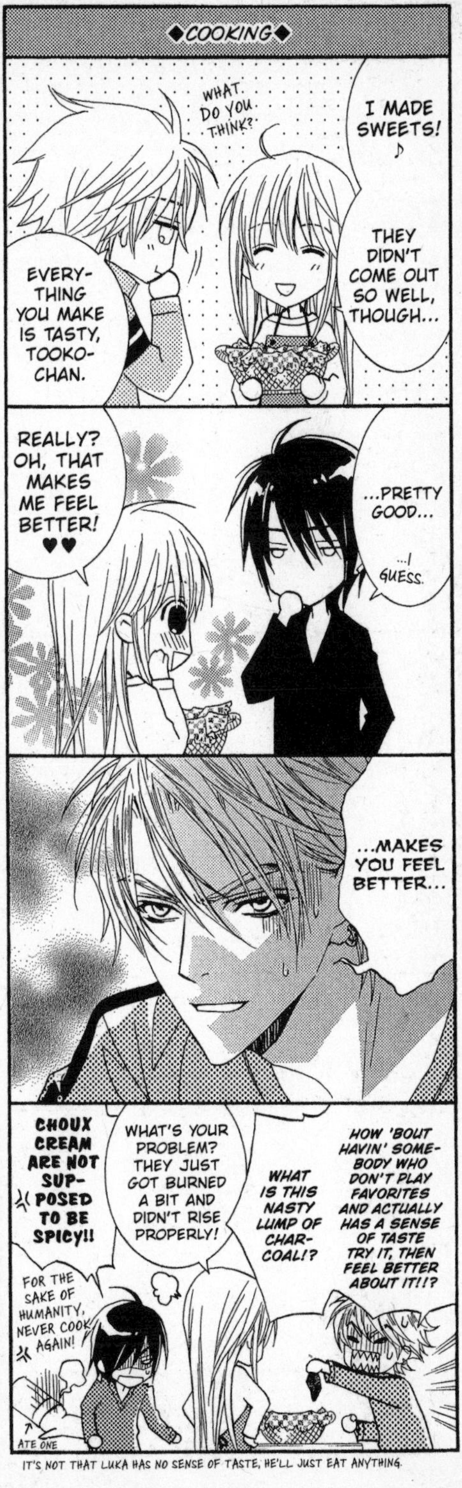
I MADE SWEETS! ♪
THEY DIDN'T COME OUT SO WELL, THOUGH...
WHAT. DO YOU THINK?
EVERYTHING YOU MAKE IS TASTY, TOOKO-CHAN.
...PRETTY GOOD...
...I GUESS.
REALLY? OH, THAT MAKES ME FEEL BETTER! ♥♥
...MAKES YOU FEEL BETTER...
HOW 'BOUT HAVIN' SOMEBODY WHO DON'T PLAY FAVORITES AND ACTUALLY HAS A SENSE OF TASTE TRY IT, THEN FEEL BETTER ABOUT IT!!?
WHAT IS THIS NASTY LUMP OF CHARCOAL!?
WHAT'S YOUR PROBLEM? THEY JUST GOT BURNED A BIT AND DIDN'T RISE PROPERLY!
CHOUX CREAM ARE NOT SUPPOSED TO BE SPICY!!
FOR THE SAKE OF HUMANITY, NEVER COOK AGAIN!
ATE ONE

IT'S NOT THAT LUKA HAS NO SENSE OF TASTE, HE'LL JUST EAT ANYTHING.

◆SOUVENIR GIFTS◆

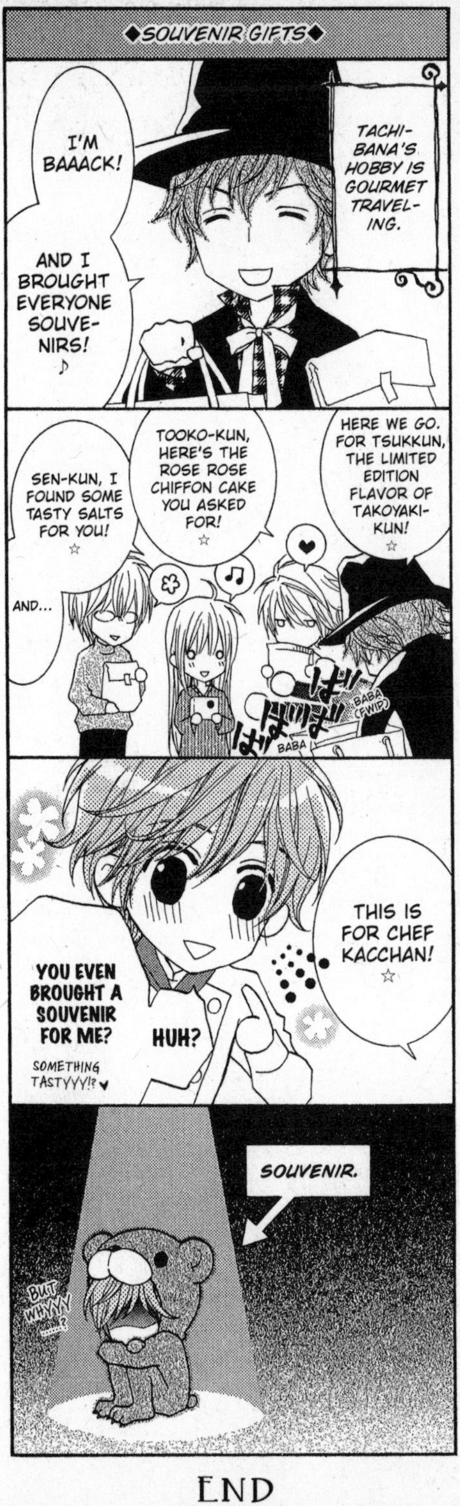
TACHIBANA'S HOBBY IS GOURMET TRAVELING.
I'M BAAACK!
AND I BROUGHT EVERYONE SOUVENIRS! ♪
HERE WE GO. FOR TSUKKUN, THE LIMITED EDITION FLAVOR OF TAKOYAKI-KUN! ☆
TOOKO-KUN, HERE'S THE ROSE ROSE CHIFFON CAKE YOU ASKED FOR! ☆
SEN-KUN, I FOUND SOME TASTY SALTS FOR YOU! ☆
BABA (FWIP)
BABA
AND...
THIS IS FOR CHEF KACCHAN! ☆
HUH?
YOU EVEN BROUGHT A SOUVENIR FOR ME?
SOMETHING TASTYYY!? ♥
SOUVENIR.
BUT WHYYY ......?

END

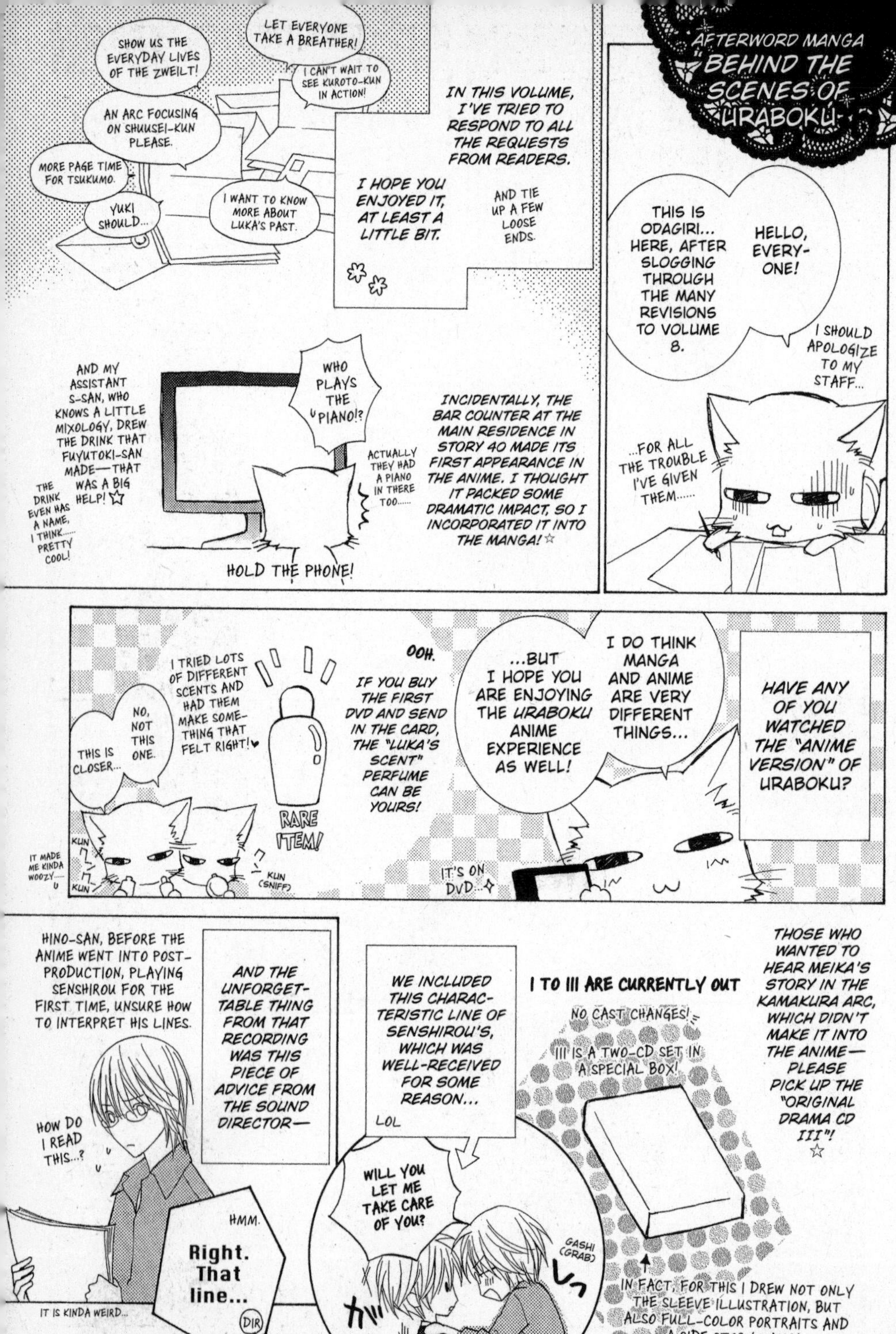
AFTERWORD MANGA
BEHIND THE SCENES OF URABOKU
HELLO, EVERYONE!
THIS IS ODAGIRI... HERE, AFTER SLOGGING THROUGH THE MANY REVISIONS TO VOLUME 8.
I SHOULD APOLOGIZE TO MY STAFF...
...FOR ALL THE TROUBLE I'VE GIVEN THEM......
IN THIS VOLUME, I'VE TRIED TO RESPOND TO ALL THE REQUESTS FROM READERS.
AND TIE UP A FEW LOOSE ENDS.
I HOPE YOU ENJOYED IT, AT LEAST A LITTLE BIT.
LET EVERYONE TAKE A BREATHER!
I CAN'T WAIT TO SEE KUROTO-KUN IN ACTION!
SHOW US THE EVERYDAY LIVES OF THE ZWEILT!
AN ARC FOCUSING ON SHUUSEI-KUN PLEASE.
I WANT TO KNOW MORE ABOUT LUKA'S PAST.
MORE PAGE TIME FOR TSUKUMO.
YUKI SHOULD...
INCIDENTALLY, THE BAR COUNTER AT THE MAIN RESIDENCE IN STORY 40 MADE ITS FIRST APPEARANCE IN THE ANIME. I THOUGHT IT PACKED SOME DRAMATIC IMPACT, SO I INCORPORATED IT INTO THE MANGA! ☆
ACTUALLY THEY HAD A PIANO IN THERE TOO......
WHO PLAYS THE PIANO!?
HOLD THE PHONE!
AND MY ASSISTANT S-SAN, WHO KNOWS A LITTLE MIXOLOGY, DREW THE DRINK THAT FUYUTOKI-SAN MADE—THAT WAS A BIG HELP! ☆
THE DRINK EVEN HAS A NAME, I THINK...... PRETTY COOL!
HAVE ANY OF YOU WATCHED THE "ANIME VERSION" OF URABOKU?
I DO THINK MANGA AND ANIME ARE VERY DIFFERENT THINGS...
...BUT I HOPE YOU ARE ENJOYING THE URABOKU ANIME EXPERIENCE AS WELL!
IT'S ON DVD...
OOH.
IF YOU BUY THE FIRST DVD AND SEND IN THE CARD, THE "LUKA'S SCENT" PERFUME CAN BE YOURS!
RARE ITEM!
I TRIED LOTS OF DIFFERENT SCENTS AND HAD THEM MAKE SOMETHING THAT FELT RIGHT! ♥
NO, NOT THIS ONE.
THIS IS CLOSER...
KUN (SNIFF)
KUN
KUN
IT MADE ME KINDA WOOZY......
THOSE WHO WANTED TO HEAR MEIKA'S STORY IN THE KAMAKURA ARC, WHICH DIDN'T MAKE IT INTO THE ANIME—PLEASE PICK UP THE "ORIGINAL DRAMA CD III"! ☆
I TO III ARE CURRENTLY OUT
NO CAST CHANGES!
III IS A TWO-CD SET IN A SPECIAL BOX!
IN FACT, FOR THIS I DREW NOT ONLY THE SLEEVE ILLUSTRATION, BUT ALSO FULL-COLOR PORTRAITS AND A SIDE STORY MANGA.
WE INCLUDED THIS CHARACTERISTIC LINE OF SENSHIROU'S, WHICH WAS WELL-RECEIVED FOR SOME REASON...
LOL
WILL YOU LET ME TAKE CARE OF YOU?
GASHI (GRAB)
HINO-SAN, BEFORE THE ANIME WENT INTO POST-PRODUCTION, PLAYING SENSHIROU FOR THE FIRST TIME, UNSURE HOW TO INTERPRET HIS LINES.
AND THE UNFORGETTABLE THING FROM THAT RECORDING WAS THIS PIECE OF ADVICE FROM THE SOUND DIRECTOR—
HOW DO I READ THIS...?
HMM.
Right. That line...
DIR
IT IS KINDA WEIRD...

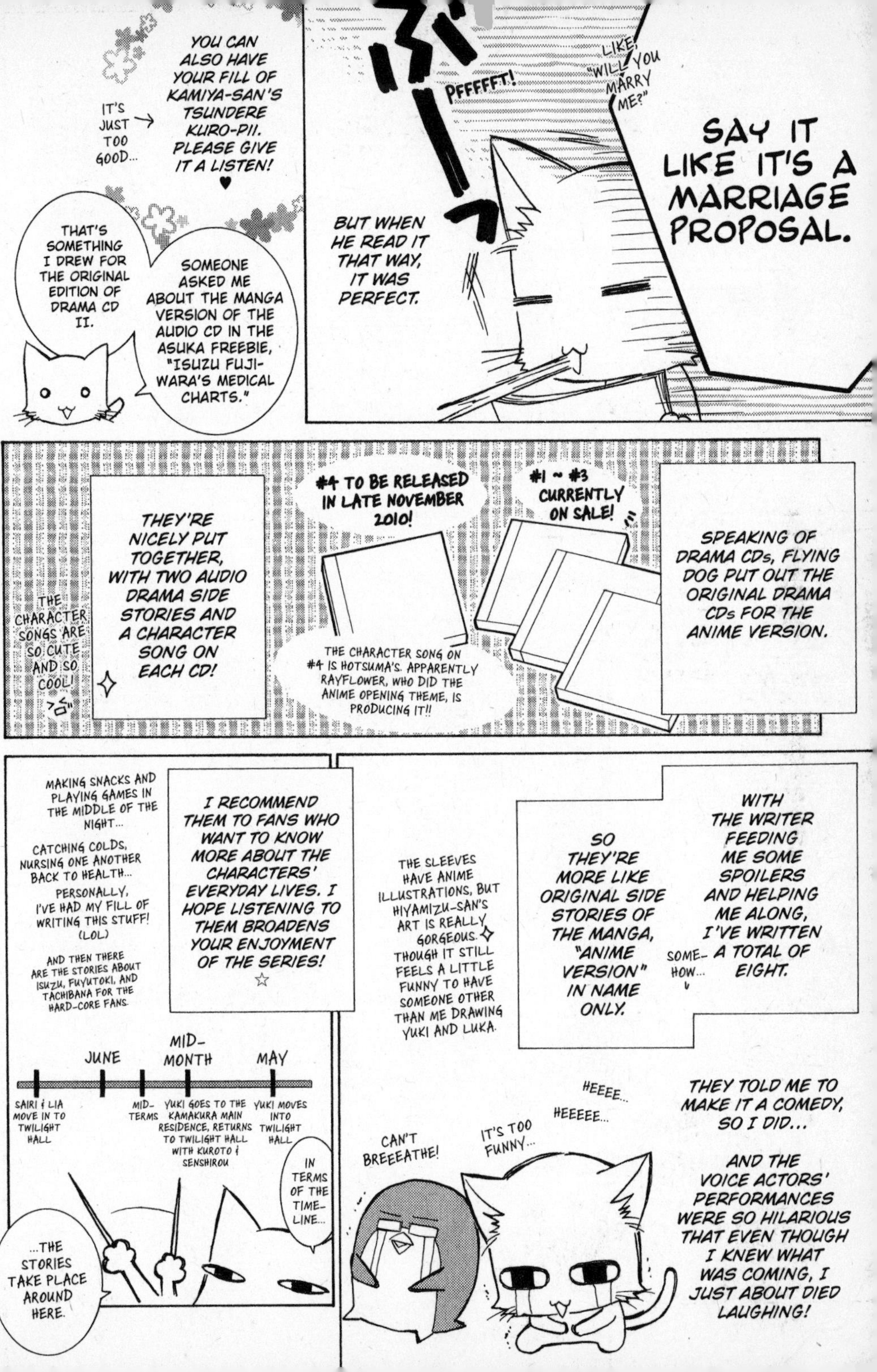
SAY IT LIKE IT'S A MARRIAGE PROPOSAL.
LIKE, "WILL YOU MARRY ME?"
PFFFFFT!
BUT WHEN HE READ IT THAT WAY, IT WAS PERFECT.
YOU CAN ALSO HAVE YOUR FILL OF KAMIYA-SAN'S TSUNDERE KURO-PII. PLEASE GIVE IT A LISTEN! ♥
IT'S JUST TOO GOOD...
SOMEONE ASKED ME ABOUT THE MANGA VERSION OF THE AUDIO CD IN THE ASUKA FREEBIE, "ISUZU FUJIWARA'S MEDICAL CHARTS."
THAT'S SOMETHING I DREW FOR THE ORIGINAL EDITION OF DRAMA CD II.
SPEAKING OF DRAMA CDs, FLYING DOG PUT OUT THE ORIGINAL DRAMA CDs FOR THE ANIME VERSION.
#1 ~ #3 CURRENTLY ON SALE!
#4 TO BE RELEASED IN LATE NOVEMBER 2010!
THE CHARACTER SONG ON #4 IS HOTSUMA'S. APPARENTLY RAYFLOWER, WHO DID THE ANIME OPENING THEME, IS PRODUCING IT!!
THEY'RE NICELY PUT TOGETHER, WITH TWO AUDIO DRAMA SIDE STORIES AND A CHARACTER SONG ON EACH CD!
THE CHARACTER SONGS ARE SO CUTE AND SO COOL!
WITH THE WRITER FEEDING ME SOME SPOILERS AND HELPING ME ALONG, I'VE WRITTEN A TOTAL OF EIGHT.
SOME-HOW...
SO THEY'RE MORE LIKE ORIGINAL SIDE STORIES OF THE MANGA, "ANIME VERSION" IN NAME ONLY.
THE SLEEVES HAVE ANIME ILLUSTRATIONS, BUT HIYAMIZU-SAN'S ART IS REALLY GORGEOUS. THOUGH IT STILL FEELS A LITTLE FUNNY TO HAVE SOMEONE OTHER THAN ME DRAWING YUKI AND LUKA.
THEY TOLD ME TO MAKE IT A COMEDY, SO I DID...
AND THE VOICE ACTORS' PERFORMANCES WERE SO HILARIOUS THAT EVEN THOUGH I KNEW WHAT WAS COMING, I JUST ABOUT DIED LAUGHING!
HEEEE...
HEEEEE...
IT'S TOO FUNNY...
CAN'T BREEEATHE!
I RECOMMEND THEM TO FANS WHO WANT TO KNOW MORE ABOUT THE CHARACTERS' EVERYDAY LIVES. I HOPE LISTENING TO THEM BROADENS YOUR ENJOYMENT OF THE SERIES! ☆
MAKING SNACKS AND PLAYING GAMES IN THE MIDDLE OF THE NIGHT...
CATCHING COLDS, NURSING ONE ANOTHER BACK TO HEALTH...
PERSONALLY, I'VE HAD MY FILL OF WRITING THIS STUFF! (LOL)
AND THEN THERE ARE THE STORIES ABOUT ISUZU, FUYUTOKI, AND TACHIBANA FOR THE HARD-CORE FANS.
MAY
MID-MONTH
JUNE
YUKI MOVES INTO TWILIGHT HALL
YUKI GOES TO THE KAMAKURA MAIN RESIDENCE, RETURNS TO TWILIGHT HALL WITH KUROTO & SENSHIROU
MID-TERMS
SAIRI & LIA MOVE IN TO TWILIGHT HALL
IN TERMS OF THE TIME-LINE...
...THE STORIES TAKE PLACE AROUND HERE.

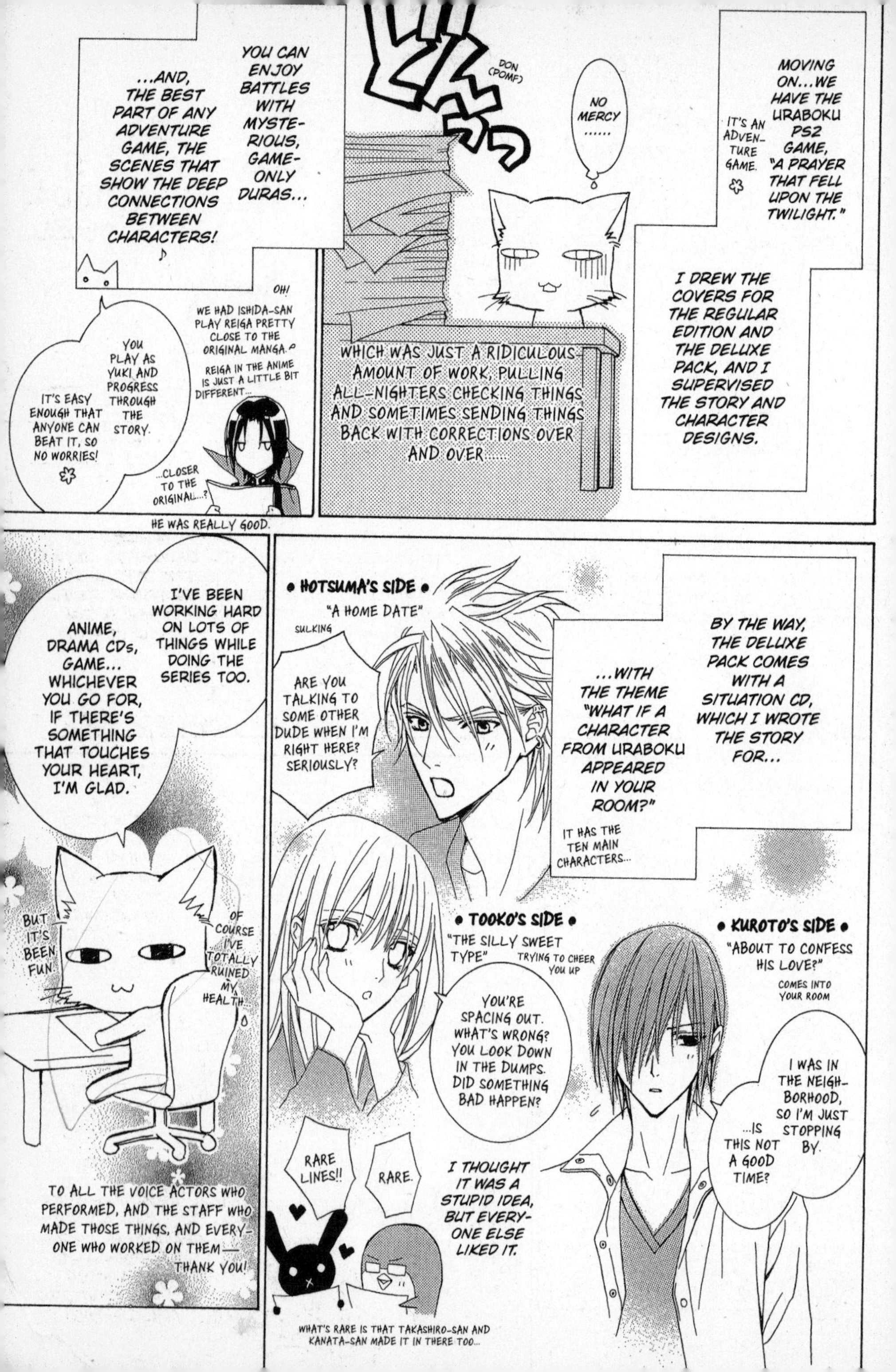
MOVING ON…WE HAVE THE URABOKU PS2 GAME, "A PRAYER THAT FELL UPON THE TWILIGHT."
IT'S AN ADVEN-TURE GAME.
I DREW THE COVERS FOR THE REGULAR EDITION AND THE DELUXE PACK, AND I SUPERVISED THE STORY AND CHARACTER DESIGNS.
NO MERCY ……
DON (POMF)
WHICH WAS JUST A RIDICULOUS AMOUNT OF WORK, PULLING ALL-NIGHTERS CHECKING THINGS AND SOMETIMES SENDING THINGS BACK WITH CORRECTIONS OVER AND OVER……
YOU CAN ENJOY BATTLES WITH MYSTE-RIOUS, GAME-ONLY DURAS…
…AND, THE BEST PART OF ANY ADVENTURE GAME, THE SCENES THAT SHOW THE DEEP CONNECTIONS BETWEEN CHARACTERS! ♪
OH!
WE HAD ISHIDA-SAN PLAY REIGA PRETTY CLOSE TO THE ORIGINAL MANGA.
REIGA IN THE ANIME IS JUST A LITTLE BIT DIFFERENT…
YOU PLAY AS YUKI AND PROGRESS THROUGH THE STORY.
IT'S EASY ENOUGH THAT ANYONE CAN BEAT IT, SO NO WORRIES!
…CLOSER TO THE ORIGINAL…?
HE WAS REALLY GOOD.
BY THE WAY, THE DELUXE PACK COMES WITH A SITUATION CD, WHICH I WROTE THE STORY FOR…
…WITH THE THEME "WHAT IF A CHARACTER FROM URABOKU APPEARED IN YOUR ROOM?"
IT HAS THE TEN MAIN CHARACTERS…
• HOTSUMA'S SIDE •
"A HOME DATE"
SULKING
ARE YOU TALKING TO SOME OTHER DUDE WHEN I'M RIGHT HERE? SERIOUSLY?
• KUROTO'S SIDE •
"ABOUT TO CONFESS HIS LOVE?"
COMES INTO YOUR ROOM
I WAS IN THE NEIGH-BORHOOD, SO I'M JUST STOPPING BY.
…IS THIS NOT A GOOD TIME?
• TOOKO'S SIDE •
"THE SILLY SWEET TYPE"
TRYING TO CHEER YOU UP
YOU'RE SPACING OUT. WHAT'S WRONG? YOU LOOK DOWN IN THE DUMPS. DID SOMETHING BAD HAPPEN?
I THOUGHT IT WAS A STUPID IDEA, BUT EVERY-ONE ELSE LIKED IT.
RARE.
RARE LINES!!
WHAT'S RARE IS THAT TAKASHIRO-SAN AND KANATA-SAN MADE IT IN THERE TOO…
I'VE BEEN WORKING HARD ON LOTS OF THINGS WHILE DOING THE SERIES TOO.
ANIME, DRAMA CDs, GAME… WHICHEVER YOU GO FOR, IF THERE'S SOMETHING THAT TOUCHES YOUR HEART, I'M GLAD.
OF COURSE I'VE TOTALLY RUINED MY HEALTH.
BUT IT'S BEEN FUN.
TO ALL THE VOICE ACTORS WHO PERFORMED, AND THE STAFF WHO MADE THOSE THINGS, AND EVERY-ONE WHO WORKED ON THEM— THANK YOU!

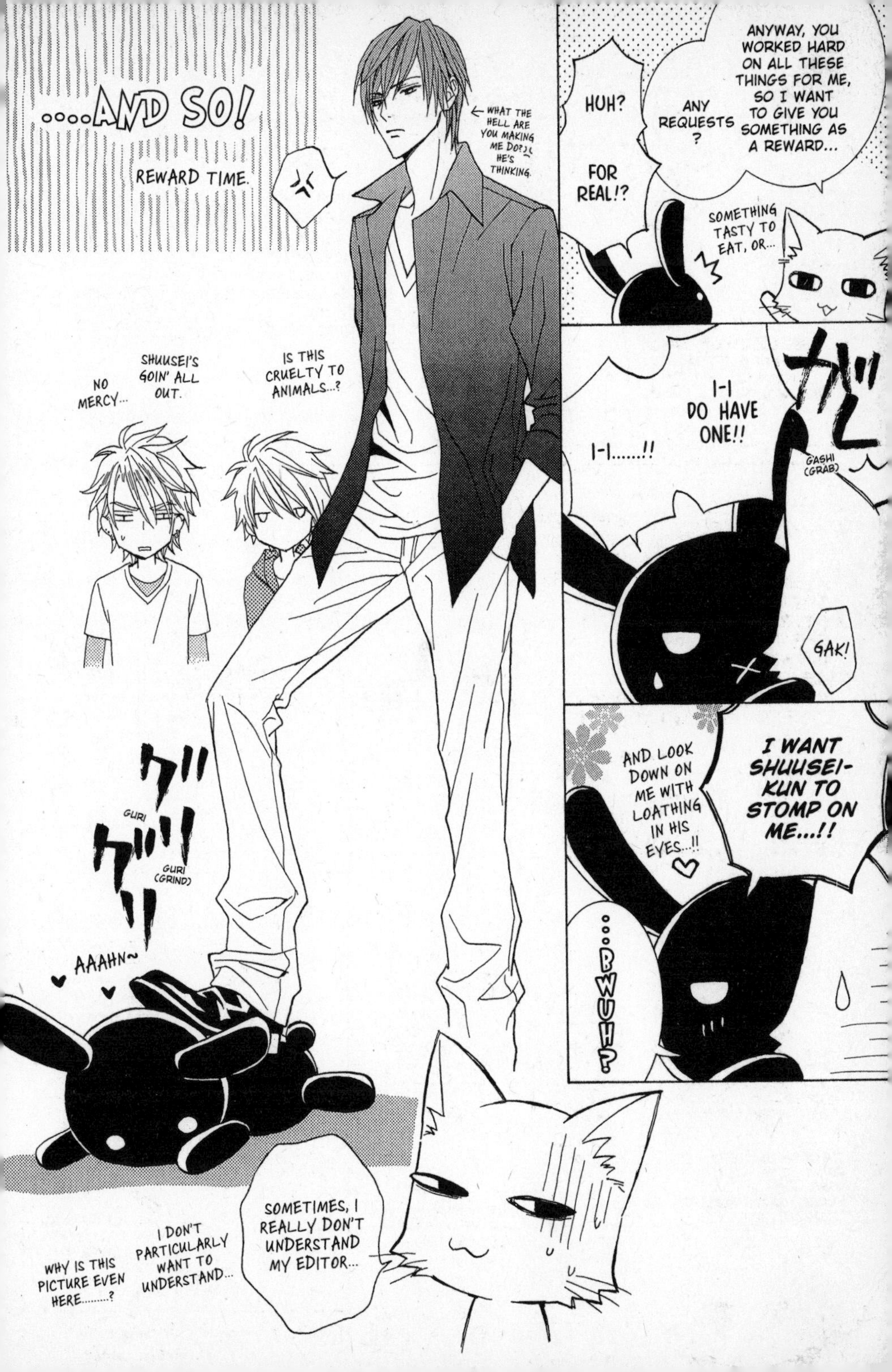
ANYWAY, YOU WORKED HARD ON ALL THESE THINGS FOR ME, SO I WANT TO GIVE YOU SOMETHING AS A REWARD...
ANY REQUESTS?
HUH?
FOR REAL!?
SOMETHING TASTY TO EAT, OR...
GASHI (GRAB)
I-I DO HAVE ONE!!
I-I......!!
GAK!
I WANT SHUUSEI-KUN TO STOMP ON ME...!!
AND LOOK DOWN ON ME WITH LOATHING IN HIS EYES...!!
...BWUH?
.....AND SO!
REWARD TIME.
← WHAT THE HELL ARE YOU MAKING ME DO?! HE'S THINKING.
IS THIS CRUELTY TO ANIMALS...?
SHUUSEI'S GOIN' ALL OUT.
NO MERCY...
GURI
GURI (GRIND)
AAAHN~
SOMETIMES, I REALLY DON'T UNDERSTAND MY EDITOR...
I DON'T PARTICULARLY WANT TO UNDERSTAND...
WHY IS THIS PICTURE EVEN HERE.........?

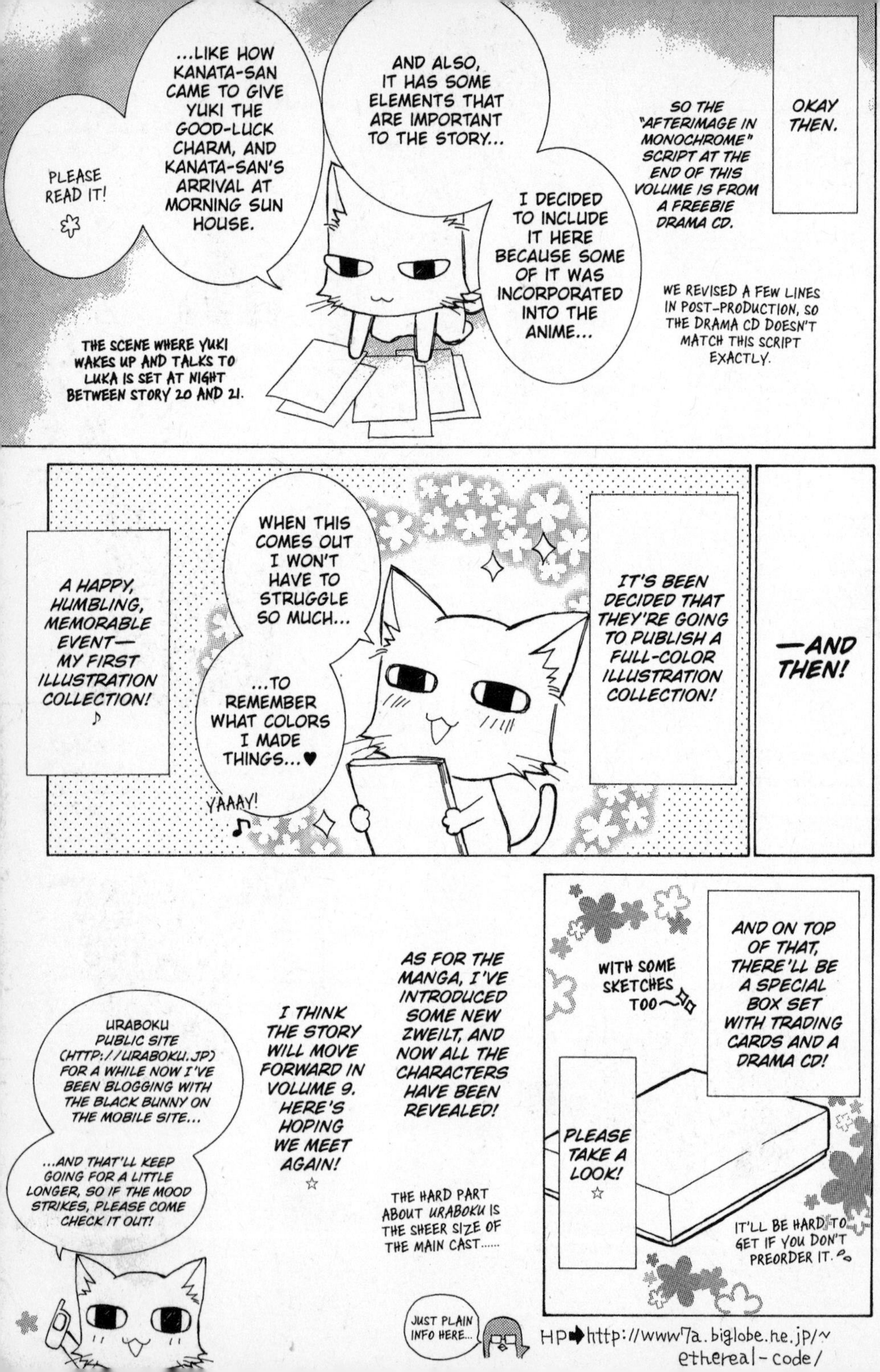
OKAY THEN.
SO THE "AFTERIMAGE IN MONOCHROME" SCRIPT AT THE END OF THIS VOLUME IS FROM A FREEBIE DRAMA CD.
WE REVISED A FEW LINES IN POST-PRODUCTION, SO THE DRAMA CD DOESN'T MATCH THIS SCRIPT EXACTLY.
I DECIDED TO INCLUDE IT HERE BECAUSE SOME OF IT WAS INCORPORATED INTO THE ANIME...
AND ALSO, IT HAS SOME ELEMENTS THAT ARE IMPORTANT TO THE STORY...
...LIKE HOW KANATA-SAN CAME TO GIVE YUKI THE GOOD-LUCK CHARM, AND KANATA-SAN'S ARRIVAL AT MORNING SUN HOUSE.
PLEASE READ IT!
THE SCENE WHERE YUKI WAKES UP AND TALKS TO LUKA IS SET AT NIGHT BETWEEN STORY 20 AND 21.
—AND THEN!
IT'S BEEN DECIDED THAT THEY'RE GOING TO PUBLISH A FULL-COLOR ILLUSTRATION COLLECTION!
WHEN THIS COMES OUT I WON'T HAVE TO STRUGGLE SO MUCH...
...TO REMEMBER WHAT COLORS I MADE THINGS...♥
YAAAY! ♪
A HAPPY, HUMBLING, MEMORABLE EVENT— MY FIRST ILLUSTRATION COLLECTION! ♪
AND ON TOP OF THAT, THERE'LL BE A SPECIAL BOX SET WITH TRADING CARDS AND A DRAMA CD!
WITH SOME SKETCHES TOO~
PLEASE TAKE A LOOK! ☆
IT'LL BE HARD TO GET IF YOU DON'T PREORDER IT.
AS FOR THE MANGA, I'VE INTRODUCED SOME NEW ZWEILT, AND NOW ALL THE CHARACTERS HAVE BEEN REVEALED!
I THINK THE STORY WILL MOVE FORWARD IN VOLUME 9. HERE'S HOPING WE MEET AGAIN! ☆
THE HARD PART ABOUT URABOKU IS THE SHEER SIZE OF THE MAIN CAST......
URABOKU PUBLIC SITE (HTTP://URABOKU.JP) FOR A WHILE NOW I'VE BEEN BLOGGING WITH THE BLACK BUNNY ON THE MOBILE SITE...
...AND THAT'LL KEEP GOING FOR A LITTLE LONGER, SO IF THE MOOD STRIKES, PLEASE COME CHECK IT OUT!
JUST PLAIN INFO HERE...
HP➡http://www7a.biglobe.ne.jp/~ethereal-code/

SPECIAL THANKS

✝

K-san
H.Sanbe
H.Matsuo
T.Kondo

K.Nobata
M.Fujikura
K.Okuda
E.Yamagishi

K.Kato

Y.Suzuki

...... and You

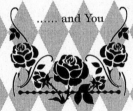

SEND LETTERS TO:

HOTARU ODAGIRI
C/O GEKKAN ASUKA EDITORIAL DEPARTMENT
KADOKAWA SHOTEN, INC.
TOKYO, JAPAN 102-8078

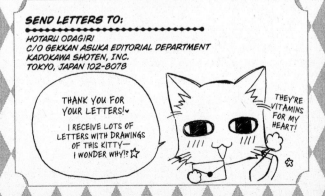

THANK YOU FOR YOUR LETTERS! ♥

I RECEIVE LOTS OF LETTERS WITH DRAWINGS OF THIS KITTY— I WONDER WHY!? ☆

THEY'RE VITAMINS FOR MY HEART!

Afterimage in Monochrome

Hotaru Odagiri

This script was originally created for the mail-away drama CD offered in
the August through September 2008 issues of *Monthly Asuka*.

||||||||||||||||||||||||||||||||||||||||||||||||||||||||||||||||||||||||||||||||||||||||||||||||||||||||||||||||||||||||||||||||||||||||||||

◆*Kanata's apartment – kitchen*
Yuki and Kanata are standing in the kitchen, doing some cooking.
Yuki has just finished chopping vegetables.

Yuki: Kanata-san, I've finished chopping all the vegetables.
Kanata: Hm? That was fast. ......Yeah, that's perfect.
Yuki: I want to live on my own when I get to high school, so I have to be able to
cook for myself. They're letting me practice at Morning Sun House. You're already
on your own, so would you mind teaching me some pointers?
Kanata: That's great, Yuki. But I don't know if there's much I could teach you.
You'll be fine with cooking, I bet. ......Remember that first time...... (nostalgic
chuckle)......
Yuki: Wh-what first time?
Kanata: I mean, back at the orphanage, when you first started helping out with the
cooking. You were still in elementary school. ......Someone handed you a kitchen
knife, and even though you didn't really know how, you were chopping through the
ingredients with such determination. And I'll never forget what you said when you
were just about finished.
Yuki: Was it something really funny?
Kanata: With the knife in your hand and your eyes all gleaming, you said, "Isn't
there anything else to chop?"

Yuki: ....
Kanata: And then I said, "Is that kid okay?" because I was actually kind of worried. (unable to hold in laughter) Ah-ha-ha-ha!
Yuki: (embarrassed) Kanata-san! That's what you thought of me!? You're so mean!

Yuki smacks Kanata on the shoulder.

Kanata: Ow......
Yuki: Oh......I-I'm sorry! I didn't mean to hit you so hard......
Kanata: ......No, that's not it. I just got a headache...... (sudden pain) Unh...... (kneels down)

Yuki stares at him, worried.

Yuki: K-Kanata-san, are you all right? Should I call a doctor?

Kanata smiles a bit through his pain for Yuki's sake.

Kanata: I'm all right...... It'll pass soon...... Don't worry......
Yuki: (worried) ......But......

Even though he still doesn't feel too great, Kanata slowly stands up.

Kanata: ......(sigh)...... Yeah, I'm......okay now. Sorry to worry you. I've had a lot of these headaches lately.
Yuki: Shouldn't you go to a hospital and get that checked out?
Kanata: Maybe, but they go away quick. I think it's just a lack of sleep. I've been having these weird dreams, so I'm not sleeping well these days.
Yuki: Weird dreams......?
Kanata: Yeah. ......I'll be wearing something that looks like a kimono from a long time ago......like maybe from the Heian period. But when I wake up, I can't really remember. It just feels like I've had a terrible nightmare. And I'm soaked in sweat.
Yuki: (worried) Kanata-san......
Kanata: (trying to laugh it off) I'm telling you not to worry. I'm okay. Don't I look fine?
Yuki: ......

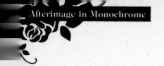

From outside, they can hear the chirping of cicadas in the evening.

Kanata: ......Cicadas....... I guess it's getting dark already. Well, let's hurry up and make dinner.

◆*Kanata's apartment – living room*
Yuki and Kanata have just put down their chopsticks.

Yuki: That was good.
Kanata: Yeah. Should I make some tea?
Yuki: Oh, I'll take care of the dishes.

He stands up and starts stacking plates.

Kanata: Okay, just leave them in the sink, and I'll wash them later.

Yuki carries them to the kitchen.

Yuki: No, I'll do it. You're helping me out and everything......
Kanata: Don't worry about it. You came to study for your exams, right?

Kanata makes tea.

Kanata: The high school you want to go to is one of the best in the prefecture, with a high rate of graduates moving on to a good college. You're competing against perfect students who pay lots of money for high-end tutors and classes. So this week you're here to study until practice questions come out your ears.

Yuki comes back and sits down.

Yuki: I'm prepared. But I'm lucky, aren't I? I have an excellent private tutor who happens to be an alum.
Kanata: You can flatter me all you want, but I won't go easy on you. You're putting your nose to the grindstone once you finish that tea!

With that, he places a teacup in front of Yuki.

Yuki: (nervous laughter) ......Thanks. I'm ready for it.
Kanata: Oh, right.

He gets up and goes to a nearby cabinet.

Kanata: There's something I wanted to give you.

He takes a good-luck charm out of a drawer.

Kanata: This is the good-luck charm I kept on me when I was taking my entrance exams. I passed both the high school and college exams, so I bet it'll help you too. Would you take it with you?

He hands it to Yuki.

Yuki: ......I can have it?
Kanata: Yeah. It'd make me happy. Even though you probably won't need it.
Yuki: No! I'm grateful! I'll treasure it. Thank you, it's just the encouragement I need.
Kanata: (kindly chuckle)......

He returns to his seat...

Kanata: (lonely sigh)

...and sits back down.

CHARM: ACADEMIC SUCCESS

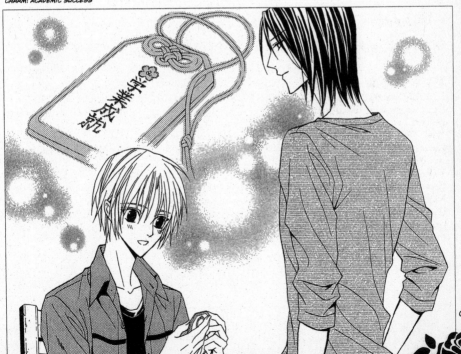

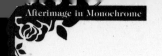

Yuki: ......Kanata-san?
Kanata: ......To be honest, Yuki, I'm a little worried about you going to high school.
Yuki: ......Why is that?
Kanata: (hesitates a little, then speaks decisively) ......In high school, there will be lots of people who came from different middle schools. You won't know most of them. And of course, there'll be cliques who, once they hear about our "situation," come and stare out of curiosity. In my case— (looking into Yuki's eyes, he says curtly) Well, it turned nasty.
Yuki: (realizing with a gasp) ......Oh......

* * *

—*Flashback.*

Yuki (elementary school-age): Kanata-san, what's that on your forehead? Did you get hurt?
Kanata (high school-age): Huh? ......Oh, someone threw a rock at me. But it's fine. It really doesn't hurt at all.

* * *

—*The present.*

Yuki (monologue): —*"It doesn't hurt." "Physical wounds don't hurt that much." That's what Kanata-san said then.*

Kanata: ......There are lots of overachievers and spoiled rich kids at that school, so I hardly ever got beaten up and stuff. But whenever anything went missing, I'd be the one getting the blame. Or I'd get ignored, or spat on...... (bitterly) It was such stupid, immature teasing, worse than in middle school.
Yuki: (heartbroken) ......Kanata-san......
Kanata: You don't have to make that face, Yuki. I'm not hurt at all. See, perfectly healthy.
Yuki: ......What about inside?
Kanata: Huh......?
Yuki: (sadly, but earnestly) Are you okay on the inside? Even if bruises on your body get better, wounds to your heart...... I don't think they ever heal. You can pretend you've forgotten, but that just means you're living with the hurt lodged deep inside you, I think......

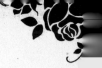

Kanata: ....
Yuki: I wonder why it's invisible when we hurt on the inside...... If people can see that you're hurt, they worry for you. They can see how bad it is...... Just because no one can see it doesn't mean that someone isn't hurting......
Yuki (monologue): *I've been bullied by classmates since way back too......at least a little bit. Even though they're half-kidding, it really hurts, deep down.*
Kanata: (pained, but harshly) ......Yuki. There are people who will come at you whether or not they can see your pain.
Yuki: ......(breath catches)
Kanata: They won't try to understand your feelings or character. They live for themselves, and sometimes they hurt others, even their own family. Humans are foolish creatures, worthless, weak and arrogant. I've always thought that. So I was even able to put up with bullying. Because I didn't expect anything from them in the first place, I had no faith to lose when classmates treated me that way. Because I always knew people were like that. ......People are...... (stares off into the distance)
Yuki: ......Kanata-san......
Kanata: (looks at Yuki) ......But those ideas of mine have changed a bit since I met you, Yuki.
Yuki: Really......?
Kanata: You've heard that my dad was a nasty drunk, right? Whenever he drank, he'd beat me up. ......The day Morning Sun House took me in too, I had bruises all over, in places you couldn't see. ......But you found them pretty easily.
Yuki: I did......?
Kanata: Yeah. You saw a bruise on my arm and asked, "Does it hurt?" And I said, "No, that's nothing." ......And then you put your tiny hand over my heart and said, "Pain, pain, fly away!" over and over......
Kanata (monologue): *It was strange. Why was this kid doing that for me? His own eyes were puffy. I could tell he'd just been crying. But there he was, this little kid, fussing over another person, and I couldn't understand it. I was just bewildered...... and then, I don't know why, but......there were tears in my eyes.*
Kanata: ......You probably don't remember it, though. Anyway, after that, bit by bit I started to think......it might be okay to have some hope in people and for the future......

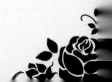

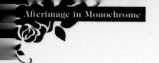

Yuki: ......Kanata-san......

Yuki (monologue): *So I did something like that...although I don't remember....... I'm glad that he has memories like that about me......*

Kanata: (lets out a deep breath, as if a little tired) But even now, I still can't like people all that much. I'm not very friendly...... Maybe people can sense those things about me somehow.

Yuki: (unsure what to say) ......That's not......

Kanata: (laughs self-deprecatingly) Sorry. I shouldn't have said all that. I've just been worried about you...... But maybe I don't have to worry. ......I bet you'll meet people who understand you, and you'll be able to make lots of friends. Yeah, I'm sure you will.

Yuki: Kanata-san......

Yuki (monologue): *He looks somehow sad saying that. Am I just imagining it......? I don't know why, but......it feels like Kanata-san is going to leave for someplace else......*

Yuki: (as if trying to keep him close, without thinking) Kanata-san! I like you, Kanata-san!

Kanata: (taken by surprise) ......Yuki?

Yuki: (choosing his words carefully) I always thought you were amazing, working so hard to make your own way...... That's why I want to go to the same high school you went to, and the same college too. But if it was just me, alone, all those goals would be too daunting......so...that's why......

Kanata: ....

Yuki: ......So, can I make you my goal? I just want to be with you...... Kanata-san, I want us to be together forever.

Kanata: Yuki......

Yuki: (gazing at him desperately) ....

Kanata stares back, then finally says,

Kanata: (soft smile) Thanks, Yuki.

Yuki: Kanata-san......

Kanata: (solemnly) —But I'm sorry. I don't think I can make that wish come true.

Kanata stands up.

Yuki: !?

Kanata is walking toward something. Confused, Yuki stands up.

Yuki: ......Kanata-san...... Kanata-san!

Standing in front of a door to Infernus, Kanata turns back to look at him.

Kanata: (sadly) Good-bye, Yuki.

He leaves through the door.

Yuki: Kanata-san!? Where are you going...

Yuki tries to follow, but the door slams shut in his face.

Yuki: —!? Kanata-san!

Agitated, he opens the door and runs down a hallway.

Yuki: Kanata-san! Kanata-san!

But there is no answer.

Yuki: (confused and distraught) Kanata-san! Where are you!? What do you mean, "goodbye"......? Kanata-san—...!!

Yuki's shouting is swallowed up by the darkness—

◆*Twilight Hall – Yuki's room*
Luka is shaking Yuki, who is in bed.

Luka: ....ki, ...Yuki, Yuki!
Yuki: (waking up) ......Oh......

Luka peers into Yuki's face with concern.

Luka: Are you all right, Yuki?
Yuki: (seems a little out of breath) ......Luka.
Luka: You were crying out in your sleep. Did you have a bad dream?

Yuki sits up heavily.

Yuki: ......That's right...... It was a dream......
Yuki (monologue): —No......until the end there, it was a conversation I really had with Kanata-san a year ago.

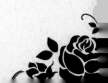

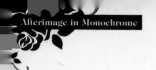

Yuki: (forcing himself to smile) ......It's nothing. I'm fine. But you were next to me this whole time, weren't you, Luka?
Luka: (looking a bit gloomy) Were you dreaming about Kanata Wakamiya?
Yuki: (startled) ......
Luka: ......You were calling his name.
Yuki: ! ......Kanata-san's name......
Luka: Yuki, why do you try to bear all your burdens alone? What do you think I'm here for?
Yuki: ....Oh...... Sorry... (tears welling up)
Luka: Yuki...
Yuki: ......Luka, I-I lied...... I was the one who told him......that I wanted us to be together forever...... But......! ...Why did this have to happen?
Luka: ....
Yuki: ......Why... (crying, trying to keep his voice in) ......(sobbing quietly)......

Luka sits beside Yuki and gently puts an arm around him.

Luka: You've been through a lot.
Yuki: .... (breath catches) ......
Luka: (calmly and gently) ......Even if I tell you not to blame yourself, it's probably difficult not to right now...... But this isn't your fault and yours alone. Do you understand? There's no one single person to blame......
Yuki: ......Luka......
Yuki (monologue): *Luka's hand on my shoulder is so gentle...... And his words— somehow they get through to me......*
Luka: (gently persuading) If you feel like crying, then cry. The Zweilt aren't here right now. ......Were you holding in your tears this whole time? ......I'm here. I will always be by your side.
Yuki: (teary-eyed) ......(crying)......

Unable to hold back, he clings to Luka.

Yuki: (crying loudly)

He keeps sobbing with all his strength—

Luka (monologue): *Cry it all out now, Yuki. In the morning, you'll smile and face everyone again. ......So at least......for now—......*

~END~

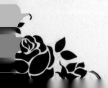

Translation Notes

Page 16
"Vil Yue" is written with the characters for "Light of God." This is the name for Yuki among the Duras.

Page 25
Onmyouji (meaning a Yin-Yang magician) was the title of a hit movie about the historical/legendary magician Abe no Seimei, hence the imagery.

Page 52
"Izanagi," the name of Kuroto's sword, is taken from one of the Shinto creation deities, but is written with the characters for *naraku*, a Buddhist word for "hell."

Page 68
The name of Cadenza's spell, "Adamrad," is written with the characters reading "boulder spear hellstorm."

Page 70
Senshirou's spell "Lev Roima" is written with the characters for "brushwork."

Page 98
"Hallow Woe" is written with the characters for "shield of holy protection."

Page 110
"Faolar" is written with the characters "summon-master." This is the Infernus word for the summoned being addressing the summoner.

Page 114
"Izarbdo" is written with the characters "freezing blast arrows."

Page 115
"Domion Scrayme" is written with the characters for "final judgment."

Page 140
"Dearg Ho" appears to be derived from Irish Gaelic.

Page 183
Katsushi Sakurabi, director at J.C. Staff, did the storyboards. Natsuko Takahashi is the script writer for the *UraBoku* anime. Seishi Yokomizu, Ranpo Edogawa were mystery writers of the early twentieth century.

Page 233
Hakama are pleated trousers worn with kimono, often donned for traditional Japanese arts such as kendo and archery.

Page 301
Fuyutoki's name is written with the characters for "winter" and "melt."

Page 321
Reiga usually refers to himself with the personal pronoun *watashi*, the formal, grown-up, gender-neutral "I." But as Kanata, he called himself *boku*, a more boyish, informal "I." Reiga used *boku* when he insisted to Yuki that making it impossible to hate him was all part of his plan in Story 34, thereby betraying Kanata's lingering feelings.

Page 342
Flying Dog is a recording company.

Page 352
"Pain, pain, fly away!" isn't Yuki being silly, but a common comforting phrase spoken, for instance, by a parent to a kid with a skinned knee.

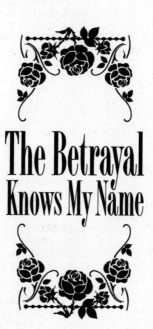

The Betrayal
Knows My Name

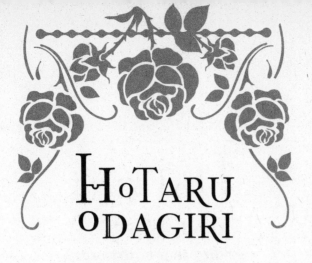

HoTaru ODAGIRI

I'm really regretting
making it canon that
"the more powerful
the Duras, the more
beautiful the form
they take." I wish
I could send the past
me a memo that there's
only so much beauty
I can draw...

MESSAGE FROM VOLUME 7
(Japanese edition)

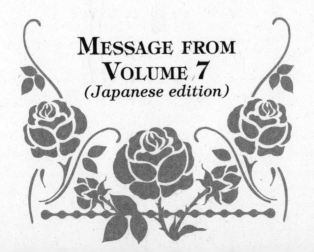

HoTaru oDagiri

Living is a continuous
battle. Sometimes, it's
so painful you just want
to give up. And yet, if
you can grasp the truth
that you're not alone,
maybe that can give you
strength. Luka and the
Zweilt pairs were born
out of that feeling.
Not that someone will
carry you, but that some-
one else can help you to
find the strength to walk
on your own two feet.

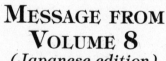

MESSAGE FROM
VOLUME 8
(Japanese edition)

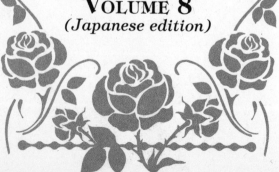

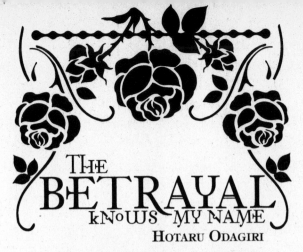

THE BETRAYAL kNoWS MY NAME

HOTARU ODAGIRI

Translation: Melissa Tanaka † Lettering: Lys Blakeslee

URAGIRI WA BOKU NO NAMAE WO SHITTEIRU Volumes 7 and 8 © Hotaru ODAGIRI 2010. First published in Japan in 2010 by KADOKAWA SHOTEN Co., Ltd., Tokyo. English translation rights arranged with KADOKAWA SHOTEN Co., Ltd., Tokyo through TUTTLE-MORI AGENCY, INC., Tokyo.

Translation © 2012 by Hachette Book Group, Inc.

Yen Press
Hachette Book Group
237 Park Avenue, New York, NY 10017

www.HachetteBookGroup.com
www.YenPress.com

Yen Press is an imprint of Hachette Book Group, Inc. The Yen Press name and logo are trademarks of Hachette Book Group, Inc.

First Yen Press Edition: August 2012

ISBN: 978-0-316-21615-9

10 9 8 7 6 5 4 3 2

BVG

Printed in the
United States of America